The Philosophy of John Dewey

Volume I
The Structure of Experience

Volume II
The Lived Experience

*Edited with an Introduction
and Commentary by*

John J. McDermott

The University of Chicago Press

Chicago and London

This book was published originally in
two volumes.

The University of Chicago Press, Chicago 60637
The University of Chicago Press, Ltd., London

Library of Congress Cataloging in Publication Data

Dewey, John, 1859–1952.
    The philosophy of John Dewey.

    Originally published in 2 vols. in 1973 by Putnam,
New York.
    CONTENTS: The structure of experience.—The
lived experience.
    1. Philosophy—Collected works. I. McDermott,
John J. II. Title.
B945.D41   1981b   191   80-39766
ISBN 0-226-14401-1 (pbk.)

FOR
Marise McDermott
1953–

*Our First Born—A Life of Loyalty
and Celebration*

AND

FOR
Michele McDermott
1954–

*Our Second Born—A Life of Integrity
and Mystery*

Contents

VOLUME I
THE STRUCTURE OF EXPERIENCE

Preface to the Phoenix Edition   ix
Preface   xi
Introduction   xv
Notes   xxxi
Chronology   xxxv
Bibliography   xxxvii
Editor's Note on the Text   xli

I. HISTORICAL ROOTS AND REFLECTIONS   1

  1. From Absolutism to Experimentalism   1
  2. Kant and Philosophic Method   13
  3. Ralph Waldo Emerson   24
  4. The Influence of Darwinism on Philosophy   31
  5. The Development of American Pragmatism   41
  6. The Need for a Recovery of Philosophy   58

II. EARLY PSYCHOLOGICAL WRITINGS   98

  7. The Psychological Standpoint   98
  8. Psychology as Philosophic Method   116
  9. The Reflex Arc Concept in Psychology   136
 10. The Psychology of Effort   148

III. THE EXPERIENCE OF KNOWING   160

 11. "Consciousness" and Experience   160
 12. The Experimental Theory of Knowledge   175
 13. Experience and Objective Idealism   193

14. The Practical Character of Reality   207
15. The Pattern of Inquiry   223

IV. THE METAPHYSICS OF EXPERIENCE   240

16. The Postulate of Immediate Empiricism   240
17. Experience and Philosophic Method   249
18. Existence as Precarious and Stable   277
19. Experience, Nature and Art   300
20. Existence, Value and Criticism   325

VOLUME II
THE LIVED EXPERIENCE

V. THE CULTURE OF INQUIRY   355

21. Escape from Peril   355
22. Philosophy's Search for the Immutable   371
23. Science and Society   388
24. Social Inquiry   397

VI. EXPERIENCE IS PEDAGOGICAL   421

25. Interest in Relation to the Training of the Will   421
26. My Pedagogic Creed   442
27. The School and Social Progress   454
28. The Child and the Curriculum   467
29. Education as Growth   483
30. Experience and Thinking   494
31. The Need of a Theory of Experience   506
32. Criteria of Experience   511

VII. EXPERIENCE AS AESTHETIC   525

33. The Live Creature   525
34. The Live Creature and "Etherial Things"   541
35. Having an Experience   554

VIII. EXPERIENCE AS PROBLEMATIC:
ETHICAL, RELIGIOUS, POLITICAL,
AND SOCIAL DIMENSIONS   575

36. The Construction of Good   575
37. The Lost Individual   598
38. Toward a New Individualism   608
39. Search for the Great Community   620
40. Renascent Liberalism   643
41. The Problem of Freedom   665
42. Culture and Human Nature   679
43. The Human Abode of the Religious Function   696
44. Morality Is Social   712

Preface to the Phoenix Edition

Almost a decade has passed since the publication of *The Philosophy of John Dewey*, in two volumes. Students and teachers of the thought of Dewey are in debt to the University of Chicago Press for its decision to reprint these writings, all of them now in a one volume edition. I am grateful, also, to the permissions' editors at G. P. Putnam's Sons for release of material published earlier in their Capricorn edition. Furthermore, I have received permission to reprint material now held by the Center for Dewey Studies at Southern Illinois University. Consequently, although for the most part the permission acknowledgments stand as stated beneath the first page of each essay, the following exceptions should be noted: chapters 4, 5, 6, 11, 12, 13, 16, 29, 30, 39, and 44 are now reprinted with the permission of the Center for Dewey Studies. In this regard, Ms. Jo Ann Boydston, editor of the superb and definitive multivolume edition of Dewey's *Works*, has been extraordinarily cooperative. As director of the Center for Dewey Studies, Ms. Boydston has thus far been responsible for the editing of fifteen volumes of Dewey's writings, a collection of his poems, and editions of both primary and secondary source bibliographies on Dewey.

The reviews of *The Philosophy of John Dewey*, with few exceptions, have been extremely favorable. The most detailed, perceptive, and affectionately critical was by Gary Brodsky in a 1975 issue of *The Transactions of the C.S. Peirce Society*. In that review, Brodsky stressed the need to emphasize Dewey's philosophy of science and his "broadly cognitive concerns." His point is well taken, and readers of this volume are encouraged to supplement the material presented by reading Dewey's *Logic: The Theory of Inquiry* and his essay on "Anti-Naturalism in Extremis" in Yervant Krikorian, ed., *Naturalism and the Human Spirit*.

A vast amount of literature on Dewey has been produced since his death, and the past ten years are no exception. I cite here only a few highlights in the continuing philosophical interest in his thought. As the editor of a 1977 volume of essays entitled *New Studies in the Philosophy of John Dewey*, Steven M. Cahn wrote that

the ideological fervor of [the makers of the British philosophical revolution] has now passed, and the last decade has witnessed a major revival of interest in central questions of personal morality and public policy. Perhaps then the time is right for a renewal of interest in Dewey's philosophy and its attempt "to interpret the conclusions of science with respect to their consequences for our beliefs and purposes and values in all phases of life."

It is significant that among the contributors to this volume of essays on the thought of Dewey are two distinguished American philosophers of the analytic persuasion, Richard Rorty and Joseph Margolis. Their interest in Dewey, although subject to dispute of interpretation, is heartening. Dewey's moral philosophy has been given careful analysis and presentation by James Gouinlock's book, *The Moral Writings of John Dewey*. In an important recent dissertation, James Campbell has detailed the complex intellectual relations between Dewey and G. H. Mead and in so doing has richly portrayed the American social ethic in the first half of this century. In this context, an original discussion of Dewey's understanding of democracy as being primarily a local face-to-face and antistate affair can be found in the writings of Peter Manicas. Finally, there is the work of Arthur Lothstein, who is rejuvenating Dewey's aesthetics in its relationship to his social and political philosophy.

As for myself, I remain committed to the position taken in the introduction to this volume. During the past decade, I have addressed the philosophical dimensions of a number of social, political, and interpersonal concerns, such as the aesthetics of the city and of institutions, the plight of the handicapped, and the experience of human death. In these endeavors, aspects of what I call "the culture of experience," Dewey's metaphysics and his use of the method of creative intelligence, have been unfailingly helpful.

In short, John Dewey takes his place in the tradition of the great philosophers, for his work maintains a creative viability, no matter the shift in linguistic or methodological fashion. The paradox is that Dewey achieved this viability, not by having written for the future, but rather by writing out of his own present experience. His attitude of affection for ordinary experience remained a lifelong characteristic of his work. He believed that ordinary experience is seeded with surprises and possibilities for enhancement, if we but allow it to bathe over us on its own terms. The key here is to avoid derision and the seduction of condescension to the seemingly obvious. In my judgment, the central text in Dewey is found late in his work, in *Experience and Education*. He writes,

We always live at the time we live and not at some other time, and only by extracting at each present time the full meaning of each present experience are we prepared for doing the same thing in the future.

The paradox here is that if we live as Dewey suggests, we may even be remembered.

Preface

Who was John Dewey? Despite a staggering output of lectures, articles, and books, an incredibly long career of almost a century, an engendering of fascination, controversy, and widespread influence in many areas of human activity, the question is difficult to answer in any depth. No modern philosopher has exerted such influence while being hidden from view. This vagueness in our grasp of the qualities of his person, his motivations, sufferings, and delights cannot proceed from his having lived a sheltered life. His personal and intellectual odyssey ranged from Burlington, Vermont, to David Dubinsky and the trade unions of New York City, from Chicago to China, the Soviet Union, Turkey, and the Trotsky Commission in Mexico.

Embroiled and embattled at every level of human endeavor, we find John Dewey responding to technical philosophical disputes, as well as to highly inflammatory issues of the public arena. Yet at this writing we have only a thin autobiographical statement, "From Absolutism to Experimentalism," and a few biographical sketches. We are promised more, with the most encouraging news being the announcement of a definitive biography by George Dykhuizen, to be published by Southern Illinois University Press as part of its distinguished series of the complete writings of John Dewey. Whether these future biographical studies will provide adequate insight into the life of this extraordinary man or whether it is of his very person to remain elusive and out of reach of such studies remains an open question.

The corollary to our limited understanding of the person of John Dewey is the acknowledgment of the importance and power of his writings. And it is with this in mind that we present these two volumes. In view of the fact that the Co-operative Research Project on Dewey publications at Southern Illinois University is now issuing critical editions of all of Dewey's writings, it has not been necessary for me to provide a full critical and bibliographical apparatus. Nor do the present volumes supplant the excellent edition of Dewey's writings by Richard

xi

J. Bernstein, *On Experience, Nature, and Freedom*, which has as its scope the development of Dewey's *Experience and Nature* after 1925.

What is needed, however, is a presentation of Dewey's thought as it has developed both chronologically and thematically. Within the omnipresent limitation of space, I have tried to offer as wide a range of Dewey's interests as possible and to set those interests into the framework of the development and growth of his thought. Given the massiveness of Dewey's bibliography, these selections, although running to approximately 1,000 pages of his own writing, constitute but a small sampling. Nonetheless, they yield access to almost every major theme in his writings, and they do this by representation of the full range of his thought. Students and teachers of all disciplines will find in these pages a renewed call to the majesty and importance of Dewey's insight into "creative intelligence." It is especially hoped that the present generation, so often fired by a sense of social responsibility and a feeling for the "lived body" but so woefully lacking in "accrued wisdom," will find in Dewey's thought a dramatic instance of their being brought together.

By way of acknowledgment, I again cite the imaginative teaching and writing of Robert C. Pollock, whose "Process and Experience" is still the best essay on the philosophy of John Dewey. Over the years, I have learned much about John Dewey from my colleagues at Queens College: Eugene Fontinell, Peter T. Manicas, John B. Noone, Jr., and especially Ralph W. Sleeper. From among the vast amount of writings about John Dewey, I am especially indebted to the work of Sidney Hook, H. S. Thayer, Richard J. Bernstein, and John Herman Randall, Jr., whose book *Nature and Historical Experience* is thus far the only successor to Dewey's *Experience and Nature*. As for all Dewey scholarship, the bibliographical research of Milton Halsey Thomas has been invaluable. And I wish to acknowledge the cooperation and good fellowship offered to me by Morris and Elizabeth Eames, Jo-Ann Boydston, Garth Gillan, George McClure, and Lewis Hahn during my visit to the Center for Dewey Studies at Southern Illinois University. I have also enjoyed a conversation with John Dewey's son, Sabino, now deceased.

With regard to the preparation of the manuscript, I am indebted to Peter T. Manicas, who facilitated its acceptance, and to Marsha Treiber, who provided expert and cordial secretarial services. Eugene Fontinell provided a perceptive critique of the Introduction. My editor, Mr. Walter C. Betkowski, has been properly firm but understanding, supremely long on patience, and kind throughout. In past work, I have acknowledged the extensive editorial assistance of my wife, Virginia.

Since that time, Deweyan by instinct as well as by learning, she has chosen to teach elementary school children in an open-corridor experiment. Her contribution has been to tell of the lives of children in a way which people who write and edit books tend to forget, if they ever knew.

JOHN J. MCDERMOTT

Huntington, New York
1972

Introduction

John Dewey: A Biographical Sketch

American philosophy of the nineteenth century is often said to lack a sense of the tragic. This charge is addressed particularly at the thought of John Dewey, so often typed for its overall optimism, its confidence in the potentialities of men, and its leaning toward an ameliorated future. If, however, we dig beneath the bland commentaries on the American philosophers and proceed to study their lives in depth, the tragic dimensions of the lives and thought of Ralph Waldo Emerson,[1] Charles Peirce,[2] William James,[3] and Josiah Royce[4] become painfully obvious. The life of Emerson reads like a long chapter from *A Cool Million* by Nathaniel West, riven throughout with illness and premature deaths, culminating in the destruction by fire of his home. William James, who lost an infant son by whooping cough, suffered all his life from severe psychoneurosis and major family crises and was plagued in the last decade of his life by increasing heart failure. Charles Peirce was a dissolute, debt-ridden public failure, whose life was capped by a lingering, painful illness. And Josiah Royce, despite the bravado of his public presence, hid from view his own considerable mental anguish and the tragic lives of some of his children. Perhaps it can be said that the confidence and optimism which characterizes their doctrines are partially in the form of compensation, as Emerson, for one, would be quick to acknowledge. Certainly, it cannot be said that these philosophers are naïve about the meaning of suffering and tragedy.

A similar judgment can be offered about the thought of John Dewey, although, with some notable exceptions, his life was not laced with the violent upheavals just cited. Further, Dewey lived so actively, for so long (1859-1952), that the major events of his life seem to fade into an almost unreal historical tapestry. Aside from Dewey's brief autobiographical piece, "From Absolutism to Experimentalism,"[4] published in 1930, and some isolated reminiscences of colleagues and friends,[5] the only substantial statement we have of Dewey's life is that of Jane Dewey,[6] who edited a brief biography written by herself and her two sisters, Evelyn and Lucy, from material provided by their father. Virtually all of the biographical material written by subsequent commentators thus far is a reduction of portions of this material. Yet, in most instances the death of two of Dewey's children and the personal stress involved in the collapse of the laboratory school at the University of Chicago are either passed over or mentioned briefly and without assessment, as though they might mar the cool logic of Dewey's thought. But Dewey's philosophy never strays from his insight into the irreducible presence of the tension between the "precarious" and the "stable," while, more than most philosophers, he integrates the experience of loss and setback with that of growth.

John Dewey was born in Burlington, Vermont, on October 20, 1859. He was the third of four sons born to Lucina Rich Dewey and Archibald Sprague Dewey. A quartermaster of a Vermont regiment during the Civil War, Dewey's father made his living in Burlington as a grocer. With the exception of a winter stay in the war-devastated area of northern Virginia, John Dewey's childhood was uneventful, and at age fifteen he entered the University of Vermont. In addition to a classical education, Dewey also studied the evolutionary thought of T. H. Huxley, which widened his outlook. He studied the reigning "Scotch realism" with H. A. P. Torrey and was introduced to German philosophy through the teaching of James Marsh. In 1879, Dewey graduated with honors and went on to teach high school for two years at Oil City, Pennsylvania. In retrospect, his experience in Oil City was very significant. He learned to live in comparative isolation, devoted to his thoughts and his teaching. And it was during this period that he resolved to continue with philosophy. His experience with the school and the children began an abiding interest in the affairs and problems of education.

In 1881 Dewey returned to Vermont, where he taught in a village school and studied philosophy on a tutorial basis with Professor Torrey. After reading *Speculative Philosophy,* a journal edited by W. T. Harris, Dewey sent off an essay on "The Metaphysical Assumptions of Materialism," asking Harris if the author should contemplate a career in philosophy. Harris answered yes and published the essay, and Dewey went to the new graduate school at Johns Hopkins University. Although Dewey studied with Charles Peirce at Johns Hopkins, he was unaware of the vast learning and importance of Peirce until many years later. The most powerful philosophical and personal influence on John Dewey at that time was that exercised by George S. Morris, who was responsible for Dewey's early interest and commitment to idealism and especially to the philosophy of Hegel. Despite subsequent vast changes in his thought, Dewey was fond of saying throughout his life that Hegel "left a permanent deposit in my thinking." Of particular importance to Dewey was Hegel's view that the individual is not isolated from history, culture, or environment, thereby providing a basis for Dewey's later fascination with social psychology.

In 1884 George Morris was influential in obtaining for Dewey an instructorship in philosophy at the University of Michigan, where, with the exception of a year at the University of Minnesota (1888-89), he taught until 1894. This period was to begin his long friendship and collaboration with the distinguished philosopher George Herbert Mead, who was to have a pervasive influence on the development of Dewey's thought. And during his stay at Michigan, on July 28, 1886, Dewey married Alice Chipman (1859-1927), a graduate of the University of Michigan. Six children were born to them: in Michigan, Frederick (1887-1967), Evelyn (1889-1965), and Morris (1893-95); and in Chicago, Gordon (1896-1904), Lucy (1897-   ), and Jane (1900-   ).

In 1894 Dewey accepted a position as professor of philosophy and chairman of the Department of Philosophy, Psychology, and Education at the University of Chicago—a most important decision. Such a troika of responsibilities might seem the height of pretense, but for Dewey it was merely a symbol of what we now call the interdisciplinary approach to human activity. He had become increasingly concerned with the social dimensions of behavior, particularly in the genetic state, and therefore wished to organize a program around the philosophical and psychological problems of inquiry as found in the education of children. Also, during his time at Michigan, Dewey's view of the meaning of psychology and its relationship to other approaches to human activity underwent a tremendous change due to the publication in 1890 of William James' *Principles of Psychology*. In a later essay on "The Development of American Pragmatism,"* Dewey details the importance of James' *Principles* both in his own thought and for the subsequent direction of American philosophy.

The Chicago years are crucially important for an understanding of Dewey's personal development and the evolution of his thought. In the first place, he gathered around him a group of philosophers and thinkers from other disciplines who, upon the publication of a group effort in 1903, *Studies in Logical Theory*, were dubbed by William James as the Chicago School.[7] Of them, Darnell Rucker writes:

Because the Chicago philosophy reflected an awareness of the interconnections among the advances being made in biology, psychology, and sociology, it was able to provide a method and a perspective for an array of disciplines. And so it was that the Chicago School was a school, not merely in the sense that several men were working together evolving (not just defending) a philosophy, but in the fuller sense that their work had effects in a cluster of fields of thought around philosophy; it was a school with a university full of its progeny.[8]

John Dewey was the acknowledged leader of the Chicago School, although in retrospect we see the pervasive influence of George Herbert Mead as well. Dewey also exercised that leadership, albeit indirectly, after he left the University of Chicago in 1904. His abrupt departure at that time also signalized the end of a second major event in Dewey's Chicago years: his founding of "the laboratory school."[9] At its maximum size in 1904, this school served well over 100 children, ranging from ages four to fifteen. Dewey saw the school as not only a laboratory for pedagogy but also a way to pursue experimentally the wider problems of inquiry in an interdisciplinary context. Dewey had great support from the parents and the community, but a combination of personal and financial strains, set in the environment of the politics of the comparatively new University of Chicago, spelled its demise. The ending of the laboratory school was a very unpleasant affair for Dewey. While he was away, the president of the University of Chicago arranged a merger of Dewey's school with the Chicago Institute under the direction of the University School of Education. He also arranged for the resignation of Mrs. Dewey as principal of the laboratory school. Upon returning home, Dewey was appalled at the high-handedness of this decision, and he promptly resigned from all three of his positions at the University of Chicago. At the age of forty-four, he accepted a position as professor of philosophy at Columbia University in New York City, which was to be his home for close to half a century.

Two other events, both catastrophic, intruded upon Dewey's life during the ten years of his Chicago period. The first, in 1895, was the death of his third child, Morris, of diphtheria in Milan at the age of two and a half. Even at such a young age, he was apparently a child of rare promise, and his tragic death inflicted a lifelong wound on John and Alice Dewey. Not quite ten years later untimely death struck again, this time felling the Dewey's fourth child, Gordon. Only eight years of age and

very gifted, Gordon was a victim of typhoid fever, dying in a hospital in
Ireland while the Deweys were vacationing before beginning their life at
Columbia University. The death of Gordon revisited the Deweys with
all the sadness and inexplicability of the death of Morris. Evelyn Dewey
writes of this event that "the blow to Mrs. Dewey was so serious that
she never fully recovered her former energy."[10]

Many years later, in *Experience and Education*, John Dewey wrote
that "We always live at the time we live and not at some other time, and
only by extracting at each present time the full meaning of each present
experience are we prepared for doing the same thing in the future. This
is the only preparation which in the long run amounts to anything."[11]
A typical interpretation of this kind of statement from Dewey holds that
he is present-minded, locked in immediacy, without adequate sense of
the ravages or joys of the past. Reading Dewey through the experience
of the death of his two sons yields a different point of view. I offer that
for Dewey the above text and many others point to the irreducible
presence of loss and suffering in all events, an experiential shadow accompanying our efforts at ". . . extracting at each present time the full
meaning of each present experience. . . ." Dewey's way of confronting
the death of Gordon was to return to Italy, the site of the earlier death
of Morris, where he and his wife adopted an orphan boy, Sabino. This
child grew wise in ways different from those anticipated for Morris and
Gordon. In some ways, however, he was distinctively a Dewey child.
Gifted with his hands, a master of the sea, Sabino taught and innovated
programs in the industrial arts. At more than seventy years of age, he
was seen picketing in New York City on behalf of a young pacifist sen-
tenced to five years for refusal to serve in the Vietnam War. The loss of
Morris and Gordon—the precarious—the adoption and odyssey of
Sabino—the stable—is what John Dewey means by the relationship
between suffering and celebration, the precarious and the stable.

The years from 1904 to his retirement in 1930 found Dewey teaching
at Columbia University and at Teachers College. He also made a series
of lecture trips and educational surveys to Japan, China, Turkey, Mexico, and the Soviet Union.[12] His involvements in public matters of a
social, political, and educational nature during this time and after his
retirement from teaching are too numerous to even list.[13] It should be
noted, however, that he was a founder and first president of the
American Association of University Professors. He was also involved in
the founding of the teacher union movement in New York City and was
a charter member of the New York Teachers' Guild of the American
Federation of Teachers.[14] In 1937, at the age of seventy-eight, John

Dewey served in Mexico City as chairman of the Commission of Inquiry into the Charges Made Against Leon Trotsky in the Moscow Trials.[15] The international observers of the trial were extremely impressed with Dewey's tact, wisdom and, not least, energy during the proceedings. Despite his extraordinary involvement in public affairs, Dewey still wrote voluminously and addressed himself to philosophical problems, both those long-standing and those emerging with each generation. He was invited to a number of prestigious lecture series, among them the Carus Lectures (*Experience and Nature*), the Gifford Lectures (*The Quest for Certainty*), and the William James Lectures (*Art as Experience*).

In 1927 Dewey's wife Alice died of arteriosclerosis. Actually, the loss of her position in the laboratory school in Chicago and the death of her two sons made even more inroads on her person than on her husband. Not having the vast distractions, which characterize the life of a public figure, her world was more inundated by the loss. After her death Dewey depended increasingly on his children for care and concern until 1946, when he remarried. His second wife was Roberta Lowitz Grant, who came originally from Oil City, Pennsylvania, and whose family knew Dewey for many years. John and Roberta Dewey adopted two children, John and Adrienne. It is of note that the first John Dewey II, Dewey's grandson, the child of Frederick and Elizabeth Dewey, was killed in an automobile accident at age thirteen in 1934.

After a series of what turned out to be premature *Festschriften* and farewell birthday celebrations in 1929,[16] 1939,[17] and 1949,[18] Dewey, publicly active to the very end, died on June 1, 1952, at his home, 1158 Fifth Avenue, New York City. He was ninety-two years of age. His second wife, Roberta Dewey, died in Florida on May 6, 1970.

This short biographical summary has no doubt failed to indicate Dewey's charm and the lighter side of his person. Although far too little of that quality of Dewey is on record, some gleaning of his person can be found in the aforementioned essay by Eastman and in the reminiscing found in Lamont's edition of the *Dialogue on John Dewey*. Most of us who are intrigued by Dewey have heard delightful stories about him, but we just as often hear them from someone else with all the data changed. The likely apocryphal nature of these stories is cautioning.

It is known that John Dewey was not an especially adept teacher if flamboyance of personal style is the criterion. But if depth of insight, concentration, loyalty to students, and original thinking in the classroom become the criteria, then Dewey was a superb teacher. And it is also known that Dewey was a man of extraordinary personal integrity, who often risked his reputation in a defense of others, even when the cause was as unpopular as it was transitory. An obvious case in point is his well-known defense of Bertrand Russell, with whom he had little personal or philosophical sympathy, when Russell was denied his appointment to City College in New York on alleged moral grounds.[19] More revealing, perhaps, of Dewey's person was his reaction to the Maxim Gorki affair. Gorki arrived in New York to obtain support for the Russian Revolution and was accompanied by his common-law wife. Under great attack by czarist elements in America, Gorki's moral character was ridiculed, and he was reportedly ousted from a number of hotels. Support for him was difficult to rally, and even Mark Twain reneged, stating that "laws can be evaded and punishment escaped, but an openly transgressed custom brings sure punishment."[20] In the midst of this public outcry, John Dewey offered his home to Gorki and his mistress. The publicity in this instance was unusual but the hospitality was not, for the Deweys often housed on a temporary basis people fleeing or making one revolution or another, be they Irish or Chinese. Of course, even without visitors the Dewey house was always filled with children and later with grandchildren. It is legend that Dewey, despite his involvements and the complexity of his domestic life, was able to persist in his work, as if his ever-present typewriter were an extension of his body, reflecting and producing all the while.

Although it is true that at the present time extensive and trustworthy information about Dewey's personal life is difficult to obtain, nonetheless one aspect of his later life has been brought posthumously to public awareness—namely, his extensive correspondence with Arthur Bentley[21] (1870-1957), which not only casts profound light on Dewey's thought and on the rigor of his mind but also tells us of his sensitivity, his modesty, and his ability to cultivate a deep friendship without any pandering or false affection. And this despite the fact that the published correspondence is that which met the criterion of philosophical viability, thereby lamentably leaving out the more personal commentary.

The story quite simply is this: When Arthur Bentley was a young lecturer in sociology in the late 1890's at the University of Chicago, he audited some of Dewey's courses. He did not make Dewey's acquaintance at that time and went on to a career in political journalism and free-lance speculation in logic and mathematics. In 1932, almost forty years later, he sent Dewey the following letter from Paoli, Indiana:

MY DEAR PROFESSOR DEWEY:

While you were at Chicago, I had a place at the outer edge
of one of your courses, where I secured a certain manner of
vision which, so far as I can appraise such things, I have long
regarded as one of the three or four most valuable aids I have
received. I have at length found a region of investigation in
which some tentative results can be secured, and I am permit-
ting myself to send you a copy of the resulting book,
Linguistic Analysis of Mathematics. I do this, I may add, entirely for my own satisfaction by way of making ac-
knowledgements.

With the strongest wishes for success in your present
political work.

Sincerely yours,
ARTHUR F. BENTLEY[22]

Some two and a half years later Dewey answered this letter. Addressed
to "Dear Mr. Bentley," the first few lines read as follows:

Some time ago I received a copy of your *Linguistic
Analysis of Mathematics*. I fear I didn't acknowledge it. At
all events as I was occupied with other matters, I didn't read
it. Recently I have read it, and am still re-reading it. It has
given me more enlightenment and intellectual help than any
book I have read for a very long time. . . .[23]

Thus began a correspondence that was to last for almost twenty
years, covering Dewey's age-span from seventy-three to ninety-two and
Bentley's from sixty-two to eighty-one. They ranged over the full spectrum of contemporary philosophy, made visits into the past, and
challenged friends and foes alike. They doubted and recast
philosophical term after term, and in passing they offered brilliant
analyses of ordinary language. Bentley, often acidic in style, was mostly
on the attack as directed to their philosophical peers. Dewey was forth-
right in opinion but gentle in manner, ever cutting through Bentley's
rhetoric to state their shared position with acumen and dignity. Slow to
be informal in address,[24] they became companions in inquiry, seemingly
sensing that the end of the correspondence would be the end of everything. In 1945, when eighty-five years of age, Dewey wrote to Bentley

that "there is no doubt you are right in feeling that we are leaving out lots of good stuff, but it isn't as if we weren't going to have a chance to write more in the future."[25] And indeed they did, publishing thirteen articles between 1945 and 1949 and revising them for their book *Knowing and the Known*. Throughout the correspondence Dewey evoked a freshness of approach and a constant willingness to begin over. In 1951 he formulated a new and massive task but hinted that he might not be able to manage it. Prescient to the end, he pointed to the problem at the center of what we now call bio-feedback in our attempt to humanize the new media. Dewey wrote to Bentley that "If I ever get the needed strength, I want to write on *knowing* as the way of behaving in which linguistic artifacts transact business with physical artifacts, tools, implements, apparatus, both kinds being planned for the purpose and rendering *inquiry* of necessity an *experimental* transaction. . . ."[26] It is then with considerable sadness that we read the opening lines of the next and last letter from Bentley to Dewey: "Dear John: I haven't heard from you for some time. In much the same figure of speech, however, I might say that I have not heard even from myself."[27] In not quite seven months from that letter John Dewey was dead.

John Dewey: A Philosophical Perspective

The selections contained in the present volumes constitute an ample representation of John Dewey's philosophy. They are chosen with both Dewey's chronological development and thematic presentation in mind. The editorial commentaries prior to each selection attempt to focus on a root concern of the piece, whether it be historical or problematic. The titles of each volume and the titles of the eight section headings have been chosen with an eye to providing an interpretive context for Dewey's philosophy.[28]

In *The Philosophy of John Dewey* I have subtitled the first volume *The Structure of Experience* and the second *The Lived Experience*. It would be an unfortunate irony if the reader took this separation to be indicative of a bifurcation in the thought of Dewey. To the contrary, Dewey held to no such separation in any fundamental sense, and indeed it can be said that the "lived experience" is precisely the ground from which the "structure of experience" is obtained. His point of departure and style of explication very much depended on the nature of the problem under consideration, although he usually found a way to integrate both concerns in even the most topical piece of writing. Consequently, although the ideal is to read these two volumes consecutively, they also stand on their merits independent of each other.

Dewey once described philosophy as "a generalized theory of criticism."[29] He also wrote that metaphysics is defined by its search for a "generic insight into existence."[30] Both of these positions indicate a concern for structure, but they also locate that structure in an ongoing process, and as a matter of fact, the attempt to delineate the meaning of existence is itself a factor to be considered. For example, in "Existence, Value and Criticism," Dewey writes that:

> The generic insight into existence which alone can define metaphysics in any empirically intelligible sense is itself an added fact of interaction, and is therefore subject to the same requirement of intelligence as any other, natural occurrence: namely, inquiry into the bearings, leadings, and consequences of what it discovers. The universe is no infinite self-representative series, if only because the addition within it of a representation makes it a different universe.[31]

From the sense of the above text, we could rightfully conclude that the search for the structure of experience *is* the lived experience. Thus for Dewey, in the most fundamental sense, philosophy deals with experience which is "had"—that is, undergone, lived. Yet, in functional terms, in this case the pedagogy of presentation, a difference does obtain between Dewey's writings on the meaning of experience and his writings on those specific clusterings of experiences which constitute problematic situations for man such that they elicit direction and possible resolution. Dewey's writings, then, on politics, the arts, society, education, and religion are not to be construed as merely applications of principles derived from his metaphysics. Rather, these writings should be seen as working from a change in venue, sensitized to the qualities of new data and new patterns of organization but nonetheless faithful to the experimental mode of inquiry, which runs consistently throughout all of his work. The "structure of experience" and "the lived experience" represent two contexts from which Dewey proceeds to articulate the nature of the human endeavor.

It is important to note that the term "experience" occurs in both subtitles and in five of the eight section headings. Indeed, it is a crucial term in most of the selections and throughout the entire corpus of Dewey's work. The very obviousness of the term "experience" makes it an unlikely candidate for a root philosophical notion, and Dewey agrees with William James that it is a double-barreled word, as with "history" and "life," referring both to *what* men do and *how* they are acted upon. The ambiguity here is not of semantic origin but is of the nature of man, who in touching is thereby touched. In "Experience and Philosophic Method"* Dewey elaborates on his comment that "experience is *of* as well as *in* nature."

> It is not experience which is experienced, but nature—stones, plants, animals, diseases, health, temperature, electricity, and so on. Things interacting in certain ways *are* experience; they are what is experienced. Linked in certain other ways with another natural object—the human organism—they are *how* things are experienced as well. Experience thus reaches down into nature; it has depth. It also has breadth and to an indefinitely elastic extent. It stretches. That stretch constitutes inference.

This text, as much as any single text can, conveys the core of Dewey's philosophy. Opening it up slightly, we have the following themes, corresponding in a general way to the concerns of the eight sections of these present volumes. The setting is the interaction of the human organism with nature or with the environment. Nature has a life of its own, undergoing its own relatings, which in turn become what we experience. Our own transaction[32] with the affairs of nature cuts across the givenness of nature and our ways of relating. This is *how* we experience *what* we experience. Dewey was a realist in the sense that the world exists independent of our thought of it, but the meaning *of* the world is inseparable from our *meaning* the world. Experience, therefore, is not headless, for it teems with relational leads, inferences, implications, comparisons, retrospections, directions, warnings, and so on. The rhythm of *how* we experience is an aesthetic, having as its major characteristic the relationship between anticipation and consummation, yet having other perturbations, as mishap, loss, boredom, and listlessness. Pedagogy becomes then the twin effort to integrate the directions of experience with the total needs of the person and to cultivate the ability of an individual to generate new potentialities in his experiencing and to make new relationships so as to foster patterns of growth. And politics is the struggle to construct an optimum environment for the realizing and sanctioning of the aesthetic processes of living. Finally, the entire human endeavor should be an effort to apply the method of creative intelligence in order to achieve optimum possibilities in the never-ending moral struggle to harmonize the means-end relationship[33] for the purpose of enhancing human life and achieving growth. In "The Construction of Good"* Dewey writes:

> The problem of restoring integration and cooperation between man's beliefs about the world in which he lives and his beliefs about the values and purposes that should direct his conduct is the deepest problem of modern life. It is the problem of any philosophy that is not isolated from that life.

Terms such as "integration," "interaction," "transaction," and "means-end relationships" are not objects of Dewey's philosophy so much as they are descriptions of both the affairs of nature and the method of inquiry. Frequently, working from two points of view or from two apparently isolated fields of inquiry, Dewey has the extraordinary capacity to cut across the conceptual and terminological gaps presented by engendering a version of the underlying problem which binds them, in a language closer to our actual experiencing.[34] This approach of Dewey finds him rarely introducing a technical term as a shortcut for the describing of the ongoing experience. The use of technical terms often gains clarity but at the price of isolating the language of the discipline from that of other disciplines and from common recognition by the larger community of inquiry. Dewey's awareness of the difficulty in achieving a rapprochement between philosophic purpose and fidelity to ordinary language is made clear in one of his letters to Arthur Bentley. Commenting on his preparation of a new edition of *Experience and Nature* in 1951, Dewey wrote that he decided to change the title to *Nature and Culture*: "I was dumb not to have seen the need for such a shift when the old text was written. I was still hopeful that the [philosophic] word 'Experience' would be redeemed by [being] returned to its idiomatic usages—which was a piece of historic folly, the hope, I mean. . . ."[35] The many critics of Dewey's prose style should be more aware that the gnarled character of some of his writing traces to a determined effort to articulate the character of our experiences in a language faithful to our way of having them and in as rich a descriptive version as possible.

A knowledge of two other general themes in Dewey's philosophy will be of assistance to the reader of these volumes. The first, which is at the center of Dewey's logic and epistemology, is his affirmation that "knowing is one mode of experiencing." Stated most clearly in "The

Postulate of Immediate Empiricism''* but often elsewhere and in different ways, Dewey's position is that the process of inquiry is that specific way of having experience in which things are ''experienced as known things,'' as ''compared with things experienced esthetically, or morally, or economically or technologically.'' Put another way, things are what they are experienced to be, only one way of which is to know them. One implication of this position taken by Dewey is that there are multiple ways of experiencing the world which do not necessarily translate into the specific conceptual apparatus that accompanies knowing about something. Without challenging, at this point, the too exhaustive distinction between the cognitive and noncognitive,[36] suffice it to say that for Dewey experiencing is a learning consistent with the variety of ways of experiencing. One such way is to experience by knowing about things and structuring their relationship in a logic of inquiry. His text in ''The Postulate of Immediate Empiricism''* will prove helpful here:

> By our postulate, things are what they are experienced to be; and unless knowing is the sole and only genuine mode of experiencing, it is fallacious to say that Reality is just and exclusively what it is or would be to an all-competent all-knower; or even that it *is* relatively and piece-meal, what it is to a finite and partial knower. Or, put more positively, knowing is one mode of experiencing, and the primary philosophic demand (from the standpoint of immediatism) is to find out *what* sort of an experience knowing is—or, concretely how things are experienced when they are experienced *as* known things.

In our discussion of approaches to these selections from the writings of John Dewey, one further general theme should be mentioned—namely, the role of the body in his philosophy. Less obvious than the concerns already examined and discussed rarely by commentators, it is nonetheless of central importance. Of course, for readers who are familiar with phenomenological and existential writings, Dewey's references to the body will seem tame and indirect. And for those who are acquainted with the work of Freud and the host of thinkers with allied concerns, the comparative absence of sexual themes in Dewey's writing may lead to the view that his interests were mainly cerebral and detached from the activities of the lived body. In effect, one does not find in Dewey's writing those hyperpersonal metaphors and descriptions that characterize so vividly the contemporary self-consciousness about bodily states and psychosexual activity. Even were Dewey to have had access to contemporary literature, it is doubtful that he would have altered his style dramatically. For one thing, despite his cosmopolitan experiences, he maintained a Yankee simplicity to his person, and the experience of the "underground" man or the world of a Kafka and Genet would be extremely peripheral to his vision. Also, Dewey was very wary of the seductive character of language and strove to avoid the use of the flamboyant phrase, choosing rather to make his point in the "plain style."

These limitations of perspective and style should not mislead us, however, into thinking that Dewey had no sense of the body or of the themes so central to contemporary thought. To the contrary, if we make some concessions to Dewey's style and allow him to speak in his own language, we discover at least three concerns that occupied him throughout his entire life and that attest dramatically to the presence of the lived body at the center of all of his philosophy. First, he insisted that the meaning of life was to be found in "growth"—that is, in an embodied process—rather than in a state of being, such as happiness or success. Second, he had unusual insight into nonsexual repression—that is, to the damage done to our person by the insensitivity, irrelevance, and manipulation of many of our institutions. As a case in point, Dewey's attempt to create a school distinctively for children, environmentally as well as intellectually, ranks with the work of Maria Montessori as one of the two early major efforts to liberate children in their bodily experience. Third, Dewey early maintained and finally articulated in detail in *Art as Experience* that the affective dimension of human activity was to be considered as central rather than peripheral in any evaluation of its worth. Further, he held that we learn of the affective not so much in the perusal of the affairs and objects of high culture but in sensitizing ourselves to the aesthetic rhythm of our bodies as we live our daily lives.

The body, then, is not alien to Dewey's philosophy. And given the rarity of his references to our sexual situation, we should remember that Dewey's philosophy had as its starting point the transaction of the organism with the world. Although agreeing to the primary role of the biological in any assessment of human life, some thinkers, such as Freud in *Civilization and Its Discontents*[37] and Norman O. Brown in *Life Against Death*,[38] are pessimistic about the outcome of such transactions. For them, and for countless other thinkers, repression and alienation necessarily dominate the life of man. John Dewey, while not pollyanna in his approach or naïve in his expectations, sees it differently. In "The Live Creature"* Dewey wrote that:

Life itself consists of phases in which the organism falls out of step with the march of surrounding things and then recovers unison with it—either through effort or by some happy chance. And, in a growing life, the recovery is never mere return to a prior state, for it is enriched by the state of disparity and resistance through which it has successfully passed. If the gap between organism and environment is too wide, the creature dies. If its activity is not enhanced by the temporary alienation, it merely subsists. Life grows when a temporary falling out is a transition to a more extensive balance of the energies of the organism with those of the conditions under which it lives.

At first glance this text may appear gentle and comforting. A closer look, however, reveals that alienation and death present themselves in the course of events, and the line between the temporary alienation necessary to the enhancement of life and the gap of permanent alienation which spells death, physical or spiritual, is a thin one. The blame for crossing it is placed not on nature, or on civilization, or on a *deus ex machina*, but on ourselves. In John Dewey's philosophy, the task of overcoming alienation and reconstituting the processes of living is one which is laced with chance, but the responsibility is ours and ours alone.

Notes

1 Cf. Ralph L. Rusk, *The Life of Ralph Waldo Emerson* (New York, Charles Scribner's Sons, 1949), and Stephen E. Whicher, "Emerson's Tragic Sense," Milton Konvitz and Stephen Whicher, eds., *Emerson* (New York, Prentice Hall 1962), pp. 39-45.

2 Until we receive the long-awaited biography of Peirce by Max H. Fisch, *cf.* Paul K. Conkin, *Puritans and Pragmatists* (New York, Dodd, Mead & Co., 1968), pp. 193-207.

3 For the literature about James, *cf.* John J. McDermott, "Introduction," *The Writings of William James* (New York, Random House, 1967), pp. xiii-xliv.

4 For the literature about Royce, *cf.* John J. McDermott, "Introduction," *The Basic Writings of Josiah Royce* (Chicago, University of Chicago Press, 1969), Vol. I, pp. 3-18.

5 *Cf. e.g.* Corliss Lamont, ed., *Dialogue on John Dewey* (New York, Horizon Press, 1959), and Max Eastman, *Great Companions* (New York, Farrar, Straus and Cudahy, 1959), pp. 249-98.

6 Jane Dewey, ed., "Biography of John Dewey," in Paul Arthur Schilpp, ed., *The Philosophy of John Dewey* (New York, Tudor Publishing Co., 1951) (1939), pp. 3-45.

7 *Cf.* Darnell Rucker, *The Chicago Pragmatists* (Minneapolis, University of Minnesota Press, 1969), for a detailed history of this movement. *Cf.* also Charles Morris, *The Pragmatic Movement* (New York, George Braziller, 1970), pp. 174-91 for a discussion of the Chicago School.

8 Rucker, *op. cit.*, p. vi.

9 *Cf.* Katherine Camp Mayhew and Anna Camp Edwards, *The Dewey School* (New York, Appleton-Century Co., 1936); Melvin C. Baker, *Foundations of John Dewey's Educational Theory* (New York, Atherton Press, 1966), pp. 136-57; and George Dykhuizen, "John Dewey: The Chicago Years," *Journal of the History of Philosophy*, II (October, 1964), pp. 227-53; "John Dewey in Chicago:

Some Biographical Notes," *Journal of the History of Philosophy*, III (October, 1965) pp. 217-33.

10 Jane Dewey, ed., "The Biography of John Dewey," p. 35. *Cf.* also Eastman, *op. cit.*, pp. 279-80.

11 John Dewey, *Experience and Education* (New York, Macmillan Co., 1956) (1938), p. 51.

12 *C.f e.g.* William W. Brickman, *John Dewey's Impressions of Soviet Russia and the Revolutionary World, Mexico—China—Turkey, 1929* (New York, Teacher's College, 1964).

13 A sample of Dewey's range of interests and the astonishing level of competence he maintained in addressing public issues can be found in Joseph Ratner, ed., *Characters and Events—Popular Essays in Social and Political Philosophy* (New York, Henry Holt and Co., 1929), 2 Vols. Much of Dewey's sensitivity to these matters can be traced to Jane Addams and her work at Hull House in Chicago.

14 Dewey participated widely in the labor movement. *Cf.* his sympathetic account of the president of the International Ladies Garment Workers Union in *David Dubinsky—A Pictorial Biography* (New York, Inter-Allied Publications, 1951), pp. 13-19, 21-28.

15 *Cf. The Case of Leon Trotsky* (New York, Merit Publishers, 1968) (1937), *passim*, and *Not Guilty* (New York, Harper and Bros., 1938).

16 *Essays in Honor of John Dewey* (New York, Henry Holt and Co., 1929). Of particular interest in this book is the large number of Columbia University colleagues and students of Dewey who join with his older Chicago colleagues in tribute. Thus, F. J. E. Woodbridge, an important philosophical influence on Dewey, and Herbert Schneider, John Herman Randall, Jr., and Sidney Hook, each to become a distinguished interpreter of Dewey's thought, are among the contributors.

17 *The Philosopher of the Common Man—Essays in Honor of John Dewey* (New York, Greenwood Press, 1968) (1940).

18 Sidney Hook, ed., *John Dewey—Philosopher of Science and Freedom* (New York, Dial Press, 1950).

19 *Cf.* John Dewey and Horace M. Kallen, ed., *The Bertrand Russell Case* (New York, Viking Press, 1941), and Bertrand Russell, *The Autobiography of Bertrand Russell—The Middle Years: 1914-1944* (New York, Bantam Books, 1969), pp. 341-44.

20 *Cf.* Howard Mumford Jones, *The Age of Energy—Varieties of American*

Experience, 1865-1915 (New York, Viking Press, 1971), p. 184. *Cf.* also, Eastman, *op. cit.*, pp. 288-89.

21 Sidney Ratner, Jules Altman, and James E. Wheeler, eds., *John Dewey and Arthur F. Bentley, A Philosophical Correspondence—1932-1951* (New Brunswick, Rutgers University Press, 1964). Surperbly introduced, edited, and printed, this book is a selection of almost 600 pages of correspondence from among 2,000 pieces collected by the editors. It also contains two previously unpublished essays by Dewey and drafts of material used subsequently in Dewey and Bentley's collaborative book, *Knowing and the Known* (Boston, Beacon Press, 1949).

22 Ratner *et. al.*, *Dewey and Bentley, op. cit.*, p. 51.

23 *Ibid.*

24 Dewey didn't drop the "Mr." in his salutation until 1939, while Bentley waited until 1942. And they did not use first names until 1945.

25 Ratner *et. al.*, *Dewey and Bentley, op. cit.*, p. 387.

26 *Ibid.*, p. 646.

27 *Ibid.*

28 There are a variety of sources available for the continued study of Dewey's thought. From among the vast array of writings about John Dewey, informative and trustworthy analyses of the philosophy can be found in Sidney Hook, Morton G. White, H. S. Thayer, and Richard J. Bernstein. Imaginative efforts to relate Dewey's thought to other philosophical and cultural traditions characterize recent work by Robert C. Pollock, Ralph W. Sleeper, Reginald Archambault, and Richard J. Bernstein. A thorough survey of Dewey's main interests is provided in Jo-Ann Boydston's *Guide to the Works of John Dewey* (Carbondale, Southern Illinois University Press, 1969).

29 John Dewey, *Experience and Nature* (New York, Dover Publications, 1958), p. xvi.

30 *Ibid.*, p. 414.

31 The criticism of a "self-representative series" refers to a doctrine held for a time by Josiah Royce.

32 In order to overcome the dualism possibly associated with the term "interaction," Dewey, late in life, came to prefer "transaction." *Cf.* Ratner *et al.*, *Dewey and Bentley, op. cit.*, pp. 613-14.

33 *Cf.* John Dewey, *Reconstruction in Philosophy* (Boston, Beacon Press, 1948), p. 73. "When we take means for ends we indeed fall into moral material-

ism. But when we take ends without regard to means we degenerate into sentimentalism. In the name of the ideal we fall back upon mere luck and chance and magic or exhortation and preaching; or else upon a fanaticism that will force the realization of preconceived ends at any cost.''

34 *Cf.* the comment on Dewey's ability to cut across different and even polarized fields of inquiry in C. Wright Mills, *Sociology and Pragmatism* (New York, Paine-Whitman Publishers, 1964), pp. 314-15.

35 Ratner *et al.*, *Dewey and Bentley, op. cit.*, p. 643.

36 Dewey did not hold to a rigid distinction between cognitive and noncognitive experiences. *Cf.* John Dewey, "Experience, Knowledge and Value," in Schilpp, *op. cit.*, pp. 532-33. "My theory of the relation of cognitive experiences to other modes of experience is based upon the fact that *connections* exist in the most immediate non-cognitive experience, and when the experienced situation becomes problematic, the connections are developed into distinctive objects of knowledge, whether of common sense or of science.''

37 Sigmund Freud, *Civilization and Its Discontents* (London, Hogarth Press, 1953) (1930).

38 Norman O. Brown, *Life Against Death* (Middletown, Wesleyan University Press, 1959).

Chronology

1859 Born on October 20, in Burlington, Vermont
1879 Graduates from University of Vermont
     Begins teaching high school at Oil City, Pennsylvania
1881 Teaches in Charlotte, Vermont, and studies philosophy with H. A.
     P. Torrey
1882 Graduate student, Johns Hopkins University
1884 PhD, Johns Hopkins University
     Begins teaching philosophy at the University of Michigan, 1884-88
1886 Marries Alice Chipman
1888 Professor of philosophy, University of Minnesota
1889 Professor of philosophy, University of Michigan, 1889-94
1894 Professor of philosophy and chairman of the Department of
     Philosophy, Psychology, and Education, University of Chicago,
     1894-1904
1899 President of the American Psychological Association, 1899-1900
1904 Professor of philosophy, Columbia University, 1904-30
1905 President of the American Philosophical Association, 1905-06
1915 A founder and first president of the American Association of
     University Professors
1919 Lectures in Japan
     Lectures in China, 1919-21
1924 Visits schools in Turkey
1926 Visits schools in Mexico
1927 Death of Alice Chipman Dewey
1928 Visits schools in Soviet Russia
1930 Professor Emeritus, Columbia
1946 Married to Roberta (Lowitz) Grant
1952 Dies on June 1, in New York City

Bibliography

Three major bibliographies of John Dewey's writing are now extant. Two of them are arranged chronologically and the third is by subject matter.

1) "Writings of John Dewey, 1882-1950," in Paul Arthur Schilipp, ed., *The Philosophy of John Dewey.* New York, Tudor Publishing Company, 1951, pp. 609-86.
2) "Writings of John Dewey," in *John Dewey: A Centennial Bibliography (1882-1962),* edited and annotated by Milton Halsey Thomas. Chicago, University of Chicago Press, 1962, pp. 1-153, 298.
3) Jo-Ann Boydston, ed., *Guide to the Works of John Dewey.* Carbondale, Southern Illinois University Press, 1970 (Paperback edition, 1972).

John Dewey's writings have been translated into many other languages. For this information, consult Jo-Ann Boydston and Robert L. Andresen, eds., *John Dewey: A Checklist of Translations, 1900-1967.* Carbondale, Southern Illinois University Press, 1969. For a list of "Writings About John Dewey" consult Thomas, *John Dewey: A Centennial Bibliography,* pp. 195-293.

The following bibliography serves as an introductory list of Dewey's most important books and collections of essays.

Writings of John Dewey
1882-98
1) *The Early Works of John Dewey.* Carbondale, Southern Illinois University Press, 1967, 1967, 1969, 1971, 1972, 5 vols.

1900
2) *The School and Society.* Chicago, University of Chicago Press, 129 pp. (Rev. ed. 1915, Paperback, Phoenix Books, 1956).

3) *The Child and the Curriculum*. Chicago, University of Chicago Press, 40 pp. (Paperback, Phoenix Books, 1956).

1910
4) *How We Think*. Boston, D. C. Heath and Co., 224 pp. (Rev. ed. 1933).
5) *The Influence of Darwin and Other Essays on Contemporary Thought*. New York, Henry Holt and Co., 309 pp. (Paperback, Midland Books, 1965).

1916
6) *Democracy and Education*. New York, Macmillan Co., 434 pp. (Macmillan Paperbacks, 1961).
7) *Essays in Experimental Logic*. Chicago, University of Chicago Press, 444 pp. (Paperback, Dover Books, n.d.).

1917
8) "The Need for a Recovery of Philosophy," in *Creative Intelligence, Essays in the Pragmatic Attitude*. New York, Henry Holt and Co., pp. 3-69.

1920
9) *Reconstruction in Philosophy*. New York, Henry Holt and Co., 224 pp. (Paperback, enlarged edition, Beacon Press, 1957).

1922
10) *Human Nature and Conduct*. New York, Henry Holt and Co., 336 pp. (Modern Library edition, 1930).

1925
11) *Experience and Nature*. Chicago, Open Court Publishing Co., 443 pp. (Rev. ed., New York, W. W. Norton and Co., 1929). (Paperback, Dover Books, 1958.)

1927
12) *The Public and Its Problems*. New York, Henry Holt and Co., 224 pp. (Paperback, Alan Swallow, 1957).

1929
13) Joseph Ratner, ed., *Characters and Events: Popular Essays in Social a...d Political Philosophy*. New York, Henry Holt and Co., 2 vols.
14) *The Quest for Certainty*. New York, Minton, Balch and Co., 318 pp. (Paperback, Capricorn Books, 1960).

1930
15) *Individualism Old and New*. New York, Minton, Balch and Co., 171 pp. (Paperback, Capricorn Books, 1962).

1931
16) *Philosophy and Civilization*. New York, Minton, Balch and Co., 334 pp. (Paperback, Capricorn Books, 1963).

1932
17) John Dewey and James H. Tufts, *Ethics—Revised Edition*. New York, Henry Holt and Co., 528 pp.

1934
18) *Art as Experience*. New York, Minton, Balch and Co., 355 pp. (Paperback, Capricorn Books, 1959).
19) *A Common Faith*. New Haven, Yale University Press, 87 pp. (Paperback, Yale, 1960).

1935
20) *Liberalism and Social Action*. New York, G. P. Putnam's Sons, 93 pp. (Paperback, Capricorn Books, 1963).

1938
21) *Logic: The Theory of Inquiry*. New York, Henry Holt and Co., 546 pp.
22) *Experience and Education*. New York, Macmillan Co., 116 pp. (Paperback, Collier Books, 1963).

1939
23) Joseph Ratner, ed., *Intelligence in the Modern World: John Dewey's Philosophy*. New York, Modern Library, 1,077 pp.
24) *Freedom and Culture*. New York, G. P. Putnam's Sons, 176 pp. (Paperback, Capricorn Books, 1963).
25) *Theory of Valuation*. Chicago, University of Chicago Press, 67 pp. (Published originally in the *International Encyclopedia of Unified Science*, Vol. II, No. 4).
26) "Experience, Knowledge and Value: A Rejoinder," in Paul Arthur Schilpp, ed., *The Philosophy of John Dewey*. Evanston, Northwestern University Press, pp. 517-608.

1946
27) *Problems of Men*. New York, Philosophical Library, 424 pp.

1949
28) John Dewey and Arthur F. Bentley, *Knowing and the Known*. Boston, Beacon Press, 334 pp. (Paperback).

1960
29) Richard J. Bernstein, ed., *Dewey on Experience, Nature and Freedom*. New York, Library of Liberal Arts, 293 pp. (Paperback).

1963
30) Joseph Ratner, ed., *Philosophy, Psychology and Social Practice*. New York, G. P. Putnam's Sons, 315 pp. (Paperback, Capricorn Books, 1965).

1964
31) Reginald D. Archambault, ed., *John Dewey on Education*. New York, Modern Library, 439 pp.
32) William W. Brickman, ed., *John Dewey's Impression of Soviet Russia and the Revolutionary World: Mexico—China—Turkey*. New York, Teachers College Publications, 178 pp. (Paperback).

33) Sidney Ratner and Jules Altman, eds., *John Dewey and Arthur Bentley: A Philosophical Correspondence, 1932-1951*. New Brunswick, Rutgers University Press, 737 pp.

1966
34) Reginald D. Archambault, ed., *John Dewey—Lectures in the Philosophy of Education: 1899*. New York, Random House, 366 pp.

1973
35) Robert W. Clopton and Tsuin-chen Ou, eds., *John Dewey, Lectures in China, 1919-1920*. Honolulu, University Press of Hawaii, 337 pp.

1976
36) Jo Ann Boydston, ed., *John Dewey: The Middle Works, 1899-1924*. Carbondale, Southern Illinois University Press (Of the fifteen volumes projected, ten have been published thus far, bringing the series to 1917).

1977
37) Sidney Morgenbesser, ed., *Dewey and His Critics: Essays from The Journal of Philosophy*. New York, *Journal of Philosophy*, 705 pp.

Editor's Note on the Text

The selections in these volumes are each complete in themselves. They were originally chapters in books or essays written for journals and collections of essays. With the exception of an occasional transitional sentence at the beginning or end of a selection, no editorial excisions have been made. A few typographical errors in the original text have been corrected.

Southern Illinois University Press is publishing a complete critical edition of Dewey's work. At this writing, four volumes have appeared, with the fifth imminent. Thus far, only three of the selections in the present volumes have been edited critically by Southern Illinois University Press. They are: "Kant and Philosophic Method," "The Psychological Standpoint," and "Psychology as Philosophic Method." These essays as printed in the critical editions of *The Early Works* are not altered in any substantial way. The critical apparatus, however, that accompanies those editions is very informative as to verifying and providing Dewey's source material. The most signal contribution of this critical apparatus is to make it clear that Dewey was notoriously careless in citing the texts of other thinkers. Serious students of John Dewey are encouraged to utilize the critical editions as they appear. It is to be hoped that the impressive work of the Center for Dewey Studies at Southern Illinois University is to be followed by similar efforts on behalf of William James and Josiah Royce.

The material in the present volumes is cited as to the edition used. If the date of this edition is later than that of the original publication, the latter date is added in parentheses. I have used the latest version of Dewey's writings except in the case of "The Reflex Arc Concept in Psychology." That was chosen for historical reasons over the later, slightly changed, retitled piece "The Unit of Behavior." When Dewey refers to previous or subsequent material, the reference is to the original source and not to the selections in these volumes, unless consecutive chapters have been reprinted. Finally, an asterisk accompanying a reference in the Preface or Introduction indicates that the selection is contained in these volumes.

Respect for experience is respect for its possibilities in thought and knowledge as well as an enforced attention to its joys and sorrows. Intellectual piety toward experience is a precondition of the direction of life and of tolerant and generous cooperation among men. Respect for the things of experience alone brings with it such a respect for others, the centres of experience, as is free from patronage, domination and the will to impose.

—JOHN DEWEY, *Experience and Nature, 1925*

Under such circumstances there is danger that the philosophy which tries to escape the form of generation by taking refuge under the form of eternity will only come under the form of a bygone generation. To try to escape from the snares and pitfalls of time by recourse to traditional problems and interests:—rather than that let the dead bury their own dead. Better it is for philosophy to err in active participation in the living struggles and issues of its own age and times than to maintain an immune monastic impeccability, without relevancy and bearing in the generating ideas of its contemporary present.

—JOHN DEWEY, "Does Reality Possess Practical Character?" *1908*

I
Historical Roots
and Reflections

With the exception of his early works on Immanuel Kant and Gott-fried Wilhelm von Leibniz and some subsequent isolated pieces, Dewey's concern with the history of philosophy was not pronounced, al-though it exercised a subtle influence on all of his writings. The material collected in this section indicates the range of Dewey's concerns and some of his judgments about prior philosophical efforts. Throughout these two columes many other *aperçus* on the history of philosophy will emerge from Dewey's point of view. It should be kept in mind that Dewey approached philosophy contextually—that is, as inseparable from wider cultural issues.

1. From Absolutism to Experimentalism*

Although sparse in detail about his personal life, this essay yields a number of judgments by Dewey which are crucial to any understanding of his life and work. In addition to the influence of some of his first teachers, Dewey stresses the significance of Hegel as "a permanent deposit" in his thinking and points especially to the work of William James as the "one specifiable philosophic factor which entered into my think-ing so as to give it a new direction and quality."

The reader should note also Dewey's admission of a "cer-tain skepticism about the depth and range of purely con-temporary issues" and his belief that on the whole, the forces that have influenced him "have come from persons and from situations more than books." Finally, as he points to the philosophical significance of his classic work on *Democracy*

* From *Contemporary American Philosophers*, George Plimpton Adams and William Pepperell Montague, eds. (New York, 1930), Vol. II, pp. 13-27.

2 THE PHILOSOPHY OF JOHN DEWEY

and Education, we should heed Dewey's chastisement that philosophers have failed to take education seriously, for this criticism is still pertinent.

In the late 'seventies, when I was an undergraduate, "electives" were still unknown in the smaller New England colleges. But in the one I attended, the University of Vermont, the tradition of a "senior-year course" still subsisted. This course was regarded as a kind of intellectual coping to the structure erected in earlier years, or, at least, as an insertion of the key-stone of the arch. It included courses in political economy, international law, history of civilization (Guizot), psychology, ethics, philosophy of religion (Butler's *Analogy*), logic, etc., not history of philosophy, save incidentally. The enumeration of these titles may not serve the purpose for which it is made; but the idea was that after three years of somewhat specialized study in languages and sciences, the last year was reserved for an introduction into serious intellectual topics of wide and deep significance—an introduction into the world of ideas. I doubt if in many cases it served its alleged end; however, it fell in with my own inclinations, and I have always been grateful for that year of my schooling. There was, however, one course in the previous year that had excited a taste that in retrospect may be called philosophical. That was a rather short course, without laboratory work, in Physiology, a book of Huxley's being the text. It is difficult to speak with exactitude about what happened to me intellectually so many years ago, but I have an impression that there was derived from that study a sense of interdependence and interrelated unity that gave form to intellectual stirrings that had been previously inchoate, and created a kind of type or model of a view of things to which material in any field ought to conform. Subconsciously, at least, I was led to desire a world and a life that would have the same properties as had the human organism in the picture of it derived from study of Huxley's treatment. At all events, I got great stimulation from the study, more than from anything I had had contact with before; and as no desire was awakened in me to continue that particular branch of learning, I date from this time the awakening of a distinctive philosophic interest.

The University of Vermont rather prided itself upon its tradition in philosophy. One of its earlier teachers, Dr. Marsh, was almost the first person in the United States to venture upon the speculative and dubiously orthodox seas of German thinking—that of Kant, Schelling, and Hegel. The venture, to be sure, was made largely by way of Coleridge; Marsh edited an American edition of Coleridge's *Aids to Reflec-*

tion. Even this degree of speculative generalization, in its somewhat obvious tendency to rationalize the body of Christian theological doctrines, created a flutter in ecclesiastical dovecots. In particular, a controversy was carried on between the Germanizing rationalizers and the orthodox representatives of the Scottish school of thought through the representatives of the latter at Princeton. I imagine—although it is a very long time since I have had any contact with this material—that the controversy still provides data for a section, if not a chapter, in the history of thought in this country.

Although the University retained pride in its pioneer work, and its atmosphere was for those days theologically "liberal"—of the Congregational type—the teaching of philosophy had become more restrained in tone, more influenced by the still dominant Scotch school. Its professor, Mr. H. A. P. Torrey, was a man of genuinely sensitive and cultivated mind, with marked esthetic interest and taste, which, in a more congenial atmosphere than that of northern New England in those days, would have achieved something significant. He was, however, constitutionally timid, and never really let his mind go. I recall that, in a conversation I had with him a few years after graduation, he said: "Undoubtedly pantheism is the most satisfactory form of metaphysics intellectually, but it goes counter to religious faith." I fancy that remark told of an inner conflict that prevented his native capacity from coming to full fruition. His interest in philosophy, however, was genuine, not perfunctory; he was an excellent teacher, and I owe to him a double debt, that of turning my thoughts definitely to the study of philosophy as a life-pursuit, and of a generous gift of time to me during a year devoted privately under his direction to a reading of classics in the history of philosophy and learning to read philosophic German. In our walks and talks during this year, after three years on my part of high-school teaching, he let his mind go much more freely than in the classroom, and revealed potentialities that might have placed him among the leaders in the development of a freer American philosophy—but the time for the latter had not yet come.

Teachers of philosophy were at that time, almost to a man, clergymen; the supposed requirements of religion, or theology, dominated the teaching of philosophy in most colleges. Just how and why Scotch philosophy lent itself so well to the exigencies of religion I cannot say; probably the causes were more extrinsic than intrinsic; but at all events there was a firm alliance established between religion and the cause of "intuition". It is probably impossible to recover at this date the almost sacrosanct air that enveloped the idea of intuitions; but somehow the cause of all holy and valuable things was supposed to stand or fall with the validity of intuitionalism; the only vital issue was that between intuitionalism and a sensational empiricism that explained away the reality of all higher objects. The story of this almost forgotten debate, once so urgent, is probably a factor in developing in me a certain scepticism about the depth and range of purely contemporary issues; it is likely that many of those which seem highly important to-day will also in a generation have receded to the status of the local and provincial. It also aided in generating a sense of the value of the history of philosophy; some of the claims made for this as a sole avenue of approach to the study of philosophic problems seem to me misdirected and injurious. But its value in giving perspective and a sense of proportion in relation to immediate contemporary issues can hardly be overestimated.

I do not mention this theological and intuitional phase because it had any lasting influence upon my own development, except negatively. I learned the terminology of an intuitional philosophy, but it did not go deep, and in no way did it satisfy what I was dimly reaching for. I was brought up in a conventionally evangelical atmosphere of the more "liberal" sort; and the struggles that later arose between acceptance of that faith and the discarding of traditional and institutional creeds came from personal experiences and not from the effects of philosophical teaching. It was not, in other words, in this respect that philosophy either appealed to me or influenced me—though I am not sure that Butler's *Analogy*, with its cold logic and acute analysis, was not, in a reversed way, a factor in developing "scepticism".

During the year of private study, of which mention has been made, I decided to make philosophy my life-study, and accordingly went to Johns Hopkins the next year (1884) to enter upon that new thing, "graduate work". It was something of a risk; the work offered there was almost the only indication that there were likely to be any self-supporting jobs in the field of philosophy for others than clergymen. Aside from the effect of my study with Professor Torrey, another influence moved me to undertake the risk. During the years after graduation I had kept up philosophical readings and I had even written a few articles which I sent to Dr. W. T. Harris, the well-known Hegelian, and the editor of the *Journal of Speculative Philosophy*, the only philosophic journal in the country at that time, as he and his group formed almost the only group of laymen devoted to philosophy for non-theological reasons. In sending an article I asked Dr. Harris for advice as to the possibility of my successfully prosecuting philosophic studies. His reply was so encouraging that it was a distinct factor in deciding me to try philosophy as a professional career.

The articles sent were, as I recall them, highly schematic and formal; they were couched in the language of intuitionalism; of Hegel I was then ignorant. My deeper interests had not as yet been met, and in the absence of subject-matter that would correspond to them, the only topics at my command were such as were capable of a merely formal treatment. I imagine that my development has been controlled largely by a struggle between a native inclination toward the schematic and formally logical, and those incidents of personal experience that compelled me to take account of actual material. Probably there is in the consciously articulated ideas of every thinker an over-weighting of just those things that are contrary to his natural tendencies, an emphasis upon those things that are contrary to his intrinsic bent, and which, therefore, he has to struggle to bring to expression, while the native bent, on the other hand, can take care of itself. Anyway, a case might be made out for the proposition that the emphasis upon the concrete, empirical, and "practical" in my later writings is partly due to considerations of this nature. It was a reaction against what was more natural, and it served as a protest and protection against something in myself which, in the pressure of the weight of actual experiences, I knew to be a weakness. It is, I suppose, becoming a commonplace that when anyone is unduly concerned with controversy, the remarks that seem to be directed against others are really concerned with a struggle that is going on inside himself. The marks, the stigmata, of the struggle to weld together the characteristics of a formal, theoretic interest and the material of a maturing experience of contacts with realities also showed themselves, naturally, in style of writing and manner of presentation. During the time when the schematic interest predominated, writing was comparatively easy; there were even compliments upon the clearness of my style. Since then thinking and writing have been hard work. It is easy to give way to the dialectic development of a theme; the pressure of concrete experiences was, however, sufficiently heavy, so that a sense of intellectual honesty prevented a surrender to that course. But, on the other hand, the formal interest persisted, so that there was an inner demand for an intellectual technique that would be consistent and yet capable of flexible adaptation to the concrete diversity of experienced things. It is hardly necessary to say that I have not been among those to whom the union of abilities to satisfy these two opposed requirements, the formal and the material, came easily. For that very reason I have been acutely aware, too much so, doubtless, of a tendency of other thinkers and writers to achieve a specious lucidity and simplicity by the mere process of ignoring considerations which a greater respect for concrete materials of experience would have forced upon them.

It is a commonplace of educational history that the opening of Johns Hopkins University marked a new epoch in higher education in the United States. We are probably not in a condition as yet to estimate the extent to which its foundation and the development of graduate schools in other universities, following its example, mark a turn in our American culture. The 'eighties and 'nineties seem to mark the definitive close of our pioneer period, and the turn from the civil war era into the new industrialized and commercial age. In philosophy, at least, the influence of Johns Hopkins was not due to the size of the provision that was made. There was a half-year of lecturing and seminar work given by Professor George Sylvester Morris, of the University of Michigan; belief in the "demonstrated" (a favourite word of his) truth of the substance of German idealism, and of belief in its competency to give direction to a life of aspiring thought, emotion, and action. I have never known a more single-hearted and whole-souled man—a man of a single piece all the way through; while I long since deviated from his philosophic faith, I should be happy to believe that the influence of the spirit of his teaching has been an enduring influence.

While it was impossible that a young and impressionable student, unacquainted with any system of thought that satisfied his head and heart, should not have been deeply affected, to the point of at least a temporary conversion, by the enthusiastic and scholarly devotion of Mr. Morris, this effect was far from being the only source of my own "Hegelianism". The 'eighties and 'nineties were a time of new ferment in English thought; the reaction against atomic individualism and sensationalistic empiricism was in full swing. It was the time of Thomas Hill Green, of the two Cairds, of Wallace, of the appearance of the *Essays in Philosophical Criticism,* co-operatively produced by a younger group under the leadership of the late Lord Haldane. This movement was at the time the vital and constructive one in philosophy. Naturally its influence fell in with and reinforced that of Professor Morris. There was but one marked difference, and that, I think, was in favour of Mr. Morris. He came to Kant through Hegel instead of to Hegel by way of Kant, so that his attitude toward Kant was the critical one expressed by Hegel himself. Moreover, he retained something of his early Scotch philosophical training in a common-sense belief in the existence of the external world. He used to make merry over those who thought the *existence* of this world and of matter were things to be proved by philosophy. To him the only philosophical question was as to the *meaning* of this existence; his idealism was wholly of the objective type. Like his contemporary, Professor John Watson, of Kingston, he combined a logical and idealistic metaphysics with a realistic epistemology. Through his teacher at Berlin, Trendelenburg, he had acquired a great reverence for Aristotle, and he had no difficulty in uniting Aristoteleanism with Hegelianism.

There were, however, also "subjective" reasons for the appeal that Hegel's thought made to me; it supplied a demand for unification that was doubtless an intense emotional craving, and yet was a hunger that only an intellectualized subject-matter could satisfy. It is more than difficult, it is impossible, to recover that early mood. But the sense of divisions and separations that were, I suppose, borne in upon me as a consequence of a heritage of New England culture, divisions by way of isolation of self from the world, of soul from body, of nature from God, brought a painful oppression—or, rather, they were an inward laceration. My earlier philosophic study had been an intellectual gymnastic. Hegel's synthesis of subject and object, matter and spirit, the divine and the human, was, however, no mere intellectual formula; it operated as an immense release, a liberation. Hegel's treatment of human culture, of institutions and the arts, involved the same dissolution of hard-and-fast dividing walls, and had a special attraction for me.

As I have already intimated, while the conflict of traditional religious beliefs with opinions that I could myself honestly entertain was the source of a trying personal crisis, it did not at any time constitute a leading philosophical problem. This might look as if the two things were kept apart; in reality it was due to a feeling that any genuinely sound religious experience could and should adapt itself to whatever beliefs one found oneself intellectually entitled to hold—a half unconscious sense at first, but one which ensuing years have deepened into a fundamental conviction. In consequence, while I have, I hope, a due degree of personal sympathy with individuals who are undergoing the throes of a personal change of attitude, I have not been able to attach much importance to religion as a philosophic problem; for the effect of that attachment seems to be in the end a subornation of candid philosophic thinking to the alleged but factitious needs of some special set of convictions. I have enough faith in the depth of the religious tendencies of men to believe that they will adapt themselves to any required intellectual change, and that it is futile (and likely to be dishonest) to forecast prematurely just what forms the religious interest will take as a final consequence of the great intellectual transformation that is going on. As I have been frequently criticized for undue reticence about the problems of religion, I insert this explanation: it seems to me that the great solicitude of many persons, professing belief in the universality of the need for religion, about the present and future of religion proves that in fact they are moved more by partisan interest in a particular religion than by interest in religious experience.

The chief reason, however, for inserting these remarks at this point is to bring out a contrast effect. Social interests and problems from an early period had to me the intellectual appeal and provided the intellectual sustenance that many seem to have found primarily in religious questions. In undergraduate days I had run across, in the college library, Harriet Martineau's exposition of Comte. I cannot remember that his law of "the three stages" affected me particularly; but his idea of the disorganized character of Western modern culture, due to a disintegrative "individualism", and his idea of a synthesis of science that should be a regulative method of an organized social life, impressed me deeply. I found, as I thought, the same criticisms combined with a deeper and more far-reaching integration in Hegel. I did not, in those days when I read Francis Bacon, detect the origin of the Comtean idea in him, and I had not made acquaintance with Condorcet, the connecting link.

I drifted away from Hegeliansim in the next fifteen years; the word "drifting" expresses the slow and, for a long time, imperceptible character of the movement, though it does not convey the impression that there was an adequate cause for the change. Nevertheless I should never think of ignoring, much less denying, what an astute critic occasionally refers to as a novel discovery—that acquaintance with Hegel has left a permanent deposit in my thinking. The form, the schematism, of his system now seems to me artificial to the last degree. But in the content of his ideas there is often an extraordinary depth; in many of his analyses, taken out of their mechanical dialectical setting, an extraordinary acuteness. Were it possible for me to be a devotee of any system, I still should believe that there is greater richness and greater variety of insight in Hegel than in any other single systematic philosopher—though when I say this I exclude Plato, who still provides my favourite philosophic reading. For I am unable to find in him that all-comprehensive and overriding system which later interpretation has, as it seems to me, conferred upon him as a dubious boon. The ancient sceptics overworked another aspect of Plato's thought when they treated him as their spiritual father, but they were nearer the truth, I think, than those who force him into the frame of a rigidly systematized doctrine. Although I have not the aversion to system as such that is sometimes attributed to me, I am dubious of my own ability to reach inclusive systematic unity, and in consequence, perhaps, of that fact also dubious about my contemporaries. Nothing could be more helpful to present philosophizing than a "Back to Plato" movement; but it would have to be back to the dramatic, restless, co-operatively inquiring Plato of the Dialogues, trying one mode of attack after another to see what it might yield; back to the Plato whose highest flight of metaphysics always terminated with a social and practical turn, and not to the artificial Plato constructed by unimaginative commentators who treat him as the original university professor.

The rest of the story of my intellectual development I am unable to record without more faking than I care to indulge in. What I have so far related is so far removed in time that I can talk about myself as another person; and much has faded, so that a few points stand out without my having to force them into the foreground. The philosopher, if I may apply that word to myself, that I became as I moved away from German idealism, is too much the self that I still am and is still too much in process of change to lend itself to record. I envy, up to a certain point, those who can write their intellectual biography in a unified pattern, woven out of a few distinctly discernible strands of interest and influence. By contrast, I seem to be unstable, chameleon-like, yielding one after another to many diverse and even incompatible influences; struggling to assimilate something from each and yet striving to carry it forward in a way that is logically consistent with what has been learned from its predecessors. Upon the whole, the forces that have influenced me have come from persons and from situations more than from books—not that I have not, I hope, learned a great deal from philosophical writings, but that what I have learned from them has been technical in comparison with what I have been forced to think upon and about because of some experience in which I found myself entangled. It is for this reason that I cannot say with candour that I envy completely, or envy beyond a certain point, those to whom I have referred. I like to think, though it may be a defence reaction, that with all the inconveniences of the road I have been forced to travel, it has the compensatory advantage of not inducing an immunity of thought to experiences—which perhaps, after all should not be treated even by a philosopher as the germ of a disease to which he needs to develop resistance.

While I cannot write an account of intellectual development without giving it the semblance of a continuity that it does not in fact own, there are four special points that seem to stand out. One is the importance that the practice and theory of education have had for me: especially the education of the young, for I have never been able to feel much optimism regarding the possibilities of "higher" education when it is built upon warped and weak foundations. This interest fused with and brought together what might otherwise have been separate interests— that in psychology and that in social institutions and social life. I can recall but one critic who has suggested that my thinking has been too much permeated by interest in education. Although a book called *Democracy and Education* was for many years that in which my philosophy, such as it is, was most fully expounded, I do not know that philosophic critics, as distinct from teachers, have ever had recourse to it. I have wondered whether such facts signified that philosophers in general, although they are themselves usually teachers, have not taken education with sufficient seriousness for it to occur to them that any rational person could actually think it possible that philosophizing should focus about education as the supreme human interest in which, moreover, other problems, cosmological, moral, logical, come to a head. At all events, this handle is offered to any subsequent critic who may wish to lay hold of it.

A second point is that as my study and thinking progressed, I became more and more troubled by the intellectual scandal that seemed to me involved in the current (and traditional) dualism in logical standpoint and method between something called "science" on the one hand and something called "morals" on the other. I have long felt that the construction of a logic, that is, a method of effective inquiry, which would apply without abrupt breach of continuity to the fields designated by both of these words, is at once our needed theoretical solvent and the supply of our greatest practical want. This belief has had much more to do with the development of what I termed, for lack of a better word, "instrumentalism", than have most of the reasons that have been assigned.

The third point forms the great exception to what was said about no very fundamental vital influence issuing from books; it concerns the influence of William James. As far as I can discover, one specifiable philosophic factor which entered into my thinking so as to give it a new direction and quality, it is this one. To say that it proceeded from his *Psychology* rather than from the essays collected in the volume called *Will to Believe*, his *Pluralistic Universe*, or *Pragmatism*, is to say something that needs explanation. For there are, I think, two unreconciled strains in the *Psychology*. One is found in the adoption of the subjective tenor of prior psychological tradition; even when the special tenets of that tradition are radically criticized, an underlying subjectivism is retained, at least in vocabulary—and the difficulty in finding a vocabulary which will intelligibly convey a genuinely new idea is perhaps the obstacle that most retards the easy progress of philosophy. I may cite as an illustration the substitution of the "stream of consciousness" for discrete elementary states: the advance made was enormous. Nevertheless the point of view remained that of a realm of consciousness set off by itself. The other strain is objective, having its roots in a return to the earlier biological conception of the *psyche,* but a return possessed of a new force and value due to the immense progress made by biology since the time of Aristotle. I doubt if we have as yet begun to realize all that is due to William James for the introduction and use of this idea; as I have already intimated, I do not think that he fully and consistently realized it himself. Anyway, it worked its way more and more into all my ideas and acted as a ferment to transform old beliefs.

If this biological conception and mode of approach had been prematurely hardened by James, its effect might have been merely to substitute one schematism for another. But it is not tautology to say that James's sense of life was itself vital. He had a profound sense, in origin artistic and moral, perhaps, rather than "scientific", of the difference between the categories of the living and of the mechanical; some time, I think, someone may write an essay that will show how the most distinctive factors in his general philosophic view, pluralism, novelty, freedom, individuality, are all connected with his feeling for the qualities and traits of that which lives. Many philosophers have had much to say about the idea of organism; but they have taken it structurally and hence statically. It was reserved for James to think of life in terms of life in action. This point, and that about the objective biological factor in James's conception of thought (discrimination, abstraction, conception, generalization), is fundamental when the rôle of psychology in philosophy comes under consideration. It is true that the effect of its introduction into philosophy has often, usually, been to dilute and distort the latter. But that is because the psychology was bad psychology.

I do not mean that I think that in the end the connection of psychology with philosophy is, in the abstract, closer than is that of other branches of science. Logically it stands on the same plane with them. But historically and at the present juncture the revolution introduced by James had, and still has, a peculiar significance. On the negative side it is important, for it is indispensable as a purge of the heavy charge of bad psychology that is so embedded in the philosophical tradition that it is not generally recognized to be psychology at all. As an example, I would say that the problem of "sense data", which occupies such a great bulk in recent British thinking, has to my mind no significance other than as a survival of an old and outworn psychological doctrine—although those who deal with the problem are for the most part among those who stoutly assert the complete irrelevance of psychology to philosophy. On the positive side we have the obverse of this situation. The newer objective psychology supplies the easiest way, pedagogically if not in the abstract, by which to reach a fruitful conception of thought and its work, and thus to better our logical theories—provided thought and logic have anything to do with one another. And in the present state of men's minds the linking of philosophy to the significant issues of actual experience is facilitated by constant interaction with the methods and conclusions of psychology. The more abstract sciences, mathematics and physics, for example, have left their impress deep upon traditional philosophy. The former, in connection with an exaggerated anxiety about formal certainty, has more than once operated to divorce philosophic thinking from connection with questions that have a source in existence. The remoteness of psychology from such abstractions, its nearness to what is distinctively human, gives it an emphatic claim for a sympathetic hearing at the present time.

In connection with an increasing recognition of this human aspect, there developed the influence which forms the fourth heading of this recital. The objective biological approach of the Jamesian psychology led straight to the perception of the importance of distinctive social categories, especially communication and participation. It is my conviction that a great deal of our philosophizing needs to be done over again from this point of view, and that there will ultimately result an integrated synthesis in a philosophy congruous with modern science and related to actual needs in education, morals, and religion. One has to take a broad survey in detachment from immediate prepossessions to realize the extent to which the characteristic traits of the science of to-day are connected with the development of social subjects—anthropology, history, politics, economics, language and literature, social and abnormal psychology, and so on. The movement is both so new, in an intellectual sense, and we are so much of it and it so much of us, that it escapes definite notice. Technically the influence of mathematics upon philosophy is more obvious; the great change that has taken place in recent years in the ruling ideas and methods of the physical sciences attracts attention much more easily than does the growth of the social subjects, just because it is farther away from impact upon us. Intellectual prophecy is dangerous; but if I read the cultural signs of the times aright, the next synthetic movement in philosophy will emerge when the significance of the social sciences and arts has become an object of reflective attention in the same way that mathematical and physical sciences have been made the objects of thought in the past, and when their full import is grasped. If I read these signs wrongly, nevertheless the statement may stand as a token of a factor significant in my own intellectual development.

In any case, I think it shows a deplorable deadness of imagination to suppose that philosophy will indefinitely revolve within the scope of the problems and systems that two thousand years of European history have bequeathed to us. Seen in the long perspective of the future, the whole of western European history is a provincial episode. I do not expect to see in my day a genuine, as distinct from a forced and artificial, integration of thought. But a mind that is not too egotistically impatient can have faith that this unification will issue in its season. Meantime a chief task of those who call themselves philosophers is to help get rid of the useless lumber that blocks our highways of thought, and strive to make straight and open the paths that lead to the future. Forty years spent in wandering in a wilderness like that of the present is not a sad fate—unless one attempts to make himself believe that the wilderness is after all itself the promised land.

2. Kant and Philosophic Method*

Written when he was a young graduate student at Johns Hopkins University, this essay of Dewey's attempts to locate a mooring point, a point of departure, for philosophic method. This piece is very cluttered and Dewey is yet to discover the importance of William James, who this very year, 1884, was to publish "On Some Omissions of Introspective Psychology," but even at this early date it is clear that for Dewey "experience" is a key term, and he is wary of abstract schema in philosophical inquiry.

On its subjective side, so far as individuals are concerned, philosophy comes into existence when men are confronted with problems and contradictions which common sense and the special sciences are able neither to solve nor resolve. There is felt the need of going deeper into

* From *Journal of Speculative Philosophy*, XVIII (April, 1884), pp. 162-74.

things, of not being content with haphazard views or opinions derived from this or that science, but of having some principle which, true on its account, may also serve to judge the truth of all besides. It is no matter of accident that modern philosophy begins, in Descartes, with a method which doubts all, that it may find that wherewith to judge all; nor is it meaningless that Kant, the founder of modernist philosophy, commences his first great work with a similar demand, and "calls upon Reason to undertake the most difficult of tasks, self-knowledge, and establish a tribunal to decide all questions according to its own eternal and unchangeable laws." This self-knowledge of Reason, then, is the Method and criterion which Kant offers.

Before we may see what is involved in this, it is necessary to see what in gist the previous methods had been, and why they had failed. The method of "intellectualism" begun by Descartes and presented to Kant through Wolff was (in one word): Analysis of conceptions, with the law of identity or non-contradiction for criterion. To discover truth is to analyze the problem down to those simple elements which cannot be thought away, and reach a judgment whose predicate may be clearly and distinctly seen to be identical with its subject. Analytic thought, proceeding by the law of identity, gives the method for philosophic procedure. Now, Kant in his pre-critical period[1] had become convinced that analysis does not explain such a conception as that which we have of causation: "How one thing should arise out of another, when it is not connected with it, according to the law of identity, this is a thing which I should much like to have explained." Nor again, while it may be, and undoubtedly is, the method for pure thought, does it give any means for passing from thought to existence. This, he would say, is no predicate of anything; it is part of no conception, and can be got by no analysis. Reality is added to our notions from without, not evolved from them. But, if logical thought is not adequate to such notions as cause, nor able to reach existence, it can be no method for discovering Absolute truth.

So Kant finds himself thrown into the arms of the Empiricists. It is experience which shows us the origin of an effect in a cause, and experience which adds reality or existence to our thoughts. What, then, is the method of "Empiricism"? Beginning with Bacon, at first it merely asserted that the mind must be freed from all subjective elements, and become a mirror, to reflect the world of reality. But this, as criterion, is purely negative, and required the positive complement of Locke. This

[1] See especially his essay on attempt to introduce the idea of negative quantity into philosophy.

method in a word is, *Analysis of perceptions with agreement as criterion*. In contrast with the intellectual school, which began with conceptions supposed to be found ready-made in the human mind, it begins with the perceptions impressed upon that blank tablet, the Mind, by external objects, and finds "knowledge to consist in the perception of the connection or agreement or disagreement of these ideas." But two questions arise: If truth or knowledge consists in perceptions, how, any more than from conceptions, shall we get to an external world? This question was answered by Berkeley in showing that, if knowledge were what this theory made it to be, the external world was just that whose *esse* is *percipi*. The second question is: What is agreement of perception? Agreement certainly means, as Locke said, "connexion," that is, mutual reference, or Synthesis. But how can this synthesis occur? The mind is a blank, a wax tablet, a *tabula rasa*, whose sole nature is receptivity, and certainly it can furnish no synthesis. Locke had avoided the difficulty by assuming that ideas come to us or are "given" more or less conjoined—that one has naturally some bond of union with another. But this, of course, cannot be. Simple impressions or perceptions are, as Hume stated, such as admit of no distinction or separation, and these are the ultimate sensations. These have no connection with each other, except perhaps the accidental one of following or occurring together in time, and so it is that "every distinct perception is a separate existence." Necessary connection among them, therefore, there can be none. Sensations are purely contingent, accidental, and external in their relations to each other, with no bonds of union. Any agreement is the result of chance or blind custom. Knowledge as the necessary connection of perceptions does not exist.

Kant consequently discovers, by a more thorough study of empiricism, that it too betrays him. It, no more than his former guides, can furnish him with a way of getting to an external world nor to knowledge at all. Nay, even self, some ghost of which was left him by the other method, has disappeared too.

What has been the difficulty? Descartes did not come to a standstill at once, for he had tacitly presupposed the synthetic power of thought in itself—had even laid the ground for a theory of it in his reference to the Ego, or self-consciousness. But his successors, neglecting this, and developing only the analytic aspect of thought, had produced a vacuum, where no step to existence or actual relations, being synthetic, could be taken. "Conceptions are empty." Nor had Locke been estopped immediately, for he presupposed some synthesis in the objective world; but it turns out that he had no right to it, and world, self, and all actual relations, being synthetic, have gone. "Perceptions are blind." The problem, then, is clearly before Kant, as is the key to its solution. Synthesis is the *sine qua non*. Knowledge is synthesis, and the explanation of knowledge or truth must be found in the explanation of synthesis. Hence the question of Method is now the question: How are synthetic judgments *a priori* possible? *A priori* means simply belonging to Reason in its own nature, so the question is, How and to what extent is Reason the source of synthesis?

The case stands thus: Pure thought is purely analytic; experience *per se* gives only a blind rhapsody of particulars, without meaning or connection—actual experience, or knowledge involves, *is* synthesis. How shall it be got? One path remains open. We may suppose that while thought *in itself* is analytic, it is synthetic when applied to a material given it, and that from this material, by its functions, it forms the objects which it knows. And such, in its lowest terms, is the contribution Kant makes. The material, the manifold, the particulars, are furnished by Sense in perception; the conceptions, the synthetic functions from Reason itself, and the union of these two elements are required, as well for the formation of the object known, as for its knowing.

To characterize Kant's contribution to Method, it remains to briefly examine these two sides of his theory: First, for the part played by the synthetic functions or the categories. These, in first intention, are so many conceptions of the understanding, and, as such, subject to analysis according to the law of identity, and thus furnish the subject matter of Logic. But they also have relation to objects, and as such, are synthetic and furnish the subject matter of Transcendental Logic, whose work is to demonstrate and explain their objective validity. This is done by showing that "the categories make experience and its objects for the first time possible." That is to say, Kant, after showing that the principles of identity and contradiction, though the highest criteria of logical thought, can give no aid in determining the truths of actual experience, inquires what is the criterion of truth for the latter, or what comes to the same thing, of the synthetic use of the categories as Transcendental Logic—and the answer he finds to be "possible experience" itself. In other words, the categories have objective validity or synthetic use because without them no experience would be possible. If Hume, for example, asks how we can have assurance that the notion of causality has any worth when applied to objects, he is answered by showing that without this notion experience as an intelligible connected system would not exist. By the categories the objects of experience are constituted, and hence their objective validity.

It follows, accordingly, that the system of experience may be determined, as to its form, by a completely made out system of categories. In them, as synthetic functions, constituting experience, we find the criterion of truth. But they themselves have a higher condition. As synthetic functions, they must all be functions of a higher unity which is subject to none of them. And this Kant calls the synthetic *unity* of Apperception or, in brief, self-consciousness. This is the highest condition of experience, and in the developed notion of self-consciousness we find the criterion of truth. The theory of self-consciousness is Method.

But this abstract statement must be further developed. It comes to saying, on the one hand, that the criterion of the categories is possible experience, and on the other, that the criterion of possible experience is the categories and their supreme condition. This is evidently a circle, yet a circle which, Kant would say, exists in the case itself, which expresses the very nature of knowledge. It but states that in knowledge there is naught but knowledge which knows or is known—the only judge of knowledge, of experience, is experience itself. And experience is a system, a real whole made up of real parts. It as a whole is necessarily implied in every fact of experience, while it is constituted in and through these facts. In other terms, the relation of categories to experience is the relation of members of an organism to a whole. The criterion of knowledge is neither anything outside of knowledge, nor a particular conception within the sphere of knowledge which is not subject to the system as a whole; it is just this system which is constituted, so far as its form is concerned, by the categories.

Philosophic Method, or the discovering of the criterion of truth, will consist, then, in no setting up of a transcendent object as the empiricists did, or of an abstract principle after the manner of the intellectual school. Since the categories, in and through self-consciousness, constitute experience, Method will consist in making out a complete table of these categories in all their mutual relations, giving each its proper placing, with the full confidence that when so placed each will have its proper place in experience, *i.e.*, its capacity for expressing reality determined.

But we have now strayed far from Kant. While having said nothing which is not deducible from his Transcendental Logic, we have abstracted from the fact that this holds only of the *form* of our knowledge; that there is also an *aesthetic*, and that thought is synthetic, not in itself, but only upon a material supplied to it from without. Turning to this, we find the aspect of affairs changed. Though the categories make experience, they make it out of a foreign material to which they bear a purely external relation. They constitute objects, but these objects are not such in universal reference, but only to beings of like capacities of receptivity as ourselves. They respect not existence in itself, but ourselves as *affected* by that existence. The system of categories furnished the criterion for all the knowledge we have, but this turns out to be no real knowledge. It is, Hegel says, as if one ascribed correct insight to a person, and then added that he could see only into the untruth, not the truth. Nor does the deficiency of our method end here. We had previously assumed that the categories as a system, or in their organic relation to self-consciousness, could be known. But it now turns out that nothing can be known except that to which this feeling of external matter through sensibility is given. To know this subject, or self-consciousness, is to make an object of it, and every object is sensible, that is, has a feeling which tells us how we are affected. But such a knowledge is evidently no knowledge of self-consciousness in its own nature. Thus, so far as knowledge is concerned, it must remain a bare form of self-identity, of "I = I," into definite organic relations with which the categories can never be brought. Hence, it appears that our picture of a method was doubly false—false in that after all it could not reach truth; false in that after all no such method was in itself possible. Our organic system of categories cannot constitute absolute truth—and no such organic system is itself knowable. Criterion and method we are still without. The golden prize, which seemed just within our hands as long as we confined ourselves to the Transcendental Logic, turns out to be a tinsel superfluity.

Yet, none the less, there was the suggestion of a method there, which is exactly what we wish. The only question is: Is its reference to the Aesthetic necessary? Is the latter a necessary part of Kant's theory, or, so far as it concerns the reception of external matter, an excrescence? The question is just here: Previous methods failed because they made no allowance for synthesis—Kant's because the synthesis can occur only upon matter foreign to it. Thought in the previous theories was *purely* analytic; in Kant's it is *purely* synthetic, in that it is synthesis of foreign material. Were thought at once synthetic *and* analytic, differentiating and integrating in its own nature, both affirmative and negative, relating to self at the same time that it related to other—indeed, through this relation to other—the difficulty would not have arisen.

Is the state of the case as Kant supposes? Must we say that Reason is synthetic only upon condition that material be given it to act upon, or, may it be, that while we must say that for the individual the material, nay, the form as indissolubly connected with the material, is given, yet, to Reason itself, nothing is given in the sense of being foreign to it? A slight examination will show us that, at least as far as Kant is concerned, the former supposition is but an arbitrary limitation or assumption which Kant imposed upon himself, or received without question from previous philosophy. On one side, he had learned that pure thought is analytic; on the other, that the individual is affected with sensations impressed upon it by external objects. At the same that he corrects both of these doctrines with his own deduction of the categories, he formally retains both errors.

So we have him asking at the very outset, as a matter of course: "In what other way is it to be conceived that the knowing power can be excited to activity, except by objects which affect our senses?" That is to say, he assumes at the outset that there is something external to Reason by which it must be excited. He perceives, what all admit, that an individual organized in a certain specific way with certain senses, and external things acting upon these senses, are conditions to our knowledge, and then proceeds to identify respectively this individual with the subject, and these things with the object, in the process of knowledge. But here it is that we ask with what right does he make this identification. If it is made, then surely the case stands with Reason as he says it does—it acts only upon a material foreign to it. Yet this individual and these things are but known objects already constituted by the categories, and existing only for the synthetic unity of apperception or self-consciousness. This, then, is the real subject, and the so-called subject and object are but the forms in which it expresses its own activity. In short, the relation of subject and object is not a "transcendent" one, but an "immanent," and is but the first form in which Reason manifests that it is both synthetic and analytic; that it separates itself from itself, that it may thereby reach higher unity with itself. It is the highest type of the law which Reason follows everywhere. The material which was supposed to confront Reason as foreign to it is but the manifestation of Reason itself. Such, at least, are the results which we reach in the Transcendental Deduction, and such are the results we consider ourselves justified to keep in opposition to Kant's pure assumptions.

We see the same thing in Kant's theory of phenomenon. Just as, concerning the process of knowledge, he assumes that subject and object are in external relation to each other, and hence Reason in contact with a foreign material, so here he assumes that the character of phenomenality consists in relation to an unknowable noumenon. The phenomenon is referred to something outside of experience, instead of being defined by its relation within experience—in which case it would be seen to be a phenomenon in its own nature, in that the categories which constitute it as such are not adequate to truth.

We have but to turn to Kant's derivation of the categories, to be again assured that Kant's theory of Reason as synthetic only in reference to foreign material is one purely assumed. As is notorious, these he took from the Logic of the School, which he held to give a complete table of all the forms of pure thought. When we turn to this table we find the highest point reached in it to be reciprocity. Now, reciprocity is precisely that external relation of two things to each other that we have already found existing, in Kant's theory, between subject and object in Knowledge—the relations of things that are independent of each other but mutually act upon each other. So, too, it is but another way of stating that Thought, analytic in itself, is synthetic when applied to an external material, or that this material, blind and haphazard in itself, is formed by something acting upon it. When Kant tells us, therefore, that the categories are not limited in their own nature, but become so when applied, as they must be, to determine space and time, we have in our hands the means of correcting him. They are limited, and express just the limitation of Kant himself. And Kant confesses their insufficiency as soon as he takes up the questions of moral and aesthetic experience and of life itself. Here we find the categories of freedom determined by ends, free production, organism to be everywhere present, while all through his *Critiques* is woven in the notion of an intuitive understanding which is the ultimate criterion of all truth, and this understanding is just what we have already met as the organic system of experience or self-consciousness.

Whether we consider the relations of subject and object, or the nature of the categories, we find ourselves forced into the presence of the notion of organic relation. The relation between subject and object is not an external one; it is one in a higher unity which is itself constituted by this relation. The only conception adequate to experience as a whole is organism. What is involved in the notion of organism? Why, precisely the Idea which we had formerly reached of a Reason which is both analytic and synthetic, a Reason which differentiates itself that it may integrate itself into fuller riches, a Reason that denies itself that it may become itself. Such a Reason, and neither an analytic Thought, nor an analytic Experience, nor a Reason which is analytic in itself, and synthetic for something else, is the ultimate criterion of truth, and the theory of this Reason is the Philosophic Method.

The two defects which we found before in Kant's theory now vanish. The method is no longer one which can reach untruth only, nor is it a method which cannot be made out. The track which we were upon in-following the course of the Transcendental Deduction was the right one. The criterion of experience is the system of categories in their organic unity in self-consciousness, and the method consists in determining this system and the part each plays in constituting it. The method takes the totality of experience to pieces, and brings before us its conditions in their entirety. The relations of its content, through which alone this content has character and meaning, whereby it becomes an intelligible, connected whole, must be made to appear.

It was the suggestion of this method, it was the suggestion of so many means for its execution, it was the actual carrying of it out in so many points that makes Kant's *Philosophy* the *critical* philosophy, and his work the *crisis,* the separating, dividing, turning point of modern philosophy, and this hurried sketch would not be complete if we did not briefly point out what steps have been taken toward the fulfilling of the Ideal. This is found chiefly in Hegel and his *Logic*. We can only discuss in the light of what has already been said why Hegel begins with Logic; why the negative plays so important a part in his philosophy, and what is the meaning of Dialectic. (1) Logic. One of Hegel's repeated charges against Kant is, that he examines the categories with reference to their *objective* character, and not to determine their own meaning and worth. At first it might seem as if this were the best way to determine their worth, but it ought now to be evident that such a procedure is both to presuppose that they are subjective in themselves, and that we have a ready-made conception of object by which to judge them—in short, it amounts to saying that these conceptions are purely analytic, and have meaning only in relation to an external material. Hence the method must examine the categories without any reference to subjective or objective existences; or, to speak properly, since we now see that there are no purely subjective or objective existences, without any relation to things and thoughts as two distinct spheres. The antithesis between them is not to be blinked out of sight, but it must be treated as one which exists within Reason, and not one with one term in and the other out. The categories which, for the individual, determine the nature of the object, and those which state how the object is brought into the subjective form of cognition, must be deduced from Reason alone. A theory performing this task is what Hegel calls Logic, and is needed not only to overcome Kant's defects, but is immediately suggested by his positive accomplishments. In our account of the Transcendental Deduction we saw that self-consciousness was the supreme condition of all the categories, and hence can be subject in itself to none of them. When it is made subject we have no longer the absolute self-consciousness, but the empirical ego, the object of the inner sense. In short, the categories constitute the individuals as an object of experience, just as much as they do the material known. Hence they are no more subjective than objective. We may call them indifferently neither or both. The truth is, they belong to a sphere where the antithesis between subject and object is still potential, or *an sich*. It is evident, therefore, that logic, in the Hegelian use, is just that criterion of truth which we thought at first to find in Kant's transcendental Logic—it is an account of the conceptions or categories of Reason which constitute experience, internal and external, subjective and objective, and an account of them as a system, an organic unity in which each has its own place fixed. It is the completed Method of Philosophy.

(2) The Negative in Hegel. It ought now to be evident that any Philosophy which can pretend to be a Method of Truth must show Reason as both Analytic *and* Synthetic. If History can demonstrate anything, it has demonstrated this, both by its successes and its failures. Reason must be that which separates itself, which differentiates, goes forth into differences, that it may then grasp these differences into a unity of its own. It cannot unite unless there be difference; there can be no synthesis where there is not analysis. On the other hand, the differences must remain forever foreign to Reason unless it brings them together; there can be no analysis where there is not synthesis, or a unity to be dirempted. If there be no synthesis in Reason, we end in the impotence of the former school of intellectualism, or in the helpless skepticism of Hume; if Reason be synthetic only upon a foreign material, we end in the contradictions of Kant. If there is to be *knowledge,* Reason must include both elements within herself. It is Hegel's thorough recognition of this fact that causes him to lay such emphasis on the negative. Pure affirmation or identity reaches its summit in Spinoza, where all is lost in the infinite substance of infinite attributes, as waves in the sea. Yet even Spinoza was obliged to introduce the negative, the determinations, the modes, though he never could succeed in getting them by any means from his pure affirmation. In Hume we find pure difference or negation, the manifold particularization of sensations, but even he is obliged to introduce synthetic principles in the laws of association, though he never succeeds in legitimately deriving them from sensations, for a "consistent sensationalism is speechless." Kant had tried a compromise of the principle, synthesis from within, difference from without. That, too, failed to give us knowledge or a criterion of Truth. Hegel comprehends the problem, and offers us Reason af-

firmative *and* negative, and affirmative only in and through its own negations, as the solution.

(3) Dialectic. We have now the notion of Dialectic before us in its essential features. We have seen that the desired object is a theory of the Conceptions of Reason in an organic system, and that Reason is itself both integrating and differentiating. Dialectic is the construction by Reason, through its successive differentiations and resumptions of these differences into higher unities, of just this system. If we take any single category of Reason—that is to say, some conception which we find involved in the system of experience—this is one specific form into which Reason has unified or "synthesized" itself. Reason itself is immanent in this category; but, since Reason is also differentiating or analytic, Reason must reveal itself as such in this category, which accordingly passes, or is reflected, or develops into its opposite, while the two conceptions are then resumed into the higher unity of a more concrete conception.

Since the system of knowledge is implicit in each of its members, each category must judge itself, or rather, Reason, in its successive forms, passes judgment on its own inadequacy until the adequate is reached—and this can be nothing but Reason no longer implicit, but developed into its completed system. Reason must everywhere, and in all its forms, propose itself as what it is, *viz.*, absolute or adequate to the entire truth of experience; but, since at first its *form* is still inadequate, it must show what is absolutely implicit in it, *viz.*, the entire system. That at first it does, by doing what it is the nature of the Reason which it manifests to do, by differencing itself, or passing into its opposite, its other; but, since Reason is also synthetic, grasping together, these differences must resolve themselves into a higher unity. Thus, Reason continues until it has developed itself into the conception which is in form equal to what itself is in content, or, until it has manifested all that it is implicitly. A twofold process has occurred. On the one hand, each special form of Reason or Category has been placed; that is, its degree of ability to state absolute truth fixed by its place in the whole organic system. On the other, the system itself has been developed; that is to say, as Reason goes on manifesting its own nature through successive differences and unities, each lower category is not destroyed, but retained—but retained at its proper value. Each, since it is Reason, has its relative *truth;* but each, since Reason is not yet adequately manifested, has only a *relative* truth. The Idea is the completed category, and this has for its meaning or content Reason made explicit or manifested; that is, all the stages or types of Reason employed in reaching it. "The categories are not errors, which one goes through on the way to the truth, but phases of truth. Their completed system in its organic wholeness is *the* Truth." And such a system is at once philosophic Method and Criterion; method, because it shows us not only the way to reach truth, but truth itself in construction; criterion, because it gives us the form of experience to which all the facts of experience as organic members must conform.

It will be seen, I hope, that we have not left our subject, "Kant's Relation to Philosophic Method"; for a crisis in nothing in itself. It is a crisis only as it is the turning point; and a turning point is the old passing into the new, and can be understood only as the old and the new are understood. The criterion of Kant is just this turning point; it is the transition of the old abstract thought, the old meaningless conception of experience, into the new concrete thought, the ever growing, ever rich experience.

3. Ralph Waldo Emerson*

In 1907, when commenting on Santayana's multivolumed *Life of Reason,* John Dewey wrote that "we are grateful to Mr. Santayana for what he has given us, the most adequate contribution America has yet made, always excepting Emerson, to moral philosophy." Although this essay on Emerson was first written in 1903, readers of the later John Dewey will be struck by the anticipation here of Deweyan themes: the affection for the ordinary, a logic of inquiry, and the close relationship of philosophy and poetry.

It is said that Emerson is not a philosopher. I find this denegation false or true according as it is said in blame or praise—according to the reasons proffered. When the critic writes of lack of method, of the absence of continuity, of coherent logic, and, with the old story of the string of pearls loosely strung, puts Emerson away as a writer of maxims and proverbs, a recorder of brilliant insights and abrupt aphorisms,

* From John Dewey, *Characters and Events: Popular Essays in Social and Political Philosophy*, Joseph Ratner, ed., Vol. I, pp. 69-77. Copyright 1929 by Holt, Rinehart and Winston, Inc. Copyright © 1957 by Joseph Ratner. Reprinted by permission of Holt, Rinehart and Winston, Inc. (Published originally in 1903.)

the critic, to my mind, but writes down his own incapacity to follow a logic that is finely wrought. "We want in every man a logic; we cannot pardon the absence of it, but it must not be spoken. Logic is the procession or proportionate unfolding of the intuition; but its virtue is as silent method; the moment it would appear as propositions and have a separate value, it is worthless." Emerson fulfills his own requisition. The critic needs the method separately propounded, and not finding his wonted leading-string is all lost. Again, says Emerson, "There is no compliment like the addressing to the human being thoughts out of certain heights and presupposing his intelligence"—a compliment which Emerson's critics have mostly hastened to avert. But to make this short, I am not acquainted with any writer, no matter how assured his position in treatises upon the history of philosophy, whose movement of thought is more compact and unified, nor one who combines more adequately diversity of intellectual attack with concentration of form and effect. I recently read a letter from a gentleman, himself a distinguished writer of philosophy, in which he remarked that philosophers are a stupid class, since they want every reason carefully pointed out and labelled, and are incapable of taking anything for granted. The condescending patronage by literary critics of Emerson's lack of cohesiveness may remind us that philosophers have no monopoly of this particular form of stupidity.

Perhaps those are nearer right, however, who deny that Emerson is a philosopher, because he is more than a philosopher. He would work, he says, by art, not by metaphysics, finding truth "in the sonnet and the play." "I am," to quote him again, "in all my theories, ethics and politics, a poet"; and we may, I think, safely take his word for it that he meant to be a maker rather than a reflector. His own preference was to be ranked with the seers rather than with the reasoners of the race, for he says, "I think that philosophy is still rude and elementary; it will one day be taught by poets. The poet is in the right attitude; he is believing; the philosopher, after some struggle, having only reasons for believing." Nor do I regard it as impertinent to place by the side of this utterance, that other in which he said, "We have yet to learn that the thing uttered in words is not therefore affirmed. It must affirm itself or no forms of grammar and no plausibility can give it evidence and no array of arguments." To Emerson, perception was more potent than reasoning; the deliverances of intercourse more to be desired than the chains of discourse; the surprise of reception more demonstrative than the conclusions of intentional proof. As he said, "Good as is discourse, silence is better, and shames it. The length of discourse indicates the distance of thought betwixt the speaker and the hearer." And again, "If I speak, I define and confine, and am less." "Silence is a solvent that destroys personality and gives us leave to be great and universal."

I would not make hard and fast lines between philosopher and poet, yet there is some distinction of accent in thought and of rhythm in speech. The desire for an articulate, not for silent, logic is intrinsic with philosophy. The unfolding of the perception must be stated, not merely followed and understood. Such conscious method is, one might say, the only thing of ultimate concern to the abstract thinker. Not thought, but reasoned thought, not things, but the ways of things, interest him; not even truth, but the paths by which truth is sought. He construes elaborately the symbols of thinking. He is given over to manufacturing and sharpening the weapons of the spirit. Outcomes, interpretations, victories, are indifferent. Otherwise is it with art. That, as Emerson says, is "the path of the Creator to his work"; and again "a habitual respect to the whole by an eye loving beauty in detail." Affection is towards the meaning of the symbol, not to its constitution. Only as he wields them, does the artist forge the sword and buckler of the spirit. His affair is to uncover rather than to analyze; to discern rather than to classify. He reads but does not compose.

One, however, has no sooner drawn such lines than one is ashamed and begins to retract. Euripides and Plato, Dante and Bruno, Bacon and Milton, Spinoza and Goethe, rise in rebuke. The spirit of Emerson rises to protest against exaggerating his ultimate value by trying to place him upon a plane of art higher than a philosophic platform. Literary critics admit his philosophy and deny his literature. And if philosophers extol his keen, calm art and speak with some depreciation of his metaphysic, it also is perhaps because Emerson knew something deeper than our conventional definitions. It is indeed true that reflective thinkers have taken the way to truth for their truth; the method of life for the conduct of life—in short, have taken means for end. But it is also assured that in the completeness of their devotion, they have expiated their transgression; means become identified with end, thought turns to life, and wisdom is justified not of herself but of her children. Language justly preserves the difference between philosopher and sophist. It is no more possible to eliminate love and generation from the definition of the thinker than it is to eliminate thought and limits from the conception of the artist. It is interest, concern, caring, which makes the one as it makes the other. It is significant irony that the old quarrel of philosopher and poet was brought off by one who united in himself more than has another individual the qualities of both artist and metaphysician. At bottom the quarrel is not one of objectives nor yet of methods, but of the affections. And in the divisions of love, there always abides the unity of him who loves. Because Plato was so great he was divided in his affections. A lesser man could not brook that torn love, because of which he set poet and philosopher over against one another. Looked at in the open, our fences between literature and metaphysics appear petty—signs of an attempt to affix the legalities and formularies of property to the things of the spirit. If ever there lived not only a metaphysician but a professor of metaphysics it was Immanuel Kant. Yet he declares that he should account himself more unworthy than the day laborer in the field if he did not believe that somehow, even in his technical classifications and remote distinctions, he too, was carrying forward the struggle of humanity for freedom—that is for illumination.

And for Emerson of all others, there is a one-sidedness and exaggeration, which he would have been the first to scorn, in exalting overmuch his creative substance at the expense of his reflective procedure. He says in effect somewhere that the individual man is only a method, a plan of arrangement. The saying is amply descriptive of Emerson. His idealism is the faith of the thinker in his thought raised to its *nth* power. "History," he says, "and the state of the world at any one time is directly dependent on the intellectual classification then existing in the minds of men." Again, "Beware when the great God lets loose a thinker on this planet. Then all things are at risk. The very hopes of man, the thoughts of his heart, the religion of nations, the manner and morals of mankind are all at the mercy of a new generalization." And again, "Everything looks permanent until its secret is known. Nature looks provokingly stable and secular, but it has a cause like all the rest; and when once I comprehend that, will these fields stretch so immovably wide, these leaves hang so individually considerable?" And finally, "In history an idea always overhangs like a moon and rules the tide which rises simultaneously in all the souls of a generation." There are times, indeed, when one is inclined to regard Emerson's whole work as a hymn to intelligence, a paean to the all-creating, all-disturbing power of thought.

And so, with an expiatory offering to the Manes of Emerson, one may proceed to characterize his thought, his method, yea, even his system. I find it in the fact that he takes the distinctions and classifications which to most philosophers are true in and of and because of their systems, and makes them true of life, of the common experience of the everyday man. To take his own words for it, "There are degrees in idealism. We learn first to play with it academically, as the magnet was once a toy. Then we see, in the hey-day of youth and poetry, that it may be true, that it is true in gleams and fragments. Then, its countenance waxes stern and grand, and we see that it must be true. It now shows itself ethical and practical.'' The idealism which is a thing of the academic intellect to the professor, a hope to the generous youth, an inspiration to the genial projector, is to Emerson a narrowly accurate description of the facts of the most real world in which all earn their living.

Such reference to the immediate life is the text by which he tries every philosopher. "Each new mind we approach seems to require," he says, "an abdication of all our past and present possessions. A new doctrine seems at first a subversion of all our opinions, tastes and manner of living." But while one gives himself "up unreservedly to that which draws him, because that is his own, he is to refuse himself to that which draws him not, because it is not his own. I were a fool not to sacrifice a thousand Aeschyluses to my intellectual integrity. Especially take the same ground in regard to abstract truth, the science of the mind. The Bacon, the Spinoza, the Hume, Schelling, Kant, is only a more or less awkward translator of things in your consciousness. Say, then, instead of too timidly poring into his obscure sense, that he has not succeeded in rendering back to you your consciousness. Anyhow, when at last, it is done, you will find it is not recondite, but a simple, natural state which the writer restores to you." And again, take this other saying, "Aristotle or Bacon or Kant propound some maxim which is the key-note of philosophy thenceforward, but I am more interested to know that when at last they have hurled out their grand word, it is only some familiar experience of every man on the street." I fancy he reads the so-called eclecticism of Emerson wrongly who does not see that it is reduction of all the philosophers of the race, even the prophets like Plato and Proclus whom Emerson holds most dear, to the test of trial by the service rendered the present and immediate experience. As for those who condemn Emerson for superficial pedantry because of the strings of names he is wont to flash like beads before our eyes, they but voice their own pedantry, not seeing, in their literalness, that all such things are with Emerson symbols of various uses administered to the common soul.

As Emerson treated the philosophers, so he treats their doctrines. The Platonist teaches the immanence of absolute ideas in the World and in Man, that every thing and every man participates in an absolute Meaning, individualized in him and through which one has community with others. Yet by the time this truth of the universe has become proper and fit for teaching, it has somehow become a truth of philosophy, a truth of private interpretation, reached by some men, not others, and consequently true for some, but not true for all, and hence not wholly true for any. But to Emerson all "truth lies on the highway." Emerson says, "We lie in the lap of immense intelligence which makes us organs of its activity and receivers of its truth," and the Idea is no longer either an academic toy nor even a gleam of poetry, but a literal report of the experience of the hour as that is enriched and reinforced for the individual through the tale of history, the appliance of science, the gossip of conversation and the exchange of commerce. That every individual is at once the focus and the channel of mankind's long and wide endeavor, that all nature exists for the education of the human soul—such things, as we read Emerson, cease to be statements of a separated philosophy and become natural transcripts of the course of events and of the rights of man.

Emerson's philosophy has this in common with that of the transcendentalists; he prefers to borrow from them rather than from others certain pigments and delineations. But he finds truth in the highway, in the untaught endeavor, the unexpected idea, and this removes him from their remotenesses. His ideas are not fixed upon any Reality that is beyond or behind or in any way apart, and hence they do not have to be bent. They are versions of the Here and the Now, and flow freely. The reputed transcendental worth of an overweening Beyond and Away, Emerson, jealous for spiritual democracy, finds to be the possession of the unquestionable Present. When Emerson, speaking of the chronology of history, designated the There and Then as "wild, savage and preposterous," he also drew the line which marks him off from transcendentalism—which is the idealism of a Class. In sorry truth, the idealist has too frequently conspired with the sensualist to deprive the pressing and so the passing Now of value which is spiritual. Through the joint work of such malign conspiracy, the common man is not, or at least does not know himself for, an idealist. It is such disinherited of the earth that Emerson summons to their own. "If man is sick, is unable, is mean-spirited and odious, it is because there is so much of his nature which is unlawfully withholden from him."

Against creed and system, convention and institution, Emerson stands for restoring to the common man that which in the name of religion, of philosophy, of art and of morality, has been embezzled from the common store and appropriated to sectarian and class use. Beyond any one we know of, Emerson has comprehended and declared how such malversation makes truth decline from its simplicity, and in becoming partial and owned, become a puzzle of and trick for theologian, metaphysician and litterateur—a puzzle of an imposed law, of an unwished for and refused goodness, of a romantic ideal gleaming only from afar, and a trick of manipular skill, of specialized performance.

For such reasons, the coming century may well make evident what is just now dawning, that Emerson is not only a philosopher, but that he is the Philosopher of Democracy. Plato's own generation would, I think, have found it difficult to class Plato. Was he an inept visionary or a subtle dialectician? A political reformer or a founder of the new type of literary art? Was he a moral exhorter, or an instructor in an Academy? Was he a theorist upon education, or the inventor of a method of knowledge? We, looking at Plato through the centuries of exposition and interpretation, find no difficulty in placing Plato as a philosopher and in attributing to him a system of thought. We dispute about the nature and content of this system, but we do not doubt it is there. It is the intervening centuries which have furnished Plato with his technique and which have developed and wrought Plato to a system. One century bears but a slender ratio to twenty-five; it is not safe to predict. But at least, thinking of Emerson as the one citizen of the New World fit to have his name uttered in the same breath with that of Plato, one may without presumption believe that even if Emerson has no system, none the less he is the prophet and herald of any system which democracy may henceforth construct and hold by, and that when democracy has articulated itself, it will have no difficulty in finding itself already proposed in Emerson. It is as true to-day as when he said it: "It is not propositions, not new dogmas and the logical exposition of the world that are our first need, but to watch and continually cherish the intellectual and moral sensibilities and woo them to stay and make their homes with us. Whilst they abide with us, we shall not think amiss." We are moved to say that Emerson is the first and as yet almost the only Christian of the Intellect. From out such reverence for the instinct and impulse of our common nature shall emerge in their due season propositions, systems and logical expositions of the world. Then shall we have a philosophy which religion has no call to chide and which knows its friendship with science and with art.

Emerson wrote of a certain type of mind: "This tranquil, well-founded, wide-seeing soul is no express-rider, no attorney, no magistrate. It lies in the sun and broods on the world." It is the soul of Emerson which these words describe. Yet this is no private merit nor personal credit. For thousands of earth's children, Emerson has taken away the barriers that shut out the sun and has secured the unimpeded, cheerful circulation of the light of heaven, and the wholesome air of day. For such, content to endure without contriving and contending, at the last all express-riders journey, since to them comes the final service of all commodity. For them, careless to make out their own case, all attorneys plead in the day of final judgment; for though falsehoods pile mountain high, truth is the only deposit that nature tolerates. To them who refuse to be called "master, master," all magistracies in the end defer, for theirs is the common cause for which dominion, power and principality is put under foot. Before such successes, even the worshipers of that which to-day goes by the name of success, those who bend to millions and incline to imperialisms, may lower their standard, and give at least a passing assent to the final word of Emerson's philosophy, the identity of Being, unqualified and immutable, with Character.

4. The Influence of Darwinism on Philosophy*

The doctrine of evolution was of central importance to the development of classical American philosophy, particularly as found in the writings of C. S. Peirce, William James, G. H. Mead, and John Dewey. In this essay, Dewey sketches the climate of opinion which contexts the publication of the *Origin of the Species,* and he points to the new mode of inquiry that has emerged from the controversy about evolution. Of particular interest to present readers is Dewey's last paragraph, where he stresses the social-psychological character of the struggle over ideas and, in a vein anticipatory of recent work by Thomas Kuhn, contends that "in fact intellectual progress usually occurs through sheer abandonment of questions together with both of the alternatives they assume—an abandonment that results from their decreasing vitality and a change of urgent interest. We do not solve them: we get over them."

I

That the publication of the "Origin of Species" marked an epoch in

* From John Dewey, *The Influence of Darwin on Philosophy: And Other Essays in Contemporary Thought*, pp. 1-19. Copyright 1910 by Holt, Rinehart and Winston, Inc. Copyright 1938 by John Dewey. Reprinted by permission of Holt, Rinehart and Winston, Inc.

the development of the natural sciences is well known to the layman. That the combination of the very words origin and species embodied an intellectual revolt and introduced a new intellectual temper is easily overlooked by the expert. The conceptions that had reigned in the philosophy of nature and knowledge for two thousand years, the conceptions that had become the familiar furniture of the mind, rested on the assumption of the superiority of the fixed and final; they rested upon treating change and origin as signs of defect and unreality. In laying hands upon the sacred ark of absolute permanency, in treating the forms that had been regarded as types of fixity and perfection as originating and passing away, the "Origin of Species" introduced a mode of thinking that in the end was bound to transform the logic of knowledge, and hence the treatment of morals, politics, and religion.

No wonder, then, that the publication of Darwin's book, a half century ago, precipitated a crisis. The true nature of the controversy is easily concealed from us, however, by the theological clamor that attended it. The vivid and popular features of the anti-Darwinian row tended to leave the impression that the issue was between science on one side and theology on the other. Such was not the case—the issue lay primarily within science itself, as Darwin himself early recognized. The theological outcry he discounted from the start, hardly noticing it save as it bore upon the "feelings of his female relatives." But for two decades before final publication he contemplated the possibility of being put down by his scientific peers as a fool or as crazy; and he set, as the measure of his success, the degree in which he should affect three men of science: Lyell in geology, Hooker in botany, and Huxley in zoology.

Religious considerations lent fervor to the controversy, but they did not provoke it. Intellectually, religious emotions are not creative but conservative. They attach themselves readily to the current view of the world and consecrate it. They steep and dye intellectual fabrics in the seething vat of emotions; they do not form their warp and woof. There is not, I think, an instance of any large idea about the world being independently generated by religion. Although the ideas that rose up like armed men against Darwinism owed their intensity to religious associations, their origin and meaning are to be sought in science and philosophy, not in religion.

II

Few words in our language foreshorten intellectual history as much as does the word species. The Greeks, in initiating the intellectual life of Europe, were impressed by characteristic traits of the life of plants and animals; so impressed indeed that they made these traits the key to defining nature and to explaining mind and society. And truly, life is so wonderful that a seemingly successful reading of its mystery might well lead men to believe that the key to the secrets of heaven and earth was in their hands. The Greek rendering of this mystery, the Greek formulation of the aim and standard of knowledge, was in the course of time embodied in the word species, and it controlled philosophy for two thousand years. To understand the intellectual face-about expressed in the phrase "Origin of Species," we must, then, understand the long dominant idea against which it is a protest.

Consider how men were impressed by the facts of life. Their eyes fell upon certain things slight in bulk, and frail in structure. To every appearance, these perceived things were inert and passive. Suddenly, under certain circumstances, these things—henceforth known as seeds or eggs or germs—begin to change, to change rapidly in size, form, and qualities. Rapid and extensive changes occur, however, in many things—as when wood is touched by fire. But the changes in the living thing are orderly; they are cumulative; they tend constantly in one direction; they do not, like other changes, destroy or consume, or pass fruitless into wandering flux; they realize and fulfil. Each successive stage, no matter how unlike its predecessor, preserves its net effect and also prepares the way for a fuller activity on the part of its successor. In living beings, changes do not happen as they seem to happen elsewhere, any which way; the earlier changes are regulated in view of later results. This progressive organization does not cease till there is achieved a true final term, a *telos,* a completed, perfected end. This final form exercises in turn a plentitude of functions, not the least noteworthy of which is production of germs like those from which it took its own origin, germs capable of the same cycle of self-fulfilling activity.

But the whole miraculous tale is not yet told. The same drama is enacted to the same destiny in countless myriads of individuals so sundered in time, so severed in space, that they have no opportunity for mutual consultation and no means of interaction. As an old writer quaintly said, "things of the same kind go through the same formalities"—celebrate, as it were, the same ceremonial rites.

This formal activity which operates throughout a series of changes and holds them to a single course; which subordinates their aimless flux to its own perfect manifestation; which, leaping the boundaries of space and time, keeps individuals distant in space and remote in time to a uniform type of structure and function: this principle seemed to give insight into the very nature of reality itself. To it Aristotle gave the name, *eidos*. This term the scholastics translated as *species*.

The force of this term was deepened by its application to everything in the universe that observes order in flux and manifests constancy through change. From the casual drift of daily weather, through the uneven recurrence of seasons and unequal return of seed time and harvest, up to the majestic sweep of the heavens—the image of eternity in time—and from this to the unchanging pure and contemplative intelligence beyond nature lies one unbroken fulfilment of ends. Nature as a whole is a progressive realization of purpose strictly comparable to the realization of purpose in any single plant or animal.

The conception of *eidos*, species, a fixed form and final cause, was the central principle of knowledge as well as of nature. Upon it rested the logic of science. Change as change is mere flux and lapse; it insults intelligence. Genuinely to know is to grasp a permanent end that realizes itself through changes, holding them thereby within the metes and bounds of fixed truth. Completely to know is to relate all special forms to their one single end and good: pure contemplative intelligence. Since, however, the scene of nature which directly confronts us is in change, nature as directly and practically experienced does not satisfy the conditions of knowledge. Human experience is in flux, and hence the instrumentalities of sense-perception and of inference based upon observation are condemned in advance. Science is compelled to aim at realities lying behind and beyond the processes of nature, and to carry on its search for these realities by means of rational forms transcending ordinary modes of perception and inference.

There are, indeed, but two alternative courses. We must either find the appropriate objects and organs of knowledge in the mutual interactions of changing things; or else, to escape the infection of change, we *must* seek them in some transcendent and supernal region. The human mind, deliberately as it were, exhausted the logic of the changeless, the final, and the transcendent, before it essayed adventure on the pathless wastes of generation and transformation. We dispose all too easily of the efforts of the schoolmen to interpret nature and mind in terms of real essences, hidden forms, and occult faculties, forgetful of the seriousness and dignity of the ideas that lay behind. We dispose of them by laughing at the famous gentleman who accounted for the fact that opium put people to sleep on the ground it had a dormitive faculty. But the doctrine, held in our own day, that knowledge of the plant that yields the poppy consists in referring the peculiarities of an individual to a type, to a universal form, a doctrine so firmly established that any other method of knowing was conceived to be unphilosophical and unscientific, is a survival of precisely the same logic. This identity of conception in the scholastic and anti-Darwinian theory may well suggest greater sympathy for what has become unfamiliar as well as greater humility regarding the further unfamiliarities that history has in store.

Darwin was not, of course, the first to question the classic philosophy of nature and of knowledge. The beginnings of the revolution are in the physical science of the sixteenth and seventeenth centuries. When Galileo said: "It is my opinion that the earth is very noble and admirable by reason of so many and so different alterations and generations which are incessantly made therein," he expressed the changed temper that was coming over the world; the transfer of interest from the permanent to the changing. When Descartes said: "The nature of physical things is much more easily conceived when they are beheld coming gradually into existence, than when they are only considered as produced at once in a finished and perfect state," the modern world became self-conscious of the logic that was henceforth to control it, the logic of which Darwin's "Origin of Species" is the latest scientific achievement. Without the methods of Copernicus, Kepler, Galileo, and their successors in astronomy, physics, and chemistry, Darwin would have been helpless in the organic sciences. But prior to Darwin the impact of the new scientific method upon life, mind, and politics, had been arrested, because between these ideal or moral interests and the inorganic world intervened the kingdom of plants and animals. The gates of the garden of life were barred to the new ideas; and only through this garden was there access to mind and politics. The influence of Darwin upon philosophy resides in his having conquered the phenomena of life for the principle of transition, and thereby freed the new logic for application to mind and morals and life. When he said of species what Galileo had said of the earth, *e pur se muove,* he emancipated, once for all, genetic and experimental ideas as an organon of asking questions and looking for explanations.

III

The exact bearings upon philosophy of the new logical outlook are, of course, as yet, uncertain and inchoate. We live in the twilight of intellectual transition. One must add the rashness of the prophet to the stubbornness of the partizan to venture a systematic exposition of the influence upon philosophy of the Darwinian method. At best, we can but inquire as to its general bearing—the effect upon mental temper and complexion, upon that body of half-conscious, half-instinctive intellectual aversions and preferences which determine, after all, our more deliberate intellectual enterprises. In this vague inquiry there happens to exist as a kind of touchstone a problem of long historic currency that has also been much discussed in Darwinian literature. I refer to the old problem of design *versus* chance, mind *versus* matter, as the casual explanation, first or final, of things.

As we have already seen, the classic notion of species carried with it the idea of purpose. In all living forms, a specific type is present directing the earlier stages of growth to the realization of its own perfection. Since this purposive regulative principle is not visible to the senses, it follows that it must be an ideal or rational force. Since, however, the perfect form is gradually approximated through the sensible changes, it also follows that in and through a sensible realm a rational ideal force is working out its own ultimate manifestation. These inferences were extended to nature: (*a*) She does nothing in vain; but all for an ulterior purpose. (*b*) Within natural sensible events there is therefore contained a spiritual causal force, which as spiritual escapes perception, but is apprehended by an enlightened reason. (*c*) The manifestation of this principle brings about a subordination of matter and sense to its own realization, and this ultimate fulfilment is the goal of nature and of man. The design argument thus operated in two directions. Purposefulness accounted for the intelligibility of nature and the possibility of science, while the absolute or cosmic character of this purposefulness gave sanction and worth to the moral and religious endeavors of man. Science was underpinned and morals authorized by one and the same principle, and their mutual agreement was eternally guaranteed.

This philosophy remained, in spite of sceptical and polemic outbursts, the official and the regnant philosophy of Europe for over two thousand years. The expulsion of fixed first and final causes from astronomy, physics, and chemistry had indeed given the doctrine something of a shock. But, on the other hand, increased acquaintance with the details of plant and animal life operated as a counterbalance and perhaps even strengthened the argument from design. The marvelous adaptations of organisms to their environment, of organs to the organism, of unlike parts of a complex organ—like the eye—to the organ itself; the foreshadowing by lower forms of the higher; the preparation in earlier stages of growth for organs that only later had their functioning—these things were increasingly recognized with the progress of botany, zoology, paleontology, and embryology. Together, they added such prestige to the design argument that by the late eighteenth century it was, as approved by the sciences of organic life, the central point of theistic and idealistic philosophy.

The Darwinian principle of natural selection cut straight under this philosophy. If all organic adaptations are due simply to constant variation and the elimination of those variations which are harmful in the struggle for existence that is brought about by excessive reproduction, there is no call for a prior intelligent causal force to plan and preordain them. Hostile critics charged Darwin with materialism and with making chance the cause of the universe.

Some naturalists, like Asa Gray, favored the Darwinian principle and attempted to reconcile it with design. Gray held to what may be called design on the installment plan. If we conceive the "stream of variations" to be itself intended, we may suppose that each successive variation was designed from the first to be selected. In that case, variation, struggle, and selection simply define the mechanism of "secondary causes" through which the "first cause" acts; and the doctrine of design is none the worse off because we know more of its *modus operandi.*

Darwin could not accept this mediating proposal. He admits or rather he asserts that it is "impossible to conceive this immense and wonderful universe including man with his capacity of looking far backwards and far into futurity as the result of blind chance or necessity."[1]. But nevertheless he holds that since variations are in useless as well as useful directions, and since the latter are sifted out simply by the stress of the conditions of struggle for existence, the design argument as applied to living beings is unjustifiable; and its lack of support there deprives it of scientific value as applied to nature in general. If the variations of the pigeon, which under artificial selection give the pouter pigeon, are not pre-ordained for the sake of the breeder, by what logic do we argue that variations resulting in natural species are pre-designed?[2].

---

[1] "Life and Letters," Vol. I., p. 282; cf. 285.
[2] "Life and Letters," Vol. II., pp. 146, 170, 245; Vol. I., pp. 283-84. See also the closing portion of his "Variations of Animals and Plants under Domestication."

IV

So much for some of the more obvious facts of the discussion of design *versus* chance, as causal principles of nature and of life as a whole. We brought up this discussion, you recall, as a crucial instance. What does our touchstone indicate as to the bearing of Darwinian ideas upon philosophy? In the first place, the new logic outlaws, flanks, dismisses—what you will—one type of problems and substitutes for it another type. Philosophy foreswears inquiry after absolute origins and absolute finalities in order to explore specific values and the specific conditions that generate them.

Darwin concluded that the impossibility of assigning the world to chance as a whole and to design in its parts indicated the insolubility of the question. Two radically different reasons, however, may be given as to why a problem is insoluble. One reason is that the problem is too high for intelligence; the other is that the question in its very asking makes assumptions that render the question meaningless. The latter alternative is unerringly pointed to in the celebrated case of design *versus* chance. Once admit that the sole verifiable or fruitful object of knowledge is the particular set of changes that generate the object of study together with the consequences that then flow from it, and no intelligible question can be asked about what, by assumption, lies outside. To assert—as is often asserted—that specific values of particular truth, social bonds and forms of beauty, if they can be shown to be generated by concretely knowable conditions, are meaningless and in vain; to assert that they are justified only when they and their particular causes and effects have all at once been gathered up into some inclusive first cause and some exhaustive final goal, is intellectual atavism. Such argumentation is reversion to the logic that explained the extinction of fire by water through the formal essence of aqueousness and the quenching of thirst by water through the final cause of aqueousness. Whether used in the case of the special event or that of life as a whole, such logic only abstracts some aspect of the existing course of events in order to reduplicate it as a petrified eternal principle by which to explain the very changes of which it is the formalization.

When Henry Sidgwick casually remarked in a letter that as he grew older his interest in what or who made the world was altered into interest in what kind of a world it is anyway, his voicing of a common experience of our own day illustrates also the nature of that intellectual transformation effected by the Darwinian logic. Interest shifts from the wholesale essence back of special changes to the question of how special changes serve and defeat concrete purposes; shifts from an intelligence that shaped things once for all to the particular intelligences which things are even now shaping; shifts from an ultimate goal of good to the direct increments of justice and happiness that intelligent administration of existent conditions may beget and that present carelessness or stupidity will destroy or forego.

In the second place, the classic type of logic inevitably set philosophy upon proving that life *must* have certain qualities and values—no matter how experience presents the matter—because of some remote cause and eventual goal. The duty of wholesale justification inevitably accompanies all thinking that makes the meaning of special occurrences depend upon something that once and for all lies behind them. The habit of derogating from present meanings and uses prevents our looking the facts of experience in the face; it prevents serious acknowledgment of the evils they present and serious concern with the goods they promise but do not as yet fulfil. It turns thought to the business of finding a wholesale transcendent remedy for the one and guarantee for the other. One is reminded of the way many moralists and theologians greeted Herbert Spencer's recognition of an unknowable energy from which welled up the phenomenal physical processes without and the conscious operations within. Merely because Spencer labeled his unknowable energy "God," this faded piece of metaphysical goods was greeted as an important and grateful concession to the reality of the spiritual realm. Were it not for the deep hold of the habit of seeking justification for ideal values in the remote and transcendent, surely this reference of them to an unknowable absolute would be despised in comparison with the demonstrations of experience that knowable energies are daily generating about us precious values.

The displacing of this wholesale type of philosophy will doubtless not arrive by sheer logical disproof, but rather by growing recognition of its futility. Were it a thousand times true that opium produces sleep because of its dormitive energy, yet the inducing of sleep in the tired, and the recovery to waking life of the poisoned, would not be thereby one least step forwarded. And were it a thousand times dialectically demonstrated that life as a whole is regulated by a transcendent principle to a final inclusive goal, none the less truth and error, health and disease, good and evil, hope and fear in the concrete, would remain just what and where they now are. To improve our education, to advance our politics, we must have recourse to specific conditions of generation.

Finally, the new logic introduces responsibility into the intellectual life. To idealize and rationalize the universe at large is after all a confession of inability to master the courses of things that specifically concern us. As long as mankind suffered from this impotency, it naturally shifted a burden of responsibility that it could not carry over to the more competent shoulders of the transcendent cause. But if insight into specific conditions of value and into specific consequences of ideas is possible, philosophy must in time become a method of locating and interpreting the more serious of the conflicts that occur in life, and a method of projecting ways for dealing with them: a method of moral and political diagnosis and prognosis.

The claim to formulate *a priori* the legislative constitution of the universe is by its nature a claim that may lead to elaborate dialectic developments. But it is also one that removes these very conclusions from subjection to experimental test, for, by definition, these results make no differences in the detailed course of events. But a philosophy that humbles its pretensions to the work of projecting hypotheses for the education and conduct of mind, individual and social, is thereby subjected to test by the way in which the ideas it propounds work out in practice. In having modesty forced upon it, philosophy also acquires responsibility.

Doubtless I seem to have violated the implied promise of my earlier remarks and to have turned both prophet and partisan. But in anticipating the direction of the transformations in philosophy to be wrought by the Darwinian genetic and experimental logic, I do not profess to speak for any save those who yield themselves consciously or unconsciously to this logic. No one can fairly deny that at present there are two effects of the Darwinian mode of thinking. On the one hand, there are making many sincere and vital efforts to revise our traditional philosophic conceptions in accordance with its demands. On the other hand, there is as definitely a recrudescence of absolutistic philosophies; an assertion of a type of philosophic knowing distinct from that of the sciences, one which opens to us another kind of reality from that to which the sciences give access; an appeal through experience to something that essentially goes beyond experience. This reaction affects popular creeds and religious movements as well as technical philosophies. The very conquest of the biological sciences by the new ideas has led many to proclaim an explicit and rigid separation of philosophy from science.

Old ideas give way slowly; for they are more than abstract logical forms and categories. They are habits, predispositions, deeply engrained attitudes of aversion and preference. Moreover, the conviction persists—though history shows it to be a hallucination—that all the questions that the human mind has asked are questions that can be answered in terms of the alternatives that the questions themselves present. But in fact intellectual progress usually occurs through sheer abandonment of questions together with both of the alternatives they assume—an abandonment that results from their decreasing vitality and a change of urgent interest. We do not solve them: we get over them. Old questions are solved by disappearing, evaporating, while new questions corresponding to the changed attitude of endeavor and preference take their place. Doubtless the greatest dissolvent in contemporary thought of old questions, the greatest precipitant of new methods, new intentions, new problems, is the one effected by the scientific revolution that found its climax in the "Origin of Species."

5. The Development of American Pragmatism*

John Dewey once wrote "that we are no longer a colony of any European nation nor of them all collectively. We are a new body and a new spirit in the world." In the present essay, Dewey gives a balanced account of the European origins as well as the originality of American philosophy, particularly as found in the work of William James. Dewey also denies that pragmatism is simply a philosophical version of the popular American mind, seeing it rather as a method for bringing intelligence to bear on the problems of moral and social life and as an antidote to the often "unreflective and brutal" individualism which pervades American life.

The purpose of this article is to define the principal theories of the philosophical movements known under the names of Pragmatism, Instrumentalism, or Experimentalism. To do this we must trace their historical development; for this method seems to present the simplest way of comprehending these movements, and at the same time avoiding certain current misunderstandings of their doctrines and their aims.

The origin of Pragmatism goes back to Charles Sanders Peirce, the son of one of the most celebrated mathematicians of the United States, and himself very proficient in the science of mathematics; he is one of the founders of the modern symbolic logic of relations. Unfortunately

* From John Dewey, *Philosophy and Civilization* (New York, Capricorn Books, 1963) (1931), pp. 13-35. Reprinted by permission of G. P. Putnam's Sons. (Published originally in French in 1922 and then in English, as translated by Herbert W. Schneider, 1925.)

Peirce was not at all a systematic writer and never expounded his ideas in a single system. The pragmatic method which he developed applies only to a very narrow and limited universe of discourse. After William James had extended the scope of the method, Peirce wrote an exposition of the origin of pragmatism as he had first conceived it; it is from this exposition that we take the following passages.

The term "pragmatic," contrary to the opinion of those who regard pragmatism as an exclusively American conception, was suggested to him by the study of Kant. In the *Metaphysic of Morals* Kant established a distinction between *pragmatic* and *practical*. The latter term applies to moral laws which Kant regards as *a priori*, whereas the former term applies to the rules of art and technique which are based on experience and are applicable to experience. Peirce, who was an empiricist, with the habits of mind, as he put it, of the laboratory, consequently refused to call his system "practicalism," as some of his friends suggested. As a logician he was interested in the art and technique of real thinking, and especially interested, as far as pragmatic method is concerned, in the art of making concepts clear, or of construing adequate and effective definitions in accord with the spirit of scientific method.

Following his own words, for a person "who still thought in Kantian terms most readily, *"praktisch"* and *"pragmatisch"* were as far apart as the two poles; the former belonging in a region of thought where no mind of the experimental type can ever make sure of solid ground under his feet, the latter expressing relation to some definite human purpose. Now quite the most striking feature of the new theory was its recognition of an inseparable connection between rational cognition and rational purpose."[1]

In alluding to the experimental type of mind, we are brought to the exact meaning given by Peirce to the word "pragmatic." In speaking of an experimentalist as a man whose intelligence is formed in the laboratory, he said: "Whatever assertion you may make to him, he will either understand as meaning that if a given prescription for an experiment ever can be and ever is carried out in act, an experience of a given description will result, or else he will see no sense at all in what you say." And thus Peirce developed the theory that "the rational purport of a word or other expression, lies exclusively in its conceivable bearing upon the conduct of life; so that, since obviously nothing that might not result from experiment can have any direct bearing upon conduct, if one can define accurately all the conceivable experimental phenomena

[1] *Monist*, vol. 15, p. 163.

which the affirmation or denial of a concept could imply, one will have therein a complete definition of the concept.[2]

The essay in which Peirce developed his theory bears the title: *How to Make Our Ideas Clear*.[3] There is a remarkable similarity here to Kant's doctrine. Peirce's effort was to interpret the universality of concepts in the domain of *experience* in the same way in which Kant established the law of practical reason in the domain of the *a priori*. "The rational meaning of every proposition lies in the future. . . . But of the myriads of forms into which a proposition may be translated, what is that one which is to be called its very meaning? It is, according to the pragmatist, that form in which the proposition becomes applicable to human conduct, not in these or those special circumstances, nor when one entertains this or that special design, but that form which is most directly applicable to self-control under every situation, and to every purpose."[4] So also, "the pragmatist does not make the *summum bonum* to consist in action, but makes it to consist in that process of evolution whereby the existent comes more and more to embody generals . . ."[5] in other words—the process whereby the existent becomes, with the aid of action, a body of rational tendencies or of habits generalized as much as possible. These statements of Peirce are quite conclusive with respect to two errors which are commonly committed in regard to the ideas of the founder of pragmatism. It is often said of pragmatism that it makes action the end of life. It is also said of pragmatism that it subordinates thought and rational activity to particular ends of interest and profit. It is true that the theory according to Peirce's conception implies essentially a certain relation to action, to human conduct. But the rôle of action is that of an intermediary. In order to be able to attribute a meaning to concepts, one must be able to apply them to existence. Now it is by means of action that this application is made possible. And the modification of existence which results from this application constitutes the true meaning of concepts. Pragmatism is, therefore, far from being that glorification of action for its own sake which is regarded as the peculiar characteristic of American life.

It is also to be noted that there is a scale of possible applications of concepts to existence, and hence a diversity of meanings. The greater the extension of the concepts, the more they are freed from the restric-

[2] *Ibid.*, p. 162.
[3] *Popular Science Monthly*, 1878.
[4] *Monist*, vol. 15, pp. 173-4.
[5] *Ibid.*, p. 178.

tions which limit them to particular cases, the more is it possible for us to attribute the greatest generality of meaning to a term. Thus the theory of Peirce is opposed to every restriction of the meaning of a concept to the achievement of a particular end, and still more to a personal aim. It is still more strongly opposed to the idea that reason or thought should be reduced to being a servant of any interest which is pecuniary or narrow. This theory was American in its origin in so far as it insisted on the necessity of human conduct and the fulfillment of some aim in order to clarify thought. But at the same time, it disapproves of those aspects of American life which make action an end in itself, and which conceive ends too narrowly and too "practically." In considering a system of philosophy in its relation to national factors it is necessary to keep in mind not only the aspects of life which are incorporated in the system, but also the aspects against which the system is a protest. There never was a philosopher who has merited the name for the simple reason that he glorified the tendencies and characteristics of his social environment; just as it is also true that there never has been a philosopher who has not seized upon certain aspects of the life of his time and idealized them.

The work commenced by Peirce was continued by William James. In one sense James narrowed the application of Peirce's pragmatic method, but at the same time he extended it. The articles which Peirce wrote in 1878 commanded almost no attention from philosophical circles, which were then under the dominating influence of the neo-kantian idealism of Green, of Caird, and of the Oxford School, excepting those circles in which the Scottish philosophy of common sense maintained its supremacy. In 1898 James inaugurated the new pragmatic movement in an address entitled, "Philosophical Conceptions and Practical Results," later reprinted in the volume, *Collected Essays and Reviews*. Even in this early study one can easily notice the presence of those two tendencies to restrict and at the same time to extend early pragmatism. After having quoted the psychological remark of Peirce that "beliefs are really rules for action, and the whole function of thinking is but one step in the production of habits of action," and that every idea which we frame for ourselves of an object is really an idea of the possible effects of that object, he expressed the opinion that all these principles could be expressed more broadly than Peirce expressed them. "The ultimate test for us of what a truth means is indeed the conduct it dictates or inspires. But it inspires that conduct because it first foretells some particular turn to our experience which shall call for just that conduct from us. And I should prefer to express Peirce's principle by saying that the effective meaning of any philosophic proposition can always be brought down to some particular consequence, in our future practical experience, whether active or passive; the point lying rather in the fact that the experience must be particular, than in the fact that it must be active."[6] In an essay written in 1908 James repeats this statement and states that whenever he employs the term "the practical," he means by it, "the distinctively concrete, the individual, the particular and effective as opposed to the abstract, general and inert—'Pragmata' are things in their plurality—particular consequences can perfectly well be of a theoretic nature."[7]

William James alluded to the development which he gave to Peirce's expression of the principle. In one sense, one can say that he enlarged the bearing of the principle by the substitution of particular consequences for the general rule or method applicable to future experience. But in another sense this substitution limited the application of the principle, since it destroyed the importance attached by Peirce to the greatest possible application of the rule, or the habit of conduct—its extension to universality. That is to say, William James was much more of a nominalist than Peirce.

One can notice an extension of pragmatism in the above passage. James there alludes to the use of a method of determining the meaning of truth. Since truth is a term and has consequently a meaning, this extension is a legitimate application of pragmatic method. But it should be remarked that here this method serves only to make clear the meaning of the term "truth," and has nothing to do with the truth of a particular judgment. The principal reason which led James to give a new color to pragmatic method was that he was preoccupied with applying the method to determine the meaning of philosophical problems and questions, and that moreover, he chose to submit to examination philosophical notions of a theological or religious nature. He wished to establish a criterion which

[6] *Collected Essays and Reviews*, p. 412.

[7] *The Meaning of Truth*, pp. 209-210. In a footnote James gave an example of the errors which are committed in connection with the term "Practical," quoting M. Bourdeau who had written that "Pragmatism is an Anglo Saxon reaction against the intellectualism and rationalism of the Latin mind. . . . It is a philosophy without words, a philosophy of gestures and of facts, which abandons what is general and holds only to what is particular." In his lecture at California, James brought out the idea that his pragmatism was inspired to a considerable extent by the thought of the British philosophers, Locke, Berkeley, Hume, Mill, Bain, and Shadworth Hodgson. But he contrasted this method with German transcendentalism, and particularly with that of Kant. It is especially interesting to notice this difference between Peirce and James: the former attempted to give an experimental, not an *a priori* interpretation of Kant, whereas James tried to develop the point of view of the British thinkers.

would enable one to determine whether a given philosophical question has an authentic and vital meaning or whether, on the contrary, it is trivial and purely verbal; and in the former case, what interests are at stake when one accepts and affirms one or the other of two theses in dispute. Peirce was above all a logician; whereas James was an educator and humanist and wished to force the general public to realize that certain problems, certain philosophical debates, have a real importance for mankind, because the beliefs which they bring into play lead to very different modes of conduct. If this important distinction is not grasped, it is impossible to understand the majority of the ambiguities and errors which belong to the later period of the pragmatic movement.

James took as an example the controversy between theism and materialism. It follows from this principle that if the course of the world is considered as completed, it is equally legitimate to assert that God or matter is its cause. Whether one way or the other, the facts are what they are, and it is they which determine whatever meaning is to be given to their cause. Consequently the name which we can give to this cause is entirely arbitrary. It is entirely different if we take the future into account. God then has the meaning of a power concerned with assuring the final triumph of ideal and spiritual values, and matter becomes a power indifferent to the triumph or defeat of these values. And our life takes a different direction according as we adopt one or the other of these alternatives. In the lectures on pragmatism published in 1907, he applies the same criticism to the philosophical problem of the One and the Many, that is to say of Monism and Pluralism, as well as to other questions. Thus he shows that Monism is equivalent to a rigid universe where everything is fixed and immutably united to others, where indetermination, free choice, novelty, and the unforeseen in experience have no place; a universe which demands the sacrifice of the concrete and complex diversity of things to the simplicity and nobility of an architectural structure. In what concerns our beliefs, Monism demands a rationalistic temperament leading to a fixed and dogmatic attitude. Pluralism, on the other hand, leaves room for contingence, liberty, novelty, and gives complete liberty of action to the empirical method, which can be indefinitely extended. It accepts unity where it finds it, but it does not attempt to force the vast diversity of events and things into a single rational mold.

From the point of view of an educator or of a student or, if you will, of those who are thoroughly interested in these problems, in philosophical discussions and controversies, there is no reason for contesting the value of this application of pragmatic method, but it is no less important to determine the nature of this application. It affords a means of discovering the implications for human life of philosophical conceptions which are often treated as of no importance and of a purely dialectical nature. It furnishes a criterion for determining the vital implications of beliefs which present themselves as alternatives in any theory. Thus as he himself said, "the whole function of philosophy ought to be to find the characteristic influences which you and I would undergo at a determinate moment of our lives, if one or the other formula of the universe were true." However, in saying that the whole function of philosophy has this aim, it seems that he is referring rather to the teaching than to the construction of philosophy. For such a statement implies that the world formulas have already all been made, and that the necessary work of producing them has already been finished, so that there remains only to define the consequences which are reflected in life by the acceptance of one or the other of these formulas as true.

From the point of view of Peirce, the object of philosophy would be rather to give a fixed meaning to the universe by formulas which correspond to our attitudes or our most general habits of response to the environment; and this generality depends on the extension of the applicability of these formulas to specific future events. The *meaning* of concepts of "matter" and of "God" must be fixed before we can even attempt to reach an understanding concerning the *value* of our belief in these concepts. Materialism would signify that the world demands on our part a single kind of constant and general habits; and God would signify the demand for another type of habits; the difference between materialism and theism would be tantamount to the difference in the habits required to face all the detailed facts of the universe. The world would be one in so far as it would be possible for us to form a single habit of action which would take account of all future existences and would be applicable to them. It would be many in so far as it is necessary for us to form several habits, differing from each other and irreducible to each other, in order to be able to meet the events in the world and control them. In short, Peirce wrote as a logician and James as a humanist.

William James accomplished a new advance in Pragmatism by his theory of the will to believe, or as he himself later called it, the right to believe. The discovery of the fundamental consequences of one or another belief has without fail a certain influence on that belief itself. If a man cherishes novelty, risk, opportunity and a variegated esthetic reality, he will certainly reject any belief in Monism, when he clearly perceives the import of this system. But if, from the very start, he is attracted by esthetic harmony, classic proportions, fixity even to the extent of absolute security, and logical coherence, it is quite natural that he should put faith in Monism. Thus William James took into account those motives of instinctive sympathy which play a greater rôle in our choice of a philosophic system than do formal reasonings; and he thought that we should be rendering a service to the cause of philosophical sincerity if we would openly recognize the motives which inspire us. He also maintained the thesis that the greater part of philosophic problems and especially those which touch on religious fields are of such a nature that they are not susceptible of decisive evidence one way or the other. Consequently he claimed the right of a man to choose his beliefs not only in the presence of proofs or conclusive facts, but also in the absence of all such proof. Above all when he is forced to choose between one meaning or another, or when by refusing to choose he has a right to assume the risks of faith, his refusal is itself equivalent to a choice. The theory of the will to believe gives rise to misunderstandings and even to ridicule; and therefore it is necessary to understand clearly in what way James used it. We are always obliged to act in any case; our actions and with them their consequences actually change according to the beliefs which we have chosen. Moreover it may be that, in order to discover the proofs which will ultimately be the intellectual justification of certain beliefs—the belief in freedom, for example, or the belief in God—it is necessary to begin to act in accordance with this belief.

In his lectures on pragmatism, and in his volume of essays bearing the title *The Meaning of Truth,* which appeared in 1909, James extended the use of the pragmatic method to the problem of the nature of truth. So far we have considered the pragmatic method as an instrument in determining the meaning of words and the vital importance of philosophic beliefs. Now and then we have made allusion to the future consequences which are implied. James showed, among other things, that in certain philosophic conceptions, the affirmation of certain beliefs could be justified by means of the nature of their consequences, or by the differences which these beliefs make in existence. But then why not push the argument to the point of maintaining that the meaning of truth in general is determined by its consequences? We must not forget here that James was an empiricist before he was a pragmatist, and repeatedly stated that pragmatism is merely empiricism pushed to its legitimate conclusions. From a general point of view, the pragmatic attitude consists in "looking away from first things, principles, 'categories,' supposed necessities; and of looking towards last things, fruits, consequences, facts.'' It is only one step further to apply the pragmatic method to the problem of truth. In the natural sciences there is a tendency to identify truth in any particular case with a verification. The verification of a theory, or of a concept, is carried on by the observation of particular facts. Even the most scientific and harmonious physical theory is merely an hypothesis until its implications, deduced by mathematical reasoning or by any other kind of inference, are verified by observed facts. What direction, therefore, must an empirical philosopher take who wishes to arrive at a definition of truth by means of an empirical method? He must, if he wants to apply this method, and without bringing in for the present the pragmatic formula, first find particular cases from which he then generalizes. It is therefore in submitting conceptions to the control of experience, in the process of verifying them, that one finds examples of what is called truth. Therefore any philosopher who applies this empirical method without the least prejudice in favor of pragmatic doctrine, can be led to conclude that truth ''means'' verification, or if one prefers, that verification, either actual or possible, is the definition of truth.

In combining this conception of empirical method with the theory of pragmatism, we come upon other important philosophical results. The classic theories of truth in terms of the coherence or compatibility of terms, and of the correspondence of an idea with a thing, hereby receive a new interpretation. A merely mental coherence without experimental verification does not enable us to get beyond the realm of hypothesis. If a notion or a theory makes pretense of corresponding to reality or to the facts, this pretense cannot be put to the test and confirmed or refuted except by causing it to pass over into the realm of action and by noting the results which it yields in the form of the concrete observable facts to which this notion or theory leads. If, in acting upon this notion, we are brought to the fact which it implies or which it demands, then this notion is true. A theory corresponds to the facts when it leads to the facts which are its consequences, by the intermediary of experience. And from this consideration the pragmatic generalization is drawn that all knowledge is prospective in its results, except in the case where notions and theories after having been first prospective in their application, have already been tried out and verified. Theoretically, however, even such verifications or truths could not be absolute. They would be based upon practical or moral certainty, but they are always subject to being corrected by unforeseen future consequences or by observed facts which had been disregarded. Every proposition concerning truths is really in the last analysis hypothetical and provisional, although a large number of these propositions have been so frequently verified without failure that we are justified in using them as if they were absolutely true. But, logically, absolute truth is an ideal which cannot be realized, at least not until all the facts have been registered, or as James says "bagged," and until it is no longer possible to make other observations and other experiences.

Pragmatism, thus, presents itself as an extension of historical empiricism, but with this fundamental difference, that it does not insist upon antecedent phenomena but upon consequent phenomena; not upon the precedents but upon the possibilities of action. And this change in point of view is almost revolutionary in its consequences. An empiricism which is content with repeating facts already past has no place for possibility and for liberty. It cannot find room for general conceptions or ideas, at least no more than to consider them as summaries or records. But when we take the point of view of pragmatism we see that general ideas have a very different rôle to play than that of reporting and registering past experiences. They are the bases for organizing future observations and experiences. Whereas, for empiricism, in a world already constructed and determined, reason or general thought has no other meaning than that of summing up particular cases, in a world where the future is not a mere word, where theories, general notions, rational ideas have consequences for action, reason necessarily has a constructive function. Nevertheless the conceptions of reasoning have only a secondary interest in comparison with the reality of facts, since they must be confronted with concrete observations.[8]

Pragmatism thus has a metaphysical implication. The doctrine of the value of consequences leads us to take the future into consideration. And this taking into consideration of the future takes us to the conception of a universe whose evolution is not finished, of a universe which is still, in James' term, "in the making," "in the process of becoming," of a universe up to a certain point still plastic.

Consequently reason, or thought, in its more general sense, has a real, though limited, function, a creative, constructive function. If we form general ideas and if we put them in action, consequences are pro-

---

[8] William James said in a happy metaphor, that they must be "cashed in," by producing specific consequences. This expression means that they must be able to lead to concrete facts. But for those who are not familiar with American idioms, James' formula was taken to mean that the consequences themselves of our rational conceptions must be narrowly limited by their pecuniary value. Thus Mr. Bertrand Russell wrote recently that pragmatism is merely a manifestation of American commercialism.

duced which could not be produced otherwise. Under these conditions the world will be different from what it would have been if thought had not intervened. This consideration confirms the human and moral importance of thought and of its reflective operation in experience. It is therefore not true to say that James treated reason, thought, and knowledge with contempt, or that he regarded them as mere means of gaining personal or even social profits. For him reason has a creative function, limited because specific, which helps to make the world other than it would have been without it. It makes the world really more reasonable; it gives to it an intrinsic value. One will understand the philosophy of James better if one considers it in its totality as a revision of English empiricism, a revision which replaces the value of past experience, of what is already given, by the future, by that which is as yet mere possibility.

These considerations naturally bring us to the movement called instrumentalism. The survey which we have just made of James' philosophy shows that he regarded conceptions and theories purely as instruments which can serve to constitute future facts in a specific manner. But James devoted himself primarily to the moral aspects of this theory, to the support which it gave to "meliorism" and moral idealism, and to the consequences which followed from it concerning the sentimental value and the bearing of various philosophical systems, particularly to its destructive implications for monistic rationalism and for absolutism in all its forms. He never attempted to develop a complete theory of the forms or "structures" and of the logical operations which are founded on this conception. Instrumentalism is an attempt to establish a precise logical theory of concepts, of judgments and inferences in their various forms, by considering primarily how thought functions in the experimental determinations of future consequences. That is to say, it attempts to establish universally recognized distinctions and rules of logic by deriving them from the reconstructive or mediative function ascribed to reason. It aims to constitute a theory of the general forms of conception and reasoning, and not of this or that particular judgment or concept related to its own content, or to its particular implications.

As far as the historical antecedents of instrumentalism are concerned, two factors are particularly important, over and above this matter of experimental verification which we have already mentioned in connection with James. The first of these two factors is psychological, and the second is a critique of the theory of knowledge and of logic which has resulted from the theory proposed by Neo-Kantian idealism and expounded in the logical writings of such philosophers as Lotze,

Bosanquet, and F. H. Bradley. As we have already said, Neo-Kantian influence was very marked in the United States during the last decade of the nineteenth century. I myself, and those who have collaborated with me in the exposition of instrumentalism, began by being Neo-Kantians, in the same way that Peirce's point of departure was Kantianism and that of James was the empiricism of the British School.

The psychological tendencies which have exerted an influence on instrumentalism are of a biological rather than a physiological nature. They are, more or less, closely related to the important movement whose promoter in psychology has been Doctor John Watson and to which he has given the name of Behaviorism. Briefly, the point of departure of this theory is the conception of the brain as an organ for the co-ordination of sense stimuli (to which one should add modifications caused by habit, unconscious memory, or what are called today "conditioned reflexes") for the purpose of effecting appropriate motor responses. On the basis of the theory of organic evolution it is maintained that the analysis of intelligence and of its operations should be compatible with the order of known biological facts, concerning the intermediate position occupied by the central nervous system in making possible responses to the environment adequate to the needs of the living organism. It is particularly interesting to note that in the *Studies in Logical Theory* (1903), which was their first declaration, the instrumentalists recognized how much they owed to William James for having forged the instruments which they used, while at the same time, in the course of the studies, the authors constantly declared their belief in a close union of the "normative" principles of logic and the real processes of thought, in so far as these are determined by an objective or biological psychology and not by an introspective psychology of states of consciousness. But it is curious to note that the "instruments" to which allusion is made, are not the considerations which were of the greatest service to James. They precede his pragmatism and it is among some of the pages of his *Principles of Psychology* that one must look for them. This important work (1890) really developed two distinct theses.

The one is a re-interpretation of introspective psychology, in which James denies that sensations, images and ideas are discrete and in which he replaces them by a continuous stream which he calls "the stream of consciousness." This conception necessitates a consideration of relations as an immediate part of the field of consciousness, having the same status as qualities. And throughout his *Psychology* James gives a philosophical tinge to this conception by using it in criticizing the atomism of Locke and of Hume as well as the *a-priorism* of the synthesis of rational principles by Kant and his successors, among whom should be mentioned in England, Thomas Hill Green, who was then at the height of his influence.

The other aspect of his *Principles of Psychology* is of a biological nature. It shows itself in its full force in the criterion which James established for discovering the existence of mind. "The pursuance of future ends and the choice of means for their attainment are thus the mark and criterion of the presence of mentality in a phenomenon."[9] The force of this criterion is plainly shown in the chapter on Attention, and its relation to Interest considered as the force which controls it, and its teleological function of selection and integration; in the chapter on Discrimination and Comparison (Analysis and Abstraction), where he discusses the way in which ends to be attained and the means for attaining them evoke and control intellectual analysis; and in the chapter on Conception, where he shows that a general idea is a mode of signifying particular things and not merely an abstraction from particular cases or a super-empirical function,—that it is a teleological instrument. James then develops this idea in the chapter on reasoning where he says that "the only meaning of essence is teleological, and that classification and conception are purely teleological weapons of mind."

One might complete this brief enumeration by mentioning also the chapter of James' book in which he discusses the Nature of Necessary Truths and the Rôle of Experience, and affirms in opposition to Herbert Spencer, that many of our most important modes of perception and conception of the world of sensible objects are not the cumulative products of particular experience, but rather original biological sports, spontaneous variations, which are maintained because of their applicability to concrete experiences after once having been created. Number, space, time, resemblance and other important "categories" could have been brought into existence, he says, as a consequence of some particular cerebral instability, but they could by no means have been registered on the mind by outside influence. Many significant and useless concepts also arise in the same manner. But the fundamental categories have been cumulatively extended and reinforced because of their value when applied to concrete instances and things of experience. It is therefore not the origin of a concept, it is its application which becomes the criterion of its value; and here we have the whole of pragmatism in embryo. A phrase of James' very well summarizes its import: "the popular notion that 'Science' is forced on the mind *ab extra*,

[9] *Psychology*, vol. I, p. 8.

and that our interests have nothing to do with its constructions, is utterly absurd.''

Given the point of view which we have just specified, and the interest attaching to a logical theory of conception and judgment, and there results a theory of the following description. The adaptations made by inferior organisms, for example their effective and co-ordinated responses to stimuli, become teleological in man and therefore give occasion to thought. Reflection is an indirect response to the environment, and the element of indirection can itself become great and very complicated. But it has its origin in biological adaptive behavior and the ultimate function of its cognitive aspect is a prospective control of the conditions of the environment. The function of intelligence is therefore not that of copying the objects of the environment, but rather of taking account of the way in which more effective and more profitable relations with these objects may be established in the future.

How this point of view has been applied to the theory of judgment is too long a story to be told here. We shall confine ourselves here to saying that, in general, the "subject" of a judgment represents that portion of the environment to which a reaction must be made; the predicate represents the possible response or habit or manner in which one should behave towards the environment; the copula represents the organic and concrete act by which the connection is made between the fact and its signification; and finally the conclusion, or the definitive object of judgment, is simply the original situation transformed, a situation which implies a change as well in the original subject (including its mind) as in the environment itself. The new and harmonious unity thus attained verifies the bearing of the data which were at first chosen to serve as subject and of the concepts introduced into the situation during the process as teleological instruments for its elaboration. Until this final unification is attained the perceptual data and the conceptual principles, theories, are merely hypotheses from a logical point of view. Moreover, affirmation and negation are intrinsically a-logical: they are acts.

Such a summary survey can hardly pretend to be either convincing or suggestive. However, in noting the points of resemblance and difference between this phase of pragmatism and the logic of Neo-Hegelian idealism, we are bringing out a point of great importance. According to the latter logic, thought constitutes in the last analysis its object and even the universe. It is necessary to affirm the existence of a series of forms of judgment, because our first judgments, which are nearest to sense, succeed in constituting objects in only a partial and fragmentary fashion, even to the extent of involving in their nature an element of contradiction. There results a dialectic which permits each inferior and partial type of judgment to pass into a more complete form until we finally arrive at the total judgment, where the thought which comprehends the entire object or the universe is an organic whole of interrelated mental distinctions. It is evident that this theory magnifies the rôle of thought beyond all proportion. It is an objective and rational idealism which is opposed to and distinct from the subjective and perceptual idealism of Berkeley's school. Instrumentalism, however, assigns a positive function to thought, that of *re*constituting the present stage of things instead of merely knowing it. As a consequence, there cannot be intrinsic degrees, or a hierarchy of forms of judgment. Each type has its own end, and its validity is entirely determined by its efficacy in the pursuit of its end. A limited perceptual judgment, adapted to the situation which has given it birth, is as true in its place as is the most complete and significant philosophic or scientific judgment. Logic, therefore, leads to a realistic metaphysics in so far as it accepts things and events for what they are independently of thought, and to an idealistic metaphysics in so far as it contends that thought gives birth to distinctive acts which modify future facts and events in such a way as to render them more reasonable, that is to say, more adequate to the ends which we propose for ourselves. This ideal element is more and more accentuated by the inclusion progressively of social factors in human environment over and above natural factors; so that the needs which are fulfilled, the ends which are attained are no longer of a merely biological or particular character, but include also the ends and activities of other members of society.

It is natural that continental thinkers should be interested in American philosophy as it reflects, in a certain sense, American life. Thus it should be clear after this rapid survey of the history of pragmatism that American thought continues European thought. We have imported our language, our laws, our institutions, our morals, and our religion from Europe, and we have adapted them to the new conditions of our life. The same is true of our ideas. For long years our philosophical thought was merely an echo of European thought. The pragmatic movement which we have traced in the present essay, as well as neo-realism, behaviorism, the absolute idealism of Royce, the naturalistic idealism of Santayana, are all attempts at re-adaptation; but they are not creations *de novo*. They have their roots in British and European thought. Since these systems are re-adaptations they take into consideration the distinctive traits of the environment of American life. But as has already been said, they are not limited to reproducing what is worn and imperfect in this environment. They do not aim to glorify the energy and the love of action which the new conditions of American life exaggerated. They do not reflect the excessive mercantilism of American life. Without doubt all these traits of the environment have not been without a certain influence on American philosophical thought; our philosophy would not be national or spontaneous if it were not subject to this influence. But the fundamental idea which the movements of which we have just spoken have attempted to express, is the idea that action and opportunity justify themselves only to the degree in which they render life more reasonable and increase its value. Instrumentalism maintains in opposition to many contrary tendencies in the American environment, that action should be intelligent and reflective, and that thought should occupy a central position in life. That is the reason for our insistence on the teleological phase of thought and knowledge. If it must be teleological in particular and not merely true in the abstract, that is probably due to the practical element which is found in all phases of American life. However that may be, what we insist upon above all else is that intelligence be regarded as the only source and sole guarantee of a desirable and happy future. It is beyond doubt that the progressive and unstable character of American life and civilization has facilitated the birth of a philosophy which regards the world as being in continuous formation, where there is still place for indeterminism, for the new, and for a real future. But this idea is not exclusively American, although the conditions of American life have aided this idea in becoming self-conscious. It is also true that Americans tend to underestimate the value of tradition and of rationality considered as an achievement of the past. But the world has also given proof of irrationality in the past and this irrationality is incorporated in our beliefs and our institutions. There are bad traditions as there are good ones: it is always important to distinguish. Our neglect of the traditions of the past, with whatever this negligence implies in the way of spiritual impoverishment of our life, has its compensation in the idea that the world is recommencing and being remade under our eyes. The future as well as the past can be a source of interest and consolation and give meaning to the present. Pragmatism and instrumental experimentalism bring into prominence the importance of the individual. It is he who is the carrier of creative thought, the author of action, and of its application. Subjectivism is an old story in philosophy; a story which began in Europe and not in America. But American philosophy, in the systems which we have expounded, has given to the subject, to the individual mind, a practical rather than an epistemological function.

The individual mind is important because only the individual mind is the organ of modifications in traditions and institutions, the vehicle of experimental creation. One-sided and egoistic individualism in American life has left its imprint on our practices. For better or for worse, depending on the point of view, it has transformed the esthetic and fixed individualism of the old European culture into an active individualism. But the idea of a society of individuals is not foreign to American thought; it penetrates even our current individualism which is unreflective and brutal. And the individual which American thought idealizes is not an individual *per se,* an individual fixed in isolation and set up for himself, but an individual who evolves and develops in a natural and human environment, an individual who can be educated.

If I were asked to give an historical parallel to this movement in American thought I would remind my reader of the French philosophy of the enlightenment. Every one knows that the thinkers who made that movement illustrious were inspired by Bacon, Locke, and Newton; what interested them was the application of scientific method and the conclusions of an experimental theory of knowledge to human affairs, the critique and reconstruction of beliefs and institutions. As Höffding writes, they were animated "by a fervent faith in intelligence, progress, and humanity." And certainly they are not accused to-day, just because of their educational and social significance, of having sought to subordinate intelligence and science to ordinary utilitarian aims. They merely sought to free intelligence from its impurities and to render it sovereign. One can scarcely say that those who glorify intelligence and reason in the abstract, because of their value for those who find personal satisfaction in their possession, estimate intelligence more truly than those who wish to make it the indispensable guide of intellectual and social life. When an American critic says of instrumentalism that it regards ideas as mere servants which make for success in life, he only reacts, without reflection, to the ordinary verbal associations of the word "instrumental," as many others have reacted in the same manner to the use of the word "practical." Similarly a recent Italian writer, after having said that pragmatism and instrumentalism are characteristic products of American thought, adds that these systems "regard intelligence as a mere mechanism of belief, and consequently attempt to re-establish the dignity of reason by making of it a machine for the production of beliefs useful to morals and society." This criticism does not hold. It is by no means the production of beliefs useful to morals and society which these systems pursue. It is the formation of a faith in intelligence, as the one and indispensable belief necessary to moral and social life. The more one appreciates the intrinsic esthetic, immediate value of thought and of science, the more one takes into account what intelligence itself adds to the joy and dignity of life, the more one should feel grieved at a situation in which the exercise and joy of reason are limited to a narrow, closed and technical social group and the more one should ask how it is possible to make all men participators in this inestimable wealth.

6. The Need for a Recovery of Philosophy*

With the exception of his major work on *Experience and Nature*, this is Dewey's most extensive effort to locate experience as the central concern of philosophical method. Paramount to this consideration is Dewey's effort to distinguish by virtue of five comparisons the "orthodox description of experience and that congenial to present conditions." Dewey is also prescient about contemporary philosophy in America when he writes: "I believe that philosophy in America will be lost between chewing a historic cud long since reduced to woody fiber, or an apologetics for lost causes (lost to natural science), or a scholastic, schematic formalism, unless it can somehow bring to consciousness America's own needs and its own implicit principle of successful action."

Intellectual advance occurs in two ways. At times increase of knowledge is organized about old conceptions, while these are expanded, elaborated and refined, but not seriously revised, much less abandoned. At other times, the increase of knowledge demands qualitative rather than quantitative change; alteration, not addition. Men's minds grow cold to their former intellectual concerns; ideas that were burning fade; interests that were urgent seem remote. Men face in another direction; their older perplexities are unreal; considerations passed over as negligible loom up. Former problems may not have been solved, but they no longer press for solution.

Philosophy is no exception to the rule. But it is unusually conservative—not, necessarily, in proffering solutions, but in clinging to problems. It has been so allied with theology and theological morals as

* From John Dewey *Creative Intelligence: Essays in the Pragmatic Attitude*, et al., pp. 3-69. Copyright 1945 by John Dewey. Reprinted by permission of Holt, Rinehart and Winston, Inc. (Published originally in 1917.)

representative of men's chief interests, that radical alteration has been shocking. Men's activities took a decidedly new turn, for example, in the seventeenth century, and it seemed as if philosophy, under the lead of thinkers like Bacon and Descartes, was to execute an about-face. But, in spite of the ferment, it turned out that many of the older problems were but translated from Latin into the vernacular or into the new terminology furnished by science.

The association of philosophy with academic teaching has reinforced this intrinsic conservatism. Scholastic philosophy persisted in universities after men's thoughts outside of the walls of colleges had moved in other directions. In the last hundred years intellectual advances of science and politics have in like fashion been crystallized into material of instruction and now resist further change. I would not say that the spirit of teaching is hostile to that of liberal inquiry, but a philosophy which exists largely as something to be taught rather than wholly as something to be reflected upon is conducive to discussion of views held by others rather than to immediate response. Philosophy when taught inevitably magnifies the history of past thought, and leads professional philosophers to approach their subject matter through its formulation in received systems. It tends, also, to emphasize points upon which men have divided into schools, for these lend themselves to retrospective definition and elaboration. Consequently, philosophical discussion is likely to be a dressing out of antithetical traditions, where criticism of one view is thought to afford proof of the truth of its opposite (as if formulation of views guaranteed logical exclusives). Direct preoccupation with contemporary difficulties is left to literature and politics.

If changing conduct and expanding knowledge ever required a willingness to surrender not merely old solutions but old problems it is now. I do not mean that we can turn abruptly away from all traditional issues. This is impossible; it would be the undoing of the one who attempted it. Irrespective of the professionalizing of philosophy, the ideas philosophers discuss are still those in which Western civilization has been bred. They are in the backs of the heads of educated people. But what serious-minded men not engaged in the professional business of philosophy most want to know is what modifications and abandonments of intellectual inheritance are required by the newer industrial, political, and scientific movements. They want to know what these newer movements mean when translated into general ideas. Unless professional philosophy can mobilize itself sufficiently to assist in this clarification and redirection of men's thoughts, it is likely to get more and more sidetracked from the main currents of contemporary life.

This essay may, then, be looked upon as an attempt to forward the emancipation of philosophy from too intimate and exclusive attachment to traditional problems. It is not in intent a criticism of various solutions that have been offered, but raises a question *as to the genuineness, under the present conditions of science and social life, of the problems*.

The limited object of my discussion will, doubtless, give an exaggerated impression of my conviction as to the artificiality of much recent philosophizing. Not that I have wilfully exaggerated in what I have said, but that the limitations of my purpose have led me not to say many things pertinent to a broader purpose. A discussion less restricted would strive to enforce the genuineness, in their own context, of questions now discussed mainly because they have been discussed rather than because contemporary conditions of life suggest them. It would also be a grateful task to dwell upon the precious contributions made by philosophic systems which as a whole are impossible. In the course of the development of unreal premises and the discussion of artificial problems, points of view have emerged which are indispensable possessions of culture. The horizon has been widened; ideas of great fecundity struck out; imagination quickened; a sense of the meaning of things created. It may even be asked whether these accompaniments of classic systems have not often been treated as a kind of guarantee of the systems themselves. But while it is a sign of an illiberal mind to throw away the fertile and ample ideas of a Spinoza, a Kant, or a Hegel, because their setting is not logically adequate, it is surely a sign of an undisciplined one to treat their contributions to culture as confirmations of premises with which they have no necessary connection.

I

A criticism of current philosophizing from the standpoint of the traditional quality of its problems must begin somewhere, and the choice of a beginning is arbitrary. It has appeared to me that the notion of experience implied in the questions most actively discussed gives a natural point of departure. For, if I mistake not, it is just the inherited view of experience common to the empirical school and its opponents which keeps alive many discussions even of matters that on their face are quite remote from it, while it is also this view which is most untenable in the light of existing science and social practice. Accordingly I set out with a brief statement of some of the chief contrasts between the orthodox description of experience and that congenial to present conditions.

(i) In the orthodox view, experience is regarded primarily as a knowledge-affair. But to eyes not looking through ancient spectacles, it assuredly appears as an affair of the intercourse of a living being with its physical and social environment. (ii) According to tradition experience is (at least primarily) a psychical thing, infected throughout by "subjectivity." What experience suggests about itself is a genuinely objective world which enters into the actions and sufferings of men and undergoes modifications through their responses. (iii) So far as anything beyond a bare present is recognized by the established doctrine, the past exclusively counts. Registration of what has taken place, reference to precedent, is believed to be the essence of experience. Empiricism is conceived of as tied up to what has been, or is, "given." But experience in its vital form is experimental, an effort to change the given; it is characterized by projection, by reaching forward into the unknown; connection with a future is its salient trait. (iv) The empirical tradition is committed to particularism. Connections and continuities are supposed to be foreign to experience, to be by-products of dubious validity. An experience that is an undergoing of an environment and a striving for its control in new directions is pregnant with connections. (v) In the traditional notion experience and thought are antithetical terms. Inference, so far as it is other than a revival of what has been given in the past, goes beyond experience; hence it is either invalid, or else a measure of desperation by which, using experience as a springboard, we jump out to a world of stable things and other selves. But experience, taken free of the restrictions imposed by the older concept, is full of inference. There is, apparently, no conscious experience without inference; reflection is native and constant.

These contrasts, with a consideration of the effect of substituting the account of experience relevant to modern life for the inherited account, afford the subject matter of the following discussion.

Suppose we take seriously the contribution made to our idea of experience by biology—not that recent biological science discovered the facts, but that it has so emphasized them that there is no longer an excuse for ignoring them or treating them as negligible. Any account of experience must now fit into the consideration that experiencing means living; and that living goes on in and because of an environing medium, not in a vacuum. Where there is experience, there is a living being. Where there is life, there is a double connection maintained with the environment. In part, environmental energies constitute organic functions; they enter into them. Life is not possible without such direct support by the environment. But while all organic changes depend upon the natural energies of the environment for their origination and occurrence, the natural energies sometimes carry the organic functions prosperously forward, and sometimes act counter to their continuance. Growth and decay, health and disease, are alike continuous with activities of the natural surroundings. The difference lies in the bearing of what happens upon future life activity. From the standpoint of this future reference environmental incidents fall into groups: those favorable-to-life activities, and those hostile.

The successful activities of the organism, those within which environmental assistance is incorporated, react upon the environment to bring about modifications favorable to their own future. The human being has upon his hands the problem of responding to what is going on around him so that these changes will take one turn rather than another, namely, that required by its own future functioning. While backed in part by the environment, its life is anything but a peaceful exhalation of environment. It is obliged to struggle—that is to say, to employ the direct support given by the environment in order indirectly to effect changes that would not otherwise occur. In this sense, life goes on by means of controlling the environment. Its activities must change the changes going on around it; they must neutralize hostile occurrences; they must transform neutral events into co-operative factors or into an efflorescence of new features.

Dialectic developments of the notion of self-preservation, of the *conatus essendi,* often ignore all the important facts of the actual process. They argue as if self-control, self-development, went on directly as a sort of unrolling push from within. But life endures only in virtue of the support of the environment. And since the environment is only incompletely enlisted in our behalf, self-preservation—or self-realization or whatever—is always indirect—always an affair of the way in which our present activities affect the direction taken by independent changes in the surroundings. Hindrances must be turned into means.

We are also given to playing loose with the conception of adjustment, as if that meant something fixed—a kind of accommodation once for all (ideally at least) of the organism *to* an environment. But as life requires the fitness of the environment to the organic functions, adjustment to the environment means not passive acceptance of the latter, but acting so that the environing changes take a certain turn. The "higher" the type of life, the more adjustment takes the form of an adjusting of the factors of the environment to one another in the interest of life; the less the significance of living, the more it becomes an adjustment to a given environment till at the lower end of the scale the differences between living and the nonliving disappear.

These statements are of an external kind. They are about the conditions of experience, rather than about experiencing itself. But assuredly experience as it concretely takes place bears out the statements. Experience is primarily a process of undergoing: a process of standing something; of suffering and passion, of affection, in the literal sense of these words. The organism has to endure, to undergo, the consequences of its own actions. Experience is no slipping along in a path fixed by inner consciousness. Private consciousness is an incidental outcome of experience of a vital objective sort; it is not its source. Undergoing, however, is never mere passivity. The most patient patient is more than a receptor. He is also an agent—a reactor, one trying experiments, one concerned with undergoing in a way which may influence what is still to happen. Sheer endurance, side-stepping evasions, are, after all, ways of treating the environment with a view to what such treatment will accomplish. Even if we shut ourselves up in the most clam-like fashion, we are doing something; our passivity is an active attitude, not an extinction of response. Just as there is no assertive action, no aggressive attack upon things as they are, which is all action, so there is no undergoing which is not on our part also a going on and a going through.

Experience, in other words, is a matter of *simultaneous* doings and sufferings. Our undergoings are experiments in varying the course of events; our active tryings are trials and tests of ourselves. This duplicity of experience shows itself in our happiness and misery, our successes and failures. Triumphs are dangerous when dwelt upon or lived off from; successes use themselves up. Any achieved equilibrium of adjustment with the environment is precarious because we cannot evenly keep pace with changes in the environment. These are so opposed in direction that we must choose. We must take the risk of casting in our lot with one movement or the other. Nothing can eliminate all risk, all adventure; the one thing doomed to failure is to try to keep even with the whole environment at once—that is to say, to maintain the happy moment when all things go our way.

The obstacles which confront us are stimuli to variation, to novel response, and hence are occasions of progress. If a favor done us by the environment conceals a threat, so its disfavor is a potential means of hitherto unexperienced modes of success. To treat misery as anything but misery, as for example a blessing in disguise or a necessary factor in good, is disingenuous apologetics. But to say that the progress of the race has been stimulated by ills undergone, and that men have been moved by what they suffer to search out new and better courses of action is to speak veraciously.

The preoccupation of experience with things which are coming (are now coming, not just to come) is obvious to any one whose interest in experience is empirical. Since we live forward; since we live in a world where changes are going on whose issue means our weal or woe; since every act of ours modifies these changes and hence is fraught with promise, or charged with hostile energies—what should experience be but a future implicated in a present! Adjustment is no timeless state; it is a continuing process. To say that a change takes time may be to say something about the event which is external and uninstructive. But adjustment of organism to environment takes time in the pregnant sense; every step in the process is conditioned by reference to further changes which it effects. What is going on in the environment is the concern of the organism; not what is already "there" in accomplished and finished form. In so far as the issue of what is going on may be affected by intervention of the organism, the moving event is a challenge which stretches the agent-patient to meet what is coming. Experiencing exhibits things in their unterminated aspect moving toward determinate conclusions. The finished and done with is of import as affecting the future, not on its own account: in short, because it is not, really, done with.

Anticipation is therefore more primary than recollection; projection than summoning of the past; the prospective than the retrospective. Given a world like that in which we live, a world in which environing changes are partly favorable and partly callously indifferent, and experience is bound to be prospective in import; for any control attainable by the living creature depends upon what is done to alter the state of things. Success and failure are the primary "categories" of life; achieving of good and averting of ill are its supreme interests; hope and anxiety (which are not self-enclosed states of feeling, but active attitudes of welcome and wariness) are dominant qualities of experience. Imaginative forecast of the future is this forerunning quality of behavior rendered available for guidance in the present. Day-dreaming and castle-building and esthetic realization of what is not practically achieved are offshoots of this practical trait, or else practical intelligence is a chastened fantasy. It makes little difference. Imaginative recovery of the bygone is indispensable to successful invasion of the future, but its status is that of an instrument. To ignore its import is the sign of an undisciplined agent; but to isolate the past, dwelling upon it for its own sake and giving it the eulogistic name of knowledge, is to substitute the reminiscence of old age for effective intelligence. The movement of the agent-patient to meet the future is partial and passionate; yet detached and impartial study of the past is the only alternative to luck in assuring success to passion.

II

This description of experience would be but a rhapsodic celebration of the commonplace were it not in marked contrast to orthodox philosophical accounts. The contrast indicates that traditional accounts have not been empirical, but have been deductions, from unnamed premises, of what experience *must* be. Historic empiricism has been empirical in a technical and controversial sense. It has said, Lord, Lord, Experience, Experience; but in practice it has served ideas *forced into* experience, not *gathered from* it.

The confusion and artificiality thereby introduced into philosophical thought is nowhere more evident than in the empirical treatment of relations or dynamic continuities. The experience of a living being struggling to hold its own and make its way in an environment, physical and social, partly facilitating and partly obstructing its actions, is of necessity a matter of ties and connections, of bearings and uses. The very point of experience, so to say, is that it doesn't occur in a vacuum; its agent-patient instead of being insulated and disconnected is bound up with the movement of things by most intimate and pervasive bonds. Only because the organism is in and of the world, and its activities correlated with those of other things in multiple ways, is it susceptible to undergoing things and capable of trying to reduce objects to means of securing its good fortune. That these connections are of diverse kinds is irresistibly proved by the fluctuations which occur in its career. Help and hindrance, stimulation and inhibition, success and failure mean specifically different modes of correlation. Although the actions of things in the world are taking place in one continuous stretch of existence, there are all kinds of specific affinities, repulsions, and relative indifferencies.

Dynamic connections are qualitatively diverse, just as are the centers of action. *In this sense,* pluralism, not monism, is an established empirical fact. The attempt to establish monism from consideration of the very nature of a relation is a mere piece of dialectics. Equally dialectical is the effort to establish by a consideration of the nature of relations an ontological Pluralism of Ultimates: *simple and independent beings.* To attempt to get results from a consideration of the "external" nature of relations is of a piece with the attempt to deduce results from their "internal" character. Some things are relatively insulated from the influence of other things; some things are easily invaded by others; some things are fiercely attracted to conjoin their activities with those of others. Experience exhibits every kind of connection[1] from the most intimate to mere external juxtaposition.

Empirically, then, active bonds of continuities of all kinds, together with static discontinuities, characterize existence. To deny this qualitative heterogeneity is to reduce the struggles and difficulties of life, its comedies and tragedies, to illusion: to the nonbeing of the Greeks or to its modern counterpart, the "subjective." Experience is an affair of facilitations and checks, of being sustained and disrupted, being let alone, being helped and troubled, of good fortune and defeat in all the countless qualitative modes which these words pallidly suggest. The existence of genuine connections of all manner of heterogeneity cannot be doubted. Such words as conjoining, disjoining, resisting, modifying, saltatory, and ambulatory (to use James's picturesque term) only hint at their actual heterogeneity.

Among the revisions and surrenders of historic problems demanded by this feature of empirical situations, those centering in the rationalistic-empirical controversy may be selected for attention. The implications of this controversy are two-fold: First, that connections are as homogeneous in fact as in name; and, secondly, if genuine, are all due to thought, or, if empirical, are arbitrary by-products of past particulars. The stubborn particularism of orthodox empiricism is its outstanding trait; consequently the opposed rationalism found no justification of bearings, continuities, and ties save to refer them in gross to the work of a hyper-empirical Reason.

Of course, not all empiricism prior to Hume and Kant was sensationalistic, pulverizing "experience" into isolated sensory qualities or simple ideas. It did not all follow Locke's lead in regarding the entire content of generalization as the "workmanship of the understanding." On the Continent, prior to Kant, philosophers were content to draw a line between empirical generalizations regarding matters of fact and

[1] The word relation suffers from ambiguity. I am speaking here of *connection*, dynamic and functional interaction. "Relation" is a term used also to express logical reference. I suspect that much of the controversy about internal and external relations is due to this ambiguity. One passes at will from existential connections of things to logical relationship of terms. Such an identification of existences with *terms* is congenial to idealism, but is paradoxical in a professed realism.

necessary universals applying to truths of reason. But logical atomism was implicit even in this theory. Statements referring to empirical fact were mere quantitative summaries of particular instances. In the sensationalism which sprang from Hume (and which was left unquestioned by Kant as far as any strictly empirical element was concerned) the implicit particularism was made explicit. But the doctrine that sensations and ideas are so many separate existences was not derived from observation nor from experiment. It was a logical deduction from a prior unexamined concept of the nature of experience. From the same concept it followed that the appearance of stable objects and of general principles of connection was but an appearance.[2]

Kantianism, then, naturally invoked universal bonds to restore objectivity. But, in so doing, it accepted the particularism of experience and proceeded to supplement it from nonempirical sources. A sensory manifold being all which is really empirical in experience, a reason which transcends experience must provide synthesis. The net outcome might have suggested a correct account of experience. For we have only to forget the apparatus by which the net outcome is arrived at, to have before us the experience of the plain man—a diversity of ceaseless changes connected in all kinds of ways, static and dynamic. This conclusion would deal a deathblow to both empiricism and rationalism. For, making clear the nonempirical character of the alleged manifold of unconnected particulars, it would render unnecessary the appeal to functions of the understanding in order to connect them. With the downfall of the traditional notion of experience, the appeal to reason to supplement its defects becomes superfluous.

The tradition was, however, too strongly entrenched; especially as it furnished the subject matter of an alleged science of states of mind which were directly known in their very presence. The historic outcome was a new crop of artificial puzzles about relations; it fastened upon philosophy for a long time the quarrel about the *a priori* and the *a posteriori* as its chief issue. The controversy is today quiescent. Yet it is not at all uncommon to find thinkers modern in tone and intent who regard any philosophy of experience as necessarily committed to denial of the existence of genuinely general propositions, and who take empiricism to be inherently averse to the recognition of the importance of an organizing and constructive intelligence.

[2] There is some gain in substituting a doctrine of flux and interpenetration of psychical states *à la* Bergson, for that of rigid discontinuity. But the substitution leaves untouched the fundamental misstatement of experience, the conception of experience as directly and primarily ''inner'' and psychical.

The quiescence alluded to is in part due, I think, to sheer weariness. But it is also due to a change of standpoint introduced by biological conceptions; and particularly the discovery of biological continuity from the lower organisms to man. For a short period, Spencerians might connect the doctrine of evolution with the old problem, and use the long temporal accumulation of "experiences" to generate something which, for human experience, is *a priori*. But the tendency of the biological way of thinking is neither to confirm or negate the Spencerian doctrine, but to shift the issue. In the orthodox position *a posteriori* and *a priori* were affairs of knowledge. But it soon becomes obvious that while there is assuredly something *a priori*—that is to say, native, unlearned, original—in human experience, that something is *not* knowledge, but is activities made possible by means of established connections of neurones. This empirical fact does not solve the orthodox problem; it dissolves it. It shows that the problem was misconceived, and solution sought by both parties in the wrong direction.

Organic instincts and organic retention, or habit-forming, are undeniable factors in actual experience. They are factors which effect organization and secure continuity. They are among the specific facts which a description of experience cognizant of the correlation of organic action with the action of other natural objects will include. But while fortunately the contribution of biological science to a truly empirical description of experiencing has outlawed the discussion of the *a priori* and *a posteriori*, the transforming effect of the same contributions upon other issues has gone unnoticed, save as pragmatism has made an effort to bring them to recognition.

III

The point seriously at issue in the notion of experience common to both sides in the older controversy thus turns out to be the place of thought or intelligence in experience. Does reason have a distinctive office? Is there a characteristic order of relations contributed by it?

Experience, to return to our positive conception, is primarily what is undergone in connection with activities whose import lies in their objective consequences—their bearing upon future experiences. Organic functions deal with things as things in course, in operation, in a state of affairs not yet given or completed. What is done with, what is just "there," is of concern only in the potentialities which it may indicate. As ended, as wholly given, it is of no account. But as a sign of what may come, it becomes an indispensable factor in behavior dealing with changes, the outcome of which is not yet determined.

The only power the organism possesses to control its own future depends upon the way its present responses modify changes which are taking place in its medium. A living being may be comparatively impotent, or comparatively free. It is all a matter of the way in which its present reactions to things influence the future reactions of things upon it. Without regard to its wish or intent every act it performs makes some difference in the environment. The change may be trivial as respects its own career and fortune. But it may also be of incalculable importance; it may import harm, destruction, or it may procure well-being.

Is it possible for a living being to increase its control of welfare and success? Can it manage, in any degree, to assure its future? Or does the amount of security depend wholly upon the accidents of the situation? Can it learn? Can it gain ability to assure its future in the present? These questions center attention upon the significance of reflective intelligence in the process of experience. The extent of an agent's capacity for inference, its power to use a given fact as a sign of something not yet given, measures the extent of its ability systematically to enlarge its control of the future.

A being which can use given and finished facts as signs of things to come; which can take given things as evidences of absent things, can, in that degree, forecast the future; it can form reasonable expectations. It is capable of achieving ideas; it is possessed of intelligence. For use of the given or finished to anticipate the consequence of processes going on is precisely what is meant by "ideas," by "intelligence."

As we have already noted, the environment is rarely all of a kind in its bearing upon organic welfare; its most wholehearted support of life activities is precarious and temporary. Some environmental changes are auspicious; others are menacing. The secret of success—that is, of the greatest attainable success—is for the organic response to cast in its lot with present auspicious changes to strengthen them and thus to avert the consequences flowing from occurrences of ill-omen. Any reaction is a venture; it involves risk. We always build better or worse than we can foretell. But the organism's fateful intervention in the course of events is blind, its choice is random, except as it can employ what happens to it as a basis of inferring what is likely to happen later. In the degree in which it can read future results in present on-goings, its responsive choice, its partiality to this condition or that, become intelligent. Its bias grows reasonable. It can deliberately, intentionally, participate in the direction of the course of affairs. Its foresight of different futures which result according as this or that present factor predominates in the shaping of affairs permits it to partake intelligently instead of blindly and fatally in the consequences its reactions give rise to. Participate it must, and to its own weal or woe. Inference, the use of what happens, to anticipate what will—or at least may—happen, makes the difference between directed and undirected participation. And this capacity for inferring is precisely the same as that use of natural occurrences for the discovery and determination of consequences—the formation of new dynamic connections—which constitutes knowledge.

The fact that thought is an intrinsic feature of experience is fatal to the traditional empiricism which makes it an artificial by-product. But for that same reason it is fatal to the historic rationalisms whose justification was the secondary and retrospective position assigned to thought by empirical philosophy. According to the particularism of the latter, thought was inevitably only a bunching together of hard-and-fast separate items; thinking was but the gathering together and tying of items already completely given, or else an equally artificial untying—a mechanical adding and subtracting of the given. It was but a cumulative registration, a consolidated merger; generality was a matter of bulk, not of quality. Thinking was therefore treated as lacking constructive power; even its organizing capacity was but simulated, being in truth but arbitrary pigeon-holing. Genuine projection of the novel, deliberate variation and invention, are idle fictions in such a version of experience. If there ever was creation, it all took place at a remote period. Since then the world has only recited lessons.

The value of inventive construction is too precious to be disposed of in this cavalier way. Its unceremonious denial afforded an opportunity to assert that in addition to experience the subject has a ready-made faculty of thought or reason which transcends experience. Rationalism thus accepted the account of experience given by traditional empiricism, and introduced reason as extra-empirical. There are still thinkers who regard any empiricism as necessarily committed to a belief in a cut-and-dried reliance upon disconnected precedents, and who hold that all systematic organization of past experiences for new and constructive purposes is alien to strict empiricism.

Rationalism never explained, however, how a reason extraneous to experience could enter into helpful relation with concrete experiences. By definition, reason and experience were antithetical, so that the concern of reason was not the fruitful expansion and guidance of the course of experience, but a realm of considerations too sublime to touch, or be touched by, experience. Discreet rationalists confined themselves to theology and allied branches of abstruse science, and to mathematics. Rationalism would have been a doctrine reserved for academic specialists and abstract formalists had it not assumed the task of providing an apologetics for traditional morals and theology, thereby getting into touch with actual human beliefs and concerns. It is notorious that historic empiricism was strong in criticism and in demolition of outworn beliefs, but weak for purposes of constructive social direction. But we frequently overlook the fact that whenever rationalism cut free from conservative apologetics, it was also simply an instrumentality for pointing out inconsistencies and absurdities in existing beliefs—a sphere in which it was immensely useful, as the Enlightenment shows. Leibniz and Voltaire were contemporary rationalists in more senses than one.[3]

The recognition that reflection is a genuine factor within experience and an indispensable factor in that control of the world which secures a prosperous and significant expansion of experience undermines historic rationalism as assuredly as it abolishes the foundations of historic empiricism. The bearing of a correct idea of the place and office of reflection upon modern idealisms is less obvious, but no less certain.

One of the curiosities of orthodox empricism is that its outstanding speculative problem is the existence of an "external world." For in accordance with the notion that experience is attached to a private subject as its exclusive possession, a world like the one in which we appear to live must be "external" to experience instead of being its subject matter. I call it a curiosity, for if anything seems adequately grounded empirically it is the existence of a world which resists the characteristic functions of the subject of experience; which goes its way, in some respects, independently of these functions, and which frustrates our hopes and intentions. Ignorance which is fatal; disappointment; the need of adjusting means and ends to the course of nature, would seem to be facts sufficiently characterizing empirical situations as to render the existence of an external world indubitable.

That the description of experience was arrived at by forcing actual empirical facts into conformity with dialectic developments from a concept of a knower outside of the real world of nature is testified to by the

---

[3] Mathematical science in its formal aspects, or as a branch of formal logic, has been the empirical stronghold of rationalism. But an empirical empiricism, in contrast with orthodox deductive empiricism, has no difficulty in establishing its jurisdiction as to deductive functions.

historic alliance of empiricism and idealism.[4] According to the most logically consistent editions of orthodox empiricism, all that can be experienced is the fleeting, the momentary, mental state. That alone is absolutely and indubitably present; therefore, it alone is cognitively certain. It alone is *knowledge*. The existence of the past (and of the future), of a decently stable world and of other selves—indeed, of one's own self—falls outside this datum of experience. These can be arrived at only by inference which is "ejective"—a name given to an alleged type of inference that jumps from experience, as from a springboard, to something beyond experience.

I should not anticipate difficulty in showing that this doctrine is, dialectically, a mass of inconsistencies. Avowedly it is a doctrine of desperation, and as such it is cited here to show the desperate straits to which ignoring empirical facts has reduced a doctrine of experience. More positively instructive are the objective idealisms which have been the offspring of the marriage between the "reason" of historic rationalism and the alleged immediate psychical stuff of historic empiricism. These idealisms have recognized the genuineness of connections and the impotency of "feeling." They have then identified connections with logical or rational connections, and thus treated "the real World" as a synthesis of sentient consciousness by means of a rational self-consciousness introducing objectivity: stability and universality of reference.

Here again, for present purposes, criticism is unnecessary. It suffices to point out that the value of this theory is bound up with the genuineness of the problem of which it purports to be a solution. If the basic concept is a fiction, there is no call for the solution. The more important point is to perceive how far the "thought" which figures in objective idealism comes from meeting the empirical demands made upon actual thought. Idealism is much less formal than historic rationalism. It treats thought, or reason, as constitutive of experience by means of uniting and constructive functions, not as just concerned with a realm of eternal truths apart from experience. On such a view thought certainly loses its abstractness and remoteness. But, unfortunately, in thus gaining the whole world it loses its own self. A world already, in its intrinsic structure, dominated by thought is not a world in which, save by contradiction of premises, thinking has anything to do.

---

[4] It is a shame to devote the word idealism, with its latent moral, practical connotations, to a doctrine whose tenets are the denial of the existence of a physical world, and the psychical character of all objects—at least as far as they are knowable. But I am following usage, not attempting to make it.

That the doctrine logically results in making change unreal and error unaccountable are consequences of importance in the technique of professional philosophy; in the denial of empirical fact which they imply they seem to many a *reductio ad absurdum* of the premises from which they proceed. But, after all, such consequences are of only professional import. What is serious, even sinister, is the implied sophistication regarding the place and office of reflection in the scheme of things. A doctrine which exalts thought in name while ignoring its efficacy in fact (that is, its use in bettering life) is a doctrine which cannot be entertained and taught without serious peril. Those who are not concerned with professional philosophy but who are solicitous for intelligence as a factor in the amelioration of actual conditions can but look askance at any doctrine which holds that the entire scheme of things is already, if we but acquire the knack of looking at it aright, fixedly and completely rational. It is a striking manifestation of the extent in which philosophies have been compensatory in quality.[5] But the matter cannot be passed over as if it were simply a question of not grudging a certain amount of consolation to one amid the irretrievable evils of life. For as to these evils no one knows how many are retrievable; and a philosophy which proclaims the ability of a dialectic theory of knowledge to reveal the world as already and eternally a self-luminous rational whole, contaminates the scope and use of thought at its very spring. To substitute the otiose insight gained by manipulation of a formula for the slow co-operative work of a humanity guided by reflective intelligence is more than a technical blunder of speculative philosophers.

A practical crisis may throw the relationship of ideas to life into an exaggerated Brocken-like spectral relief, where exaggeration renders perceptible features not ordinarily noted. The use of force to secure narrow because exclusive aims is no novelty in human affairs. The deploying of all the intelligence at command in order to increase the effectiveness of the force used is not so common, yet presents nothing intrinsically remarkable. The identification of force—military, economic, and administrative—with moral necessity and moral culture is, however, a phenomenon not likely to exhibit itself on a wide scale except where intelligence has already been suborned by an idealism which identifies "the actual with the rational," and thus finds the measure of reason in the brute event determined by superior force. If we are to have

---

[5] See Dr. Kallen's essay . . . . ["Value and Existence in Philosophy, Art and Religion" in *Creative Intelligence*.]

a philosophy which will intervene between attachment to rule of thumb muddling and devotion to a systematized subordination of intelligence to pre-existent ends, it can be found only in a philosophy which finds the ultimate measure of intelligence in consideration of a desirable future and in search for the means of bringing it progressively into existence. When professed idealism turns out to be a narrow pragmatism—narrow because taking for granted the finality of ends determined by historic conditions—the time has arrived for a pragmatism which shall be empirically idealistic, proclaiming the essential connection of intelligence with the unachieved future—with possibilities involving a transfiguration.

IV

Why has the description of experience been so remote from the facts of empirical situations? To answer this question throws light upon the submergence of recent philosophizing in epistemology—that is, in discussions of the nature, possibility, and limits of knowledge in general, and in the attempt to reach conclusions regarding the ultimate nature of reality from the answers given to such questions.

The reply to the query regarding the currency of a nonempirical doctrine of experience (even among professed empiricists) is that the traditional account is derived from a conception once universally entertained regarding the subject or bearer or center of experience. The description of experience has been forced into conformity with this prior conception; it has been primarily a deduction from it, actual empirical facts being poured into the moulds of the deductions. The characteristic feature of this prior notion is the assumption that experience centers in, or gathers about, or proceeds from a center or subject which is outside the course of natural existence, and set over against it—it being of no importance, for present purposes, whether this antithetical subject is termed soul, or spirit, or mind, or ego, or consciousness, or just knower or knowing subject.

There are plausible grounds for thinking that the currency of the idea in question lies in the form which men's religious preoccupations took for many centuries. These were deliberately and systematically otherworldly. They centered about a Fall which was not an event in nature, but an aboriginal catastrophe that corrupted Nature; about a redemption made possible by supernatural means; about a life in another world—essentially, not merely spatially, Other. The supreme drama of destiny took place in a soul or spirit which, under the circumstances, could not be conceived other than as nonnatural—extranatural, if not, strictly speaking, supernatural. When Descartes and others broke away from medieval interests, they retained as commonplaces its intellectual apparatus: Such as, knowledge is exercised by a power that is extranatural and set over against the world to be known. Even if they had wished to make a complete break, they had nothing to put as knower in the place of the soul. It may be doubted whether there was any available empirical substitute until science worked out the fact that physical changes are functional correlations of energies, and that man is continuous with other forms of life, and until social life had developed an intellectually free and responsible individual as its agent.

But my main point is not dependent upon any particular theory as to the historic origin of the notion about the bearer of experience. The point is there on its own account. The essential thing is that the bearer was conceived as outside of the world; so that experience consisted in the bearer's being affected through a type of operations not found anywhere in the world, while knowledge consists in surveying the world, looking at it, getting the view of a spectator.

The theological problem of attaining knowledge of God as ultimate reality was transformed in effect into the philosophical problem of the possibility of attaining knowledge of reality. For how is one to get beyond the limits of the subject and subjective occurrences? Familiarity breeds credulity oftener than contempt. How can a problem be artificial when men have been busy discussing it almost for three hundred years? But if the assumption that experience is something set over against the world is contrary to fact, then the problem of how self or mind or subjective experience or consciousness can reach knowledge of an external world is assuredly a meaningless problem. Whatever questions there may be about knowledge, they will not be the kind of problems which have formed epistemology.

The problem of knowledge as conceived in the industry of epistemology is the problem of knowledge *in general*—of the possibility, extent, and validity of knowledge in general. What does this "in general" mean? In ordinary life there are problems a-plenty of knowledge in particular; every conclusion we try to reach, theoretical or practical, affords such a problem. But there is no problem of knowledge in general. I do not mean, of course, that general statements cannot be made about knowledge, or that the problem of attaining these general statements is not a genuine one. On the contrary, specific instances of success and failure in inquiry exist, and are of such a character that one can discover the conditions conducing to success and failure. Statement of these conditions constitutes logic, and is capable of being an important aid in proper guidance of further attempts at knowing. But this logical problem of knowledge is at the opposite pole from the epistemological. Specific problems are about right conclusions to be reached—which means, in effect, right ways of going about the business of inquiry. They imply a difference between knowledge and error consequent upon right and wrong methods of inquiry and testing; not a difference between experience and the world. The problem of knowledge *überhaupt* exists because it is assumed that there is a knower in general, who is outside of the world to be known, and who is defined in terms antithetical to the traits of the world. With analogous assumptions, we could invent and discuss a problem of digestion in general. All that would be required would be to conceive the stomach and food material as inhabiting different worlds. Such an assumption would leave on our hands the question of the possibility, extent, nature, and genuineness of any transaction between stomach and food.

But because the stomach and food inhabit a continuous stretch of existence, because digestion is but a correlation of diverse activities in one world, the problems of digestion are specific and plural: What are the particular correlations which constitute it? How does it proceed in different situations? What is favorable and what unfavorable to its best performance?—and so on. Can one deny that if we were to take our clue from the present empirical situation, including the scientific notion of evolution (biological continuity) and the existing arts of control of nature, subject and object would be treated as occupying the same natural world as unhesitatingly as we assume the natural conjunction of an animal and its food? Would it not follow that knowledge is one way in which natural energies co-operate? Would there be any problem save discovery of the peculiar structure of this co-operation, the conditions under which it occurs to best effect, and the consequences which issue from its occurrence?

It is a commonplace that the chief divisions of modern philosophy, idealism in its different kinds, realisms of various brands, so-called common-sense dualism, agnosticism, relativism, phenomenalism, have grown up around the epistemological problem of the general relation of subject and object. Problems not openly epistemological, such as whether the relation of changes in consciousness to physical changes is one of interaction, parallelism, or automatism have the same origin. What becomes of philosophy, consisting largely as it does of different answers to these questions, in case the assumptions which generate the questions have no empirical standing? Is it not time that philosophers turned from the attempt to determine the comparative merits of various replies to the questions to a consideration of the claims of the questions?

When dominating religious ideas were built up about the idea that the self is a stranger and pilgrim in this world; when morals, falling in line, found true good only in inner states of a self inaccessible to anything but its own private introspection; when political theory assumed the finality of disconnected and mutually exclusive personalities, the notion that the bearer of experience is antithetical to the world instead of being in and of it was congenial. It at least had the warrant of other beliefs and aspirations. But the doctrine of biological continuity or organic evolution has destroyed the scientific basis of the conception. Morally, men are now concerned with the amelioration of the conditions of the common lot in this world. Social sciences recognize that associated life is not a matter of physical juxtaposition, but of genuine intercourse—of community of experience in a non-metaphorical sense of community. Why should we longer try to patch up and refine and stretch the old solutions till they seem to cover the change of thought and practice? Why not recognize that the trouble is with the problem?

A belief in organic evolution which does not extend unreservedly to the way in which the subject of experience is thought of, and which does not strive to bring the entire theory of experience and knowing into line with biological and social facts, is hardly more than Pickwickian. There are many, for example, who hold that dreams, hallucinations, and errors cannot be accounted for at all except on the theory that a self (or "consciousness") exercises a modifying influence upon the "real object." The logical assumption is that consciousness is outside of the real object; that it is something different in kind, and therefore has the power of changing "reality" into appearance, of introducing "relativities" into things as they are in themselves—in short, of infecting real things with subjectivity. Such writers seem unaware of the fact that this assumption makes consciousness supernatural in the literal sense of the word; and that, to say the least, the conception can be accepted by one who accepts the doctrine of biological continuity only after every other way of dealing with the facts has been exhausted.

Realists, of course (at least some of the Neorealists), deny any such miraculous intervention of consciousness. But they[6] admit the reality of

[6] The "they" means the "some" of the prior sentence—those whose realism is epistemological, instead of being a plea for taking the facts of experience as we find them without refraction through epistemological apparatus.

the problem; denying only this particular solution, they try to find some other way out, which will still preserve intact the notion of knowledge as a relationship of a general sort between subject and object.

Now dreams and hallucinations, errors, pleasures, and pains, possibly "secondary" qualities, do not occur save where there are organic centers of experience. They cluster about a subject. But to treat them as things which inhere exclusively in the subject; or as posing the problem of a distortion of *the* real object by a knower set over against the world, or as presenting facts to be explained primarily as cases of contemplative knowledge, is to testify that one has still to learn the lesson of evolution in its application to the affairs in hand.

If biological development be accepted, the subject of experience is at least an animal, continuous with other organic forms in a process of more complex organization. An animal in turn is at least continuous with chemico-physical processes which, in living things, are so organized as really to constitute the activities of life with all their defining traits. And experience is not identical with brain action; it is the entire organic agent-patient in all its interaction with the environment, natural and social. The brain is primarily an organ of a certain kind of behavior, not of knowing the world. And to repeat what has already been said, experiencing *is* just certain modes of interaction, of correlation, of natural objects among which the organism happens, so to say, to be one. It follows with equal force that experience means primarily not knowledge, but ways of doing and suffering. Knowing must be described by discovering what particular mode—qualitatively unique—of doing and suffering it is. As it is, we find experience assimilated to a nonempirical concept of knowledge, derived from an antecedent notion of a spectator outside of the world.[7]

In short, the epistemological fashion of conceiving dreams, errors, "relativities," etc., depends upon the isolation of mind from intimate participation with other changes in the same continuous nexus. Thus it is like contending that when a bottle bursts, the bottle is, in some self-

---

[7] It is interesting to note that some of the realists who have assimilated the cognitive relation to other existential relations in the world (instead of treating it as an unique or epistemological relation) have been forced in support of their conception of knowledge as a "presentative" or spectatorial affair to extend the defining features of the latter to all relations among things, and hence to make all the "real" things in the world pure "simples," wholly independent of one another. So conceived the doctrine of external relations appears to be rather the doctrine of complete externality of *things*. Aside from this point, the doctrine is interesting for its dialectical ingenuity and for the elegant development of assumed premises, rather than convincing on account of empirical evidence supporting it.

contained miraculous way, exclusively responsible. Since it is the nature of a bottle to be whole so as to retain fluids, bursting is an abnormal event—comparable to a hallucination. Hence it cannot belong to the "real" bottle; the "subjectivity" of glass is the cause. It is obvious that since the breaking of glass is a case of specific correlation of natural energies, its accidental and abnormal character has to do with *consequences,* not with causation. Accident is interference with the consequences for which the bottle is intended. The bursting considered apart from its bearing on these consequences is on a plane with any other occurrence in the wide world. But from the standpoint of a desired future, bursting is an anomaly, an interruption of the course of events.

The analogy with the occurrence of dreams, hallucinations, etc., seems to me exact. Dreams are not something outside of the regular course of events; they are in and of it. They are not cognitive distortions of real things; they are *more* real things. There is nothing abnormal in their existence, any more than there is in the bursting of a bottle.[8] But they may be abnormal, from the standpoint of their influence, of their operation as stimuli in calling out responses to modify the future. Dreams have often been taken as prognostics of what is to happen; they have modified conduct. A hallucination may lead a man to consult a doctor; such a consequence is right and proper. But the consultation indicates that the subject regarded it as an indication of consequences which he feared: as a symptom of a disturbed life. Or the hallucination may lead him to anticipate consequences which in fact flow only from the possession of great wealth. Then the hallucination is a disturbance of the normal course of events; the occurrence is wrongly *used* with reference to eventualities.

To regard reference to use and to desired and intended consequences as involving a "subjective" factor is to miss the point, for this has regard to the future. The uses to which a bottle are put are not mental; they do not consist of physical states; they are further correlations of natural existences. Consequences in use are genuine natural events; but they do not occur without the intervention of behavior involving anticipation of a future. The case is not otherwise with a hallucination. The differences it makes are in any case differences in the course of the one continuous world. The important point is whether they are good or bad differences. To use the hallucination as a sign of organic lesions that menace health means the beneficial result of seeing a physician; to respond to it as a

---

[8] In other words, there is a general "problem of error" only because there is a general problem of evil, concerning which see Dr. Kallen's essay . . . . [*Loc. cit.*]

sign of consequences such as actually follow only from being persecuted is to fall into error—to be abnormal. The persecutors are "unreal"; that is, there are no things which act as persecutors act; but the hallucination exists. Given its conditions it is as natural as any other event, and poses only the same kind of problem as is put by the occurrence of, say, a thunderstorm. The "unreality" of persecution is not, however, a subjective matter; it means that conditions do not exist for producing the *future* consequences which are now anticipated and reacted to. Ability to anticipate future consequences and to respond to them as stimuli to present behavior may well *define* what is meant by a mind or by "consciousness."[9] But this is only a way of saying just what kind of a real or natural existence the subject is; it is not to fall back on a preconception about an unnatural subject in order to characterize the occurrence of error.

Although the discussion may be already labored, let us take another example—the occurrence of disease. By definition it is pathological, abnormal. At one time in human history this abnormality was taken to be something dwelling in the intrinsic nature of the event—in its existence irrespective of future consequences. Disease was literally extranatural and to be referred to demons or to magic. No one today questions its naturalness—its place in the order of natural events. Yet it is abnormal—for it operates to effect results different from those which follow from health. The difference is a genuine empirical difference, not a mere mental distinction. From the standpoint of bearing on a subsequent course of events disease is unnatural, in spite of the naturalness of its occurrence and origin.

The habit of ignoring reference to the future is responsible for the assumption that to admit human participation in any form is to admit the "subjective" in a sense which alters the objective into the phenomenal. There have been those who, like Spinoza, regarded health and disease, good and ill, as equally real and equally unreal. However, only a few consistent materialists have included truth along with error as merely phenomenal and subjective. But if one does not regard movement toward possible consequences as genuine, wholesale denial of existential validity to all these distinctions is the only logical course. To select truth as objective and error as "subjective" is, on this basis, an unjustifiably partial procedure. Take everything as fixedly given, and

[9] Compare the paper by Professor Bode. ["Consciousness and Psychology" in *Creative Intelligence*.]

both truth and error are arbitrary insertions into fact. Admit the genuineness of changes going on, and capacity for its direction through organic action based on foresight, and both truth and falsity are alike existential. It is human to regard the course of events which is in line with our own efforts as the *regular* course of events, and interruptions as abnormal, but this partiality of human desire is itself a part of what actually takes place.

It is now proposed to take a particular case of the alleged epistemological predicament for discussion, since the entire ground cannot be covered. I think, however, the instance chosen is typical, so that the conclusion reached may be generalized.

The instance is that of so-called relativity in perception. There are almost endless instances; the stick bent in water; the whistle changing pitch with change of distance from the ear; objects doubled when the eye is pushed; the destroyed star still visible, etc., etc. For our consideration we may take the case of a spherical object that presents itself to one observer as a flat circle, to another as a somewhat distorted elliptical surface. This situation gives empirical proof, so it is argued, of the difference between a real object and mere appearance. Since there is but one object, the existence of two *subjects* is the sole differentiating factor. Hence the two appearances of the one real object [are] proof of the intervening distorting action of the subject. And many of the Neorealists who deny the difference in question, admit the case to be one of knowledge and accordingly to constitute an epistemological problem. They have in consequence developed wonderfully elaborate schemes of sundry kinds to maintain "epistemological monism" intact.

Let us try to keep close to empirical facts. In the first place the two unlike appearances of the one sphere are physically necessary because of the laws of reaction of light. If the one sphere did *not* assume these two appearances under given conditions, we should be confronted with a hopelessly irreconcilable discrepancy in the behavior of natural energy. That the result is natural is evidenced by the fact that two cameras—or other arrangements of apparatus for reflecting light—yield precisely the same results. Photographs are as genuinely physical existence as the original sphere; and they exhibit the two geometrical forms.

The statement of these facts makes no impression upon the confirmed epistemologist; he merely retorts that as long as it is admitted that the organism is the cause of a sphere being seen, from different points, as a circular and as an elliptical surface, the essence of his contention—the modification of the real object by the subject—is admitted. To the question why the same logic does not apply to photographic records he makes, as far as I know, no reply at all.

The source of the difficulty is not hard to see. The objection assumes that the alleged modifications of *the* real object are cases of *knowing* and hence attributable to the influence of a *knower*. Statements which set forth the doctrine will always be found to refer to the organic factor, to the eye, as an observer or a percipient. Even when reference is made to a lens or a mirror, language is sometimes used which suggests that the writer's näiveté is sufficiently gross to treat these physical factors as if they were engaged in perceiving the sphere. But as it is evident that the lens operates as a physical factor in correlation with other physical factors—notably light—so it ought to be evident that the intervention of the optical apparatus of the eye is a purely noncognitive matter. The relation in question is not one between a sphere and a would-be knower of it, unfortunately condemned by the nature of the knowing apparatus to alter the thing he would know; it is an affair of the dynamic interaction of two physical agents in producing a third thing, an effect—an affair of precisely the same kind as in any physical conjoint action, say the operation of hydrogen and oxygen in producing water. To regard the eye as primarily a knower, an observer, of things, is as crass as to assign that function to a camera. But unless the eye (or optical apparatus, or brain, or organism) be so regarded, there is absolutely no problem of observation or of knowledge in the case of the occurrence of elliptical and circular surfaces. Knowledge does not enter into the affair at all till *after* these forms of refracted light have been produced. About them there is nothing unreal. Light is really, physically, existentially, refracted into these forms. If the same spherical form upon refracting light to physical objects in two quite different positions produced the same geometric forms, there would, indeed, be something to marvel at—as there would be if wax produced the same results in contact simultaneously with a cold body and with a warm one. Why talk about *the real* object in relation to *a knower* when what is given is one real thing in dynamic connection with another real thing?

The way of dealing with the case will probably meet with a retort; at least, it has done so before. It has been said that the account given above and the account of traditional subjectivism differ only verbally. The essential thing in both, so it is said, is the admission that an activity of a self or subject or organism makes a difference in the real object. Whether the subject makes this difference in the very process of knowing or makes it prior to the act of knowing is a minor matter; what is important is that the known thing has, by the time it is known, been "subjectified."

The objection gives a convenient occasion for summarizing the main points of the argument. On the one hand, the retort of the objector depends upon talking about *the* real object. Employ the term "*a* real object," and the change produced by the activity characteristic of the optical apparatus is of just the same kind as that of the camera lens or that of any other physical agency. Every event in the world marks a difference made to one existence in active conjunction with some other existence. And, as for the alleged subjectivity, if subjective is used merely as an adjective to designate the specific activity of a particular existence, comparable, say, to the term feral, applied to tiger, or metallic, applied to iron, then of course reference to subjective is legitimate. But it is also tautological. It is like saying that flesh eaters are carnivorous. But the term "subjective" is so consecrated to other uses, usually implying invidious contrast with objectivity (while subjective in the sense just suggested means specific mode *of* objectivity), that it is difficult to maintain this innocent sense. Its use in any disparaging way in the situation before us—any sense implicating contrast with a real object—assumes that the organism *ought* not to make any difference when it operates in conjunction with other things. Thus we run to earth that assumption that the subject is heterogeneous from every other natural existence; it is to be the one otiose, inoperative thing in a moving world—our old assumption of the self as outside of things.[10]

What and where is knowledge in the case we have been considering? Not, as we have already seen, in the production of forms of light having a circular and elliptical surface. These forms are natural happenings. They may enter into knowledge or they may not, according to circumstances. Countless such refractive changes take place without being noted.[11] When they become subject matter for knowledge, the inquiry

[10] As the attempt to retain the epistemological problem and yet to reject idealistic and relativistic solutions has forced some Neorealists into the doctrine of isolated and independent simples, so it has also led to a doctrine of Eleatic pluralism. In order to maintain the doctrine [that] the subject makes no difference to anything else, it is held that *no* ultimate real makes any difference to anything else—all this rather than surrender once for all the genuineness of the problem and to follow the lead of empirical subject matter.

[11] There is almost no end to the various dialectic developments of the epistemological situation. When it is held that all the relations of the type in question are cognitive, and yet it is recognized (as it must be) that many such "transformations" go unremarked, the theory is supplemented by introducing "unconscious" psychical modifications.

they set on foot may take on an indefinite variety of forms. One may be interested in ascertaining more about the structural peculiarities of the forms themselves; one may be interested in the mechanism of their production; one may find problems in projective geometry, or in drawing and painting—all depending upon the specific matter-of-fact context. The forms may be *objectives* of knowledge—of reflective examination—or they may be means of knowing something else. It may happen—under some circumstances it does happen—that the objective of inquiry is the nature of the geometric form which, when refracting light, gives rise to these other forms. In this case the sphere is the thing known, and in this case, the forms of light are signs or evidence of the conclusion to be drawn. There is no more reason for supposing that they *are* (mis)knowledges of the sphere—that the sphere is necessarily and from the start what one is trying to know—than for supposing that the position of the mercury in the thermometer tube is a cognitive distortion of atmospheric pressure. In each case (that of the mercury and that of, say, a circular surface) the primary datum is a physical happening. In each case it may be used, upon occasion, as a sign or evidence of the nature of the causes which brought it about. Given the position in question, the circular form would be an intrinsically *unreliable* evidence of the nature and position of the spherical body only in case it, as the direct datum of perception, were *not* what it is—a circular form.

I confess that all this seems so obvious that the reader is entitled to inquire into the motive for reciting such plain facts. Were it not for the persistence of the epistemological problem it would be an affront to the reader's intelligence to dwell upon them. But as long as such facts as we have been discussing furnish the subject matter with which philosophizing is peculiarly concerned, these commonplaces must be urged and reiterated. They bear out two contentions which are important at the juncture, although they will lose special significance as soon as these are habitually recognized: Negatively, a prior and nonempirical notion of the self is the source of the prevailing belief that experience as such is primarily cognitional—a knowledge affair; positively, *knowledge is always a matter of the use that is made of experienced natural events*, a use in which given things are treated as indications of what will be experienced under different conditions.

Let us make one effort more to clear up these points. Suppose it is a question of knowledge of water. The thing to be known does not present itself primarily as a matter of knowledge-and-ignorance at all. It occurs as a stimulus to action and as the source of certain undergoings. It is something to react to—to drink, to wash with, to put out fire with, and also something that reacts unexpectedly to our reactions, that makes us undergo disease, suffocation, drowning. In this two-fold way, water or anything else enters into experience. Such presence in experience has of itself nothing to do with knowledge or consciousness; nothing that is in the sense of depending upon them, though it has everything to do with knowledge and consciousness in the sense that the latter depends upon prior experience of this noncognitive sort. Man's experience is what it is because his response to things (even successful response) and the reactions of things to his life, are so radically different from knowledge. The difficulties and tragedies of life, the stimuli to acquiring knowledge, lie in the radical disparity of presence-in-experience and presence-in-knowing. Yet the immense importance of knowledge experience, the fact that turning presence-in-experience over into presence-in-a-knowledge-experience is the sole mode of control of nature, has systematically hypnotized European philosophy since the time of Socrates into thinking that all experiencing is a mode of knowing, if not good knowledge, then a low-grade or confused or implicit knowledge.

When water is an adequate stimulus to action or when its reactions oppress and overwhelm us, it remains outside the scope of knowledge. When, however, the bare presence of the thing (say, as optical stimulus) ceases to operate directly as stimulus to response and begins to operate in connection with a forecast of the consequences it will effect when responded to, it begins to acquire meaning—to be known, to be an object. It is noted as something which is wet, fluid, satisfies thirst, allays uneasiness, etc. The conception that we begin with a known visual quality which is thereafter enlarged by adding on qualities apprehended by the other senses does not rest upon experience; it rests upon making experience conform to the notion that every experience *must* be a cognitive noting. As long as the visual stimulus operates as a stimulus on its own account, there is no apprehension, no noting, of color or light at all. To much the greater portion of sensory stimuli we react in precisely this wholly noncognitive way. In the attitude of suspended response in which consequences are anticipated, the direct stimulus becomes a sign or index of something else—and thus matter of noting or apprehension or acquaintance, or whatever term may be employed. This difference (together, of course, with the consequences which go with it) is the difference which the natural event of knowing makes to the natural event of direct organic stimulation. It is no change of a reality into an unreality, of an object into something subjective; it is no secret, illicit, or epistemological transformation; it is a genuine acquisition of new and distinctive features through entering into relations with things with which it was not formerly connected—namely, possible and future things.

But, replies some one so obsessed with the epistemological point of view that he assumes that the prior account is a rival epistemology in disguise, all this involves no change in Reality, no difference made to Reality. Water was all the time all the things it is ever found out to be. Its real nature has not been altered by knowing it; any such alteration means a misknowing.

In reply let it be said—once more and finally—there is no assertion or implication about *the* real object or *the* real world or *the* reality. Such an assumption goes with that epistemological universe of discourse which has to be abandoned in an empirical universe of discourse. The change is of *a* real object. An incident of the world operating as a physiologically direct stimulus is assuredly a reality. Responded to, it produces specific consequences in virtue of the response. Water is not drunk unless somebody drinks it; it does not quench thirst unless a thirsty person drinks it—and so on. Consequences occur whether one is aware of them or not; they are integral facts in experience. But let one of these consequences be anticipated and let it, as anticipated, become an indispensable element in the stimulus, and then there is a known object. It is not that knowing *produces* a change, but that it *is* a change of the specific kind described. A serial process, the successive portions of which are as such incapable of simultaneous occurrence, is telescoped and condensed into an object, a unified interreference of con-temporaneous properties, most of which express potentialities rather than completed data.

Because of this change, an *object* possesses truth or error (which the physical occurrence as such never has); it is classifiable as fact or fantasy; it is of a sort or kind, expresses an essence or nature, possesses implications, etc., etc. That is to say, it is marked by specifiable *logical* traits not found in physical occurrences as such. Because objective idealisms have seized upon these traits as constituting the very essence of Reality is no reason for proclaiming that they are ready-made features of physical happenings, and hence for maintaining that know-ing is nothing but an appearance of things on a stage for which "consciousness" supplies the footlights. For only the epistemological predicament leads to "presentations" being regarded as cognitions of things which were previously unpresented. In any empirical situation of everyday life or of science, knowledge signifies something stated or in-ferred of another thing. Visible water is not a more or less erroneous presentation of H_2O, but H_2O is a knowledge about the thing we see, drink, wash with, sail on, and use for power.

A further point and the present phase of discussion terminates. Treating knowledge as a presentative relation between the knower and object makes it necessary to regard the mechanism of *presentation* as constituting the act of knowing. Since things may be presented in sense-perception, in recollection, in imagination and in conception, and since the mechanism in every one of these four styles of presentation is sensory-cerebral the problem of knowing becomes a mind-body problem.[12] The psychological, or physiological, mechanism of presentation involved in seeing a chair, remembering what I ate yesterday for luncheon, imagining the moon the size of a cart wheel, conceiving a mathematical continuum is identified with the operation of knowing. The evil consequences are two-fold. The problem of the relation of mind and body has become a part of the problem of the possibility of knowledge in general, to the further complication of a matter already hopelessly constrained. Meantime the actual process of knowing, namely, operations of controlled observation, inference, reasoning, and testing, the only process with *intellectual* import, is dismissed as irrelevant to the theory of knowing. The methods of knowing practiced in daily life and science are excluded from consideration in the philosophical theory of knowing. Hence the constructions of the latter become more and more elaborately artificial because there is no definite check upon them. It would be easy to quote from epistemological writers statements to the effect that these processes (which supply the only empirically verifiable facts of knowing) are *merely* inductive in character, or even that they are of purely psychological significance. It would be difficult to find a more complete inversion of the facts than in the latter statement, since presentation constitutes in fact the psychological affair. A confusion of logic with physiological [psychology] has bred hybrid epistemology, with the amazing result that the technique of effective inquiry is rendered irrelevant to the theory of knowing, and those physical events involved in the occurrence of data for knowing are treated as if they constituted the act of knowing.

---

[12] Conception-presentation has, of course, been made by many in the history of speculation an exception to this statement: "pure" memory is also made an exception by Bergson. To take cognizance of this matter would, of course, accentuate, not relieve, the difficulty remarked upon in the text.

V

What are the bearings of our discussion upon the conception of the present scope and office of philosophy? What do our conclusions indicate and demand with reference to philosophy itself? For the philosophy which reaches such conclusions regarding knowledge and mind must apply them, sincerely and wholeheartedly, to its idea of its own nature. For philosophy claims to be one form or mode of knowing. If, then, the conclusion is reached that knowing is a way of employing empirical occurrences with respect to increasing power to direct the consequences which flow from things, the application of the conclusion must be made to philosophy itself. It, too, becomes not a contemplative survey of existence nor an analysis of what is past and done with, but an outlook upon future possibilities with reference to attaining the better and averting the worse. Philosophy must take, with good grace, its own medicine.

It is easier to state the negative results of the changed idea of philosophy than the positive ones. The point that occurs to mind most readily is that philosophy will have to surrender all pretension to be peculiarly concerned with ultimate reality, or with reality as a complete (i.e., completed) whole: with *the* real object. The surrender is not easy of achievement. The philosophic tradition that comes to us from classic Greek thought and that was reinforced by Christian philosophy in the Middle Ages discriminates philosophical knowing from other modes of knowing by means of an alleged peculiarly intimate concern with supreme, ultimate, true reality. To deny this trait to philosophy seems to many to be the suicide of philosophy; to be a systematic adoption of skepticism or agnostic positivism.

The pervasiveness of the tradition is shown in the fact that so vitally a contemporary thinker as Bergson, who finds a philosophic revolution involved in abandonment of the traditional identification of the truly real with the fixed (an identification inherited from Greek thought), does not find it in his heart to abandon the counterpart identification of philosophy with search for the truly Real; and hence he finds it necessary to substitute an ultimate and absolute flux for an ultimate and absolute permanence. Thus his great empirical services in calling attention to the fundamental importance of considerations of time for problems of life and mind get compromised with a mystic, nonempirical "Intuition"; and we find him preoccupied with solving, by means of his new idea of ultimate reality, the traditional problems of realities-in-themselves and phenomena, matter and mind, free will and determinism, God and the world. Is not that another evidence of the influence of the classic idea about philosophy?

Even the new realists are not content to take their realism as a plea for approaching subject matter directly instead of through the intervention of epistemological apparatus; they find it necessary first to determine the status of *the* real object. Thus they too become entangled in the problem of the possibility of error, dreams, hallucinations, etc., in short, the problem of evil. For I take it that an uncorrupted realism would accept such things as real events, and find in them no other problems than those attending the consideration of any real occurrence—namely, problems of structure, origin, and operation.

It is often said that pragmatism, unless it is content to be a contribution to mere methodology, must develop a theory of Reality. But the chief characteristic trait of the pragmatic notion of reality is precisely that no theory of Reality in general, *überhaupt*, is possible or needed. It occupies the position of an emancipated empiricism or a thoroughgoing naïve realism. It finds that "reality" is a *denotative* term, a word used to designate indifferently everything that happens. Lies, dreams, insanities, deceptions, myths, theories are all of them just the events which they specifically are. Pragmatism is content to take its stand with science; for science finds all such events to be subject matter of description and inquiry—just like stars and fossils, mosquitoes and malaria, circulation and vision. It also takes its stand with daily life, which finds that such things really have to be reckoned with as they occur interwoven in the texture of events.

The only way in which the term reality can ever become more than a blanket denotative term is through recourse to specific events in all their diversity and thatness. Speaking summarily, I find that the retention by philosophy of the notion of a Reality feudally superior to the events of everyday occurrence is the chief source of the increasing isolation of philosophy from common sense and science. For the latter do not operate in any such region. As with them of old, philosophy in dealing with real difficulties finds itself still hampered by reference to realities more real, more ultimate, than those which directly happen.

I have said that identifying the cause of philosophy with the notion of superior reality is the cause of an *increasing* isolation from science and practical life. The phrase reminds us that there was a time when the enterprise of science and the moral interests of men both moved in a universe invidiously distinguished from that of ordinary occurrence. While all that happens is equally real—since it really happens—happenings are not of equal worth. Their respective consequences, their import, varies tremendously. Counterfeit money, although real (or rather *because* real) is really different from valid circulatory medium, just as disease is really different from health; different in specific structure and so different in consequences. In occidental thought, the Greeks were the first to draw the distinction between the genuine and the spurious in a generalized fashion and to formulate and enforce its tremendous significance for the conduct of life. But since they had at command no technique of experimental analysis and no adequate technique of mathematical analysis, they were compelled to treat the difference of the true and the false, the dependable and the deceptive, as signifying two kinds of existence, the truly real and the apparently real.

Two points can hardly be asserted with too much emphasis. The Greeks were wholly right in the feeling that questions of good and ill, as far as they fall within human control, are bound up with discrimination of the genuine from the spurious, of "being" from what only pretends to be. But because they lacked adequate instrumentalities for coping with this difference in specific situations, they were forced to treat the difference as a wholesale and rigid one. Science was concerned with vision of ultimate and true reality; opinion was concerned with getting along with apparent realities. Each had its appropriate region permanently marked off. Matters of opinion could never become matters of science; their intrinsic nature forbade. When the practice of science went on under such conditions, science and philosophy were one and the same thing. Both had to do with ultimate reality in its rigid and insuperable difference from ordinary occurrences.

We have only to refer to the way in which medieval life wrought the philosophy of an ultimate and supreme reality into the context of practical life to realize that for centuries political and moral interests were bound up with the distinction between the absolutely real and the relatively real. The difference was no matter of a remote technical philosophy, but one which controlled life from the cradle to the grave, from the grave to the endless life after death. By means of a vast institution, which in effect was state as well as church, the claims of ultimate reality were enforced; means of access to it were provided. Acknowledgment of The Reality brought security in this world and salvation in the next. It is not necessary to report the story of the change which has since taken place. It is enough for our purposes to note that none of the modern philosophies of a superior reality, or *the* real object, idealistic or realistic, holds that its insight makes a difference like that between sin and holiness, eternal condemnation and eternal bliss. While in its own context the philosophy of ultimate reality entered into the vital concerns of men, it now tends to be an ingenious dialectic exercised in professorial corners by a few who have retained ancient premises while rejecting their application to the conduct of life.

The increased isolation from science of any philosophy identified with the problem of *the* real is equally marked. For the growth of science has consisted precisely in the invention of an equipment, a technique of appliances and procedures, which, accepting all occurrences as homogeneously real, proceeds to distinguish the authenticated from the spurious, the true from the false, by specific modes of treatment in specific situations. The procedures of the trained engineer, of the competent physician, of the laboratory expert, have turned out to be the only ways of discriminating the counterfeit from the valid. And they have revealed that the difference is not one of antecedent fixity of existence, but one of mode of treatment and of the consequences thereon attendant. After mankind has learned to put its trust in specific procedures in order to make its discriminations between the false and the true, philosophy arrogates to itself the enforcement of the distinction at its own cost.

More than once, this essay has intimated that the counterpart of the idea of invidiously real reality is the spectator notion of knowledge. If the knower, however defined, is set over against the world to be known, knowing consists in possessing a transcript, more or less accurate but otiose, of real things. Whether this transcript is presentative in character (as realists say) or whether it is by means of states of consciousness which represent things (as subjectivists say), is a matter of great importance in its own context. But, in another regard, this difference is negligible in comparison with the point in which both agree. Knowing is viewing from outside. But if it be true that the self or subject of experience is part and parcel of the course of events, it follows that the self *becomes* a knower. It becomes a mind in virtue of a distinctive way of partaking in the course of events. The significant distinction is no longer between the knower *and* the world; it is between different ways of being in and of the movement of things; between a brute physical way and a purposive, intelligent way.

There is no call to repeat in detail the statements which have been advanced. Their net purport is that the directive presence of future possibilities in dealing with existent conditions is what is meant by knowing; that the self becomes a knower or mind when anticipation of future consequences operates as its stimulus. What we are now concerned with is the effect of this conception upon the nature of philosophic knowing.

As far as I can judge, popular response to pragmatic philosophy was moved by two quite different considerations. By some it was thought to provide a new species of sanctions, a new mode of apologetics, for certain religious ideas whose standing had been threatened. By others, it was welcomed because it was taken as a sign that philosophy was about to surrender its otiose and speculative remoteness; that philosophers were beginning to recognize that philosophy is of account only if, like everyday knowing and like science, it affords guidance to action and thereby makes a difference in the event. It was welcomed as a sign that philosophers were willing to have the worth of their philosophizing measured by responsible tests.

I have not seen this point of view emphasized, or hardly recognized, by professional critics. The difference of attitude can probably be easily explained. The epistemological universe of discourse is so highly technical that only those who have been trained in the history of thought think in terms of it. It did not occur, accordingly, to nontechnical readers to interpret the doctrine that the meaning and validity of thought are fixed by differences made in consequences and in satisfactoriness, to mean consequences in personal feelings. Those who were professionally trained, however, took the statement to mean that consciousness or mind in the mere act of looking at things modifies them. It understood the doctrine of test of validity by consequences to mean that apprehensions and conceptions are true if the modifications affected by them were of an emotionally desirable tone.

Prior discussion should have made it reasonably clear that the source of this misunderstanding lies in the neglect of temporal considerations. The change made in things by the self in knowing is not immediate and, so to say, cross-sectional. It is longitudinal—in the redirection given to changes already going on. Its analogue is found in the changes which take place in the development of, say, iron ore into a watch spring, not in those of the miracle of transubstantiation. For the static, cross-sectional, nontemporal relation of subject and object, the pragmatic hypothesis substitutes apprehension of a thing in terms of the results in other things which it is tending to effect. For the unique epistemological relation, it substitutes a practical relation of a familiar type—responsive behavior which changes in time the subject matter to which it applies. The unique thing about the responsible behavior which constitutes knowing is the specific difference which marks it off from other modes of response, namely, the part played in it by anticipation and prediction. Knowing is the act, stimulated by this foresight, of securing and averting consequences. The success of the achievement measures the standing of the foresight by which response is directed. The popular impression that pragmatic philosophy means that philosophy shall develop ideas relevant to the actual crises of life, ideas influential in dealing with them and tested by the assistance they afford, is correct.

Reference to practical response suggests, however, another misapprehension. Many critics have jumped at the obvious association of the word pragmatic with practical. They have assumed that the intent is to limit all knowledge, philosophic included, to promoting "action," understanding by action either just any bodily movement, or those bodily movements which conduce to the preservation and grosser well-being of the body. James's statement that general conceptions must "cash in" has been taken (especially by European critics) to mean that the end and measure of intelligence lies in the narrow and coarse utilities which it produces. Even an acute American thinker, after first criticizing pragmatism as a kind of idealistic epistemology, goes on to treat it as a doctrine which regards intelligence as a lubricating oil facilitating the workings of the body.

One source of the misunderstanding is suggested by the fact that "cashing in" to James meant that a general idea must always be capable of verification in specific existential cases. The notion of "cashing in" says nothing about the breadth or depth of the specific consequences. As an empirical doctrine, it could not say anything about them in general; the specific cases must speak for themselves. If one conception is verified in terms of eating beefsteak, and another in terms of a favorable credit balance in the bank, that is not because of anything in the theory, but because of the specific nature of the conceptions in question, and because there exist particular events like hunger and trade. If there are also existences in which the most liberal esthetic ideas and the most generous moral conceptions can be verified by specific embodiment, assuredly so much the better. The fact that a strictly empirical philosophy was taken by so many critics to imply an *a priori* dogma about the kind of consequences capable of existence is evidence, I think, of the inability of many philosophers to think in concretely empirical terms. Since the critics were themselves accustomed to get results by manipulating the concepts of "consequences" and of "practice," they assumed that even a would-be empiricist must be doing the same sort of thing. It will, I suppose, remain for a long time incredible to some that a philosopher should really intend to go to specific experiences to determine of what scope and depth practice admits, and what sort of consequences the world permits to come into being. Concepts are so clear; it takes so little time to develop their implications; experiences are so confused, and it requires so much time and energy to lay hold of them. And yet these same critics charge pragmatism with adopting subjective and emotional standards!

As a matter of fact, the pragmatic theory of intelligence means that the function of mind is to project new and more complex ends—to free experience from routine and from caprice. Not the use of thought to accomplish purposes already given either in the mechanism of the body or in that of the existent state of society, but the use of intelligence to liberate and liberalize action, is the pragmatic lesson. Action restricted to given and fixed ends may attain great technical efficiency; but efficiency is the only quality to which it can lay claim. Such action is mechanical (or becomes so), no matter what the scope of the preformed end, be it the Will of God or *Kultur*. But the doctrine that intelligence develops within the sphere of action for the sake of possibilities not yet given is the opposite of a doctrine of mechanical efficiency. Intelligence *as* intelligence is inherently forward-looking; only by ignoring its primary function does it become a mere means for an end already given. The latter *is* servile, even when the end is labeled moral, religious, or esthetic. But action directed to ends to which the agent has not previously been attached inevitably carries with it a quickened and enlarged spirit. A pragmatic intelligence is a creative intelligence, not a routine mechanic.

All this may read like a defense of pragmatism by one concerned to make out for it the best case possible. Such is not, however, the intention. The purpose is to indicate the extent to which intelligence frees action from a mechanically instrumental character. Intelligence is, indeed, instrumental *through* action to the determination of the qualities of future experience. But the very fact that the concern of intelligence is with the future, with the as-yet-unrealized (and with the given and the established only as conditions of the realization of possibilities), makes the action in which it takes effect generous and liberal; free of spirit. Just that action which extends and approves intelligence has an intrinsic value of its own in being instrumental—the intrinsic value of being informed with intelligence in behalf of the enrichment of life. By the same stroke, intelligence becomes truly liberal: knowing is a human undertaking, not an esthetic appreciation carried on by a refined class or a capitalistic possession of a few learned specialists, whether men of science or of philosophy.

More emphasis has been put upon what philosophy is not than upon what it may become. But it is not necessary, it is not even desirable, to set forth philosophy as a scheduled program. There are human difficulties of an urgent, deep-seated kind which may be clarified by trained reflection, and whose solution may be forwarded by the careful development of hypotheses. When it is understood that philosophic thinking is caught up in the actual course of events, having the office of guiding them toward a prosperous issue, problems will abundantly present themselves. Philosophy will not solve these problems; philosophy is vision, imagination, reflection—and these functions, apart from action, modify nothing and hence resolve nothing. But in a complicated and perverse world, action which is not informed with vision, imagination, and reflection, is more likely to increase confusion and conflict than to straighten things out. It is not easy for generous and sustained reflection to become a guiding and illuminating method in action. Until it frees itself from identification with problems which are supposed to depend upon Reality as such, or its distinction from a world of Appearance, or its relation to a Knower as such, the hands of philosophy are tied. Having no chance to link its fortunes with a responsible career by suggesting things to be tried, it cannot identify itself with questions which actually arise in the vicissitudes of life. Philosophy recovers itself when it ceases to be a device for dealing with the problems of philosophers and becomes a method, cultivated by philosophers, for dealing with the problems of men.

Emphasis must vary with the stress and special impact of the troubles which perplex men. Each age knows its own ills, and seeks its own remedies. One does not have to forecast a particular program to note that the central need of any program at the present day is an adequate conception of the nature of intelligence and its place in action. Philosophy cannot disavow responsibility for many misconceptions of the nature of intelligence which now hamper its efficacious operation. It has at least a negative task imposed upon it. It must take away the burdens which it has laid upon the intelligence of the common man in struggling with his difficulties. It must deny and eject that intelligence which is naught but a distant eye, registering in a remote and alien medium the spectacle of nature and life. To enforce the fact that the emergence of imagination and thought is relative to the connection of the sufferings of men with their doings is of itself to illuminate those sufferings and to instruct those doings. To catch mind in its connection with the entrance of the novel into the course of the world is to be on the road to see that intelligence is itself the most promising of all novelties, the revelation of the meaning of that transformation of past into future which is the reality of every present. To reveal intelligence as the organ for the guidance of this transformation, the sole director of its quality, is to make a declaration of present untold significance for action. To elaborate these convictions of the connection of intelligence with what men undergo because of their doings and with the emergence and direction of the creative, the novel, in the world is of itself a program which will keep philosophers busy until something more worth while is forced upon them. For the elaboration has to be made through application to all the disciplines which have an intimate connection with human conduct: to logic, ethics, esthetics, economics, and the procedure of the sciences formal and natural.

I also believe that there is a genuine sense in which the enforcement of the pivotal position of intelligence in the world and thereby in control of human fortunes (so far as they are manageable) is the peculiar problem in the problems of life which come home most closely to ourselves—to ourselves living not merely in the early twentieth century but in the United States. It is easy to be foolish about the connection of thought with national life. But I do not see how any one can question the distinctively national color of English, or French, or German philosophies. And if of late the history of thought has come under the domination of the German dogma of an inner evolution of ideas, it requires but a little inquiry to convince oneself that that dogma itself testifies to a particularly nationalistic need and origin. I believe that philosophy in America will be lost between chewing a historic cud long since reduced to woody fiber, or an apologetics for lost causes (lost to natural science), or a scholastic, schematic formalism, unless it can somehow bring to consciousness America's own needs and its own implicit principle of successful action.

This need and principle, I am convinced, is the necessity of a deliberate control of policies by the method of intelligence, an intelligence which is not the faculty of intellect honored in textbooks and neglected elsewhere, but which is the sum-total of impulses, habits, emotions, records, and discoveries which forecast what is desirable and undesirable in future possibilities, and which contrive ingeniously in behalf of imagined good. Our life has no background of sanctified categories upon which we may fall back; we rely upon precedent as authority only to our own undoing—for with us there is such a continuously novel situation that final reliance upon precedent entails some class interest guiding us by the nose whither it will. British empiricism, with its appeal to what has been in the past, is, after all, only a kind of *a priorism*. For it lays down a fixed rule for future intelligence to follow; and only the immersion of philosophy in technical learning prevents our seeing that this is the essence of *a priorism*.

We pride ourselves upon being realistic, desiring a hard-headed cognizance of facts, and devoted to mastering the means of life. We pride ourselves upon a practical idealism, a lively and easily moved faith in possibilities as yet unrealized, in willingness to make sacrifice for their realization. Idealism easily becomes a sanction of waste and carelessness, and realism a sanction of legal formalism in behalf of things as they are—the rights of the possessor. We thus tend to combine a loose and ineffective optimism with assent to the doctrine of take who take can: a deification of power. All peoples at all times have been narrowly realistic in practice and have then employed idealization to cover up in sentiment and theory their brutalities. But never, perhaps, has the tendency been so dangerous and so tempting as with ourselves. Faith in the power of intelligence to imagine a future which is the projection of the desirable in the present, and to invent the instrumentalities of its realization, is our salvation. And it is a faith which must be nurtured and made articulate: surely a sufficiently large task for our philosophy.

II

Earlier Psychological
Writings

The material in this section illustrates Dewey's philosophical development from the perspective of his concern with psychology. In his attempt to bring the concerns and methods of psychology to bear upon philosophical issues, Dewey himself undergoes significant changes in outlook, methodology, and above all, terminology. These essays provide us not only with an insight into the evolution of Dewey's thought but also into the impact of the new psychology, particularly that of William James, on philosophical language at the turn of the century.

7. The Psychological Standpoint*

In this early essay (1886) Dewey's position is that British philosophy has deserted the psychological standpoint. He laments this, for he contends that "the nature of all objects of philosophical inquiry is to be fixed by finding out what experience says about them. And psychology is the scientific and systematic account of this experience." Of course, at that time Dewey's understanding of psychology, even when dealing with British philosophy, was still characterized by the problems germane to philosophical idealism, such as the unity of consciousness and the "thing in itself." And despite his attempt to abandon the "old ontological man," he can still say that "the individual consciousness is but the process of realization of the universal consciousness through itself." At this point in his career Dewey's approach was empirical, but he lacked the behavioral data to make a real break with the language of idealism.

* From *Mind*, XI (January, 1886), pp. 1-19.

1

It is a good omen for the future of philosophy that there is now a disposition to avoid discussion of particular cases in dispute, and to examine instead the fundamental presuppositions and method. This is the sole condition of discussion which shall be fruitful, and not word-bandying. It is the sole way of discovering whatever of fundamental agreement there is between different tendencies of thought, as well as of showing on what grounds the radical differences are based. It is therefore a most auspicious sign that, instead of eagerly clamoring forth our views on various subjects, we are now trying to show *why* we hold them and *why* we reject others. It is hardly too much to say that it is only within the past ten years that what is vaguely called Transcendentalism has shown to the English reading world just why it holds what it does, and just what are its objections to the method most characteristically associated with English thinking. Assertion of its results, accompanied with attacks upon the results of Empiricism, and *vice versa*, we had before; but it is only recently that the grounds, the reasons, the method, have been stated. And no one can deny that the work has been done well, clearly, conscientiously, and thoroughly. English philosophy cannot now be what it would have been, if (to name only one of the writers) the late Professor Green had not written. And now that the differences and the grounds for them have been so definitely and clearly stated, we are in a condition, I think, to see a fundamental agreement, and that just where the difference has been most insisted upon, *viz.*, in the standpoint. It is the *psychological* standpoint which is the root of all the difference, as Professor Green has shown with such admirable lucidity and force. Yet I hope to be able to suggest, if not to show, that after all the psychological standpoint is what both sides have in common. In this present paper, I wish to point out that the defects and contradictions so powerfully urged against the characteristic tendency of British Philosophy are due—not to its psychological standpoint but—to its *desertion* of it. In short, the psychological basis of English philosophy has been its strength: its weakness has been that it has left this basis—that it has not been psychological enough.

In stating what is the psychological standpoint, care has to be taken that it be not so stated as to prejudge at the outset the whole matter. This can be avoided only by stating it in a very general manner. Let Locke do it. "I thought that the first step towards satisfying several inquiries the mind of man was very apt to run into was to take a view of our own understandings, examine our own powers, and see to what things they were adapted." This, with the further statement that "Whatsoever is the object of the understanding when a man thinks" is an Idea, fixed the method of philosophy. We are not to determine the nature of reality or of any object of philosophical inquiry by examining it as it is in itself, but only as it is an element in our knowledge, in our experience, only as it is related to our mind, or is an "idea." As Professor Fraser well puts it, Locke's way of stating the question "involves the fundamental assumption of philosophy, that real things as well as imaginary things, whatever their absolute existence may involve, exist for us only through becoming involved in what we mentally experience in the course of our self-conscious lives." Or, in the ordinary way of putting it, the nature of all objects of philosophical inquiry is to be fixed by finding out what experience says about them. And psychology is the scientific and systematic account of this experience. This and this only do I understand to be essential to the psychological standpoint, and, to avoid misunderstanding from the start, I shall ask the reader not to think any more into it, and especially to avoid reading into it any assumption regarding its "individual" and "introspective" character. The further development of the standpoint can come only in the course of the article.

Now that Locke, having stated his method, immediately deserted it will, I suppose, be admitted by all. Instead of determining the nature of objects of experience by an account of our knowledge, he proceeded to explain our knowledge by reference to certain unknowable substances, called by the name of matter, making impressions on an unknowable substance, called mind. While, by his method, he should explain the nature of "matter" and of "mind"—two "inquiries the mind of man is very apt to run into"—from our own understandings, from "ideas," he actually explains the nature of our ideas, of our consciousness, whether sensitive or reflective, from that whose characteristic, whether mind or matter, is to be *not* ideas nor consciousness nor in any possible relation thereto, because utterly unknowable. Berkeley, in effect, though not necessarily, as it seems to me, in intention, deserted the method in his reference of ideas to a purely transcendent spirit. Whether or not he conceived it as purely transcendent, yet at all events, he did not show its necessary immanence *in* our conscious experience. But Hume? Hume, it must be confessed, is generally thought to stand on purely psychological ground. This is asserted as his merit by those who regard the theory of the association of ideas as the basis of all philosophy; it is asserted as his defect by those who look at his skeptical mocking of knowledge as following necessarily from his method. But according to both, he, at least, was consistently psychological. Now the psychological standpoint is this: nothing shall be admitted into philosophy which does not show itself in experience, and its nature, that is, its place in experience, shall be fixed by an account of the process of knowledge—by Psychology. Hume reversed this. He started with a theory as to the nature of reality and determined experience from that. The only reals for him were certain irrelated sensations and out of these knowledge arises or becomes. But if knowledge or experience becomes from them, then *they* are never known and never can be. If experience *originates from* them, they never were and never can be elements *in* experience. Sensations as known or experienced are always related, classified sensations. That which is known as existing only in experience, which has its existence only as an element of knowledge, cannot be the same when transported out of knowledge, and made its origin. A known sensation has its sole existence *as* known; and to suppose that it can be regarded as *not* known, as prior to knowledge, and still be what it is *as* known, is a logical feat which it is hoped few are capable of. Hume, just as much as Locke, assumes that something exists out of relation to knowledge or consciousness, and that this something is ultimately the only real, and that from it knowledge, consciousness, experience, come to be. If this is not giving up the psychological standpoint, it would be difficult to tell what is. Hume's "distinct perceptions which are distinct existences," and which give rise to knowledge only as they are related to each other, are so many things-in-themselves. They existed prior to knowledge, and therefore are not for or within it.

But it will be objected that all this is a total misapprehension. Hume did not assume them *because* they were prior to and beyond knowledge. He examined experience and found, as any one does who analyzes it, that it is made up of sensations; that, however complex or immediate it appears to be, on analysis it is always found to be but an aggregate of grouped sensations. Having found this by analysis, it was his business, as it is that of every psychologist, to show *how* by composition these sensations produce knowledge and experience. To call them things-in-themselves is absurd—they are the simplest and best-known things in all our experience. Now this answer, natural as it is, and conclusive as it seems, only brings out the radical defect of the procedure. The dependence of our knowledge upon sensations—or rather that knowledge is nothing but sensations as related to each other—is not denied. What is denied is the correctness of the procedure which, discovering a certain element *in* knowledge to be necessary for knowledge, therefore concludes that this element has an existence prior to or apart from knowledge. The alternative is not complex. Either these sensations are the sensations which are known—sensations which are elements in knowledge—and then they cannot be employed to account for its origin; or they can be employed to account for its origin, and then are not sensations as they are known. In this case, they must be something of which nothing can be said except that they are *not* known, *are* not in consciousness—that they are things-in-themselves. If, in short, these sensations are not to be made "ontological," they must be sensations known, sensations which are elements in experience; and if they exist only for knowledge, then knowledge is wherever they are, and they cannot account for its origin. The supposed objection rests upon a distinction between sensations as they are known, and sensations as they exist. And this means simply that existence—the only real existence—is not for consciousness, but that consciousness comes about from it; it makes no difference that one calls it sensations, and another the "real existence" of mind or matter. If one is anxious for a thing-in-itself in one's philosophy, this will be no objection. But we who are psychological, who believe in the relativity of knowledge, should we not make a halt before we declare a fundamental disparity between a thing as it is and a thing as it is known—whether that thing be sensation or what not?

As this point is fundamental, let me dwell upon it a little. All our knowledge originates from sensations. Very good. But what are these sensations? Are they the sensations which we know: the classified related sensations; *this* smell, or *this* color? No, these are the results of knowledge. They too presuppose sensations as their origin. What about these original sensations? They existed before knowledge, and knowledge originated and was developed by their grouping themselves together. Now, waiving the point that knowledge *is* precisely this grouping together and that therefore to tell us that it originated from grouping sensations is a good deal like telling us that knowledge originated knowledge, that experience is the result of experience—I must inquire again what these sensations are. And I can see but this simple alternative: either they are known, are, from the first, elements in knowledge, and hence cannot be used to account for the origin of knowledge; or they are not, and, what is more to the point, they never can be. As soon as they are known, they cease to be the pure sensation we are after and become an element *in* experience, *of* knowledge. The conclusion of the matter is, that sensations which can be used to account for the *origin* of knowledge or experience, are sensations which cannot be known, are things-in-themselves which are not relative to consciousness. I do not here say that there are not such: I only say that, if there are, we have given up our psychological standpoint and have become "ontologists" of the most pronounced character.

But the confusion is deeply rooted, and I cannot hope that I have yet shown that any attempt to show the *origin* of knowledge or of conscious experience presupposes a division between things as they are for knowledge or experience and as they are in themselves, and is therefore non-psychological in character. I shall be told that I am making the whole difficulty for myself; that I persist in taking the standpoint of an adult whose experience is already formed; that I must become as an infant to enter the true psychological kingdom. If I will only go back to that stage, I shall find a point where knowledge has not yet begun, but where sensations must be supposed to exist. Owing to our different standing, since these sensations have to us been covered with the residues of thousands of others and have become symbolic of them, we cannot tell what these sensations are; though in all probability they are to be conceived in some analogy to nervous shocks. But the truth of our psychological analysis does not depend upon this. The fact that sensations exist before knowledge and that knowledge comes about by their organic registration and integration is undisputed. And I can imagine that I am told that if I would but confine myself to the analysis of given facts, I should find this whole matter perfectly simple—that the sensations have not the remotest connection with any sort of "metaphysics" or analogy with things-in-themselves, and that we are all the time on positive scientific ground. I hope so. We are certainly approaching some degree of definiteness in our conception of what constitutes a sensation. But I am afraid that in thus defining the nature of a sensation, in taking it out of the region of vagueness, my objector has taken from it all those qualities which would enable it to serve as the origin of knowledge or of conscious experience. It is no longer a thing-in-itself, but neither is it, I fear, capable of accounting for experience. For, alas, we have to use experience to account for it. An infant, whether I think myself back to my early days or select some other baby, is, I suppose, a known object existing in the world of experience; and his nervous organism and the objects which affect it, these too, I suppose, are known objects which exist for consciousness. Surely it is not a baby thing-in-itself which is affected, nor a world thing-in-itself which calls forth the sensation. It is the known baby and a known world in definite action and reaction upon each other, and this definite relation is precisely a sensation. Yes, we are on positive scientific ground, and for that very reason we are on ground where the origin of knowledge and experience cannot be accounted for. Such a sensation I can easily form some conception of. I can even imagine how such sensations may by their organic registration and integration bring about that knowledge which I may myself possess. But such a sensation is not prior to consciousness or knowledge. It is but an element in the world of conscious experience. Far from being that from which all relations spring, it is itself but one relation—the relation between an organic body, and one acting upon it. Such a sensation, a sensation which exists only within and for experience, is not one which can be used to account for experience. It is but one element in an organic whole, and can no more account for the whole, than a given digestive act can account for the existence of a living body, although this digestive act and others similar to it may no doubt be shown to be all-important in the formation of a given living body. In short, we have finally arrived at the root of the difficulty. Our objector has been supposing that he could account for the origin of consciousness or knowledge because he could account for the process by which the given knowledge of a given individual came about. But if he accounts for this by something which is not known, which does not exist for consciousness, he is leaving the psychological standpoint to take the ontological; if he accounts for it by a known something, as a sensation produced by the reaction of a nervous organism upon a stimulus, he is accounting for its origin from something which exists only for and within consciousness. Consequently he is not accounting for the origin of consciousness or knowledge as such at all. He is simply accounting for the origin of an individual consciousness, or a specific group of known facts, by reference to the larger group of known facts or universal consciousness. Hence also the historic impotency of all forms of materialism. For either this matter is unknown, is a thing-in-itself, and hence may be called anything else as well as matter; or it is known, and then becomes but one set of the relations which in their completeness constitute mind—when to account for mind from it is to assume as ultimate reality that which has existence only as substantiated by mind. To the relations of the individual to the universal consciousness, I shall return later. At present, I am concerned only to point out that, if a man comes to the conclusion that *all* knowledge is relative, that existence means existence for consciousness, he is bound to apply this conclusion to his starting point and to his process. If he does this, he sees that the starting point (in this case, sensations) and the process (in this case, integration of sensations) exist for consciousness also—in short, that the *becoming* of consciousness exists for consciousness only, and hence that consciousness can never have become at all. That for which all origin and change exists, can never have originated or changed.

I hope that my objector and myself have now got within sight of each other so that we can see our common ground, and the cause of our difference. We both admit that the becoming of certain definite forms of knowledge, say Space, Time, Body, External World, etc., etc., may (in ideal, at least, if not yet as matter of actual fact) be accounted for as the product of a series of events. Now he supposes that, because the origin of some or all of our knowledge or conscious experience, knowledge of all particular things and of all general relations, can be thus accounted for, he has thereby accounted for the origin of consciousness or knowledge itself. All I desire to point out is that he is always accounting for their origin *within* knowledge or conscious experience, and that he cannot take his first step or develop this into the next, cannot have either beginning or process, without presupposing known elements—the whole sphere of consciousness, in fact. In short, what he has been doing is not to show the origin of consciousness or knowledge, but simply how consciousness or knowledge has differentiated itself into various forms. It is indeed the business of the psychologist to show how (not the *ideas of* space and time, etc., but) space, time, etc., arise, but since this origin is only within or for consciousness, it is but the showing of how knowledge develops *itself;* it is but the showing of how consciousness specifies itself into various given forms. He has not been telling us how knowledge became, but how it came to be in a certain way, that is, in a certain set of relations. In making out the origin of any or all particular knowledges (if I may be allowed the word), he is but showing the elements of knowledge. And in doing this, he is performing a twofold task. He is showing on the one hand what place they hold within experience, *i.e.,* he is showing their special adequacy or validity, and on the other he is explicating the nature of consciousness or experience. He is showing that it is not a bare form, but that, since these different elements arise necessarily within it, it is an infinite richness of relations. Let not the psychologist imagine then that he is showing the *origin* of consciousness, or of experience. There is nothing but themselves from which they can originate. He is but showing *what they are,* and, since they *are,* what they always have been.

I hope that it has now been made plain that the polemic against the attempt of the psychologist to account for the origin of conscious experience does not originate in any desire to limit his sphere but simply to call him away from a meaningless and self-contradictory conception of the psychological standpoint to an infinitely fruitful one. The psychological standpoint as it has developed itself is this: all that is, is for consciousness or knowledge. The business of the psychologist is to give a genetic account of the various elements within this consciousness, and thereby fix their place, determine their validity, and at the same time show definitely what the real and eternal nature of this consciousness is. If we actually believe in experience, let us be in earnest with it, and believe also that if we only ask, instead of assuming at the outset, we shall find what the infinite content of experience is. How experience became we shall never find out, for the reason that experience always is. We shall never account for it by referring it to something else, for "something else" always is only for and in experience. *Why* it is, we shall never discover, for it is a whole. But how the elements within the whole become we may find out, and thereby account for them by referring them to each other and to the whole, and thereby also discover why they are.

We have now reached positive ground, and, in the remainder of the paper, I wish to consider the relations, within this whole, of various specific elements which have always been "inquiries into which the mind of man was very apt to run," *viz.*: the relations of Subject and Object, and the relations of Universal and Individual, or Absolute and Finite.

II

From the psychological standpoint the relation of Subject and Object is one which exists within consciousness. And its nature or meaning must be determined by an examination of consciousness itself. The duty of the psychologist is to show how it arises for consciousness. Put from the positive side, he must point out how consciousness differentiates itself so as to give rise to the existence within, that is for, itself of subject and object. This operation fixes the nature of the two (for they have no nature aside from their relation in consciousness), and at the same time explicates or develops the nature of consciousness itself. In this case, it reveals that consciousness is precisely the unity of subject and object.

Now psychology has never been so false to itself as to utterly forget that this is its task. From Locke downwards we find it dealing with the problems of the origin of space, time, the "ideas" of the external world, of matter, of body, of the *Ego,* etc., etc. But it has interpreted its results so as to deprive them of all their meaning. It has most successfully avoided seeing the necessary implications of its own procedure. There are in particular two interpretations by which it has evaded the necessary meaning of its own work.

The first of these I may now deal with shortly, as it is nothing but our old friend x, the thing-in-itself in a new guise. It is Reasoned or Transfigured Realism. It sees clearly enough that everything which we know is relative to our consciousness, and it sees also clearly enough that *our* consciousness is also relative. All that we can know exists for our consciousness; but when we come to account for our consciousness we find that this too is dependent. It is dependent on a nervous organism; it is dependent upon objects which affect this organism. It is dependent upon a whole series of past events formulated by the doctrine of evolution. But this body, these objects, this series of events, they too exist but for our consciousness. Now there is no *"metaphysics"* about all this. It is positive science. Still there is a contradiction. Consciousness at once depends upon objects and events, and these depend upon, or are relative to consciousness. Hence the fact of the case must be this: The nervous organism, the objects, the series of events *as known*, are relative to our consciousness, but since this itself is dependent, is a product, there is a reality behind the processes, behind our consciousness, which has produced them both. Subject and object as known *are* relative to consciousness, but there is a larger circle, a real object from which both of them emerge, but which can never be known, since to know is to relate to our consciousness. This is the problem: on one hand, the relativity of all knowledge to our consciousness; on the other, the dependence of our consciousness on something not itself. And this is the solution: a real not related to consciousness, but which has produced both consciousness itself, and the objects which as known are relative to consciousness. Now all that has been said in the first part of this article has gone for naught if it is not seen that such an argument is not a solution of the contradiction, but a statement of it. The problem is to reconcile the undoubted relativity of all existence as known, to consciousness, and the undoubted dependence of our own consciousness. And it ought to be evident that the only way to reconcile the apparent contradiction, to give each its rights without denying the truth of the other, is to think them together. If this is done, it will be seen that the solution is that the consciousness to which all existence is relative is not our consciousness, and that our consciousness is itself relative to consciousness in general. But Reasoned Realism attempts to solve the problem not by bringing the elements together, but by holding them apart. It does not seek the higher unity which enables each to be seen as indeed true, but it attempts to divide. It attributes one element of the contradiction to our consciousness, and another to a thing-in-itself—the unknown reality. But this is only an express statement of the contradiction. If all *be* relative to consciousness, there is no thing-in-itself, just consciousness itself. If there be a thing-in-itself then all is not relative to consciousness. Let a man hold the latter if he will, but let him expressly recognize that thereby he has put himself on "ontological" ground and adopted an "ontological" method. Psychology he has forever abandoned.

The other evasion is much more subtle and "reasoned." It is a genuine attempt to untie the Gordian knot, as the other was a slashing attempt to cut it with the sword of a thing-in-itself. It is Subjective Idealism. And I wish now to show that Subjective Idealism is *not* the meaning of the psychological standpoint applied to the relation of subject and object. It is rather a misinterpretation of it based upon the same refusal to think two undoubted facts in their unity, the same attempt to divide the contradiction instead of solving it, which we have seen in the case of attempts to determine the origin of knowledge, and of Transfigured Realism. The position is this: The necessary relation of the world of existences to consciousness is recognized. [Thus Bain:] "There is no possible knowledge of a world except in reference to our minds—knowledge is a state of mind. The notion of material things is a mental fact. We are incapable even of discussing the existence of an independent material world; the very fact is a contradiction. We can speak only of a world presented to our own minds." But this being stated, consciousness is now separated into two parts—one of which is the subject, which is identified with mind, *Ego*, the Internal; while the other is the object, which is identified with the External, the *Non-Ego*, Matter. "Mind is definable, in the first instance, by the *method of contrast,* or as a remainder arising from *subtracting the object world from the totality of conscious experience.*" "The totality of our mental life is made up of *two kinds* of consciousness—the object consciousness and the subject consciousness. The first is the external world, or *Non-Ego;* the second is our *Ego*, or mind proper." Consciousness "includes our object states as well as our subject states. The object and subject are *both parts* of our being, as I conceive, and hence we have a subject consciousness, which is in a special sense Mind (*the scope of mental science*), and an object consciousness in which all other sentient beings participate, and which gives us the extended and material universe." It is, of course, still kept in view (which constitutes the logical superiority of Subjective Idealism over Realism) that "the object consciousness, which we call Externality, is still a mode of self in the most comprehensive sense." "Object experience is still conscious experience, that is Mind." I have quoted at this length because the above passages seem to me an admirable statement of a representative type of Subjective Idealism.

The logic of the process seems to be as follows. It is recognized that all existence with which philosophy or anything else has to do must be known existence—that is, that all existence is for consciousness. If we examine this consciousness, we shall find it testifying to "two kinds of consciousness"—one, a series of sensations, emotions, and ideas, etc., the other, objects determined by spatial relations. We have to recognize then two parts in consciousness, a subject part, mind more strictly speaking, and an object part, commonly called the external world or matter. But it must not be forgotten that this after all is a part of my own being, my consciousness. The subject swallows up the object. But this subject, again, "segregates" itself into "two antithetical halves," into "two parts," the subject and the object. Then again the object vanishes into the subject, and again the subject divides itself. And forever the process is kept up. Now the point I wish to make is that consciousness is here used in two entirely different senses, and that the apparent plausibility of the argument rests upon their confusion. There is consciousness in the broad sense, consciousness which includes subject and object; and there is consciousness in the narrow sense, in which it is equivalent to "mind," "*Ego*," that is, to the series of conscious states. The whole validity of the argument rests, of course, upon the supposition that ultimately these two are just the same—that it is the individual consciousness, the "*Ego*" which differentiates itself into the "two kinds of consciousness," subject and object. If not, "mind," as well as "matter"—the series of psychical states or events which constitute the *Ego* and are "the scope of mental science," as well as that in which all "sentient beings participate"—is but an element *in* consciousness. If this be so, Subjective Idealism is abandoned and Absolute Idealism (to which I hardly need say this article has been constantly pointing) is assumed. The essence of Subjective Idealism is that the subject consciousness or mind, which remains after the "object world has been subtracted," is that for which after all this object world exists. Were this not so—were it admitted that this subject, mind, and the object, matter, are both but *elements within,* and both exist only *for,* consciousness—we should be in the sphere of an eternal absolute consciousness, whose partial realization both the individual "subject" and the "external world" are. And I wish to show that this is the only meaning of the facts of the case; that Subjective Idealism is but the bald statement of a contradiction.

This brief digression is for the purpose of showing that, to Subjective

Idealism, the consciousness for which all exists is the consciousness which is called mind, *Ego*, "my being." The point which I wished to make was that this identification is self-contradictory, although it is absolutely necessary to this form of Idealism. I shall be brief here in order not to make a simple matter appear complicated. How can consciousness which gives rise to the "two kinds" of consciousness which in its primary aspect exists in time as a series of psychical events or states be the consciousness for which a permanent world of spatially related objects, in which "all sentient beings participate," exists? How can the "mind" which is defined by way of "contrast," which exists after the object world has been "subtracted," be the mind which is the whole, of which subject and object are alike elements? To state that the mind, in the first instance, is but the remainder from the totality of conscious experience "minus the object world," and to state also "that this object world is itself a part of mind"—what is that but to state in terms a self-contradiction? Unless it be to state that this way of looking at mind, "in the first instance," is but a partial and unreal way of looking at it, and that mind in truth is the unity of subject and object, one of which cannot be subtracted from the other, because it has absolutely no existence without the other. Is it not a self-contradiction to declare that the "scope of mental science" is subject consciousness or mind, and at the same time to declare that "both subject and object are parts of our being," are but "two kinds" of consciousness? Surely Psychology ought to be the science of our whole being, and of the whole consciousness. But no words can make the contradiction clearer than the mere statement of it. The only possible hypothesis upon which to reconcile the two statements that mind is consciousness with the object world subtracted, and that it is the whole of our conscious experience, including both subject and object world, is that the term "Mind" is used in two entirely different senses in the two cases. In the first it must be individual mind, or consciousness, and in the second it must be absolute mind or consciousness, for and in which alone the individual or subject consciousness and the external world or object consciousness exist and get their reality.

The root of the whole difficulty is this. It is the business of Psychology to take the whole of conscious experience for its scope. It is its business to determine within this whole what the nature of subject and object are. Now Subjective Idealism identifies at the outset, as may be seen in the passages quoted, subject with "Mind," "*Ego*," and object with "Matter," "*Non-Ego*," "External World," and then goes on to hold that the "scope" of Psychology is the former only. In short, the psychological standpoint, according to which the nature of subject and object was to be determined from the nature of conscious experience, was abandoned at the outset. It is presumed that we already know what the "subject" is, and Psychology is confined to treatment of that. It is assumed that we know already what the "object" is, and Psychology is defined by its elimination. This method, as psychology, has two vices. It is "ontological," for it sets up some external test to fix upon the nature of subject and object; and it is arbitrary, for it dogmatically presupposes the limitation of Psychology to a series of subjective states. It assumes that Psychology instead of being the criterion of all, has some outside criterion from which its own place and subject matter is determined, and more specifically, *it assumes that the standpoint of Psychology is necessarily individual or subjective*. Why should we be told that the scope of Psychology is subject consciousness, and subject consciousness be defined as the totality of conscious experience *minus* the object world, unless there is presupposed a knowledge of what subject and object are? How different is the method of the true psychological standpoint! It shows how subject and object arise within conscious experience, and thereby develops the nature of consciousness. It shows it to be the unity of subject and object. It shows therefore that there cannot be "two kinds" of consciousness, one subject, the other object, but that all consciousness whether of "Mind," or of "Matter," is, *since* consciousness, the unity of subject and object. Consciousness may, and undoubtedly does, have two aspects—one aspect in which it appears as an individual, and another in which it appears as an external world over against the individual. But there are not two kinds of consciousness, one of which may be subtracted from the whole and leave the other. They are but consciousness in one phase, and how it is that consciousness assumes this phase, how it is that this division into the individual and the external world arises for consciousness (in short, how consciousness in one stage appears as perception)—that is precisely the business of Psychology to determine. But it does not determine it by assuming at the outset that the subject is "me," and the object is the world. And if this be not assumed at the outset it certainly will not be reached at the conclusion. The conclusion will show that the distinction of consciousness into the individual and the world is but one form in which the *relation* of subject and object, which everywhere constitutes consciousness, appears. This brings us definitely to the relation of the individual and the universal consciousness.

III

We have seen that the attempt to account for the origin of knowledge, at bottom, rests on the undoubted fact that the individual consciousness does become, but also that the only way to account for this becoming, without self-contradiction, is by the postulate of a universal consciousness. We have seen again that the truth at the bottom of subjective idealism is the undoubted fact that all existence is relative to our consciousness, but also that the only consistent meaning of this fact is that our consciousness as individual is itself relative to a universal consciousness. And now I am sure that my objector, for some time silent, will meet me with renewed vigor. He will turn one of these arguments against the other and say: "After all, this consciousness for which all exists is your individual consciousness. The universal consciousness itself exists only for it. You may say indeed that this individual consciousness, which has now absorbed the universal again, shows the universal as necessary to its own existence, but this is only to fall into the contradiction which you have already urged against a similar view on the part of Subjective Idealism. Your objection in that case was that consciousness divided into subject consciousness and object consciousness, of which the former immediately absorbed the latter, and again subdivided itself into the subject and object consciousness. You objected that this was the express statement of a contradiction—the statement that the subject consciousness was and was not the whole of conscious experience. It was only as it was asserted to be the whole that any ground was found for subjective idealism; but only as it was regarded as a remainder left over from subtraction of the object world does it correspond to actual experience. Now you have yourself fallen into precisely this contradiction. You do but state that the individual consciousness is and is not the universal consciousness. Only so far as it is not, do you escape subjective idealism; only so far as it is, do you escape the thing-in-itself. If this universal consciousness is not for our individual consciousness, if it is not a part of our conscious experience, it is unknowable, a thing-in-itself. But if it be a part of our individual consciousness, then after all the individual consciousness is the ultimate. By your own argument you have no choice except between the acceptance of an unknowable unrelated reality or of subjective idealism."

This objection amounts to the following disjunction: Either the universal consciousness is the individual and we have subjective idealism; or, it is something beyond the individual consciousness, and we have a thing-in-itself. Now this dilemma looks somewhat formidable, yet its statement shows that the objector has not yet put himself upon the psychological ground: there is something of the old "ontological" man left in him yet, for it assumes that he has, prior to its determination by Psychology, an adequate idea of what "individual" is and means. If he will take the psychological standpoint, he will see that nature of the individual as well as of the universal must be determined within and through conscious experience. And if this is so, all ground for the disjunction falls away at once. This disjunction rests upon the supposition that the individual and the universal consciousness are something opposed to each other. If one were to assert that the meaning of the individual consciousness is that it is universal, the whole objection loses not only its ground but its meaning; it becomes nonsense. But I am not concerned just at present to state this; I am concerned only to point out that, if one starts with a presupposition regarding the nature of the individual consciousness, one is leaving the psychological standpoint. In forming the parallel between the position attributed to the writer and that of subjective idealism, the supposed objector was building wiser than perhaps he knew. The trouble with the latter view is that it supposes that consciousness may be divided into "two kinds," one subjective, the other objective; that it presupposes, at the start, the nature of subject and object. The fact of the case is that, since consciousness is the unity of subject and object, there is no purely subjective or purely objective. So here. It is presupposed that there are "two kinds" of consciousness, one individual, the other universal. And the fact will be found to be, I imagine, that consciousness is the unity of the individual and the universal; that there is no purely individual or purely universal. So the disjunction made is meaningless. But however that may be, at all events it leaves the psychological basis, for it assumes that the nature of the individual is already known.

This has been said that it may be borne in mind from the outset that Psychology must determine within consciousness the nature of the individual and the universal consciousness, thereby determining at once their place within experience, and explicating the nature of consciousness itself. And this, stated in plain terms, means simply that, since consciousness does show the origin of individual and universal consciousness *within itself,* consciousness is therefore both universal and individual. *How* this is, the present article, of course, does not undertake to say. Its more modest function is simply to point out that it is the business of psychology to show the nature of the individual and the universal and of the relation existing between them. These must not be presupposed, and then imported bodily to determine the nature of psychologic experience. There has now been rendered explicit what was implied concerning the psychological standpoint from the first, *viz.*, that it is a universal standpoint. If the nature of all objects of philosophical inquiry is to be determined from fixing their place within conscious experience, then there is no criterion outside of or beyond or behind just consciousness itself. To adopt the psychological standpoint is to assume that consciousness itself is the only possible absolute. And this is tacitly assumed all the while by subjective idealism. The most obvious objection to subjective idealism is, of course, that it presupposes that, if "mind were to become extinct, the annihilation of matter, space, time would result." And the equally obvious reply of subjective idealism is: "My conception of the universe even though death may have overtaken all its inhabitants, would not be an independent reality, I should merely take on the object-consciousness of a supposed mind then present" (Bain). In short, the reality of the external world, though I should imagine all finite minds destroyed, would be that I cannot imagine consciousness destroyed. As soon as I imagine an external world, I imagine a consciousness in relation to which it exists. One may put the objection from a side which gets added force with every advance of physical science. The simplest physiology teaches that all our sensations originate from bodily states—that they are conditioned upon a nervous organism. The science of biology teaches that this nervous organism is not ultimate but had its origin; that its origin lies back in indefinite time, and that as it now exists it is a result of an almost infinite series of processes; all these events, through no one knows how much time, having been precedent to your and my mind, and being the condition of their existence. Now is all this an illusion, as it must be, if its only existence is for a consciousness which is "but a transition from one state to another"? The usual answer to this argument is that it is an *ignoratio elenchi:* that it has presupposed a consciousness for which these events existed; and that they have no meaning except when stated in terms of consciousness. This answer I have no call to rebut. But it must be pointed out that this is to suppose the individual consciousness capable of transcending itself and assuming a universal standpoint—a standpoint whence it can see its own becoming, as individual. It is this *implication* of the universal nature of the individual consciousness which has constituted the strength of English philosophy; it is its lack of *explication* which has constituted its weakness. Subjective idealism has "admitted of no answer and produced no conviction" because of just this confusion. That which has admitted of no answer is the existence of all *for* consciousness; that which has produced no conviction is the existence of all for our consciousness as merely individual. English philosophy can assume its rightful position only when it has become fully aware of its own presuppositions; only when it has become conscious of that which constitutes its essential characteristic. It must see that the psychological standpoint is necessarily a universal standpoint and consciousness necessarily the only absolute, before it can go on to develop the nature of consciousness and of experience. It must see that the individual consciousness, the consciousness which is but "transition," but a process of becoming, which, in its primary aspect, has to be defined by way of "contrast," which is but a "part" of conscious experience, nevertheless is when viewed in its finality, in a perfectly concrete way, the universal consciousness, the consciousness which has never become and which *is* the totality; and that it is only because the individual consciousness is, in its ultimate reality, the universal consciousness that it affords any basis whatever for philosophy.

The case stands thus: We are to determine the nature of everything, subject and object, individual and universal, as it is found within conscious experience. Conscious experience testifies, in the primary aspect, my individual self is a "transition," is a process of becoming. But it testifies also that this individual self is conscious of the transition, that it knows the process by which it has become. In short, the individual self can take the universal self as its standpoint, and thence know its own origin. In so doing, it knows that it has its origin in processes which exist for the universal self, and that therefore the universal self never has become. Consciousness testifies that consciousness is a result, but that it is the result of consciousness. Consciousness is the self-related. Stated from the positive side, consciousness has shown that it involves *within* itself a process of becoming, and that this process becomes conscious of itself. This process is the individual consciousness; but since it is conscious of itself, it is consciousness of the universal consciousness. All consciousness, in short, is self-consciousness, and the self is the universal consciousness, for which all process is and which, therefore, always is. The individual consciousness is but the process of realization of the universal consciousness through itself. Looked at as process, as realizing, it is individual consciousness; looked at as produced or realized, as conscious of the process, that is, of itself, it is universal consciousness.

It must not be forgotten that the object of this paper is simply to develop the presuppositions which have always been latent or implicit in the psychological standpoint. What has been said in the way of positive result has been said, therefore, only as it seemed necessary to develop the meaning of the standpoint. It must also be remembered that it is the work of Psychology itself to determine the exact and concrete relations of subject and object, individual and universal, within consciousness. What has been said here, if said only for the development of the standpoint, is therefore exceedingly formal. To some of the more concrete problems I hope to be able to return at another time.

8. Psychology as Philosophic Method*

In some ways a clarification of the previous article, "The Psychological Standpoint," Dewey, in the following selection, takes on a more positive tone in defending psychology as a viable philosophic method. Dewey reads the state of the problem in 1886 as follows: "There is an absolute self-consciousness. The science of this is philosophy. This absolute self-consciousness manifests itself in the knowing and acting of individual men. The science of this manifestation, a phenomenology, is psychology." But Dewey considers this distinction to be merely functional and not substantive, and so the burden of the present paper is to show that "what else can philosophy in its fullness be but psychology, and psychology but philosophy."

In "The Psychological Standpoint," I endeavored to point out that the characteristic English development in philosophy—the psychological movement since Locke—had been neither a "threshing of old straw," nor a movement of purely negative meaning, whose significance for us was exhausted when we had learned how it necessarily led to the movement in Germany—the so-called "transcendental" movement. Its positive significance was found to consist in the fact that it declared consciousness to be the sole content, account and criterion of all reality; and psychology, as the science of this consciousness, to be the explicit and accurate determination of the nature of reality in its wholeness, as well as the determination of the value and validity of the various elements or factors of this whole. It is the ultimate science of reality, because it declares what experience in its totality is; it fixes the worth and meaning of its various elements by showing their development and place within this whole. It is, in short,

* From *Mind*, XI (April, 1886), pp. 153-73.

philosophic method. But that paper was necessarily largely negative, for it was necessary to point out that as matter of fact the movement had not been successful in presenting psychology as the method of philosophy, for it had not been true to its own basis and ideal. Instead of determining all, both in its totality and its factors, through consciousness, it had endeavored to determine consciousness from something out of and beyond necessary relation to consciousness. It had determined its psychology from a dogmatically presupposed ontology, instead of getting at its ontology from a critical examination of the nature and contents of consciousness, as its standpoint required. It had a thing-in-itself, something whose very existence was to be opposed to consciousness, as in the unknowable "substances" of Locke, the transcendent Deity of Berkeley, the sensations or impressions of Hume and Mill, the "transfigured real" of Spencer; and it used this thing-in-itself as the cause and criterion of conscious experience. Thus it contradicted itself; for, if psychology as method of philosophy means anything, it means that nothing shall be assumed except just conscious experience itself, and that the nature of all shall be ascertained from and within this.

It is to the positive significance of psychology as philosophic method—its significance when it is allowed to develop itself free from self-contradictory assumptions—that this present paper is directed. It was suggested in the previous paper that this method, taken in its purity, would show substantial identity with the presuppositions and results of the "transcendental" movement. And as the principal attacks upon the pretensions of psychology to be method for philosophy, or anything more than one of the special sciences, have come from representatives of this movement, this paper must be occupied with treating psychology in reference to what we may call German philosophy, as the other treated it in reference to English philosophy. In so far as the criticisms from this side have been occupied with pointing out the failure of the actual English psychology to be philosophy, there is of course no difference of opinion. That arises only in so far as these criticisms have seemed (*seemed,* I repeat) to imply that the same objections must hold against every *possible* psychology; while it seems to the writer that psychology is the only *possible* method.

It is held, or seems to be held, by representatives of the post-Kantian movement, that man may be regarded in two aspects, in one of which he is an object of experience like other objects: he is a finite thing among other finite things; with these things he is in relations of action and reaction, but possesses the additional characteristic that he is a knowing, feeling, willing *phenomenon.* As such, he forms the object of a special science, psychology, which, like every other special science, deals with its material as pure object, abstracting from that creative synthesis *of subject and object*, self-consciousness, through which all things are and are known. It is therefore, like all the special sciences, partial and utterly inadequate to determining the nature and meaning of that whole with which philosophy has to deal. Nay more, it is itself ultimately dependent upon philosophy for the determination of the meaning, validity, and limits of the principles, categories, and method which it unconsciously assumes. To regard psychology therefore as philosophic method is to be guilty of the same error as it would be to regard the highest generalizations of, say, physics as adequate to determining the problems of philosophy. It is an attempt to determine the unconditioned whole, self-consciousness, by that which has no existence except as a conditioned part of this very whole.

> Metaphysics [says Professor Caird] has to deal with conditions of the knowable, and hence with self-consciousness or that unity which is implied in all that is and is known. Psychology has to inquire how this self-consciousness is realized or developed in man, in whom the consciousness of self grows with the consciousness of a world in time and space, of which he individually is only a part, and to parts of which only he stands in immediate relation. In considering the former question we are considering the sphere within which all knowledge and all objects of knowledge are contained. In considering the latter, we are selecting one particular object or class of objects within this sphere. . . . It is possible to have a *purely objective* anthropology or psychology—which abstracts from the relation of man to the mind that knows him—just as it is possible to have a purely objective science of nature.[1]

The other aspect of man is that in which he, as self-conscious, has manifested in him the unity of all being and knowing, and is not finite, *i.e.*, an object or event, but is, in virtue of his self-conscious nature, infinite, the bond, the living union of all objects and events. With this infinite, universal self-consciousness, philosophy deals; with man as the object of experience, psychology deals.

In stating the position of the post-Kantian movement, I used the

---

[1] Art. "Metaphysic," *Ency. Britt.*, xvi, 89. Cp. Professor Adamson, *Philosophy of Kant*, pp. 22 ff., *Fichte*, pp. 109 ff.; *Essays in Philosophical Criticism*, pp. 44 ff.; Professor A. Seth, *Ency. Britt.*, art. "Philosophy."

word *seemed,* and used it advisedly, as I do not conceive that at bottom there is any difference of opinion. But it seems to me that there are invariably involved in the reasonings of this school certain presuppositions regarding the real science of psychology which, probably for the reason that the writers have seen such misuse made of a false psychology, are not distinctly stated, and which, accordingly, not only lessen the convincing force with which their reasonings are received by those unacquainted with the necessity and rationality of these presuppositions, but which also, as not distinctly thought out, tend at times to involve these reasonings in unnecessary obscurity and even contradictions. It is these presuppositions regarding the nature of a real psychology, lying at the basis of all the work of the post-Kantian school, conditioning it and giving it its worth, which it is the object of this paper to examine.

The start is made accordingly from the supposed distinction of aspects in man's nature, according to one of which he is an object of experience and the subject of psychology, and according to the other of which, he, as self-consciousness, is the universal condition and unity of all experience, and hence not an object of experience. As I have already referred to Professor Adamson's treatment of this distinction, let me refer to a later writing of his which seems to retract all that gave validity to this distinction. After pointing out that the subject matter of psychology *cannot* be *pure* objects but must always be the reference of an individual subject to a content which is universal, he goes on with the following most admirable statement:

> It is in and through the conscious life of the individual that all the thinking and acting which form the material for other treatment is realised. When we isolate the content and treat it as having a *quasi*-experience *per se*, we are in the attitude of objective or natural science. When we endeavour to interpret the significance of the whole, to determine the meaning of the connective links that bind it together, we are in the attitude of philosophy. But when we regard the modes through which knowledge and acting are realised in the life of an individual subject, we are in the position of the psychological inquirer.

Now, when psychology is defined as the science of the realization of the universe in and through the individual, all pretense of regarding psychology as merely one of the special sciences, whose subject matter by necessity is simply some one department of the universe, considered out of relation to the individual, is, of course, abandoned. With this falls, as a matter of course, the supposed twofold character of man's nature. If the essence of his nature is to be the realization of the universe, there is no aspect in which, *as man*, it appears as a mere object or event in the universe. The distinction is now transferred to the two ways of looking at the same material, and no longer concerns two distinct materials. Is this distinction, however, any more valid? Is there any reason for distinguishing between the modes through which the universe is realized in an individual, and the significance of this universe as a whole? At first sight there may appear to be, but let us consider the following questions. Does the whole have any significance beyond itself? If we consider experience in its absolute totality so far as realized in the individual, can the "significance of the whole" be determined beyond what itself testifies to as a whole; and do the "connective links which bind together" have any "meaning" except just as they do bind together? And since this whole and these connective links are given to us by the science of psychology, what is this except completed philosophic method, and what more has philosophy to do except to abstract from this totality, and regard it, on its material side, as philosophy of nature, and on its formal as real logic? Psychology, as science of the realization through the individual of the universe, answers the question as to the significance of the whole, by giving that whole, and at the same time gives the meaning of the parts and of their connection by showing just their place within this whole.

It would be fatal to the existence of philosophy as well as of psychology to make any distinction here. Were not the universe realized in the individual, it would be impossible for the individual to rise to a universal point of view, and hence to philosophize. That the universe has not been completely realized in man is no more an objection to the employment of psychology as the determination of the nature of this universe, than it is to any treatment of philosophy whatever. In no way can the individual philosophize about a universe which has not been realized in his conscious experience. The universe, except as realized in an individual, has no existence. In man it is partially realized, and man has a partial science; in the absolute it is completely realized, and God has a complete science. Self-consciousness means simply an individualized universe; and if this universe has *not* been realized in man, if man be not self-conscious, then no philosophy whatever is possible. If it *has* been realized, it is in and through psychological experience that this realization has occurred. Psychology is the scientific account of this realization, of this individualized universe, of this self-consciousness.

What other account can be given? It is the object of this paper to show that no other account can be given. Not only is any final distinction or dualism, even of aspects, in man's nature utterly untenable, but no distinction even of aspects can be made in the *treatment* of man's nature. Psychology has to do with just the consciousness which constitutes man's experience, and all further determinations of experience fall within this psychological determination of it, and are hence abstract. More definitely, Psychology, and not Logic, is the method of Philosophy. Let us deal *seriatim* with these two questions.

I

No such distinction in the nature of man, as that in one aspect he is "part of the partial world," and hence the subject of a purely natural science, psychology, and in another the conscious subject for which all exists, the subject of philosophy, can be maintained. This is our first assertion. Let us turn again to that most lucid and comprehensive statement of philosophic doctrine by Professor Caird, from which extract has already been made. The distinction to be upheld is that between the "sphere in which all knowledge and all objects of knowledge are contained" and "one particular object within this sphere." The question which at once arises is, How does this distinction come about? Granted that it is valid, how is man known as requiring in his nature this distinction for his proper comprehension? There is but one possible answer: it is a distinction which has arisen within and from conscious experience itself. In the course of man's realization of the universe there is necessitated this distinction. This distinction therefore falls within the sphere of psychology, and cannot be used to fix the position of psychology. Much less can psychology be identified with some one aspect of experience which has its origin only within that experience which in its wholeness constitutes the material of psychology. The distinction, as we shall immediately see, cannot be an absolute one: by no possibility or contingency can man be regarded as *merely* one of objects of experience; but so far as the distinction has relative validity it is a purely psychological one, originating because man in his experience, at different *stages* of it, finds it necessary to regard himself in two lights—in one of which he is a particular space- and time-conditioned being (we cannot say object or event) or activity, and in the other the unconditioned eternal synthesis of all. At most the distinction is only one of various stages in one and the same experience, both of which, as stages of experience—one, indeed, of experience in its partiality and the other of experience in its totality—fall within the science of experience, *viz.*, psychology.

We will see how the question stands if we state it otherwise. Does or does not the self-consciousness of man fall within the science of psychology? What reason can be given for excluding it? Certainly few would be found so thoroughgoing as to deny that perception is a matter which that science must treat; those however who admit perception would find themselves hard put to it to give a reason for excluding memory, imagination, conception, judgment, reasoning. Why having reached the stage of reasoning, where the original implicit individual with which we began has been broken up into the greatest possible number of explicit relations, shall we rule out self-consciousness where these relations are again seen united into an individual unity? There is no possible break: either we must deny the possibility of treating perception in psychology, and then our "purely objective science of psychology" can be nothing more than a physiology; or, admitting it, we must admit what follows directly from and upon it—self-consciousness. Self-consciousness is indeed a *fact* (I do not fear the word) of experience, and must therefore find its treatment in psychology.

But this is not all. Not only does self-consciousness appear as one of the stages of psychological experience, but the explanation of the simplest psychological fact—say one of perception, or feeling, or impulse—involves necessary reference to self-consciousness. Self-consciousness is involved in every simpler process, and no one of them can be scientifically described or comprehended except as this involution is brought out. In fact, their comprehension or explanation is simply bringing to light this implication of self-consciousness within them. This would be the last thing that the upholders of self-consciousness as the final unity and synthesis, the absolute meaning of experience, could deny. The organic nature of self-consciousness being their thesis, it must indeed reveal itself in, or rather constitute, each of its members and phases. The very *existence* of any idea or feeling being ultimately its relation to self-consciousness, what other account of it can be given except its organic placing in the system? If there be such an act as perception, a candid, careful examination of it, *not of its logical conditions,* but of itself as *matter of experienced fact,* will reveal what it is; and this revelation will be the declaration of its relation to that organic system which in its wholeness is self-consciousness. We may then abstract from this relation, which constitutes its very being, and consider it as an *object of perception,* and, generalizing the case, produce a philosophy of nature; or, considering it as conditioned by thought, we may thus produce a logic. But both of these proceedings go on in abstraction from its real being, and cannot give the real method of philosophy. In short, the real *esse* of things is neither their *percipi*, nor their *intelligi* alone; it is their *experiri*. Logic may give us the science of the *intelligi*, the philosophy of nature of the *percipi*, but only psychology can give us the systematic connected account of the *experiri*, which is also in its wholeness just the *experior*—self-consciousness itself.

We may see how the matter stands by inquiring what would be the effect upon philosophy if self-consciousness were not an *experienced fact*, *i.e.*, if it were not one actual stage in that realization of the universe by an individual which is defined as constituting the sphere of psychology. The result would be again, precisely, that no such thing as philosophy, under any theory of its nature whatever, is possible. Philosophy, it cannot be too often repeated, consists simply in viewing things *sub specie aeternitatis* or *in ordine ad universum*. If man, as matter of fact, does not realize the nature of the eternal and the universal *within* himself, as the essence of his own being; if he does not at one stage of his experience consciously, and in all stages implicitly, lay hold of this universal and eternal, then it is a mere matter of words to say that he can give no account of things as they universally and eternally are. To deny, therefore, that self-consciousness is a matter of psychological experience is to deny the possibility of any philosophy.

What the denial comes to we have had historically demonstrated in Kant. He admits perception and conception as matters of experience, but he draws the line at self-consciousness. It is worth noticing that his reason for denying it is not psychological at all, but logical. It is not because self-consciousness *is* not a fact, but because it *cannot* be a fact according to his logical presuppositions. The results following the denial are worthy of notice as corresponding exactly to what we might be led to expect: first, with the denial of the fact of self-consciousness comes the impossibility of solving the problem of philosophy, expressed in the setting up of an unknown thing-in-itself as the ultimate ground and condition of experience; and, secondly, comes the failure to bring perception and conception into any organic connection with experience, that is, the failure to really comprehend and explain them, manifested in the limitation of both perception, through the forms of space and time, and thinking, through the categories, to phenomena which are in no demonstrable connection with reality. The failure to recognize self-consciousness as a stage of psychological experience leads not only to a failure to reach the alternate synthesis of experience, but renders it impossible to explain the simpler forms of psychological experience. This failure of Kant teaches us another lesson also, in that, as already stated, it was due to abandoning his real method, which was *psychological*, consisting in the self-knowledge of reason as an organic system by reason itself, and setting up a *logical* standard (in this latter case the principles of non-contradiction and identity), by which to determine the totality of experience. The work of Hegel consisted essentially in showing that Kant's *logical* standard was erroneous, and that, as matter of logic, the only true criterion or standard was the organic notion, or *Begriff*, which is a systematic totality, and accordingly able to explain both itself and also the simpler processes and principles. That Hegel accomplished this work successfully and thoroughly there can be to the writer no doubt; but it seems equally clear that the work of Kant is in need of another complement, following more closely his own conception of method and of philosophy, which shall consist in showing self-consciousness as a fact of experience, as well as perception through organic forms and thinking through organic principles. And it seems further that, only when this has been done, will, for the first time, the presuppositions latent in the work of Hegel, which give it its convincing force and validity, be brought out.

Again, it seems worthy of note that the late Professor Green (of whom the writer would not speak without expressing his deep, almost reverential gratitude), when following out Kant's work from its logical side, hardly escaped Kant's negative results. (By Kant's logical method we mean the inquiry into the *necessary conditions* of experience; by his psychological method the inquiry into the *actual nature* of experience.) After his complete demonstration of consciousness as the final condition, synthesis and unity of all that is or is knowable, he finds himself obliged to state: "As to what that consciousness in itself or in its completeness is, we can only make negative statements. *That* there is such a consciousness is implied in the existence of the world; but *what* it is we can only know through its so far acting in us as to enable us, however partially and interruptedly, to have knowledge of a world or an intelligent experience." Had he begun from the latter statement, and shown as matter of fact that this universal consciousness *had* realized itself, though only partially and interruptedly, in us, he certainly would have been able to make very positive statements regarding it, and would also have furnished a basis in fact for his logical method, which now seems to hang upon nothing but a unity of which all that can be said is that it *is* a unity, and that it *is not* anything in particular. When one reflects that it is not only upon the existence of this unity, but upon its working in and through us, that all philosophy and philosophizing depend, one cannot conceal the apprehension that too great a load of philosophy has been hung upon too feeble a peg.

So, too, after his victorious demonstration that upon the existence of this spiritual unity depends the possibility of all moral experience, he finds himself obliged to state, with that candor so characteristic of all his thinking: "Of a life of completed development, of activity with the end attained, we can only speak or think in negatives, and thus only can we speak or think of that state of being in which, according to our theory, the ultimate moral good must consist." Once more, had he started from the fact that as matter of actual realization this absolute good has been reproduced in our lives and the end attained (for surely the good is a matter of quality and not of quantity, and the end a power, not a sum), he would not have found himself in this difficulty. But with a purely logical method, one can end only with the *must be* or the *ought:* the *is* vanishes, because it has been abstracted from. The psychological method starts from the *is*, and thereby also gives the basis *and* the ideal for the *ought* and *must be.*

But it is time that we returned to our thesis, which, in brief, was that no distinction which maintains that psychology is the science of man as "part of this partial world" can be maintained. The following reasons for this denial have been given: it was pointed out that the relative validity which this distinction in man's nature undoubtedly possesses is itself the product and manifestation of psychological experience; that man as man, or as the conscious experience whose science is psychology, is self-conscious, and that therefore self-consciousness as the unity of subject and object, not as "purely objective," as the totality, not as a "part," must be included in the science of psychology; and that furthermore this treatment of self-consciousness is necessary for the explanation and comprehension of any partial fact of conscious experience. And finally, it was pointed out that the denial of self-consciousness as constituting matter of experience, and hence of psychology, was the denial of the possibility of philosophy itself; and this was illustrated by historic examples. Before passing on to the second topic, I wish briefly to return to Professor Caird's exposition, and shelter myself somewhat beneath the wings of his authority. In the article already referred to, he goes on to state that the natural objective science of man after all "omits the distinctive characteristic of man's being"; that while we may treat inorganic nature and even organic with purely natural objective methods and principles, because "they are not unities for *themselves,* but only *for us,*" such treatment cannot be applied to man, for man *is for himself, i.e.,* is not a pure object, but is self-consciousness. Thus, he continues:

> In man, in so far as he is self-conscious—*and it is self-consciousness that makes him man*—the unity through which all things are and are known is manifested. . . . Therefore to treat him as a simply natural being is *even more inaccurate and misleading* than to forget or deny his relation to nature altogether. A true psychology must avoid both errors: it must conceive man as at once spiritual and natural; it must find a reconciliation of freedom and necessity. It must face *all the difficulties involved in the conception of the absolute principle of self-consciousness*—through which all things are and are known—*as manifesting itself in the life of a being like man,* who "comes to himself" only by a long process of development out of the unconsciousness of a merely animal existence.

When it is stated, later on, that the natural science of man "is necessarily abstract and imperfect, as it omits from its view the central fact in the life of the object of which it treats," it is hardly worth while discussing whether there be any such science or not. But there is suggested for us in the quotation just made our second problem—the final relation of psychology, which confessedly must deal with self-consciousness, to philosophy. For there the problem of psychology was stated to be the question of the "absolute principle of self-consciousness, manifesting itself in the life of a being like man." That is, it is here suggested that psychology does not deal with the absolute principle in itself, but only with the modes by which this is manifested or realized in the life of man. Psychology no longer appears as an objective science; it now comes before us as a phenomenology, presupposing a science of the absolute reality itself. It is to this question that I now turn. Is psychology the science *merely* of the manifestation of the Absolute, or is it the science of the Absolute itself?

II

The relation of Psychology to Philosophy now stands, I suppose, something like this: There is an absolute self-consciousness. The science of this is philosophy. This absolute self-consciousness manifests itself in the knowing and acting of individual men. The science of this manifestation, a phenomenology, is psychology. The distinction is no longer concerned with man's being itself; it is a distinction of treatment, of ways of looking at the same material. Before going to its positive consideration the following questions may suggest the result we desire to reach. How does there come about this distinction between the "spiritual" and the "natural," between "freedom" and "necessity"? How does there come into our knowledge the notion of a distinction between the "absolute principle of self-consciousness" and "man coming to himself only by a long process of development out of the unconsciousness of a merely animal existence"? Is this a distinction which falls outside the subject matter of psychology, and which may therefore be used to determine it; or is it one which has originated *within* psychological experience, and whose nature therefore, instead of being capable of fixing the character of psychology, must itself be determined *by* psychology? Furthermore, what *is* this distinction between the absolute self-consciousness and its manifestation in a being like man? Is the absolute self-consciousness complete in itself, or does it involve this realization and manifestation in a being like man? If it is complete in itself, how can any philosophy which is limited to "this absolute principle of self-consciousness" face and solve the difficulties involved in its going beyond itself to manifest itself in self-consciousness? This cannot be what is meant. The absolute self-consciousness must involve within itself, as organic member of its very being and activity, this manifestation and revelation. Its being must be this realization and manifestation. Granted that this realization and manifestation is an act not occurring in time, but eternally completed in the nature of the Absolute, and that it occurs only "partially" and "interruptedly" *through* (not *in*) time, in a being like man—the fact none the less remains that philosophy, under any theory of its nature, can deal with this absolute self-consciousness only so far as it has partially and interruptedly realized itself in man. For man, as object of his philosophy, this Absolute has existence only so far as it has manifested itself in his conscious experience. To return to our questions: If the material of philosophy be the absolute self-consciousness, and this absolute self-consciousness *is* the realization and manifestation of itself, and as material for philosophy exists only in so far as it has realized and manifested itself in man's conscious experience, and if psychology be the science of this realization in man, what else can philosophy in its fullness be but psychology, and psychology but philosophy?

These questions are stated only to suggest the end which we shall endeavor to reach. I shall not attempt to answer them directly, but to consider first the relations of Psychology to Science, and hence to Philosophy; and secondly to Logic.

(1) *The Relation of Psychology to Science.* Psychology is the completed method of philosophy, because in it science and philosophy, fact and reason, are one. Philosophy seems to stand in a double relation to Science. In its first aspect it is *a* science—the highest of all sciences. We take one sphere of reality and ask certain questions regarding it, and the answers give us some one science; we find in the process that this sphere of reality can only artificially be thus isolated, and we broaden and deepen our question, until finally, led by the organic connection of science with science, we ask after the nature of all reality, as one connected system. The answer to this question constitutes philosophy as one science amid the circle of sciences. But to continue to regard it in this way is to fail to grasp the meaning of the process which has forced us into philosophy. At the same time that philosophy is seen as the completion of the sciences, it is seen as their basis. It is no longer *a* science; it is Scicnce. That is to say, the same movement of thought and reality which forces upon us the conception of a science which shall deal with the totality of reality forces us to recognize that no one of our previous sciences was in strict truth science. Each abstracted from certain larger aspects of reality, and was hence hypothetical. Its truth was conditioned upon the truth of its relations to that whole which that science, as special science, could not investigate without giving up its own independent existence. Only in this whole is categorical truth to be found, and only as categorical truth is found in this whole is the basis found for the special sciences. Philosophy as the science of this whole appears no longer therefore as *a* science, but as all science taken in its organic systematic wholeness—not merely to which every so-called special science is something subordinate, but of which it constitutes an organic member. Philosophy has no existence except as the organic living unity and bond of these sciences; they have no existence except through their position in this living synthesis.

Now the question is, where does psychology stand within this organism? On the one hand, psychology is certainly a positive science. It finds its materials in certain facts and events. As to systematic observation, experiment, conclusion and verification, it can differ in no essential way from any one of them. It is based upon and deals with fact, and aims at the ordered comprehension and explanation of fact as any special science does. Yet the whole drift of this paper has been to show that in some way psychology does differ very essentially from any one of them. Where shall we find this difference? In one word, its relation to them is precisely that which we have discovered philosophy to bear: it is not only *a* science, but it turns out to be science as an organic system, in which every special science has its life, and from which it must abstract when it sets up for an independent existence of its own. We begin with any special science. That turns out to be not only some one department or sphere of reality, but also some one department of conscious experience. From one science to another we go, asking for some explanation of conscious experience, until we come to psychology, which gives us an account of it, in its own behalf, as neither mathematics, nor physics, nor biology does. So far we have only *a* special science, though the highest and most concrete of all. But the very process that has made necessary this new science reveals also that each of the former sciences existed only in abstraction from it. Each dealt with some one phase of conscious experience, and for that very reason could not deal with the totality which gave it its being, consciousness. But in psychology we have the manifestation and explication of this consciousness. It gives in its wholeness what each of them would give in part, *viz.,* the nature of experience, and hence is related to them as the whole is to the part. It appears no longer, therefore, as the highest *of* sciences: it appears as Science itself, that is, as systematic account and comprehension of the nature of conscious experience. Mathematics, physics, biology, exist, because conscious experience reveals itself to be of such a nature, that one may make virtual abstraction from the whole, and consider a part by itself, without damage, so long as the treatment is purely scientific, that is, so long as the implicit connection with the whole is left undisturbed, and the attempt is not made to present this partial science as metaphysic, or as an explanation of the whole, as is the usual fashion of our uncritical so-called "scientific philosophies." Nay more, this abstraction of some one sphere is itself a living function of the psychologic experience. It is not merely something which it allows: it is something which it *does*. It is the analytic aspect of its own activity, whereby it deepens and renders explicit, realizes its own nature; just as their connection with each other is the synthetic aspect of the same self-realizing movement, whereby it returns to itself: while psychology in its completeness is the whole self-developing activity itself, which shows itself as the organic unity of both synthetic and analytic movements, and thus the condition of their possibility and ground of their validity. The analytic movement constitutes the special sciences; the synthetic constitutes the philosophy of nature; the self-developing activity itself, as psychology, constitutes philosophy.

What other position can be given psychology, so soon as we recognize the absurdity and impossibility of considering it a purely objective science? It is the science of the modes by which, in and through the individual, the universe is realized, it is said. But that the universe has no existence except as absolutely realized in an individual, *i.e.*, except as self-consciousness, is precisely the result of philosophy, and can therefore be no objection to such a consideration of the universe: in fact, such a statement only amounts to saying that psychology considers the universe as it really is. If the assertion is varied again, to read that philosophy treats of this individualized universe as it eternally *is*, while psychology can treat of it only as it partially and interruptedly *becomes*, this loses sight of two very important facts. First, philosophy can treat of absolute self-consciousness only in so far as it *has become* in a being like man, for otherwise it is not material for philosophy at all; and, secondly, it falls into the error of regarding this realization in man as a time-conditioned product, which it is not. Time is not something outside of the process of conscious experience; it is a form within it, one of the functions by which it organically constitutes its own being. In fact, psychology as philosophic method has an immense advantage at just this point over any other method of treating this problem. To any philosophy attempting to consider the absolute self-consciousness by itself, it must remain forever an insoluble problem why the *is* should ever appear as *becoming*, why the eternal should ever appear through the temporal. Psychology solves the problem by avoiding the assumption which makes it a problem. For, dealing with an individualized universe, one of whose functions of realization *is* time, it knows nothing about any consciousness which is out of relation to time. The case is just here: if philosophy will deal with the absolute consciousness conceived as purely eternal, out of relation to time, then the existence of that which constitutes the actual content of man's experience is utterly inexplicable; it is not only a mystery, but a mystery which contradicts the very nature of that which is, *ex hypothesi*, the absolute. If philosophy does deal with the eternal absolute consciousness as forever realized, yet as forever having time as one of its organic functions, it is not open to anyone to bring charges against psychology as philosophy, for this and no more psychology does.

The question just comes to this: If we start from reason alone we shall never reach fact. If we start with fact, we shall find it revealing itself as reason. The objection to an account of fact or experience as philosophy is but a prejudice, though historically considered a well-grounded one. On the one hand, it has arisen because some partial account of experience, or rather account of partial experience, has been put forth as the totality, and just because thus put forth as absolute, has lost even the relative validity which it possessed as partial. Such is the procedure of Empiricism. On the other hand, we have had put forth as matter of fact certain truths declared to be immediate and necessary and intuitive, coming no one knows whence and meaning no one knows what. The aversion to immediacy, to "undeduced" fact, as given us by the Intuitionalists, is certainly a well-grounded one. But neither of these objections lies against psychology as account of the facts of experience. Men are mortal, and every actual account of experience will suffer from the defects of mortals, and be but partial, no doubt; unfortunately we are none of us omniscient yet. But the very essence of psychology as method is that it treats of experience in its absolute totality, not setting up some one aspect of it to account for the whole, as, for example, our physical evolutionists do, nor yet attempting to determine its nature from something outside of and beyond itself, as, for example, our so-called empirical psychologists have done. The vice of the procedure of both is at bottom precisely the same—the abstracting of some one element from the organism which gives it meaning, and setting it up as absolute. It is no wonder that the organism always has its revenge by pronouncing this abstracted element "unknowable." The only wonder is that men should still bow in spirit before this creation of their own abstracting thought, and reverence it as the cause and ground of all reality and knowledge. There is indeed an anthropomorphism which is degrading, but it is the anthropormorphism which sets up the feeblest element of its own thinking, pure being, as Mr. Spencer does, or the poorest element of its own feeling, a sensation, and reverences that as its own and the universe's cause. That is the anthropomorphism of the enslaved thought which has not yet awakened to the consciousness of its own totality and spiritual freedom.

Now does the account of fact given by psychology have anything in common with the "ultimate, inexplicable, necessary" mental facts called intuitions. The fact of psychology reveals itself as precisely reason, which thereby accounts for itself, and in accounting for itself accounts for all its members. The fact of psychology is not isolated "truths," but the organic system of self-consciousness. This fact is indeed "immediate," but it is immediate only in and through a process, hence of mediation. It is indeed self-evidencing, but what it evidences is simply, of the parts, relation to and dependence upon the whole, and of the whole, that it is self-conditioned and self-related. Of the whole fact it may be said indeed that it is inexplicable. "It is true that we cannot explain the spiritual principle which is implied in all experience by reference to anything else than itself."[2] "Because all we can experience is included in this one world, and all our inferences and explanations relate only to its details, neither it as a whole, nor the one consciousness which constitutes it, can be accounted for in the ordinary sense of the word. They cannot be accounted for by what they include; and being all-inclusive, there remains nothing else by which they can be accounted for."[3] In short, any system of philosophy must ultimately fall back on the fact for which no reason can be given except precisely just that it is what it is. This implication of fact[4] is latent in all philosophy whatever, and all that psychology as philosophic method does is to render this necessary implication explicit. It alone starts from the completed fact, and it alone is therefore completed philosophy.

If it may have seemed at times in the course of the discussion that the nominal subject—the relation of psychology to science—had been left, it will now appear, I think, that we have all the time been dealing with just that subject. Science is the systematic account, or *reason* of *fact;* Psychology is the completed systematic account of the ultimate fact, which, as fact, reveals itself as reason, and hence accounts for itself, and gives the "reasons" of all sciences. The other point, the relation of psychology to logic, has already been dealt with by implication, and need not detain us long again.

(2) *The Relation of Psychology to Logic.* The whole course of philosophic thought, so far as the writer can comprehend it, has consisted in showing that any distinction between the form and the matter of philosophic truth, between the content and the method, is fatal to the reaching of truth. Self-consciousness is the final truth, and in self-consciousness the form as organic system and the content as organized system are exactly equal to each other. It is a process which, as form, has produced itself as matter. Psychology as the account of this self-consciousness must necessarily fulfill all the conditions of true method. Logic, since it necessarily abstracts from the ultimate fact, cannot reach in matter what it points to in form. While its content, if it be true philosophy, must be the whole content of self-consciousness or spirit, its form is only one process within this content, that of thought-conditions, the *Idee.* While the content is the eternal nature of the universe, its form

---

[2] Professor E. Caird, *Mind*, viii, 560.

[3] Green, *Prolegomena to Ethics*, p. 52.

[4] The insistence upon this seems to have been Lotze's great work as a philosopher.

is adequate only to "thinking what God thought and was before the creation of the world," that is, the universe in its unreality, in its abstraction. It is this contradiction between content and form in logic which makes it not philosophic method, but only one moment within that method. No contradiction results as soon as logic is given its proper place *within* the system. The contradiction occurs when, at the same moment that it is said that logic is "abstract," the logical method is still said to be the method of philosophy.

Such contradictions certainly appear to exist, for example, in the philosophy of Hegel. They have been often pointed out, and I shall only summarize them, following for the most part a recent writer.[5] There is no way of getting from logic to the philosophy of nature *logically*. The only way is to fall back upon the fact; "we know from experience" that we have nature as well as the *Idee*. In truth we do not go from logic to nature at all. The movement is a reverse movement. "In reality, the necessity for any such transition is purely factitious, because *the notions never existed otherwise than in nature and spirit*. . . . They were got by abstraction from the concrete. . . . We owe, therefore, no apology for a return to the reality from which we took them." In short, it is necessity of fact, a necessity of conscious experience, which takes us from the realm of the *Idee* to the realm of nature, from the sphere of thought-conditions to the sphere of existent relations. "The same is true when we pass to the philosophy of spirit. The general *form* of personality is deducible, but not a living human spirit with its individual thoughts, feelings and actions." This remains "the incomprehensible and inexplicable point in philosophy." And so it does undoubtedly while we regard logic as method of philosophy. But this "inexplicability" is but the express condemnation of the method, not a fact to be contented with. If we go deeper and inquire not how is the transition from logic to the philosophy of nature or to the philosophy of spirit made, but how is any transition whatever possible, we find the same difficulty. It exists only by reason of the presupposed fact. "We cannot in strictness say that the result has been independently proved, because it has been reached in this fashion by the method. It was presupposed *in* the method all along." In a definite case, how is the transition, say from the category of quality to that of quantity, made? It occurs not by virtue of the category of quality in itself, but by virtue of the fact that the whole *Idee* is implicitly contained in the principle of quality, and must manifest itself, which it does by forcing quality, as an inadequate expression of its own

[5] Professor A. Seth, "Hegel: an Exposition and Criticism," *Mind*, 24.

nature, into quantity, which expresses its being more fully. And thus the process continues until the *Idee* has manifested itself as the whole organic system, which has expressed explicitly all that which in *Idee* it is. But this movement itself depends on spirit, and on the manifestation of spirit in nature, as already seen. Every purely logical transition therefore occurs at bottom because of fact, *i.e.*, seen in its wholeness it is not a logical transition but a factual. Psychology, as philosophic method, merely starts from this everywhere presupposed fact, and by so doing, for the first time, gives logic its basis and validity.

There can be no escape from this result by saying that after all in the philosophy of spirit, spirit is shown to be the *prius* and condition of the whole, as it undoubtedly is by Hegel himself. This merely brings the contradiction itself into clearer light. For logic, being thus confessedly determined as abstract, is still retained to determine the nature of the concrete. Logic, while it is thus declared to be only one moment of spirit, is still used to determine the nature of the whole. Thus is revealed the contradiction between form and content involved in the use of logic as the method of philosophy. Spirit is reached by a *logical* process, and the *logical* result is that as fact it is not reached at all. As concrete, it is beyond the reach of any abstract process. Either one must call in the aid of the presupposed but suppressed Fact, and recognize that after all the process has been going on within a further and higher determination; or, failing to see this, must recognize Spirit as only one factor or moment of the logical movement, that is, give up the notion of self-consciousness as subject, and fall back into Spinozistic pantheism. The logical movement, considered by itself, is always balancing in unstable equilibrium between dualism and pantheism. Set up as absolute method, it either recognizes the fact, but being unable to comprehend it, has to regard this fact, as foreign element over against it, as the matter of Plato and Aristotle, the thing-in-itself of Kant, and *Anstoss* of Fichte,[6] or endeavors to absorb the Fact as a mere element in its own logical being, and falls into Pantheism.

This is the reason why Hegel, although the very center of his system is self-conditioned spirit, lends himself so easily to pantheistic treatment. Logic cannot reach, however much it may point to, an actual individual. The gathering up of the universe into the one self-conscious individuality it may assert as *necessary*, it cannot give it as *reality*. It is only as logic contradicts itself and faces back on the constant presup-

---

[6] The inability to go from the "because" of reason to the "cause" of fact, from logic to reality, when logic is not taken simply as one movement *within* reality, is clearly set forth in the closing chapters of Mr. Bradley's *Principles of Logic*.

position of this reality that it can demonstrate what it asserts. Taken purely by itself it must issue in a pantheism where the only real is the *Idee*, and where all its factors and moments, including spirit and nature, are real only at different stages or phases of the *Idee*, but vanish as imperfect ways of looking at things, or as illusions, when we reach the *Idee*. And thus the *Idee* itself vanishes, as an organic system, as a unity which lives through its distinctions, and becomes a dead identity, in no way distinguishable from the substance of Spinoza. Logic set up as absolute method reveals its self-contradiction by destroying itself. In a purely logical method the distinctions, the process, must disappear in the final unity, the product. Only a living actual Fact can preserve within its unity that organic system of differences in virtue of which it lives and moves and has its being. It is with this fact, conscious experience in its entirety, that psychology as method begins. It thus brings to clear light of day the presupposition implicit in every philosophy, and thereby affords logic, as well as the philosophy of nature, its basis, ideal and surety. If we have determined the nature of reality, by a process whose content equals its form, we can show the meaning, worth and limits of any one moment of this reality.

The conclusion of the whole matter is that a "being like man," since self-conscious, is an individualized universe, and hence that his nature is the proper material of philosophy, and in its wholeness the only material. Psychology is the science of this nature, and no dualism in it, or in ways of regarding it, is tenable. Whatever the dualism may be, it is only relative, and one which occurs within, not without, psychological experience. Psychology, as the complete systematic account of man, at the same time shows the value and meaning, and affords the condition, of the special sciences, the philosophy of nature and of logic. Or, in a word, if the reality of spirit be the presupposition, the *prius* and the goal, the condition and the end of all reality, the science of spirit must occupy a corresponding position with relation to all science. Surely then, as the Editor of *Mind* formerly urged, "the method of psychological approach is not philosophically valueless," and we have "ground for the belief that it has only to be more systematically followed out for the attaining of as great results as have been claimed for another way, while in this way the results are more likely to secure general acceptance"[7] because, we may add, it simply expresses in a scientific way that which lies at the basis of all that has been otherwise secured.

[7] "Psychology and Philosophy," *Mind*, Vol. viii, 20.

9. The Reflex Arc Concept in Psychology*

This article, with some changes, was reprinted by Dewey in *Philosophy and Civilization* (1930), under the new title of "The Unit of Behavior." We reprint the earlier version as an indication of Dewey's thought in the 1890's, although the use of the word "behavior" in the second edition is instructive, for it is precisely Dewey's awareness of the behavioral dimensions in psychology that characterizes "The Reflex Arc Conception in Psychology" and differentiates it sharply from his earlier psychological writings.

Without doubt, the decisive factor in enabling Dewey to break with the language of Kant in his consideration of psychology was the publication in 1890 of William James' *Principles of Psychology*. In "The Development of American Pragmatism," Dewey wrote that the *Principles* enabled him to criticize Locke and Hume, as well as Kant and the neo-Kantians.

As for the essay itself, regarded by Gordon W. Allport as "the most important psychological paper of the nineties" (Schilpp, p. 269), it is Dewey's effort to criticize the reflex arc concept as being inadequate as a principle of behavioral unity with regard to sensory stimulus and motor responses.

That the greater demand for a unifying principle and controlling working hypothesis in psychology should come at just the time when all generalizations and classifications are most questioned and questionable is natural enough. It is the very cumulation of discrete facts creating the demand for unification that also breaks down previous lines of classification. The material is too great in mass and too varied in style to fit into existing pigeonholes, and the cabinets of science break of their own dead weight. The idea of the reflex arc has upon the whole come nearer to meeting this demand for a general working hypothesis than any other single concept. It being admitted that the sensorimotor apparatus represents both the unit of nerve structure and the type of nerve function, the image of this relationship passed over into psychology, and became an organizing principle to hold together the multiplicity of fact.

In criticizing this conception it is not intended to make a plea for the

* From *Psychological Review*, III (July, 1896), pp. 357-70.

principles of explanation and classification which the reflex arc idea has replaced; but, on the contrary, to urge that they are not sufficiently displaced, and that in the idea of the sensorimotor circuit, conceptions of the nature of sensation and of action derived from the nominally displaced psychology are still in control.

The older dualism between sensation and idea is repeated in the current dualism of peripheral and central structures and functions; the older dualism of body and soul finds a distinct echo in the current dualism of stimulus and response. Instead of interpreting the character of sensation, idea and action from their place and function in the sensorimotor circuit, we still incline to interpret the latter from our preconceived and preformulated ideas of rigid distinctions between sensations, thoughts and acts. The sensory stimulus is one thing, the central activity, standing for the idea, is another thing, and the motor discharge, standing for the act proper, is a third. As a result, the reflex arc is not a comprehensive, or organic, unity, but a patchwork of disjointed parts, a mechanical conjunction of unallied processes. What is needed is that the principle underlying the idea of the reflex arc as the fundamental psychical unity shall react into and determine the values of its constitutive factors. More specifically, what is wanted is that sensory stimulus, central connections and motor responses shall be viewed, not as separate and complete entities in themselves, but as divisions of labor, functioning factors, within the single concrete whole, now designated the reflex arc.

What is the reality so designated? What shall we term that which is not sensation-followed-by-idea-followed-by-movement, but which is primary; which is, as it were, the psychical organism of which sensation, idea and movement are the chief organs? Stated on the physiological side, this reality may most conveniently be termed co-ordination. This is the essence of the facts held together by and subsumed under the reflex arc concept. Let us take, for our example, the familiar child-candle instance. The ordinary interpretation would say the sensation of light is a stimulus to the grasping as a response, the burn resulting is a stimulus to withdrawing the hand as response and so on. There is, of course, no doubt that is a rough practical way of representing the process. But when we ask for its psychological adequacy, the case is quite different. Upon analysis, we find that we begin not with a sensory stimulus, but with a sensorimotor co-ordination, the optical-ocular, and that in a certain sense it is the movement which is primary, and the sensation which is secondary, the movement of body, head and eye muscles determining the quality of what is experienced. In other words, the real beginning is with the act of seeing; it is looking, and not a sensation of light. The sensory quale gives the value of the act, just as the movement furnishes its mechanism and control, but both sensation and movement lie inside, not outside, the act.

Now if this act, the seeing, stimulates another act, the reaching, it is because both of these acts fall within a larger co-ordination; because seeing and grasping have been so often bound together to reinforce each other, to help each other out, that each may be considered practically a subordinate member of a bigger co-ordination. More specifically, the ability of the hand to do its work will depend, either directly or indirectly, upon its control, as well as its stimulation, by the act of vision. If the sight did not inhibit as well as excite the reaching, the latter would be purely indeterminate, it would be for anything or nothing, not for the particular object seen. The reaching, in turn, must both stimulate and control the seeing. The eye must be kept upon the candle if the arm is to do its work; let it wander and the arm takes up another task. In other words, we now have an enlarged and transformed co-ordination; the act is seeing no less than before, but it is now seeing-for-reaching purposes. There is still a sensorimotor circuit, one with more content or value, not a substitution of a motor response for a sensory stimulus.

Now take the affairs at its next state, that in which the child gets burned. It is hardly necessary to point out again that this is also a sensorimotor co-ordination and not a mere sensation. It is worth while, however, to note especially the fact that it is simply the completion, or fulfilment, of the previous eye-arm-hand co-ordination and not an entirely new occurrence. Only because the heat-pain quale enters into the same circuit of experience with the optical-ocular and muscular quales, does the child learn from the experience and get the ability to avoid the experience in the future.

More technically stated, the so-called response is not merely *to* the stimulus; it is *into* it. The burn is the original seeing, the original optical-ocular experience enlarged and transformed in its value. It is no longer mere seeing; it is seeing-of-a-light-that-means-pain-when-contact-occurs. The ordinary reflex arc theory proceeds upon the more or less tacit assumption that the outcome of the response is a totally new experience; that it is, say, the substitution of a burn sensation for a light sensation through the intervention of motion. The fact is that the sole meaning of the intervening movement is to maintain, reinforce or transform (as the case may be) the original quale; that we do not have the replacing of one sort of experience by another, but the development or (as it seems convenient to term it) the mediation of an experience.

The seeing, in a word, remains to control the reaching, and is, in turn, interpreted by the burning.[1]

The discussion up to this point may be summarized by saying that the reflex arc idea, as commonly employed, is defective in that it assumes sensory stimulus and motor response as distinct psychical existences, while in reality they are always inside a co-ordination and have their significance purely from the part played in maintaining or reconstituting the co-ordination; and (secondly) in assuming that the quale of experience which precedes the "motor" phase and that which succeeds it are two different states, instead of the last being always the first reconstituted, the motor phase coming in only for the sake of such mediation. The result is that the reflex arc idea leaves us with a disjointed psychology, whether viewed from the standpoint of development in the individual or in the race, or from that of the analysis of the mature consciousness. As to the former, in its failure to see that the arc of which it talks is virtually a circuit, a continual reconstitution, it breaks continuity and leaves us nothing but a series of jerks, the origin of each jerk to be sought outside the process of experience itself, in either an external pressure of "environment," or else in an unaccountable spontaneous variation from within the "soul" or the "organism."[2] As to the latter, failing to see the unity of activity, no matter how much it may prate of unity, it still leaves us with sensation or peripheral stimulus; idea, or central process (the equivalent of attention); and motor response, or act, as three disconnected existences, having to be somehow adjusted to each other, whether through the intervention of an extra-experimental soul, or by mechanical push and pull.

Before proceeding to a consideration of the general meaning for psychology of the summary, it may be well to give another descriptive analysis, as the value of the statement depends entirely upon the universality of its range of application. For such an instance we may conveniently take Baldwin's analysis of the reactive consciousness. In this there are, he says, "three elements corresponding to the three elements of the nervous arc. First, the receiving consciousness, the stimulus—say

[1] See, for a further statement of mediation, my *Syllabus of Ethics*, p. 15.

[2] It is not too much to say that the whole controversy in biology regarding the source of variation, represented by Weismann and Spencer respectively, arises from beginning with stimulus or response instead of with the co-ordination with reference to which stimulus or response are functional divisions of labor. The same may be said, on the psychological side, of the controversy between the Wundtian "apperceptionists" and their opponents. Each has a *disjectum membrum* of the same organic whole, whichever is selected being an arbitrary matter of personal taste.

a loud, unexpected sound; second, the attention involuntarily drawn, the registering element; and, third, the muscular reaction following upon the sound—say flight from fancied danger." Now, in the first place, such an analysis is incomplete; it ignores the status prior to hearing the sound. Of course, if this status is irrelevant to what happens afterwards, such ignoring is quite legitimate. But is it irrelevant either to the quantity or the quality of the stimulus?

If one is reading a book, if one is hunting, if one is watching in a dark place on a lonely night, if one is performing a chemical experiment; in each case, the noise has a very different psychical value; it is a different experience. In any case, what proceeds the "stimulus" is a whole act, a sensorimotor co-ordination. What is more to the point, the "stimulus" emerges out of this co-ordination; it is born from it as its matrix; it represents as it were an escape from it. I might here fall back upon authority, and refer to the widely accepted sensation continuum theory, according to which the sound cannot be absolutely *ex abrupto* from the outside, but is simply a shifting of focus of emphasis, a redistribution of tensions within the former act; and declare that unless the sound activity had been present to some extent in the prior co-ordination, it would be impossible for it now to come to prominence in consciousness. And such a reference would be only an amplification of what has already been said concerning the way in which the prior activity influences the value of the sound sensation. Or, we might point to cases of hypnotism, mono-ideism and absent-mindedness, like that of Archimedes, as evidences that if the previous co-ordination is such as rigidly to lock the door, the auditory disturbance will knock in vain for admission to consciousness. Or, to speak more truly in the metaphor, the auditory activity must already have one foot over the threshold, if it is ever to gain admittance.

But it will be more satisfactory, probably, to refer to the biological side of the case, and point out that as the ear activity has been evolved on account of the advantage gained by the whole organism, it must stand in the strictest histological and physiological connection with the eye, or hand, or leg, or whatever other organ has been the overt center of action. It is absolutely impossible to think of the eye center as monopolizing consciousness and the ear apparatus as wholly quiescent. What happens is a certain relative prominence and subsidence as between the various organs which maintain the organic equilibrium.

Furthermore, the sound is not a mere stimulus, or mere sensation; it again is an act, that of hearing. The muscular response is involved in this as well as sensory stimulus; that is, there is a certain definite set of the motor apparatus involved in hearing just as much as there is in subsequent running away. The movement and posture of the head, the tension of the ear muscles, are required for the "reception" of the sound. It is just as true to say that the sensation of sound arises from a motor response as that the running away is a response to the sound. This may be brought out by reference to the fact that Professor Baldwin, in the passage quoted, has inverted the real order as between his first and second elements. We do not have first a sound and then activity of attention, unless sound is taken as mere nervous shock or physical event, not as conscious value. The conscious sensation of sound depends upon the motor response having already taken place; or, in terms of the previous statement (if stimulus is used as a conscious fact, and not as a mere physical event) it is the motor response or attention which constitutes that which finally becomes the stimulus to another act. Once more, the final "element," the running away, is not merely motor, but is sensorimotor, having its sensory value and its muscular mechanism. It is also a co-ordination. And, finally, this sensorimotor co-ordination is not a new act, supervening upon what preceded. Just as the "response" is necessary to constitute the stimulus, to determine it as sound and as this kind of sound, of wild beast or robber, so the sound experience must persist as a value in the running, to keep it up, to control it. The motor reaction involved in the running is, once more, into, not merely to, the sound. It occurs to change the sound, to get rid of it. The resulting quale, whatever it may be, has its meaning wholly determined by reference to the hearing of the sound. It is that experience mediated.[3] What we have is a circuit; not an arc or broken segment of a circle. This circuit is more truly termed organic than reflex, because the motor response determines the stimulus, just as truly as sensory stimulus determines movement. Indeed, the movement is only for the sake of determining the stimulus, of fixing what kind of a stimulus it is, of interpreting it.

I hope it will not appear that I am introducing needless refinements and distinctions into what, it may be urged, is after all an undoubted

---

[3] In other words, every reaction is of the same type as that which Professor Baldwin ascribes to imitation alone, viz., circular. Imitation is simply that particular form of the circuit in which the "response" lends itself to comparatively unchanged maintenance of the prior experience. I say comparatively unchanged, for as far as this maintenance means additional control over the experience, it is being psychically changed, becoming more distinct. It is safe to suppose, moreover, that the "repetition" is kept up only so long as this growth or mediation goes on. There is the new-in-the-old, if it is only the new sense of power.

fact, that movement as response follows sensation as stimulus. It is not a question of making the account of the process more complicated, though it is always wise to beware of that false simplicity which is reached by leaving out of account a large part of the problem. It is a question of finding out what stimulus or sensation, what movement and response mean; a question of seeing that they mean distinctions of flexible function only, not of fixed existence; that one and the same occurrence plays either or both parts, according to the shift of interest; and that because of this functional distinction and relationship, the supposed problem of the adjustment of one to the other, whether by superior force in the stimulus or an agency *ad hoc* in the center or the soul, is a purely self-created problem.

We may see the disjointed character of the present theory, by calling to mind that it is impossible to apply the phrase "sensorimotor" to the occurrence as a simple phrase of description; it has validity only as a term of interpretation, only, that is, as defining various functions exercised. In terms of description, the whole process may be sensory or it may be motor, but it cannot be sensorimotor. The "stimulus," the excitation of the nerve ending and of the sensory nerve, the central change, are just as much, or just as little, motion as the events taking place in the motor nerve and the muscles. It is one uninterrupted, continuous redistribution of mass in motion. And there is nothing in the process, from the standpoint of description, which entitles us to call this reflex. It is redistribution pure and simple; as much so as the burning of a log, or the falling of a house or the movement of the wind. In the physical process, as physical, there is nothing which can be set off as stimulus, nothing which reacts, nothing which is response. There is just a change in the system of tensions.

The same sort of thing is true when we describe the process purely from the psychical side. It is now all sensation, all sensory quale; the motion, as psychically described, is just as much sensation as is sound or light or burn. Take the withdrawing of the hand from the candle flame as example. What we have is a certain visual-heat-pain-muscular-quale, transformed into another visual-touch-muscular-quale—the flame now being visible only at a distance, or not at all, the touch sensation being altered, etc. If we symbolize the original visual quale by v, the temperature by h, the accompanying muscular sensation by m, the whole experience may be stated as vhm-vh*m*-*vhm'*; *m* being the quale of withdrawing, *m'* the sense of the status after the withdrawal. The motion is not a certain kind of existence; it is a sort of sensory experience interpreted, just as is candle flame, or burn from candle flame. All are on a par.

But, in spite of all this, it will be urged, there is a distinction between stimulus and response, between sensation and motion. Precisely; but we ought now to be in a condition to ask of what nature is the distinction, instead of taking it for granted as a distinction somehow lying in the existence of the facts themselves. We ought to be able to see that the ordinary conception of the reflex arc theory, instead of being a case of plain science, is a survival of the metaphysical dualism, first formulated by Plato, according to which the sensation is an ambiguous dweller on the borderland of soul and body, the idea (or central process) is purely psychical, and the act (or movement) purely physical. Thus the reflex arc formulation is neither physical (or physiological) nor psychological; it is a mixed materialistic-spiritualistic assumption.

If the previous descriptive analysis has made obvious the need of a reconsideration of the reflex arc idea, of the nest of difficulties and assumptions in the apparently simple statement, it is now time to undertake an explanatory analysis. The fact is that stimulus and response are not distinctions of existence, but teleological distinctions, that is, distinctions of function, or part played, with reference to reaching or maintaining an end. With respect to this teleological process, two stages should be discriminated, as their confusion is one cause of the confusion attending the whole matter. In one case, the relation represents an organization of means with reference to a comprehensive end. It represents an accomplished adaptation. Such is the case in all well developed instincts, as when we say that the contact of eggs is a stimulus to the hen to set; or the sight of corn a stimulus to pick; such also is the case with all thoroughly formed habits, as when the contact with the floor stimulates walking. In these instances there is no question of consciousness of stimulus *as* stimulus, of response *as* response. There is simply a continuously ordered sequence of acts, all adapted in themselves and in the order of their sequence, to reach a certain objective end, the reproduction of the species, the preservation of life, locomotion to a certain place. The end has got thoroughly organized into the means. In calling one stimulus, another response, we mean nothing more than that such an orderly sequence of acts is taking place. The same sort of statement might be made equally well with reference to the succession of changes in a plant, so far as these are considered with reference to their adaptation to, say, producing seed. It is equally applicable to the series of events in the circulation of the blood, or the sequence of acts occurring in a self-binding reaper.[4]

Regarding such cases of organization viewed as already attained, we may say, positively, that it is only the assumed common reference to an inclusive end which marks each member off as stimulus and response, that apart from such reference we have only antecedent and consequent;[5] in other words, the distinction is one of interpretation. Negatively, it must be pointed out that it is not legitimate to carry over, without change, exactly the same order of considerations to cases where it is a question of *conscious* stimulation and response. We may, in the above case, regard, if we please, stimulus and response each as an entire act, having an individuality of its own, subject even here to the qualification that individuality means not an entirely independent whole, but a division of labor as regards maintaining or reaching an end. But in any case, it is an act, a sensorimotor co-ordination, which stimulates the response, itself in turn sensorimotor, not a sensation which stimulates a movement. Hence the illegitimacy of identifying, as is so often done, such cases of organized instincts or habits with the so-called reflex arc, or of transferring, without modification, considerations valid of this serial co-ordination of acts to the sensation-movement case.

The fallacy that arises when this is done is virtually the psychological or historical fallacy. A set of considerations which hold good only because of a completed process, is read into the content of the process which conditions this completed result. A state of things characterizing an outcome is regarded as a true description of the events which led up to this outcome; when, as a matter of fact, if this outcome had already been in existence, there would have been no necessity for the process. Or, to make the application to the case in hand, considerations valid of an attained organization or co-ordination, the orderly sequence of minor acts in a comprehensive co-ordination, are used to describe a process, *viz.*, the distinction of mere sensation as stimulus and of mere

---

[4] To avoid misapprehension, I would say that I am not raising the question as to how far this teleology is real in any one of these cases; real or unreal, my point holds equally well. It is only when we regard the sequence of acts *as if* they were adapted to reach some end that it occurs to us to speak of one as stimulus and the other as response. Otherwise, we look at them as a *mere* series.

[5] Whether, even in such a determination, there is still not a reference of a more latent kind to an end is, of course, left open.

movement as response, which takes place only because such an attained organization is no longer at hand, but is in process of constitution. Neither mere sensation, nor mere movement, can ever be either stimulus or response; only an act can be that; the *sensation* as stimulus means the lack of and search for such an objective stimulus, or orderly placing of an act; just as mere movement as response means the lack of and search for the right act to complete a given co-ordination.

A recurrence to our example will make these formulae clearer. As long as the seeing is an unbroken act, which is as experienced no more mere sensation than it is mere motion (though the onlooker or psychological observer can interpret it into sensation and movement), it is in no sense the sensation which stimulates the reaching; we have, as already sufficiently indicated, only the serial steps in a co-ordination of *acts*. But now take a child who, upon reaching for bright light (that is, exercising the seeing-reaching co-ordination), has sometimes had a delightful exercise, sometimes found something good to eat and sometimes burned himself. *Now the response is not only uncertain, but the stimulus is equally uncertain; one is uncertain only in so far as the other is.* The real problem may be equally well stated as either to discover the right stimulus, to constitute the stimulus, or to discover, to constitute, the response. The question of whether to reach or to abstain from reaching is the question what sort of a bright light have we here? Is it the one which means playing with one's hands, eating milk, or burning one's fingers? The stimulus must be constituted for the response to occur. Now it is at precisely this juncture and because of it that the distinction of sensation as stimulus and motion as response arises.

The sensation or conscious stimulus is not a thing or existence by itself; it is that phase of a co-ordination requiring attention because, by reason of the conflict within the co-ordination, it is uncertain how to complete it. It is doubt as to the next act, whether to reach or no, which gives the motive to examining the act. The end to follow is, in this sense, the stimulus. It furnishes the motivation to attend to what has just taken place; to define it more carefully. From this point of view the discovery of the stimulus is the "response" to possible movement as "stimulus." We must have an anticipatory sensation, an image, of the movements that may occur, together with their respective values, before attention will go to the seeing to break it up as a sensation of light, and of light of this particular kind. It is the initiated activities of reaching, which, inhibited by the conflict in the co-ordination, turn round, as it were, upon the seeing, and hold it from passing over into further act until its quality is determined. Just here the act as objective stimulus becomes transformed into sensation as possible, as conscious, stimulus. Just here also, motion as conscious response emerges.

In other words, sensation as stimulus does not mean any particular psychical *existence*. It means simply a function, and will have its value shift according to the special work requiring to be done. At one moment the various activities of reaching and withdrawing will be the sensation, because they are that phase of activity which sets the problem, or creates the demand for, the next act. At the next moment the previous act of seeing will furnish the sensation, being, in turn, that phase of activity which sets the pace upon which depends further action. Generalized, sensation as stimulus is always that phase of activity requiring to be defined in order that a co-ordination may be completed. What the sensation will be in particular at a given time, therefore, will depend entirely upon the way in which an activity is being used. It has no fixed quality of its own. The search for the stimulus is the search for exact conditions of action; that is, for the state of things which decides how a beginning co-ordination should be completed.

Similarly, motion, as response, has only a functional value. It is whatever will serve to complete the disintegrating co-ordination. Just as the discovery of the sensation marks the establishing of the problem, so the constitution of the response marks the solution of this problem. At one time, fixing attention, holding the eye fixed, upon the seeing and thus bringing out a certain quale of light is the response, because that is the particular act called for just then; at another time, the movement of the arm away from the light is the response. There is nothing in itself which may be labeled response. That one certain set of sensory quales should be marked off by themselves as "motion" and put in antithesis to such sensory quales as those of color, sound and contact, as legitimate claimants to the title of sensation, is wholly inexplicable unless we keep the difference of function in view. It is the eye and ear sensations which fix for us the problem; which report to us the conditions which have to be met if the co-ordination is to be successfully completed; and just the moment we need to know about our movements to get an adequate report, just that moment, motion miraculously (from the ordinary standpoint) ceases to be motion and become "muscular sensation." On the other hand, take the change in values of experience, the transformation of sensory quales. Whether this change will or will not be interpreted as movement, whether or not any consciousness of movement will arise, will depend upon whether this change is satisfactory, whether or not it is regarded as a harmonious development of a co-ordination, or whether the change is regarded as simply a means in solving a problem, an instrument in reaching a more satisfactory co-ordination. So long as our experience runs smoothly we are no more conscious of motion as motion than we are of this or that color or sound by itself.

To sum up: the distinction of sensation and movement as stimulus and response respectively is not a distinction which can be regarded as descriptive of anything which holds of psychical events or existences as such. The only events to which the terms stimulus and response can be descriptively applied are to minor acts serving by their respective positions to the maintenance of some organized co-ordination. The conscious stimulus or sensation, and the conscious response of motion, have a special genesis or motivation, and a special end or function. The reflex arc theory, by neglecting, by abstracting from, this genesis and this function gives us one disjointed part of a process as if it were the whole. It gives us literally an arc, instead of the circuit; and not giving us the circuit of which it is an arc, does not enable us to place, to center, the arc. This arc, again, falls apart into two separate existences having to be either mechanically or externally adjusted to each other.

The circle is a co-ordination, some of whose members have come into conflict with each other. It is the temporary disintegration and need of reconstitution which occasions, which affords the genesis of, the conscious distinction into sensory stimulus on one side and motor response on the other. The stimulus is that phase of the forming co-ordination which represents the conditions which have to be met in bringing it to a successful issue; the response is that phase of one and the same forming co-ordination which gives the key to meeting these conditions, which serves as instrument in effecting the successful co-ordination. They are therefore strictly correlative and contemporaneous. The stimulus is something to be discovered; to be made out; if the activity affords its own adequate stimulation, there is no stimulus save in the objective sense already referred to. As soon as it is adequately determined, then and then only is the response also complete. To attain either, means that the co-ordination has completed itself. Moreover, it is the motor response which assists in discovering and constituting the stimulus. It is the holding of the movement at a certain stage which creates the sensation, which throws it into relief.

It is the co-ordination which unifies that which the reflex arc concept gives us only in disjointed fragments. It is the circuit within which fall distinctions of stimulus and response as functional phases of its own mediation or completion. The point of this story is in its application; but the application of it to the question of the nature of psychical evolution, to the distinction between sensational and rational consciousness, and the nature of judgment must be deferred to a more favorable opportunity.

10. The Psychology of Effort*

This essay should be read as more than an isolated piece of technical analysis of an aspect of human activity, for Dewey here prefigures a lifelong concern. He was extremely fascinated with the problematic character of human life and with the process of bringing something off—that is, of harmonizing means and ends. He writes in this essay of the effort involved in "the mastery of novel acts," while in his later works on education he focuses on the stresses involved while inquiring into new areas, and in his writing on art he points to the tension between anticipation and consummation. In this essay, the language is of a descriptive psychology but the setting is one that he returns to over and over—namely, the description of man as struggling to achieve a functional resolution of a problem, whether it be of immediate or more extensive significance.

There are three distinguishable views regarding the psychical quales experienced in cases of effort. One is the conception that effort, as such, is strictly "spiritual" or "intellectual," unmediated by any sensational element whatever; it being admitted, of course, that the expression or putting forth of effort, in so far as it occurs through the muscular system, has sensational correlates. This view shades into the next in so far as its upholders separate "physical" from "moral" effort, and admit that in the former the consciousness of effort is more or less sensational in character, while in the latter remaining wholly non-sensuous in quality. The third view declines to accept the distinction made between moral and physical effort as a distinction of genesis, and holds that all sense of effort is sensationally (peripherally) determined. For example, the first theory, in its extreme or typical form, would say that when we put forth effort, whether to lift a stone, to solve a refractory problem, or to resist temptation, the sense of effort is the consciousness of pure psychical activity, to be carefully distinguished from any sense of the

* From *Philosophical Review* VI (January, 1897), pp. 43-56.

muscular and organic changes occurring from the actual putting forth of effort, the latter being a return wave of resulting sensations. The second view would discriminate between the cases alluded to, drawing a line between effort in lifting the stone, which is considered as itself due to sense of strain and tension arising from the actual putting forth of energy (and hence sensuously conditioned), and the two other cases. Various writers would, however, apparently draw the line at different places, some conceding the sense of effort in intellectual attention to be sensational, mediated through feeling the contraction of muscles of forehead, fixation of eyes, changes in breathing, etc. Others would make the attention, as such, purely spiritual (*i.e.*, in this use, non-sensational), independently of whether the outcome is intellectual or moral in value. But the third view declares unambiguously that the sense of effort is, in any case, due to the organic reverberations of the act itself, the "muscular," visceral, and breathing sensations.[1]

In the following paper I propose, for the most part, to approach this question indirectly rather than directly, my underlying conviction being that the difference between the "sensational" and "spiritual" schools is due to the fact that one is thinking of a distinctly psychological fact, the way in which the sense or *consciousness* of effort is mediated, while the other is, in reality, discussing a logical or moral problem—the interpretation of the category of effort, the value which it has as a part of experience. To the point that the distinction between "physical" and "spiritual" effort is one of interpretation, of function, rather than of kind of existence, I shall return to the sequel. Meantime, I wish to present a certain amount of introspective evidence for the position that the sense of effort (as distinguished from the fact or the category) is sensationally mediated; and then to point out that if this is admitted, the real problem of the psychology of effort is only stated, not solved; this problem being to find the sensational *differentia* between the cases in which there is, and those in which there is not, a sense of effort.

The following material was gathered, it may be said, not with reference to the conscious examination of the case in hand, but in the course of a study of the facts of choice; this indirect origin makes it, I believe, all the more valuable. The cases not quoted are identical in kind

[1] Professor James, to whom, along with Ferrier, we owe, for the most part the express recognition of the sensational quales concerned in effort, appears to accept the second of these three types of views. I do not know that the question has been raised as to how this distinction is reconcilable with his general theory of emotion; nor yet how his ground for making it—the superiority of the spiritual over the physical—is to be adjusted to his assertion (*Psychology*, II, p. 453) that the sensational theory of emotions does not detract from their spiritual significance.

with those quoted, there being no reports of a contrary sense. "In deciding a question that had to be settled in five minutes, I found myself turned in the chair, till I was sitting on its edge, with the left arm on the back of the chair, hand clenched so tightly that the marks on the nails were left in the palm, breathing so rapid that it was oppressive, winking rapid, jaws clenched, leaning far forward and supporting my head by the right hand. The question was whether I should go to the city that day. When I decided to go I felt more like resting than starting."

The next instance relates to an attempt to recall lines of poetry formerly memorized. "There is a feeling of strain. This I found to be immediately dependent upon a hard knitting of the brows and forehead—especially upon a fixing and converging of the eyes. At the same time there is a general contraction of the system as a whole. The breathing is quiet, slow, and regular, save where emotional accompaniments break it up. The meter is usually kept by a slight movement of the toes in the shoes or by a finger of the hand. As the recollection proceeds, there is a sensation of peering, of viewing the whole scene. The fixation exhausts the eyes much more than hard reading."

The succeeding instance relates to the effort involved in understanding an author. "First, I am conscious of drawing myself together, my forehead contracts, my eyes and ears seem to draw themselves in and shut themselves off. There is tension of the muscles of limbs. Secondly, a feeling of movement or plunge forward occurs. My particular sensations differ in different cases, but all have this in common: First, a feeling of tension, and then movement forward. Sometimes the forward movement is accompanied by a muscular feeling in the arms as if throwing things to right and left, in clearing a road to a desired object. Sometimes it is a feeling of climbing, and planting my foot firmly as on a height attained."[2]

Now of course I am far from thinking that these cases, or any number of such cases, prove the sensational character of the consciousness of effort. Logically, the statements are all open to the interpretation that we are concerned here with products or incidental *sequelae* of effort, rather than with its essence. But I have yet to find a student who, with growing power of introspection, did not report that to him such sensations seemed to constitute the "feel" of effort. Moreover, the cumulative force of such statements is very great, if not logically conclusive. Many state that if they relax their muscles entirely it is impossi-

---

[2] A number of cases, on further questioning, reported a similar rhythm of contraction and movement accompanying mental effort. This topic would stand special inquiry.

ble to keep up the effort. Sensations frequently mentioned are those connected with breathing—stopping the respiration, breathing more rapidly, contracted chest and throat; others are contraction of brow, holding head fixed, or twisting it, compression of lips, clenching of fist, contraction of jaws, sensations in pit of stomach, goneness in legs, shoulders higher, head lower than usual, fogginess or mistiness in visual field, trying to see something which eludes vision, etc.

But upon the whole I intend rather to assume that the sense of effort is, in all its forms, sensationally conditioned. We have in this fact (if it be a fact) no adequate psychology of effort, but only the preliminary of such theory. The conception up to this point has, for theoretical purposes, negative value only; it is useful in overthrowing other theories of effort, but throws no positive light upon its nature. The problem of interest, as soon as the rival theories are dismissed, comes to be this: Granted the sensational character of the consciousness of effort, what is its specific *differentia?* What we wish now to know is what set of sensory values marks off experiences of effort from those closely resembling, but not felt as cases of effort. So far as I know this question has not been raised.

How then does, say, a case of perception with effort differ from a case of "easy" or effortless perception? The difference, I repeat, shall be wholly in sensory quale; but in *what* sensory quale?

At this point a reversion to a different point of view, and the introduction of a different order of ideas is likely to occur. We may be told, as an explanation of the difference, that in one case we have a feeling of activity, a feeling of the putting forth of energy. I found that persons who in special cases have become thoroughly convinced of the sensational quality of all consciousness of effort, will make this answer. The explanation is, I think, that the point of view unconsciously shifts from effort as a psychical fact, as fact of direct consciousness, to effort as an objective or teleological fact. We stop thinking of the sense of effort, and think of the reference or import of the experience. Effort, as putting forth of energy, is involved equally in all psychical occurrences. It exists with a sense of ease just as much as with a sense of strain. There may be more of it in cases of extreme absorption and interest, where no effort is felt, than in cases of extreme sense of effort. Compare, for example, the psychophysical energy put forth in listening to a symphony, or in viewing a picture gallery, with that exercised in trying to fix a small moving speck on the wall; compare the energy, that is, as objectively measured. In the former case, the whole being may be intensely active, and yet there may be, at the time, absolutely no con-

sciousness of effort or strain. The latter may be, objectively, a very trivial activity, and yet the consciousness of strain may be the chief thing
in the conscious experience. In some cases it seems almost as if the relation between effort as an objective fact, and effort as a psychical fact,
were an inverse one. If a monotonous physical movement be indefinitely repeated, it will generally be found that as long as "activity"
is put forth, and accomplishes something objectively (as measured in
some dynometric register), there is little sense of effort. Let the energy
be temporarily exhausted and action practically cease, then the sense of
effort will be at its maximum. Let a wave of energy recur, and there is at
once a sense of lightness, of ease. And in all cases, the sense of effort
and ease follows, never precedes, the change in activity as objectively
measured.

We are not concerned, accordingly, with any question of the existence or non-existence of spiritual activity, or even of psychophysical
activity. The reference to this, as furnishing the *differentia* of cases of
consciousness of effort from those of ease, is not so much false as irrelevant.

Where, then, shall we locate the discriminative factor? Take the
simplest possible case: I try to make out the exact form, or the nature,
of a faint marking on a piece of paper a few feet off, at about the limit
of distinct vision. What is the special sensation carrier of the sense of effort here? Introspectively I believe the answer is very simple. In the case
of felt effort, certain sensory quales, usually fused, fall apart in consciousness, and there is an alternation, an oscillation, between them, accompanied by a disagreeable tone when they are apart, and an
agreeable tone when they become fused again. Moreover, the separation
in consciousness during the period when the quales are apart is not complete, but the image of the fused quale is at least dimly present.
Specifically, in ordinary or normal vision, there is no distinction within
consciousness of the ocular-motor sensation which corresponds to fixation, from the optical sensations of light and color. The two are so intimately fused that there is but one quale in consciousness. In these
cases, there is feeling of ease, or at least absence of sense of effort. In
other cases, the sensations corresponding to frowning, to holding the
head steady, the breathing fixed—the whole adjustment of motor apparatus—come into consciousness of themselves on their own account.
Now we are not accustomed to find satisfaction in the experience of
motor adjustment; the relevant sensations have value and interest, not
in themselves, but in the specific quales of sound, color, touch, or
whatever they customarily introduce. In at least ninety-nine one-

hundreths of our experience, the "muscular" sensations are felt simply as passing over into some other experience which is either aimed at, or which, when experienced, affords satisfaction. A habit of expectation, of looking forward to some other experience, thus comes to be the normal associate of motor experience. It is felt as fringe, as "tendency," not as psychical resting place. Whenever it persists as motor, whenever the expectation of other sensory quales of positive value is not met, there is at least a transitory feeling of futility, of thwartedness, or of irritation at a failure. Hence the disagreeable tone referred to. But in the type of cases taken as our illustration, more is true than a failure of an expected consequent through mere inertia of habit. The image of the end aimed at persists, and, through its contrast with the partial motor quale, emphasizes and reinforces the sense of incompleteness. That is to say, one is continually imaging the speck as having some particular form—an oval or an angular form; as having a certain nature—an inkspot, a flyspeck. Then this image is as continually interfered with by the sensations of motor adjustment coming to consciousness by themselves. Each experience breaks into, and breaks up, the other before it has attained fullness. Let the image of a five-sided inkspot be acquiesced in apart from the motor adjustment (in other words, let one pass into the state of reverie), or let the "muscular" sensations be given complete sway by themselves (as when one begins to study them in his capacity as psychologist), and all sense of effort disappears. It is the rivalry, with the accompanying disagreeable tone due to failure of habit, that constitutes the sense of effort.

It will be useful to apply the terms of this analysis to some attendant phenomena of effort. First, it enables us to account for the growing sense of effort with fatigue, without having to resort to a set of conceptions lying outside the previously used ideas. The sense of fatigue increases effort, just because it marks the emergence into consciousness of a distinct new set of sensations which resist absorption into, or fusion with, the dominant images of the current habit or purpose. Upon the basis of other theories of effort, fatigue increases sense of effort because of sheer exhaustion; upon this theory, because of the elements introduced which distract attention. Other theories, in other words, have to fall back upon an extrapsychical factor, and something which is heterogeneous with the other factors concerned. Moreover, they fail to account for the fact that if the feeling of fatigue is surrendered to, it ceases to be disagreeable, and may become a delicious languor.

In a similar way certain facts connected with sense of effort, as related to the mastery of novel acts, may be explained. Take the alternation of ridiculous excess of effort, with total collapse of effort in learning to ride a bicycle. Before one mounts one has perhaps a pretty definite visual image of himself in balance and in motion. This image persists as a desirability. On the other hand, there comes into play at once the consciousness of the familiar motor adjustments—for the most part, related to walking. The two sets of sensations refuse to coincide, and the result is an amount of stress and strain relevant to the most serious problems of the universe. Or, again, the conflict becomes so unregulated that the image of the balance disappears, and one finds himself with only a lot of "muscular" sensations at hand; the effort entirely vanishes. I have taken an extreme case, but surely everyone is familiar, in dealing with unfamiliar occupations, of precisely this alternation of effort, out of all proportion to the objective significance of the end, with the complete mind-wandering and failure of endeavor. If the sense of effort is the sense of incompatibility between two sets of sensory images, one of which stands for an end to be reached, or a fulfillment of a habit, while the other represents the experiences which intervene in reaching the end, these phenomena are only what are to be expected. But if we start from a "spiritual" theory of effort, I know of no explanation which is anything more than an hypostatized repetition of the facts to be explained.

It probably has already occurred to the reader, that when the theory of the sensational character of the consciousness of effort is analyzed, instead of being merely thrown out at large, the feeling that it deals common sense a blow in the face disappears. If we state the foregoing analysis in objective, instead of in psychical, terms, it just says that effort is the feeling of opposition existing between end and means. The kinesthetic image of qualitative nature (i.e., of color, sound, contact) stands for the end, whether consciously desired, or as furnishing the culmination of habit. The "muscular" sensations[3] represent the means, the experiences to which value is not attached on their own account, but as intermediaries to an intrinsically valuable consciousness.

Practically stated, this means that effort is nothing more, and also nothing less, than tension between means and ends in action, and that the sense of effort is the awareness of this conflict. The sensational character of this experience, which has been such a stumbling block to some, means that this tension of adjustment is not merely ideal, but is actual (i.e., practical); it is one which goes on in a struggle for existence. Be-

---

[3] Perhaps it would be well to state that sensations of tendons, joints, internal contacts, etc., are what is meant by this term—the whole report of the motor adjustment.

ing a struggle for realization in the world of concrete quales and values, it makes itself felt in the only media possible—specific sensations, on the one hand, and muscular sensations, on the other. Instead of denying, or slurring over, effort, such an account brings it into prominence. Surely what common sense values in effort is not some transcendental act, occurring before any change in the actual world of qualities, but precisely this readjustment within the concrete region. And if one is somewhat scandalized at being told that the awareness of effort is a sense of changes of breathing, of muscular tensions, etc., it is not, I conceive, because of what is said, but rather because of what is left unsaid—that these sensations report the state of things as regards effective realization.

It is difficult to see, upon a more analytic consideration than common sense is called upon to make, what is gained for the "spiritual" nature of effort by relegating it to a purely extrasensational region. That "spiritual" is to be so interpreted as to mean existence in a sphere transcending space and time determinations is, at best, a piece of metaphysics, and not a piece of psychology; and as a piece of metaphysics, it cannot escape competition with the theory which finds the meaning of the spiritual in the whole process of realizing the concrete values of life. I do not find that any of the upholders of the non-sensational quality of effort has ever made a very specific analysis of the experience. Professor Baldwin's account, however, being perhaps the most thoroughgoing statement of effort as preceding sensation, in "physical" as well as "spiritual" effort, is, perhaps, as explicit as any. In one passage, effort is "distinct consciousness of opposition between what we call self and muscular resistance." Now a consciousness of muscular resistance, whatever else it may or may not be, would seem to involve sensations, and the consciousness of effort to be, so far forth, sensationally mediated—which is contrary to the hypothesis. Moreover, it is extremely difficult to see how there can be any consciousness of opposition between the self in general, and the muscles in general. Until the "self" actually starts to do something (and then, of course, there are sensations), how can the muscles offer any opposition to it? And even when it does begin to do something, how can the muscles, as muscles, offer opposition? If because the act is unfamiliar, then certainly what we get is simply a case of difficulty in the having of a unified consciousness—the kinesthetic image of the habitual movement will not unify with the proposed sensory image, and there is rivalry. But this is not a case of muscles resisting the self; it is a case of divided activity of the self. It means that the activity already going on (and, therefore, reporting itself sensationally) resists displacement, or transformation, by or into another activity which is beginning, and thus making its sensational report.

But Professor Baldwin gives another statement which is apparently different. "In all voluntary movement, therefore, there is an earlier fiat than the will to move, *i.e.*, the fiat of attention to the particular idea of movement." And it is repeatedly intimated that the real difficulty in effort is, not in the muscular execution, but in holding a given idea in consciousness. (In fact, it is distinctly stated that, even in muscular effort, the real effort is found in "attending" to the idea.) Now, this statement is certainly preferable to the other, in that it avoids the appearance of making the muscles offer resistance to the self. But now, what has become of the resistance, and, hence, of the effort? Is there anything left to offer opposition *to* the self? Can an idea, *qua* pure idea, offer resistance and demand effort? And is it the self, as barely self, to which resistance is made? Such questions may, perhaps, serve to indicate the abstractness of the account, and suggest the fact that effort is never felt, save when a *change of existing activity is proposed*. In this case, the effort may be centered in the introduction of the new idea as against the persistence of the present doing, or it may be to maintain the existing habit against the suggested change. In the former, the new activity will probably be categorized as duty; in the latter case, as temptation or distraction. But in either alternative, effort is felt with reference to the adjustment of factors in an action. Neither of these is exclusively self, neither the old nor the new factor; and the one which happens to be especially selected as self varies with the state of action. At one period, the end or aim is regarded as self, and the existing habit, or mode of action, as the obstruction to the realization of the desired self; at the next stage, the end having been pretty well defined, the habit, or existing line of action, since the only means or instrument for attaining this end, is conceived as self, and the ideal as "beyond," and at once as resisting and as soliciting the self.

I do not suppose anyone will question this account, so far as relates to the fact that the sense of effort arises only with reference to a proposed change in the existing activity, and that at least the existing activity has its sensational counterpart. Doubt is more likely to arise as regards the proposed end, or the intruding distraction. This, it may be said, is pure idea, not activity, and, hence, has no sensational report. But whoever takes this position must be able to explain the *differentia* between instances of logical manipulation of an idea, aesthetic contemplation, and cases of sense of effort. I may take the idea of something I ought to do, but which is repulsive to me; may say that I ought to do it, and may then hold the idea as an idea or object in consciousness, may revolve it in all lights, may turn it over and over, may chew it as a sweet or a bitter cud, and yet have absolutely no sense of effort. It is only, so far as I can trust my own observation, when this idea passes into at least nascent or partial action, and thus comes head up against some other line of action, that the sense of effort arises.

In other words, the sense of effort arises, not because there is an activity struggling against resistance, or a self which is endeavoring to overcome obstacles outside of it; but it arises within activity, marking the attempt to co-ordinate separate factors within a single whole. Activity is here taken not as formal, but as actual and specific. It means an act, definitely doing something definite. An act, as something which occupies time, necessarily means conflict of acts. The demand for time is simply the result of a lack of unity. The intervening process of execution, the use of means, is the process of disintegrating acts hitherto separate and independent, and putting together the result, or fragments, into a single piece of conduct. Were it not for the division of acts and results in conflict, the deed, or co-ordination, would be accomplished at once.

One of the conflicting acts stands for the end or aim. This, at first, is the sensory image which gives the cue and motive to the reaction or response. In the case previously cited, it is the image of the colored speck, as determining the movements of the head and eye muscles.[4] That we are inclined to view only the motor response as act, and regard the image, either as alone psychical, or as pure idea, is because the image is already in existence, and, therefore, its active side may be safely neglected. Being already in possession of the field, it does not require any conscious activity to keep it in existence. The movement of the muscles, being the means by which the desired end may be reached, becomes the all-important thing, or *the* act; in accordance with the general principle that attention always goes to the weakest part of a co-ordination in process of formation, meaning by weakest, that part least under the immediate control of habit. This being conceived alone as act, everything lying outside of it is conceived as resistance; thus recognition is avoided of the fact, that the real state of things is, that there are two acts mutually opposing each other, during their transformation over into a third new and inclusive act.

We have here, I think, an adequate explanation of all that can be said

---

[4] It must not be forgotten that both sensory stimulus and motor response are both in reality sensorimotor, and, therefore, each is itself an act or psychical whole. On this point, see my "The Reflex Arc Concept."

about the tremendous importance of effort, of all that Professor James has so conclusively said. This importance is not due to the fact that effort is the one sole evidence of a free spiritual activity struggling against outward and material resistance. It is due to the fact that effort is the critical point of progress in action, arising whenever old habits are in process of reconstruction, or of adaptation to new conditions; unless they are so readapted, life is given over to the rule of conservatism, routine, and over-inertia. To make a new co-ordination the old co-ordination must, to some extent, be broken up, and the only way of breaking it up is for it to come into conflict with some other co-ordination; that is, a conflict of two acts, each representing a habit, or end, is the necessary condition of reaching a new act which shall have a more comprehensive end. That sensations of the bodily state report to us this conflict and readjustment, merely indicates that the reconstruction going on is one of acts, and not mere ideas. The whole prejudice which supposes that the spiritual sense of effort is lost when it is given sensational quality, is simply a survival of the notion that an idea is somehow more spiritual than an act.

Up to this time I have purposely avoided any reference to the attempt to explain effort by attention. My experience has been that this mode of explanation does not explain, but simply shifts the difficulty, at the same time making it more obscure by claiming to solve it. There is some danger that attention may become a psychological pool of Bethesda. If we have escaped the clutch of associationalism, only to fall into attentionalism, we have hardly bettered our condition in psychology. But the preceding account would apply to any concrete analyses of effort in terms of attention. The psychological fallacy besets us here. We confuse attention as an objective fact, attention for the observer, with attention as consciously experienced. During complete absorption an onlooker may remark how attentive such a person is, or after such an absorption one may look back and say how attentive one was; but taking the absorption when it occurs, it means that only the subject matter is present in consciousness, not attention itself. We are conscious of being attentive only when our attention is divided, only when there are two centers of attention competing with each other, only when there is an oscillation from one group of ideas to another, together with a tendency to a third group of ideas, in which the two previous groups are included. The sense of strain in attention, instead of being coincident with the activity of attention, is proof that attention itself is not yet complete.

To establish the identity of attention with the formation of a new act, through the mutual adaptation of two existing habits, would take us too far away from our present purpose; but there need be no hesitation, I believe, in admitting that the sense of attention arises only under the conditions of conflict already stated.

III

The Experience
of Knowing

The five essays in this section present the origins and development of Dewey's pragmatic epistemology. The early essays show Dewey's struggle to divest himself of the absolutistic claims of objective idealism and to move in the direction of a logic of inquiry in which the experience of knowing becomes as much the focus of concern as that which is known. This position is presented clearly in the last essay of this section, "The Pattern of Inquiry."

11. "Consciousness" and Experience*

At the turn of the century, Dewey was still very much concerned with the relative responsibilities of psychology and philosophy. In this essay, he attempts to bring their functions close together while being especially critical of that type of philosophy which continues to make judgments about human behavior, although innocent of important behavioral data. In a note at the conclusion of this essay, Dewey points to the developments in the first decade of the twentieth century, which bear out his earlier judgments and which provide the basis for a "pragmatic empiricism." Dewey, of course, participated in those developments, and several of the essays in which he articulated his positions are reprinted below—namely, "The Experimental Theory of Knowledge," "Experience and Objective Idealism," and "The Postulate of Immediate Empiricism."

* From John Dewey, *The Influence of Darwin on Philosophy: And Other Essays on Contemporary Thought*, pp. 242-270. Copyright 1910 by Holt, Rinehart and Winston, Inc. Copyright 1938 by John Dewey. Reprinted by permission of Holt, Rinehart and Winston, Inc. (Published originally as "Psychology and Philosophic Method," May, 1899.)

Every science in its final standpoint and working aims is controlled by conditions lying outside itself—conditions that subsist in the practical life of the time. With no science is this as obviously true as with psychology. Taken without nicety of analysis, no one would deny that psychology is specially occupied with the individual; that it wishes to find out those things that proceed peculiarly from the individual, and the mode of their connection with him. Now, the way in which the individual is conceived, the value that is attributed to him, the things in his make-up that arouse interest, are not due at the outset to psychology. The scientific view regards these matters in a reflected, a borrowed, medium. They are revealed in the light of social life. An autocratic, an aristocratic, a democratic society propound such different estimates of the worth and place of individuality; they procure for the individual as an individual such different sorts of experience; they aim at arousing such different impulses and at organizing them according to such different purposes, that the psychology arising in each must show a different temper.

In this sense, psychology is a political science. While the professed psychologist, in his conscious procedure, may easily cut his subject-matter loose from these practical ties and references, yet the starting point and goal of his course are none the less socially set. In this conviction I venture to introduce to an audience that could hardly be expected to be interested in the technique of psychology, a technical subject, hoping that the human meaning may yet appear.

There is at present a strong, apparently a growing tendency to conceive of psychology as an account of the consciousness of the individual, considered as something in and by itself; consciousness, the assumption virtually runs, being of such an order that it may be analyzed, described, and explained in terms of just itself. The statement, as commonly made, is that psychology is an account of consciousness, *qua* consciousness; and the phrase is supposed to limit psychology to a certain definite sphere of fact that may receive adequate discussion for scientific purposes, without troubling itself with what lies outside. Now if this conception be true, there is no intimate, no important connection of psychology and philosophy at large. That philosophy, whose range is comprehensive, whose problems are catholic, should be held down by a discipline whose voice is as partial as its material is limited, is out of the range of intelligent discussion.

But there is another possibility. If the individual of whom psychology treats be, after all, a social individual, any absolute setting off and apart of a sphere of consciousness as, even for scientific purposes, self-

sufficient, is condemned in advance. All such limitation, and all inquiries, descriptions, explanations that go with it, are only preliminary.
"Consciousness" is but a symbol, an anatomy whose life is in natural
and social operations. To know the symbol, the psychical letter, is important; but its necessity lies not within itself, but in the need of a
language for reading the things signified. If this view be correct, we cannot be so sure that psychology is without large philosophic significance.
Whatever meaning the individual has for the social life that he both incorporates and animates, that meaning has psychology for philosophy.

This problem is too important and too large to suffer attack in an
evening's address. Yet I venture to consider a portion of it, hoping that
such things as appear will be useful clues in entering wider territory. We
may ask what is the effect upon psychology of considering its material
as something so distinct as to be capable of treatment without involving
larger issues. In this inquiry we take as representative some such account of the science as this: Psychology deals with consciousness "as
such" in its various modes and processes. It aims at an isolation of each
such as will permit accurate description: at statement of its place in the
serial order such as will enable us to state the laws by which one calls
another into being, or as will give the natural history of its origin,
maturing, and dissolution. It is both analytic and synthetic—analytic in
that it resolves each state into its constituent elements; synthetic in that
it discovers the processes by which these elements combine into complex wholes and series. It leaves alone—it shuts out—questions concerning the validity, the objective import of these modifications: of their
value in conveying truth, in effecting goodness, in constituting beauty.
For it is just with such questions of worth, of validity, that philosophy
has to do.

Some such view as this is held by the great majority of working psychologists to-day. A variety of reasons have conspired to bring about
general acceptance. Such a view seems to enroll one in the ranks of the
scientific men rather than of the metaphysicians—and there are those
who distrust the metaphysicians. Others desire to take problems piecemeal and in detail, avoiding that excursion into ultimates, into that
never-ending panorama of new questions and new possibilities that
seems to be the fate of the philosopher. While no temperate mind can
do other than sympathize with this view, it is hardly more than an expedient. For, as Mr. James remarks, after disposing of the question of
free-will by relegating it to the domain of the metaphysician:—"Metaphysics means only an unusually obstinate attempt to

think clearly and consistently''—and clearness and consistency are not things to be put off beyond a certain point. When the metaphysician chimes in with this new-found modesty of the psychologist, so different from the disposition of Locke and Hume and the Mills, salving his metaphysical conscience with the remark—it hardly possesses the dignity of a conviction—that the partial sciences, just because they are partial, are not expected to be coherent with themselves nor with one another; when the metaphysician, I say, praises the psychologist for sticking to his last, we are reminded that another motive is also at work. There is a half-conscious irony in this abnegation of psychology. It is not the first time that science has assumed the work of Cinderella; and, since Mr. Huxley has happily reminded her, she is not altogether oblivious, in her modesty, of a possible future check to the pride of her haughty sister, and of a certain coronation that shall mark her coming to her own.

But, be the reasons as they may, there is little doubt of the fact. Almost all our working psychologists admit, nay, herald this limitation of their work. I am not presumptuous enough to set myself against this array. I too proclaim myself of those who believe that psychology has to do (at a certain point, that is) with ''consciousness as such.'' But I do not believe that the limitation is final. Quite the contrary: if ''consciousness'' or ''state of consciousness'' be given intelligible meaning, I believe that this conception is the open gateway into the fair fields of philosophy. For, note you, the phrase is an ambiguous one. It may mean one thing to the metaphysician who proclaims: Here finally we have psychology recognizing her due metes and bounds, giving bonds to trespass no more. It may mean quite another thing to the psychologist in his work—whatever he may happen to say about it. It may be that the psychologist deals with states of consciousness as the significant, the analyzable and describable form, to which he reduces the things he is studying. Not that they *are* that existence, but that they are its indications, its clues, in shape for handling by scientific methods. So, for example, does the paleontologist work. Those curiously shaped and marked forms to which he is devoted are not life, nor are they the literal termini of his endeavor; but through them as signs and records he construes a life. And again, the painter-artist might well say that he is concerned only with colored paints as such. Yet none the less through them as registers and indices, he reveals to us the mysteries of sunny meadow, shady forest, and twilight wave. These are the things-in-themselves of which the oils on his palette are phenomena.

So the preoccupation of the psychologist with states of consciousness may signify that they are the media, the concrete conditions to which he purposely reduces his material, in order, *through them*, as methodological helps, to get at and understand that which is anything but a state of consciousness. To him, however, who insists upon the fixed and final limitation of psychology, the state of consciousness is not the shape some fact takes from the exigency of investigation; it is literally the full fact itself. It is not an intervening term; it bounds the horizon. Here, then, the issue defines itself. I conceive that states of consciousness (and I hope you will take the phrase broadly enough to cover all the specific data of psychology) have no existence before the psychologist begins to work. He brings them into existence. What we are really after is the process of experience, the way in which it arises and behaves. We want to know its course, its history, its laws. We want to know its various typical forms; how each originates; how it is related to others; the part it plays in maintaining an inclusive, expanding, connected course of experience. Our problem as psychologists is to learn its *modus operandi*, its method.

The paleontologist is again summoned to our aid. In a given district he finds a great number and variety of footprints. From these he goes to work to construct the structure and the life habits of the animals that made them. The tracks exist undoubtedly; they are there; but yet he deals with them not as final existences but as signs, phenomena in the literal sense. Imagine the hearing that the critic would receive who should inform the paleontologist that he is transcending his field of scientific activity; that his concern is with footprints as such, aiming to describe each, to analyze it into its simplest forms, to compare the different kinds with one another so as to detect common elements, and finally, thereby, to discover the laws of their arrangement in space!

Yet the immediate data are footprints, and footprints only. The paleontologist does in a way do all these things that our imaginary critic is urging upon him. The difference is not that he arbitrarily lugs in other data; that he invents entities and faculties that are not there. The difference is in his standpoint. His interest is in the animals, and the data are treated in whatever way seems likely to serve this interest. So with the psychologist. He is continually and perforce occupied with minute and empirical investigation of special facts—states of consciousness, if you please. But these neither define nor exhaust his scientific problem. They are his footprints, his clues through which he places before himself the life-process he is studying—with the further difference that his footprints are not after all given to him, but are developed by his investigation.[1]

The supposition that these states are somehow existent by themselves and in this existence provide the psychologist with ready-made material is just the supreme case of the "psychological fallacy": the confusion of experience as it is to the one experiencing with what the psychologist makes out of it with his reflective analysis.

The psychologist begins with certain operations, acts, functions as his data. If these fall out of sight in the course of discussion, it is only because having been taken for granted, they remain to control the whole development of the inquiry, and to afford the sterling medium of redemption. Acts such as perceiving, remembering, intending, loving give the points of departure; they alone are concrete experiences. To understand these experiences, under what conditions they arise, and what effects they produce, analysis into states of consciousness occurs. And the modes of consciousness that are figured remain unarranged and unimportant, save as they may be translated back into acts.

To remember is to do something, as much as to shoe a horse, or to cherish a keepsake. To propose, to observe, to be kindly affectioned, are terms of value, of practice, of operation; just as digestion, respiration, locomotion express functions, not observable "objects." But there is an object that may be described: lungs, stomach, leg-muscles, or whatever. Through the structure we present to ourselves the function; it appears laid out before us, spread forth in detail—objectified in a word. The anatomist who devotes himself to this detail may, if he please (and he probably does please to concentrate his devotion) ignore the function: to discover what is there, to analyze, to measure, to describe, gives him outlet enough. But nevertheless it is the function that fixed the point of departure, that prescribed the problem and that set the limits, physical as well as intellectual, of subsequent investigation. Reference to function makes the details discovered other than a jumble of in-

---

[1] This is a fact not without its bearings upon the question of the nature and value of introspection. The objection that introspection "alters" the reality and hence is untrustworthy, most writers dispose of by saying that, after all, it need not alter the reality so very much—not beyond repair— and that, moreover, memory assists in restoring the ruins. It would be simpler to admit the fact: that the purpose of introspection is precisely to effect the right sort of alteration. If introspection should give us the original experience again, we should just be living through the experience over again in direct fashion; as psychologists we should not be forwarded one bit. Reflection upon this obvious proposition may bring to light various other matters worthy of note.

coherent trivialities. One might as well devote himself to the minute description of a square yard of desert soil were it not for this translation. States of consciousness are the morphology of certain functions.[2] What is true of analysis, of description, is true equally of classification. Knowing, willing, feeling, name states of consciousness not in terms of themselves, but in terms of acts, attitudes, found in experience.[3]

Explanation, even of an "empirical sort" is as impossible as determination of a "state" and its classification, when we rigidly confine ourselves to modifications of consciousness as a self-existent. Sensations are always defined, classified, and explained by reference to conditions which, according to the theory, are extraneous—sense-organs and stimuli. The whole physiological side assumes a ludicrously anomalous aspect on this basis.[4] While experimentation is retained, and even made much of, it is at the cost of logical coherence. To experiment with reference to a bare state of consciousness is a performance of which one cannot imagine the nature, to say nothing of doing it; while to experiment with reference to acts and the conditions of their occurrence is a natural and straightforward undertaking. Such simple processes as association are concretely inexplicable when we assume states of consciousness as existences by themselves. As recent psychology testifies,

---

[2] Thus to divorce "structure psychology" from "function psychology" is to leave us without possibility of scientific comprehension of function, while it deprives us of all standard of reference in selecting, observing, and explaining the structure.

[3] The following answer may fairly be anticipated: "This is true of the operations cited, but only because complex processes have been selected. Such a term as 'knowing' does of course express a function involving a system of intricate references. But, for that very reason, we go back to the sensation which is the genuine type of the 'state of consciousness' as such, pure and unadulterate and unsophisticated." The point is large for a footnote, but the following considerations are instructive: (1) The same psychologist will go on to inform us that sensations, as we experience them, are networks of reference—they are perceptual, and more or less conceptual even. From which it would appear that whatever else they are or are not, the sensations, for which self-inclosed existence is claimed, are not states of consciousness. And (2) we are told that these are reached by scientific abstraction in order to account for complex forms. From which it would appear that they are hypothecated as products of interpretation and for purposes of further interpretation. Only the delusion that the more complex forms are just aggregates (instead of being acts, like seeing, hoping, etc.) prevents recognition of the point in question—that the "state of consciousness" is an instrument of inquiry or methodological appliance.

[4] On the other hand, if what we are trying to get at is just the course and procedure of experiencing, of course any consideration that helps distinguish and make comprehensible that process is thoroughly pertinent.

we again have to resort to conditions that have no place nor calling on the basis of the theory—the principle of habit, of neural action, or else some connection in the object.[5]

We have only to note that there are two opposing schools in psychology to see in what an unscientific status is the subject. We have only to consider that these two schools are the result of assuming states of consciousness as existences *per se* to locate the source of the scientific scandal. No matter what the topic, whether memory or association or attention or effort, the same dualisms present themselves, the same necessity of choosing between two schools. One, lost in the distinctions that it has developed, denies the function because it can find objectively presented only states of consciousness. So it abrogates the function, regarding it as a mere aggregate of such states, or as a purely external and factitious relation between them. The other school, recognizing that this procedure explains away rather than explains, the values of experience, attempts to even up by declaring that certain functions are themselves immediately given data of consciousness, existing side by side with the "states," but indefinitely transcending them in worth, and apprehended by some higher organ. So against the elementary contents and external associations of the analytic school in psychology, we have the complicated machinery of the intellectualist school, with its pure self-consciousness as a source of ultimate truths, its hierarchy of intuitions, its ready-made faculties. To be sure, these "spiritual faculties" are now largely reduced to some one comprehensive form—Apperception, or Will, or Attention, or whatever the fashionable term may be. But the principle remains the same; the assumption of a function as a given existent, distinguishable in itself and acting upon other existences—as if the functions digestion and vision were regarded as separate from organic structures, somehow acting upon them from the outside so as to bring co-operation and harmony into them![6] This division into psychological schools is as reasonable as would be one of botanists into rootists and flowerists; of those proclaiming the root to be the rudimentary and essential structure, and those asserting that since

[5] It may avoid misunderstanding if I anticipate here a subsequent remark: that my point is not in the least that "states of consciousness" require some "synthetic unity" or faculty of substantial mind to effect their association. Quite the contrary; for this theory also admits the "states of consciousness" as existences in themselves also. My contention is that the "state of consciousness" as such is always a methodological product, developed in the course and for the purposes of psychological analysis.

[6] The "functions" are in truth ordinary everyday acts and attitudes: seeing, smelling, talking, listening, remembering, hoping, loving, fearing.

the function of seed-bearing is the main thing, the flower is really the controlling "synthetic" principle. Both sensationalist and intellectualist suppose that psychology has some special sphere of "reality" or of experience marked off for it within which the data are just lying around, self-existent and ready-made, to be picked up and assorted as pebbles await the visitor on the beach. Both alike fail to recognize that the psychologist first has experience to deal with; the same experience that the zoologist, geologist, chemist, mathematician, and historian deal with, and that what characterizes his specialty is not some data or existences which he may call uniquely his own; but the problem raised—the problem of the *course* of the acts that constitute experiencing.

Here psychology gets its revenge upon those who would rule it out of possession of important philosophical bearing. As a matter of fact, the larger part of the questions that are being discussed in current epistemology and what is termed metaphysic of logic and ethic arise out of (and are hopelessly compromised by) this original assumption of "consciousness as such"—in other words, are provoked by the exact reason that is given for denying to psychology any essential meaning for epistemology and metaphysic. Such is the irony of the situation. The epistemologist's problem is, indeed, usually put as the question of how the subject can so far "transcend" itself as to get valid assurance of the objective world. The very phraseology in which the problem is put reveals the thoroughness of the psychologist's revenge. Just and only because experience has been reduced to "states of consciousness" as independent existences, does the question of self-transcendence have any meaning. The entire epistemological industry is one—shall I say it—of a Sisyphean nature. *Mutatis mutandis*, the same holds of the metaphysic of logic, ethic, and esthetic. In each case, the basic problem has come to be how a mere state of consciousness can be the vehicle of a system of truth, of an objectively valid good, of beauty which is other than agreeable feeling. We may, indeed, excuse the psychologist for not carrying on the special inquiries that are the business of logical, ethical, and esthetical philosophy; but can we excuse ourselves for forcing his results into such a shape as to make philosophic problems so arbitrary that they are soluble only by arbitrarily wrenching scientific facts?

Undoubtedly we are between two fires. In placing upon psychology the responsibility of discovering the method of experience, as a sequence of acts and passions, do we not destroy just that limitation to concrete detail which now constitutes it a science? Will not the psychologist be the first to repudiate this attempt to mix him up in matters philosophical? We need only to keep in mind the specific facts involved in the term Course or Process of Experience to avoid this danger. The immediate preoccupation of the psychologist is with very definite and empirical facts—questions like the limits of audition, of the origin of pitch, of the structure and conditions of the musical scale, etc. Just so the immediate affair of the geologist is with particular rock-structures, of the botanist with particular plants, and so on. But through the collection, description, location, classification of rocks the geologist is led to the splendid story of world-forming. The limited, fixed, and separate piece of work is dissolved away in the fluent and dynamic drama of the earth. So, the plant leads with inevitableness to the whole process of life and its evolution.

In form, the botanist still studies the genus, the species, the plant—hardly, indeed, that; rather the special parts, the structural elements, of the plant. In reality, he studies life itself; the structures are the indications, the signature through which he renders transparent the mystery of life growing in the changing world. It was doubtless necessary for the botanist to go through the Linnean period—the period of engagement with rigid detail and fixed classifications; of tearing apart and piecing together; of throwing all emphasis upon peculiarities of number, size, and appearance of matured structure; of regarding change, growth, and function as external, more or less interesting, attachments to form. Examination of this period is instructive; there is much in contemporary investigation and discussion that is almost unpleasantly reminiscent in its suggestiveness. The psychologist should profit by the intervening history of science. The conception of evolution is not so much an additional law as it is a face-about. The fixed structure, the separate form, the isolated element, is henceforth at best a mere stepping-stone to knowledge of process, and when not at its best, marks the end of comprehension, and betokens failure to grasp the problem.

With the change in standpoint from self-included existence to including process, from structural unit of composition to controlling unity of function, from changeless form to movement in growth, the whole scheme of values is transformed. Faculties are definite directions of development; elements are products that are starting-points for new processes; bare facts are indices of change; static conditions are modes of accomplished adjustment. Not that the concrete, empirical phenomenon loses in worth, much less that unverifiable "metaphysical" entities are impertinently introduced; but that our aim is the discovery of a process of actions in its adaptations to circumstance. If we apply this evolutionary logic in psychology, where shall we stop? Questions of limits of stimuli in a given sense, say hearing, are in reality questions of temporary arrests, adjustments marking the favorable equilibrium of the whole organism; they connect with the question of the use of sensation in general and auditory sensations in particular for life-habits; of the origin and use of localized and distinguished perception; and this, in turn, involves within itself the whole question of space and time recognition; the significance of the thing-and-quality experience, and so on. And when we are told that the question of the origin of space experience has nothing at all to do with the question of the nature and significance of the space experienced, the statement is simply evidence that the one who makes it is still at the static standpoint; he believes that things, that relations, have existence and significance apart from the particular conditions under which they come into experience, and apart from the special service rendered in those particular conditions.

Of course, I am far from saying that every psychologist must make the whole journey. Each individual may contract, as he pleases, for any section or subsection he prefers; and undoubtedly the well-being of the science is advanced by such division of labor. But psychology goes over the whole ground from detecting every distinct act of experiencing, to seeing what need calls out the special organ fitted to cope with the situation, and discovering the machinery through which it operates to keep a-going the course of action.

But, I shall be told, the wall that divides psychology from philosophy cannot be so easily treated as non-existent. Psychology is a matter of natural history, even though it may be admitted that it is the natural history of the course of experience. But philosophy is a matter of values; of the criticism and justification of certain validities. One deals, it is said, with genesis, with conditions of temporal origin and transition; the other with analysis, with eternal constitution. I shall have to repeat that just this rigid separation of genesis and analysis seems to me a survival from a pre-evolutionary, a pre-historic age. It indicates not so much an assured barrier between philosophy and psychology as the distance dividing philosophy from all science. For the lesson that mathematicians first learned, that physics and chemistry pondered over, in which the biological disciplines were finally tutored, is that sure and delicate analysis is possible only through the patient study of conditions of origin and development. The method of analysis in mathematics is the method of construction. The experimental method is the method of making, of following the history of production; the term "cause" that has (when taken as an existent entity) so hung on the heels of science as to impede its progress, has universal meaning when read as condition of appearance in a process. And, as already intimated, the conception of evolution is no more and no less the discovery of a general law of life than it is the generalization of all scientific method. Everywhere analysis that cannot proceed by examining the successive stages of its subject, from its beginning up to its culmination, that cannot control this examination by discovering the conditions under which successive stages appear, is only preliminary. It may further the invention of proper tools of inquiry, it may help define problems, it may serve to suggest valuable hypotheses. But as science it breathes an air already tainted. There is no way to sort out the results flowing from the subject-matter itself from those introduced by the assumptions and presumptions of our own reflection. Not so with natural history when it is worthy of its name. Here the analysis is the unfolding of the existence itself. Its distinctions are not pigeon-holes of our convenience; they are stakes that mark the parting of the ways in the process itself. Its classifications are not a grasp at factors resisting further analysis; they are the patient tracings of the paths pursued. Nothing is more out of date than to suppose that interest in genesis is interest in reducing higher forms to cruder ones: it is interest in locating the exact and objective conditions under which a given fact appears, and in relation to which accordingly it has its meaning. Nothing is more naïve than to suppose that in pursuing "natural history" (term of scorn in which yet resides the dignity of the world-drama) we simply learn something of the temporal conditions under which a given value appears, while its own eternal essential quality remains as opaque as before. Nature knows no such divorce of quality and circumstance. Things come when they are wanted and as they are wanted; their quality is precisely the response they give to the conditions that call for them, while the furtherance they afford to the movement of their whole is their meaning. The severance of analysis and genesis, instead of serving as a ready-made test by which to try out the empirical, temporal events of psychology from the rational abiding constitution of philosophy, is a brand of philosophic dualism: the supposition that values are externally obtruded and statically set is irrelevant rubbish.

There are those who will admit that "states of consciousness" are but the cross-sections of flow of behavior, arrested for inspection, made in order that we may reconstruct experience in its life-history. Yet in the knowledge of the course and method of our experience, they will hold that we are far from the domain proper of philosophy. Experience, they say, is just the historic achievement of finite individuals; it tells the tale of approach to the treasures of truth, of partial victory, but larger defeat, in laying hold of the treasure. But, they say, reality is not the path to reality, and record of devious wanderings in the path is hardly a a safe account of the goal. Psychology, in other words, may tell us something of how we mortals lay hold of the world of things and truths; of how we appropriate and assimilate its contents; and how we react. It may trace the issues of such approaches and apprehensions upon the course of our own individual destinies. But it cannot wisely ignore nor sanely deny the distinction between these individual strivings and achievements, and the "Reality" that subsists and supports its own structure outside these finite futilities. The processes by which we turn over The Reality into terms of our fragmentary unconcluded, inconclusive experiences are so extrinsic to the Reality itself as to have no revealing power with reference to it. There is the *ordo ad universum,* the subject of philosophy; there is the *ordo ad individuum,* the subject of psychology.

Some such assumption as this lies latent, I am convinced, in all forswearings of the kinship of psychology and philosophy. Two conceptions hang together. The opinion that psychology is an account only and finally of states of consciousness, and therefore can throw no light upon the objects with which philosophy deals, is twin to the doctrine that the whole conscious life of the individual is not organic to the world. The philosophic basis and scope of this doctrine lie beyond examination here. But even in passing one cannot avoid remarking that the doctrine is almost never consistently held; the doctrine logically carried out leads so directly to intellectual and moral scepticism that the theory usually prefers to work in the dark background as a disposition and temper of thought rather than to make a frank statement of itself. Even in the half-hearted expositions of the process of human experience as something merely annexed to the reality of the universe, we are brought face to face to the consideration with which we set out: the dependence of theories of the individual upon the position at a given time of the individual practical and social. The doctrine of the accidental, futile, transitory significance of the individual's experience as compared with eternal realities; the notion that at best the individual is simply realizing for and in himself what already has fixed completeness in itself is congruous only with a certain intellectual and political scheme and must modify itself as that shifts. When such rearrangement comes, our estimate of the nature and importance of psychology will mirror the change.

When man's command of the methods that control action was precarious and disturbed; when the tools that subject the world of things and forces to use and operation were rare and clumsy, it was unavoidable that the individual should submit his perception and purpose blankly to the blank reality beyond. Under such circumstances, external authority must reign; the belief that human experience in itself is approximate, not intrinsic, is inevitable. Under such circumstances, reference to the individual, to the subject, is a resort only for explaining error, illusion, and uncertainty. The necessity of external control and external redemption of experience reports itself in a low valuation of the self, and of all the factors and phases of experience that spring from the self. That the psychology of medievalism should appear only as a portion of its theology of sin and salvation is as obvious as that the psychology of the Greeks should be a chapter of cosmology.

As against all this, the assertion is ventured that psychology, supplying us with knowledge of the behavior of experience, is a conception of democracy. Its postulate is that since experience fulfils itself in individuals, since it administers itself through their instrumentality, the account of the course and method of this achievement is a significant and indispensable affair.

Democracy is possible only because of a change in intellectual conditions. It implies tools for getting at truth in detail, and day by day, as we go along. Only such possession justifies the surrender of fixed, all-embracing principles to which, as universals, all particulars and individuals are subject for valuation and regulation. Without such possession, it is only the courage of the fool that would undertake the venture to which democracy has committed itself—the ordering of life in response to the needs of the moment in accordance with the ascertained truth of the moment. Modern life involves the deification of the here and the now; of the specific, the particular, the unique, that which happens once and has no measure of value save such as it brings with itself. Such deification is monstrous fetishism, unless the deity be there; unless the universal lives, moves, and has its being in experience as individualized.[7] This conviction of the value of the individualized finds its

---

[7] This is perhaps a suitable moment to allude to the absence, in this discussion, of reference to what is sometimes termed rational psychology—the assumption of a separate, substantialized ego, soul, or whatever, existing side by side with particular experiences and "states of consciousness," acting upon them and acted upon by them. In ignoring this and confining myself to the "states of consciousness"

further expression in psychology, which undertakes to show how this individualization proceeds, and in what aspect it presents itself.

Of course, such a conception means something for philosophy as well as for psychology; possibly it involves for philosophy the larger measure of transformation. It involves surrender of any claim on the part of philosophy to be the sole source of some truths and the exclusive guardian of some values. It means that philosophy be a method; not an assurance company, nor a knight errant. It means an alignment with science. Philosophy may not be sacrificed to the partial and superficial clamor of that which sometimes officiously and pretentiously exhibits itself as Science. But there is a sense in which philosophy must go to school to the sciences; must have no data save such as it receives at their hands; and be hospitable to no method of inquiry or reflection not akin to those in daily use among the sciences. As long as it claims for itself special territory of fact, or peculiar modes of access to truth, so long must it occupy a dubious position. Yet this claim it has to make until psychology comes to its own. There is something in experience, something in things, which the physical and the biological sciences do not touch; something, moreover, which is not just more experiences or more existences; but without which their materials are inexperienced, unrealized. Such sciences deal only with what *might* be experienced; with the content of experience, provided and assumed there be experience. It is psychology which tells us how this possible experience loses its barely hypothetical character, and is stamped with categorical unquestioned experiencedness; how, in a word, it becomes here and

---

theory and the "natural history" theory, I may appear not only to have unduly narrowed the concerns at issue, but to have weakened my own point, as this doctrine seems to offer a special vantage ground whence to defend the close relationship of psychology and philosophy. The "narrowing," if such it be, will have to pass—from limits of time and other matters. But the other point I cannot concede. The independently existing soul restricts and degrades individuality, making of it a separate thing outside of the full flow of things, alien to things experienced and consequently in either mechanical or miraculous relations to them. It is vitiated by just the quality already objected to—that psychology has a separate piece of reality apportioned to it, instead of occupying itself with the manifestation and operation of any and all existences in reference to concrete action. From this point of view, the "states of consciousness" attitude is a much more hopeful and fruitful one. It ignores certain considerations, to be sure; and when it turns its ignoring into denial, it leaves us with curious hieroglyphics. But after all, there is a key; these symbols can be read; they may be translated into terms of the course of experience. When thus translated, selfhood, individuality, is neither wiped out nor set up as a miraculous and foreign entity; it is seen as the unity of reference and function involved in all things when fully experienced—the pivot about which they turn.

now in some uniquely individualized life. Here is the necessary transition of science into philosophy; a passage that carries the verified and solid body of the one into the large and free form of the other.*

12. The Experimental Theory of Knowledge*

An earlier version of this essay appeared in *Mind* in 1906. Along with approximately a dozen other essays published between 1905 and 1907, Dewey attempts in this selection to frame out a metaphysics of experience, with particular emphasis on the meaning of relations in the knowing process. These efforts of Dewey correspond thematically with those of William James between 1904 and 1906 to also develop a metaphysics of relations, called by James a "radical empiricism."

In this essay, "The Experimental Theory of Knowledge," Dewey cites his opposition to those for whom the knowing process is "a strictly 'mental' thing" and to those for whom "our 'mental states' are bare transitory hints" of absolute reality. To the contrary, Dewey stresses the "intending" character of knowing and the relational character of truth.

* [Note: I have let this paper stand much as written, though now conscious that much more is crowded into it than could properly be presented in one paper. The drift of the ten years from '99 to '09 has made, I venture to believe, for increased clearness in the main positions of the paper: The revival of a naturalistic realism, the denial of the existence of "consciousness," the development of functional and dynamic psychology (accompanied by aversion to interpretation of functions as faculties of a soul-substance)—all of these tendencies are sympathetic with the aim of the paper. There is another reason for letting it stand: the new functional and pragmatic empiricism proffered in this volume has been constantly objected to on the ground that its conceptions of knowledge and verification lead only to subjectivism and solipsism. The paper may indicate that the identification of experience with bare states of consciousness represents the standpoint of the critic, not of the empiricism criticised, and that it is for him, not for me, to fear the subjective implications of such a position. The paper also clearly raises the question as to how far the isolation of "consciousness" from nature and social life, which characterizes the procedure of many psychologists of to-day, is responsible for keeping alive quite unreal problems in philosophy.]

* From John Dewey, *The Influence of Darwin on Philosophy: And Other Essays in Contemporary Thought*, pp. 77-111. Copyright 1910 by Holt, Rinehart and Winston, Inc. Copyright 1938 by John Dewey. Reprinted by permission of Holt, Rinehart and Winston, Inc. (Published originally in July, 1906.)

Dewey writes that "fulfillment, completion are always relative terms. Hence the criterion of the truth or falsity of the meaning, of the adequacy, of the cognitional thing lies within the relationships of the situation and not without." He prefers the adverb "truly" to the abstract noun "truth," but perhaps it can be said that what he points to are our attempts at "trueing."

It should be possible to discern and describe a knowing as one identifies any object, concern, or event. It must have its own marks; it must offer characteristic features—as much so as a thunder-storm, the constitution of a State, or a leopard. In the search for this affair, we are first of all desirous for something which is for itself, contemporaneously with its occurrence, a cognition, not something called knowledge by another and from without—whether this other be logician, psychologist, or epistemologist. The "knowledge" may turn out false, and hence no knowledge; but this is an after-affair; it may prove to be rich in fruitage of wisdom, but if this outcome be only wisdom after the event, it does not concern us. What we want is just something which takes itself as knowledge, rightly or wrongly.

I

This means a specific case, a sample. Yet instances are proverbially dangerous—so naïvely and graciously may they beg the questions at issue. Our recourse is to an example so simple, so much on its face as to be as innocent as may be of assumptions. This case we shall gradually complicate, mindful at each step to state just what new elements are introduced. Let us suppose a smell, just a floating odor. This odor may be anchored by supposing that it moves to action; it starts changes that end in picking and enjoying a rose. This description is intended to apply to the course of events witnessed and recounted from without. What sort of a course must it be to constitute a knowledge, or to have somewhere within its career that which deserves this title? The smell, *imprimis*, is there; the movements that it excites are there; the final plucking and gratification are experienced. But, let us say, the smell is not the smell *of* the rose; the resulting change of the organism is not a sense of walking and reaching; the delicious finale is not the fulfilment of the movement, and, through that, of the original smell; "is not," in each case meaning is "not experienced as" such. We may take, in short, these experiences in a brutely serial fashion. The smell, S, is replaced (and displaced) by a felt movement, K, this is replaced by the gratification, G. Viewed from without, as we are now regarding it, there is S-K-G. But from within, for itself, it is now S, now K, now G, and so on to the end of the chapter. Nowhere is there looking before and after; memory and anticipation are not born. Such an experience neither is, in whole or in part, a knowledge, nor does it exercise a cognitive function.

Here, however, we may be halted. If there is anything present in "consciousness" at all, we may be told (at least we constantly are so told) there must be knowledge of it as present—present, at all events, in "consciousness." There is, so it is argued, knowledge at least of a simple apprehensive type, knowledge of the acquaintance order, knowledge *that*, even though not knowledge *what*. The smell, it is admitted, does not know *about* anything else, nor is anything known *about* the smell (the same thing, perhaps); but the smell is known, either by itself, or by the mind, or by some subject, some unwinking, unremitting eye. No, we must reply; there is no apprehension without some (however slight) context; no acquaintance which is not either recognition or expectation. Acquaintance is presence honored with an escort; presence is introduced as familiar, or an associate springs up to greet it. Acquaintance always implies a little friendliness; a trace of re-knowing, of anticipatory welcome or dread of the trait to follow.

This claim cannot be dismissed as trivial. If valid, it carries with it the distance between being and knowing: and the recognition of an element of mediation, that is, of art, in all knowledge. This disparity, this transcendence, is not something which holds of *our* knowledge, of finite knowledge, just marking the gap between our type of consciousness and some other with which we may contrast it after the manner of the agnostic or the transcendentalist (who hold so much property in joint ownership!), but exists because knowing is knowing, that way of bringing things to bear upon things which we call reflection—a manipulation of things experienced in the light one of another.

"Feeling," I read in a recent article, "feeling is immediately acquainted with its own quality, with its own subjective being."[1] How

---

[1] I must remind the reader again of a point already suggested. It is the identification of presence in consciousness with knowledge as such that leads to setting up *a* mind (*ego*, subject) which has the peculiar property of knowing (only so often it knows wrong!), or else that leads to supplying "sensations" with the peculiar property of surveying their own entrails. Given the correct feeling that knowledge involves relationship, there being, by supposition, no other *thing* to which the thing in consciousness is related, it is forthwith related to a soul substance, or to its ghostly offspring, a "subject," or to "consciousness" itself.

and whence this duplication in the inwards of feeling into feeling the knower and feeling the known? into feeling as being and feeling as acquaintance? Let us frankly deny such monsters. Feeling *is* its own quality; is its own *specific* (whence and why, once more, *subjective?*) being. If this statement be dogmatism, it is at least worth insistent declaration, were it only by way of counter-irritant to that other dogmatism which asserts that being in "consciousness" is always presence for or in knowledge. So let us repeat once more, that to *be* a smell (or anything else) is one thing, to be *known* as smell, another; to be a "feeling" one thing, to be *known* as a "feeling" another.[2] The first is thinghood; existence indubitable, direct; in this way all things *are* that are in "consciousness" at all.[3] The second is *reflected* being, things indicating and calling for other things—something offering the possibility of truth and hence of falsity. The first is genuine immediacy; the second is (in the instance discussed) a pseudo-immediacy, which in the same breath that it proclaims its immediacy smuggles in another term (and one which is unexperienced both in itself and in its relation) the subject or "consciousness," to which the immediate is related.[4]

But we need not remain with dogmatic assertions. To be acquainted with a thing or with a person has a definite empirical meaning; we have only to call to mind what it is to be genuinely and empirically acquainted, to have done forever with this uncanny presence which, though bare and simple presence, is yet known, and thus is clothed upon and complicated. To be acquainted with a thing is to be assured (from the standpoint of the experience itself) that it is of such and such a character; that it will behave, if given an opportunity, in such and such a

[2] Let us further recall that this theory requires either that things present shall already be psychical things (feelings, sensations, etc.), in order to be assimilated to the knowing mind, subject to consciousness; or else translates genuinely naïve realism into the miracle of a mind that gets outside itself to lay its ghostly hands upon the things of an external world.

[3] This means that things may be present *as* known, just as they be present as hard or soft, agreeable or disgusting, hoped for or dreaded. The mediacy, or the art of intervention, which characterizes knowledge, indicates precisely the way in which known things as known are immediately present.

[4] If Hume had had a tithe of the interest in the *flux* of perceptions and in *habit*—principles of continuity and of organization—which he had in distinct and isolated existences, he might have saved us both from German *Erkenntnisstheorie*, and from that modern miracle play, the psychology of elements of consciousness, that under the aegis of science, does not hesitate to have psychical elements compound and breed, and in their agile intangibility put to shame the performances of their less acrobatic cousins, physical atoms.

way; that the obviously and flagrantly present trait is associated with fellow traits that will show themselves, if the leadings of the present trait are followed out. To be acquainted is to anticipate to some extent, on the basis of prior experience. I am, say, barely acquainted with Mr. Smith: then I have no extended body of associated qualities along with those palpably present, but at least some one suggested trait occurs; his nose, his tone of voice, the place where I saw him, his calling in life, an interesting anecdote about him, etc. To be acquainted is to know what a thing is *like* in some particular. If one is acquainted with the smell of a flower it means that the smell is not just smell, but reminds one of some other experienced thing which stands in continuity with the smell. There is thus supplied a condition of control over or purchase upon what is present, the possibility of translating it into terms of some other trait not now sensibly present.

Let us return to our example. Let us suppose that S is not just displaced by K and then by G. Let us suppose it persists; and persists not as an unchanged S alongside K and G, nor yet as fused with them into a new further quale J. For in such events, we have only the type already considered and rejected. For an observer the new quale might be more complex, or fuller of meaning, than the original S, K, or G, but might not be experienced *as* complex. We might thus suppose a composite photograph which should suggest nothing of the complexity of its origin and structure. In this case we should have simply another picture.

But we may also suppose that the blur of the photograph suggests the superimposition of pictures and something of their character. Then we get another, and for our problem, much more fruitful kind of persistence. We will imagine that the final G assumes this form: Gratification-terminating-movement-induced-by-smell. The smell is still present; it has persisted. It is not present in its original form, but is represented with a quality; an office, that of having excited activity and thereby terminating its career in a certain quale of gratification. It is not S, but Σ; that is S with an increment of meaning due to maintenance and fulfilment through a process. S is no longer just smell, but smell which has excited and thereby secured.

Here we have a cognitive, but not a cognitional thing. In saying that the smell is finally experienced as *meaning* gratification (through intervening handling, seeing, etc.) and meaning it not in a hapless way, but in a fashion which operates to effect what is meant, we retrospectively attribute intellectual force and function to the smell—and this is what is signified by "cognitive." Yet the smell is not cognitional, because it did not knowingly intend to mean this; but is found, after the event, to have meant it. Nor again is the final experience, the Σ or transformed S, a knowledge.

Here again the statement may be challenged. Those who agree with the denial that bare presence of a quale in "consciousness" constitutes acquaintance and simple apprehension, may now turn against us, saying that experience of fulfilment of meaning is just what we mean by knowledge, and this is just what the Σ of our illustration is. The point is fundamental. As the smell at first was presence or being, less than knowing, so the fulfilment is an experience that is more than knowing. Seeing and handling the flower, enjoying the full meaning of the smell as the odor of just this beautiful thing, is not knowledge because it is more than knowledge.

As this may seem dogmatic, let us suppose that the fulfilment, the realization, experience, is a knowledge. Then how shall it be distinguished from and yet classed with other things called knowledge, viz., reflective, discursive cognitions? Such knowledges are what they are precisely because they are not fulfilments, but intentions, aims, schemes, symbols of overt fulfilment. Knowledge, perceptual and conceptual, of a hunting dog is prerequisite in order that I may really hunt with the hounds. The hunting in turn may increase my knowledge of dogs and their ways. But the knowledge of the dog, *qua* knowledge, remains characteristically marked off from the use of that knowledge in the fulfilment experience, the hunt. The hunt is a *realization* of knowledge; it alone, if you please, verifies, validates, knowledge, or supplies tests of truth. The prior knowledge of the dog, was, if you wish, hypothetical, lacking in assurance or categorical certainty. The hunting, the fulfilling, realizing experience alone *gives* knowledge, because it alone completely assures; makes faith good in works.

Now there is and can be no objection to this definition of knowledge, *provided it is consistently adhered to*. One has as much right to identify knowledge with complete assurance, as I have to identify it with anything else. Considerable justification in the common use of language, in common sense, may be found for defining knowledge as complete assurance. But even upon this definition, the fulfilling experience is not, as such, complete assurance, and hence not a knowledge. Assurance, cognitive validation, and guaranteeship, follow from it, but are not coincident with its occurrence. It *gives*, but *is* not, assurance. The concrete construction of a story, the manipulation of a machine, the hunting with the dogs, is not, so far as it *is* fulfilment, a confirmation of meanings previously entertained as cognitional; that is, is not contemporaneously experienced as such. To think of prior schemes, symbols, meanings, as fulfilled in a subsequent experience, is reflectively to present in their relations to one another both the meanings and the experiences in which they are, as a matter of fact, embodied. This reflective attitude cannot be identical with the fulfilment experience itself; it occurs only in retrospect when the worth of the meanings, or cognitive ideas, is critically inspected in the light of their fulfilment; or it occurs as an interruption of the fulfilling experience. The hunter stops his hunting as a fulfilment to reflect that he made a mistake in his idea of his dog, or again, that his dog is everything he thought he was—that his notion of him is confirmed. Or, the man stops the actual construction of his machine and turns back upon his plan in correction or in admiring estimate of its value. *The fulfilling experience is not of itself knowledge*, then, even if we identify knowledge with fulness of assurance or guarantee. Moreover it gives, affords, assurance only in reference to a situation which we have not yet considered.[5]

Before the category of confirmation or refutation can be introduced, there must be something which *means* to mean something and which therefore can be guaranteed or nullified by the issue—and this is precisely what we have not as yet found. We must return to our instance and introduce a further complication. Let us suppose that the smell quale recurs at a later date, and that it recurs neither as the original S nor yet as the final Σ, but as an S' which is fated or charged with the sense of the possibility of a fulfilment like unto Σ. The S' that recurs is aware of something else which it means, which it intends to effect through an operation incited by it and without which its own presence is abortive, and, so to say, unjustified, senseless. Now we have an experience which is *cognitional*, not merely cognitive; which is contemporaneously aware of meaning something beyond itself, instead of having this meaning ascribed by another at a later period. *The odor knows the rose; the rose is known by the odor; and the import of each term is constituted by the relationship in which it stands to the other.* That is, the import of the smell is the indicating and demanding relation which it sustains to the enjoyment of the rose as its fulfilling experience; while this enjoyment is just the content or definition of what the smell consciously meant, *i.e.*, meant to mean. Both the thing meaning and the thing meant are elements in the same situation. Both are present, but both are not present in the same way. In fact, one is present as-*not*-

---

[5] In other words, the situation as described is not to be confused with the case of hunting on purpose to test an idea regarding the dog.

present-in-the-same-way-in-which-the-other-is. It is present as something to be rendered present in the same way through the intervention of an operation. We must not balk at a purely verbal difficulty. It suggests a verbal inconsistency to speak of a thing present-as-absent. But all ideal contents, all aims (that is, things aimed at) are present in just such fashion. Things can be presented as absent, just as they can be presented as hard or soft, black or white, six inches or fifty rods away from the body. The assumption that an ideal content must be either totally absent, or else present *in just the same fashion* as it will be when it is realized, is not only dogmatic, but self-contradictory. The only way in which an ideal content can be experienced at all is to be presented as *not-present-in-the-same-way* in which something else is present, the latter kind of presence affording the standard or type of *satisfactory* presence. When present in the same way it ceases to be an ideal content. Not a contrast of bare existence over against non-existence, or of present consciousness over against reality out of present consciousness, but of a satisfactory with an unsatisfactory mode of presence makes the difference between the "really" and the "ideally" present.

In terms of our illustration, handling and enjoying the rose are present, but they are not present in the same way that the smell is present. They are present as *going* to be there in the same way, through an operation which the smell stands sponsor for. The situation is inherently an uneasy one—one in which everything hangs upon the performance of the operation indicated; upon the adequacy of movement as a connecting link, or real adjustment of the thing meaning and the thing meant. Generalizing from the instance, we get the following definition: An experience is a knowledge, if in its quale there is an experienced distinction and connection of two elements of the following sort: *one means or intends the presence of the other in the same fashion in which itself is already present, while the other is that which, while not present in the same fashion, must become so present if the meaning or intention of its companion or yoke-fellow is to be fulfilled through the operation it sets up.*

II

We now return briefly to the question of knowledge as acquaintance, and at greater length to that of knowledge as assurance, or as fulfilment which confirms and validates. With the recurrence of the odor as meaning something beyond itself, there is apprehension, knowledge *that*. One may now say I know what a *rose* smells like; or I know what *this* smell is like; I am acquainted with the rose's agreeable odor. In short, on the basis of a present quality, the odor anticipates and forestalls some further trait.

We have also the conditions of knowledge of the confirmation and refutation type. In the working out of the situation just described, in the transformation, self-indicated and self-demanded, of the tensional into a harmonious or satisfactory situation, fulfilment *or* disappointment results. The odor either does or does not fulfil itself in the rose. The smell as intention is borne out by the facts, or is nullified. As has already been pointed out, the subsequent experience of the fulfilment type is not primarily a confirmation or refutation. Its import is too vital, too urgent to be reduced *in itself* just to the value of testing an intention or meaning.[6] But it gets *in reflection* just such verificatory significance. If the smell's intention is unfulfilled, the discrepancy may throw one back, in reflection, upon the original situation. Interesting developments then occur. The smell meant a rose; and yet it did not (so it turns out) mean a rose; it meant another flower, or something, one can't just tell what. Clearly there is *something else* which enters in; something else beyond the odor as it was first experienced determined the validity of its meaning. Here then, perhaps, we have a transcendental, as distinct from an experimental reference? *Only if this something else makes no difference, or no detectable difference, in the smell itself.* If the utmost observation and reflection can find no difference in the smell quales that fail and those that succeed in executing their intentions, then there is an outside controlling and disturbing factor, which, since it is outside of the situation, can never be utilized in knowledge, and hence can never be employed in any concrete testing or verifying. In this case, knowing depends upon an extra-experimental or transcendental factor. But this very transcendental quality makes both confirmation and refutation, correction, criticism, of the pretensions or meanings of things, impossible. For the conceptions of truth and error, we must, upon the transcendental basis, substitute those of accidental success or

---

[6] Dr. Moore, in an essay in "Contributions to Logical Theory" has brought out clearly, on the basis of a criticism of the theory of meaning and fulfilment advanced in Royce's "World and Individual," the full consequences of this distinction. I quote one sentence (p. 350): "Surely there is a pretty discernible difference between experience as a purposive idea, and the experience which fulfils this purpose. To call them both 'ideas' is at least confusing." The text above simply adds that there is also a discernible and important difference between experiences which, *de facto*, are purposing and fulfilling (that is, are seen to be such *ab extra*), and those which meant to be such, and are found to be what they meant.

failure. Sometimes the intention chances upon one, sometimes upon another. Why or how, the gods only know—and they only if to them the extra-experimental factor is not extra-experimental, but makes a concrete ·difference in the concrete smell. But fortunately the situation is not one to be thus described. The factor that determines the success or failure, does institute a difference in the thing which means the object, and this difference is detectable, once attention, through failure, has been called to the need of its discovery. At the very least, it makes this difference: the smell is infected with an element of uncertainty of meaning—and this as a part of the thing experienced, not for an observer. This additional *awareness* at least brings about an additional *wariness*. Meaning is more critical, and operation more cautious.

But we need not stop here. Attention may be fully directed to the subject of smells. Smells may become the object of knowledge. They may take, *pro tempore*,[7] the place which the rose formerly occupied. One may, that is, observe the cases in which odors mean other things than just roses, may voluntarily produce new cases for the sake of further inspection, and thus account for the cases where meanings had been falsified in the issue; discriminate more carefully the peculiarities of those meanings which the event verified, and thus safeguard and bulwark to some extent the employing of similar meanings in the future. Superficially, it may then seem as if odors were treated after the fashion of Locke's simple ideas, or Hume's "distinct ideas which are separate existences." Smells apparently assume an independent, isolated status during this period of investigation. "Sensations," as the laboratory psychologist and the analytic psychologist generally study them, are examples of just such detached things. But egregious error results if we forget that this seeming isolation and detachment is the outcome of a deliberate scientific device—that it is simply a part of the scientific technique of an inquiry directed upon securing *tested* conclusions. Just and only because odors (or any group of qualities) are parts of a connected world are they signs of things beyond themselves; and only because they are signs is it profitable and necessary to study them *as if* they were complete, self-enclosed entities.

In the reflective determination of things with reference to their specifically meaning other things, experiences of fulfilment, disap-

---

[7] The association of science and philosophy with leisure, with a certain economic surplus, is not accidental. It is practically worth while to postpone practice; to substitute theorizing, to develop a new and fascinating mode of practice. But it is the excess achievement of practice which makes this postponement and substitution possible.

pointment, and going astray inevitably play an important and recurrent *rôle*. They also are realistic facts, related in realistic ways to the things that intend to mean other things and to the things intended. When these fulfilments and refusals *are reflected upon* in the determinate relations in which they stand to their relevant meanings, they obtain a quality which is quite lacking to them in their immediate occurrence as just fulfilments or disappointments; viz., the property of affording assurance and correction—of confirming and refuting. Truth and falsity are not properties of any experience or thing, in and of itself or in its first intention; *but of things where the problem of assurance consciously enters in. Truth and falsity present themselves as significant facts only in situations in which specific meanings and their already experienced fulfilments and non-fulfilments are intentionally compared and contrasted with reference to the question of the worth, as to reliability of meaning, of the given meaning or class of meanings.* Like knowledge itself, truth is an experienced relation of things, and it has no meaning outside of such relation,[8] any more than such adjectives as comfortable applied to a lodging, correct applied to speech, persuasive applied to an orator, etc., have worth apart from the *specific* things to which they are applied. It would be a great gain for logic and epistemology, if we were always to translate the noun "truth" back into the adjective "true," and this back into the adverb "truly"; at least, if we were to do so until we have familiarized ourselves thoroughly with the fact that "truth" is an abstract noun, summarizing a quality presented by specific affairs in their own specific contents.

III

I have attempted, in the foregoing pages, a description of the function of knowledge in its own terms and on its merits—a description which in intention is realistic, if by realistic we are content to mean naturalistic, a description undertaken on the basis of what Mr. Santayana has well called "following the lead of the subject-matter." Unfortunately at the present time all such undertakings contend with a serious extraneous obstacle. Accomplishing the undertaking has difficulties enough of its

[8] It is the failure to grasp the coupling of truth of meaning with a *specific* promise, undertaking, or intention expressed by a thing which underlies, so far as I can see, the criticisms passed upon the experimental or pragmatic view of the truth. It is the same failure which is responsible for the wholly *at large* view of truth which characterizes the absolutists.

own to reckon with; and first attempts are sure to be imperfect, if not radically wrong. But at present the attempts are not, for the most part, even listened to on their own account, they are not examined and criticised as naturalistic attempts. *They are compared with undertakings of a wholly different nature, with an epistemological theory of knowledge, and the assumptions of this extraneous theory are taken as a ready-made standard by which to test their validity.* Literally of course, "epistemology" means only theory of knowledge; the term *might* therefore have been employed simply as a synonym for a descriptive logic; for a theory that takes knowledge as it finds it and attempts to give the same kind of an account of it that would be given of any other natural function or occurrence. But the mere mention of what *might* have been only accentuates what is. The things that pass for epistemology all assume that knowledge is not a natural function or event, but a mystery.

Epistemology starts from the assumption that certain conditions lie back of knowledge. The mystery would be great enough if knowledge were constituted by non-natural conditions back of knowledge, but the mystery is increased by the fact that the conditions are defined so as to be incompatible with knowledge. Hence the primary problem of epistemology is: How is knowledge *überhaupt*, knowledge at large, *possible?* Because of the incompatibility between the concrete occurrence and function of knowledge and the conditions back of it to which it must conform, a second problem arises: How is knowledge in general, knowledge *überhaupt, valid?* Hence the complete divorce in contemporary thought between epistemology as theory of knowledge and logic as an account of the specific ways in which particular beliefs that are better than other alternative beliefs regarding the same matters are formed; and also the complete divorce between a naturalistic, a biological and social psychology, setting forth how the function of knowledge is evolved out of other natural activities, and epistemology as an account of how knowledge is possible anyhow.

It is out of the question to set forth in this place in detail the contrast between transcendental epistemology and an experimental theory of knowledge. It may assist the understanding of the latter, however, if I point out, baldly and briefly, how, *out of the distinctively empirical situation*, there arise those assumptions which make knowledge a mystery, and hence a topic for a peculiar branch of philosophizing.

As just pointed out, epistemology makes the possibility of knowledge a problem, because it assumes back of knowledge conditions incompatible with the obvious traits of knowledge as it empirically exists. These assumptions are that the organ or instrument of knowledge is not a natural object, but some ready-made state of mind or consciousness, something purely "subjective," a peculiar kind of existence which lives, moves, and has its being in a realm different from things to be known; and that the ultimate goal and content of knowledge is a fixed, ready-made thing which has no organic connections with the origin, purpose, and growth of the attempt to know it, some kind of *Ding-an-sich* or absolute, extra-empirical "Reality."

(1) It is not difficult to see at what point in the development of natural knowledge, or the signifying of one thing by another, there arises the notion of the knowing medium as something radically different in the order of existence from the thing to be known. It arises subsequent to the repeated experience of non-fulfilment, of frustration and disappointment. The odor did not after all mean the rose; it meant something quite different; and yet its indicative function was exercised so forcibly that we could not help—or at least *did* not help—believing in the existence of the rose. This is a familiar and typical kind of experience, one which very early leads to the recognition that "things are not what they seem." There are two contrasted methods of dealing with this recognition: one is the method indicated above. We go more thoroughly, patiently, and carefully into the facts of the case. We employ all sorts of methods, invented for the purpose, of examining the things that are signs and the things that are signified, and we experimentally produce various situations, in order that we may tell *what* smells mean roses *when* roses are meant, what it is about the smell and the rose that led us into error; and that we may be able to discriminate those cases in which a suspended conclusion is all that circumstances admit. We simply do the best we can to regulate our system of signs so that they become as instructive as possible, utilizing for this purpose (as indicated above) all possible experiences of success and of failure, and deliberately instituting cases which will throw light on the specific empirical causes of success and failure.

Now it so happens that when the facts of error were consciously generalized and formulated, namely in Greek thought, such a technique of specific inquiry and rectification did not exist—in fact, it hardly could come into existence until *after* error had been seized upon as constituting a fundamental anomaly. Hence the method just outlined of dealing with the situation was impossible. We can imagine disconsolate ghosts willing to postpone any professed solution of the difficulty till subsequent generations have thrown more light on the question itself; we can hardly imagine passionate human beings exercising such reserve.

At all events, Greek thought provided what seemed a satisfactory way out: there are two orders of existence, one permanent and complete, the noumenal region, to which alone the characteristic of Being is properly applicable, the other transitory, phenomenal, sensible, a region of non-Being, or at least of mere Coming-to-be, a region in which Being is hopelessly mixed with non-Being, with the unreal. The former alone is the domain of knowledge, of truth; the latter is the territory of opinion, confusion, and error. In short, the contrast *within* experience of the cases in which things successfully and unsuccessfully maintained and executed the meanings of other things was erected into a wholesale difference of status in the intrinsic characters of the things involved in the two types of cases.

With the beginnings of modern thought, the region of the "unreal," the source of opinion and error, was located exclusively in the individual. The object was *all* real and *all* satisfactory, but the "subect" could approach the object only through his own subjective states, his "sensations" and "ideas." The Greek conception of two orders of existence was retained, but instead of the two orders characterizing the "universe" itself, one *was* the universe, the other was the individual mind trying to know that universe. This scheme would obviously easily account for error and hallucination; but how could *knowledge*, truth, ever come about on such a basis? The Greek problem of the possibility of error became the modern problem of the possibility of knowledge.

Putting the matter in terms that are independent of history, experiences of failure, disappointment, non-fulfilment of the function of meaning and contention may lead the individual to the path of science—to more careful and extensive investigation of the things themselves, with a view to detecting specific sources of error, and guarding against them, and regulating, so far as possible, the conditions under which objects are bearers of meanings beyond themselves. But impatient of such slow and tentative methods (which insure not infallibility but increased probability of valid conclusions), by reason of disappointment a person may turn epistemologist. He may then take the discrepancy, the failure of the smell to execute its own intended meaning, as a wholesale, rather than as a specific fact: as evidence of a contrast in general between things meaning and things meant, instead of as evidence of the need of a more cautious and thorough inspection of odors and execution of operations indicated by them. One may then say: Woe is me; smells are only *my* smells, subjective states existing in an order of being made out of consciousness, while roses exist in another order made out of a radically different sort of stuff; or, odors are made out of "finite" consciousness as their stuff, while the real things, the objects which fulfil them, are made out of an "infinite" consciousness as their material. Hence some purely metaphysical tie has to be called in to bring them into connection with each other. And yet this tie does not concern knowledge; it does not make the meaning of one odor any more correct than that of another, nor enable us to discriminate relative degrees of correctness. As a principle of control, this transcendental connection is related to all alike, and hence condemns and justifies all alike.[9]

It is interesting to note that the transcendentalist almost invariably first falls into the psychological fallacy; and then having himself taken the psychologist's attitude (the attitude which is interested in meanings as themselves self-inclosed "ideas") accuses the empiricist whom he criticises of having confused mere psychological existence with logical validity. That is, he begins by supposing that the smell of our illustration (and all the cognitional objects for which this is used as a symbol) is a purely mental or psychical state, so that the question of logical reference or intention is the problem of how the merely mental can "know" the extra mental. But from a strictly empirical point of view, the smell which knows is no more merely mental than is the rose known. We may, if we please, say that the smell when involving conscious meaning or intention is "mental," but this term "mental" does not denote some separate type of existence—existence as a state of consciousness. It denotes only the fact that the smell, a real and nonpsychical object, now exercises an intellectual *function*. This new property involves, as James has pointed out, an *additive* relation—a new

[10] The belief in the *metaphysical* transcendence of the object of knowledge seems to have its real origin in an *empirical* transcendence of a very specific and describable sort. The thing meaning is one thing; the thing meant is another thing, and is (as already pointed out) a thing presented as not given in the same way as is the thing which means. It is something *to be* so given. No amount of careful and thorough inspection of the indicating and signifying things can remove or annihilate this gap. The *probability* of correct meaning may be increased in varying degrees—and this is what we mean by control. But final certitude can never be reached except experimentally—except by performing the operations indicated and discovering whether or no the intended meaning is fulfilled *in propria persona*. In this experimental sense, truth or the object of any given meaning is always beyond or outside of the cognitional thing that means it. Error as well as truth is a necessary function of knowing. But the non-empirical account of this transcendent (or beyond) relationship puts *all* the error in one place (*our* knowledge), and *all* the truth in another (absolute consciousness or else a thing-in-itself).

property possessed by a non-mental object, when that object, occurring in a new context, assumes a further office and use.[10] To be "in the mind" means to be in a situation in which the function of intending is directly concerned.[11] Will not some one who believes that the knowing experience is *ab origine* a strictly "mental" thing, explain how, as matter of fact, it does get a specific, extra-mental reference, capable of being tested, confirmed, or refuted? Or, if he believes that viewing it as merely mental expresses only the form it takes for psychological analysis, will he not explain why he so persistently attributes the inherently "mental" characterization of it to the empiricist whom he criticises? An object *becomes* meaning when used empirically in a certain way; and, under certain circumstances, the exact character and worth of this meaning *becomes* an object of solicitude. But the transcendental epistemologist with his purely psychical "meanings" and his purely extra-empirical "truths" assumes a *Deus ex Machina* whose mechanism is preserved a secret. And as if to add to the arbitrary character of his assumption, he has to admit that the transcendental *a priori* faculty by which mental states get objective reference does not in the least help us to discriminate, *in the concrete*, between an objective reference that is false and one that is valid.

(2) The counterpart assumption to that of pure aboriginal "mental states" is, of course, that of an Absolute Reality, fixed and complete in itself, of which our "mental states" are bare transitory hints, their true meaning and their transcendent goal being the Truth *in rerum natura*. If the organ and medium of knowing is a self-inclosed order of existence different in kind from the Object to be known, then that Object must stand out there in complete aloofness from the concrete purpose and procedure of knowing it. But if we go back to the knowing as a natural occurrence, capable of description, we find that just as a smell does not mean Rose in general (or anything else at large), but means a *specific* group of qualities whose experience is intended and anticipated, so the function of knowing is always expressed in connections between a given experience and a specific possible wanted experience. The "rose" that is meant in a particular situation *is* the rose of that situation. When this experience is consummated, it is achieved as the fulfilment of the conditions in which just *that* intention was entertained—not as the

[10] Compare his essay, "Does Consciousness Exist?" in the *Journal of Philosophy, Psychology, and Scientific Methods*, Vol. I., p. 480.

[11] Compare the essay on the "Problem of Consciousness," by Professor Woodbridge, in the Garman Memorial Volume, entitled "Studies in Philosophy and Psychology."

fulfilment of a faculty of knowledge or a meaning in general. Subsequent meanings and subsequent fulfilments may increase, may enrich the consummating experience; the object or content of the rose as known may be other and fuller next time and so on. But we have no right to set up "a rose" at large or in general as the object of the knowing odor; the object of a knowledge is always strictly correlative to that particular thing which means it. It is not something which can be put in a wholesale way over against that which cognitively refers to it, as when the epistemologist puts the "real" rose (object) over against a merely phenomenal or empirical rose which *this* smell happens to mean. As the meaning gets more complex, fuller, more finely discriminated, the object which realizes or fulfils the meaning grows similarly in quality. But we cannot set up a rose, an object of fullest, complete, and exhaustive content as that which is really meant by any and every odor of a rose, whether it consciously meant to mean it or not. The test of the cognitional rectitude of the odor lies in the *specific* object which it sets out to secure. This is the meaning of the statement that the import of *each* term is found in its relationship to the other. It applies to object meant as well as to the meaning. Fulfilment, completion are always relative terms. *Hence the criterion of the truth or falsity of the meaning, of the adequacy, of the cognitional thing lies within the relationships of the situation and not without.* The thing that means another by means of an intervening operation either succeeds or fails in accomplishing the operation indicated, while this operation either gives or fails to give the object meant. Hence the truth or falsity of the original cognitional object.

IV

From this excursion, I return in conclusion to a brief general characterization of those situations in which we are aware that things mean other things and are so critically aware of it that, in order to increase the probability of fulfilment and to decrease the chance of frustration, all possible pains are taken to regulate the meanings that attach to things. These situations define that type of knowing which we call *scientific*. There are things that claim to mean other experiences; in which the trait of meaning other objects is not discovered *ab extra*, and after the event, but is part of the thing itself. This trait of the thing is as realistic, as specific, as any other of its traits. It is, therefore, as open to inspection and determination as to its nature, as is any other trait. Moreover, since

it is upon this trait that assurance (as distinct from accident) of fulfilment depends, an especial interest, an absorbing interest, attaches to its
determination. Hence the scientific type of knowledge and its growing
domination over other sorts.

We *employ* meanings in all intentional constructions of experience—in all anticipations, whether artistic, utilitarian or technological, social or moral. The success of the anticipation is found to depend upon
the character of the meaning. Hence the stress upon a right determination of these meanings. Since they are the instruments upon which fulfilment depends *so far as that is controlled* or other than accidental, they
become themselves objects of surpassing interest. For all persons at
some times, and for one class of persons (scientists) at almost all times,
the determination of the meanings employed in the control of fulfilments (of acting upon meanings) is central. The experimental or
pragmatic theory of knowledge explains the dominating importance of
science; it does not depreciate it or explain it away.

Possibly pragmatic writers are to blame for the tendency of their
critics to assume that the practice they have in mind is utilitarian in
some narrow sense, referring to some preconceived and inferior
use—though I cannot recall any evidence for this admission. But what
the pragmatic theory has in mind is precisely the fact that all the affairs
of life which need regulation—*all values of all types*—depend upon
utilizations of meanings. Action is not to be limited to anything less
than the carrying out of ideas, than the execution, whether strenuous or
easeful, of meanings. Hence the surpassing importance which comes to
attach to the careful, impartial construction of the meanings, and to
their constant survey and resurvey with reference to their value as
evidenced by experiences of fulfilment and deviation.

That truth denotes *truths*, that is, specific verifications, combinations
of meanings and outcomes reflectively viewed, is, one may say, the central point of the experimental theory. Truth, in general or in the
abstract, is a just name for an experienced relation among the things of
experience: that sort of relation in which intents are retrospectively
viewed from the standpoint of the fulfilment which they secure through
their own natural operation or incitement. Thus the experimental theory
explains directly and simply the absolutistic tendency to translate concrete true things into the general relationship, Truth, and then to
hypostatize this abstraction into identity with real being, Truth *per se*
and *in se*, of which all transitory things and events—that is, all experienced realities—are only shadowy futile approximations. This type

of relationship is central for man's will, for man's conscious endeavor. To select, to conserve, to extend, to propagate those meanings which the course of events has generated, to note their peculiarities, to be in advance on the alert for them, to search for them anxiously, to substitute them for meanings that eat up our energy in vain, defines the aim of rational effort and the goal of legitimate ambition. The absolutistic theory is the transfer of this moral or voluntary law of selective action into a quasi-physical (that is, metaphysical) law of indiscriminate being. Identify metaphysical being with *significant excellent being*—that is, with those relationships of things which, in our moments of deepest insight and largest survey, we would continue and reproduce—and the experimentalist, rather than the absolutist, is he who has a right to proclaim the supremacy of Truth, and the superiority of the life devoted to Truth for its own sake over that of "mere" activity. But to read back into an order of things which exists without the participation of our reflection and aim, the quality which defines the purpose of our thought and endeavor is at one and the same stroke to mythologize reality and to deprive the life of thoughtful endeavor of its ground for being.

13. Experience and Objective Idealism*

This essay is extremely telescoped in style, as witness the fact that some twenty years later Dewey devoted several hundred pages of *Experience and Nature* to an explication of the same themes. His fundamental concern is with the misleading presentation of the meaning of "experience" in the history of philosophy. Dewey believes that objective idealism owes its influence in great measure to its description of experiencing as a purely subjective human activity. Dewey denies this allegation and cites Locke, Peirce, and James to support his position. He points to a mediation between idealism seen as a process of "idealization" and an empiricism that acknowledges "the transitive character of experience" and "the possible control of the character of the transition by means of intelligent effort." Students who have found irreducible

* From John Dewey, *The Influence of Darwin on Philosophy: And Other Essays in Contemporary Thought*, pp. 198-225. Copyright 1910 by Holt, Rinehart and Winston, Inc. Copyright 1938 by John Dewey. Reprinted by permission of Holt, Rinehart and Winston, Inc. (Originally published in 1906.)

strains of idealism in the development of pragmatism will find this essay a primary source for such a claim.

I

Idealism as a philosophic system stands in such a delicate relation to experience as to invite attention. In its subjective form, or sensationalism, it claims to be the last word of empiricism. In its objective, or rational form, it claims to make good the deficiencies of the subjective type, by emphasizing the work of thought that supplies the factors of objectivity and universality lacking in sensationalism. With reference to experience *as it now is*, such idealism is half opposed to empiricism and half committed to it,—antagonistic, so far as existing experience is regarded as tainted with a sensational character; favorable, so far as this experience is even now prophetic of some final, all-comprehensive, or absolute experience, which in truth is one with reality.

That this combination of opposition to present experience with devotion to the cause of experience in the abstract leaves objective idealism in a position of unstable equilibrium from which it can find release only by euthanasia in a thorough-going empiricism seems evident. Some of the reasons for this belief may be readily approached by a summary sketch of three historic episodes in which have emerged important conceptions of experience and its relation to reason. The first takes us to classic Greek thought. Here experience means the preservation, through memory, of the net result of a multiplicity of particular doings and sufferings; a preservation that affords positive skill in maintaining further practice, and promise of success in new emergencies. The craft of the carpenter, the art of the physician are standing examples of its nature. It differs from instinct and blind routine or servile practice because there is some knowledge of materials, methods, and aims, in their adjustment to one another. Yet the marks of its passive, habitual origin are indelibly stamped upon it. On the knowledge side it can never aspire beyond opinion, and if true opinion be achieved, it is only by happy chance. On the active side it is limited to the accomplishment of a special work or a particular product, following some unjustified, because assumed, method. Thus it contrasts with the true knowledge of reason, which is direct apprehension, self-revealing and self-validating, of an eternal and harmonious content. The regions in which experience and reason respectively hold sway are thus explained. Experience has to do with production, which, in turn, is relative to decay. It deals with generation, becoming, not with finality, being. Hence it is infected with the trait of relative non-being, of mere imitativeness; hence its multiplicity, its logical inadequacy, its relativity to a standard and end beyond itself. Reason, *per contra*, has to do with meaning, with significance (ideas, forms), that is eternal and ultimate. Since the meaning of anything is the worth, the good, the end of that thing, experience presents us with partial and tentative efforts to achieve the embodiment of purpose, under conditions that doom the attempt to inconclusiveness. It has, however, its meed of reality in the degree in which its results *participate* in meaning, the good, reason.

From this classic period, then, comes the antithesis of experience as the historically achieved *embodiments* of meaning, partial, multiple, insecure, to reason as the source, author, and container of *meaning*, permanent, assured, unified. Idealism means ideality, experience means brute and broken facts. That things exist because of and for the sake of meaning, and that experience gives us meaning in a servile, interrupted, and inherently deficient way—such is the standpoint. Experience gives us meaning in process of becoming; special and isolated instances in which it *happens*, temporally, to appear, rather than meaning pure, undefiled, independent. Experience presents purpose, the good, struggling against obstacles, "involved in matter."

Just how much the vogue of modern Neo-Kantian idealism, professedly built upon a strictly epistemological instead of upon a cosmological basis, is due, in days of a declining theology, to a vague sense that affirming the function of reason in the constitution of a knowable world (which in its own constitution as logically knowable may be, morally and spiritually, anything you please), carries with it an assurance of the superior reality of the good and the beautiful as well as of the "true," it would be hard to say. Certainly unction seems to have descended upon epistemology, in apostolic succession, from classic idealism; so that neo-Kantianism is rarely without a tone of edification, as if feeling itself the patron of man's spiritual interests in contrast to the supposed crudeness and insensitiveness of naturalism and empiricism. At all events, we find here one element in our problem: Experience considered as the summary of past episodic adventures and happenings in relation to fulfilled and adequately expressed meaning.

The second historic event centers about the controversy of innate ideas, or pure concepts. The issue is between empiricism and rationalism as theories of the origin and validation of scientific knowledge. The empiricist is he who feels that the chief obstacle which prevents scientific method from making way is the belief in pure thoughts, not derived from particular observations and hence not responsible to the course of experience. His objection to the "high *a priori* road" is that it introduces in irresponsible fashion a mode of presumed knowledge which may be used at any turn to stand sponsor for mere tradition and prejudice, and thus to nullify the results of science resting upon and verified by observable facts. Experience thus comes to mean, to use the words of Peirce, "that which is forced upon a man's recognition will-he, nill-he, and shapes his thoughts to something quite different from what they naturally would have taken."[1] The same definition is found in James, in his chapter on Necessary Truths: "Experience means experience of something foreign supposed to impress us whether spontaneously or in consequence of our own exertions and acts."[2] As Peirce points out, this notion of experience as the foreign element that forces the hand of thought and controls its efficacy, goes back to Locke. Experience is "observation employed either about external sensible objects, or about the internal operations of our minds"[3] as furnishing in short all the valid data and tests of thinking and knowledge. This meaning, thinks Peirce, should be accepted "as a landmark which it would be a crime to disturb or displace."

The contention of idealism, here bound up with rationalism, is that perception and observation cannot guarantee knowledge in its honorific sense (science); that the peculiar differentia of scientific knowledge is a constancy, a universality, and necessity that contrast at every point with perceptual data, and that indispensably require the function of conception.[4] In short, *qualitative transformation of facts* (data of perception), not their mechanical subtraction and recombination, is the difference between scientific and perceptual knowledge. Here the problem which emerges is, of course, the significance of perception and of conception in respect to experience.[5]

The third episode reverses in a curious manner (which confuses pres-

[1] C. S. Peirce, *Monist*, Vol. XVI., p. 150.

[2] *Psychology*, Vol. II., p. 618.

[3] "Essay concerning Human Understanding," Book II, Chapter II, §2. Locke doubtless derived this notion from Bacon.

[4] It is hardly necessary to refer to the stress placed upon mathematics, as well as upon fundamental propositions in logic, ethics, and cosmology.

[5] Of course there are internal historic connections between experience as effective "memory," and experience as "observation." But the motivation and stress, the problem, has quite shifted. It may be remarked that Hobbes still writes under the influence of the Aristotelian conception. "Experience is nothing but Memory" ("Elements of Philosophy," Part I, Chapter I, §2), and hence is opposed to science.

ent discussion) the notion of experience as a foreign, alien, coercive material. It regards experience as a fortuitous association, by merely psychic connections, of individualistic states of consciousness. This is due to the Humian development of Locke. The "objects" and "operations," which to Locke were just given and secured in observation, become shifting complexes of subjective sensations and ideas, whose apparent permanency is due to discoverable illusions. This, of course, is the empiricism which made Kant so uneasily toss in his dogmatic slumbers (a tossing that he took for an awakening); and which, by reaction, called out the conception of thought as a function operating both to elevate perceptual data to scientific status, and also to confer objective status, or knowable character, upon even sensational data and their associative combinations.[6] Here emerges the third element in our problem: The function of thought as furnishing objectivity to any experience that claims cognitive reference or capacity.

Summing up the matter, idealism stands forth with its assertion of thought or reason as (1) the sponsor for all significance, ideality, purpose, in experience,—the author of the good and the beautiful as well as the true; (2) the power, located in pure conceptions, required to elevate perceptive or observational material to the plane of science; and (3) the constitution that gives objectivity, even the semblance of order, system, connection, mutual reference, to sensory data that without its assistance are mere subjective flux.

[6] There are, of course, anticipations of Hume in Locke. But to regard Lockeian experience as equivalent to Humian is to pervert history. Locke, as he was to himself and to the century succeeding him, was not a subjectivist, but in the main a common sense objectivist. It was this that gave him his historic influence. But so completely has the Hume-Kant controversy dominated recent thinking that it is constantly projected backward. Within a few weeks I have seen three articles, all insisting that the meaning of the term experience must be subjective, and stating or implying that those who take the term objectively are subverters of established usage! But a casual study of the dictionary will reveal that experience has always meant "*what* is experienced," observation as a source of knowledge, as well as the act, fact, or mode of experiencing. In the Oxford Dictionary, the (obsolete) sense of "experimental testing," of actual "observation of facts and events," and "the fact of being consciously affected by an act" have almost contemporaneous datings, viz., 1384, 1377, and 1382 respectively. A usage almost more objective than the second, the Baconian use, is "what has been experienced; the events that have taken place within the knowledge of an individual, a community, mankind at large, either during a particular period or generally." This dates back to 1607. Let us have no more captious criticisms and plaints based on ignorance of linguistic usage. [This pious wish has not been met. J. D., 1909.]

II

I begin the discussion with the last-named function. Thought is here conceived as *a priori*, not in the sense of particular innate ideas, but of a function that constitutes the very possibility of any objective experience, any experience involving reference beyond its own mere subjective happening. I shall try to show that idealism is condemned to move back and forth between two inconsistent interpretations of this *a priori* thought. It is taken to mean both the organized, the regulated, the informed, established character of experience, an order immanent and constitutional; and an agency which organizes, regulates, forms, synthesizes, a power operative and constructive. And the oscillation between and confusion of these two diverse senses is necessary to Neo-Kantian idealism.

When Kant compared his work in philosophy to that of the men who introduced construction into geometry, and experimentation into physics and chemistry, the point of his remarks depends upon taking the *a priori* worth of thought in a regulative, directive, controlling sense, thought as consciously, intentionally, making an experience *different* in a *determinate* sense and manner. But the point of his answer to Hume consists in taking the *a priori* in the other sense, as something which is *already* immanent in *any* experience, and which accordingly makes no determinate difference to any one experience as compared with any other, or with any past or future form of itself. The concept is treated first as that which makes an experience actually different, controlling its evolution towards consistency, coherency, and objective reliability; then, it is treated as that which has already effected the organization of any and every experience that comes to recognition at all. The fallacy from which he never emerges consists in vibrating between the definition of a concept as a rule of constructive synthesis in a *differential* sense, and the definition of it as a static endowment lurking in "mind," and giving automatically a hard and fixed law for the determination of every experienced object. The *a priori* conceptions of Kant as immanent fall, like the rain, upon the just and the unjust; upon error, opinion, and hallucination. But Kant slides into these *a priori* functions the preferential values exercised by empirical reflective thought. The concept of triangle, taken geometrically, means doubtless a determinate method of construing space elements; but to Kant it also means something that exists in the mind *prior* to all such geometrical constructions and that unconsciously lays down the law not only for their conscious elaboration, but also for any space perception, even for that which takes a rectangle to be a triangle. The first of the meanings is intelligible, and marks a definite contribution to the logic of science. But it is not "objective idealism"; it is a contribution to a revised empiricism. The second is a dark saying.

That organization of some sort exists in every experience I make no doubt. That isolation, discrepancy, the fragmentary, the incompatible, are brought to recognition and to logical function only with reference to some prior existential mode of organization seems clear. And it seems equally clear that reflection goes on with profit only because the materials with which it deals have already some degree of organization, or exemplify various relationships. As against Hume, or even Locke, we may be duly grateful to Kant for enforcing acknowledgment of these facts. But the acknowledgment means simply an improved and revised empiricism.

For, be it noted, this organization, first, is not the work of reason or thought, unless "reason" be stretched beyond all identification; and, secondly, it has no sacrosanct or finally valid and worthful character. (1) Experience always carries with it and within it certain systematized arrangements, certain classifications (using the term without intellectualistic prejudice), coexistent and serial. If we attribute these to "thought" then the structure of the brain of a Mozart which hears and combines sounds in certain groupings, the psycho-physical visual habit of the Greek, the locomotor apparatus of the human body in the laying-out and plotting of space is "thought." Social institutions, established political customs, effect and perpetuate modes of reaction and of perception that compel a certain grouping of objects, elements, and values. A national constitution brings about a definite arrangement of the factors of human action which holds even physical things together in certain determinate orders. Every successful economic process, with its elaborate divisions and adjustments of labor, of materials and instruments, is just such an objective organization. Now it is one thing to say that thought has played a part in the origin and development of such organizations, and continues to have a rôle in their judicious employment and application; it is another to say that these organizations *are* thought, or are its exclusive product. Thought that functions in these ways is distinctively *reflective* thought, thought as practical, volitional, deliberately exercised for specific aims—thought as an act, an art of skilled mediation. As *reflective* thought, its end is to terminate its own first and experimental forms, and to secure an organization which, while it may evoke new reflective thinking, puts an end to the thinking that secured the organization. *As organizations*, as established, effectively controlling arrangements of objects in experience, their mark is that they are not thoughts, but habits, customs of action.[7]

Moreover, such reflective thought as does intervene in the formation and maintenance of these practical organizations harks back to prior practical organizations, biological and social in nature. It serves to *valuate* organizations already existent as biological functions and instincts, while, as itself a biological activity, it redirects them to new conditions and results. Recognize, for example, that a geometric concept is a practical locomotor function of arranging stimuli in reference to maintenance of life activities *brought into consciousness*, and then serving as a center of reorganization of such activities to freer, more varied flexible and valuable forms; recognize this, and we have the truth of the Kantian idea, without its excrescences and miracles. The concept is the practical activity doing consciously and artfully what it had aforetime done blindly and aimlessly, and thereby not only doing it better but opening up a freer world of significant activities. Thought as such a reorganization of natural functions does naturally what Kantian forms and schematizations do only supernaturally. In a word, the constructive or organizing activity of "thought" does not inhere in thought as a transcendental function, a form or mode of some supra-empirical ego, mind, or consciousness, but in thought as itself vital activity. And in any case we have passed to the idea of thought as reflectively reconstructive and directive, and away from the notion of thought as immanently constitutional and organizational. To make this passage and yet to ignore its existence and import is essential to objective idealism.

(2) No final or ultimate validity attaches to these original arrangements and institutionalizations in any case. Their value is teleological and experimental, not fixedly ontological. "Law and order" are good things, but not when they become rigidity, and create mechanical uniformity or routine. Prejudice is the acme of the *a priori*. Of the *a priori* in this sense we may say what is always to be said of habits and institutions: They are good servants, but harsh and futile masters. Organization as already effected is always in danger of becoming a *mortmain*; it may be a way of sacrificing novelty, flexibility, freedom, creation to static standards. The curious inefficiency of idealism at this point is evident in the fact that genuine thought, empirical reflective

---

[7] The relationship of organization and thought is precisely that which we find psychologically typified by the rhythmic functions of habit and attention, attention being always, *ab quo*, a sign of the failure of habit, and, *ad quem*, a reconstructive modification of habit.

thought, is required precisely for the purpose of re-forming established and set formations.

In short, (a) a priori character is no exclusive function of thought. Every biological function, every motor attitude, every vital impulse as the carrying vehicle of experience is thus apriorily regulative in prospective reference; what we call apperception, expectation, anticipation, desire, demand, choice, are pregnant with this constitutive and organizing power. (b) In so far as "thought" does exercise such reorganizing power, it is because thought is itself still a vital function. (c) Objective idealism depends not only upon ignoring the existence and capacity of vital functions, but upon a profound confusion of the constitutional a priori, the unconsciously dominant, with empirically reflective thought. In the sense in which the a priori is worth while as an attribute of thought, thought cannot be what the objective idealist defines it as being. Plain, ordinary, everyday empirical reflections, operating as centers of inquiry, of suggestion, of experimentation, exercise the valuable function of regulation, in an auspicious direction, of subsequent experiences.

The categories of accomplished systematization cover alike the just and the unjust, the false and the true, while (unlike God's rain) they exercise no specific or differential activity of stimulation and control. Error and inefficiency, as well as value and energy, are embodied in our objective institutional classifications. As a special favor, will not the objective idealist show how, in some one single instance, his immanent "reason" makes any difference as respects the detection and elimination of error, or gives even the slightest assistance in discovering and validating the truly worthful? This practical work, the life blood of intelligence in everyday life and in critical science, is done by the despised and rejected matter of concrete empirical contexts and functions. Generalizing the issue: If the immanent organization be ascribed to thought, why should its work be such as to demand continuous correction and revision? If specific reflective thought, as empirical, be subject to all the limitations supposed to inhere in experience as such, how can it assume the burden of making good, of supplementing, reconstructing, and developing meanings? The logic of the case seems to be that Neo-Kantian idealism gets its status against empiricism by first accepting the Humian idea of experience, while the express import of its positive contribution is to show the non-existence (not merely the cognitive invalidity) of anything describable as mere states of subjective consciousness. Thus in the end it tends to destroy itself and to make way for a more adequate empiricism.

III

In the above discussion, I have unavoidably anticipated the second problem: the relation of conceptual thought to perceptual data. A distinct aspect still remains, however. Perception, as well as apriority, is a term harboring a fundamental ambiguity. It may mean (1) a distinct type of activity, predominantly practical in character, though carrying at its heart important cognitive and esthetic qualities; or (2) a distinctively cognitional experience, the function of observation as explicitly logical—a factor in science *qua* science.

In the first sense, as recent functional empiricism (working in harmony with psychology, but not itself peculiarly psychological) has abundantly shown, perception is primarily an act of adjustment of organism and environment, differing from a mere reflex or instinctive adaptation in that, in order to compensate for the failure of the instinctive adjustment, it requires an objective or discriminative presentation of conditions of action: the negative conditions or obstacles, and the positive conditions or means and resources.[8] This, of course, is its cognitive phase. In so far as the material thus presented not only serves as a direct cue to further successful activity (successful in the overcoming of obstacles to the maintenance of the function entered upon) but presents auxiliary collateral objects and qualities that give additional range and depth of meaning to the activity of adjustment, perceiving is esthetic as well as intellectual.[9]

Now such perception cannot be made antithetical to thought, for it may itself be surcharged with any amount of imaginatively supplied and reflectively sustained ideal factors—such as are needed to determine and select relevant stimuli and to suggest and develop an appropriate plan and course of behavior. The amount of such saturating intellectual material depends upon the complexity and maturity of the behaving agent. Such perception, moreover, is strictly teleological, since it arises from an experienced need and functions to fulfil the purpose indicated by this need. The cognitional content is, indeed, carried by affectional and intentional contexts.

[8] Compare, for example, Dr. Stuart's paper in the "Studies in Logical Theory," pp. 253-256. I may here remark that I remain totally unable to see how the *interpretation* of objectivity to mean controlling conditions of action (negative and positive as above) derogates at all from its naïve objectivity, or how it connotes cognitive subjectivity, or is in any way incompatible with a common-sense realistic theory of perception.

[9] For this suggested interpretation of the esthetic as surprising, or unintended, gratuitous collateral reinforcement, see Gordon, "Psychology of Meaning."

Then we have perception as scientific observation. This involves the deliberate, artful exclusion of affectional and purposive factors as exercising mayhap a vitiating influence upon the cognitive or objective content; or, more strictly speaking, a transformation of the more ordinary or "natural" emotional and purposive concomitants, into what Bain calls "neutral" emotion, and a purpose of finding out what the present conditions of the problem are. (The practical feature is not thus denied or eliminated, but the overweening influence of a present dominating end is avoided, so that *change of the character of the end* may be effected, if found desirable.) Here observation may be opposed to thought, in the sense that exact and minute description may be set over against interpretation, explanation, theorizing, and inference. In the wider sense of thought as equaling reflective process, the work of observation and description forms a constituent division of labor *within* thought. The impersonal demarcation and accurate registration of what is objectively there or present occurs for the sake (*a*) of eliminating meaning which is habitually but uncritically referred, and (*b*) of getting a basis for a meaning (at first purely inferential or hypothetical) that may be consistently referred; and that (*c*), resting upon examination and not upon mere *a priori* custom, may weather the strain of subsequent experiences. But in so far as thought is identified with the conceptual phase as such of the entire logical function, observation is, of course, set over against thought: deliberately, purposely, and artfully so.

It is not uncommon to hear it said that the Lockeian movement was all well enough for psychology, but went astray because it invaded the field of logic. If we mean by psychology a natural history of what at any time *passes* for knowledge, and by logic conscious control in the direction of grounded assurance, this remark appears to reverse the truth. As a natural history of knowledge in the sense of opinion and belief, Locke's account of discrete, simple ideas or meanings, which are compounded and then distributed, does palpable violence to the facts. But every line of Locke shows that he was interested in knowledge in its honorific sense—controlled certainty, or, where this is not feasible, measured probability. And to logic as an account of the way in which we by art build up a *tested* assurance, a rationalized conviction, Locke makes an important positive contribution. The pity is that he inclined to take it for the whole of the logic of science,[10] not seeing that it was but a correlative division of labor to the work of hypotheses or inference; and that he

---

[10] This, however, is not strictly true, since Locke goes far to supply the means of his own correction in his account of the "workmanship of the understanding."

tended to identify it with a natural history or psychology. The latter tendency exposed Locke to the Humian interpretation, and permanently sidetracked the positive contribution of his theory to logic, while it led to that confusion of an untrue psychology with a logic valid within limits, of which Mill is the standard example.

In analytic observation, it is a positive object to strip off all inferential meaning so far as may be—to reduce the facts as nearly as may be to derationalized data, in order to make possible a new and better rationalization. In and because of this process, the perceptual data approach the limit of a disconnected manifold, of the brutely given, of the merely sensibly present; while meaning stands out as a searched for principle of unification and explanation, that is, as a thought, a concept, an hypothesis. The extent to which this is carried depends wholly upon the character of the specific situation and problem; but, speaking generally, or of limiting tendencies, one may say it is carried to mere observation, pure brute description, on the one side, and to mere thought, that is hypothetical inference, on the other.

So far as Locke ignored this instrumental character of observation, he naturally evoked and strengthened rationalistic idealism; he called forth its assertion of the need of reason, of concepts, of universals, to constitute knowledge in its eulogistic sense. But two contrary errors do not make a truth, although they suggest and determine the nature of some relevant truth. This truth is the empirical origin, in a determinate type of situation, of the contrast of observation and conception, the empirical relevancy and the empirical worth of this contrast in controlling the character of subsequent experiences. To suppose that perception as it concretely exists, either in the early experiences of the animal, the race, or the individual, or in its later refined and expanded experiences, is identical with the sharply analyzed, objectively discriminated and internally disintegrated elements of scientific observation, is a perversion of experience; a perversion for which, indeed, professed empiricists set the example, but which idealism must perpetuate if it is not to find its end in an improved, functional empiricism.[11]

---

[11] Plato, especially in his "Theaetetus," seems to have begun the procedure of blasting the good name of perceptive experience by identifying a late and instrumental distinction, having to do with logical control, with all experience whatsoever.

IV

We come now to the consideration of the third element in our problem; identity, important and normative value, in relation to experience; the antithesis of experience as a tentative, fragmentary, and ineffectual embodiment of meaning over against the perfect, eternal system of meanings which experience suggests even in nullifying and mutilating.

That from the *memory* standpoint experience presents itself as a multiplicity of episodic events with just enough continuity among them to suggest principles true "on the whole" or usually, but without furnishing instruction as to their exact range and bearing, seems obvious enough. Why should it not? The motive which leads to reflection on *past* experience could be satisfied in no other way. Continuities, connecting links, dynamic transitions drop out because, for the purpose of the recollection, they would be hindrances if now repeated; or because they are now available only when themselves objectified in definite terms and thus given a *quasi* atomistic standing of their own. This is the only alternative to what the psychologists term "total reminiscence," which, so far as total, leave us with an elephant on our hands. Unless we are going to have a wholesale revivification of the past, giving us just another embarrassing present experience, illusory because irrelevant, memory must work by retail—by summoning *distinct* cases, events, sequences, precedents. Dis-membering is a positively necessary part of remembering. But the resulting *disjecta membra* are in no sense experience as it was or is; they are simply elements held apart, and yet tentatively implicated together, in present experience for the sake of its most favorable evolution; evolution in the direction of the most excellent meaning or value conceived. If the remembering is efficacious and pertinent, it reveals the possibilities of the present; that is to say, it clarifies the transitive, transforming character that belongs inherently to the present. The dismembering of the vital present into the disconnected past is correlative to an anticipation, an idealization of the future.

Moreover, the contingent character of the principle or rule that emerges from a survey of cases, instances, as distinct from a fixed or necessary character, secures just what is wanted in the exigency of a prospective idealization, or refinement of excellence. It is just this character that secures flexibility and variety of outlook, that makes possible a consideration of alternatives and an attempt to select and to execute the more worthy among them. The fixed or necessary law would mean a future like the past—a dead, an unidealized future. It is exasperating to imagine how completely different would have been Aristotle's valuation of "experience" with respect to its contingency, if he had but once employed the function of developing and perfecting value, instead of the function of knowing an unalterable object, as the standard by which to estimate and measure intelligence.

The one constant trait of experience from its crudest to its most mature forms is that its contents undergo change of meaning, and of meaning in the sense of excellence, value. Every experience is in-course,[12] in course of becoming worse or better as to its contents, or in course of conscious endeavor to sustain some satisfactory level of value against encroachment or lapse. In this effort, both precedent, the reduction of the present idealization, the anticipation of the possible, though doubtful, future, emerge. Without idealization, that is, without conception of the favorable issue that the present, defined in terms of precedents, may portend in its transition, the recollection of precedents, and the formulation of tentative rules is nonsense. But without the identification of the present in terms of elements suggested by the past, without recognition, the ideal, the value projected as end, remains inert, helpless, sentimental, without means of realization. Resembling cases and anticipation, memory and idealization, are the corresponding terms in which a present experience has its transitive force analyzed into reciprocally pertinent means and ends.

That an experience will change in content and value is the one thing certain. *How* it will change is the one thing naturally uncertain. Hence the import of the art of reflection and invention. Control of the character of the change in the direction of the worthful is the common business of theory and practice. Here is the province of the episodic recollection of past history and of the idealized foresight of possibilities. The irrelevancy of an objective idealism lies in the fact that it totally ignores the position and function of ideality in sustained and serious endeavor. Were values automatically injected and kept in the world of experience by any force not reflected in human memories and projects, it would make no difference whether this force were a Spencerian environment

---

[12] Compare James, "Continuous transition is one sort of conjunctive relation; and to be a radical empiricist means to hold fast to this conjunctive relation of all others, for this is the strategic point, the position through which, if a hole be made, all the corruptions of dialectics and all the metaphysical fictions pour into our philosophy."—*Journal of Philosophy, Psychology, and Scientific Methods*, Vol. I, p. 536.

or an Absolute Reason. Did purpose ride in a cosmic automobile toward a predestined goal, it would not cease to be physical and mechanical in quality because labeled Divine Idea, or Perfect Reason. The moral would be "let us eat, drink, and be merry," for to-morrow—or if not this to-morrow, then upon some to-morrow, unaffected by our empirical memories, reflections, inventions, and idealizations—the cosmic automobile arrives. Spirituality, ideality, meaning as purpose, would be the last things to present themselves if objective idealism were true. Values cannot be both ideal and given, and their "given" character is emphasized, not transformed, when they are called eternal and absolute. But natural values become ideal the moment their maintenance is dependent upon the intentional activities of an empirical agent. To suppose that values are ideal because they are so eternally given is the contradiction in which objective idealism has intrenched itself. Objective ontological teleology spells machinery. Reflective and volitional, experimental teleology alone spells ideality.[13] Objective, rationalistic idealism breaks upon the fact that it can have no intermediary between a brutely achieved embodiment of meaning (physical in character or else of that peculiar quasi-physical character which goes generally by the name of metaphysical) and a total opposition of the given and the ideal, connoting their mutal indifference and incapacity. An empiricism that acknowledges the transitive character of experience, and that acknowledges the possible control of the character of the transition by means of intelligent effort, has abundant opportunity to celebrate in productive art, genial morals, and impartial inquiry the grace and the severity of the ideal.

14. The Practical Character of Reality*

In 1908, one year after the publication of *Pragmatism* by William James, John Dewey published the original version of this essay under the title "Does Reality Possess Practical Character?" In part, this essay was a defense of pragmatism, then defined tentatively by Dewey as "the doctrine that

[13] One of the not least of the many merits of Santayana's "Life of Reason" is the consistency and vigor with which is upheld the doctrine that significant idealism means idealization.

* From John Dewey, *Philosophy and Civilization* (New York, Capricorn Books, 1963) (1931), pp. 36-55.Reprinted by permission of G. P. Putnam's Sons. (Published originally as "Does Reality Possess Practical Character?" in 1908.)

reality possess practical character and that this character is most efficaciously expressed in the function of intelligence. . . ." But Dewey was concerned also with the heightening of his ‚attack on traditional epistemology, which he judged to be suffering from "intellectual lock-jaw." From Dewey's point of view, the process of knowing is not simply a way to guide us to an already existing "final term." To the contrary, it is the changes generated by our inquiry which should occupy our attention, although these changes are neither "total" nor "miraculous." Dewey states the mediating ground of pragmatic epistemology as follows: "Transformation, readjustment, reconstruction, all imply prior existences; existences which have characters and behavior of their own which must be accepted, consulted, humored, manipulated, or made light of, in all kinds of differing ways in the different contexts of different problems." And in a rhetorical conclusion, Dewey challenges philosophy to assume the risks and instability involved in devoting itself to these shifts in context, rather than to an abstract delineation of "prior existences."

I

Recently I have had an experience which, insignificant in itself, seems to mean something as an index-figure of the present philosophic situation. In a criticism of the neo-Kantian conception that *a priori* functions of thought are necessary to constitute knowledge, it became relevant to deny its underlying postulates: viz., the existence of anything properly called mental states or subjective impressions precedent to all objective recognitions, and which accordingly needed some transcendental function to order them into a world of stable and consistent reference. It was argued that such so-called original mental data are in truth turning points of the readjustment, or making over, through a state of incompatibility and shock, of objective affairs. This doctrine was met by the cry of "Subjectivism!" It had seemed to its author to be a criticism, on ground at once naturalistic and ethical, of the ground proposition of subjectivism. Why this diversity of interpretations? So far as the writer can judge, it is due to the fact that certain things characteristic of practical life, such things as lack and need, conflict and clash, desire and effort, loss and satisfaction, had been frankly referred to reality; and to the further fact that the function and structure of knowing had been systematically connected with these practical features. These conceptions are doubtless radical enough; the latter was perhaps more or less revolutionary. The probability, the antecedent probability, was that hostile critics would have easy work in pointing out specific errors of fact and interpretation. But no: the simpler, the more effective method, was to dismiss the whole thing as anarchic subjectivism.

This was and remains food for thought. I have been able to find but one explanation: In current philosophy, everything of a practical nature is regarded as "merely" personal, and the "merely" has the force of denying legitimate standing in the court of cosmic jurisdiction. This conception seems to me the great and the ignored assumption in contemporary philosophy; many who might shrink from the doctrine were it expressly formulated hang desperately to its implications. Yet as an underlying assumption, it is surely sheer prejudice, a culture-survival. If we suppose the traditions of philosophic discussion wiped out and philosophy starting afresh from the most active tendencies of to-day,—those striving in social life, in science, in literature, and art,—one can hardly imagine any philosophic view springing up and gaining credence, which did not give large place, in its scheme of things, to the practical and personal, and to them without employing disparaging terms, such as phenomenal, merely subjective, and so on. Why, putting it mildly, should what gives tragedy, comedy, and poignancy to life, be excluded from things? Doubtless, what we call life, what we take to be genuinely vital, is not all of things. But it is a part of things; and is that part which counts most with the philosopher—unless he has quite parted with his ancient dignity of lover of wisdom. What becomes of philosophy as far as humane and liberal interests are concerned, if, in an age when the person and the personal loom large in politics, industry, religion, art, and science, it contents itself with this parrot cry of phenomenalism, whenever the personal comes into view? When science is led by the idea of evolution to introduce into the world the principles of initiative, variation, struggle, and selection; and when social forces have driven into bankruptcy absolutistic and static dogmas as authorities for the conduct of life, it is trifling for philosophy to decline to look the situation in the face. The relegation, as matter of course, of need, of stress and strain, strife and satisfaction, to the merely personal and the merely personal to the limbo of something which is neither flesh, fowl, nor good red herring, seems the thoughtless rehearsal of ancestral prejudice.

When we get beyond the echoing of tradition, the sticking point seems to be the relation of knowledge to the practical function of things. Let reality be in itself as "practical" as you please, but let not this practical character lay profane hands on the ark of truth! Every new mode of interpreting life—every new gospel—is met with the charge of antinomianism. Imagination when bound by custom apprehends the restrictions that are relaxed and the checks that are removed, but not the inevitable responsibilities and tests that the new idea brings in. And so the conception that knowledge makes a difference in and to things looks licentious to those who fail to see that the necessity of doing this business well, of making the *right* difference, puts intelligence under bonds it never yet has known: most of all in philosophy, the most gayly irresponsible of the procedures, and the most irresponsively sullen, of the historic fruits of intelligence.

Why should the idea that knowledge makes a difference to and in things be antecedently objectionable? If one is already committed to a belief that Reality is neatly and finally tied up in a packet without loose ends, unfinished issues or new departures, one would object to knowledge making a difference just as one would object to any other impertinent obtruder. But if one believes that the world itself is in transformation, why should the notion that knowledge is the most important mode of its modification and the only organ of its guidance be *a priori* obnoxious?

There is, I think, no answer save that the theory of knowledge has been systematically built up on the notion of a static universe, so that even those perfectly free to feel the lessons of physics and biology concerning moving energy and evolution, and of history concerning the constant transformation of man's affairs (science included), retain an unquestioning belief in a theory of knowledge which is out of any possible harmony with their own theory of the matters to be known. Modern epistemology, having created the idea that the way to frame right conceptions is to analyze knowledge, has strengthened this view. For it at once leads to the view that realities must themselves have a theoretic and intellectual complexion—not a practical one. This view is naturally congenial to idealists; but that realists should so readily play into the hands of idealists by asserting what, on the basis of a formal theory of knowledge, realities must be, instead of accepting the guidance of things in divining what knowledge *is*, is an anomaly so striking as to support the view that the notion of static reality has taken its last stand in ideas about knowledge. Take, for example, the most striking, because the extreme case—knowledge of a past event. It is absurd to suppose that knowledge makes a difference to the final or appropriate content of knowledge: to the subject-matter which fulfils the requirements of knowing. In this case, it would get in its own way and trip itself up in endless regress. But it seems the very superstition of intellectualism to suppose that this fact about knowledge can decide what is the nature of that reference to the past which, when rightly made, is final. No doctrine about knowledge can hinder the belief—if there be sufficient specific evidence for it—that what we know as past may be something which has *irretrievably* undergone just the difference which knowledge makes.

Now arguments against pragmatism—by which I mean the doctrine that reality possesses practical character and that this character is most efficaciously expressed in the function of intelligence[1]—seem to fall blandly into this fallacy. They assume that to hold that knowledge makes a difference in existences is equivalent to holding that it makes a difference in the object *to be* known, thus defeating its own purpose; witless that the reality which is the appropriate object of knowledge in a given case may be precisely a reality in which knowing has succeeded in making the needed difference. This question is not one to be settled by manipulation of the concept of knowledge, nor by dialectic discussion of its essence or nature. It is a question of facts, a question of what knowing exists as in the scheme of existence. If things undergo change without thereby ceasing to be real, there can be no *formal* bar to knowing being one specific kind of change in things, nor to its test being found in the successful carrying into effect of the kind of change intended. If knowing be a change in a reality, then the more knowing reveals this change, the more transparent, the more adequate, it is. And if all existences are in transition, then the knowledge which treats them as if they were something of which knowledge is a kodak fixation is just the kind of knowledge which refracts and perverts them. And by the same token a knowing which actively participates in a change in the way to effect it in the needed fashion would be the type of knowing which is valid. If reality be itself in transition—and this doctrine originated not with the objectionable pragmatist but with the physicist and naturalist and historian—then the doctrine that knowledge *is* reality making a par-

---

[1] This definition, in the present state of discussion, is an arbitrary or personal one. The text does not mean that "pragmatism" is currently used exclusively in this sense; obviously there are other senses. It does not mean it is the sense in which it *ought* to be used. I have no wish to legislate either for language or for philosophy. But it marks the sense in which *is* is used in this paper; and the pragmatic movement is still so loose and variable that I judge one has a right to fix his own meaning, provided he serves notice and adheres to it.

ticular and specified sort of change in itself seems to have the best
chance at maintaining a theory of knowing which is in wholesome touch
with the genuine and valid.

II

If the ground be cleared of *a priori* objections, and if it be evident
that pragmatism cannot be disposed of by any formal or dialectic
manipulations of "knowledge" or "truth," but only by showing that
some specific things are not of the sort claimed, we may consider some
common sense affiliations of pragmatism. Common sense regards intelligence as having a purpose, and knowledge as amounting to something. I once heard a physicist, quite innocent of the pragmatic controversy, remark that the knowledge of a mechanic or farmer was what
the Yankee calls gumption—acknowledgment of things in their belong-
ings and uses, and that to his mind natural science was gumption on a
larger scale: the convenient cataloguing and arranging of a whole lot of
things with reference to their most efficacious services. Popularly, good
judgment is judgment as to the relative values of things: good sense is
horse sense, ability to take hold of things right end up, to fit an instrument to an obstacle, to select resources apt for a task. To be reasonable
is to recognize things in their office as obstacles and as resources. Intelligence, in its ordinary use, is a practical term; ability to size up matters with respect to the needs and possibilities of the various situations
in which one is called to do something; capacity to envisage things in
terms of the adjustments and adaptations they make possible or hinder.
One objective test of the presence or absence of intelligence is influence
upon behavior. No capacity to make adjustments means no intelligence;
conduct evincing management of complex and novel conditions means
a high degree of reason. Such conditions at least suggest that a reality-
to-be-known, a reality which is the appropriate subject-matter of
knowledge is reality-of-use-and-in-use, direct or indirect, and that a
reality which is not in any sort of use, or bearing upon use, may go
hang, *so far as knowledge is concerned*.

No one, I suppose, would deny that knowledge *issues* in some action
which changes things to some extent—be the action only a more
deliberate maintenance of a course of conduct already instinctively entered upon. When I see a sign on the street corner I can turn or go on,
knowing what I am about. The perceptions of the scientist need have no
such overt or "utilitarian" uses, but surely after them he behaves dif-

ferently, as an inquirer if in no other way; and the cumulative effect of such changes finally modifies the overt action of the ordinary man. That knowing, *after the event,* makes a difference of this sort, few I suppose would deny: if that were all pragmatism means, it would perhaps be accepted as a harmless truism. But there is a further question of fact: just how is the "consequent" action related to the "precedent" knowledge? When *is* "after the event"? What degree of continuity exists? Is the difference between knowing and acting intelligently one of kind or simply one of dominant quality? How does a thing, if it is not already in change in the knowing, manage to issue at its term in action? Moreover, do not the changes actively effected constitute the whole *import* of the knowledge, and hence its final measure and test of validity? If it merely *happens* that knowing when it is done with passes into some action, by what miracle is the subsequent action so pat to the situation? Is it not rather true that the "knowledge" is instituted and framed in anticipation of the consequent issue, and, in the degree in which it is wise and prudent, is held open to revision during it? Certainly the moralist (one might quote, for example, Goethe, Carlyle, and Mazzini) and the common man often agree that full knowledge, adequate assurance of reality is found only in the issue which fulfills ideas; that we have to do a doctrine to *know* its truth; otherwise it is only dogma or doctrinaire program. Experimental science is a recognition that no idea is entitled to be termed knowledge till it has passed into such overt manipulation of physical conditions as constructs the object to which the idea refers. If one could get rid of one's traditional logical theories and set to work afresh to frame a theory of knowledge on the basis of the procedure of the common man, the moralist, and the experimentalist, would it be the forced or the natural procedure to say that the realities which we *know*, which we are sure of, are precisely those realities that have taken shape in and through the active procedures of knowing?

I turn to another type of consideration. Certainly one of the most genuine problems of modern life is the reconciliation of the scientific view of the universe with the claims of the moral life. Are judgments in terms of the redistribution of matter in motion (or some other closed formula) alone valid? Or are accounts of the universe in terms of possibility and desirability, of initiative and responsibility, also valid? There is no occasion to expatiate on the importance of the moral life, nor upon the supreme importance of intelligence within the moral life. But there does seem to be occasion for asking how moral judgments—judgments of the would and should—relate themselves to the world of scientific knowledge. To frame a theory of knowledge which makes it necessary to deny the validity of moral ideas, or else to refer them to some other and separate kind of universe from that of common sense and science, is both provincial and arbitrary. The pragmatist has at least tried to face, and not to dodge, the question of how it is that moral and scientific "knowledge" can both hold of one and the same world. And whatever the difficulties in his proffered solution, the conception that scientific judgments are to be assimilated to moral is closer to common sense than is the theory that validity is to be denied to moral judgments because they do not square with a preconceived theory of the nature of the world to which scientific judgments must refer. And all moral judgments are about changes to be made.

III

I turn to one affiliation of the pragmatic theory with the results of recent science. The necessity, for the occurrence of an event in the way of knowledge, of an organism which reacts or behaves in a specific way, would seem to be as well established as any specific proposition. It is a peculiar fact, a fact fit to stir curiosity, that the rational function seems to be intercalated in a scheme of practical adjustments. The parts and members of the organism are certainly not there primarily for pure intellection or for theoretic contemplation. The brain, the last physical organ of thought, is a part of the same practical machinery for bringing about adaptation of the environment to the life requirements of the organism, to which belong legs and hand and eye. That the brain frees organic behavior from complete servitude to immediate physical conditions, that it makes possible the liberation of energy for remote and ever expanding ends is, indeed, a precious fact, but not one which removes the brain from the category of organic devices of behavior.[2] That the organ of thinking, of knowledge, was at least originally an organ of conduct, few, I imagine, will deny. And even if we try to believe that the cognitive function has supervened as a different operation, it is difficult to believe that the transfiguration has been so radical that knowing has lost all traces of its connection with vital impulse. But unless we so assume, have we any alternatives except to hold that this continual

[2] It is interesting to note how the metaphysical puzzles regarding "parallelism," "interaction," "automatism," the relation of "consciousness" to "body," evaporate when one ceases isolating the brain into a peculiar physical substrate of mind at large, and treats it simply as one portion of the body which is the instrumentality of adaptive behavior.

presence of vital impulse is a disturbing and refracting factor, which forever prevents knowledge from reaching its own aim; or else that a certain promoting, a certain carrying forward of the vital impulse, importing certain differences in things, *is* the aim of knowledge?

The problem cannot be evaded—save ostrich wise—by saying that such considerations are "merely genetic," or "psychological," having to do only with the origin and natural history of knowing. For the point is that the organic reaction, the behavior of the organism, affects the *content* of awareness. The subject-matter of all awareness is thing-related-to-organism—related as stimulus direct or indirect or as material of response, present or remote, ulterior or achieved.

No one—so far as I know—denies this with respect to the perceptual field of awareness. Pains, pleasures, hunger, and thirst, all "secondary" qualities, involve inextricably the "interaction" of organism and environment. The perceptual field is distributed and arranged as the possible field of selective reactions of the organism at its center. Up and down, far and near, before and behind, right and left, hard and soft (as well as white and black, bass and alto), involve reference to a center of behavior.

This material has so long been the stock in trade of both idealistic arguments and proclamations of the agnostic "relativity" of knowledge that philosophers have grown aweary of listening. But even this lethargy might be quickened by a moderate hospitality to the pragmatic interpretation. That red, or far and near, or hard and soft, or big and little, involves a relation between organism and environment, is no more an argument for idealism than is the fact that water involves a relation between hydrogen and oxygen.[3] It is, however, an argument for the ultimately practical value of these distinctions—that they are *differences* made in what things would have been without organic behavior —differences made not by "consciousness" or "mind," but by the organism as the active center of a system of activities. Moreover, the whole agnostic sting of the doctrine of "relativity" lies in the assumption that the ideal or aim of knowledge is to repeat or copy a prior existence—in which case, of course, the making of contemporaneous differences by the organism in the very fact of awareness would get in the way and forever hinder the knowledge function from the fulfillment of its proper end. Knowledge, awareness, in this case suffers from an impediment which no surgery can better. But if the aim of knowing be precisely to make *certain* differences in an environment, to carry on to

[3] I owe this illustration to my colleague, Dr. Montague.

favorable issue, by the readjustment of the organism, certain changes going on indifferently in the environment, then the fact that the changes of thȩ organism enter pervasively into the subject-matter of awareness is no restriction or perversion of knowledge, but part of the fulfillment of its office.

The only question would then be whether *proper* reactions take place. The whole agnostic, positivistic controversy is flanked by a single move. The issue is no longer an ideally necessary but actually impossible copying, *versus* an improper but unavoidable modification of reality through organic inhibitions and stimulations: but it is the right, the economical, the effective, and, if one may venture, the useful and satisfactory reaction *versus* the wasteful, the enslaving, the misleading, and the confusing reaction. The presence of organic responses, influencing and modifying every content, every subject-matter of awareness, is the undoubted fact. But the significant thing is the *way* organic behavior enters in—the *way* it influences and modifies. We assign very different values to different types of "knowledge,"—or subject-matters involving organic attitudes and operations. Some are only guesses, opinions, suspicious characters; others are "knowledge" in the honorific and eulogistic sense—science; some turn out mistakes, blunders, errors. Whence and how this discrimination of quality in what is taken at its own time to be good knowledge? Why and how is the content of some "knowledge" genuine-knowing and of other mis-knowing? Awareness is itself a blanket term, covering, in the same bed, delusion, doubt, confusion, ambiguity, and definition, organization, logical conclusiveness assured by evidence and reason. Any naturalistic or realistic theory is committed to the idea that all of these terms bear impartially the same relation to things considered as sheer existence. What we must have in any case is the same existences—the same in kind—only differently arranged or linked up. But why then the tremendous difference in value? And if the un-naturalist, the non-realist, says the difference is one of exististial kind, made by the working here malign, there benign, of "consciousness," "psychical" operations and states, upon the existences which are the direct subject-matter of knowledge, there is still the problem of discriminating the conditions and nature of the respective beneficent and malicious interventions of the peculiar "existence" labeled consciousness.[4] The realness of error, ambiguity, doubt and guess poses a problem. It is a problem which has perplexed philosophy

---

[4] Of course on the theory I am interested in expounding, the so-called action of "consciousness" means simply the organic releases in the way of behavior which are the conditions of awareness, and which also modify its content.

so long and has led to so many speculative adventures, that it would seem worth while, were it only for the sake of variety, to listen to the pragmatic solution according to which it is the business of the organic adaptation involved in all knowing to make a *certain* difference in reality, but *not* to make any old or casual difference. The right, the true and good, difference is that which carries out satisfactorily the specific purpose for the sake of which knowing occurs. All manufactures are the product of an activity, but it does not follow that all manufactures are equally good. And so all "knowledges" are differences made in things by knowing, but some differences are not calculated or wanted in the knowing, and hence are disturbers and interlopers when they come— while others fulfill the intent of the knowing, being in harmony with the consistent behavior of the organism and re-inforcing and enlarging its function. A mistake is literally a mishandling; a doubt is a temporary suspense and vacillation of reactions; an ambiguity is the tension of alternative but incompatible mode of responsive treatment; an inquiry is a tentative and retrievable (because intra-organic) mode of activity, entered upon prior to launching upon a knowledge which is public, ineluctable—without anchors to windward—since it has taken physical effect through overt action.

It is practically all one to say that the norm of honorable knowing is to make no difference in *its* object, and that its aim is to attain and buttress a specific kind of difference in reality. Knowing fails in its business if it makes a change in its *own* object—that is a mistake; but its own object is none the less a prior existence changed in a certain way. Nor is this a play upon the two senses—end and subject-matter—of "object." The organism has its appropriate functions. To maintain, to expand, adequate functioning is its business. This functioning does not occur *in vacuo*. It involves co-operative and readjusted changes in the cosmic medium. Hence the appropriate subject-matter of awareness is not reality at large, a metaphysical heaven to be mimeographed at many removes upon a badly constructed mental carbon paper which yields at best only fragmentary, blurred, and erroneous copies. Its proper and legitimate object is that relationship of organism and environment in which functioning is most amply and effectively attained; or by which, in case of obstruction and consequent needed experimentation, its later eventual free course is most facilitated. As for the other reality, metaphysical reality *at large*, it may, so far as awareness is concerned, go to its own place.

For ordinary purposes, that is for practical purposes, the truth and the realness of things are synonymous. We are all children who say "really and truly." A reality which is taken in organic response so as to lead to subsequent reactions that are off the track and aside from the mark, while it is, existentially speaking, perfectly real, is not *good* reality. It lacks the hallmark of value. Since it is a certain *kind* of object which we want, one which will be as favorable as possible to a consistent and liberal or growing functioning, it is this kind, the *true* kind, which for us monopolizes the title of reality. Pragmatically, teleologically, this identification of truth and "reality" is sound and reasonable: rationalistically, it leads to the notion of the duplicate versions of reality, one absolute and static because exhausted; the other phenomenal and kept continually on the jump because otherwise its own inherent nothingness would lead to its total annihilation. Since it is only genuine or sincere things, things which are good for what they lay claim to in the way of consequences, which we want or are after, *morally* they alone are "real."

IV

So far we have been dealing with awareness as a fact—a fact there like any fact—and have been concerned to show that the subject-matter of awareness is, in any case, things in process of change; and in such change that the knowing function takes a hand in trying to guide it or steer it, so that *some* (and *not* other) consequences accrue. But what about the awareness itself? What happens when it is made the subject-matter of awareness? What sort of a thing is it? It is, I submit, mere sophistication (futile at that), to argue either that we cannot become aware of awareness without involving ourselves in an endless regress, or that whenever we are aware of anything we are thereby necessarily aware of awareness once for all, so that it has no character save a purely formal and empty one. Taken concretely, awareness is an event with certain specifiable conditions. We may indeed be aware of it formally, as a bare fact, just as we may be cognizant of an explosion without knowing anything of its nature. But we may also be aware of it in a curious and analytic spirit, undertaking to study it in detail. This inquiry, like any other inquiry, proceeds by determining conditions and consequences. Here awareness is a characteristic fact, presenting to inquiry its own characteristic ear-marks, and a valid knowledge of awareness is the same sort of thing as valid knowledge of the spectrum or of a trotting horse; it proceeds generically in the same way and must satisfy the same generic tests.

What, then, is awareness found to be? The following answer, dogmatically summary in form, involves positive difficulties, and glides over many points where our ignorance is still too great. But it represents a general trend of scientific inquiry, carried on, I hardly need say, on its own merits without respect to the pragmatic controversy. Awareness means *attention,* and attention means a crisis of some sort in an existent situation; a forking of the roads of some material, a tendency to go this way and that. It represents something the matter, something out of gear, or in some way menaced, insecure, problematical and strained. This state of tension, of ambiguous indications, projects and tendencies, is not merely in the "mind," it is nothing merely emotional. It is in the facts of the situation as transitive facts; the emotional or "subjective" disturbance is just a part of the larger disturbance. And if, employing the *language* of psychology, we say that attention is a phenomenon of conflicting habits, being the process of resolving this conflict by finding an act which functions for all the factors concerned, this language does not make the facts "merely psychological"—whatever that means.[5] The habits are as biologic as they are "personal," and as cosmic as they are biologic. They are the total order of things expressed in one way; just as a physical or chemical phenomenon is the same order expressed in another way. The statement in terms of conflict and readjustment of habits is at most one way of locating the disturbance in *things;* it furnishes no substitute for, or rival of, reality, and no "psychical" duplication.

If this be true, then awareness, even in its most perplexed and confused state, that of maximum doubt and precariousness of subject-matter, means things entering, *via* the particular thing known as organism, into a peculiar condition of differential—or additive—change. How can we refuse to raise and consider the question of how things in this condition are related to the prior state which emerges into it, and to the subsequent state of things into which it issues?[6]

Suppose the case to be awareness of a chair. Suppose that this

[5] What does it mean? Does the objectivity of fact disappear when the biologist gives it a biological statement? Why not object to his conclusions on the ground that they are "merely" biological?

[6] It is this question *of the relation to one another of different successive states of things* which the pragmatic method substitutes for the epistemological inquiry of how one sort of existence, purely mental, temporal but not spatial, immaterial, made of sublimated gaseous consciousness, can get beyond itself and have valid reference to a totally different kind of existence—spatial and extended; and how it can receive impressions from the latter, etc.,—all the questions which constitute that species of confirmed intellectual lock-jaw called epistemology.

awareness comes only when there is some problematic affair with which the chair is in some way—in whatever degree of remoteness—concerned. It may be a wonder whether it is a chair at all; or whether it is strong enough to stand on; or where I shall put it; or whether it is worth what I paid for it; or, as not infrequently happens, the situation involved in uncertainty may be some philosophic matter in which the perception of the chair is cited as evidence of illustration. (Humorously enough, awareness of it may even be cited in the course of a philosophic argument intended to show that awareness has nothing to do with situations of incompleteness and ambiguity.) Now what of the change the chair undergoes in entering this way into a situation of perplexed inquiry? Is this any part of the genuineness of that chair with which we are concerned? If not, where is the change found? In something totally different called "consciousness"? In that case how can the operations of inquiry, of observation and memory and reflection, ever have any assurance of getting referred back to the *right* object? Positively the presumption is that the *chair-of-which-we-are-speaking is* the chair *of-which-we-are-speaking;* it is the *same* thing that is out there which is also involved in the doubtful situation. Moreover, the reference to "consciousness" as the exclusive locus of the doubt only repeats the problem, for "consciousness," by the theory under consideration, means, after all, only the chair *as* concerned in the problematical situation. The *physical* chair remains unchanged, you say. Surely, if, as is altogether likely, what is *meant by* physical is precisely *that part* of the chair as object of total awareness which remains unaffected, for certain possible purposes, by entering for certain other actual purposes into the situation of awareness. But how can we segregate, *antecedently* to experimental inquiry, the "physical" chair from the chair which is now the object to be known; into what contradictions do we fall when we attempt to define the object of one awareness not in its own terms, but in terms of a selected type of object which is the appropriate subject-matter of some other cognizance!

But awareness means inquiry as well as doubt—there are the negative and positive, the retrospective and the prospective relationships of the thing. This means a genuinely *additive* quality—one of readjustment in prior things.[7] I know the dialectic argument that nothing can assume a new relation, because in order to do so it must

---

[7] We have arrived here, upon a more analytic platform, at the point made earlier concerning the fact that knowing *issues* in action which changes things.

already be completely related—when it comes from an absolutist I can understand why he holds it, even if I cannot understand the idea itself. But apart from this conceptual reasoning we must follow the lead of our subject-matter; and when we find a thing assuming new relations in the process of inquiry, must accept the fact, and frame our theory of things and of knowing to include it, not assert that it is impossible because we already have a theory of knowledge which precludes it. In inquiry, the existence which has become doubtful always undergoes experimental reconstruction. This may be largely imaginative or "speculative." We may view certain things *as if* placed under varying conditions, and consider what then happens to them. But such differences are really transformative as far as they go,—and besides, such inquiries never reach conclusions finally justifiable. In important and persistent inquiry, we insist upon something in the way of actual physical making—be it only a diagram. In other words, *science,* or knowing in its honorific sense, is experimental, involving physical construction. We insist upon something being *done about* it, that we may see how the idea when carried into effect comports with the other things through which our activities are hedged in and released. To avoid this conclusion by saying that knowing makes no difference in the "truth," but merely is the preliminary exercise which discovers it, is that old friend whose acquaintance we have repeatedly made in this discussion: the fallacy of confusing an existence anteceding knowing with the object which terminates and fulfills it. For knowing to make a difference in its own final term is gross self-stultification; it is none the less so when the aim of knowing is precisely to guide things straight up to this term. When "truth" means the accomplished introduction of certain new differences into conditions, why be foolish enough to introduce other differences, which are not wanted since they are irrelevant and misleading?

Were it not for the teachings of sad experience, it would not be necessary to add that the change in environment made by knowing is not a total or miraculous change. Transformation, readjustment, reconstruction, all imply prior existences: existences which have characters and behaviors of their own which must be accepted, consulted, humored, manipulated or made light of, in all kinds of differing ways in the different contexts of different problems. Making a difference in reality does not mean making any more difference than we find by experimentation can be made under the given conditions—even though we may still hope for different fortune another time under other circumstances. Still less does it mean making a thing into an unreality, though the pragmatist is sometimes criticized as if any change in reality must be a change into non-reality. There are difficulties, indeed, both dialectic, and real or practical, in the fact of change—in the fact that only a permanent can change and that change is alteration of a permanent. But till we enjoin botanists and chemists from referring to changes and transformations in their subject-matter on the ground that for anything to change means for it to part with its reality, we may as well permit the logician to make similar references.

V

Sub specie aeternitatis? or *sub specie generationis?* I am susceptible to the esthetic charm of the former ideal—who is not? There are moments of relaxation: there are moments when the demand for peace, to be let alone and relieved from the continual claim of the world in which we live that we be up and doing something about it, seems irresistible; when the responsibilities imposed by living in a moving universe seem intolerable. We contemplate with equal mind the thought of the eternal sleep. But, after all, this is a matter in which reality and not the philosopher is the court of final jurisdiction. Outside of philosophy, the question seems fairly settled; in science, in poetry, in social organization, in religion—wherever religion is not hopelessly at the mercy of a Frankenstein philosophy which it originally called into being to be its own slave. Under such circumstances there is danger that the philosophy which tries to escape the form of generation by taking refuge under the form of eternity will only come under the form of a bygone generation. To try to escape from the snares and pitfalls of time by recourse to traditional problems and interests:—rather than that let the dead bury their own dead. Better it is for philosophy to err in active participation in the living struggles and issues of its own age and times than to maintain an immune monastic impeccability, without relevancy and bearing in the generating ideas of its contemporary present. In the one case, it will be respected, as we respect all virtue that attests its sincerity by sharing in the perplexities and failures, as well as in the joys and triumphs, of endeavor. In the other case, it bids fair to share the fate of whatever preserves its gentility, but not its activity, in descent from better days; namely, to be snugly ensconced in the consciousness of its own respectability.

15. The Pattern of Inquiry*

At the beginning of Part II of his *Logic: The Theory of Inquiry*, John Dewey attempts to lay the groundwork for his operational approach to the problem of inquiry. He defines inquiry as "the controlled or directed transformation of an indeterminate situation into one that is so determinate in its constituent distinctions and relations as to convert the elements of the original situation into a unified whole."

Continuous with the theme of his earlier writings, several of which are reprinted above, Dewey focuses on the functional character of logical forms. He holds that "formal conceptions arise out of the ordinary transactions; they are not imposed upon them from on high or from any external and *a priori* source." And reminiscent of his views on "conclusions" and "consummations" in *Art as Experience*, Dewey contends that "objects" are not fixed things to be thought about but are both "outcomes of inquiries" and "*means* of attaining knowledge of something else." This chapter is the key to Dewey's book on *Logic* and in summary fashion contains the major themes and judgments of his mature theory of knowing.

The first chapter set forth the fundamental thesis of this volume: Logical forms accrue to subject-matter when the latter is subjected to controlled inquiry. It also set forth some of the implications of this thesis for the nature of logical theory. The second and third chapters stated the independent grounds, biological and cultural, for holding that logic is a theory of experiential naturalistic subject-matter. The first of the next two chapters developed the theme with reference to the relations of the logic of common sense and science, while the second discussed Aristotelian logic as the organized formulation of the language of Greek life, when that language is regarded as the expression of the meanings of Greek culture and of the significance attributed to various forms of natural existence. It was held throughout these chap-

* From John Dewey, *Logic: The Theory of Inquiry*, pp. 101-119. Copyright 1938 by Holt, Rinehart and Winston, Inc. Copyright © 1966 by Roberta L. Dewey. Reprinted by permission of Holt, Rinehart and Winston, Inc.

ters that inquiry, in spite of the diverse subjects to which it applies, and the consequent diversity of its special techniques has a common structure or pattern: that this common structure is applied both in common sense and science, although because of the nature of the problems with which they are concerned, the emphasis upon the factors involved varies·widely in the two modes. We now come to the consideration of the common pattern.

The fact that new formal properties accrue to subject-matter in virtue of its subjection to certain types of operation is familiar to us in certain fields, even though the idea corresponding to this fact is unfamiliar in logic. Two outstanding instances are provided by art and law. In music, the dance, painting, sculpture, literature and the other fine arts, subject-matters of everyday experience are *trans*formed by the development of forms which render certain products of doing and making objects of fine art. The materials of legal regulations are transactions occurring in the ordinary activities of human beings and groups of human beings; transactions of a sort that are engaged in apart from law. As certain aspects and phases of these transactions are legally formalized, conceptions such as misdemeanor, crime, torts, contracts and so on arise. These formal conceptions arise out of the ordinary transactions; they are not imposed upon them from on high or from any external and *a priori* source. But when they are formed they are also *formative*; they regulate the proper conduct of the activities out of which they develop.

All of these formal legal conceptions are operational in nature. They formulate and define *ways* of operation on the part of those engaged in the transactions into which a number of persons or groups enter as "parties," and the ways of operation followed by those who have jurisdiction in deciding whether established forms have been complied with, together with the existential consequences of failure of observation. The forms in question are not fixed and eternal. They change, though as a rule too slowly, with changes in the habitual transactions in which individuals and groups engage and the changes that occur in the consequences of these transactions. However hypothetical may be the conception that *logical* forms accrue to existential materials in virtue of the control exercised over inquiries in order that they may fulfil their end, the conception is descriptive of something that verifiably exists. The development of forms in consequence of operations is an established fact in some fields; it is not invented *ad hoc* in relation to logical forms.

The existence of inquiries is not a matter of doubt. They enter into every area of life and into every aspect of every area. In everyday living, men examine; they turn things over intellectually; they infer and judge as "naturally" as they reap and sow, produce and exchange commodities. As a mode of conduct, inquiry is as accessible to objective study as are these other modes of behavior. Because of the intimate and decisive way in which inquiry and its conclusions enter into the management of all affairs of life, no study of the latter is adequate save as it is noted how they are affected by the methods and instruments of inquiry that currently obtain. Quite apart, then, from the particular hypothesis about logical forms that is put forth, study of the objective facts of inquiry is a matter of tremendous import, practically and intellectually. These materials provide the theory of logical forms with a subject-matter that is not only objective but is objective in a fashion that enables logic to avoid the three mistakes most characteristic of its history.

1. In virtue of its concern with objectively observable subject-matter by reference to which reflective conclusions can be tried and tested, dependence upon subjective and "mentalistic" states and processes is eliminated.

2. The distinctive existence and nature of forms is acknowledged. Logic is not compelled, as historic "empirical" logic felt compelled to do, to reduce logical forms to mere transcripts of the empirical materials that antecede the existence of the former. Just as art-forms and legal forms are capable of independent discussion and development, so are logical forms, even though the "independence" in question is intermediate, not final and complete. As in the case of these other forms, they originate *out* of experiential material, and when constituted introduce new ways of operating with prior materials, which ways modify the material out of which they develop.

3. Logical theory is liberated from the unobservable, transcendental and "intuitional."

When methods and results of inquiry are studied as objective data, the distinction that has often been drawn between noting and reporting the ways in which men *do* think, and prescribing the ways in which they *ought* to think, takes on a very different interpretation from that usually given. The usual interpretation is in terms of the difference between the psychological and the logical, the latter consisting of "norms" provided from some source wholly outside of and independent of "experience."

The way in which men *do* "think" denotes, as it is *here* interpreted, simply the ways in which men at a given time carry on their inquiries. So far as it is used to register a difference from the ways in which they *ought* to think, it denotes a difference like that between good and bad farming or good and bad medical practice. Men think in ways they should not when they follow methods of inquiry that experience of past inquiries shows are not competent to reach the intended end of the inquiries in question.

Everybody knows that today there are in vogue methods of farming generally followed in the past which compare very unfavorably in their results with those obtained by practices that have already been introduced and tested. When an expert tells a farmer he *should* do thus and so, he is not setting up for a bad farmer an ideal drawn from the blue. He is instructing him in methods that have been tried and that have proved successful in procuring results. In a similar way we are able to contrast various kinds of inquiry that are in use or that have been used in respect to their economy and efficiency in reaching warranted conclusions. We know that some methods of inquiry are better than others in just the same way in which we know that some methods of surgery, farming, road-making, navigating or what-not are better than others. It does not follow in any of these cases that the "better" methods are ideally perfect, or that they are regulative or "normative" because of conformity to some absolute form. They are the methods which experience up to the present time shows to be the best methods available for achieving certain results, while abstraction of these methods does supply a (relative) norm or standard for further undertakings.

The search for the pattern of inquiry is, accordingly, not one instituted in the dark or at large. It is checked and controlled by knowledge of the kinds of inquiry that have and that have not worked; methods which, as was pointed out earlier, can be so compared as to yield reasoned or rational conclusions. For, through comparison-contrast, we ascertain *how and why* certain means and agencies have provided warrantably assertible conclusions, while others have not and *cannot* do so in the sense in which "cannot" expresses an intrinsic incompatibility between means used and consequences attained.

We may now ask: What is the *definition* of Inquiry? That is, what is the most highly generalized conception of inquiry which can be justifiably formulated? The definition that will be expanded, directly in the present chapter and indirectly in the following chapters, is as follows: *Inquiry is the controlled or directed transformation of an indeterminate situation into one that is so determinate in its constituent distinctions and relations as to convert the elements of the original situation into a unified whole.*[1]

---

[1] The word "situation" is to be understood in the sense already expounded.

The orginal indeterminate situation is not only "open" to inquiry, but it is open in the sense that its constituents do not hang together. The determinate situtation on the other hand, *qua* outcome of inquiry, is a closed and, as it were, finished situation or "universe of experience." "Controlled or directed" in the above formula refers to the fact that inquiry is competent in any given case in the degree in which the operations involved in it actually do terminate in the establishment of an objectively unified existential situation. In the intermediate course of transition and transformation of the indeterminate situation, *discourse* through use of symbols is employed as means. In received logical terminology, propositions, or terms and the relations between them, are instrinsically involved.

I. *The Antecedent Conditions of Inquiry: The Indeterminate Situation.* Inquiry and questioning, up to a certain point, are synonymous terms. We inquire when we question; and we inquire when we seek for whatever will provide an answer to a question asked. Thus it is of the very nature of the indeterminate situation which evokes inquiry to be *questionable;* or, in terms of actuality instead of potentiality, to be uncertain, unsettled, disturbed. The peculiar quality of what pervades the given materials, constituting them a situation, is not just uncertainty at large; it is a unique doubtfulness which makes that situation to be just and only the situation it is. It is this unique quality that not only evokes the particular inquiry engaged in but that exercises control over its special procedures. Otherwise, one procedure in inquiry would be as likely to occur and to be effective as any other. Unless a situation is uniquely qualified in its very indeterminateness, there is a condition of complete panic; response to it takes the form of blind and wild overt activities. Stating the matter from the personal side, we have "lost our heads." A variety of names serves to characterize indeterminate situations. They are disturbed, troubled, ambiguous, confused, full of conflicting tendencies, obscure, etc.

It is the *situation* that has these traits. *We* are doubtful because the situation is inherently doubtful. Personal states of doubt that are not evoked by and are not relative to some existential situation are pathological; when they are extreme they constitute the mania of doubting. Consequently, situations that are disturbed and troubled, confused or obscure, cannot be straightened out, cleared up and put in order, by manipulation of our personal states of mind. The attempt to settle them by such manipulations involves what psychiatrists call "withdrawal from reality." Such an attempt is pathological as far as it goes, and when it goes far it is the source of some form of actual insanity. The habit of disposing of the doubtful as if it belonged only to *us* rather than to the existential situation in which we are caught and implicated is an inheritance from subjectivisitic psychology. The biological antecedent conditions of an unsettled situation are involved in that state of imbalance in organic-environmental interactions which has already been described. Restoration of integration can be effected, in one case as in the other, only by operations which actually modify existing conditions, not by merely "mental" processes.

It is, accordingly, a mistake to suppose that a situation is doubtful only in a "subjective" sense. The notion that in actual existence everything is completely determinate has been rendered questionable by the progress of physical science itself. Even if it had not been, complete determination would not hold of existences as an *environment*. For Nature is an environment only as it is involved in interaction with an organism, or self, or whatever name be used.[2]

Every such interaction is a temporal process, not a momentary cross-sectional occurrence. The situation in which it occurs is indeterminate, therefore, with respect to its *issue*. If we call it *confused*, then it is meant that its outcome cannot be anticipated. It is called *obscure* when its course of movement permits of final consequences that cannot be clearly made out. It is called *conflicting* when it tends to evoke discordant responses. Even were existential conditions unqualifiedly determinate in and of themselves, they are indeterminate in *significance:* that is, in what they import and portend in their interaction with the organism. The organic responses that enter into the production of the state of affairs that is temporally later and sequential are just as existential as are environing conditions.

The immediate *locus* of the problem concerns, then, what kind of responses the organism shall make. It concerns the interaction of organic responses and environing conditions in their movement toward an existential issue. It is a commonplace that in any troubled state of affairs *things* will come out differently according to what is done. The farmer won't get grain unless he plants and tills; the general will win or lose the battle according to the way he conducts it, and so on. Neither

---

[2] Except of course a purely mentalistic name, like *consciousness*. The alleged problem of "interactionism" versus automatism, parallelism, etc., is a problem (and an insoluble one) because of the assumption involved in its statement—the assumption, namely, that the interaction in question is with something mental instead of with biological-cultural human beings.

the grain nor the tilling, neither the outcome of the battle nor the conduct of it, are "mental" events. Organic interaction becomes inquiry when existential consequences are anticipated; when environing conditions are examined with reference to their potentialities; and when responsive activities are selected and ordered with reference to actualization of some of the potentialities, rather than others, in a final existential situation. Resolution of the indeterminate situation is active and operational. If the inquiry is adequately directed, the final issue is the unified situation that has been mentioned.

II. *Institution of a Problem.* The unsettled or indeterminate situation might have been called a *problematic* situation. This name would have been, however, proleptic and anticipatory. The indeterminate situation becomes problematic in the very process of being subjected to inquiry. The indeterminate situation comes into existence from existential causes, just as does, say, the organic imbalance of hunger. There is nothing intellectual or cognitive in the existence of such situations, although they are the necessary condition of cognitive operations or inquiry. In themselves they are precognitive. The first result of evocation of inquiry is that the situation is taken, adjudged, to be problematic. To see that a situation requires inquiry is the initial step in inquiry.[3]

Qualification of a situation as problematic does not, however, carry inquiry far. It is but an initial step in institution of a problem. A problem is not a task to be performed which a person puts upon himself or that is placed upon him by others—like a so-called arithmetical "problem" in school work. A problem represents the partial transformation by inquiry of a problematic situation into a determinate situation. It is a familiar and significant saying that a problem well put is half-solved. To find out *what* the problem and problems are which a problematic situation presents to be inquired into, is to be well along in inquiry. To mistake the problem involved is to cause subsequent inquiry to be irrelevant or to go astray. Without a problem, there is blind groping in the dark. The way in which the problem is conceived decides what specific suggestions are entertained and which are dismissed; what data are selected and which rejected; it is the criterion for relevancy and irrelevancy of hypotheses and conceptual structures. On the other hand,

---

[3] If by "two-valued logic" is meant a logic that regards "true and false" as the sole logical values, then such a logic is necessarily so truncated that clearness and consistency in logical doctrine are impossible. Being the matter of a problem is a primary logical property.

to set up a problem that does not grow out of an actual situation is to start on a course of dead work, nonetheless dead because the work is "busy work." Problems that are self-set are mere excuses for seeming to do something intellectual, something that has the semblance but not the substance of scientific activity.

III. *The Determination of a Problem-Solution.* Statement of a problematic situation in terms of a problem has no meaning save as the problem instituted has, in the very terms of its statement, reference to a possible solution. Just because a problem well stated is on its way to solution, the determining of a genuine problem is a *progressive* inquiry; the cases in which a problem and its probable solution flash upon an inquirer are cases where much prior ingestion and digestion have occurred. If we assume, prematurely, that the problem involved is definite and clear, subsequent inquiry proceeds on the wrong track. Hence the question arises: How is the formation of a genuine problem so controlled that further inquiries will move toward a solution?

The first step in answering this question is to recognize that no situation which is *completely* indeterminate can possibly be converted into a problem having definite constituents. The first step then is to search out the *constituents* of a given situation which, as constituents, are settled. When an alarm of fire is sounded in a crowded assembly hall, there is much that is indeterminate as regards the activities that may produce a favorable issue. One may get out safely or one may be trampled and burned. The fire is characterized, however, by some settled traits. It is, for example, located *somewhere*. Then the aisles and exits are at fixed places. Since they are settled or determinate in *existence*, the first step in institution of a problem is to settle them in *observation*. There are other factors which, while they are not as temporally and spatially fixed, are yet observable constituents; for example, the behavior and movements of other members of the audience. All of these observed conditions taken together constitute "the facts of the case." They constitute the terms of the problem, because they are conditions that must be reckoned with or taken account of in any relevant solution that is proposed.

A *possible* relevant solution is then suggested by the determination of factual conditions which are secured by observation. The possible solution presents itself, therefore, as an *idea*, just as the terms of the problem (which are facts) are instituted by observation. Ideas are anticipated consequences (forecasts) of what will happen when certain operations are executed under and with respect to observed conditions.[4] Observation of facts and suggested meanings or ideas arise and develop in correspondence with each other. The more the facts of the case come to light in consequence of being subjected to observation, the clearer and more pertinent become the conceptions of the way the problem constituted by these facts is to be dealt with. On the other side, the clearer the idea, the more definite, as a truism, become the operations of observation and of execution that must be performed in order to resolve the situation.

An idea is first of all an anticipation of something that may happen; it marks a *possibility*. When it is said, as it sometimes is, that science is *prediction*, the anticipation that constitutes every idea an idea is grounded in a set of controlled observations and of regulated conceptual ways of interpreting them. Because inquiry is a progressive determination of a problem and its possible solution, ideas differ in grade according to the stage of inquiry reached. At first, save in highly familiar matters, they are vague. They occur at first simply as suggestions; suggestions just spring up, flash upon us, occur to us. They may then become stimuli to direct an overt activity but they have as yet no logical status. Every idea originates as a suggestion, but not every suggestion is an idea. The suggestion becomes an idea when it is examined with reference to its functional fitness; its capacity as a means of resolving the given situation.

This examination takes the form of reasoning, as a result of which we are able to appraise better than we were at the outset, the pertinency and weight of the meaning now entertained with respect to its functional capacity. But the final test of its possession of these properties is determined when it actually functions—that is, when it is put into operation so as to institute by means of observations facts not previously observed, and is then used to organize them with other facts into a coherent whole.

Because suggestions and ideas are of that which is not present in given existence, the meanings which they involve must be embodied in some symbol. Without some kind of symbol no idea; a meaning that is

[4] The theory of *ideas* that has been held in psychology and epistemology since the time of Locke's successors is completely irrelevant and obstructive in logical theory. For in treating them as copies of perceptions or "impressions," it ignores the prospective and anticipatory character that defines *being* an idea. Failure to define ideas functionally, in the reference they have to a solution of a problem, is one reason they have been treated as merely "mental." The notion, on the other hand, that ideas are fantasies is a derivative. Fantasies arise when the function an idea performs is ruled out when it is entertained and developed.

completely disembodied can not be entertained or used. Since an existence (which *is* an existence) is the support and vehicle of a meaning and is a symbol instead of a merely physical existence only in this respect, embodied meanings or ideas are capable of objective survey and development. To "look at an idea" is not a mere literary figure of speech.

"Suggestions" have received scant courtesy in logical theory. It is true that when they just "pop into our heads," because of the workings of the psycho-physical organism, they are not logical. But they are both the conditions and the primary stuff of logical ideas. The traditional empiristic theory reduced them, as has already been pointed out, to mental copies of physical things and assumed that they were *per se* identical with ideas. Consequently it ignored the function of ideas in directing observation and in ascertaining relevant facts. The rationalistic school, on the other hand, saw clearly that "facts" apart from ideas are trivial, that they acquire import and significance only in relation to ideas. But at the same time it failed to attend to the operative and functional nature of the latter. Hence, it treated ideas as equivalent to the ultimate structure of "Reality." The Kantian formula that apart from each other "perceptions are blind and conceptions empty" marks a profound logical insight. The insight, however, was radically distorted because perceptual and conceptual contents were supposed to originate from different sources and thus required a third activity, that of synthetic understanding, to bring them together. In logical fact, perceptual and conceptual materials are instituted in functional correlativity with each other, in such a manner that the former locates and describes the problem while the latter represents a possible method of solution. Both are determinations in and by inquiry of the original problematic situation whose pervasive quality controls their institution and their contents. Both are finally checked by their capacity to work together to introduce a resolved unified situation. As distinctions they represent logical divisions of labor.

IV. *Reasoning*. The necessity of developing the meaning-contents of ideas in their relations to one another has been incidentally noted. This process, operating with symbols (constituting propositions) is reasoning in the sense of ratiocination or rational discourse.[5] When a suggested meaning is immediately accepted, inquiry is cut short. Hence the conclusion reached is not grounded, even if it happens to be correct. The

---

[5] "Reasoning" is sometimes used to designate *inference* as well as ratiocination. When so used in logic the tendency is to identify inference and implication and thereby seriously to confuse logical theory.

check upon immediate acceptance is the examination of the meaning as a meaning. This examination consists in noting what the meaning in question implies in relation to other meanings in the system of which it is a member, the formulated relation constituting a proposition. If such and such a relation of meanings is accepted, then we are committed to such and such other relations of meanings because of their membership in the same system. Through a series of intermediate meanings, a meaning is finally reached which is more clearly *relevant* to the problem in hand than the originally suggested idea. It indicates operations which can be performed to test its applicability, whereas the original idea is usually too vague to determine crucial operations. In other words, the idea or meaning when developed in discourse directs the activities which, when executed, provide needed evidential material.

The point made can be most readily appreciated in connection with scientific reasoning. An hypothesis, once suggested and entertained, is developed in relation to other conceptual structures until it receives a form in which it can instigate and direct an experiment that will disclose precisely those conditions which have the maximum possible force in determining whether the hypothesis should be accepted or rejected. Or it may be that the experiment will indicate what modifications are required in the hypothesis so that it may be applicable, i.e., suited to interpret and organize the facts of the case. In many familiar situations, the meaning that is most relevant has been settled because of the eventuations of experiments in prior cases so that it is applicable almost immediately upon its occurrence. But, indirectly, if not directly, an idea or suggestion that is not developed in terms of the constellation of meanings to which it belongs can lead only to overt response. Since the latter terminates inquiry, there is then no adequate inquiry into the meaning that is used to settle the given situation, and the conclusion is in so far logically ungrounded.

V. *The Operational Character of Facts-Meanings.* It was stated that the observed facts of the case and the ideational contents expressed in ideas are related to each other, as, respectively, a clarification of the problem involved and the proposal of some possible solution; that they are, accordingly, functional divisions in the work of inquiry. Observed facts in their office of locating and describing the problem are existential; ideational subject-matter is non-existential. How, then, do they cooperate with each other in the resolution of an existential situation? The problem is insoluble save as it is recognized that both observed facts and entertained ideas are operational. Ideas are operational in that they instigate and direct further operations of observation; they are proposals and plans for acting upon existing conditions to bring new facts to light and to organize all the selected facts into a coherent whole.

What is meant by calling facts operational? Upon the negative side what is meant is that they are not self-sufficient and complete in themselves. They are selected and described, as we have seen, for a purpose, namely statement of the problem involved in such a way that its material both indicates a meaning relevant to resolution of the difficulty and serves to test its worth and validity. In regulated inquiry facts are selected and arranged with the express intent of fulfilling this office. They are not merely *results* of operations of observation which are executed with the aid of bodily organs and auxiliary instruments of art, but they are the particular facts and kinds of facts that will link up with one another in the definite ways that are required to produce a definite end. Those not found to connect with others in furtherance of this end are dropped and others are sought for. Being functional, they are necessarily operational. Their function is to serve as evidence and their evidential quality is judged on the basis of their capacity to form an ordered whole in response to operations prescribed by the ideas they occasion and support. If "the facts of the case" were final and complete in themselves, if they did not have a special operative force in resolution of the problematic situation, they could not serve as evidence.

The operative force of facts is apparent when we consider that no fact in isolation has evidential potency. Facts are evidential and are tests of an idea in so far as they are capable of being organized with one another. The organization can be achieved only as they *interact* with one another. When the problematic situation is such as to require extensive inquiries to effect its resolution, a series of interactions intervenes. Some observed facts point to an idea that stands for a possible solution. This idea evokes more observations. Some of the newly observed facts link up with those previously observed and are such as to rule out other observed things with respect to their evidential function. The new order of facts suggests a modified idea (or hypothesis) which occasions new observations whose result again determines a new order of facts, and so on until the existing order is both unified and complete. In the course of this serial process, the ideas that represent possible solutions are tested or "proved."

Meantime, the orders of fact, which present themselves in consequence of the experimental observations the ideas call out and direct, are *trial* facts. They are provisional. They are "facts" if they are observed by sound organs and techniques. But they are not on that account the *facts of the case*. They are tested or "proved" with respect to their evidential function just as much as ideas (hypotheses) are tested with reference to their power to exercise the function of resolution. The operative force of both ideas and facts is thus practically recognized in the degree in which they are connected with *experiment*. Naming them "operational" is but a theoretical recognition of what is involved when inquiry satisfies the conditions imposed by the necessity for experiment.

I recur, in this connection, to what has been said about the necessity for symbols in inquiry. It is obvious, on the face of matters, that a possible mode of solution must be carried in symbolic form since it is a possibility, not an assured present existence. Observed facts, on the other hand, are existentially present. It might seem therefore, that symbols are not required for referring to them. But if they are not carried and treated by means of symbols, they lose their provisional character, and in losing this character they are categorically asserted and inquiry comes to an end. The carrying on of inquiry requires that the facts be taken as *re*presentative and not just as *pre*-sented. This demand is met by formulating them in propositions—that is, by means of symbols. Unless they are so represented they relapse into the total qualitative situation.

VI. *Common Sense and Scientific Inquiry*. The discussion up to this point has proceeded in general terms which recognize no distinction between common sense and scientific inquiry. We have now reached a point where the community of pattern in these two distinctive modes of inquiry should receive explicit attention. It was said in earlier chapters that the difference between them resides in their respective subject-matters, not in their basic logical forms and relations; that the difference in subject-matters is due to the difference in the problems respectively involved; and, finally, that this difference sets up a difference in the ends or objective consequences they are concerned to achieve. Because common sense problems and inquiries have to do with the interactions into which living creatures enter in connection with environing conditions in order to establish objects of use and enjoyment, the symbols employed are those which have been determined in the habitual culture of a group. They form a system but the system is practical rather than intellectual. It is constituted by the traditions, occupations, techniques, interests, and established institutions of the group. The meanings that compose it are carried in the common everyday language of communication between members of the group. The meanings involved in this common language system determine what individuals of the group may and may not do in relation to physical objects and in relations to one another. They regulate *what* can be used and enjoyed and *how* use and enjoyment shall occur.

Because the symbol-meaning systems involved are connected directly with cultural life-activities and are related to each other in virtue of this connection, the specific meanings which are present have reference to the specific and limited environing conditions under which the group lives. Only those things of the environment that are taken, according to custom and tradition, as having connection with and bearing upon this life, enter into the meaning system. There is no such thing as disinterested intellectual concern with either physical or social matters. For, until the rise of science, there were no problems of common sense that called for such inquiry. Disinterestedness existed practically in the demand that group interests and concerns be put above private needs and interests. But there was no intellectual disinterestedness beyond the activities, interests and concerns of the group. In other words, there was no science as such, although, as was earlier pointed out, there did exist information and techniques which were available for the purposes of scientific inquiry and out of which the latter subsequently grew.

In scientific inquiry, then, meanings are related to one another on the ground of their character *as* meanings, freed from direct reference to the concerns of a limited group. Their intellectual abstractness is a product of this liberation, just as the "concrete" is practically identified by directness of connection with environmental interactions. Consequently a new language, a new system of symbols related together on a new basis, comes into existence, and in this new language semantic coherence, as such, is the controlling consideration. To repeat what has already been said, connection with problems of use and enjoyment is the source of the dominant role of qualities, sensible and moral, and of ends in common sense.

In science, since meanings are determined on the ground of their relation as meanings to one another, *relations* become the objects of inquiry and qualities are relegated to a secondary status, playing a part only as far as they assist in institution of relations. They are subordinate because they have an instrumental office, instead of being themselves, as in prescientific common sense, the matters of final importance. The enduring hold of common sense is testified to historically by the long time it took before it was seen that scientific objects are strictly relational. First tertiary qualities were eliminated; it was recognized that moral qualities are not agencies in determining the structure of nature. Then secondary qualities, the wet-dry, hot-cold, light-heavy, which were the explanatory principles of physical phenomena in Greek science, were ejected. But so-called primary qualities took their place, as with Newton and the Lockeian formulation of Newtonian existential postulates. It was not until the threshold of our time was reached that scientific inquiries perceived that their own problems and methods required an interpretation of "primary qualities" in terms of relations, such as position, motion and temporal span. In the structure of distinctively scientific objects these relations are indifferent to qualities.

The foregoing is intended to indicate that the different objectives of common sense and of scientific inquiry demand different subject-matters and that this difference in subject-matters is not incompatible with the existence of a common pattern in both types. There are, of course, secondary logical forms which reflect the distinction of properties involved in the change from qualitative and teleological subject-matter to non-qualitative and non-teleological relations. But they occur and operate within the described community of pattern. They are explicable, and explicable only, on the ground of the distinctive problems generated by scientific subject-matter. The independence of scientific objects from limited and fairly direct reference to the environment as a factor in activities of use and enjoyment, is equivalent, as has already been intimated, to their *abstract* character. It is also equivalent to their *general* character in the sense in which the generalizations of science are different from the generalizations with which common sense is familiar. The generality of *all* scientific subject-matter as such means that it is freed from restriction to conditions which present themselves at particular times and places. Their reference is to *any* set of time and place conditions—a statement which is not to be confused with the doctrine that they have no reference to actual existential occasions. Reference to time-place of existence is necessarily involved, but it is reference to whatever set of existences fulfils the general relations laid down in and by the constitution of the scientific object.[6]

Summary. Since a number of points have been discussed, it will be well to round up conclusions reached about them in a summary statement of the structure of the common pattern of inquiry. Inquiry is the directed or controlled transformation of an indeterminate situation into

---

[6] The consequences that follow are directly related to the statement in Ch. IV that the elimination of qualities and ends is intermediate; that, in fact, the construction of purely relational objects has enormously liberated and expanded common sense uses and enjoyments by conferring control over production of qualities, by enabling new ends to be realistically instituted, and by providing competent means for achieving them.

a determinately unified one. The transition is achieved by means of operations of two kinds which are in functional correspondence with each other. One kind of operations deals with ideational or conceptual subject-matter. This subject-matter stands for possible ways and ends of resolution. It anticipates a solution, and is marked off from fancy because, or, in so far as, it becomes operative in instigation and direction of new observations yielding new factual material. The other kind of operations is made up of activities involving the techniques and organs of observation. Since these operations are existential they modify the prior existential situation, bring into high relief conditions previously obscure, and relegate to the background other aspects that were at the outset conspicuous. The ground and criterion of the execution of this work of emphasis, selection and arrangement is to delimit the problem in such a way that existential material may be provided with which to test the ideas that represent possible modes of solution. Symbols, defining terms and propositions, are necessarily required in order to retain and carry forward both ideational and existential subject-matters in order that they may serve their proper functions in the control of inquiry. Otherwise the problem is taken to be closed and inquiry ceases.

One fundamentally important phase of the transformation of the situation which constitutes inquiry is central in the treatment of judgment and its functions. The transformation is existential and hence temporal. The pre-cognitive unsettled situation can be settled only by modification of its constituents. Experimental operations change existing conditions. Reasoning, as such, can provide means for effecting the change of conditions but by itself cannot effect it. Only execution of existential operations directed by an idea in which ratiocination terminates can bring about the re-ordering of environing conditions required to produce a settled and unified situation. Since this principle also applies to the meanings that are elaborated in science, the experimental production and re-arrangement of physical conditions involved in natural science is further evidence of the unity of the pattern of inquiry. The temporal quality of inquiry means, then, something quite other than that the process of inquiry takes time. It means that the objective subject-matter of inquiry undergoes temporal modification.

Terminological. Were it not that knowledge is related to inquiry as a product to the operations by which it is produced, no distinctions requiring special differentiating designations would exist. Material would merely be a matter of knowledge or of ignorance and error; that would be all that could be said. The content of any given proposition would have the values "true" and "false" as final and exclusive attributes. But if knowledge is related to inquiry as its warrantably assertible product, and if inquiry is progressive and temporal, then the material inquired into reveals distinctive properties which need to be designated by distinctive names. As *undergoing* inquiry, the material has a different logical import from that which it has as the *outcome* of inquiry. In its first capacity and status, it will be called by the general name *subject-matter*. When it is necessary to refer to subject-matter in the context of either observation or ideation, the name *content* will be used, and, particularly on account of its *representative* character, content of propositions.

The name *objects* will be reserved for subject-matter so far as it has been produced and ordered in settled form by means of inquiry; proleptically, objects are the *objectives* of inquiry. The apparent ambiguity of using "objects" for this purpose (since the word is regularly applied to things that are observed or thought of) is only apparent. For things exist *as* objects for us only as they have been previously determined as outcomes of inquiries. When used in carrying on new inquiries in new problematic situations, they are known as objects in virtue of prior inquiries which warrant their assertibility. In the new situation, they are *means* of attaining knowledge of something else. In the strict sense, they are part of the *contents* of inquiry as the word content was defined above. But retrospectively (that is, as products of prior determination in inquiry) they are objects.

IV

The Metaphysics
of Experience

With the exception of the essay on "The Postulate of Immediate Empiricism," which acts as a transition between Dewey's early pragmatic epistemology and his mature philosophy of experience, the material in this section is from *Experience and Nature*. Delivered originally as the Carus Lectures in 1922, this book stands as Dewey's major effort to present a full-scale analysis of traditional philosophical concerns in the context of his own metaphysics of experience.

16. The Postulate of Immediate Empiricism*

Although written during the time when Dewey was attempting to frame out a pragmatic epistemology, this essay is characterized by an emphasis on the meaning of experience and thereby serves as a transition to his later views in *Experience and Nature*. Entitling his own version of the new movement in philosophy during the first decade of this century as "immediate empiricism," Dewey postulates that things—anything, everything, in the ordinary or nontechnical use of the term 'thing'—are what they are experienced as." This is not to be confused with the contention that things are what they are "known" as, for in Dewey's view, "knowing is one mode of experiencing" but not the sole or only genuine mode.

Now, more so than finding out what we know about, the primary philosophical question is "to find out *what* sort of experience knowing is—or, concretely how things are ex-

* From John Dewey, *The Influence of Darwin on Philosophy: And Other Essays on Contemporary Thought*, pp. 226-41. Copyright 1910 by Holt, Rinehart and Winston, Inc. Copyright 1938 by John Dewey. Reprinted by permission of Holt, Rinehart and Winston, Inc. (Published originally in 1905.)

perienced when they are experienced *as* known things.''
Implicit, but left undeveloped in this essay, is Dewey's corollary view that experience is cognitive in a wider sense than
that conveyed by speaking of "known objects," as witness his
subsequent views on aesthetic and religious experience.

The criticisms made upon that vital but still unformed movement
variously termed radical empiricism, pragmatism, humanism, func-
tionalism, according as one or another aspect of it is uppermost, have
left me with a conviction that the *fundamental* difference is not so much
in matters overtly discussed as in a presupposition that remains tacit: a
presupposition as to what experience is and means. To do my little part
in clearing up the confusion, I shall try to make my own presupposition
explicit. The object of this paper is, then, to set forth what I understand
to be the postulate and the criterion of *immediate empiricism*.[1]

Immediate empiricism postulates that things—anything, everything,
in the ordinary or non-technical use of the term "thing"—are what they
are experienced as. Hence, if one wishes to describe anything truly, his
task is to tell what it is experienced as being. If it is a horse that is to be
described, or the *equus* that is to be defined, then must the horse-trader,
or the jockey, or the timid family man who wants a "safe driver," or the
zoologist or the paleontologist tell us what the horse is which is experienced. If these accounts turn out different in some respects, as well
as congruous in others, this is no reason for assuming the content of one
to be exclusively "real," and that of others to be "phenomenal"; for
each account of what is experienced will manifest that it is the account
of the horse-dealer, or *of* the zoologist, and hence will give the conditions requisite for understanding the differences as well as the agreements of the various accounts. And the principle varies not a whit if we
bring in the psychologist's horse, the logician's horse, or the metaphysician's horse.

[1] All labels are, of course, obnoxious and misleading. I hope, however, the term
will be taken by the reader in the sense in which it is forthwith explained, and not
in some more usual and familiar sense. Empiricism, as herein used, is as antipodal
to sensationalistic empiricism, as it is to transcendentalism, and for the same
reason. Both of these systems fall back on something which is defined in non-
directly-experienced terms in order to justify that which is directly experienced.
Hence I have criticized such empiricism (*Philosophical Review*, Vol. XI, No. 4, p.
364) as essentially absolutistic in character; and also ("Studies in Logical Theory,"
pp. 30, 58) as an attempt to build up experience in terms of certain methodological
checks and cues of attaining *certainty*.

In each case, the nub of the question is, *what sort of experience* is denoted or indicated: a concrete and determinate experience, varying, when it varies, in specific real elements, and agreeing, when it agrees, in specific real elements, so that we have a contrast, not between *a* Reality, and various approximations to, or phenomenal representations of Reality, but between different reals of experience. And the reader is begged to bear in mind that from this standpoint, when "an experience" or "some sort of experience" is referred to, "some thing" or "some sort of thing" is always meant.

Now, this statement that things are what they are experienced to be is usually translated into the statement that things (or, ultimately, Reality, Being) *are* only and just what they are *known* to be or that things are, or Reality *is*, what it is for a conscious knower—whether the knower be conceived primarily as a perceiver or as a thinker being a further, and secondary, question. This is the root-paralogism of all idealisms, whether subjective or objective, psychological or epistemological. By our postulate, things are what they are experienced to be; and, unless knowing is the sole and only genuine mode of experiencing, it is fallacious to say that Reality is just and exclusively what it is or would be to an all-competent all-knower; or even that it *is*, relatively and piecemeal, what it is to a finite and partial knower. Or, put more positively, knowing is one mode of experiencing, and the primary philosophic demand (from the standpoint of immediatism) is to find out *what* sort of an experience knowing is—or, concretely how things are experienced when they are experienced *as* known things.[2] By concretely is meant, obviously enough (among other things), such an account of the experience of things as known that will bring out the characteristic traits and distinctions they possess as things of a knowing experience, as compared with things experienced esthetically, or morally, or economically, or technologically. To assume that, because from the *standpoint of the knowledge experience* things *are* what they are known to be, therefore, metaphysically, absolutely, without qualification, everything in its reality (as distinct from its "appearance,"

---

[2] I hope the reader will not therefore assume that from the empiricist's standpoint knowledge is of small worth or import. On the contrary, from the empiricist's standpoint it has *all* the worth which it is concretely experienced as possessing—which is simply tremendous. But the exact *nature* of this worth is a thing to be found out in describing what we mean by experiencing objects as known—the actual differences made or found in experience.

or phenomenal occurrence) is what a knower would find it to be, is, from the immediatist's standpoint, if not the root of all philosophic evil, at least one of its main roots. For this leaves out of account what the knowledge standpoint is itself *experienced as*.

I start and am flustered by a noise heard. Empirically, that noise *is* fearsome; it *really* is, not merely phenomenally or subjectively so. That *is what* it is experienced as being. But, when I experience the noise as a *known* thing, I find it to be innocent of harm. It is the tapping of a shade against the window, owing to movements of the wind. The experience has changed; that is, the thing experienced has changed—not that an unreality has given place to a reality, nor that some transcendental (unexperienced) Reality has changed,[3] not that truth has changed, but just and only the concrete reality experienced has changed. I now feel ashamed of my fright; and the noise as fearsome is changed to noise as a wind-curtain fact, and hence practically indifferent to my welfare. This is a change of experienced existence effected through the medium of cognition. The content of the latter experience cognitively regarded is doubtless *truer* than the content of the earlier; but it is in no sense more real. To call it truer, moreover, must, from the empirical standpoint, mean a concrete *difference* in actual things experienced.[4] Again, in many cases, only in retrospect is the prior experience cognitionally regarded at all. In such cases, it is only in regard to contrasted content *in* a subsequent experience that the determination "truer" has force.

Perhaps some reader may now object that as matter of fact the entire experience *is* cognitive, but that the earlier parts of it are only imperfectly so, resulting in a phenomenon that is not real; while the latter

[3] Since the non-empiricist believes in things-in-themselves (which he may term "atoms," "sensations," transcendental unities, *a priori* concepts, *an* absolute experience, or whatever), and since he finds that the empiricist makes much of change (as he must, since change is continuously experienced) he assumes that the empiricist means *his own* non-empirical Realities are in continual flux, and he naturally shudders at having his divinities so violently treated. But, once recognize that the empiricist doesn't have any such Realities at all, and the entire problem of the relation of change to reality takes a very different aspect.

[4] It would lead us aside from the point to try to tell just what is the nature of the experienced difference we call truth. Professor James's recent articles may well be consulted. The point to bear in mind here is just what sort of a thing the empiricist must mean by true, or truer (the noun of Truth is, of course, a generic name for all cases of "Trues"). The adequacy of any particular account is not a matter to be settled by general reasoning, but by finding out what sort of an experience the truth-experience actually is.

part, being a more complete cognition, results in what is relatively, at least, more real.[5] In short, a critic may say that, when I was frightened by the noise, I *knew* I was frightened; otherwise there would have been no experience at all. At this point, it is necessary to make a distinction so simple and yet so all-fundamental that I am afraid the reader will be inclined to pooh-pooh it away as a mere verbal distinction. But to see that to the empiricist this distinction is not verbal, but genuine, is the precondition of any understanding of him. The immediatist must, by his postulate, ask what is the fright experienced *as*. Is what is actually experienced, I-know-I-am-frightened, or I-*am*-frightened? I see absolutely no reason for claiming that the experience *must* be described by the former phrase. In all probability (and all the empiricist logically needs is just one case of this sort) the experience is simply and just of fright-at-the-noise. Later one may (or may not) have an experience describable *as* I-know-I-am- (or-was) and improperly or properly, frightened. But this is a different experience—that is, a different *thing*. And if the critic goes on to urge that the person "*really*" must have known that he was frightened, I can only point out that the critic is shifting the venue. He may be right, but, if so, it is only because the "really" is something not concretely experienced (whose nature accordingly is the critic's business); and this is to depart from the empiricist's point of view, to attribute to him a postulate he expressly repudiates.

The material point may come out more clearly if I say that we must make a distinction between a thing as *cognitive*, and one as *cognized*.[6] I should define a cognitive experience as one that has certain bearings or implications which induce, and fulfil themselves in, a subsequent experience in which the relevant thing is experienced *as* cognized, *as* a known object, and is thereby transformed, or reorganized. The fright-at-the-noise in the case cited is obviously *cognitive*, in this sense. By description, it induces an investigation or inquiry in which both noise and fright are objectively stated or presented—the noise as a shade-wind fact, the fright as an organic reaction to a sudden acoustic stimulus, a reaction that under the given circumstances was useless or

---

[5] I say, "relatively," because the transcendentalist still holds that finally the cognition is imperfect, giving us only some symbol or phenomenon of Reality (which *is* only in the Absolute or in some Thing-in-Itself)—otherwise the curtain-wind fact would have as much ontological reality as the existence of the Absolute itself: a conclusion at which the non-empiricist perhorresces, for no reason obvious to me—save that it would put an end to his transcendentalism.

[6] In general, I think the distinction between -*ive* and -*ed* one of the most fundamental of philosophic distinctions, and one of the most neglected. The same holds of -*tion* and -*ing*.

even detrimental, a maladaptation. Now, pretty much all of experience is of this sort (the "is" meaning, of course, is experienced *as*), and the empiricist is false to his principle if he does not duly note this fact.[7] But he is equally false to his principle if he permits himself to be confused as to the concrete differences in the two things experienced.

There are two little words through explication of which the empiricist's position may be brought out—"*as*" and "*that*." We may express his presupposition by saying that things are what they are experienced *as* being; or that to give a just account of anything is to tell what *that* thing is experienced to be. By these words I want to indicate the absolute, final, irreducible, and inexpugnable concrete *quale* which everything experienced not so much *has* as *is*. To grasp this aspect of empiricism is to see what the empiricist means by objectivity, by the element of control. Suppose we take, as a crucial case for the empiricist, an out and out illusion, say of Zöllner's lines. These are experienced as convergent; they are "truly" parallel. If things are what they are experienced as being, how can the distinction be drawn between illusion and the true state of the case? There is no answer to this question except by sticking to the fact that the experience of the lines as divergent is a concrete qualitative thing or *that*. It is *that* experience which it is, and no other. And if the reader rebels at the iteration of such obvious tautology, I can only reiterate that the realization of the *meaning* of this tautology is the key to the whole question of the objectivity of experience, as that stands to the empiricist. The lines of *that* experience *are* divergent; not merely *seem* so. The question of truth is not as to whether Being or Non-Being, Reality or mere Appearance, is experienced, but as to the *worth* of a certain concretely experienced thing. The only way of passing upon this question is by sticking in the most uncompromising fashion to *that* experience as real. *That* experience is that two lines with certain cross-hatchings are apprehended as convergent; only by taking that experience as real and as fully real, is there any basis for, or way of going to, an experienced knowledge that the lines are parallel. It is in the concrete thing *as experienced* that all the grounds and clues to its own intellectual or logical rectification are contained. It is because this thing, afterwards adjudged false, is a concrete *that*, that it develops into a corrected experience (that is, experience of a corrected thing—we reform things just as we reform ourselves or a bad

---

[7] What is criticised, now as "geneticism" (if I may coin the word) and now as "pragmatism" is, in its truth, just the fact that the empiricist does take account of the experienced "drift, occasion, and contexture" of things experienced—to use Hobbes's phrase.

boy) whose full content is not a whit more real, but which is true or truer.[8]

If *any* experience, then a *determinate* experience; and this determinateness is the only, and is the adequate, principle of control, or "objectivity." The experience may be of the vaguest sort. I may not see anything which I can identify as a familiar object—a table, a chair, etc. It may be dark; I may have only the vaguest impression that there is something which looks like a table. Or I may be completely befogged and confused, as when one rises quickly from sleep in a pitch-dark room. But this vagueness, this doubtfulness, this confusion is the thing experienced, and, *qua* real, is as "good" a reality as the self-luminous vision of an Absolute. It is not just vagueness, doubtfulness, confusion, at large or in general. It is *this* vagueness, and no other; absolutely unique, absolutely what *it* is.[9] Whatever gain in clearness, in fullness, in trueness of content is experienced must grow out of some element in the experience of *this* experienced *as* what it is. To return to the illusion: If the experience of the lines as convergent is illusory, it is because of some elements in the thing as experienced, not because of something defined in terms of externality to this particular experience. If the illusoriness can be detected, it is because the thing experienced is real, having within its experienced reality elements whose *own mutual* tension effects its reconstruction. Taken concretely, the experience of convergent lines contains within itself the elements of the transformation of its own content. It is *this* thing, and not some separate truth, that clamors for its own reform. There is, then, from the empiricist's point of view, no need to search for some aboriginal *that* to which all successive experiences are attached, and which is somehow thereby undergoing continuous change. Experience is always of *thats*; and the most comprehensive and inclusive experience of the universe that the philosopher himself can obtain is the experience of a characteristic *that*. From the empiricist's point of view, this is as true of the exhaustive and complete insight of a hypothetical all-knower as of the vague, blind experience of the awakened sleeper. As reals, they stand on the same level. As trues,

---

[8] Perhaps the point would be clearer if expressed in this way: Except as subsequent estimates of *worth* are introduced, "real" means only existent. The eulogistic connotation that makes the term Reality equivalent to *true* or *genuine* being has great pragmatic significance, but its confusion with reality as existence is the point aimed at in the above paragraph.

[9] One does not so easily escape medieval Realism as one thinks. Either every experienced thing has its own determinateness, its own unsubstitutable, unredeemable reality, or else "generals" *are* separate existences after all.

the latter has by definition the better of it; but if this insight is in any way the truth of the blind awakening, it is because the latter has, in its *own* determinate *quale*, elements of real continuity with the former; it is, *ex hypothesi*, transformable through a series of experienced reals without break of continuity, into the absolute thought-experience. There is no need of logical manipulation to effect the transformation, nor *could* any logical consideration effect it. If effected at all it is just by immediate experiences, each of which is just as real (no more, no less) as either of the two terms between which they lie. Such, at least, is the meaning of the empiricist's contention. So, when he talks of experience, he does not mean some grandiose, remote affair that is cast like a net around a succession of fleeting experiences; he does not mean an indefinite total, comprehensive experience which somehow engirdles an endless flux; he means that *things* are what they are experienced to be, and that every experience is *some* thing.

From the postulate of empiricism, then (or, what is the same thing, from a *general* consideration of the concept of experience), nothing can be deduced, not a single philosophical proposition.[10] The reader may hence conclude that all this just comes to the truism that experience is experience, or is what it is. If one attempts to draw conclusions from the bare concept of experience, the reader is quite right. But the real significance of the principle is that of a method of philosophical analysis—a method identical in kind (but differing in problem and hence in operation) with that of the scientist. If you wish to find out what subjective, objective, physical, mental, cosmic, psychic, cause, substance, purpose, activity, evil, being, quality—any philosophic term, in short—means, go to experience and see what the thing is experienced *as*.

Such a method is not spectacular; it permits of no offhand demonstrations of God, freedom, immortality, nor of the exclusive reality of matter, or ideas, or consciousness, etc. But it supplies a way of telling what all these terms mean. It may seem insignificant, or chillingly disap-

---

[10] Excepting, of course, some negative ones. One could say that certain views are certainly *not* true, because, by hypothesis, they refer to nonentities, *i.e.*, nonempiricals. But even here the empiricist must go slowly. From his own standpoint, even the most professedly transcendental statements are, after all, real as experiences, and hence negotiate some transaction with facts. For this reason, he cannot, in theory, reject them *in toto*, but has to show concretely how they arose and how they are to be corrected. In a word, his logical relationship to statements that profess to relate to things-in-themselves, unknowables, inexperienced substances, etc., is precisely that of the psychologist to the Zollner lines. .

pointing, but only upon condition that it be not worked. Philosophic conceptions have, I believe, outlived their usefulness considered as stimulants to emotion, or as a species of sanctions; and a larger, more fruitful and more valuable career awaits them considered as specifically experienced meanings.*

* [Note: The reception of this essay proved that I was unreasonably sanguine in thinking that the foot-note of warning, appended to the title, would forfend radical misapprehension. I see now that it was unreasonable to expect that the word "immediate" in a philosophic writing could be generally understood to apply to anything except *knowledge*, even though the body of the essay is a protest against such limitation. But I venture to repeat that the essay is not a denial of the necessity of "mediation," or reflection, in knowledge, but is an assertion that the inferential factor must *exist*, or must occur, and that all existence is direct and vital, so that philosophy can pass upon its nature—as upon the nature of all of the rest of its subject-matter—only by first ascertaining what it exists or occurs *as*.

I venture to repeat also another statement of the text: I do not mean by "immediate experience" any aboriginal stuff out of which things are evolved, but I use the term to indicate the necessity of employing in philosophy the direct descriptive method that has now made its way in all the natural sciences, with such modifications, of course, as the subject itself entails.

There is nothing in the text to imply that things exist in experience atomically or in isolation. When it is said that a thing as cognized is *different* from an earlier non-cognitionally experienced thing, the saying no more implies lack of continuity between the things, than the obvious remark that a seed is different from a flower or a leaf denies their continuity. The amount and kind of continuity or discreteness that exists is to be discovered by recurring to what actually occurs in experience.

Finally, there is nothing in the text that denies the existence of things temporally prior to human experiencing of them. Indeed, I should think it fairly obvious that we experience most things *as* temporally prior to our experiencing of them. The import of the article is to the effect that we are not entitled to draw philosophic (as distinct from scientific) conclusions as to the meaning of prior temporal existence till we have ascertained what it is to experience a thing as past. These four disclaimers cover, I think, all the misapprehensions disclosed in the four or five controversial articles (noted below) that the original essay evoked. One of these articles (that of Professor Woodbridge), raised a point of fact, holding that cognitional experience tells us, without alteration, just what the things of other types of experience are, and in that sense transcend other experiences. This is too fundamental an issue to discuss in a note, and I content myself with remarking that with respect to it, the bearing of the article is that the issue must be settled by a careful descriptive survey of things as experienced, to see whether modifications do not occur in existences when they are experienced *as* known; *i.e.*, as true or false in character. The reader interested in following up this discussion is referred to the following articles: Vol. II of the *Journal of Philosophy, Psychology, and Scientific Methods*, two articles by Bakewell, p. 520 and p. 687; one by Bode, p. 658; one by Woodbridge, p. 573; Vol. III of the same *Journal*, by Leighton, p. 174.]

17. Experience and Philosophic Method*

This selection, from *Experience and Nature*, repeats in a detailed and passionate manner one of Dewey's lifelong concerns, the irreducible importance of everyday experience for philosophical method. Proceeding from his assertion of the continuity between experience and nature, Dewey affirms the relevance of the commonplace to the most profound philosophical speculation; indeed, as cut off from the use of experiences undergone, speculation becomes first incestuous and then trite.

In commenting on the riches of ordinary experience, for our understanding of nature as revealed in our interactions with the world, Dewey writes again and again of the reach of experience, its depth and its inferential power. To bypass the qualities revealed in the experience of "enjoyment and trouble, friendship and human association, art and industry" for the niceties of the language of reflection is to court disaster by playing into the hands of those who respond to the everyday with "cynicism, indifference and pessimism." In Dewey's version, philosophy has the task of "creating and promoting a respect for concrete human experience and its potentialities."

The title of this volume, *Experience and Nature*, is intended to signify that the philosophy here presented may be termed either empirical naturalism or naturalistic empiricism, or, taking "experience" in its usual signification, naturalistic humanism.

To many the associating of the two words will seem like talking of a round square, so engrained is the notion of the separation of man and experience from nature. Experience, they say, is important for those beings who have it, but is too casual and sporadic in its occurrence to carry with it any important implications regarding the nature of Nature. Nature, on the other hand, is said to be complete apart from experience. Indeed, according to some thinkers the case is even in worse plight: Experience to them is not only something extraneous which is occasionally super-imposed upon nature, but it forms a veil or screen which shuts us

* From John Dewey, *Experience and Nature* (New York, 1958) (1929), 2nd ed., Chap. 1.

off from nature, unless in some way it can be "transcended." So something non-natural by way of reason or intuition is introduced, something supra-empirical. According to an opposite school experience fares as badly, nature being thought to signify something wholly material and mechanistic; to frame a theory of experience in naturalistic terms is, accordingly, to degrade and deny the noble and ideal values that characterize experience.

I know of no route by which dialectical argument can answer such objections. They arise from associations with words and cannot be dealt with argumentatively. One can only hope in the course of the whole discussion to disclose the meanings which are attached to "experience" and "nature," and thus insensibly produce, if one is fortunate, a change in the significations previously attached to them. This process of change may be hastened by calling attention to another context in which nature and experience get on harmoniously together—wherein experience presents itself as the method, and the only method, for getting at nature, penetrating its secrets, and wherein nature empirically disclosed (by the use of empirical method in natural science) deepens, enriches and directs the further development of experience.

In the natural sciences there is a union of experience and nature which is not greeted as a monstrosity; on the contrary, the inquirer must use empirical method if his findings are to be treated as genuinely scientific. The investigator assumes as a matter of course that experience, controlled in specifiable ways, is the avenue that leads to the facts and laws of nature. He uses reason and calculation freely; he could not get along without them. But he sees to it that ventures of this theoretical sort start from and terminate in directly experienced subject-matter. Theory may intervene in a long course of reasoning, many portions of which are remote from what is directly experienced. But the vine of pendant theory is attached at both ends to the pillars of observed subject-matter. And this experienced material is the same for the scientific man and the man in the street. The latter cannot follow the intervening reasoning without special preparation. But stars, rocks, trees, and creeping things are the same material of experience for both.

These commonplaces take on significance when the relation of experience to the formation of a philosophic theory of nature is in question. They indicate that experience, if scientific inquiry is justified, is no infinitesimally thin layer or foreground of nature, but that it penetrates into it, reaching down into its depths, and in such a way that its grasp is capable of expansion; it tunnels in all directions and in so doing brings to the surface things at first hidden—as miners pile high on the surface of the earth treasures brought from below. Unless we are prepared to deny all validity to scientific inquiry, these facts have a value that cannot be ignored for the general theory of the relation of nature and experience.

It is sometimes contended, for example, that since experience is a late comer in the history of our solar system and planet, and since these occupy a trivial place in the wide areas of celestial space, experience is at most a slight and insignificant incident in nature. No one with an honest respect for scientific conclusions can deny that experience as an existence is something that occurs only under highly specialized conditions, such as are found in a highly organized creature which in turn requires a specialized environment. There is no evidence that experience occurs everywhere and everywhen. But candid regard for scientific inquiry also compels the recognition that when experience does occur, no matter at what limited portion of time and space, it enters into possession of some portion of nature and in such a manner as to render other of its precincts accessible.

A geologist living in 1928 tells us about events that happened not only before he was born but millions of years before any human being came into existence on this earth. He does so by starting from things that are now the material of experience. Lyell revolutionized geology by perceiving that the sort of thing that can be experienced now in the operations of fire, water, pressure, is the sort of thing by which the earth took on its present structural forms. Visiting a natural history museum, one beholds a mass of rock and, reading a label, finds that it comes from a tree that grew, so it is affirmed, five million years ago. The geologist did not leap from the thing he can see and touch to some event in by-gone ages; he collated this observed thing with many others, of different kinds, found all over the globe; the results of his comparisons he then compared with data of other experiences, say, the astronomer's. He translates, that is, observed coexistences into non-observed, inferred sequences. Finally he dates his object, placing it in an order of events. By the same sort of method he predicts that at certain places some things not yet experienced will be observed, and then he takes pains to bring them within the scope of experience. The scientific conscience is, moreover, so sensitive with respect to the necessity of experience that when it reconstructs the past it is not fully satisfied with inferences drawn from even a large and cumulative mass of uncontradicted evidence; it sets to work to institute conditions of heat and pressure and moisture, etc., so as actually to reproduce in experiment that which he has inferred.

These commonplaces prove that experience is *of* as well as *in* nature. It is not experience which is experienced, but nature—stones, plants, animals, diseases, health, temperature, electricity, and so on. Things interacting in certain ways *are* experience; they are what is experienced. Linked in certain other ways with another natural object—the human organism—they are *how* things are experienced as well. Experience thus reaches down into nature; it has depth. It also has breadth and to an indefinitely elastic extent. It stretches. That stretch constitutes inference.

Dialectical difficulties, perplexities due to definitions given to the concepts that enter into the discussion, may be raised. It is said to be absurd that what is only a tiny part of nature should be competent to incorporate vast reaches of nature within itself. But even were it logically absurd one would be bound to cleave to it as a fact. Logic, however, is not put under a strain. The fact that something is an occurrence does not decide what kind of an occurrence it is; that can be found out only by examination. To argue from an experience "being an experience" to what it is of and about is warranted by no logic, even though modern thought has attempted it a thousand times. A bare event is no event at all; *something* happens. What that something is, is found out by actual study. This applies to seeing a flash of lightning and holds of the longer event called experience. The very existence of science is evidence that experience is such an occurrence that it penetrates into nature and expands without limit through it.

These remarks are not supposed to prove anything about experience and nature for philosophical doctrine; they are not supposed to settle anything about the worth of empirical naturalism. But they do show that in the case of natural science we habitually treat experience as starting-point, and as method for dealing with nature, and as the goal in which nature is disclosed for what it is. To realize this fact is at least to weaken those verbal associations which stand in the way of apprehending the force of empirical method in philosophy.

The same considerations apply to the other objection that was suggested: namely, that to view experience naturalistically is to reduce it to something materialistic, depriving it of all ideal significance. If experience actually presents esthetic and moral traits, then these traits may also be supposed to reach down into nature, and to testify to something that belongs to nature as truly as does the mechanical structure attributed to it in physical science. To rule out that possibility by some general reasoning is to forget that the very meaning and purport of empirical method is that things are to be studied on their own account, so as to find out what is revealed when they are experienced. The traits possessed by the subject-matters of experience are as genuine as the characteristics of sun and electron. They are *found*, experienced, and are not to be shoved out of being by some trick of logic. When found, their ideal qualities are as relevant to the philosophic theory of nature as are the traits found by physical inquiry.

To discover some of these general features of experienced things and to interpret their significance for a philosophic theory of the universe in which we live is the aim of this volume. From the point of view adopted, the theory of empirical method in philosophy does for experienced subject-matter on a liberal scale what it does for special sciences on a technical scale. It is this aspect of method with which we are especially concerned in the present chapter.

If the empirical method were universally or even generally adopted in philosophizing, there would be no need of referring to experience. The scientific inquirer talks and writes about particular observed events and qualities, about specific calculations and reasonings. He makes no allusion to experience; one would probably have to search a long time through reports of special researches in order to find the word. The reason is that everything designated by the word "experience" is so adequately incorporated into scientific procedures and subject-matter that to mention experience would be only to duplicate in a general term what is already covered in definite terms.

Yet this was not always so. Before the technique of empirical method was developed and generally adopted, it was necessary to dwell explicitly upon the importance of "experience" as a starting point and terminal point, as setting problems and as testing proposed solutions. We need not be content with the conventional allusion to Roger Bacon and Francis Bacon. The followers of Newton and the followers of the Cartesian school carried on a definite controversy as to the place occupied by experience and experiment in science as compared with intuitive concepts and with reasoning from them. The Cartesian school relegated experience to a secondary and almost accidental place, and only when the Galilean-Newtonian method had wholly triumphed did it cease to be necessary to mention the importance of experience. We may, if sufficiently hopeful, anticipate a similar outcome in philosophy. But the date does not appear to be close at hand; we are nearer in philosophic theory to the time of Roger Bacon than to that of Newton.

In short, it is the contrast of empirical method with other methods employed in philosophizing, together with the striking dissimilarity of results yielded by an empirical method and professed non-empirical methods that make the discussion of the methodological import of "experience" for philosophy pertinent and indeed indispensable.

This consideration of method may suitably begin with the contrast between gross, macroscopic, crude subject-matters in primary experience and the refined, derived objects of reflection. The distinction is one between what is experienced as the result of a minimum of incidental reflection and what is experienced in consequence of continued and regulated reflective inquiry. For derived and refined products are experienced only because of the intervention of systematic thinking. The objects of both science and philosphy obviously belong chiefly to the secondary and refined system. But at this point we come to a marked divergence between science and philosophy. For the natural sciences not only draw their material from primary experience, but they refer it back again for test. Darwin began with the pigeons, cattle and plants of breeders and gardeners. Some of the conclusions he reached were so contrary to accepted beliefs that they were condemned as absurd, contrary to common-sense, etc. But scientific men, whether they accepted his theories or not, employed his hypotheses as directive ideas for making new observations and experiments among the things of raw experience—just as the metallurgist who extracts refined metal from crude ore makes tools that are then set to work to control and use other crude materials. An Einstein working by highly elaborate methods of reflection, calculates theoretically certain results in the deflection of light by the presence of the sun. A technically equipped expedition is sent to South Africa so that by means of experiencing a thing—an eclipse—in crude, primary, experience, observations can be secured to compare with, and test the theory implied in, the calculated result.

The facts are familiar enough. They are cited in order to invite attention to the relationship between the objects of primary and of secondary or reflective experience. That the subject-matter of primary experience sets the problems and furnishes the first data of the reflection which constructs the secondary objects is evident; it is also obvious that test and verification of the latter is secured only by return to things of crude or macroscopic experience—the sun, earth, plants and animals of common, every-day life. But just what rôle do the objects attained in reflection play? Where do they come in? They *explain* the primary objects, they enable us to grasp them with *understanding*, instead of just having sense-contact with them. But how?

Well, they define or lay out a path by which return to experienced things is of such a sort that the meaning, the significant content, of what is experienced gains an enriched and expanded force because of the path or method by which it was reached. Directly, in immediate contact it may be just what it was before—hard, colored, odorous, etc. But when the secondary objects, the refined objects, are employed as a method or road for coming at them, these qualities cease to be isolated details; they get the meaning contained in a whole system of related objects; they are rendered continuous with the rest of nature and take on the import of the things they are now seen to be continuous with. The phenomena observed in the eclipse tested and, as far as they went, confirmed Einstein's theory of deflection of light by mass. But that is far from being the whole story. The phenomena themselves got a far-reaching significance they did not previously have. Perhaps they would not even have been noticed if the theory had not been employed as a guide or road to observation of them. But even if they had been noticed, they would have been dismissed as of no importance, just as we daily drop from attention hundreds of perceived details for which we have no intellectual use. But approached by means of theory these lines of slight deflection take on a significance as large as that of the revolutionary theory that lead to their being experienced.

This empirical method I shall call the *denotative* method. That philosophy is a mode of reflection, often of a subtle and penetrating sort, goes without saying. The charge that is brought against the non-empirical method of philosophizing is not that it depends upon theorizing, but that it fails to use refined, secondary products as a path pointing and leading back to something in primary experience. The resulting failure is three-fold.

First, there is no verification, no effort even to test and check. What is even worse, secondly, is that the things of ordinary experience do not get enlargement and enrichment of meaning as they do when approached through the medium of scientific principles and reasonings. This lack of function reacts, in the third place, back upon the philosophic subject-matter in itself. Not tested by being employed to see what it leads to in ordinary experience and what new meanings it contributes, this subject-matter becomes arbitrary, aloof—what is called "abstract" when that word is used in a bad sense to designate something which exclusively occupies a realm of its own without contact with the things of ordinary experience.

As the net outcome of these three evils, we find that extraordinary phenomenon which accounts for the revulsion of many cultivated persons from any form of philosophy. The objects of reflection in philosophy, being reached by methods that seem to those who employ them rationally mandatory are taken to be "real" in and of themselves—and supremely real. Then it becomes an insoluble problem why the things of gross, primary experience, should be what they are, or indeed why they should be at all. The refined objects of reflection in the natural sciences, however, never end by rendering the subject-matter from which they are derived a problem; rather, when used to describe a path by which some goal in primary experience is designated or denoted, they solve perplexities to which that crude material gives rise but which it cannot resolve of itself. They become means of control, of enlarged use and enjoyment of ordinary things. They may generate new problems, but these are problems of the same sort, to be dealt with by further use of the same methods of inquiry and experimentation. The problems to which empirical method gives rise afford, in a word, opportunities for more investigations yielding fruit in new and enriched experiences. But the problems to which non-empirical method gives rise in philosophy are blocks to inquiry, blind alleys; they are puzzles rather than problems, solved only by calling the original material of primary experience, "phenomenal," mere appearance, mere impressions, or by some other disparaging name.

Thus there is here supplied, I think, a first-rate test of the value of any philosophy which is offered us: Does it end in conclusions which, when they are referred back to ordinary life-experiences and their predicaments, render them more significant, more luminous to us, and make our dealings with them more fruitful? Or does it terminate in rendering the things of ordinary experience more opaque than they were before, and in depriving them of having in "reality" even the significance they had previously seemed to have? Does it yield the enrichment and increase of power of ordinary things which the results of physical science afford when applied in every-day affairs? Or does it become a mystery that these ordinary things should be what they are; and are philosophic concepts left to dwell in separation in some technical realm of their own? It is the fact, I repeat, that so many philosophies terminate in conclusions that make it necessary to disparage and condemn primary experience, leading those who hold them to measure the sublimity of their "realities" as philosophically defined by remoteness from the concerns of daily life, which leads cultivated common-sense to look askance at philosophy.

These general statements must be made more definite. We must illustrate the meaning of empirical method by seeing some of its results in contrast with those to which non-empirical philosophies conduct us. We begin by noting that "experience" is what James called a double-barrelled word. Like its congeners, life and history, it includes *what* men do and suffer, *what* they strive for, love, believe and endure, and also *how* men act and are acted upon, the ways in which they do and suffer, desire and enjoy, see, believe, imagine—in short, processes of *experiencing*. "Experience" denotes the planted field, the sowed seeds, the reaped harvests, the changes of night and day, spring and autumn, wet and dry, heat and cold, that are observed, feared, longed for; it also denotes the one who plants and reaps, who works and rejoices, hopes, fears, plans, invokes magic or chemistry to aid him, who is downcast or triumphant. It is "double-barrelled" in that it recognizes in its primary integrity no division between act and material, subject and object, but contains them both in an unanalyzed totality. "Thing" and "thought," as James says in the same connection, are single-barrelled; they refer to products discriminated by reflection out of primary experience.[2]

It is significant that "life" and "history" have the same fullness of undivided meaning. Life denotes a function, a comprehensive activity, in which organism and environment are included. Only upon reflective analysis does it break up into external conditions—air breathed, food taken, ground walked upon—and internal structures—lungs respiring, stomach digesting, legs walking. The scope of "history" is notorious: it is the deeds enacted, the tragedies undergone; and it is the human comment, record, and interpretation that inevitably follow. Objectively, history takes in rivers, mountains, fields and forests, laws and institutions; subjectively it includes the purposes and plans, the desires and emotions, through which these things are administered and transformed.

Now empirical method is the only method which can do justice to this inclusive integrity of "experience." It alone takes this integrated unity as the starting point for philosophic thought. Other methods begin with results of a reflection that has already torn in two the subject-matter experienced and the operations and states of experiencing. The problem is then to get together again what has been sundered—which is as if the king's men started with the fragments of the egg and tried to construct the whole egg out of them. For empirical method the problem is nothing so impossible of solution. Its problem is to note how and why the whole is distinguished into subject and object, nature and mental operations. Having done this, it is in a position to see *to what effect* the distinction

---

[1] Essays in Radical Empiricism, p. 10.

[2] It is not intended, however, to attribute to James precisely the interpretation given in the text.

is made: how the distinguished factors function in the further control and enrichment of the subject-matters of crude but total experience. Non-empirical method starts with a reflective product as if it were primary, as if it were the originally "given." To non-empirical method, therefore, object and subject, mind and matter (or whatever words and ideas are used) are separate and independent. Therefore it has upon its hands the problem of how it is possible to know at all; how an outer world can affect an inner mind; how the acts of mind can reach out and lay hold of objects defined in antithesis to them. Naturally it is at a loss for an answer, since its premises make the fact of knowledge both unnatural and unempirical. One thinker turns metaphysical materialist and denies reality to the mental; another turns psychological idealist, and holds that matter and force are merely disguised psychical events. Solutions are given up as a hopeless task, or else different schools pile one intellectual complication on another only to arrive by a long and tortuous course at that which naïve experience aleady has in its own possession.

The first and perhaps the greatest difference made in philosophy by adoption respectively of empirical or non-empirical method is, thus, the difference made in what is selected as original material. To a truly naturalistic empiricism, the moot problem of the relation of subject and object is the problem of what consequences follow in and for primary experience from the distinction of the physical and the psychological or mental from each other. The answer is not far to seek. To distinguish in reflection the physical and to hold it in temporary detachment is to be set upon the road that conducts to tools and technologies, to construction of mechanisms, to the arts that ensue in the wake of the sciences. That these constructions make possible a better regulation of the affairs of primary experience is evident. Engineering and medicine, all the utilities that make for expansion of life, are the answer. There is better administration of old familiar things, and there is invention of new objects and satisfactions. Along with this added ability in regulation goes enriched meaning and value in things, clarification, increased depth and continuity—a result even more precious than is the added power of control.

The history of the development of the physical sciences is the story of the enlarging possession by mankind of more efficacious instrumentalities for dealing with the conditions of life and action. But when one neglects the connection of these scientific objects with the affairs of primary experience, the result is a picture of a world of things indifferent to human interests because it is wholly apart from experience. It is more than merely isolated, for it is set in opposition. Hence when it is viewed as fixed and final in itself it is a source of oppression to the heart and paralysis to imagination. Since this picture of the physical universe and philosophy of the character of physical objects is contradicted by every engineering project and every intelligent measure of public hygiene, it would seem to be time to examine the foundations upon which it rests, and find out how and why such conclusions are come to.

When objects are isolated from the experience through which they are reached and in which they function, experience itself becomes reduced to the mere process of experiencing, and experiencing is therefore treated as if it were also complete in itself. We get the absurdity of an experiencing which experiences only itself, states and processes of consciousness, instead of the things of nature. Since the seventeenth century this conception of experience as the equivalent of subjective private consciousness set over against nature, which consists wholly of physical objects, has wrought havoc in philosophy. It is responsible for the feeling mentioned at the outset that "nature" and "experience" are names for things which have nothing to do with each other.

Let us inquire how the matter stands when these mental and psychical objects are looked at in their connection with experience in its primary and vital modes. As has been suggested, these objects are not original, isolated and self-sufficient. They represent the discriminated analysis of the process of experiencing from subject-matter experienced. Although breathing is in fact a function that includes both air and the operations of the lungs, we may detach the latter for study, even though we cannot separate it in fact. So while we always know, love, act for and against *things*, instead of experiencing ideas, emotions and mental intents, the attitudes themselves may be made a special object of attention, and thus come to form a distinctive subject-matter of reflective, although not of primary, experience.

We primarily observe things, not observations. But the *act* of observation may be inquired into and form a subject of study and become thereby a refined object; so may the acts of thinking, desire, purposing, the state of affection, reverie, etc. Now just as long as these attitudes are not distinguished and abstracted, they are incorporated into subject-matter. It is a notorious fact that the one who hates finds the one hated an obnoxious and despicable character; to the lover his adored one is full of intrinsically delightful and wonderful qualities. The connection between such facts and the fact of animism is direct.

The natural and original bias of man is all toward the objective; whatever is experienced is taken to be there independent of the attitude and act of the self. Its "thereness," its independence of emotion and volition, render the properties of things, whatever they are, cosmic. Only when vanity, prestige, rights of possession are involved does an individual tend to separate off from the environment and the group in which he, quite literally, lives, some things as being peculiarly himself. It is obvious that a total, unanalyzed world does not lend itself to control; that, on the contrary it is equivalent to the subjection of man to whatever occurs, as if to fate. Until some acts and their consequences are discriminatingly referred to the human organism and other energies and effects are referred to other bodies, there is no leverage, no purchase, with which to regulate the course of experience. The abstraction of certain qualities of things as due to human acts and states is the *pou sto* of ability in control. There can be no doubt that the long period of human arrest at a low level of culture was largely the result of failure to select the human being and his acts as a special kind of object, having his own characteristic activities that condition specifiable consequences.

In this sense, the recognition of "subjects" as centres of experience together with the development of "subjectivism" marks a great advance. It is equivalent to the emergence of agencies equipped with special powers of observation and experiment, and with emotions and desires that are efficacious for production of chosen modifications of nature. For otherwise the agencies are submerged in nature and produce qualities of things which must be accepted and submitted to. It is no mere play on words to say that recognition of subjective minds having a special equipment of psychological abilities is a necessary factor in subjecting the energies of nature to use as instrumentalities for ends.

Out of the indefinite number of possible illustrations of the consequences of reflective analysis yielding personal or "subjective" minds we cite one case. It concerns the influence of habitual beliefs and expectations in their social generation upon *what* is experienced. The things of primary experience are so arresting and engrossing that we tend to accept them just as they are—the flat earth, the march of the sun from east to west and its sinking under the earth. Current beliefs in morals, religion and politics similarly reflect the social conditions which present themselves. Only analysis shows that the *ways* in which we believe and expect have a tremendous affect upon *what* we believe and expect. We have discovered at last that these ways are set, almost abjectly so, by social factors, by tradition and the influence of education. Thus we discover that we believe many things not because the things are so, but because we have become habituated through the weight of authority, by imitation, prestige, instruction, the unconscious effect of language, etc.

We learn, in short, that qualities which we attribute to objects ought to be imputed to our own ways of experiencing them, and that these in turn are due to the force of intercourse and custom. This discovery marks an emancipation; it purifies and remakes the objects of our direct or primary experience. The power of custom and tradition in scientific as well as in moral beliefs never suffered a serious check until analysis revealed the effect of personal ways of believing upon things believed, and the extent to which these ways are unwittingly fixed by social custom and tradition. In spite of the acute and penetrating powers of observation among the Greeks, their "science" is a monument of the extent to which the effects of acquired social habits as well as of organic constitution were attributed directly to natural events. The de-personalizing and de-socializing of some objects, to be henceforth the objects of physical science, was a necessary precondition of ability to regulate experience by directing the attitudes and objects that enter into it.

This great emancipation was coincident with the rise of "individualism," which was in effect identical with the reflective discovery of the part played in experience by concrete selves, with their ways of acting, thinking and desiring. The results would have been all to the good if they had been interpreted by empirical method. For this would have kept the eye of thinkers constantly upon the origin of the "subjective" out of primary experience, and then directed it to the function of discriminating what is usable in the management of experienced objects. But for lack of such a method, because of isolation from empirical origin and instrumental use, the results of psychological inquiry were conceived to form a separate and isolated mental world in and of itself, self-sufficient and self-enclosed. Since the psychological movement necessarily coincided with that which set up physical objects as correspondingly complete and self-enclosed, there resulted that dualism of mind and matter, of a physical and a psychical world, which from the day of Descartes to the present dominates the formulation of philosophical problems.

With the dualism we are not here concerned, beyond pointing out that it is the inevitable result, logically, of the abandoning of acknowledgment of the primacy and ultimacy of gross experience —primary as it is given in an uncontrolled form, ultimate as it is given in a more regulated and significant form—a form made possible by the methods and results of reflective experience. But what we are directly concerned with at this stage of discussion is the result of the discovery of subjective objects upon philosophy in creation of wholesale subjectivism. The outcome was, that while in actual life the discovery of personal attitudes and their consequences was a great liberating instrument, psychology became for philosophy, as Santayana has well put it, "malicious." That is, mental attitudes, *ways* of experiencing, were treated as self-sufficient and complete in themselves, as that which is primarily *given*, the sole original and therefore indubitable data. Thus the traits of genuine primary experience, in which natural things are the determining factors in production of all change, were regarded either as not-given dubious things that could be reached only by endowing the only certain thing, the mental, with some miraculous power, or else were denied all existence save as complexes of mental states, of impressions, sensations, feelings.[3]

One illustration out of the multitude available follows. It is taken almost at random, because it is both simple and typical. To illustrate the nature of experience, what experience really is, an author writes: "When I look at a chair, I say I experience it. But what I actually experience is only a very few of the elements that go to make up a chair, namely the color that belongs to the chair under these particular conditions of light, the shape which the chair displays when viewed from this angle, etc." Two points are involved in any such statement. One is that "experience" is reduced to the traits connected with the *act of experiencing*, in this case the act of seeing. Certain patches of color, for example, assume a certain shape or form in connection with qualities connected with the muscular strains and adjustments of seeing. These qualities, which define the act of seeing when it is made an object of reflective inquiry, *over against what is seen*, thus become the chair itself for immediate or direct experience. Logically, the chair disappears and is replaced by certain qualities of sense attending the act of vision. There is no longer any other object, much less the chair which was bought, that is placed in a room and that is used to sit in, etc. If we ever get back to this total chair, it will not be the chair of direct experience, of use and enjoyment, a thing with its own independent origin, history and career; it will be only a complex of directly "given" sense qualities

---

[3] Because of this identification of the mental as the sole "given" in a primary, original way, appeal to experience by a philosopher is treated by many as necessarily committing one to subjectivism. It accounts for the alleged antithesis between nature and experience mentioned in the opening paragraph. It has become so deeply engrained that the empirical method employed in this volume has been taken by critics to be simply a re-statement of a purely subjective philosophy, although in fact it is wholly contrary to such a philosophy.

as a core, plus a surrounding cluster of other qualities revived imaginatively as "ideas."

The other point is that, even in such a brief statement as that just quoted, there is compelled recognition of an *object* of experience which is infinitely other and more than what is asserted to be alone experienced. There is the *chair* which is looked at; the *chair displaying* certain colors, the *light* in which they are displayed; the angle of vision implying reference to an organism that possesses an optical apparatus. Reference to these *things* is compulsory, because otherwise there would be no meaning assignable to the sense qualities—which are, nevertheless, affirmed to be the sole data experienced. It would be hard to find a more complete recognition, although an unavowed one, of the fact that in reality the account given concerns only a selected portion of the actual experience, namely that part which defines the act of experiencing, to the deliberate omission, *for the purpose of the inquiry in hand*, of *what* is experienced.

The instance cited is typical of all "subjectivism" as a philosophic position. Reflective analysis of one element in actual experience is undertaken; its result is then taken to be primary; as a consequence the subject-matter of actual experience from which the analytic result was derived is rendered dubious and problematic, although it is assumed at every step of the analysis. Genuine empirical method sets out from the actual subject-matter of primary experience, recognizes that reflection discriminates a new factor in it, the *act* of seeing, makes an object of that, and then uses that new object, the organic response to light, to regulate, when needed, further experiences of the subject-matter already contained in primary experience.

The topics just dealt with, segregation of physical and mental objects, will receive extended attention in the body of this volume. As respects *method*, however, it is pertinent at this point to summarize our results. Reference to the primacy and ultimacy of the material of ordinary experience protects us, in the first place, from creating artificial problems which deflect the energy and attention of philosophers from the real problems that arise out of actual subject-matter. In the second place, it provides a check or test for the conclusions of philosophic inquiry; it is a constant reminder that we must replace them, as secondary reflective products, in the experience out of which they arose, so that they may be confirmed or modified by the new order and clarity they introduce into it, and the new significantly experienced objects for which they furnish a method. In the third place, in seeing how they thus function in further experiences, the philosophical results themselves acquire empirical value; they are what they contribute to the common experience of man, instead of being curiosities to be deposited, with appropriate labels, in a metaphysical museum.

There is another important result for philosophy of the use of empirical method which, when it is developed, introduces our next topic. Philosophy, like all forms of reflective analysis, takes us away, for the time being, from the things had in primary experience as they directly act and are acted upon, used and enjoyed. Now the standing temptation of philosophy, as its course abundantly demonstrates, is to regard the results of reflection as having, in and of themselves, a reality superior to that of the material of any other mode of experience. The commonest assumption of philosophies, common even to philosophies very different from one another, is the assumption of the identity of objects of knowledge and ultimately real objects. The assumption is so deep that it is usually not expressed; it is taken for granted as something so fundamental that it does not need to be stated. A technical example of the view is found in the contention of the Cartesian school—including Spinoza—that emotion as well as sense is but confused thought which when it becomes clear and definite or reaches its goal is *cognition*. That esthetic and moral experience reveal traits of real things as truly as does intellectual experience, that poetry may have a metaphysical import as well as science, is rarely affirmed, and when it is asserted, the statement is likely to be meant in some mystical or esoteric sense rather than in a straightforward everyday sense.

Suppose however that we start with no presuppositions save that what is experienced, since it is a manifestation of nature, may, and indeed, must be used as testimony of the characteristics of natural events. Upon this basis, reverie and desire are pertinent for a philosophic theory of the true nature of things; the possibilities present in imagination that are not found in observation, are something to be taken into account. The features of objects reached by scientific or reflective experiencing are important, but so are all the phenomena of magic, myth, politics, painting, and penitentiaries. The phenomena of social life are as relevant to the problem of the relation of the individual and universal as are those of logic; the existence in political organization of boundaries and barriers, of centralization, of interaction across boundaries, of expansion and absorption, will be quite as important for metaphysical theories of the discrete and the continuous as is anything derived from chemical analysis. The existence of ignorance as well as of wisdom, of error and even insanity as well as of truth will be taken into account.

That is to say, nature is construed in such a way that all these things, since they are actual, are naturally possible; they are not explained away into mere "appearance" in contrast with reality. Illusions are illusions, but the occurrence of illusions is not an illusion, but a genuine reality. What is really "in" experience extends much further than that which at any time is *known*. From the standpoint of knowledge, objects must be distinct; their traits must be explicit; the vague and unrevealed is a limitation. Hence whenever the habit of identifying reality with the object of knowledge as such prevails, the obscure and vague are explained away. It is important for philosophic theory to be aware that the distinct and evident are prized and why they are. But it is equally important to note that the dark and twilight abound. For in any object of primary experience there are always potentialities which are not explicit; any object that is overt is charged with possible consequences that are hidden; the most overt act has factors which are not explicit. Strain thought as far as we may and not all consequences can be foreseen or made an express or known part of reflection and decision. In the face of such empirical facts, the assumption that nature in itself is all of the same kind, all distinct, explicit and evident, having no hidden possibilities, no novelties or obscurities, is possible only on the basis of a philosophy which at some point draws an arbitrary line between nature and experience.

In the assertion (implied here) that the great vice of philosophy is an arbitrary "intellectualism," there is no slight cast upon intelligence and reason. By "intellectualism" as an indictment is meant the theory that all experiencing is a mode of knowing, and that all subject-matter, all nature, is, in principle, to be reduced and transformed till it is defined in terms identical with the characteristics presented by refined objects of science as such. The assumption of "intellectualism" goes contrary to the facts of what is primarily experienced. For things are objects to be treated, used, acted upon and with, enjoyed and endured, even more than things to be known. They are things *had* before they are things cognized.

The isolation of traits characteristic of objects known, and then defined as the sole ultimate realities, accounts for the denial to nature of the characters which make things lovable and contemptible, beautiful and ugly, adorable and awful. It accounts for the belief that nature is an indifferent, dead mechanism; it explains why characteristics that are the valuable and valued traits of objects in actual experience are thought to create a fundamentally troublesome philosophical problem. Recognition of their genuine and primary reality does not signify that no thought and knowledge enter in when things are loved, desired and striven for; it signifies that the former are subordinate, so that the genuine problem is how and why, to what effect, things thus experienced are transformed into objects in which cognized traits are supreme and affectional and volitional traits incidental and subsidiary.

"Intellectualism" as a sovereign method of philosophy is so foreign to the facts of primary experience that it not only compels recourse to non-empirical method, but it ends in making knowledge, conceived as ubiquitous, itself inexplicable. If we start from primary experience, occurring as it does chiefly in modes of action and undergoing, it is easy to see what knowledge contributes—namely, the possibility of intelligent administration of the elements of doing and suffering. We are about something, and it is well to know what we are about, as the common phrase has it. To be intelligent in action and in suffering (enjoyment too) yields satisfaction even when conditions cannot be controlled. But when there is possibility of control, knowledge is the sole agency of its realization. Given this element of knowledge in primary experience, it is not difficult to understand how it may develop from a subdued and subsidiary factor into a dominant character. Doing and suffering, experimenting and putting ourselves in the way of having our sense and nervous system acted upon in ways that yield material for reflection, may reverse the original situation in which knowing and thinking were subservient to action-undergoing. And when we trace the genesis of knowing along this line, we also see that knowledge has a function and office in bettering and enriching the subject-matters of crude experience. We are prepared to understand what we are about on a grander scale, and to understand what happens even when we seem to be the hapless puppets of uncontrollable fate. But knowledge that is ubiquitous, all-inclusive and all-monopolizing, ceases to have meaning in losing all context; that it does not appear to do so when made supreme and self-sufficient is because it is literally impossible to exclude that context of non-cognitive but experienced subject-matter which gives what is *known* its import.

While this matter is dealt with at some length in further chapters of this volume, there is one point worth mentioning here. When intellectual experience and its material are taken to be primary, the cord that binds experience and nature is cut. That the physiological organism with its structures, whether in man or in the lower animals, is concerned with making adaptations and uses of material in the interest of maintenance of the life-process, cannot be denied. The brain and nervous system are primarily organs of action-undergoing; biologically, it can be asserted without contravention that primary experience is of a corresponding type. Hence, unless there is breach of historic and natural continuity, cognitive experience must originate within that of a non-cognitive sort. And unless we start from knowing as a factor in action and undergoing we are inevitably committed to the intrusion of an extra-natural, if not a supernatural, agency and principle. That professed non-supernaturalists so readily endow the organism with powers that have no basis in natural events is a fact so peculiar that it would be inexplicable were it not for the inertia of the traditional schools. Otherwise it would be evident that the only way to maintain the doctrine of natural continuity is to recognize the secondary and derived character aspects of experience of the intellectual or cognitive. But so deeply grounded is the opposite position in the entire philosophic tradition, that it is probably not surprising that philosophers are loath to admit a fact which when admitted compels an extensive reconstruction in form and content.

We have spoken of the difference which acceptance of empirical method in philosophy makes in the problem of subject-object and in that of the alleged all-inclusiveness of cognitive experience.[4] There is an intimate connection between these two problems. When real objects are identified, point for point, with knowledge-objects, all affectional and volitional objects are inevitably excluded from the "real" world, and are compelled to find refuge in the privacy of an experiencing subject or mind. Thus the notion of the ubiquity of all comprehensive cognitive experience results by a necessary logic in setting up a hard and fast wall between the experiencing subject and that nature which is experienced. The self becomes not merely a pilgrim but an unnaturalized and unnaturalizable alien in the world. The only way to avoid a sharp separation between the mind which is the centre of the processes of experiencing and the natural world which is experienced is to acknowledge that

[4] To avoid misapprehension, it may be well to add a statement on the latter point. It is not denied that any experienced subject-matter whatever may *become* an object of reflection and cognitive inspection. But the emphasis is upon "become"; the cognitive never *is* all-inclusive: that is, when the material of a prior non-cognitive experience is the object of knowledge, it and the act of knowing are themselves included within a new and wider non-cognitive experience—and *this* situation can never be transcended. It is only when the temporal character of experienced things is forgotten that the idea of the total "transcendence" of knowledge is asserted.

all modes of experiencing are ways in which some genuine traits of nature come to manifest realization.

The favoring of cognitive objects and their characteristics at the expense of traits that excite desire, command action and produce passion, is a special instance of a principle of selective emphasis which introduces partiality and partisanship into philosophy. Selective emphasis, with accompanying omission and rejection, is the heart-beat of mental life. To object to the operation is to discard all thinking. But in ordinary matters and in scientific inquiries, we always retain the sense that the material chosen is selected for a purpose; there is no idea of denying what is left out, for what is omitted is merely that which is not relevant to the particular problem and purpose in hand.

But in philosophies, this limiting condition is often wholly ignored. It is not noted and remembered that the favored subject-matter is chosen for a purpose and that what is left out is just as real and important in its own characteristic context. It tends to be assumed that because qualities that figure in poetical discourse and those that are central in friendship do not figure in scientific inquiry, they have no reality, at least not the kind of unquestionable reality attributed to the mathematical, mechanical or magneto-electric properties that constitute matter. It is natural to men to take that which is of chief value to them at the time as *the* real. Reality and superior value are equated. In ordinary experience this fact does no particular harm; it is at once compensated for by turning to other things which since they also present value are equally real. But philosophy often exhibits a cataleptic rigidity in attachment to that phase of the total objects of experience which has become especially dear to a philosopher. *It* is real at all hazards and only it; other things are real only in some secondary and Pickwickian sense.

For example, certainty, assurance, is immensely valuable in a world as full of uncertainty and peril as that in which we live. As a result whatever is capable of certainty is assumed to constitute ultimate Being, and everything else is said to be merely phenomenal, or, in extreme cases, illusory. The arbitrary character of the "reality" that emerges is seen in the fact that very different objects are selected by different philosophers. These may be mathematical entities, states of consciousness, or sense data. That is, whatever strikes a philosopher from the angle of the particular problem that presses on him as being self-evident and hence completely assured, is selected by him to constitute reality. The honorable and dignified have ranked with the mundanely certain in determining philosophic definitions of the real. Scholasticism considered that the True and the Good, along with Unity, were the marks of Being as such. In the face of a problem, thought always seeks to unify things otherwise fragmentary and discrepant. Deliberately action strives to attain the good; knowledge is reached when truth is grasped. Then the goals of our efforts, the things that afford satisfaction and peace under conditions of tension and unrest, are converted into that which alone is ultimate real Being. Ulterior functions are treated as original properties.

Another aspect of the same erection of objects of selective preference into exclusive realities is seen in the addiction of philosophers to what is simple, their love for "elements." Gross experience is loaded with the tangled and complex; hence philosophy hurries away from it to search out something so simple that the mind can rest trustfully in it, knowing that it has no surprises in store, that it will not spring anything to make trouble, that it will stay put, having no potentialities in reserve. There is again the predilection for mathematical objects; there is Spinoza with his assurance that a true idea carries truth intrinsic in its bosom; Locke with his "simple idea"; Hume with his "impression"; the English neo-realist with his ultimate atomic data; the American neo-realist with his ready-made essences.

Another striking example of the fallacy of selective emphasis is found in the hypnotic influence exercised by the conception of the eternal. The permanent enables us to rest, it gives peace; the variable, the changing, is a constant challenge. Where things change something is hanging over us. It is a threat of trouble. Even when change is marked by hope of better things to come, that hope tends to project its object as something to stay once for all when it arrives. Moreover we can deal with the variable and precarious only by means of the stable and constant; "invariants"—for the time being—are as much a necessity in practice for bringing something to pass as they are in mathematical functions. The permanent answers genuine emotional, practical and intellectual requirements. But the demand and the response which meets it are empirically always found in a special context; they arise because of a particular need and in order to effect specifiable consequences. Philosophy, thinking at large, allows itself to be diverted into absurd search for an intellectual philosopher's stone of absolutely wholesale generalizations, thus isolating that which is permanent in a function and for a purpose, and converting it into the intrinsically eternal, conceived either (as Aristotle conceived it) as that which is the same at all times, or as that which is indifferent to time, out of time.

This bias toward treating objects selected because of their value in some special context as the "real," in a superior and invidious sense, testifies to an empirical fact of importance. Philosophical simplifications are due to choice, and choice marks an interest *moral* in the broad sense of concern for what is good. Our constant and unescapable concern is with prosperity and adversity, success and failure, achievement and frustration, good and bad. Since we are creatures with lives to live, and find ourselves within an uncertain environment, we are constructed to note and judge in terms of bearing upon weal and woe—upon value. Acknowledgment of this fact is a very different thing, however, from the transformation effected by philosophers of the traits they find good (simplicity, certainty, nobility, permanence, etc.) into fixed traits of real Being. The former presents something *to be accomplished*, to be brought about by the *actions* in which choice is manifested and made genuine. The latter ignores the need of action to effect the better and to prove the honesty of choice; it converts what is desired into antecedent and final features of a reality which is supposed to need only logical warrant in order to be contemplatively enjoyed as true Being.

For reflection the eventual is always better or worse than the given. But since it would also be better if the eventual good were now given, the philosopher, belonging by status to a leisure class relieved from the urgent necessity of dealing with conditions, converts the eventual into some kind of Being, something which *is*, even if it does not *exist*. Permanence, real essence, totality, order, unity, rationality, the *unum, verum et bonum* of the classic tradition, are eulogistic predicates. When we find such terms used to describe the foundations and proper conclusions of a philosophic system, there is ground for suspecting that an artificial simplification of existence has been performed. Reflection determining preference for an eventual good has dialectically wrought a miracle of transubstantiation.

Selective emphasis, choice, is inevitable whenever reflection occurs. This is not an evil. Deception comes only when the presence and operation of choice is concealed, disguised, denied. Empirical method finds and points to the operation of choice as it does to any other event. Thus it protects us from conversion of eventual functions into antecedent existence: a conversion that may be said to be *the* philosophic fallacy, whether it be performed in behalf of mathematical subsistences, esthetic essences, the purely physical order of nature, or God. The present writer does not profess any greater candor of intent than animates fellow philosophers. But the pursuance of an empirical method, is, he submits, the only way to secure execution of candid intent. Whatever enters into choice, determining its need and giving it guidance, an empirical method frankly indicates what it is for; and the fact of choice, with its workings and consequences, an empirical method points out with equal openness.

The adoption of an empirical method is no guarantee that all the things relevant to any particular conclusion will actually be found, or that when found they will be correctly shown and communicated. But empirical method points out when and where and how things of a designated description have been arrived at. It places before others a map of the road that has been travelled; they may accordingly, if they will, re-travel the road to inspect the landscape for themselves. Thus the findings of one may be rectified and extended by the findings of others, with as much assurance as is humanly possible of confirmation, extension and rectification. The adoption of empirical method thus procures for philosophic reflection something of that cooperative tendency toward consensus which marks inquiry in the natural sciences. The scientific investigator convinces others not by the plausibility of his definitions and the cogency of his dialectic, but by placing before them the specified course of searchings, doings and arrivals, in consequence of which certain things have been found. His appeal is for others to traverse a similar course, so as to see how what they find corresponds with his report.

Honest empirical method will state when and where and why the act of selection took place, and thus enable others to repeat it and test its worth. Selective choice, denoted as an empirical event, reveals the basis and bearing of intellectual simplifications; they then cease to be of such a self-enclosed nature as to be affairs only of opinion and argument, admitting no alternatives save complete acceptance or rejection. Choice that is disguised or denied is the source of those astounding differences of philosophic belief that startle the beginner and that become the plaything of the expert. Choice that is avowed is an experiment to be tried on its merits and tested by its results. Under all the captions that are called immediate knowledge, or self-sufficient certitude of belief, whether logical, esthetic or epistemological, there is something selected for a purpose, and hence not simple, not self-evident and not intrinsically eulogizable. State the purpose so that it may be re-experienced, and its value and the pertinency of selection undertaken in its behalf may be tested. The purport of thinking, scientific and philosophic, is not to eliminate choice but to render it less arbitrary and more significant. It loses its arbitrary character when its quality and consequences are such as to commend themselves to the reflection of others after they have betaken themselves to the situations indicated; it becomes significant when reason for the choice is found to be weighty and its consequences momentous. When choice is avowed, others can repeat the course of the experience; it is an experiment to be tried, not an automatic safety device.

This particular affair is referred to here not so much as matter of doctrine as to afford an illustration of the nature of empirical method. Truth or falsity depends upon what men find when they warily perform the experiment of observing reflective events. An empirical finding is refuted not by denial that one finds things to be thus and so, but by giving directions for a course of experience that results in finding its opposite to be the case. To convince of error as well as to lead to truth is to assist another to see and find something which he hitherto has failed to find and recognize. All of the wit and subtlety of reflection and logic find scope in the elaboration and conveying of directions that intelligibly point out a course to be followed. Every system of philosophy presents the consequences of some such experiment. As experiments, each has contributed something of worth to our observation of the events and qualities of experienceable objects. Some harsh criticisms of traditional philosophy have already been suggested; others will doubtless follow. But the criticism is not directed at the experiments; it is aimed at the denial to them by the philosophic tradition of selective experimental quality, a denial which has isolated them from their actual context and function, and has thereby converted potential illuminations into arbitrary assertions.

This discussion of empirical method has had a double content. On one hand, it has tried to make clear, from the analogy of empirical method in scientific inquiry, what the method signifies (and does *not* signify) for philosophy. Such a discussion would, however, have little definite import unless the *difference* that is made in philosophy by the adoption of empirical method is pointed out. For that reason, we have considered some typical ways and important places in which traditional philosophies have gone astray through failure to connect their reflective results with the affairs of everyday primary experience. Three sources of large fallacies have been mentioned, each containing within itself many more sub-varieties than have been hinted at. The three are the complete separation of subject and object (of *what* is experienced from *how* it is experienced); the exaggeration of the features of known objects at the expense of the qualities of objects of enjoyment and trouble, friendship and human association, art and industry; and the exclusive isolation of the results of various types of selective simplification which are undertaken for diverse unavowed purposes.

It does not follow that the products of these philosophies which have taken the wrong, because non-empirical, method are of no value or little worth for a philosophy that pursues a strictly empirical method. The contrary is the case, for no philosopher can get away from experience even if he wants to. The most fantastic views ever entertained by superstitious people had some basis in experienced fact; they can be explained by one who knows enough about them and about the conditions under which they were formed. And philosophers have been not more but less superstitious than their fellows; they have been, as a class, unusually reflective and inquiring. If some of their products have been fantasies, it was not because they did not, even unwittingly, start from empirical method; it was not wholly because they substituted unchecked imagination for thought. No, the trouble has been that they have failed to note the empirical needs that generate their problems, and have failed to return the refined products back to the context of actual experience, there to receive their check, inherit their full content of meaning, and give illumination and guidance in the immediate perplexities which originally occasioned reflection.

The chapters which follow make no pretence, accordingly, of starting to philosophize afresh as if there were no philosophies already in existence, or as if their conclusions were empirically worthless. Rather the subsequent discussions rely, perhaps excessively so, upon the main results of great philosophic systems, endeavoring to point out their elements of strength and of weakness when their conclusions are employed (as the refined objects of all reflection must be employed) as guides back to the subject-matter of crude, everyday experience.

Our primary experience as it comes is of little value for purposes of analysis and control, crammed as it is with things that need analysis and control. The very existence of reflection is proof of its deficiencies. Just as ancient astronomy and physics were of little scientific worth, because, owing to the lack of apparatus and techniques of experimental analysis, they had to take the things of primary observation at their face value, so "common-sense" philosophy usually repeats current conventionalities. What is averred to be implicit reliance upon what is given in common experience is likely to be merely an appeal to prejudice to gain support for some fanaticism or defence for some relic of conservative tradition which is beginning to be questioned.

The trouble, then, with the conclusions of philosophy is not in the least that they are results of reflection and theorizing. It is rather that philosophers have borrowed from various sources the conclusions of special analyses, particularly of some ruling science of the day, and imported them direct into philosophy, with no check by either the empirical objects from which they arose or those to which the conclusions in question point. Thus Plato trafficked with the Pythagoreans and imported mathematical concepts; Descartes and Spinoza took over the presuppositions of geometrical reasoning; Locke imported into the theory of mind the Newtonian physical corpuscles, converting them into given "simple ideas"; Hegel borrowed and generalized without limit the rising historical method of his day; contemporary English philosophy has imported from mathematics the notion of primitive indefinable propositions, and given them a content from Locke's simple ideas, which had in the meantime become part of the stock in trade of psychological science.

Well, why not, as long as what is borrowed has a sound scientific status? Because in scientific inquiry, refined methods justify themselves by opening up new fields of subject-matter for exploration; they create new techniques of observation and experimentation. Thus when the Michelson-Moley experiment disclosed, as a matter of gross experience, facts which did not agree with the results of accepted physical laws, physicists did not think for a moment of denying the validity of what was found in that experience, even though it rendered questionable an elaborate intellectual apparatus and system. The coincidence of the bands of the interferometer was accepted at its face value in spite of its incompatibility with Newtonian physics. Because scientific inquirers accepted it at its face value they at once set to work to reconstruct their theories; they questioned their reflective premises, not the full "reality" of what they saw. This task of re-adjustment compelled not only new reasonings and calculations in the development of a more comprehensive theory, but opened up new ways of inquiry into experienced subject-matter. Not for a moment did they think of explaining away the features of an object in gross experience because it was not in logical harmony with theory—as philosophers have so often done. Had they done so, they would have stultified science and shut themselves off from new problems and new findings in subject-matter. In short, the material of refined scientific method is continuous with that of the actual world as it is concretely experienced.

But when philosophers transfer into their theories bodily and as finalities the refined conclusions they borrow from the sciences, whether logic, mathematics or physics, these results are not employed to reveal new subject-matters and illuminate old ones of gross experience; they are employed to cast discredit on the latter and to generate new and artificial problems regarding the reality and validity of the things of gross experience. Thus the discoveries of psychologies taken out of their own empirical context are in philosophy employed to cast doubt upon the reality of things external to mind and to selves, things and properties that are perhaps the most salient characteristics of ordinary experience. Similarly, the discoveries and methods of physical science, the concepts of mass, space, motion, have been adopted wholesale in isolation by philosophers in such a way as to make dubious and even incredible the reality of the affections, purposes and enjoyments of concrete experience. The objects of mathematics, symbols of relations having no explicit reference to actual existence, efficacious in the territory to which mathematical technique applies, have been employed in philosophy to determine the priority of essences to existence, and to create the insoluble problem of why pure essence ever descends into the tangles and tortuosities of existence.

What empirical method exacts of philosophy is two things: First, that refined methods and products be traced back to their origin in primary experience, in all its heterogeneity and fullness; so that the needs and problems out of which they arise and which they have to satisfy be acknowledged. Secondly, that the secondary methods and conclusions be brought back to the things of ordinary experience, in all their coarseness and crudity, for verification. In this way, the methods of analytic reflection yield material which form the ingredients of a method of designation, denotation, in philosophy. A scientific work in physics or astronomy gives a record of calculations and deductions that were derived from past observations and experiments. But it is more than a record; it is also an indication, an assignment, of further observations and experiments to be performed. No scientific report would get a hearing if it did not describe the apparatus by means of which experiments were carried on and results obtained; not that apparatus is worshipped, but because this procedure tells other inquirers how they are to go to work to get results which will agree or disagree in their experience with those previously arrived at, and thus confirm, modify and rectify the latter. The recorded scientific result is in effect a *designation* of a method to be followed and a *prediction* of what will be found when specified observations are set on foot. That is all a philosophy can be or do. In the chapters that follow I have undertaken a revision and reconstruction of the conclusions, the reports, of a number of historic philosophic systems, in order that they may be usable methods by which one may go to his own experience, and, discerning what is found by use of the method, come to understand better what is already within the common experience of mankind.

There is a special service which the study of philosophy may render.

Empirically pursued it will not be a study of philosophy but a study, by means of philosophy, of life-experience. But this experience is already overlaid and saturated with the products of the reflection of past generations and by-gone ages. It is filled with interpretations, classifications, due to sophisticated thought, which have become incorporated into what seems to be fresh, naïve empirical material. It would take more wisdom than is possessed by the wisest historic scholar to track all of these absorbed borrowings to their original sources. If we may for the moment call these materials prejudices (even if they are true, as long as their source and authority is unknown), then philosophy is a critique of prejudices. These incorporated results of past reflection, welded into the genuine materials of first-hand experience, may become organs of enrichment if they are detected and reflected upon. If they are not detected, they often obfuscate and distort. Clarification and emancipation follow when they are detected and cast out; and one great object of philosophy is to accomplish this task.

An empirical philosophy is in any case a kind of intellectual disrobing. We cannot permanently divest ourselves of the intellectual habits we take on and wear when we assimilate the culture of our own time and place. But intelligent furthering of culture demands that we take some of them off, that we inspect them critically to see what they are made of and what wearing them does to us. We cannot achieve recovery of primitive naïveté. But there is attainable a cultivated naïveté of eye, ear and thought, one that can be acquired only through the discipline of severe thought. If the chapters which follow contribute to an artful innocence and simplicity they will have served their purpose.

I am loath to conclude without reference to the larger liberal humane value of philosophy when pursued with empirical method. The most serious indictment to be brought against non-empirical philosophies is that they have cast a cloud over the things of ordinary experience. They have not been content to rectify them. They have discredited them at large. In casting aspersion upon the things of everyday experience, the things of action and affection and social intercourse, they have done something worse than fail to give these affairs the intelligent direction they so much need. It would not matter much if philosophy had been reserved as a luxury of only a few thinkers. We endure many luxuries. The serious matter is that philosophies have denied that common experience is capable of developing from within itself methods which will secure direction for itself and will create inherent standards of judgment and value. No one knows how many of the evils and deficiencies that are pointed to as reasons for flight from experience are themselves due to the disregard of experience shown by those peculiarly reflective. To waste of time and energy, to disillusionment with life that attends every deviation from concrete experience must be added the tragic failure to realize the value that intelligent search could reveal and mature among the things of ordinary experience. I cannot calculate how much of current cynicism, indifference and pessimism is due to these causes in the deflection of intelligence they have brought about. It has even become in many circles a sign of lack of sophistication to imagine that life is or can be a fountain of cheer and happiness. Philosophies no more than religions can be acquitted of responsibility for bringing this result to pass. The transcendental philosopher has probably done more than the professed sensualist and materialist to obscure the potentialities of daily experience for joy and for self-regulation. If what is written in these pages has no other result than creating and promoting a respect for concrete human experience and its potentialities, I shall be content.

18. Existence as Precarious and Stable*

In this second chapter of *Experience and Nature*, Dewey fleshes out his notion of ordinary experience by virtue of his concentration on the "precarious." He states that "man finds himself living in an aleatory world; his existence involves, to put it baldly, a gamble. The world is a scene of risk; it is uncertain, unstable, uncannily unstable." Dewey then contends that with few exceptions, traditional philosophy has been unable or unwilling to deal adequately with the precarious, the ambiguous, or the contingent aspects of experience, preferring to dismiss them or buy them off by overarching classificatory systems. But however clever the dialectic or imposing the system, philosophy must never forget that "incompleteness and precariousness is a trait that must be given footing of the same rank as the finished and fixed."

It was suggested in the last chapter that experience has its equivalents in such affairs as history, life, culture. Reference to these other affairs enables us to put to one side the reminiscences which so readily give the

* From John Dewey, *Experience and Nature* (New York, 1958) (1929), 2nd ed., Chap. 10.

word experience a sectarian and provincial content. According to Tylor, culture is "that complex whole which includes knowledge, belief, art, morals, custom, and any other capabilities acquired by a man as a member of society." It is, in some sense, a whole, but it is a complex, a diversified whole. It is differentiated into religion, magic, law, fine and useful art, science, philosophy, language, domestic and political relations, etc. Consider the following words of an anthropologist and ask if they do not fairly define the problem of philosophy, although intended for another purpose. "Cultural reality is never wholly deterministic nor yet wholly objective, never wholly of yesterday nor yet wholly of today, but combines all of these in its existential reality. . . . A reconstructive synthesis re-establishes the synthetic unity necessarily lost in the process of analytic dismemberment."[1] I do not mean that philosophy is to be merged in an anthropological view of culture. But in a different context and by a different method, it has the task of analytic dismemberment and synthetic reconstruction of experience; the phenomena of culture as presented by the anthropologist provide, moreover, precious material to aid the performance of this office, material more pertinent to the task of philosophizing than that of psychology isolated from a theory of culture.

A feature of existence which is emphasized by cultural phenomena is the precarious and perilous. Sumner refers to Grimm as authority for the statement that the Germanic tribes had over a thousand distinct sayings, proverbs and apothegms, concerning luck. Time is brief, and this statement must stand instead of the discourse which the subject deserves. Man finds himself living in an aleatory world; his existence involves, to put it baldly, a gamble. The world is a scene of risk; it is uncertain, unstable, uncannily unstable. Its dangers are irregular, inconstant, not to be counted upon as to their times and seasons. Although persistent, they are sporadic, episodic. It is darkest just before dawn; pride goes before a fall; the moment of greatest prosperity is the moment most charged with ill-omen, most opportune for the evil eye. Plague, famine, failure of crops, disease, death, defeat in battle, are always just around the corner, and so are abundance, strength, victory, festival and song. Luck is proverbially both good and bad in its distributions. The sacred and the accursed are potentialities of the same situation; and there is no category of things which has not embodied the sacred and accursed: persons, words, places, times, directions in space, stones, winds, animals, stars.

[1] Goldenweiser.

Anthropologists have shown incontrovertibly the part played by the precarious aspect of the world in generating religion with its ceremonies, rites, cults, myths, magic; and it has shown the pervasive penetration of these affairs into morals, law, art, and industry. Beliefs and dispositions connected with them are the background out of which philosophy and secular morals slowly developed, as well as more slowly those late inventions, art for art's sake, and business is business. Interesting and instructive as is this fact, it is not the ramifications which here concern us. We must not be diverted to consider the consequences for philosophy, even for doctrines reigning today, of facts concerning the origin of philosophies. We confine ourselves to one outstanding fact: the evidence that the world of empirical things includes the uncertain, unpredictable, uncontrollable, and hazardous.

It is an old saying that the gods were born of fear. The saying is only too likely to strengthen a misconception bred by confirmed subjective habits. We first endow man in isolation with an instinct of fear and then we imagine him irrationally ejecting that fear into the environment, scattering broadcast as it were, the fruits of his own purely personal limitations, and thereby creating superstition. But fear, whether an instinct or an acquisition, is a function of the environment. Man fears because he exists in a fearful, an awful world. The *world* is precarious and perilous. It is as easily accessible and striking evidence of this fact that primitive experience is cited. The voice is that of early man; but the hand is that of nature, the nature in which we still live. It was not fear of gods that created the gods.

For if the life of early man is filled with expiations and propitiations, if in his feasts and festivals what is enjoyed is gratefully shared with his gods, it is not because a belief in supernatural powers created a need for expiatory, propitiatory and communal offerings. Everything that man achieves and possesses is got by actions that may involve him in other and obnoxious consequences in addition to those wanted and enjoyed. His acts are trespasses upon the domain of the unknown; and hence atonement, if offered in season, may ward off direful consequences that haunt even the moment of prosperity—or that most haunt that moment. While unknown consequences flowing from the past dog the present, the future is even more unknown and perilous; the present by that fact is ominous. If unknown forces that decide future destiny can be placated, the man who will not study the methods of securing their favor is incredibly flippant. In enjoyment of present food and companionship, nature, tradition and social organization have coöperated, thereby supplementing our own endeavors so petty and so feeble without this extraneous reinforcement. Goods are by grace not of ourselves. He is a dangerous churl who will not gratefully acknowledge by means of free-will offerings the help that sustains him.

These things are as true today as they were in the days of early culture. It is not the facts which have changed, but the methods of insurance, regulation and acknowledgment. Herbert Spencer sometimes colored his devotion to symbolic experiences with a fact of dire experience. When he says that every fact has two opposite sides, "the one its near or visible side and the other its remote or invisible side," he expresses a persistent trait of every object in experience. The visible is set in the invisible; and in the end what is unseen decides what happens in the seen; the tangible rests precariously upon the untouched and ungrasped. The contrast and the potential maladjustment of the immediate, the conspicuous and focal phase of things, with those indirect and hidden factors which determine the origin and career of what is present, are indestructible features of any and every experience. We may term the way in which our ancestors dealt with the contrast superstitious, but the contrast is no superstition. It is a primary datum in any experience.

We have substituted sophistication for superstition, at least measurably so. But the sophistication is often as irrational and as much at the mercy of words as the superstition it replaces. Our magical safeguard against the uncertain character of the world is to deny the existence of chance, to mumble universal and necessary law, the ubiquity of cause and effect, the uniformity of nature, universal progress, and the inherent rationality of the universe. These magic formulae borrow their potency from conditions that are not magical. Through science we have secured a degree of power of prediction and of control; through tools, machinery and an accompanying technique we have made the world more conformable to our needs, a more secure abode. We have heaped up riches and means of comfort between ourselves and the risks of the world. We have professionalized amusement as an agency of escape and forgetfulness. But when all is said and done, the fundamentally hazardous character of the world is not seriously modified, much less eliminated. Such an incident as the last war and preparations for a future war remind us that it is easy to overlook the extent to which, after all, our attainments are only devices for blurring the disagreeable recognition of a fact, instead of means of altering the fact itself.

What has been said sounds pessimistic. But the concern is not with morals but with metaphysics, with, that is to say, the nature of the existential world in which we live. It would have been as easy and more comfortable to emphasize good luck, grace, unexpected and unwon joys, those unsought for happenings which we so significantly call happiness. We might have appealed to good fortune as evidence of this important trait of hazard in nature. Comedy is as genuine as tragedy. But it is traditional that comedy strikes a more superficial note than tragedy. And there is an even better reason for appealing to misfortunes and mistakes as evidence of the precarious nature of the world. The problem of evil is a well recognized problem, while we rarely or never hear of a problem of good. Goods we take for granted; they are as they should be; they are natural and proper. The good is a recognition of our deserts. When we pull out a plum we treat it as evidence of the *real* order of cause and effect in the world. For this reason it is difficult for the goods of existence to furnish as convincing evidence of the uncertain character of nature as do evils. It is the latter we term accidents, not the former, even when their adventitious character is as certain.

What of it all, it may be asked? In the sense in which an assertion is true that uncontrolled distribution of good and evil is evidence of the precarious, uncertain nature of existence, it is a truism, and no problem is forwarded by its reiteration. But it is submitted that just this predicament of the inextricable mixture of stability and uncertainty gives rise to philosophy, and that it is reflected in all its recurrent problems and issues. If classic philosophy says so much about unity and so little about unreconciled diversity, so much about the eternal and permanent, and so little about change (save as something to be resolved into combinations of the permanent), so much about necessity and so little about contingency, so much about the comprehending universal and so little about the recalcitrant particular, it may well be because the ambiguousness and ambivalence of reality are actually so pervasive. Since these things form the problem, solution is more apparent (although not more actual), in the degree in which whatever of stability and assurance the world presents is fastened upon and asserted.

Upon their surface, the reports of the world which form our different philosophies are various to the point of stark contrariness. They range from spiritualism to materialism, from absolutism to relativistic phenomenalism, from transcendentalism to positivism, from rationalism to sensationalism, from idealism to realism, from subjectivism to bald objectivism, from Platonic realism to nominalism. The array of contradictions is so imposing as to suggest to sceptics that the mind of man has tackled an impossible job, or that philosophers have abandoned themselves to vagary. These radical oppositions in philosophers suggest however another consideration. They suggest that all their different philosophies have a common premise, and that their diversity is due to acceptance of a common premise. Variant philosophies may be looked at as different ways of supplying recipes for denying to the universe the character of contingency which it possesses so integrally that its denial leaves the reflecting mind without a clew, and puts subsequent philosophising at the mercy of temperament, interest and local surroundings.

Quarrels among conflicting types of philosphy are thus family quarrels. They go on within the limits of a too domestic circle, and can be settled only by venturing further afield, and out of doors. Concerned with imputing complete, finished and sure character to the world of real existence, even if things have to be broken into two disconnected pieces in order to accomplish the result, the character desiderated can plausibly be found in reason or in mechanism; in rational conceptions like those of mathematics, or brute things like sensory data; in atoms or in essences; in consciousness or in a physical externality which forces and overrides consciousness.

As against this common identification of reality with what is sure, regular and finished, experience in unsophisticated forms gives evidence of a different world and points to a different metaphysics. We live in a world which is an impressive and irresistible mixture of sufficiencies, tight completenesses, order, recurrences which make possible prediction and control, and singularities, ambiguities, uncertain possibilities, processes going on to consequences as yet indeterminate. They are mixed not mechanically but vitally like the wheat and tares of the parable. We may recognize them separately but we cannot divide them, for unlike wheat and tares they grow from the same root. Qualities have defects as necessary conditions of their excellencies; the instrumentalities of truth are the causes of error; change gives meaning to permanence and recurrence makes novelty possible. A world that was wholly risky would be a world in which adventure is impossible, and only a living world can include death. Such facts have been celebrated by thinkers like Heracleitus and Laotze; they have been greeted by theologians as furnishing occasions for exercise of divine grace; they have been elaborately formulated by various schools under a principle of relativity, so defined as to become itself final and absolute. They have rarely been frankly recognized as fundamentally significant for the formation of a naturalistic metaphysics.

Aristotle perhaps came the nearest to a start in that direction. But his thought did not go far on the road, though it may be used to suggest the road which he failed to take. Aristotle acknowledges contingency, but he never surrenders his bias in favor of the fixed, certain and finished.

His whole theory of forms and ends is a theory of the superiority in Being of rounded-out fixities. His physics is a fixation of ranks or grades of necessity and contingency so sorted that necessity measures dignity and equals degree of reality, while contingency and change measure degrees of deficiency of Being. The empirical impact and sting of the mixture of universality and singularity and chance is evaded by parcelling out the regions of space so that they have their natural abode in different portions of nature. His logic is one of definition and classification, so that its task is completed when changing and contingent things are distinguished from the necessary, universal and fixed, by attribution to inferior species of things. Chance appears in thought not as a calculus of probabilities in predicting the observable occurrence of any and every event, but as marking an inferior type of syllogism. Things that move are intrinsically different from things that exhibit eternal regularity. Change is honestly recognized as a genuine feature of *some* things, but the point of the recognition is avoided by imputing alteration to inherent deficiency of Being over against complete Being which never changes. Changing things belong to a purgatorial realm, where they wander aimlessly until redeemed by love of finality of form, the acquisition of which lifts them to a paradise of self-sufficient Being. With slight exaggeration, it may be said that the thoroughgoing way in which Aristotle defined, distinguished and classified rest and movement, the finished and the incomplete, the actual and potential, did more to fix tradition, *the* genteel tradition one is tempted to add, which identifies the fixed and regular with reality of Being and the changing and hazardous with deficiency of Being than ever was accomplished by those who took the shorter path of asserting that change is illusory.

His philosophy was closer to empirical facts than most modern philosophies, in that it was neither monistic nor dualistic but openly pluralistic. His plurals fall however, within a grammatical system, to each portion of which a corresponding cosmic status is allotted. Thus his pluralism solved the problem of how to have your cake and eat it too, for a classified and hierarchically ordered set of pluralities, of variants, has none of the sting of the miscellaneous and uncoördinated plurals of our actual world. In this classificatory scheme of separation he has been followed, though perhaps unwittingly, by many philosophers of different import. Thus Kant assigns all that is manifold and chaotic to one realm, that of sense, and all that is uniform and regular to that of reason. A single and all embracing dialectic problem of the combination of sense and thought is thereby substituted for the concrete problems that arise through the mixed and varied union in existence of the variable and the constant, the necessary and that which proceeds uncertainly.

The device is characteristic of a conversion such as has already been commented upon of a moral insight to be made good in action into an antecedent metaphysics of existence or a general theory of knowledge. The striving to make stability of meaning prevail over the instability of events is the main task of intelligent human effort. But when the function is dropped from the province of art and treated as a property of given things, whether cosmological or logical, effort is rendered useless, and a premium is put upon the accidental good-fortune of a class that happens to be furnished by the toil of another class with products that give to life its dignity and leisurely stability.

The argument is not forgetful that there are, from Heracleitus to Bergson, philosophies, metaphysics, of change. One is grateful to them for keeping alive a sense of what classic, orthodox philosophies have whisked out of sight. But the philosophies of flux also indicate the intensity of the craving for the sure and fixed. They have deified change by making it universal, regular, sure. To say this is not, I hope, verbal by-play. Consider the wholly eulogistic fashion in which Hegel and Bergson, and the professedly evolutionary philosophers of becoming, have taken change. With Hegel becoming is a rational process which defines logic although a new and strange logic, and an absolute, although new and strange, God. With Spencer, evolution is but the transitional process of attaining a fixed and universal equilibrium of harmonious adjustment. With Bergson, change is the creative operation of God, or *is* God—one is not quite sure which. The change of change is not only cosmic pyrotechnics, but is a process of divine, spiritual, energy. We are here in the presence of prescription, not description. Romanticism is an evangel in the garb of metaphysics. It sidesteps the painful, toilsome labor of understanding and of control which change sets us, by glorifying it for its own sake. Flux is made something to revere, something profoundly akin to what is best within ourselves, will and creative energy. It is not, as it is in experience, a call to effort, a challenge to investigation, a potential doom of disaster and death.

If we follow classical terminology, philosophy is love of wisdom, while metaphysics is cognizance of the generic traits of existence. In this sense of metaphysics, incompleteness and precariousness is a trait that must be given footing of the same rank as the finished and fixed. Love of wisdom is concerned with finding its implications for the conduct of life, in devotion to what is good. On the cognitive side, the issue is largely that of measure, of the ratio one bears to others in the situations of life. On the practical side, it is a question of the use to be made of each, of turning each to best account. Man is naturally philosophic, rather than metaphysical or coldly scientific, noting and describing. Concerned with prudence if not with what is honorifically called wisdom, man naturally prizes knowledge only for the sake of its bearing upon success and failure in attaining goods and avoiding evils. This is a fact of our structure and nothing is gained by recommending it as an ideal truth, and equally nothing is gained by attributing to intellect an intrinsic relationship to pure truth for its own sake or bare fact on its own account. The first method encourages dogma, and the second expresses a myth. The love of knowledge for its own sake is an ideal of morals; it is an integral condition of the wisdom that rightly conceives and effectually pursues the good. For wisdom as to ends depends upon acquaintance with conditions and means, and unless the acquaintance is adequate and fair, wisdom becomes a sublimated folly of self-deception.

Denial of an inherent relation of mind to truth or fact for its own sake, apart from insight into what the fact or truth exacts of us in behavior and imposes upon us in joy and suffering; and simultaneous affirmation that devotion to fact, to truth, is a necessary moral demand, involve no inconsistency. .Denial relates to natural events as independent of choice and endeavor; affirmation relates to choice and action. But choice and the reflective effort involved in it are themselves such contingent events and so bound up with the precarious uncertainty of other events, that philosophers have too readily assumed that metaphysics, and science of fact and truth, are themselves wisdom, thinking thus to avoid the necessity of either exercising or recognizing choice. The consequence is that conversion of unavowed morals or wisdom into cosmology, and into a metaphysics of nature, which was termed in the last chapter *the* philosophic fallacy. It supplies the formula of the technique by which thinkers have relegated the uncertain and unfinished to an invidious state of unreal being, while they have systematically exalted the assured and complete to the rank of true Being.

Upon the side of wisdom, as human beings interested in good and bad things in their connection with human conduct, thinkers are concerned to mitigate the instability of life, to introduce moderation, temper and economy, and when worst comes to worst to suggest consolations and compensations. They are concerned with rendering more stable good things, and more unstable bad things; they are interested in how changes may be turned to account in the consequences to which they contribute. The facts of the ungoing, unfinished and ambiguously potential world give point and poignancy to the search for absolutes and finalities. Then when philosophers have hit in reflection upon a thing which is stably good in quality and hence worthy of persistent and continued choice, they hesitate, and withdraw from the effort and struggle that choice demands:—namely, from the effort to give it some such stability in observed existence as it possesses in quality when thought of. Thus it becomes a refuge, an asylum for contemplation, or a theme for dialectical elaboration, instead of an ideal to inspire and guide conduct.

Since thinkers claim to be concerned with knowledge of existence, rather than with imagination, they have to make good the pretention to knowledge. Hence they transmute the imaginative perception of the stably good object into a definition and description of true reality in contrast with lower and specious existence, which, being precarious and incomplete, alone involves us in the necessity of choice and active struggle. Thus they remove from actual existence the very traits which generate philosophic reflection and which give point and bearing to its conclusions. In briefest formula, "reality" becomes what we wish existence to be, after we have analyzed its defects and decided upon what would remove them; "reality" is what existence would be if our reasonably justified preferences were so completely established in nature as to exhaust and define its entire being and thereby render search and struggle unnecessary. What is left over, (and since trouble, struggle, conflict, and error still empirically exist, something *is* left over) being excluded by definition from full reality is assigned to a grade or order of being which is asserted to be metaphysically inferior; an order variously called appearance, illusion, mortal mind, or the merely empirical, against what really and truly is. Then the problem of metaphysics alters: instead of being a detection and description of the generic traits of existence, it becomes an endeavor to adjust or reconcile to each other two separate realms of being. Empirically we have just what we started with: the mixture of the precarious and problematic with the assured and complete. But a classificatory device, based on desire and elaborated in reflective imagination, has been introduced by which the two traits are torn apart, one of them being labelled reality and the other appearance. The genuinely moral problem of mitigating and regulating the troublesome factor by active employment of the stable factor then drops out of sight. The dialectic problem of logical reconciliation of two notions has taken its place.

The most widespread of these classificatory devices, the one of greatest popular appeal, is that which divides existence into the supernatural and the natural. Men may fear the gods but it is axiomatic that the gods have nothing to fear. They lead a life of untroubled serenity, the life that pleases them. There is a long story between the primitive forms of this division of objects of experience and the dialectical imputation to the divine of omnipotence, omniscience, eternity and infinity, in contrast with the attribution to man and experienced nature of finitude, weakness, limitation, struggle and change. But in the make-up of human psychology the later history is implicit in the early crude division. One realm is the home of assured appropriation and possession; the other of striving, transiency and frustration. How many persons are there today who conceive that they have disposed of ignorance, struggle and disappointment by pointing to man's "finite" nature—as if finitude signifies anything else but an abstract classificatory naming of certain concrete and discriminable traits of nature itself—traits of nature which generate ignorance, arbitrary appearance and disappearance, failure and striving. It pleases man to substitute the dialectic exercise of showing how the "finite" can exist with or within the "infinite" for the problem of dealing with the contingent, thinking to solve the problem by distinguishing and naming its factors. Failure of the exercise is certain, but the failure can be flourished as one more proof of the finitude of man's intellect, and the needlessness because impotency of endeavor of "finite" creatures to attack ignorance and oppressive fatalities. Wisdom then consists in administration of the temporal, finite and human in its relation to the eternal and infinite, by means of dogma and cult, rather than in regulation of the events of life by understanding of actual conditions.

It does not demand great ingenuity to detect the inversion here. The starting point is precisely the existing mixture of the regular and dependable and the unsettled and uncertain. There are a multitude of recipes for obtaining a vicarious possession of the stable and final without getting involved in the labor and pain of intellectual effort attending regulation of the conditions upon which these fruits depend.

This situation is worthy of remark as an exemplification of how easy it is to arrive at a description of existence via a theory of wisdom, of reflective insight into goods. It has a direct bearing upon a metaphysical doctrine which is not popular, like the division into the supernatural, and natural, but which is learned and technical. The philosopher may have little esteem for the crude forms assumed by the popular metaphysics of earth and heaven, of God, nature, and man. But the philosopher has often proceeded in a manner analogous to that which resulted in this popular metaphysics; some of the most cherished metaphysical distinctions seem to be but learned counterparts, dependent upon an elaborate intellectual technique, for these rough, crude notions of supernatural and natural, divine and human, in popular belief. I refer to such things as the Platonic division into ideal archetypes and physical events; the Aristotelian division into form which is actuality and matter which is potential, when that is understood as a distinction of ranks of reality; the noumenal things, things-in-themselves of Kant in contrast with natural objects as phenomenal; the distinction, current among contemporary absolute idealists, of reality and appearance.

The division however is not confined to philosophers with leanings toward spiritualistic philosophies. There is some evidence that Plato got the term Idea, as a name for essential form, from Democritus. Whether this be the case or no, the Idea of Democritus, though having a radically diverse structure from the Platonic Idea, had the same function of designating a finished, complete, stable, wholly unprecarious reality. Both philosophers craved solidity and both found it; corresponding to the Platonic phenomenal flux are the Democritean things as they are in custom or ordinary experience: corresponding to the ideal archetypes are substantial indivisible atoms. Corresponding, again to the Platonic theory of Ideas is the modern theory of mathematical structures which are alone independently real, while the empirical impressions and suggestions to which they give rise is the counterpart of his realm of phenomena.

Apart from the materialistic and spiritualistic schools, there is the Spinozistic division into attributes and modes; the old division of essence and existence, and its modern counterpart subsistence and existence. It is impossible to force Mr. Bertrand Russell into any one of the pigeonholes of the cabinet of conventional philosophic schools. But moral, or philosophical, motivation is obvious in his metaphysics when he says that mathematics takes us "into the region of absolute necessity, to which not only the actual world but every possible world must conform." Indeed with his usual lucidity, he says, mathematics "finds a habitation eternally standing, where our ideals are fully satisfied and our best hopes are not thwarted." When he adds that contemplation of such objects is the "chief means of overcoming the terrible sense of impotence, of weakness, of exile amid hostile power, which is too apt to result from acknowledging the all but omnipotence of alien forces," the presence of moral origin is explicit.

No modern thinker has pointed out so persuasively as Santayana that "every phase of the ideal world emanates from the natural," that "sense, art, religion, society express nature exuberantly." And yet unless one reads him wrong, he then confounds his would-be disciples and confuses his critics by holding that nature is *truly* presented only in an esthetic contemplation of essences reached by physical science, an envisagement reached through a dialectic which "is a transubstantiation of matter, a passage from existence to eternity." This passage moreover is so utter that there is no road back. The stable ideal meanings which are the fruit of nature are forbidden, in the degree in which they are its highest and truest fruits, from dropping seeds in nature to its further fructification.

The perception of genetic continuity between the dynamic flux of nature and an eternity of static ideal forms thus terminate in a sharp division, in reiteration of the old tradition. Perhaps it is a caricature to say that the ultimate of reason is held to be ability to behold nature as a complete mechanism which generates and sustains the beholding of the mechanism, but the caricature is not wilful. If the separation of contingency and necessity is abandoned, what is there to exclude a belief that science, while it is grasp of the regular and stable mechanism of nature, is also an organ of regulating and enriching, through its own expansion, the more exuberant and irregular expressions of nature in human intercourse, the arts, religion, industry, and politics?

To follow out the latter suggestion would take us to a theme reserved for later consideration. We are here concerned with the fact that it is the intricate mixture of the stable and the precarious, the fixed and the unpredictably novel, the assured and the uncertain, in existence which sets mankind upon that love of wisdom which forms philosophy. Yet too commonly, although in a great variety of technical modes, the result of the search is converted into a metaphysics which denies or conceals from acknowledgment the very characters of existence which initiated it, and which give significance to its conclusions. The form assumed by the denial is, most frequently, that striking division into a superior true realm of being and lower illusory, insignificant or phenomenal realm which characterizes metaphysical systems as unlike as those of Plato and Democritus, St. Thomas and Spinoza, Aristotle and Kant, Descartes and Comte, Haeckel and Mrs. Eddy.

The same jumble of acknowledgment and denial attends the conception of Absolute Experience: as if any experience could be more absolutely experience than that which marks the life of humanity. This conception constitutes the most recent device for first admitting and then denying the combinedly stable and unstable nature of the world. Its plaintive recognition of our experience as finite and temporal, as full of error, conflict and contradiction, is an acknowledgment of the precarious uncertainty of the objects and connections that constitute nature as it emerges in history. Human experience however has also the pathetic longing for truth, beauty and order. There is more than the longing: there are moments of achievement. Experience exhibits ability to possess harmonious objects. It evinces an ability, within limits, to safeguard the excellent objects and to deflect and reduce the obnoxious ones. The concept of an absolute experience which is only and always perfect and good, first explicates these desirable implications of things of actual experience, and then asserts that they alone are real. The experienced occurrences which give poignancy and pertinency to the longing for a better world, the experimental endeavors and plans which make possible actual betterments within the objects of actual experience, are thus swept out of real Being into a limbo of appearances.

The notion of Absolute Experience thus serves as a symbol of two facts. One is the ineradicable union in nature of the relatively stable and the relatively contingent. The division of the movement and leadings of things which are experienced into two parts, such that one set constitutes and defines absolute and eternal experience, while the other set constitutes and defines finite experience, tells us nothing about absolute experience. It tells us a good deal about experience as it exists: namely, that it is such as to involve permanent and general objects of reference as well as temporally changing events; the possibility of truth as well as error; conclusive objects and goods as well as things whose purport and nature is determinable only in an indeterminate future. Nothing is gained—except the delights of a dialectic problem—in labelling one assortment absolute experience and the other finite experience. Since the appeal of the adherents of the philosophy of absolute and phenomenal experience is to a logical criterion, namely, to the implication in every judgment, however erroneous, of a standard of consistency which excludes any possibility of contradictoriness, the inherent logical contradictions in the doctrine itself are worth noting.

In the first place, the contents as well as the form of ultimate Absolute Experience are derived from and based upon the natures of actual experience, the very experience which is then relegated to unreality by the supreme reality derived from its unreality. It is "real" just long enough to afford a spring-board into ultimate reality and to afford a hint of the essential contents of the latter and then it obligingly dissolves into mere appearance. If we start from the standpoint of the Absolute Experience thus reached, the contradiction is repeated from its side. Although absolute, eternal, all-comprehensive, and pervasively integrated into a whole so logically perfect that no separate patterns, to say nothing of seams and holes, can exist in it, it proceeds to play a tragic joke upon itself—for there is nothing else to be fooled—by appearing in a queer combination of rags and glittering gew-gaws, in the garb of the temporal, partial and conflicting things, mental as well as physical, of ordinary experience. I do not cite these dialectic contradictions as having an inherent importance. But the fact that a doctrine which avowedly takes logical consistence for its method and criterion, whose adherents are noteworthy for dialectic acumen in specific issues, should terminate in such thoroughgoing contradictions may be cited as evidence that after all the doctrine is merely engaged in an arbitrary sorting out of characters of things which in nature are always present in conjunction and interpenetration.

The union of the hazardous and the stable, of the incomplete and the recurrent, is the condition of all experienced satisfaction as truly as of our predicaments and problems. While it is the source of ignorance, error and failure of expectation, it is the source of the delight which fulfillments bring. For if there were nothing in the way, if there were no deviations and resistances, fulfillment would be at once, and in so being would fulfill nothing, but merely be. It would not be in connection with desire or satisfaction. Moreover when a fulfillment comes and is pronounced good, it is *judged* good, distinguished and asserted, simply because it is in jeopardy, because it occurs amid indifferent and divergent things. Because of this mixture of the regular and that which cuts across stability, a good object once experienced acquires ideal quality and attracts demand and effort to itself. A particular ideal may be an illusion, but having ideals is no illusion. It embodies features of existence. Although imagination is often fantastic it is also an organ of nature; for it is the appropriate phase of indeterminate events moving toward eventualities that are now but possibilities. A purely stable world permits of no illusions, but neither is it clothed with ideals. It just exists. To be good is to be better than; and there can be no better except where there is shock and discord combined with enough assured order to make attainment of harmony possible. Better objects when brought into existence are existent not ideal; they retain ideal quality only retrospectively as commemorative of issue from prior conflict and prospectively, in contrast with forces which make for their destruction. Water that slakes thirst, or a conclusion that solves a problem have ideal character as long as thirst or problem persists in a way which qualifies the result. But water that is not a satisfaction of need has no more ideal quality than water running through pipes into a reservoir; a solution ceases to be a solution and becomes a bare incident of existence when its antecedent generating conditions of doubt, ambiguity and search are lost from its context. While the precarious nature of existence is indeed the source of all trouble, it is also an indispensable condition of ideality, becoming a sufficient condition when conjoined with the regular and assured.

We long, amid a troubled world, for perfect being. We forget that what gives meaning to the notion of perfection is the events that create longing, and that, apart from them, a "perfect" world would mean just an unchanging brute existential thing. The ideal significance of esthetic objects is no exception to this principle. Their satisfying quality, their power to compose while they arouse, is not dependent upon definite prior desire and effort as is the case with the ideally satisfying quality of practical and scientific objects. It is part of their peculiar satisfying quality to be gratuitous, not purchased by endeavor. The contrast to other things of this detachment from toil and labor in a world where most realizations have to be bought, as well as the contrast to trouble and uncertainty, give esthetic objects their peculiar traits. If all things came to us in the way our esthetic objects do, none of them would be a source of esthetic delight.

Some phases of recent philosophy have made much of need, desire and satisfaction. Critics have frequently held that the outcome is only recurrence to an older subjective empiricism, though with substitution of affections and volitional states for cognitive sensory states. But need and desire are exponents of natural being. They are, if we use Aristotelian phraseology, actualizations of its contingencies and incompletenesses; as such nature itself is wistful and pathetic, turbulent and passionate. Were it not, the existence of wants would be a miracle. In a world where everything is complete, nothing requires anything else for its completion. A world in which events can be carried to a finish only through the coinciding assistance of other transitory events, is already necessitous, a world of begging as well as of beggarly elements. If human experience is to express and reflect this world, it must be marked by needs; in becoming aware of the needful and needed quality of things it must project satisfactions or completions. For irrespective of whether a satisfaction is conscious, a satisfaction or non-satisfaction is an objective thing with objective conditions. It means fulfillment of the demands of objective factors. Happiness may *mark* an awareness of such satisfaction, and it may *be* its culminating form. But satisfaction is not subjective, private or personal: it is conditioned by objective partialities and defections and made real by objective situations and completions.

By the same logic, necessity implies the precarious and contingent. A world that was all necessity would not be a world of necessity; it would just be. For in its being, nothing would be necessary for anything else. But where some things are indigent, other things are necessary if demands are to be met. The common failure to note the fact that a world of complete being would be a world in which necessity is meaningless is due to a rapid shift from one universe of discourse to another. First we postulate a whole of Being; then we shift to a part; now since a "part" is logically dependent as such in its existence and its properties, it is necessitated by other parts. But we have unwittingly introduced contingency in the very fact of marking off something as just a part. If the logical implications of the original notion are held to firmly, a part is already a part-of-a-whole. Its being what it is, is not necessitated by the whole or by other parts: its being what it is, is just a name for the whole being what it is. Whole and parts alike are but names for existence there as just what it is. But wherever we can say *if* so-and-so, then something else, there is necessity, because partialities are implied which are not just parts-of-a-whole. A world of "ifs" is alone a world of "musts"—the "ifs" express real differences; the "musts" real connections. The stable and recurrent is needed for the fulfillment of the possible; the doubtful can be settled only through its adaptation to stable objects. The necessary is always necessary for, not necessary in and of itself; it is conditioned by the contingent, although itself a condition of the full determination of the latter.

One of the most striking phases of the history of philosophic thought is the recurrent grouping together of unity, permanence (or "the eternal"), completeness and rational thought, while upon another side full multiplicity, change and the temporal, the partial, defective, sense and desire. This division is obviously but another case of violent separation of the precarious and unsettled from the regular and determinate. One aspect of it, however, is worthy of particular attention: the connection of thought and unity. Empirically, all reflection sets out from the problematic and confused. Its aim is to clarify and ascertain. When thinking is successful, its career closes in transforming the disordered into the orderly, the mixed-up into the distinguished or placed, the unclear and ambiguous into the defined and unequivocal, the disconnected into the systematized. It is empirically assured that the goal of thinking does not remain a mere ideal, but is attained often enough so as to render reasonable additional efforts to achieve it.

In these facts we have, I think, the empirical basis of the philosophic doctrines which assert that reality is really and truly a rational system, a coherent whole of relations that cannot be conceived otherwise than in terms of intellect. Reflective inquiry moves in each particular case from differences toward unity; from indeterminate and ambiguous position to clear determination, from confusion and disorder to system. When thought in a given case has reached its goal of organized totality, of definite relations of distinctly placed elements, its object is the accepted starting point, the defined subject matter, of further experiences; antecedent and outgrown conditions of darkness and of unreconciled differences are dismissed as a transitory state of ignorance and inadequate apprehensions. Retain connection of the goal with the thinking by which it is reached, and then identify it with true reality in contrast with the merely phenomenal, and the outline of the logic of rational and "objective" idealisms is before us. Thought like Being, has two forms, one real; the other phenomenal. It is compelled to take on *reflective* form, it involves doubt, inquiry and hypothesis, because it sets out from a subject-matter conditioned by sense, a fact which proves that thought, intellect, is not pure in man, but restricted by an animal organism that is but one part linked with other parts, of nature. But the conclusion of reflection affords us a pattern and guarantee of thought which is *constitutive;* one with the system of objective reality. Such in outline is the procedure of all ontological logics.

A philosophy which accepts the denotative or empirical method accepts at full value the fact that reflective thinking transforms confusion, ambiguity and discrepancy into illumination, definiteness and consistency. But it also points to the contextual situation in which thinking occurs. It notes that the starting point is the actually *problematic*, and that the problematic phase resides in some actual and specifiable situation.

It notes that the means of converting the dubious into the assured, and the incomplete into the determinate, is use of assured and established things, which are just as empirical and as indicative of the nature of experienced things as is the uncertain. It thus notes that thinking is no different in kind from the use of natural materials and energies, say fire and tools, to refine, re-order, and shape other natural materials, say ore. In both cases, there are matters which as they stand are unsatisfactory and there are also adequate agencies for dealing with them and connecting them. At no point or place is there any jump outside empirical, natural objects and their relations. Thought and reason are not specific powers. They consist of the procedures intentionally employed in the application to each other of the unsatisfactorily confused and indeterminate on one side and the regular and stable on the other. Generalizing from such observations, empirical philosophy perceives that thinking is a continuous process of temporal re-organization within one and the same world of experienced things, not a jump from the latter world into one of objects constituted once for all by thought. It discovers thereby the empirical basis of rational idealism, and the point at which it empirically goes astray. Idealism fails to take into account the specified or concrete character of the uncertain situation in which thought occurs; it fails to note the empirically concrete nature of the subject-matter, acts, and tools by which determination and consistency are reached; it fails to note that the conclusive eventual objects having the latter properties are themselves as many as the situations dealt with. The conversion of the logic of reflection into an ontology of rational being is thus due to arbitrary conversion of an eventual natural function of unification into a causal antecedent reality; this in turn is due to the tendency of the imagination working under the influence of emotion to carry unification from an actual, objective and experimental enterprise, limited to particular situations where it is needed, into an unrestricted, wholesale movement which ends in an all-absorbing dream.

The occurrence of reflection is crucial for dualistic metaphysics as well as for idealistic ontologies. Reflection occurs only in situations qualified by uncertainty, alternatives, questioning, search, hypotheses, tentative trials or experiments which test the worth of thinking. A naturalistic metaphysics is bound to consider reflection as itself a natural event occurring *within* nature because of traits of the latter. It is bound to inference from the empirical traits of thinking in precisely the same way as the sciences make inferences from the happening of suns, radio-activity, thunder-storms or any other natural event. Traits of reflection are as truly indicative or evidential of the traits of *other* things as are the traits of these events. A theory of the nature of the occurrence and career of a sun reached by denial of the obvious traits of the sun, or by denial that these traits are so connected with the traits of other natural events that they can be used as evidence concerning the nature of these other things, would hardly possess scientific standing. Yet philosophers, and strangely enough philosophers who call themselves realists, have constantly held that the traits which are characteristic of thinking, namely, uncertainty, ambiguity, alternatives, inquiring, search, selection, experimental reshaping of external conditions, do not possess the same existential character as do the objects of valid knowledge. They have denied that these traits are evidential of the character of the world within which thinking occurs. They have not, as realists, asserted that these traits are mere appearances; but they have often asserted and implied that such things are only personal or psychological in contrast with a world of objective nature. But the interests of empirical and denotative method and of naturalistic metaphysics wholly coincide. The world must actually be such as to generate ignorance and inquiry; doubt and hypothesis, trial and temporal conclusions; the latter being such that they develop out of existences which while wholly "real" are not as satisfactory, as good, or as significant, as those into which they are eventually re-organized. The ultimate evidence of genuine hazard, contingency, irregularity and indeterminateness in nature is thus found in the occurrence of thinking. The traits of natural existence which generate the fears and adorations of superstitious barbarians generate the scientific procedures of disciplined civilization. The superiority of the latter does not consist in the fact that they are based on "real" existence, while the former depend wholly upon a human nature different from nature in general. It consists in the fact that scientific inquiries reach *objects* which are better, because reached by method which controls them and which adds greater control to life itself, method which mitigates accident, turns contingency to account, and releases thought and other forms of endeavor.

The conjunction of problematic and determinate characters in nature renders every existence, as well as every idea and human act, an experiment in fact, even though not in design. To be intelligently experimental is but to be conscious of this intersection of natural conditions so as to profit by it instead of being at its mercy. The Christian idea of this world and this life as a probation is a kind of distorted recognition of the situation; distorted because it applied wholesale to one stretch of existence in contrast with another, regarded as original and final. But in truth anything which can exist at any place and at any time occurs subject to tests imposed upon it by surroundings, which are only in part compatible and reinforcing. These surroundings test its strength and measure its endurance. As we can discourse of change only in terms of velocity and acceleration which involve relations to other things, so assertion of the permanent and enduring is comparative. The stablest thing we can speak of is not free from conditions set to it by other things. That even the solid earth mountains, the emblems of constancy, appear and disappear like the clouds is an old theme of moralists and poets. The fixed and unchanged being of the Democritean atom is now reported by inquirers to possess some of the traits of his non-being, and to embody a temporary equilibrium in the economy of nature's compromises and adjustments. A thing may endure *secula seculorum* and yet not be everlasting; it will crumble before the gnawing tooth of time, as it exceeds a certain measure. Every existence is an event.

This fact is nothing at which to repine and nothing to gloat over. It is something to be noted and used. If it is discomfiting when applied to good things, to our friends, possessions and precious selves, it is consoling also to know that no evil endures forever; that the longest lane turns sometime, and that the memory of loss of nearest and dearest grows dim in time. The eventful character of all existences is no reason for consigning them to the realm of mere appearance any more than it is a reason for idealizing flux into a deity. The important thing is measure, relation, ratio, knowledge of the comparative tempos of change. In mathematics some variables are constants in some problems; so it is in nature and life. The rate of change of some things is so slow, or is so rhythmic, that these changes have all the advantages of stability in dealing with more transitory and irregular happenings—if we know enough. Indeed, if any one thing that concerns us is subject to change, it is fortunate that all other things change. A thing "absolutely" stable and unchangeable would be out of the range of the principle of action and reaction, of resistance and leverage as well as of friction. Here it would have no applicability, no potentiality of use as measure and control of other events. To designate the slower and the regular rhythmic events structure, and more rapid and irregular ones process, is sound practical sense. It expresses the function of one in respect to the other.

But spiritualistic idealism and materialism alike treat this relational and functional distinction as something fixed and absolute. One doctrine finds structure in a framework of ideal forms, the other finds it in matter. They agree in supposing that structure has some superlative reality. This supposition is another form taken by preference for the stable over the precarious and uncompleted. The fact is that all structure is structure *of* something; anything defined as structure is a character of *events*, not something intrinsic and *per se*. A set of traits is called structure, because of its limiting function in relation to other traits of events. A house has a structure; in comparison with the disintegration and collapse that would occur without its presence, this structure is fixed. Yet it is not something external to which the changes involved in building and using the house have to submit. It is rather an arrangement of changing events such that properties which change slowly, limit and direct a series of quick changes and give them an order which they do not otherwise possess. Structure is constancy of means, of things used for consequences, not of things taken by themselves or absolutely.

Structure is what makes construction possible and cannot be discovered or defined except in some realized construction, construction being, of course, an evident order of changes. The isolation of structure from the changes whose stable ordering it is, renders it mysterious—something that is metaphysical in the popular sense of the word, a kind of ghostly queerness.

The "matter" of materialists and the "spirit" of idealists is a creature similar to the constitution of the United States in the minds of unimaginative persons. Obviously the real constitution is certain basic relationships among the activities of the citizens of the country; it is a property or phase of these processes, so connected with them as to influence their rate and direction of change. But by literalists it is often conceived of as something external to them; in itself fixed, a rigid framework to which *all* changes must accommodate themselves. Similarly what we call matter is that character of natural events which is so tied up with changes that are sufficiently rapid to be perceptible as to give the latter a characteristic rhythmic order, the causal sequence. It is no cause or source of events or processes; no absolute monarch; no principle of explanation; no substance behind or underlying changes—save in that sense of substance in which a man well fortified with this world's goods, and hence able to maintain himself through vicissitudes of surroundings, is a man of substance. The name designates a character in operation, not an entity.

That structure, whether of the kind called material or of the kind summed up in the word mental, is stable or permanent relationally and in its office, may be shown in another way. There is no action without reaction; there is no exclusively one-way exercise of conditioning power, no mode of regulation that operates wholly from above to below or from within outwards or from without inwards. Whatever influences the changes of other things is itself changed. The idea of an activity proceeding only in one direction, of an unmoved mover, is a survival of Greek physics. It has been banished from science, but remains to haunt philosophy. The vague and mysterious properties assigned to mind and matter, the very conceptions of mind and matter in traditional thought, are ghosts walking underground. The notion of matter actually found in the practice of science has nothing in common with the matter of materialists—and almost everybody is still a materialist as to matter, to which he merely adds a second rigid structure which he calls mind. The matter of science is a character of natural events and changes as they change; their character of regular and stable order.

Natural events are so complex and varied that there is nothing surprising in their possession of different characterizations, characters so different that they can be easily treated as opposites.

Nothing but unfamiliarity stands in the way of thinking of both mind and matter as different characters of natural events, in which matter expresses their sequential order, and mind the order of their meanings in their logical connections and dependencies. Processes may be eventful for functions which taken in abstract separation are at opposite poles, just as physiological processes eventuate in both anabolic and katabolic functions. The idea that matter and mind are two sides or "aspects" of the same things, like the convex and the concave in a curve, is literally unthinkable.

A curve is an intelligible object and concave and convex are defined in terms of this object; they are indeed but names for properties involved in its meaning. We do not start with convexity and concavity as two independent things and then set up an unknown *tertium quid* to unite two disparate things. In spite of the literal absurdity of the comparison, it may be understood however in a way which conveys an inkling of the truth. That to which both mind and matter belong is the complex of events that constitute nature. This becomes a mysterious *tertium quid*, incapable of designation, only when mind and matter are taken to be static structures instead of functional characters. It is a plausible prediction that if there were an interdict placed for a generation upon the use of mind, matter, consciousness as nouns, and we were obliged to employ adjectives and adverbs, conscious and consciously, mental and mentally, material and physically, we should find many of our problems much simplified.

We have selected only a few of the variety of the illustrations that might be used in support of the idea that the significant problems and issues of life and philosophy concern the rate and mode of the conjunction of the precarious and the assured, the incomplete and the finished, the repetitious and the varying, the safe and sane and the hazardous. If we trust to the evidence of experienced things, these traits, and the modes and tempos of their interaction with each other, are fundamental features of natural existence. The experience of their various consequences, according as they are relatively isolated, unhappily or happily combined, is evidence that wisdom, and hence that love of wisdom which is philosophy, is concerned with choice and administration of their proportioned union. Structure and process, substance and accident, matter and energy, permanence and flux, one and many, continuity and discreteness, order and progress, law and liberty, uniformity and growth, tradition and innovation, rational will and impelling desires, proof and discovery, the actual and the possible, are names given to various phases of their conjunction, and the issue of living depends upon the art with which these things are adjusted to each other.

While metaphysics may stop short with noting and registering these traits, man is not contemplatively detached from them. They involve him in his perplexities and troubles, and are the source of his joys and achievements. The situation is not indifferent to man, because it forms man as a desiring, striving, thinking, feeling creature. It is not egotism that leads man from contemplative registration of these traits to interest in managing them, to intelligence and purposive art. Interest, thinking, planning, striving, consummation and frustration are a drama enacted by these forces and conditions. A particular choice may be arbitrary; this is only to say that it does not approve itself to reflection. But choice is not arbitrary, not in a universe like this one, a world which is not finished and which has not consistently made up its mind where it is going and what it is going to do. Or, if we call it arbitrary, the arbitrariness is not ours but that of existence itself. And to call existence arbitrary or by any moral name, whether disparaging or honorific, is to patronize nature. To assume an attitude of condescension toward existence is perhaps a natural human compensation for the straits of life. But it is an ultimate source of the covert, uncandid and cheap in philosophy. This compensatory disposition it is which forgets that reflection exists to guide choice and effort. Hence its love of wisdom is but an unlaborious transformation of existence by dialectic, instead of an opening and enlarging of the ways of nature in man. A true wisdom, devoted to the latter task, discovers in thoughtful observation and experiment the method of administering the unfinished processes of existence so that frail goods shall be substantiated, secure goods be extended, and the precarious promises of good that haunt experienced things be more liberally fulfilled.

19. Experience, Nature and Art*

This selection can be read from several points of view. Taken from *Experience and Nature*, it continues a major theme of that book, the attack on dualism. Specifically Dewey opposes the "division of everything into nature *and* experience, of experi-

* From John Dewey, *Experience and Nature* (New York, 1958) (1929), 2nd ed., Chap. 9.

ence into practice *and* theory, art *and* science, of art into useful *and* fine, menial *and* free.'' In fact, Dewey sees an analysis of art as providing a microcosm of the pattern of relations at work in the doing and reflecting which characterizes the human endeavor overall. Taken in this wide, philosophical sense, art is so revealing for Dewey that he can write, ''in short, the history of human experience is a history of the development of the arts.''

From another point of view, however, this chapter can be read as a prelude to Dewey's later effort, in *Art as Experience* (1934), to develop a full-scale aesthetics. In this regard, Dewey makes a beginning here, although undeveloped, by insisting on the distinction between art and aesthetic experience, a distinction that is central to his later aesthetics. But again, both art and aesthetic experience are revelatory of a morphology of experience. In Dewey's judgment, ''the doings and sufferings that form experience are, in the degree in which experience is intelligent or charged with meanings, a union of the precarious, novel, irregular with the settled, assured and uniform—a union which also defines the artistic and esthetic.''

Experience, with the Greeks, signified a store of practical wisdom, a fund of insights useful in conducting the affairs of life. Sensation and perception were its occasion and supplied it with pertinent materials, but did not of themselves constitute it. They generated experience when retention was added and when a common factor in the multitude of felt and perceived cases detached itself so as to become available in judgment and exertion. Thus understood, experience is exemplified in the discrimination and skill of the good carpenter, pilot, physician, captain-at-arms; experience is equivalent to art. Modern theory has quite properly extended the application of the term to cover many things that the Greeks would hardly have called ''experience,'' the bare having of aches and pains, or a play of colors before the eyes. But even those who hold this larger signification would admit, I suppose, that such ''experiences'' count only when they result in insight, or in an enjoyed perception, and that only thus do they define experience in its honorific sense.

Greek thinkers nevertheless disparaged experience in comparison with something called reason and science. The ground for depreciation was not that usually assigned in modern philosophy; it was not that experience is ''subjective.'' On the contrary, experience was considered to be a

genuine expression of cosmic forces, not an exclusive attribute or possession of animal or of human nature. It was taken to be a realization of
inferior portions of nature, those infected with chance and change, the
less *Being* part of the cosmos. Thus while experience meant art, art
reflected the contingencies and partialities of nature, while science
—theory—exhibited its necessities and universalities. Art was born of
need, lack, deprivation, incompleteness, while science—theory
—manifested fullness and totality of Being. Thus the depreciatory view
of experience was identical with a conception that placed practical activity below theoretical activity, finding the former dependent, impelled
from outside, marked by deficiency of real being, while the latter was
independent and free because complete and self-sufficing: that is perfect.

In contrast with this self-consistent position we find a curious mixture
in modern thinking. The latter feels under no obligation to present a
theory of natural existence that links art with nature; on the contrary,
it usually holds that science or knowledge is the only *authentic* expression
of nature, in which case art must be an arbitrary addition to nature. But
modern thought also combines exaltation of science with eulogistic
appreciation of art, especially of fine or creative art. At the same time
it retains the substance of the classic disparagement of the practical in
contrast with the theoretical, although formulating it in somewhat different language: to the effect that knowledge deals with objective reality
as it is in itself, while in what is "practical," objective reality is altered
and cognitively distorted by subjective factors of want, emotion and striving. And yet in its encomium of art, it fails to note the commonplace
of Greek observation—that the fine arts as well as the industrial
technologies are affairs of practice.

This confused plight is partly cause and partly effect of an almost universal confusion of the artistic and the esthetic. On one hand, there is
action that deals with materials and energies outside the body, assembling, refining, combining, manipulating them until their new state yields
a satisfaction not afforded by their crude condition—a formula that
applies to fine and useful art alike. On the other hand, there is the delight
that attends vision and hearing, an enhancement of the receptive appreciation and assimilation of objects irrespective of participation in the operations of production. Provided the difference of the two things is recognized, it is no matter whether the words "esthetic" and "artistic" or
other terms be used to designate the distinction, for the difference is not
one of words but of objects. But in some form the difference must be
acknowledged.

The community in which Greek art was produced was small; numerous and complicated intermediaries between production and consumption were lacking; producers had a virtually servile status. Because of the close connection between production and enjoyable fruition, the Greeks in their perceptive uses and enjoyments were never wholly unconscious of the artisan and his work, not even when they personally were exclusively concerned with delightful contemplation. But since the artist was an artisan (the term artist having none of the eulogistic connotations of present usage), and since the artisan occupied an inferior position, the enjoyment of works of any art did not stand upon the same level as enjoyment of those objects for the realization of which manual activity was not needed. Objects of rational thought, of contemplative insight were the only things that met the specification of freedom from need, labor, and matter. They alone were self-sufficient, self-existent, and self-explanatory, and hence enjoyment of *them* was on a higher plane than enjoyment of works of art.

These conceptions were consistent with one another and with the conditions of social life at the time. Nowadays we have a messy conjunction of notions that are consistent neither with one another nor with the tenor of our actual life. Knowledge is still regarded by most thinkers as direct grasp of ultimate reality, although the practice of knowing has been assimilated to the procedure of the useful arts;—involving, that is to say, doing that manipulates and arranges natural energies. Again while science is said to lay hold of reality, yet "art" instead of being assigned a lower rank is equally esteemed and honored. And when within art a distinction is drawn between production and appreciation, the chief honor usually goes to the former on the ground that it is "creative," while taste is relatively possessive and passive, dependent for its material upon the activities of the creative artist.

If Greek philosophy was correct in thinking of knowledge as contemplation rather than as a productive art, and if modern philosophy accepts this conclusion, then the only logical course is relative disparagement of all forms of production, since they are modes of practice which is by conception inferior to contemplation. The artistic is then secondary to the esthetic: "creation," to "taste," and the scientific *worker*—as we significantly say—is subordinate in rank and worth to the dilettante who enjoys the results of his labors. But if modern tendencies are justified in putting art and creation first, then the implications of this position should be avowed and carried through. It would then be seen that science is an art, that art is practice, and that the only distinction worth drawing is not between practice and theory, but between those modes of practice that are not intelligent, not inherently and immediately enjoyable, and those which are full of enjoyed meanings. When this perception dawns, it will be a commonplace that art—the mode of activity that is charged with meanings capable of immediately enjoyed possession—is the complete culmination of nature, and that "science" is properly a handmaiden that conducts natural events to this happy issue. Thus would disappear the separations that trouble present thinking: division of everything into nature *and* experience, of experience into practice *and* theory, art *and* science, of art into useful *and* fine, menial *and* free.

Thus the issue involved in experience as art in its pregnant sense and in art as processes and materials of nature continued by direction into achieved and enjoyed meanings, sums up in itself all the issues which have been previously considered. Thought, intelligence, science is the intentional direction of natural events to meanings capable of immediate possession and enjoyment; this direction—which is operative art—is itself a natural event in which nature otherwise partial and incomplete comes fully to itself; so that objects of conscious experience when reflectively chosen, form the "end" of nature. The doings and sufferings that form experience are, in the degree in which experience is intelligent or charged with meanings, a union of the precarious, novel, irregular with the settled, assured and uniform—a union which also defines the artistic and the esthetic. For wherever there is art the contingent and ongoing no longer work at cross purposes with the formal and recurrent but commingle in harmony. And the distinguishing feature of conscious experience, of what for short is often called "consciousness," is that in it the instrumental and the final, meanings that are signs and clews and meanings that are immediately possessed, suffered and enjoyed, come together in one. And all of these things are preëminently true of art.

First, then, art is solvent union of the generic, recurrent, ordered, established phase of nature with its phase that is incomplete, going on, and hence still uncertain, contingent, novel, particular; or as certain systems of esthetic theory have truly declared, though without empirical basis and import in their words, a union of necessity and freedom, a harmony of the many and one, a reconciliation of sensuous and ideal. Of any artistic act and product it may be said both that it is inevitable in its rightness, that nothing in it can be altered without altering all, and that its occurrence is spontaneous, unexpected, fresh, unpredictable. The presence in art, whether as an act or a product, of proportion, economy, order, symmetry, composition, is such a commonplace that it does not need to be dwelt upon. But equally necessary is unexpected combination, and the consequent revelation of possibilities hitherto unrealized. "Repose in stimulation" characterizes art. Order and proportion when they are the whole story are soon exhausted; economy in itself is a tiresome and restrictive taskmaster. It is artistic when it releases.

The more extensive and repeated are the basic uniformities of nature that give form to art, the "greater" is the art, provided—and it is this proviso that distinguishes art—they are indistinguishably fused with the wonder of the new and the grace of the gratuitous. "Creation" may be asserted vaguely and mystically; but it denotes something genuine and indispensable in art. The merely finished is not fine but ended, done with, and the merely "fresh" is that bumptious impertinence indicated by the slang use of the word. The "magic" of poetry—and pregnant experience has poetical quality—is precisely the revelation of meaning in the old effected by its presentation through the new. It radiates the light that never was on land and sea but that is henceforth an abiding illumination of objects. Music in its immediate occurrence is the most varied and ethereal of the arts, but is in its conditions and structure the most mechanical. These things are commonplaces; but until they are commonly employed in their evidential significance for a theory of nature's nature, there is no cause to apologize for their citation.

The limiting terms that define art are routine at one extreme and capricious impulse at the other. It is hardly worth while to oppose science and art sharply to one another, when the deficiencies and troubles of life are so evidently due to separation between art and blind routine and blind impulse. Routine exemplifies the uniformities and recurrences of nature, caprice expresses its inchoate initiations and deviations. Each in isolation is unnatural as well as inartistic, for nature is an intersection of spontaneity and necessity, the regular and the novel, the finished and the beginning. It is right to object to much of current practice on the ground that it is routine, just as it is right to object to much of our current enjoyments on the ground that they are spasms of excited escape from the thraldom of enforced work. But to transform a just objection against the quality of much of our practical life into a description and definition of practice is on the same plane as to convert legitimate objection to trivial distraction, senseless amusement, and sensual absorption, into a Puritanical aversion to happiness. The idea that work, productive activity, signifies action carried on for merely extraneous ends, and the idea that happiness signifies surrender of mind to the thrills and excitations of the body are one and the same idea. The first notion marks the separation of activity from meaning, and the second marks the separation of receptivity from meaning. Both separations are inevitable as far as experience fails to be art:—when the regular, repetitious, and the novel, contingent in nature fail to sustain and inform each other in a productive activity possessed of immanent and directly enjoyed meaning.

Thus the theme has insensibly passed over into that of the relation of means and consequence, process and product, the instrumental and consummatory. Any activity that is simultaneously both, rather than in alternation and displacement, is art. Disunion of production and consumption is a common enough occurrence. But emphasis upon this separation in order to exalt the consummatory does not define or interpret either art or experience. It obscures their meaning, resulting in a division of art into useful and fine, adjectives which, when they are prefixed to "art," corrupt and destroy its intrinsic significance. For arts that are merely useful are not arts but routines; and arts that are merely final are not arts but passive amusements and distractions, different from other indulgent dissipations only in dependence upon a certain acquired refinement or "cultivation."

The existence of activities that have no immediate enjoyed intrinsic meaning is undeniable. They include much of our labors in home, factory, laboratory and study. By no stretch of language can they be termed either artistic or esthetic. Yet they exist, and are so coercive that they require some attentive recognition. So we optimistically call them "useful" and let it go at that, thinking that by calling them useful we have somehow justified and explained their occurrence. If we were to ask useful for what? we should be obliged to examine their actual consequences, and when we once honestly and fully faced these consequences we should probably find ground for calling such activities detrimental rather than useful.

We call them useful because we arbitrarily cut short our consideration of consequences. We bring into view simply their efficacy in bringing into existence certain commodities; we do not ask for their effect upon the quality of human life and experience. They are useful to make shoes, houses, motor cars, money, and other things which *may* then be put to use; here inquiry and imagination stop. What they also *make* by way of narrowed, embittered, and crippled life, of congested, hurried, confused and extravagant life, is left in oblivion. But to be useful is to fulfill need. The characteristic human need is for possession and appreciation of the meaning of things, and this need is ignored and unsatisfied in the traditional notion of the useful. We identify utility with the external relationship that some events and acts bear to other things that are their products, and thus leave out the only thing that is essential to the idea of utility, inherent place and bearing in experience. Our classificatory use of the conception of some arts as merely instrumental so as to dispose of a large part of human activity is no solving definition; it rather conveys an immense and urgent problem.

The same statement applies to the conception of merely fine or final arts and works of art. In point of fact, the things designated by the phrase fall under three captions. There are activities and receptivities to which the name of "self-expression" is often applied as a eulogistic qualification, in which one indulges himself by giving free outward exhibition to his own states without reference to the conditions upon which intelligible communication depends—an act also sometimes known as "expression of emotion," which is then set up for definition of all fine art. It is easy to dispose of this art by calling it a product of egotism due to balked activity in other occupations. But this treatment misses a more significant point. For all art is a process of making the world a different place in which to live, and involves a phase of protest and of compensatory response. Such art as there is in these manifestations lies in this factor. It is owing to frustration in communication of meanings that the protest becomes arbitrary and the compensatory response wilfully eccentric.

In addition to this type—and frequently mingled with it—there is experimentation in new modes or craftsmanship, cases where the seemingly bizarre and over-individualistic character of the products is due to discontent with existing technique, and is associated with an attempt to find new modes of language. It is aside from the point either to greet these manifestations as if they constituted art for the first time in human history, or to condemn them as not art because of their violent departures from received canons and methods. Some movement in this direction has always been a condition of growth of new forms, a condition of salvation from that mortal arrest and decay called academic art.

Then there is that which in quantity bulks most largely as fine art: the production of buildings in the name of the art of architecture; of pictures in the name of the art of painting; of novels, dramas, etc., in the name of literary art; a production which in reality is largely a form of commercialized industry in production of a class of commodities that find their sale among well-to-do persons desirous of maintaining a conventionally approved status. As the first two modes carry to disproportionate excess that factor of particularity, contingency and difference which is indispensable in all art, deliberately flaunting avoidance of the repetitions and order of nature; so this mode celebrates the regular and finished. It is reminiscent rather than commemorative of the meanings of experienced things. Its products remind their owner of things pleasant in memory though hard in direct-undergoing, and remind others that their owner has achieved an economic standard which makes possible cultivation and decoration of leisure.

Obviously no one of these classes of activity and product or all of them put together, mark off anything that can be called distinctively fine art. They share their qualities and defects with many other acts and objects. But, fortunately, there may be mixed with any one of them, and, still more fortunately, there may occur without mixture, process and product that are characteristically excellent. This occurs when activity is productive of an object that affords continuously renewed delight. This condition requires that the object be, with its successive consequences, indefinitely instrumental to *new* satisfying events. For otherwise the object is quickly exhausted and satiety sets in. Anyone, who reflects upon the commonplace that a measure of artistic products is their capacity to attract and retain observation with satisfaction under whatever conditions they are approached, while things of less quality soon lose capacity to hold attention becoming indifferent or repellent upon subsequent approach, has a sure demonstration that a genuinely esthetic object is not exclusively consummatory but is causally productive as well. A consummatory object that is not also instrumental turns in time to the dust and ashes of boredom. The "eternal" quality of great art is its renewed instrumentality for further consummatory experiences.

When this fact is noted, it is also seen that limitation of fineness of art to paintings, statues, poems, songs and symphonies is conventional, or even verbal. Any activity that is productive of objects whose perception is an immediate good, and whose operation is a continual source of enjoyable perception of other events exhibits fineness of art. There are acts of all kinds that directly refresh and enlarge the spirit and that are instrumental to the production of new objects and dispositions which are in turn productive of further refinements and replenishments. Frequently moralists make the acts *they* find excellent or virtuous wholly final, and treat art and affection as mere means. Estheticians reverse the performance, and see in good *acts* means to an ulterior external happiness, while esthetic appreciation is called a good in itself, or that strange thing an end in itself. But on both sides it is true that in being preëminently fructifying the things designated means are immediate satisfactions. They are their own excuses for being just because they are charged with an office in quickening apprehension, enlarging the horizon of vision, refining discrimination, creating standards of appreciation which are confirmed and deepened by further experiences. It would almost seem when their non-instrumental character is insisted upon as if what was meant were an indefinitely expansive and radiating instrumental efficacy.

The source of the error lies in the habit of calling by the name of means things that are not means at all; things that are only external and accidental antecedents of the happening of something else. Similarly things are called ends that are not ends save accidentally, since they are not fulfilments, consummatory, of means, but merely last terms closing a process. Thus it is often said that a laborer's toil is the means of his livelihood, although except in the most tenuous and arbitrary way it bears no relationship to his real living. Even his wage is hardly an end or consequence of his labor. He might—and frequently does—equally well or ill—perform any one of a hundred other tasks as a condition of receiving payment. The prevailing conception of instrumentality is profoundly vitiated by the habit of applying it to cases like the above, where, instead of an operation of means, there is an enforced necessity of doing one thing as a coerced antecedent of the occurrence of another thing which is wanted.

Means are always at least causal conditions; but causal conditions are means only when they possess an added qualification; that, namely, of being freely used, because of perceived connection with chosen consequences. To entertain, choose and accomplish anything as an end or consequence is to be committed to a like love and care for whatever events and acts are its means. Similarly, consequences, ends, are at least effects; but effects are not ends unless thought has perceived and freely chosen the conditions and processes that are their conditions. The notion that means are menial, instrumentalities servile, is more than a degradation of means to the rank of coercive and external necessities. It renders all things upon which the name of end is bestowed accompaniments of privilege, while the name of utility becomes an apologetic justification for things that are not portions of a good and reasonable life. Livelihood is at present not so much the consequence of a wage-earner's labor as it is the effect of other causes forming the economic régime, labor being merely an accidental appendage of these other causes.

Paints and skill in manipulative arrangement are means of a picture as end, because the picture is *their* assemblage and organization. Tones and susceptibility of the ear when properly interacting are the means of music, because they constitute, make, are, music. A disposition of virtue is a means to a certain quality of happiness because it is a constituent of that good, while such happiness is means in turn to virtue, as the sustaining of good in being. Flour, water, yeast are means of bread because they are ingredients of bread; while bread is a factor *in* life, not just *to* it. A good political constitution, honest police-system, and competent judiciary, are means of the prosperous life of the community because they are integrated portions of that life. Science is an instrumentality of and for art because it is the intelligent factor *in* art. The trite saying that a hand is not a hand except as an organ of the living body —except as a working coördinated part of a balanced system of activities—applies untritely to all things that are means. The connection of means-consequences is never one of bare succession in time, such that the element that is means is past and gone when the end is instituted. An active process is strung out temporarily, but there is a deposit at each stage and point entering cumulatively and constitutively into the outcome. A genuine instrumentality *for* is always an organ *of* an end. It confers continued efficacy upon the object in which it is embodied.

The traditional separation between some things as mere means and others as mere ends is a reflection of the insulated existence of working and leisure classes, of production that is not also consummatory, and consummation that is not productive. This division is not a *merely* social phenomenon. It embodies a perpetuation upon the human plane of a division between need and satisfaction belonging to brute life. And this separation expresses in turn the mechanically external relationship that exists in nature between situations of disturbed equilibrium, of stress, and strain, and achieved equilibrium. For in nature, outside of man, except when events eventuate in "development" or "evolution" (in which a cumulative carrying forward of consequences of past histories in new efficiencies occurs) antecedent events are external transitive conditions of the occurrence of an event having immediate and static qualities. To animals to whom acts have no meaning, the change in the environment required to satisfy needs has no significance on its own account; such change is a mere incident of ego-centric satisfactions. This physically external relationship of antecedents and consequents is perpetuated; it continues to hold true of human industry wherever labor and its materials and products are externally enforced necessities for securing a living. Because Greek industry was so largely upon this plane of servile labor, all industrial activity was regarded by Greek thought as a *mere* means, an extraneous necessity. Hence satisfactions due to it were conceived to be the ends or goods of purely animal nature in isolation. With respect to a truly human and rational life, they were not ends or goods at all, but merely "means," that is to say, external conditions that were antecedently enforced requisites of the life conducted and enjoyed by free men, especially by those devoted to the acme of freedom, pure thinking. As Aristotle asserted, drawing a just conclusion from the assumed premises, there are classes of men who are necessary materials of society but who are not integral parts of it. And he summed up the whole theory of the external and coerced relationship of means and ends when he said in this very connection that: "When there is one thing that is means and another thing that is end, there is *nothing common* between them, except in so far as the one, the means, produces, and the other, the end, receives the product."

It would thus seem almost self-evident that the distinction between the instrumental and the final adopted in philosophic tradition as a solving word presents in truth a problem, a problem so deep-seated and far-reaching that it may be said to be *the* problem of experience. For all the intelligent activities of men, no matter whether expressed in science, fine arts, or social relationships, have for their task the conversion of causal bonds, relations of succession, into a connection of means-consequence, into meanings. When the task is achieved the result is art: and in art everything is common between means and ends. Whenever so-called means remain external and servile, and so-called ends are enjoyed objects whose further causative status is unperceived, ignored or denied, the situation is proof positive of limitations of art. Such a situation consists of affairs in which the problem has *not* been solved; namely that of converting physical and brute relationships into connections of meanings characteristic of the possibilities of nature.

It goes without saying that man begins as a part of physical and animal nature. In as far as he reacts to physical things on a strictly physical level, he is pulled and pushed about, overwhelmed, broken to pieces, lifted on the crest of the wave of things, like anything else. His contacts, his sufferings and doings, are matters of direct interaction only. He is in a "state of nature." As an animal, even upon the brute level, he manages to subordinate some physical things to his needs, converting them into materials sustaining life and growth. But in so far things that serve as material of satisfaction and the acts that procure and utilize them are not objects, or things-with-meanings. That appetite as such is blind, is notorious; it may push us into a comfortable result instead of into disaster; but we are pushed just the same. When appetite is perceived in its meanings, in the consequences it induces, and these consequences are experimented with in reflective imagination, some being seen to be consistent with one another, and hence capable of co-existence and of serially ordered achievement, others being incompatible, forbidding conjunction at one time, and getting in one another's way serially—when this estate is attained, we live on the human plane, responding to things in their meanings. A relationship of cause-effect has been transformed into one of means-consequence. Then consequences belong *integrally* to the conditions which may produce them, and the latter possess character and distinction. The meaning of causal conditions is carried over also into the consequence, so that the latter is no longer a mere end, a last and closing term of arrest. It is marked out in perception, distinguished by the efficacy of the conditions which have entered into it. Its value as fulfilling and consummatory is measurable by subsequent fulfillments and frustrations to which it is contributory in virtue of the causal means which compose it.

Thus to be conscious of meanings or to have an idea, marks a fruition, an enjoyed or suffered arrest of the flux of events. But there are all kinds of ways of perceiving meanings, all kinds of ideas. Meaning may be determined in terms of consequences hastily snatched at and torn loose from their connections; then is prevented the formation of wider and more enduring ideas. Or, we may be aware of meanings, may achieve ideas, that unite wide and enduring scope with richness of distinctions. The latter sort of consciousness is more than a passing and superficial consummation or end: it takes up into itself meanings covering stretches of existence wrought into consistency. It marks the conclusion of long continued endeavor; of patient and indefatigable search and test. The idea is, in short, art and a work of art. As a work of art, it directly liberates subsequent action and makes it more fruitful in a creation of more meanings and more perceptions.

It is the part of wisdom to recognize how sparse and insecure are such accomplishments in comparison with experience in which physical and animal nature largely have their way. Our liberal and rich ideas, our adequate appreciations, due to productive art are hemmed in by an unconquered domain in which we are everywhere exposed to the incidence of unknown forces and hurried fatally to unforeseen consequences. Here indeed we live servilely, menially, mechanically; and we so live as much when forces blindly lead to us ends that are liked as when we are caught in conditions and ends against which we blindly rebel. To call satisfactions which happen in this blind way "ends" in a eulogistic sense, as did classic thought, is to proclaim in effect our servile submission to accident. We may indeed enjoy the goods the gods of fortune send us, but we should recognize them for what they are, not asserting them to be good and righteous *altogether*. For, since they have not been achieved by any art involving deliberate selection and arrangement of forces, we do not know with what they are charged. It is an old true tale that the god of fortune is capricious, and delights to destroy his darlings after having made them drunk with prosperity. The goods of art are not the less good in their goodness than the gifts of nature; while in addition they are such as to bring with themselves open-eyed confidence. They are fruits of means consciously employed; fulfillments whose further consequences are secured by conscious control of the causal conditions which enter into them. Art is the sole alternative to luck; and divorce from each other of the meaning and value of instrumentalities and ends is the essence of luck. The esoteric character of culture and the supernatural quality of religion are both expressions of the divorce.

The modern mind has formally abjured belief in natural teleology because it found Greek and medieval teleology juvenile and superstitious. Yet facts have a way of compelling recognition of themselves. There is little scientific writing which does not introduce at some point or other the idea of tendency. The idea of tendency unites in itself exclusion of prior design and inclusion of movement in a particular direction, a direction that may be either furthered or counteracted and frustrated, but which is intrinsic. Direction involves a limiting position, a point or goal of culminating stoppage, as well as an initial starting point. To assert a tendency and to be fore-conscious of a possible terminus of movement are two names of the same fact. Such a consciousness may be fatalistic; a sense of inevitable march toward impending doom. But it may also contain a perception of meanings such as flexibly directs a forward movement. The end is then an end-in-view and is in constant and cumulative reënactment at each stage of forward movement. It is no longer a terminal point, external to the conditions that have led up to it; it is the continually developing meaning of present tendencies—the very things which as directed we call "means." The process is art and its product, no matter at what stage it be taken, is a work of art.

To a person building a house, the end-in-view is not just a remote and final goal to be hit upon after a sufficiently great number of coerced motions have been duly performed. The end-in-view is a plan which is *contemporaneously* operative in selecting and arranging materials. The latter, brick, stone, wood and mortar, are means only as the end-in-view is actually incarnate in them, in forming them. Literally, they *are* the end in its present stage of realization. The end-in-view is present at each stage of the process; it is present as the *meaning* of the materials used and acts done; without its informing presence, the latter are in no sense "means;" they are merely extrinsic causal conditions. The statement is generic; it applies equally at every stage. The house itself, when building is complete, is "end" in no exclusive sense. It marks the conclusion of the organization of certain materials and events into effective means; but these material and events still exist in causal interaction with other things. New consequences are foreseen; new purposes, ends-in-view, are entertained; they are embodied in the coördination of the thing built, now reduced to material, although significant material, along with other materials, and thus transmuted into means. The case is still clearer, when instead of considering a process subject to as many rigid external conditions as is the building of a house, we take for illustration a flexibly and freely moving process, such as painting a picture or thinking out a scientific process, when these operations are carried on artistically. Every process of free art proves that the difference between means and end is analytic, formal, not material and chronologic.

What has been said enables us to re-define the distinction drawn between the artistic, as objectively productive, and the esthetic. Both involve a perception of meanings in which the instrumental and the consummatory peculiarly intersect. In esthetic perceptions an object interpenetrated with meanings is given; it may be taken for granted; it invites and awaits the act of appropriative enjoyment. In the esthetic object tendencies are sensed as brought to fruition; in it is embodied a means-consequence relationship, as the past work of his hands was surveyed by the Lord and pronounced good. This good differs from those gratifications to which the name sensual rather than sensuous is given, since the former are pleasing endings that occur in ways not informed with the meaning of materials and acts integrated into them. In appreciative possession, perception goes out to tendencies which *have* been brought to happy fruition in such a way as to release and arouse.

Artistic sense on the other hand grasps tendencies as possibilities; the invitation of these possibilities to perception is more urgent and compelling than that of the given already achieved. While the means-consequence relationship is directly sensed, felt, in both appreciation and artistic production, in the former the scale descends upon the side of the attained; in the latter there predominates the invitation of an existent consummation to bring into existence further perceptions. Art in being, the active productive process, may thus be defined as an esthetic perception together with an *operative* perception of the efficiencies of the esthetic object. In many persons with respect to most kinds of enjoyed perceptions, the sense of possibilities, the arousal or excitation attendant upon appreciation of poetry, music, painting, architecture or landscape remains diffuse and inchoate; it takes effect only in direct and undefined channels. The enjoyed perception of a visual scene is in any case a function of that scene in its total connections, but it does not link up adequately. In some happily constituted persons, this effect is adequately coördinated with other endowments and habits; it becomes an integral part of craft, taking effect in the creation of a new object of appreciation. The integration is, however, progressive and experimental, not momentarily accomplished. Thus every creative effort is temporal, subject to risk and deflection. In that sense the difference between the diffuse and postponed change of action due in an ordinary person to release of energies by an esthetic object, and the special and axial direction of subsequent action in a gifted person is, after all, a matter of degree.

Without a sense of moving tendencies which are operative in conjunction with a state of fruition, there is appetitive gratification, but nothing that may be termed appreciation. Sense of moving tendencies supplies thrill, stimulation, excitation; sense of completion, consummation, affords composure, form, measure, composition. Emphasize the latter, and appreciation is of the classic type. This type fits conditions where production is professionalized among technical craftsmen, as among the Greeks; it is adapted to a contemplative enjoyment of the achievements of past ages or remote places, where conditions forbid urge to emulation or productive activity of a similar kind. Any work of art that persistently retains its power to generate enjoyed perception or appreciation becomes in time classic.

In so-called romantic art, the sense of tendencies operative beyond the limits of consummation is in excess; a lively sense of unrealized potentialities attaches to the object; but it is employed to enhance immediate appreciation, not to promote further productive achievement. Whatever is peculiarly romantic excites a feeling that the possibilities suggested go beyond not merely actual present realization, but are beyond effective attainment in any experience. In so far intentionally romantic art is wilful, and in so far not art. Excited and uneasy perceptual enjoyment is made ultimate, and the work of art is accommodated to production of these feelings. The sense of unachieved possibilities is employed as a compensatory equivalent for endeavor in achievement. Thus when the romantic spirit invades philosophy the possibilities present in imaginative sentiment are declared to be the real, although "transcendental," substance of Being itself. In complete art, appreciation follows the object and moves with it to its completion; romanticism reverses the process and degrades the object to an occasion for arousing a predetermined type of appreciation. In classicism, objective achievement is primary, and appreciation not only conforms to the object, but the object is employed to compose sentiment and give it distinction. Its vice, as an 'ism, is that it turns the mind to what is given; the given is taken as if it were eternal and wholly separate from generation and movement. Art free from subjection to any "ism" has movement, creation, as well as order, finality.

To institute a difference of *kind* between useful and fine arts is, there-fore, absurd, since art involves a peculiar interpenetration of means and ends. Many things are termed useful for reasons of social status, implying deprecation and contempt. Things are sometimes said to belong to the menial arts merely because they are cheap and used familiarly by com-mon people. These things of daily use for ordinary ends may survive in later periods, or be transported to another culture, as from Japan and China to America, and being rare and sought by connoisseurs, rank forth-with as works of fine art. Other things may be called fine because their manner of use is decorative or socially ostentatious. It is tempting to make a distinction of degree and say that a thing belongs to the sphere of use when perception of its meaning is incidental to something else; and that a thing belongs to fine art when its other uses are subordinate to its use in perception. The distinction has a rough practical value, but cannot be pressed too far. For in production of a painting or a poem, as well as in making a vase or a temple, a perception is also employed as means for something beyond itself. Moreover, the perception of urns, pots and pans as commodities may be intrinsically enjoyable, although these things are primarily perceived with reference to some use to which they are put. The only *basic* distinction is that between bad art and good art, and this distinction, between things that meet the requirements of art and those that do not, applies equally to things of use and of beauty. Capacity to offer to perception meaning in which fruition and efficacy interpenetrate is met by different products in various degrees of fulness; it may be missed altogether by pans and poems alike. The difference between the ugliness of a mechanically conceived and executed utensil and of a meretricious and pretentious painting is one only of content or material; in form, both are articles, and bad articles.

Thinking is pre-eminently an art; knowledge and propositions which are the products of thinking, are works of art, as much so as statuary and symphonies. Every successive stage of thinking is a conclusion in which the meaning of what has produced it is condensed; and it is no sooner stated than it is a light radiating to other things—unless it be a fog which obscures them. The antecedents of a conclusion are as causal and existential as those of a building. They are not logical or dialectical, or an affair of ideas. While a conclusion follows from antecedents, it does not follow from "premises," in the strict, formal sense. Premises are the analysis of a conclusion into its logically justifying grounds; there are no premises till there is a conclusion. Conclusion and premise are reached by a procedure comparable to the use of boards and nails in making a box; or of paint and canvas in making a picture. If defective materials are employed or if they are put together carelessly and awkwardly, the result is defective. In some cases the result is called unworthy, in others, ugly; in others, inept; in others, wasteful, inefficient, and in still others untrue, false. But in each case, the condemnatory adjective refers to the resulting work judged in the light of its method of production. Scientific method or the art of constructing true perceptions is ascertained in the course of experience to occupy a privileged position in undertaking other arts. But this unique position only places it the more securely as an art; it does not set its product, knowledge, apart from other works of art.

The existential origin of valid cognitive perceptions is sometimes recognized in form and denied in substance; the name "psychological" is given to the events which generate valid beliefs. Then a sharp distinction is made between genesis as psychological and validity as logical. Of course lexicographic names are of no special moment; if any one wishes to call the efficient causes of knowledge and truth psychological, he is entitled to do so—provided the actual traits of these causative events are recognized. Such a recognition will note however that psychological does not mean psychic, or refer to events going on exclusively within the head or "subcutaneously." To become aware of an object cognitively as distinct from esthetically, involves external physical movements and external physical appliances physically manipulated. Some of these active changes result in unsound and defective perceptions; some have been ascertained to result usually in valid perceptions. The difference is precisely that which takes place when the art of architecture or sculpture is skilfully conducted or is carried on carelessly, and without adequate appliances. Sometimes the operations productive of tested beliefs are called "inductive;" with an implication in the naming, of discrediting them, as compared with deductive functions, which are assigned a superior exclusive status. Of deduction, when thus defined, the following assertions may be made. First, it has nothing to do with truth about any matter of existence. Secondly, it is not even concerned with consistency or correctness, save in a formal sense whose opposite (as has been previously pointed out) is not inconsistency but nonsense. Thirdly, the meanings which figure in it are the conclusions of prior inquiries which are "inductive," that is, are products of an experimental art of changing external things by appropriate external movements and appliances.

Deduction as it actually occurs in science is *not* deduction as deduction should be according to a common definition. Deduction deals directly with meanings in their relations to one another, rather than with meanings directly referred to existence. But these meanings are what they are in themselves and are related to one another by means of acts of taking and manipulating—an art of discourse. They possess intellectual import and enter fruitfully into scientific method only because they are selected, employed, separated and combined by acts extraneous to them, acts which are as existential and causative as those concerned in the experimental use of apparatus and other physical things. The *act* of knowing, whether solicitous about inference or about demonstration, is always inductive. There is only one mode of thinking, the inductive, when thinking denotes anything that actually happens. The notion that there is another kind called deduction is another evidence of the prevalent tendency in philosophy to treat functions as antecedent operations, and to take essential meanings *of* existence as if they were a kind of Being. As a concrete operation, deduction is generative, not sterile; but as a concrete operation, it contains an extraneous act of taking and using which is selective, experimental and checked constantly by consequences.

Knowledge or science, as a work of art, like any other work of art, confers upon things traits and potentialities which did not *previously* belong to them. Objection from the side of alleged realism to this statement springs from a confusion of tenses. Knowledge is not a distortion or perversion which confers upon *its* subject-matter traits which *do* not belong to it, but is an act which confers upon non-cognitive material traits which *did* not belong to it. It marks a change by which physical events exhibiting properties of mechanical energy, connected by relations of push and pull, hitting, rebounding, splitting and consolidating, realize characters, meanings and relations of meanings *hitherto* not possessed by them. Architecture does not add to stone and wood something which does not belong to them, but it does add to them properties and efficacies which they did not possess in their earlier state. It adds them by means of engaging them in new modes of interaction, having a new order of consequences. Neither engineering nor fine art limits itself to imitative reproduction or copying of antecedent conditions. Their products may nevertheless be more effectively natural, more "life like," than were antecedent states of natural existence. So it is with the art of knowing and its works.

The failure to recognize that knowledge is a product of art accounts for an otherwise inexplicable fact: that science lies today like an incubus upon such a wide area of beliefs and aspirations. To remove the deadweight, however, recognition that it is an art will have to be more than a theoretical avowal that science is made by man for man, although such recognition is probably an initial preliminary step. But the real source of the difficulty is that the art of knowing is limited to such a narrow area. Like everything precious and scarce, it has been artificially protected; and through this very protection it has been dehumanized and appropriated by a class. As costly jewels of jade and pearl belong only to a few, so with the jewels of science. The philosophic theories which have set science on an altar in a temple remote from the arts of life, to be approached only with peculiar rites, are a part of the technique of retaining a secluded monopoly of belief and intellectual authority. Till the art of achieving adequate and liberal perceptions of the meanings of events is incarnate in education, morals and industry, science will remain a special luxury for a few; for the mass, it will consist of a remote and abstruse body of curious propositions having little to do with life, except where it lays the heavy hand of law upon spontaneity, and invokes necessity and mechanism to witness against generous and free aspiration.

Every error is attended with a contrary and compensatory error, for otherwise it would soon be self-revealing. The conception that causes are metaphysically superior to effects is compensated for by the conception that ends are superior esthetically and morally to means. The two beliefs can be maintained together only by removing "ends" out of the region of the causal and efficacious. This is accomplished nowadays by first calling ends intrinsic values, and then by making a gulf between value and existence. The consequence is that science, dealing as it must, with existence, becomes brutal and mechanical, while criticism of values, whether moral or esthetic, becomes pedantic or effeminate, expressing either personal likes and dislikes, or building up a cumbrous array of rules and authorities. The thing that is needful, discriminating judgment by methods whose consequences improve the art, easily slips through such coarse meshes, and by far the greater part of life goes on in a darkness unillumined by thoughtful inquiry. As long as such a state of thing persists, the argument of this chapter that science is art—like many other propositions of this book—is largely prophetic, or more or less dialectical. When an art of thinking as appropriate to human and social affairs has grown up as that used in dealing with distant stars, it will not be necessary to argue that science is one among the arts and among the works of art. It will be enough to point to observable situations. The separation of science from art, and the division of arts into those concerned with mere means and those concerned with ends in themselves, is a mask for lack of conjunction between power and the goods of life. It will lose plausibility in the degree in which foresight of good informs the display of power.

Evidence of the interpenetration of the efficacious with the final in art is found in the slow emancipation of art from magical rite and cult, and the emergence of science from superstition. For magic and superstition could never have dominated human culture, nor poetry have been treated as insight into natural causes, if means and ends were empirically marked off from each other. The intimacy of their union in one and the same object is that which makes it easy to impute to whatever is consummatory a kind of efficacy which it does not possess. Whatever is final is important; to say this is to enunciate a truism. Lack of instrumentalities and of skill by which to analyze and follow the particular efficacies of the immediately enjoyed object lead to imputation to it of wholesale efficacy in the degree of its importance. To the short-cut pragmatism congenial to natural man, importance measures "reality" and reality in turn defines efficacious power. Loyalties evoked in the passionate citizen by sight of the flag or in the devout Christian by the cross are attributed directly to the intrinsic nature of these objects. Their share in a consummatory experience is translated into a mysterious inner sacred power, an indwelling efficacy. Thus a souvenir of the beloved one, arousing in the lover enjoyment similar to that awakened by the precious one to whom it belonged, possesses delightful, exciting, and consoling efficacies. No matter what things are directly implicated in a consummatory situation, they gain potencies for weal or woe similar to the good or evil which directly marks the situation. Obviously error here resides in the gross and undiscriminating way in which power is attributed; inquiry to reveal the specified elements which form the sequential order is lacking.

It is a commonplace of anthropologists that for the most part clothing originated in situations of unusual awe or prestigious display, rather than as a utility or protection. It was part of a consummatory object, rather than a means to specified consequences. Like the robes of priests, clothes were vestments, and investiture was believed to convey directly to the one ceremonially garbed dread potency or fascinating charm. Clothes were worn to confer authority; a man did not lend his significance to them. Similarly, a victorious hunter and warrior celebrated a triumphant return to camp by affixing to his person in conspicuous fashion claws and teeth of the wild beast or enemy that his prowess had subjugated. These signal proofs of power were integral portions of the object of admiration, loyalty and reverence. Thus the trophy became an emblem, and the emblem was endowed with mystic force. From a sign of glory it became a cause of glorification, and even when worn by another aroused the acclaim due to a hero. In time such trophies became the documented seal of prestigious authority. They had an intrinsic causal potency of their own. Legal history is full of like instances. Acts originally performed in connection with, say, the exchange of property, performed as part of the dramatic ceremony of taking possession of land, were not treated as mere evidences of title, but as having a mystic power to confer title.

Later, when such things lose their original power and become "mere matters of form," they may still be essential to the legal force of a transaction, as seals have had to be affixed to a contract to give it force, even though there was no longer sense or reason in their use. Things which have an efficacy imputed to them simply because they have shared in some eminent consummatory experience are symbols. They are called symbols, however, only afterwards and from without. To the devout in politics and religion they are other than symbols; they are articles possessed of occult potency. To one man, two crossed lines are an indication of an arithmetical operation to be performed; to another, they are evidence of the existence of Christianity as a historic fact, as a crescent is a reminder of the existence of Islam. But to another, a cross is more than a poignant reminder of a tragically significant death; it has intrinsic sacred power to protect and to bless. Since a flag stirs passionate loyalty to sudden and pervasive ebullition, the flag must have properties and potencies not possessed by other and differently configured pieces of cloth; it must be handled with reverence; it is the natural object of ceremonial adoration.

Phenomena like these when manifested in primitive culture are often interpreted as if they were attempts at a causal explanation of natural occurrences; magic is said to be science gone wrong. In reality, they are facts of direct emotional and practical response; beliefs, ideas, interpretations, only come later when responses not being direct and inevitably appropriate seem to demand explanation. As immediate responses they exemplify the fact that anything involved, no matter how incidentally, in a consummatory situation has the power of arousing the awe, excitement, relief, admiration belonging to the situation as a whole. Industry displaces magic, and science reduces myth, when the elements that enter into the constitution of the consummatory whole are discriminated, and each one has its own particular place in sequential order assigned it. Thus materials and efficacies characteristic of different kinds of arts are distinguished. But because the ceremonial, literary and poetic arts have quite other ways of working and other consequences, than industrial and scientific arts, it is far from following, as current theories assume, that they have no instrumental power at all, or that a sense of their instrumental agency is not involved in their appreciative perception. The pervasive operation of symbolism in human culture is all the proof that is needed to show that an intimate and direct sense of place and connection in a prolonged history enters into the enjoyed and suffered constituents of the history, and especially into the final or terminal members.

Further confirmation of this proposition is found in classic philosophy itself, in its theory that essential forms "make" things *what* they are, even though not causing them to occur. "Essence," as it figures in Greek theory, represents the mysterious potency of earlier "symbols" emancipated from their superstitious context and envisaged in a dialectic and reflective context. The essences of Greek-medieval science were in short poetic objects, treated as objects of demonstrative science, used to explain and understand the inner and ultimate constitution of things. While Greek thought was sufficiently emancipated from magic to deny "efficient" causality to formal and final essences, yet the latter were conceived of as making particular things to be *what* they are, members of natural kinds. Moreover, by a reversal of causal residence, intrinsic seeking for such forms was imputed to changing events. Thus the ground was prepared for the later frank return of patristic and scholastic thought to a frank animistic supernaturalism. The philosophic theory erred, as did magic and myth, regarding the nature of the efficacy involved in ends; and the error was due to the same causes, namely, failure of analysis into elements. It could not have occurred, were there that sharp division between means and ends, fruitions and instrumentalities, assumed by current thought.

In short, the history of human experience is a history of the development of arts. The history of science in its distinct emergence from religious, ceremonial and poetic arts is the record of a differentiation of arts, not a record of separation from art. The chief significance of the account just given, lies, for our present purpose, in its bearing upon the theory of experience and nature. It is not, however, without import for a theory of criticism. The present confusion, deemed chaos by some, in the fine arts and esthetic criticism seems to be an inevitable consequence of the underlying, even if unavowed, separation of the instrumental and the consummatory. The further men go in the concrete the more they are forced to recognize the logical consequence of their controlling assumptions. We owe it to theories of art prevalent to-day in one school of critics that certain implications, long obscured, of the traditional theory of art and nature have been brought to light. Gratitude for this debt should not be stinted because the adherents of the traditional theory regarding the newer views as capricious heresies, wild aberrations. For these critics, in proclaiming that esthetic qualities in works of fine art are unique, in asserting their separation from not only every thing that is existential in nature but also from all other forms of good, in proclaiming that such arts as music, poetry, painting have characters unshared with any natural things whatsoever:—in asserting such things the critics carry to its conclusion the isolation of fine art from the useful, of the final from efficacious. They thus prove that the separation of the consummation from the instrumental makes art wholly esoteric.

There are substantially but two alternatives. Either art is a continuation, by means of intelligent selection and arrangement, of natural tendencies of natural events; or art is a peculiar addition to nature springing from something dwelling exclusively within the breast of man, whatever name be given the latter. In the former case, delightfully enhanced perception or esthetic appreciation is of the same nature as enjoyment of any object that is consummatory. It is the outcome of a skilled and intelligent art of dealing with natural things for the sake of intensifying, purifying, prolonging and deepening the satisfactions which they spontaneously afford. That, in this process, new meanings develop, and that these afford uniquely new traits and modes of enjoyment is but what happens everywhere in emergent growths.

But if fine art has nothing to do with other activities and products, then of course it has nothing inherently to do with the objects, physical and social, experienced in other situations. It has an occult source and an esoteric character. It makes little difference what the source and the character be called. By strict logic it makes literally no difference. For if the quality of the esthetic experience is by conception unique, then the words employed to describe it have no significance derived from or comparable to the qualities of other experiences; their signification is hidden and specialized to a degree. Consider some of the terms which are in more or less current use among the critics who carry the isolation of art and the esthetic to its limit. It is sometimes said that art is the expression of the emotions; with the implication that, because of this fact, subject-matter is of no significance except as material through which emotion is expressed. Hence art becomes unique. For in works of science, utility and morals the character of the objects forming this subject-matter is all-important. But by this definition, subject-matter is stripped of all its own inherent characters in art in the degree in which it is genuine art; since a truly artistic work is manifest in the reduction of subject-matter to a mere medium of expression of emotion.

In such a statement emotion either has no significance at all, and it is mere accident that this particular combination of letters is employed; or else, if by emotion is meant the same sort of thing that is called emotion in daily life, the statement is demonstrably false. For emotion in its ordinary sense is something called out *by* objects, physical and personal; it is response *to* an objective situation. It is not something existing somewhere by itself which then employs material through which to express itself. Emotion is an indication of intimate participation, in a more or less excited way in some scene of nature or life; it is, so to speak, an attitude or disposition which is a function of objective things. It is intelligible that art should select and assemble objective things in such ways as to evoke emotional response of a refined, sensitive and enduring kind; it is intelligible that the artist himself is one capable of sustaining these emotions, under whose temper and spirit he performs his compositions of objective materials. This procedure may indeed be carried to a point such that the use of objective materials is economized to the minimum, and the evocation of the emotional response carried to its relative maximum. But it still remains true that the origin of the art-process lay in emotional responses spontaneously called out by a situation occurring without any reference to art, and without "esthetic" quality save in the sense in which all immediate enjoyment and suffering is esthetic. Economy in use of objective subject-matter may with experienced and trained minds go so far that what is ordinarily called "representation" is much reduced. But what happens is a highly funded and generalized representation of the formal sources of ordinary emotional experience.

The same sort of remark is to be made concerning "significant form" as a definition of an esthetic object. Unless the meaning of the term is so isolated as to be wholly occult, it denotes a selection, for sake of emphasis, purity, subtlety, of those forms which give consummatory significance to every-day subject-matters of experience. "Forms" are not the peculiar property or creation of the esthetic and artistic; they are characters in virtue of which anything meets the requirements of an enjoyable perception. "Art" does not create the forms; it is their selection and organization in such ways as to enhance, prolong and purify the perceptual experience. It is not by accident that some objects and situations afford marked perceptual satisfactions; they do so because of their structural properties and relations. An artist may work with a minimum of analytic recognition of these structures or "forms;" he may select them chiefly by a kind of sympathetic vibration. But they may also be discriminatively ascertained; and an artist may utilize his deliberate awareness of them to create works of art that are more formal and abstract than those to which the public is accustomed. Tendency to composition in terms of the formal characters marks much contemporary art, in poetry, painting; music, even sculpture and architecture. At their worst, these products are "scientific" rather than artistic; technical exercises, sterile and of a new kind of pedantry. At their best, they assist in ushering in new modes of art and by education of the organs of perception in new modes of consummatory objects; they enlarge and enrich the world of human vision.

Thus, by only a slight forcing of the argument, we reach a conclusion regarding the relations of instrumental and fine art which is precisely the opposite of that intended by seclusive estheticians; namely, that fine art *consciously* undertaken as such is peculiarly instrumental in quality. It is a device in experimentation carried on for the sake of education. It exists for the sake of a specialized use, use being a new training of modes of perception. The creators of such works of art are entitled, when successful, to the gratitude that we give to inventors of microscopes and microphones; in the end, they open new objects to be observed and enjoyed. This is a genuine service; but only an age of combined confusion and conceit will arrogate to works that perform this special utility the exclusive name of fine art.

Experience in the form of art, when reflected upon, we conclude by saying, solves more problems which have troubled philosophers and resolves more hard and fast dualisms than any other theme of thought. As the previous discussion has indicated, it demonstrates the intersection in nature of individual and generic; of chance and law, transforming one into opportunity and the other into liberation; of instrumental and final. More evidently still, it demonstrates the gratuitous falsity of notions that divide overt and executive activity from thought and feeling and thus separate mind and matter. In creative production, the external and physical world is more than a mere means or external condition of perceptions, ideas and emotions; it is subject-matter and sustainer of conscious activity; and thereby exhibits, so that he who runs may read, the fact that consciousness is not a separate realm of being, but is the manifest quality of existence when nature is most free and most active.

20. Existence, Value and Criticism*

In this selection, the concluding chapter of *Experience and Nature*, Dewey raises the problem of "value," only to cast

* From John Dewey, *Experience and Nature* (New York, 1958) (1929), 2nd ed., Chap. 2.

considerable doubt on the efficacy of a theory of value, at
least as it was posed at that time. In the use of the term
"value" Dewey detects a return of traditional dualism between existence and the honorific or precious. (Dewey
developed his own approach to "value" in 1939, when he
published a monograph entitled significantly *The Theory of
Valuation*.)

What does interest Dewey, however, is that "any *theory* of
values is perforce entrance into the field of criticism." And
this judgment leads to his statement that "philosophy is
inherently criticism, having its distinctive position among
various modes of criticism in its generality; a criticism of
criticisms, as it were." Dewey then proceeds to delineate the
salutary effects of philosophy utilized as the "critical method
of developing methods of criticism," all the while fending off
the more traditional claims made on behalf of philosophy.

Recent philosophy has witnessed the rise of a theory of value. Value
as it usually figures in this discussion marks a desperate attempt to combine the obvious empirical fact that objects are qualified with good and
bad, with philosophic deliverances which, in isolating man from nature,
qualitative individualities from the world, render this fact anomalous.
The philosopher erects a "realm of values" in which to place all the precious things which are extruded from natural existence because of isolations artificially introduced. Poignancy, humor, zest, tragedy, beauty,
prosperity and bafflement, although rejected from a nature which is
identified with mechanical structure, remain just what they empirically
are, and demand recognition. Hence they are gathered up into the realm
of values, contradistinguished from the realm of existence. Then the
philosopher has a new problem with which to wrestle: What is the relationship of these two "worlds"? Is the world of value that of ultimate
and transcendent Being from which the world of existence is a derivation or a fall? Or is it but a manifestation of human subjectivity, a factor
somehow miraculously supervening upon an order complete and closed
in physical structure? Or are there scattered at random through objective being, detached subsistences as "real" as are physical events, but
having no temporal dates and spatial locations, and yet at times and
places miraculously united with existences?

Choice among such notions of value is arbitrary, because the problem
is arbitrary. When we return to the conceptions of potentiality and ac-

tuality, contingency and regularity, qualitatively diverse individuality, with which Greek thought operated, we find no room for a theory of values separate from a theory of nature. Yet if we are to recur to the Greek conceptions, the return must be a return with a difference. It must surrender the identification of natural ends with good and perfection; recognizing that a natural end, apart from endeavor expressing choice, has no intrinsic eulogistic quality, but is the boundary which writes "Finis" to a chapter of history inscribed by a moving system of energies. Failure by exhaustion as well as by triumph may constitute an end; death, ignorance, as well as life, are finalities.

Again, the return must abandon the notion of a predetermined limited number of ends inherently arranged in an order of increasing comprehensiveness and finality. It will have to recognize that natural termini are as infinitely numerous and varied as are the individual systems of action they delimit; and that since there is only relative, not absolute, impermeability and fixity of structure, new individuals with novel ends emerge in irregular procession. It must recognize that limits, closures, ends are experimentally or dynamically determined, presenting, like the boundaries of political individuals or states, a moving adjustment of various energy-systems in their cooperative and competitive interactions, not something belonging to them of their own right. Consequently, it will surrender the separation in nature from each other of contingency and regularity, the hazardous and the assured; it will avoid that relegation of them to distinct orders of Being which is characteristic of the classic tradition. It will note that they intersect everywhere; that it is uncertainty and indeterminateness that create the need for and the sense of order and security; that whatever is most complete and liberal in being and possession is for that very reason most exposed to vicissitude, and most needful of watchful safeguarding art.

The connotation of "value" in recent thought contains some hint of the changes which experience has compelled in the classic notion of natural ends. For by implication at least values are recognized to be fugitive and precarious, to be negative and positive, and indefinitely diversified in quality. Even that metaphysical theory of super-idealism which finds them to be eternal, and the eternal foundation and source of shifting temporal events, bases its argument upon the undeniable insecurity, the interminable elusiveness, the appearance and disappearance, of values in actual experience. Because of this sense of the evanescence and uncertainty of what used to be called ends but are now called values, the important consideration and concern is not a theory of values but a theory of criticism; a method of discriminating among goods on the basis of the conditions of their appearance, and of their consequences.

Values are values, things immediately having certain intrinsic qualities. Of them as values there is accordingly nothing to be said; they are what they are. All that can be said of them concerns their generative conditions and the consequences to which they give rise. The notion that things as direct values lend themselves to thought and discourse rests upon a confusion of causal categories with immediate qualities. Objects, for example, may be distinguished as contributory or as fulfilling, but this is distinction of place with respect to causal relationship; it is not a distinction of values. We may be interested in a thing, be concerned with it or like it, for a reason. The reason for appreciation, for an enjoyed appropriation, is often that the object in question serves as a means to something; or the reason is that it stands as the culmination of an antecedent process. But to take into account the reason for liking and enjoyment concerns the cause of the existence of a value, and has nothing to do with the intrinsicalness or nature of the value-quality, which either does or does not exist. Things that are means and things that are fulfillments have different qualities; but so do symphonies, operas and oratorios among themselves. The difference is not one that has anything to do with the immediacy or intrinsicalness of value-quality; it is a difference between one affair and quality and another.

It is self-contradictory to suppose that when a fulfillment possesses immediate value, its means of attainment do not. The person to whom the cessation of a tooth-ache has value, by that very fact finds value in going to a dentist, or in whatever else is means of fulfillment. For fulfillment is as relative to means as means are to realization. Means-consequences constitute a single undivided situation. Consequently when thought and discussion enter, when theorizing sets in, when there is anything beyond bare immediate enjoyment and suffering, it is the means-consequence relationship that is considered. Thought goes beyond immediate existence to its relationships, the conditions which mediate it and the things to which it is in turn mediatory. And such a procedure is criticism. The all but universal confusion in theories of value of determined position in causative or sequential relationship with value proper is indirect testimony to the fact that every intelligent appreciation is also criticism, judgment, of the thing having immediate value. Any *theory* of values is perforce entrance into the field of criticism. Value as such, even things having value, cannot in their immediate existence be reflected upon; they either are or are not; are or are not enjoyed. To pass beyond direct occurrence, even though the passage be restricted to an attempt to define value, is to begin a process of discrimination which implies a reflective criterion. In themselves, values may be just pointed at; to attempt a definition by complete pointing is however bootless. Sooner or later, with respect to positive or negative value, designation will have to include everything.

These remarks are preparatory to presenting a conception of philosophy; namely, that philosophy is inherently criticism, having its distinctive position among various modes of criticism in its generality; a criticism of criticisms, as it were. Criticism is discriminating judgment, careful appraisal, and judgment is appropriately termed criticism wherever the subject-matter of discrimination concerns goods or values. Possession and enjoyment of goods passes insensibly and inevitably into appraisal. First and immature experience is content simply to enjoy. But a brief course in experience enforces reflection; it requires but brief time to teach that some things sweet in the having are bitter in after-taste and in what they lead to. Primitive innocence does not last. Enjoyment ceases to be a datum and becomes a problem. As a problem, it implies intelligent inquiry into the conditions and consequences of a value-object; that is, criticism. If values were as plentiful as huckleberries, and the huckleberry-patch were always at hand, the passage of appreciation into criticism would be a senseless procedure. If one thing tired or bored us, we should have only to turn to another. But values are as unstable as the forms of clouds. The things that possess them are exposed to all the contingencies of existence, and they are indifferent to our likings and tastes.

Good things change and vanish not only with changes in the environing medium but with changes in ourselves. Continued perception, except when it has been cultivated through prior criticism, dulls itself; it is soon satiated, exhausted, blasé. The infinite flippancy of the natural man is a standing theme for discourse by shrewd observers of human nature. Cultivated taste alone is capable of prolonged appreciation of the same object; and it is capable of it because it has been trained to a discriminating procedure which constantly uncovers in the object new meanings to be perceived and enjoyed. Add to exhaustion of the organs of perception and enjoyment, all the other organic causes which render enjoyed objects unstable, and then add the external vicissitudes to which they are subjected, and there is no cause to wonder at the evanescence of immediate goods; nor at the so-called paradoxes of pleasure and virtue, according to which they are not secured by aiming at them but by attention to other things;—a fact however, which is not a paradox in a world where nothing is attained in any other way than by attention to its causal conditions.

When criticism and the critical attitude are legitimately distinguished from appreciation and taste, we are in the presence of one case of the constant rhythm of "perchings and flights" (to borrow James' terms), characteristic of alternate emphasis upon the immediate and mediate, the consummatory and instrumental, phases of all conscious experience. If we are misled into ignoring the omnipresence in all observations and ideas of this rhythm, it is largely because, under the influence of formal theories, we attach too elaborate and too remote a signification to "appreciation" and "criticism." Values of some sort or other are not traits of rare and festal occasions; they occur whenever any object is welcomed and lingered over; whenever it arouses aversion and protest; even though the lingering be but momentary and the aversion a passing glance toward something else.

Similarly, criticism is not a matter of formal treatises, published articles, or taking up important matters for consideration in a serious way. It occurs whenever a moment is devoted to looking to see what sort of value is present; whenever instead of accepting a value-object wholeheartedly, being rapt by it, we raise even a shadow of a question about its worth, or modify our sense of it by even a passing estimate of its probable future. It is well upon the whole that we use the terms "appreciation" and "criticism" honorifically, to designate conspicuous instances. But it is fatal to any understanding of them to fail to note that formally emphatic instances are of exactly the same nature as the rhythmic alternation between slight agreeable acceptances, annoyed rejections and passing questionings and estimates, which make up the entire course of our waking experience, whether in revery, in controlled inquiry or in deliberate management of affairs.

The rhythmic succession of the two modes of perception suggests that the difference is one of emphasis, or degree. Critical appreciation, and appreciative, warmly emotionalized criticism occur in every matured sane experience. After the first dumb, formless experience of a thing as a good, subsequent perception of the good contains at least a germ of critical reflection. For this reason, and only for this reason, elaborate and formulated criticism is subsequently possible. The latter, if just and pertinent, can but develop the reflective implications found within appreciation itself. Criticism would be the most wilful of undertakings if the possession and enjoyment of good objects had no element of memory and foresight in it; if it lacked all circumspection and judgment. Criticism is reasonable and to the point, in the degree in which it extends and deepens these factors of intelligence found in immediate taste and enjoyment.

Conscience in morals, taste in fine arts and conviction in beliefs pass insensibly into critical judgments; the latter pass also into a more and more generalized form of criticism called philosophy. How is the assertion of "canons" of taste and criticism compatible with the declaration that there is no discussing tastes? What is meant by a distinction between apparent good and real good? How can the distinction between seeming and being be capable of application to what is good? Is critical appraisal possible without a standard measure of values? Is the standard of values itself a value? Is it derived from the value-objects to which it is applied? If so, what authority does it possess over and beyond that of particular cases? What right has it to pass judgment upon its own source and authors? Does a standard exist transcendentally in independence of concrete cases judged? If so, what is its source, and what is the ground and guarantee of its applicability to alien material? Is taste, immediate appreciation, sense and moral sense, ultimate, its own final judge in every case as it arises? What, in that event, saves us from chaotic anarchy? Is there among men a common measure of value? If so, is it grounded outside of man, in an independent objective form of Being?

Such questions as these, which may be multiplied as one pleases, indicate that no great difficulty would attend an effort to derive all the stock issues of philosophy from the problems of value and their relationship to critical judgment. Whether it be a question of the good and bad in conviction and opinion, or in matters of conduct, or in appreciated scenes of nature and art, there occurs in every instance a conflict between the immediate value-object and the ulterior value-object: the given good, and that reached and justified by reflection; the now apparent and the eventual. In knowledge, for example there are beliefs *de facto* and beliefs *de jure*. In morals, there are immediate goods, the desired, and reasonable goods, the desirable. In esthetics, there are the goods of an undeveloped or perverted taste and there are the goods of cultivated taste. With respect to any of these distinctions, the true, real, final, or objective good is no *more* good as an immediate existence than is the contrasting good, called false, specious, illusory, showy, meretricious, *le faux bon*. The difference in adjectives designates a difference instituted in critical judgment; the validity of the difference between good which is approved and that which is good (immediately) but is *judged bad*, depends therefore upon the value of reflection in general, and of a particular reflective operation in especial. Even if good of the reflective object is different from that of the good of the non-reflective object, it does not follow that it is a better good, much less that it is such a difference in goodness as makes the non-reflective good *bad:*—except upon one proviso, namely, that there is something unique in the value or goodness of reflection.

Either, then, the difference between genuine, valid good and a counterfeit, specious good is unreal, or it is a difference consequent upon reflection, or criticism, and the significant point is that this difference is equivalent to that made by discovery of relationships, of conditions and consequences. With this conclusion are bound up two other propositions: Of immediate values as such, values which occur and which are possessed and enjoyed, there is no theory at all; they just occur, are enjoyed, possessed; and that is all. The moment we begin to discourse about these values, to define and generalize, to make distinctions in kinds, we are passing beyond value-objects themselves; we are entering, even if only blindly, upon an inquiry into causal antecedents and causative consequents, with a view to appraising the "real," that is the eventual, goodness of the thing in question. We are criticizing, not for its own sake, but for the sake of instituting and perpetuating more enduring and extensive values.

The other proposition is that philosophy is and can be nothing but this critical operation and function become aware of itself and its implications, pursued deliberately and systematically. It starts from actual situations of belief, conduct and appreciative perception which are characterized by immediate qualities of good and bad, and from the modes of critical judgment current at any given time in all the regions of value; these are its data, its subject-matter. These values, criticisms, and critical methods, it subjects to further criticism as comprehensive and consistent as possible. The function is to regulate the further appreciation of goods and bads; to give greater freedom and security in those acts of direct selection, appropriation, identification and of rejection, elimination, destruction which enstate and which exclude objects of belief, conduct and contemplation.

Such a conclusion wears an air of strangeness. It may appear to indicate an attempt by a dialectic trick to make the category of good-and-bad supreme in its jurisdiction over intellectual life and over all objects. This impression will, I think, be readily dissipated by consideration of the actual meaning of what is said. Objects of belief and of refusals to believe are value-objects; for each object is some thing acquiesced in, accepted, adopted, appropriated. This is the same as saying it is found good or satisfactory to believe or disbelieve; truistically, whatever is accepted is as such and in so far good. There is no occult significance in this statement; it is not preliminary to an argument which shall sweep away the properties which objects possess independent of their being objects of belief, or of their being values. It does not annihilate the difference among beliefs; it does not set up the *fact* that an object believed in is perforce found good as if it were a *reason* for belief. On the contrary: the statement is preliminary. The all-important matter is what lies back of and causes acceptance and rejection; whether or no there is method of discrimination and assessment which makes a difference in what is assented to and denied. Properties and relations that *entitle* an object to be found good in belief are extraneous to the qualities that are its immediate good; they are causal, and hence found only by search into the antecedent and the eventual. The conception that there are some objects or some properties of objects which carry their own adequate credentials upon their face is the snare and delusion of the whole historic tradition regarding knowledge, infecting alike sensational and rational schools, objective realisms and introspective idealisms.

Concerning beliefs and their objects taken in their immediacy *"non-disputandum"* holds, as truly as it does concerning tastes and their objects. If a man believes in ghosts, devils, miracles, fortune-tellers, the immutable certainty of the existing economic regime, and the supreme merits of his political party and its leaders, he does so believe; these are immediate goods to him, precisely as some color and tone combinations are lovely, or the mistress of his heart is charming. When the question is raised as to the "real" value of the object for belief, the appeal is to criticism, intelligence. And the court of appeal decides by the law of conditions and consequences. Inquiry duly pursued leads to the enstatement of an object which is directly accepted, good in belief, but an object whose character now depends upon the reflective operations whose conclusion it is. Like the object of dogmatic and uncritical belief, it marks an "end," a static arrest; but unlike it, the "end" is a *conclusion;* hence it carries credentials.

Were not objects of belief immediate goods, false beliefs would not be the dangerous things which they are. For it is because these objects are good to believe, to admit and assert, that they are cherished so intolerantly and unremittingly. Beliefs about God, Nature, society and man are precisely the things that men most cling to and most ardently fight for. It is easier to wean a miser from his hoard, than a man from his deeper opinions. And the tragedy is that in so many cases the *causes* which lead to the thing in question being a value are not *reasons* for its being a good, while the fact that it is an immediate good tends to preclude that search for causes, that dispassionate judgment, which is prerequisite to the conversion of goods *de facto* into goods *de jure*. Here, again and pre-eminently, since reflection is the instrumentality of securing freer and more enduring goods, reflection is a unique intrinsic good. Its instrumental efficacy determines it to be a candidate for a distinctive position as an immediate good, since beyond other goods it has power of replenishment and fructification. In it, apparent good and real good enormously coincide.

In traditional discussion the fact is overlooked that the subject-matter of belief is a good, since belief means assimilation and assertion. It is overlooked that its immediate goodness is both the obstacle to reflective examination and the source of its necessity. The "true" is indeed set up along with the good and the beautiful as a transcendent good, but the role of empirical good, of value, in the sweep of ordinary beliefs is passed by. The counterpart of this error, which isolates the subject-matter of intellect from the scope of values and valuations, is a corresponding isolation of the subject-matter of esthetic contemplation and immediate enjoyment from judgment. Between these two realms, one of intellectual objects without value and the other of value-objects without intellect, there is an equivocal mid-country in which moral objects are placed, with rival claimants striving to annex them either to the region of purely immediate goods (in this case termed pleasures) or to that of purely rational objects. Hence the primary function of philosophy at present is to make it clear that there is no such difference as this division assumes between science, morals, and esthetic appreciation. All alike exhibit the difference between immediate goods casually occurring and immediate goods which have been reflectively determined by means of critical inquiry. If bare liking is an adequate determinant of values in one case, it is in the others. If intelligence, criticism, is required in one, it is in the others. If the end to be attained in any case is an enhanced and purified immediate appreciative, experienced object, so it is in the others. All cases manifest the same duality and present the same problem; that of embodying intelligence in action which shall convert casual natural goods, whose causes and effects are unknown, into goods valid for thought, right for conduct and cultivated for appreciation.

Philosophic discourse partakes both of scientific and literary discourse. Like literature, it is a comment on nature and life in the interest of a more intense and just appreciation of the meanings present in experience. Its business is reportorial and transcriptive only in the sense in which the drama and poetry have that office. Its primary concern is to clarify, liberate and extend the goods which inhere in the naturally generated functions of experience. It has no call to create a world of "reality" *de novo*, nor to delve into secrets of Being hidden from common-sense and science. It has no stock of information or body of knowledge peculiarly its own; if it does not always become ridiculous when it sets up as a rival of science, it is only because a particular philosopher happens to be also, as a human being, a prophetic man of science. Its business is to accept and to utilize for a purpose the best available knowledge of its own time and place. And this purpose is criticism of beliefs, institutions, customs, policies with respect to their bearing upon good. This does not mean their bearing upon *the* good, as something itself attained and formulated in philosophy. For as philosophy has no private score of knowledge or of methods for attaining truth, so it has no private access to good. As it accepts knowledge of facts and principles from those competent in inquiry and discovery, so it accepts the goods that are diffused in human experience. It has no Mosaic nor Pauline authority of revelation entrusted to it. But it has the authority of intelligence, of criticism of these common and natural goods.

At this point, it departs from the arts of literary discourse. They have a freer office to perform—to perpetuate, enhance and vivify in imagination the natural goods; all things are forgiven to him who succeeds. But philosophic criticism has a stricter task, with a greater measure of responsibility to what lies outside its own products. It has to appraise values by taking cognizance of their causes and consequences; only by this straight and narrow path may it contribute to expansion and emancipation of values. For this reason the conclusions of science about matter-of-fact efficiencies of nature are its indispensable instruments. If its eventual concern is to render goods more coherent, more secure and more significant in appreciation, its road is the subject-matter of natural existence as science discovers and depicts it.

Only in verbal form is there anything novel in this conception of philosophy. It is a version of the old saying that philosophy is love of wisdom, of wisdom which is not knowledge and which nevertheless cannot be without knowledge. The need of an organon of criticism which uses knowledge of relations among events to appraise the casual, immediate goods that obtain among men is not a fact of philosophy, but of nature and life. We can conceive a happier nature and experience than flourishes among us wherein the office of critical reflection would be carried on so continuously and in such detail that no particular apparatus would be needed. But actual experience is such a jumble that a degree of distance and detachment are a pre-requisite of vision in perspective. Thinkers often withdraw too far. But a withdrawal is necessary, unless they are to be deafened by the immediate clamor and blinded by the immediate glare of the scene. What especially makes necessary a generalized instrument of criticism, is the tendency of objects to seek rigid non-communicating compartments. It is natural that nature, variegatedly qualified, should exhibit various trends when it achieves experience of itself, so that there is a distribution of emphasis such as are designated by the adjectives scientific, industrial, political, religious, artistic, educational, moral and so on.

But however natural from the standpoint of causation may be the institutionalizing of these trends, their separation effects an isolation which is unnatural. Narrowness, superficiality, stagnation follow from lack of the nourishment which can be supplied only by generous and wide interactions. Goods isolated as professionalism and institutionalization isolate them, petrify; and in a moving world solidification is always dangerous. Resistant force is gained by precipitation, but no one thing gets strong enough to defy everything. Over-specialization and division of interests, occupations and goods create the need for a generalized medium of intercommunication, of mutual criticism through all-around translation from one separated region of experience into another. Thus philosophy as a critical organ becomes in effect a messenger, a liaison officer, making reciprocally intelligible voices speaking provincial tongues, and thereby enlarging as well as rectifying the meanings with which they are charged.

The difficulty is that philosophy, even when professing catholicity, has often been suborned. Instead of being a free messenger of communication it has been a diplomatic agent of some special and partial interest; insincere, because in the name of peace it has fostered divisions that lead to strife, and in the name of loyalty has promoted unholy alliances and secret understandings. One might say that the profuseness of attestations to supreme devotion to truth on the part of philosophy is matter to arouse suspicion. For it has usually been a preliminary to the claim of being a peculiar organ of access to highest and ultimate truth. Such it is not; and it will not lose its esoteric and insincere air until the profession is disclaimed. Truth is a collection of truths; and these constituent truths are in the keeping of the best available methods of inquiry and testing as to matters-of-fact; methods, which are, when collected under a single name, science. As to truth, then, philosophy has no pre-eminent status; it is a recipient, not a donor. But the realm of meanings is wider than that of true-and-false meanings; it is more urgent and more fertile. When the claim of meanings to truth enters in, then truth is indeed pre-eminent. But this fact is often confused with the idea that truth has a claim to enter everywhere; that it has monopolistic jurisdiction. Poetic meanings, moral meanings, a large part of the goods of life are matters of richness and freedom of meanings, rather than of truth; a large part of our life is carried on in a realm of meanings to which truth and falsity as such are irrelevant. And the claim of philosophy to rival or displace science as a purveyor of truth seems to be mostly a compensatory gesture for failure to perform its proper task of liberating and clarifying meanings, including those scientifically authenticated. For, assuredly, a student prizes historic systems rather for the meanings and shades of meanings they have brought to light than for the store of ultimate truths they have ascertained. If accomplishment of the former office were made the avowed business of philosophy, instead of an incidental by-product, its position would be clearer, more intelligent and more respected.

It is sometimes suggested, however, that such a view of philosophy derogates from its dignity, degrading it into an instrument of social reforms, and that it is a view congenial only to those who are insensitive to the positive achievements of culture and over-sensitive to its evils. Such a conception overlooks outstanding facts. "Social reform" is conceived in a Philistine spirit, if it is taken to mean anything less than precisely the liberation and expansion of the meanings of which experience is capable. No doubt many schemes of social reform are guilty of precisely this narrowing. But for that very reason they are futile; they do not succeed in even the special reforms at which they aim, except at the expense of intensifying other defects and creating new ones. Nothing but the best, the richest and fullest experience possible, is good enough for man. The attainment of such an experience is not to be conceived as the specific problem of "reformers" but as the common purpose of men. The contribution which philosophy can make to this common aim is criticism. Criticism certainly includes a heightened consciousness of deficiencies and corruptions in the scheme and distribution of values that obtains at any period.

No just or pertinent criticism in its negative phase can possibly be made, however, except upon the basis of a heightened appreciation of the positive goods which human experience has achieved and offers. Positive concrete goods of science, art and social companionship are the basic subject-matter of philosophy as criticism; and only because such positive goods already exist is their emancipation and secured extension the defining aim of intelligence. The more aware one is of the richness of meanings which experience possesses, the more will a generous and catholic thinker be conscious of the limits which prevent sharing in them; the more aware will he be of their accidental and arbitrary distribution. If instrumental efficacies need to be emphasized, it is not for the sake of instruments but for the sake of that full and more secure distribution of values which is impossible without instrumentalities.

If philosophy be criticism, what is to be said of the relation of philosophy to metaphysics? For metaphysics, as a statement of the generic traits manifested by existences of all kinds without regard to their differentiation into physical and mental, seems to have nothing to do with criticism and choice, with an effective love of wisdom. It begins and ends with analysis and definition. When it has revealed the traits and characters that are sure to turn up in every universe of discourse, its work is done. So at least an argument may run. But the very nature of the traits discovered in every theme of discourse, since they are ineluctable traits of natural existence, forbids such a conclusion. Qualitative individuality and constant relations, contingency and need, movement and arrest are common traits of all existence. This fact is source both of values and of their precariousness; both of immediate possession which is casual and of reflection which is a precondition of secure attainment and appropriation. Any theory that detects and defines these traits is therefore but a ground-map of the province of criticism, establishing base lines to be employed in more intricate triangulations.

If the general traits of nature existed in water-tight compartments, it might be enough to sort out the objects and interests of experience among them. But they are actually so intimately intermixed that all important issues are concerned with their degrees and the ratios they sustain to one another. Barely to note and register that contingency is a trait of natural events has nothing to do with wisdom. To note, however, contingency in connection with a concrete situation of life is that fear of the Lord which is at least the beginning of wisdom. The detection and definition of nature's end is in itself barren. But the undergoing that actually goes on in the light of this discovery brings one close to supreme issues: life and death.

The more sure one is that the world which encompasses human life is of such and such a character (no matter what his definition), the more one is committed to try to direct the conduct of life, that of others as well as of himself, upon the basis of the character assigned to the world. And if he finds that he cannot succeed, that the attempt lands him in confusion, inconsistency and darkness, plunging others into discord and shutting them out from participation, rudimentary precepts instruct him to surrender his assurance as a delusion; and to revise his notions of the nature of nature till he makes them more adequate to the concrete facts in which nature is embodied. Man needs the earth in order to walk, the sea to swim or sail, the air to fly. Of necessity he acts within the world, and in order to be, he must in some measure adapt himself as one part of nature to other parts.

In mind, thought, this situation, this predicament becomes aware of itself. Instead of the coerced adaptation of part to part with coerced failure or success as consequence, there is search for the meaning of things with respect to acts to be performed, plans and policies to be formed; there is search for the meaning of proposed acts with respect to objects they induce and preclude. The one cord that is never broken is that between the energies and acts which compose nature. Knowledge modifies the tie. But the idea that knowledge breaks the tie, that it inserts something opaque between the interactions of things, is hardly less than infantile. Knowledge as science modifies the particular interactions that come within its reach, because it *is* itself a modification of interactions, due to taking into account their past and future. The generic insight into existence which alone can define metaphysics in any empirically intelligible sense is itself an added fact of interaction, and is therefore subject to the same requirement of intelligence as any other natural occurrence: namely, inquiry into the bearings, leadings and consequences of what it discovers. The universe is no infinite self-representative series, if only because the addition within it of a representation makes it a different universe.

By an indirect path we are brought to a consideration of the most far-reaching question of all criticism: the relationship between existence and value, or as the problem is often put, between the real and ideal.

Philosophies have usually insisted upon a wholesale relationship. Either the goods which we most prize and which are therefore termed ideal are identified completely and throughout with real Being; or the realms of existence and of the ideal are wholly severed from each other. In the European tradition in its orthodox form the former alternative has prevailed. *Ens* and *verum, bonum* are the same. Being, in the full sense, is perfection of power to be; the measure of degrees of perfection and of degrees of reality is extent of power. Evil and error are impotences; futile gestures against omnipotence—against Being. Spinoza restated to this effect medieval theology in terms of the new outlook of science. Modern professed idealisms have taught the same doctrine. After magnifying thought and the objects of thought, after magnifying the ideals of human aspiration, they have then sought to prove that after all these things are not ideal but are real—real not *as* meanings and ideals, but as existential being. Thus the assertion of faith in the ideal belies itself in the making; these "idealists" cannot trust their ideal till they have converted it into existence—that is, into the physical or the psychical, which, since it lacks the properties of the empirically physical and psycho-physical becomes a peculiar kind of existence, called metaphysical.

There are also philosophies, rarer in occurrence, which allege that the ideal is too sacredly ideal to have any point of contact whatever with existence; they think that contact is contagion and contagion infection. At first sight such a view seems to display a certain nobility of faith and fineness of abnegation. But an ideal realm that has no roots in existence has no efficacy nor relevancy. It is a light which is darkness, for shining in the void it illumines nothing and cannot reveal even itself. It gives no instruction, for it cannot be translated into the meaning and import of what actually happens, and hence it is barren; it cannot mitigate the bleakness of existence nor modify its brutalities. It thus abnegates itself in abjuring footing in natural events, and ceases to be ideal, to become whimsical fantasy or linguistic sophistication.

These remarks are made not so much by way of hostile animadversion as by way of indicating the sterility of wholesale conceptions of the relation of existence and value. By negative implication, they reveal the only kind of doctrine that can be effectively critical, taking effect in discriminations which emancipate, extend, and clarify. Such a theory will realize that the meanings which are termed ideal as truly as those which are termed sensuous are generated by existences; that as far as they continue in being they are sustained by events; that they are indications of the possibilities of existences, and are, therefore, to be used as well as enjoyed; used to inspire action to procure and buttress their causal conditions. Such a doctrine criticizes particular occurrences by the particular meanings to which they give rise; it criticizes also particular meanings and goods as their conditions are found to be sparse, accidental, incapable of conservation, or frequent, pliant, congruous, enduring; and as their consequences are found to afford enlightenment and direction in conduct, or to darken counsel, narrow the horizon of vision, befog judgment and distort perspective. A good is a good anyhow, but to reflection those goods approve themselves, whether labelled beauty or truth or righteousness, which steady, vitalize and expand judgments in creation of new goods and conservation of old goods. To common-sense this statement is a truism. If to philosophy it is a stumbling-block, it is because tradition in philosophy has set itself in stiff-necked fashion against discriminations within the realm of existences, on account of the pluralistic implications of discrimination. It insists upon having all or none; it cannot choose in favor of some existences and against others because of prior commitment to a dogma of perfect unity. Such distinctions as it makes are therefore always hierarchical; degrees of greater and less, superior and inferior, in one homogeneous order.

I gladly borrow the glowing words of one of our greatest American philosophers; with their poetry they may succeed in conveying where dry prose fails. Justice Holmes has written: "The mode in which the inevitable comes to pass is through effort. Consciously or unconsciously we all strive to make the kind of world that we like. And although with Spinoza we may regard criticism of the past as futile, there is every reason for doing all that we can to make a future such as we desire." He then goes on to say, "there is every reason also for trying to make our desires intelligent. The trouble is that our ideals for the most part are inarticulate, and that even if we have made them definite we have very little experimental knowledge of the way to bring them about." And this effort to make our desires, our strivings and our ideals (which are as natural to man as his aches and his clothes) articulate, to define them (not in themselves which is impossible) in terms of inquiry into conditions and consequences is what I have called criticism; and when carried on in the grand manner, philosophy. In a further essay, Justice Holmes touches upon the relation of philosophy (thus conceived) to our scientific and metaphysical insight into the kind of a world in which we live.

"When we come to our attitude toward the universe I do not see any rational ground for demanding the superlative for being dissatisfied unless we are assured that our truth is cosmic truth, if there is such a thing. . . . . If a man sees no reason for believing that significance, consciousness and ideals are more than marks of the human, that does not justify what has been familiar in French sceptics; getting upon a pedestal and professing to look with haughty scorn upon a world in ruins. The real conclusion is that the part cannot swallow the whole. . . . If we believe that we came out of the universe, not it out of us, we must admit that we do not know what we are talking about when we speak of brute matter. We do know that a certain complex of energies can wag its tail and another can make syllogisms. These are among the powers of the unknown, and if, as may be, it has still greater powers that we cannot understand . . . why should we not be content? Why should we employ the energy that is furnished to us by the cosmos to defy it and to shake our fist at the sky? It seems to me silly.''

"That the universe has in it more than we understand, that the private soldiers have not been told the plan of campaign, or even that there is one . . . has no bearing on our conduct. We still shall fight—all of us because we want to live, some, at least, because we want to realize our spontaneity and prove our powers, for the joy of it, and we may leave to the unknown the supposed final valuation of that which in any event has value to us. It is enough for us that the universe has produced us and has within it, as less than it, all that we believe and love. If we think of our existence not as that of a little god outside, but as that of a ganglion within, we have the infinite behind us. It gives us our only but our adequate significance. If our imagination is strong enough to accept the vision of ourselves as parts inseparable from the rest, and to extend our final interest beyond the boundary of our skins, it justifies even the sacrifice of our lives for ends outside of ourselves. The motive to be sure is the common wants and ideals that we find in man. Philosophy does not furnish motives, but it shows men that they are not fools for doing what they already want to do. It opens to the forlorn hopes on which we throw ourselves away, the vista of the farthest stretch of human thought, the chord of a harmony that breathes from the unknown.''

Men move between extremes. They conceive of themselves as gods, or feign a powerful and cunning god as an ally who bends the world to do their bidding and meet their wishes. Disillusionized, they disown the world that disappoints them; and hugging ideals to themselves as their own possession, stand in haughty aloofness apart from the hard course of events that pays so little heed to our hopes and aspirations. But a mind that has opened itself to experience and that has ripened through its discipline knows its own littleness and impotencies; it knows that its wishes and acknowledgments are not final measures of the universe whether in knowledge or in conduct, and hence are, in the end, transient. But it also knows that its juvenile assumption of power and achievement is not a dream to be wholly forgotten. It implies a unity with the universe that is to be preserved. The belief, and the effort of thought and struggle which it inspires are also the doing of the universe, and they in some way, however slight, carry the universe forward. A chastened sense of our importance, apprehension that it is not a yardstick by which to measure the whole, is consistent with the belief that we and our endeavors are significant not only for themselves but in the whole.

Fidelity to the nature to which we belong, as parts however weak, demands that we cherish our desires and ideals till we have converted them into intelligence, revised them in terms of the ways and means which nature makes possible. When we have used our thought to its utmost and have thrown into the moving unbalanced balance of things our puny strength, we know that though the universe slay us still we may trust, for our lot is one with whatever is good in existence. We know that such thought and effort is one condition of the coming into existence of the better. As far as we are concerned it is the only condition, for it alone is in our power. To ask more than this is childish; but to ask less is a recreance no less egotistic, involving no less a cutting of ourselves from the universe than does the expectation that it meet and satisfy our every wish. To ask in good faith as much as this from ourselves is to stir into motion every capacity of imagination, and to exact from action every skill and bravery.

While, therefore, philosophy has its source not in any special impulse or staked-off section of experience, but in the entire human predicament, this human situation falls wholly within nature. It reflects the traits of nature; it gives indisputable evidence that in nature itself qualities and relations, individualities and uniformities, finalities and efficacies, contingencies and necessities are inextricably bound together. The harsh conflicts and the happy coincidences of this interpenetration make experience what it consciously is; their manifest apparition creates doubt, forces inquiry, exacts choice, and imposes liability for the choice which is made. Were there complete harmony in nature, life would be spontaneous efflorescence. If disharmony were not in both man and nature, if it were only between them, man would be the ruthless overlord of nature, or its querulous oppressed subject. It is precisely the peculiar intermixture of support and frustration of man by nature which constitutes experience. The standing antitheses of philosophic thought, purpose and mechanism, subject and object, necessity and freedom, mind and body, individual and general, are all of them attempts to formulate the fact that nature induces and partially sustains meanings and goods, and at critical junctures withdraws assistance and flouts its own creatures.

The striving of man for objects of imagination is a continuation of natural processes; it is something man has learned from the world in which he occurs, not something which he arbitrarily injects into that world. When he adds perception and ideas to these endeavors, it is not after all he who adds; the addition is again the doing of nature and a further complication of its own domain. To act, to enjoy and suffer in consequence of action, to reflect, to discriminate and make differences in what had been but gross and homogeneous good and evil, according to what inquiry reveals of causes and effects; to act upon what has been learned, thereby to plunge into new and unconsidered predicaments, to test and revise what has been learned, to engage in new goods and evils is human, the course which manifests the course of nature. They are the manifest destiny of contingency, fulfillment, qualitative individualization and generic uniformities in nature. To note, register and define the constituent structure of nature is not then an affair neutral to the office of criticism. It is a preliminary outline of the field of criticism, whose chief import is to afford understanding of the necessity and nature of the office of intelligence.

If I mistake not, the actual animus of subjectivity in modern philosophy is not where its antagonists have placed it. Its actual animus and its obnoxious burden are exemplified in the doctrine of its hostile critics. For they assign to knowledge alone valid reference to existence. Desires, beliefs, "practical" activity, values are attributed exclusively to the human subject; this division is what makes subjectivity a snare and peril. The case of belief is crucial. For it is admitted that belief involves a phase of acquiescence or assertion, it presents qualities which involve *personal* factors; and (whatever definition of value be employed) value. A sharp line of demarcation has therefore to be drawn between belief and knowledge, for the latter has been defined in terms of pure objectivity. The need to control belief is admitted; knowledge figures, even though according to these theories only *per accidens*, as the organon of such control. Practically then, in effect, knowledge, science, truth, is the method of criticizing beliefs. It is the method of determining right participation in beliefs on the part of personal factors. Why then keep up any other distinction between knowledge and beliefs, save that between methodical agencies, efficacious instrumentalities, and the accepted objects which being conclusions, are hence marked by characters due to the method of their production, in contrast with objects of belief blindly and accidentally generated? Why perturbation at the intimation that science is inherently an instrument of critically determining what is good and bad in the way of acceptance and rejection?

I can see but one answer. The realm of desire, belief, search, choice is thought of as "subjective" in a sense which isolates it from natural existence and which makes it an inexplicable irruption. This is the reason for sharp separation of belief and knowledge. Aversion to making science a means of determining the right operation of personal factors, just as the technical and material apparatus of a painter determines his product, is well grounded if the personal is outside of nature. Made a means to something personal conceived in this sense, science loses its objectivity, and becomes infected with the traits which characterize the merely private and arbitrary.

There is involved, however, in the conclusion an unexamined and uncriticized assumption. The reason for isolating doubt, striving, purpose, the variegated colored play of goods and bads, rejections and acceptances, is they do not belong in the block universe which forms the object of generalized knowledge, whether the block be conceived as mechanical or as rational in structure. The argument thus moves in a vicious circle; the question is begged at the outset. If individualized qualities, status arrests, limiting "ends," and contingent changes characterize nature, then they manifest themselves in the uses, enjoyments and sufferings, the searchings and strivings which form conscious experience. These are as realistic, as "objectively" natural, as are the constitutents of the object of cognitional experience. There is then no ground for denying or evading the full import of the fact that the latter are the means and the only means of regulative appraisals of values, of their revision, rectification, of their regulated generation and fortification.

The habitual avoidance in theories of knowledge of any reference to the fact that knowledge is a case of belief, operates as a device for ignoring the monstrous consequences of regarding the latter as existentially subjective, personal and private. No such device is available in dealing with esthetic and moral goods. Here the obnoxious one-sided conception operates in full force. The usual current procedure is to link values with likings as merely personal affairs, ignoring the inconvenient fact that the theory logically thereby makes all *beliefs* also matters of arbitrary, undiscussable preference. It is no cause for wonder therefore that there is next to no consensus in esthetic and moral theories. Since their subject-matter is totally segregated from that of science, since they are assigned to independent non-participating realms of existence, the only possible method of achieving agreement has been exiled in advance.

Practically this consequence is intolerable; accordingly it is rarely faced. "Standards" of value suddenly make their appearance to serve as criteria of taste and conscience. The distinction between likings and that which is worth liking, between the desired and the desirable, between the is and the ought, descends out of the blue. There are, it seems, immediate values, but there also are standard values, and the latter may be used to judge and measure immediate goods and bads. Thus the reflective distinction between the true and the false, the genuine and the spurious is brought upon the scene. In strict logic, however, it enters only to disappear. For if the standard is itself a value, then it is by definition only another name for the object of a particular liking, on the part of some particular subjective creature. If the liking for it conflicts with some other liking, the strongest wins. There is no question of false and true, of real and seeming, but only of stronger and weaker. The question of which one *should* be stronger is as meaningless as it would be in a cock-fight.

Such a conclusion puts an end to all attempt at consistency and organization and calls out in reaction an opposite theory. The "standard" is not, it is decided, for us at least, a good. It is rather a principle rationally apprehended. It is that which is "right" rather than that which is good; and since it is the right, it is the standard for judging all goods. If right is also good, the identification subsists in some transcendental realm; in some eternal, non-empirical realm of Being which is also a realm of values. The standard of good thus conceived as a principle of reason and as a form of supreme Being, is set over against the outside of actual desires, striving, satisfactions and frustrations. It ought to enter into their determination but for the most part it does not. The distinction between is and ought is one of kind, and a separation. It is not surprising that the wheel completes a full circle, and that the finale is a retort that the alleged standard is itself but another dignified disguise for some one's arbitrary liking—the *ipse dixit* of some one accidentally clothed with extraneous authority.

It is as irritating to have experience of beauty and moral goodness reduced to groundless whims as to have that of truth. Common-sense has an inexpugnable conviction that there are immediate goods of enjoyment and conduct, and that there are principles by which they may be appraised and rectified. Common-sense entertains this firm conviction because it is innocent of any rigid demarcation between knowledge on one side and belief, conduct and esthetic appreciation on the other. It is guiltless of the division between objective reality and subjective events. It takes striving, purposing, inquiring, wanting, the life of "practice," to be as much facts of nature as are the themes of scientific discourse; to it, indeed, the former has a more direct and urgent reality. Hence it has no difficulty with the idea of rational or objective criticism and rectification of immediate goods. If it were articulate, it would say that the same natural processes which generate goods and evils generate also the striving to secure the one and avoid the other, and generate judgments to regulate the strivings. Its weakness is that it fails to recognize that deliberate and systematized science is a precondition of adequate judgments and hence of adequate striving and adequate choice. Its organs of criticism are for the most part half-judgments, un-criticized products of custom, chance circumstance and vested interests. Hence common-sense when it begins to reflect upon its own convictions easily falls a victim to traditional theories; and the vicious circle begins over again. It is sound as to the need and possibility of objective criticism of values, it is weak as to the method of accomplishing.

Yet all this time there is an example of the way out in the case of beliefs. There was a time when beliefs about external events were largely matters of what it was found immediately good to accept or reject; as far as there was a distinction made between the immediately good in belief and the real or true, it lay chiefly in the fact that the latter was the object sanctioned by authorities of church and state. Yet it is now all but commonplace that every belief-value must be subjected to criticism; in scientific undertakings, it is a commonplace that criticism does not depend upon reference to a transcendent standard truth. The distinction between an immediate belief-value, which is but a challenge to inquiry, and an eventual object of belief that concludes critical inquiry, and has the value of fulfilling the causal relationships discovered, is made in the course of intelligent experiment. The result is a distinction between the apparent and the real good. Gradually a reluctant world is persuaded that meanings so determined define what is good for acceptance and assertion. Meantime beliefs determined by passion, class-interest, routine and authority remain sufficiently prevalent to enforce the perception that it makes all the difference in the world in the value of a belief how its object is formed and arrived at. Thus the lesson is enforced that critical valuations of immediate goods proceed in terms of the generation and consequences of objects qualified with good.

In outward forms, experimental science is infinitely varied. In principle it is simple. We know an object when we know how it is made, and we know how it is made in the degree in which we ourselves make it. Old tradition compels us to call thinking "mental." But "mental" thought is but partial experimentation, terminating in preliminary readjustments, confined within the organism. As long as thinking remained at this stage, it protected itself by regarding this introverted truncation as evidence of an immaterial reason superior to and independent of body. As long as thought was thus cooped up, overt action in the "outer" natural scene was inevitably shorn of its full meed of meaning; it was to that extent arbitrary and routine. When "outer" and "inner" activity came together in a single experimental operation, used as the only adequate method of discovery and proof, effective criticism, consistent and ordered valuation, emerged. Thought aligned itself with other arts that shape objects by informing things with meanings.

Psychology, which reflects the old dualistic separation of mind from nature, has made current the notion that the processes which terminate in knowledge fare forth from innocent sensory data, or from pure logical principles, or from both together, as original starting points and material. As a natural history of mind this notion is wholly mythological. All knowing and effort to know starts from some belief, some received and asserted meaning which is a deposit of prior experience, personal and communal. In every instance, from passing query to elaborate scientific undertaking, the art of knowing criticizes a belief which has passed current as genuine coin, with a view to its revision. It terminates when freer, richer and more secure objects of belief are instituted as goods of immediate acceptance. The operation is one of doing and making in the literal sense. Starting from one good, treated as apparent and questionable, and ending in another which is tested and substantiated, the final act of knowing is acceptance and intellectual appreciation of what is significantly conclusive.

Is there any reason for supposing that the situation is any different in the case of other values and valuations? Is there any intrinsic difference between the relation of scientific inquiry to belief-values, of esthetic criticism to esthetic values, and of moral judgments to moral goods? Is there any difference in logical method? If we adopt a current theory, and say that immediate values occur wherever there is liking, interest, bias, it is clear that this liking is an act, if not an overt one, at least a dispositional tendency and direction. But most likings, all likings in their first appearance, are blind and gross. They do not know what they are about nor why they attach themselves to this or that object.

Moreover, every such act takes a risk and assumes a liability, and does so ignorantly. For there are always in existence rival claimants for liking. To prefer *this* is to exclude *that*. Any liking is choice, unwittingly performed. There is no selection without rejection; interest and bias are selective, preferential. To take this for a good is to declare in act, though not at first in thought, that it is better than something else. This decision is arbitrary, capricious, unreasoned because made without thought of the other object, and without comparison. To say that an object is a good may seem to be an absolute and intrinsic declaration particularly when the assertion is made in direct act rather than in thought. But when we recognize that in effect the assertion is that one thing is better than another thing, the issues shift to something comparative, relational, causal, intellectual and objective. *Immediately* nothing is better or worse than anything else; it is just what it is. Comparison is comparison of things, things in their efficacies, their promotions and hindrances. The better is that which will do more in the way of security, liberation and fecundity for other likings and values.

To make a valuation, to judge appraisingly, is then to bring to conscious perception relations of productivity and resistance and thus to make value significant, intelligent and intelligible. In becoming discriminately aware of the causal conditions of the object liked and preferred, we become aware of its eventual operations. If in the case of esthetic and moral goods, the causal conditions which reflection reveals as determinants of the good object are found to lie within organic constitution in greater degree than is the case with objects of belief, this finding is of enormous importance for the technique of critical judgment. But it does not modify the logic which obtains in knowledge of the relationship of values and valuations to each other. It indicates the particular subject-matter which has to be controlled and used in the conscious art of re-making goods. As inquiries which aim at knowledge start from pre-existent beliefs, so esthetic and moral criticism start from antecedent natural goods of contemplative enjoyment and social intercourse. Its purpose is to make it possible to like and choose knowingly and with meaning, instead of blindly. All criticism worthy of the title is but another name for that revealing discovery of conditions and consequences which enables liking, bias, interest to express themselves in responsible and informed ways instead of ignorantly and fatalistically.

The meaning of the theory advanced concerning the relationship of goods and criticism may be illustrated by ethical theory. Few I suppose would deny that in spite of the attention devoted to this subject by many

minds of a high order of intention and intellectual equipment, the outcome, judged from the standpoint of scientific consensus, is rather
dismaying. The outcome is due in part to the importance of the subject,
its intimate connection with man's deepest concerns, with his most
cherished traditions and with the most acutely perplexing problems of
his contemporary social life. Objective detachment and development of
adequate intellectual instruments are necessarily difficult under such
conditions. But I think that we find, amid all the diversity, one common
intellectual preconception which inevitably defers the possibility of attainment of scientific method. This is the assumption, implicit or overt,
that moral theory is concerned with ends, values rather than with
criticism of ends and values; the latter being in fact not only independent of moral theory but not themselves having even moral
quality. To discover and define once for all the *bonum* and the *summum
bonum* in a way which rationally subserves all virtues and duties, is the
traditional task of morals; to deny that moral theory has any such office
will seem to many equivalent to denial of the possibility of moral
philosophy. Yet in other things repeated failure of achievement is
regarded as evidence that we are going at the affair in a wrong way. And
to a mind willing to surrender the traditional preconception, failure to
achieve consensus in method and even in generic conclusions in morals
as a branch of philosophy may be similarly explained.

It is not meant of course that the tradition assumes that the good and
the highest good are created by moral theory. The assumption is not so
bad as that; it is to the effect that it is the province of moral theory to reveal moral goods; to bring them to consciousness and to enforce their
character in perception. As empirical fact, however, the arts, those of
converse and the literary arts which are the enhanced continuations of
social converse, have been the means by which goods are brought home
to human perception. The writings of moralists have been efficacious in
this direction upon the whole not in their professed intent as theoretical
doctrines, but in as far as they have genially participated in the arts of
poetry, fiction, parable and drama. Conversion into doctrinal teachings
of the imaginative relations of life with which great moral artists have
dowered humanity has been the great cause of their ossification into
harsh dogmas; illuminating insight into the relations and goods of life
has been lost, and an arbitrary code of precepts and rules substituted.
Direct appeal of experience concentrated, vivified and intensified by the
insight of an artist and embodied in literary creations similar in kind to
the revelation of meanings which is the work of any artist, has been

treated as a discovery and definition of things true to scientific or philosophic reason.

Meantime the work which theoretical criticism might do has not been done; namely, discovery of the conditions and consequences, the existential relations, of goods which are accepted as goods not because of theory but because they are such in experience. The cause in large measure is doubtless because the prerequisite tools of physics, physiology and economics were not at hand. But now when these potential instrumentalities are more adequately prepared they will not be employed until it is recognized that the business of moral theory is not at all with consummations and goods as such, but with discovery of the conditions and consequences of their appearance, a work which is factual and analytic, not dialectic, hortatory, nor prescriptive. The argument does not forget that there have been would-be naturalistic and empirical ethics which have asserted that goods are such prior to moral conduct as well as to moral theory, and that they become moral only when employed in conduct as objects of reflective choice and endeavor. But the apparent exception proves the rule. For these forms of moral theory while releasing morals from the obligation of telling man what goods are, leaving that office to life itself, have failed to note that the office of moral philosophy is criticism; and that the performance of this office by discovery of existential conditions and consequences involves a qualitative transformation, a re-making in subsequent action which experimentally tests the conclusions of theory.

Therefore like the Aristotelian ethics, they have been dialectic, defining and classifying in hierarchical order antecedent goods and terminating in a notion of *the* good, the *summum bonum;* or, like hedonistic ethics, they have made a dialectic abstraction of a feature of concrete goods, their pleasantness; and instead of providing a method of analysis of concrete situations have laid down rules of calculation and prescribed policies to be pursued as fixed, not intellectually experimental, results of prior calculations. When they were, like Jeremy Bentham, persons of human sensitiveness to evils from which men suffer in virtue of institutions which may be altered; or, like John Stuart Mill, of genial insight into the constituents of a liberal and humane happiness, they have stirred their generation to beneficent action. But the connection between their theories and the practical outcome was adventitious; their ideas operated when all is said and done as literary rather than as scientific apparatus, as much so as in the case of reforms to which Charles Dickens not meanly contributed.

The implications of the position which has been taken import a "practical" element into philosophy as effective and verifiable criticism, obnoxious to the traditional view. Yet if man is within nature, not a little god outside, and is within as a mode of energy inseparably connected with other modes, interaction is the one unescapable trait of every human concern; thinking, even philosophic thinking, is not exempt. This interaction is subject to partiality because the human factor has bent and bias. But partiality is not obnoxious just because it is partial. A world characterized by qualitative histories with their own beginnings, directions and terminations is of necessity a world in which any interaction is intensive change—a world of partialities, particulars. What is obnoxious in partiality is due to the illusion that there are states and acts which are not also interactions. Immature and undisciplined mind believes in actions which have their seat and source in a particular and separate being, from which they issue. This is the very belief which the advance of intelligent criticism destroys. The latter transforms the notion of isolated one-sided acts into acknowledged interactions. The view which isolates knowledge, contemplation, liking, interest, value, or whatever from action is itself a survival of the notion that there are things which can exist and be known apart from active connection with other things.

When man finds he is not a little god in his active powers and accomplishments, he retains his former conceit by hugging to his bosom the notion that nevertheless in some realm, be it knowledge or esthetic contemplation, he is still outside of and detached from the ongoing sweep of inter-acting and changing events; and being there alone and irresponsible save to himself, is as a god. When he perceives clearly and adequately that he is within nature, a part of its interactions, he sees that the line to be drawn is not between blind, slavish, meaningless action and action that is free, significant, directed and responsible. Knowledge, like the growth of a plant and the movement of the earth, is a mode of interaction; but it is a mode which renders other modes luminous, important, valuable, capable of direction, causes being translated into means and effects into consequences.

All reason which is itself reasoned, is thus method, not substance; operative, not "end in itself." To imagine it the latter is to transport it outside the natural world, to convert it into a god, whether a big and original one or a little and derived one, outside of the contingencies of existence and untouched by its vicissitudes. This is the meaning of the "reason" which is alleged to envisage reality *sub specie aeternitatis*. It is indeed true that all relations, all universals and laws as such are timeless. Even an order of time as an order is timeless, for it is relational. But to give irrelevancy to time the name of eternal in an eulogistic sense, is but to proclaim that irrelevancy to any existence forms a higher kind of existence. Orders, relations, universals are significant and invaluable as objects of knowledge. They are so because they apply to intensive and extensive, individualized, existences; to things of spacious and temporal qualities. Application is not for the sake of something extraneous, for the sake of something designated an utility. It is for the sake of the laws, principles, ideals. Had they not been detached for the purpose of application, they would not have meaning; intent and potentiality of application in the course of events lends them all their significance. Without *actuality* of application, without effort to realise their intent, they are meanings, but they possess neither truth nor falsity, since without application they have no bearing and test. Thus they cease to be objects of knowledge, or even reflection; and become detached objects of contemplation. They may then have the esthetic value possessed by the objects of a dream. But after all we have not left temporal experience, human desire, liking, and passion behind or below us. We have merely painted nature with the colors of an all too local and transitory flight from the hardships of life. These eternal objects abstracted from the course of events, although labeled Reality, in opposition to Appearance, are in truth but the idlest and most evanescent of appearances, born of personal craving and shaped by private fantasy.

Because intelligence is critical method applied to goods of belief, appreciation and conduct, so as to construct freer and more secure goods, turning assent and assertion into free communication of shareable meanings, turning feeling into ordered and liberal sense, turning reaction into response, it is the reasonable object of our deepest faith and loyalty, the stay and support of all reasonable hopes. To utter such a statement is not to indulge in romantic idealization. It is not to assert that intelligence will ever dominate the course of events; it is not even to imply that it will save from ruin and destruction. The issue is one of choice, and choice is always a question of alternatives. What the method of intelligence, thoughtful valuation will accomplish, if once it be tried, is for the result of trial to determine. Since it is relative to the intersection in existence of hazard and rule, of contingency and order, faith in a wholesale and final triumph is fantastic. But some procedure has to be tried; for life is itself a sequence of trials. Carelessness and routine, Olympian aloofness, secluded contemplation are themselves choices. To claim that intelligence is a better method than its alternatives, authority, imitation, caprice and ignorance, prejudice and passion, is hardly an excessive claim. These procedures have been tried and have worked their will. The result is not such as to make it clear that the method of intelligence, the use of science in criticizing and recreating the casual goods of nature into intentional and conclusive goods of art, the union of knowledge and values in production, is not worth trying. There may be those to whom it is treason to think of philosophy as the critical method of developing methods of criticism. But this conception of philosophy also waits to be tried, and the trial which shall approve or condemn lies in the eventual issue. The import of such knowledge as we have acquired and such experience as has been quickened by thought is to evoke and justify the trial.

V

The Culture
of Inquiry

The following selections are instances of a theme which is central to Dewey's thought—that is, the inseparability of inquiry from the social environment in which it functions. No doubt, Dewey is in part indebted to Hegel for his sense of the relationship between knowing and events, but he profits also from the development of social psychology and from a deep experience of the entwining of attitudes and method as found in the American political community.

Not one to give academic labels to his work, nonetheless it can be said of Dewey's philosophy that it is often a masterpiece of the sociology of knowledge.

21. Escape from Peril*

John Dewey held that it was neither possible nor desirable to bypass the precarious as a dimension in the human condition. Indeed, he believed that risking one's security was often necessary in the attempt to enhance the quality of life. In "Escape from Peril," Dewey considers two of the traditional attempts to ground "certainty," the first in religion and the second in philosophy, both as originating in Greek culture. While acknowledging the differences in these two approaches, Dewey contends that they both constitute a "doctrine of escape from the vicissitudes of existence by means of measures which do not demand an active coping with conditions."

Despite his isolated and perhaps unfair attack on Aristotle

* From John Dewey, *The Quest for Certainty* (New York, Capricorn Books, 1960) (1929), pp. 3-25. Reprinted by permission of G. P. Putnam's Sons.

in this selection, Dewey's real opponent is that virulent strain which runs through all of Western culture—namely, the quest for certainty. Whether by rites and cults or by reason, the energy given over to securing the meaning of human life in an ultimate way should be better put to dealing directly with the environment for purposes of amelioration and human growth. For Dewey, if there is an ultimate meaning to human life, it is that man is finite and incapable of arriving at a principle of total accountability.

Man who lives in a world of hazards is compelled to seek for security. He has sought to attain it in two ways. One of them began with an attempt to propitiate the powers which environ him and determine his destiny. It expressed itself in supplication, sacrifice, ceremonial rite and magical cult. In time these crude methods were largely displaced. The sacrifice of a contrite heart was esteemed more pleasing than that of bulls and oxen; the inner attitude of reverence and devotion more desirable than external ceremonies. If man could not conquer destiny he could willingly ally himself with it; putting his will, even in sore affliction, on the side of the powers which dispense fortune, he could escape defeat and might triumph in the midst of destruction.

The other course is to invent arts and by their means turn the powers of nature to account; man constructs a fortress out of the very conditions and forces which threaten him. He builds shelters, weaves garments, makes flame his friend instead of his enemy, and grows into the complicated arts of associated living. This is the method of changing the world through action, as the other is the method of changing the self in emotion and idea. It is a commentary on the slight control man has obtained over himself by means of control over nature, that the method of action has been felt to manifest dangerous pride, even defiance of the powers which be. People of old wavered between thinking arts to be the gift of the gods and to be an invasion of their prerogatives. Both versions testify to the sense of something extraordinary in the arts, something either superhuman or unnatural. The souls who have predicted that by means of the arts man might establish a kingdom of order, justice and beauty through mastery of nature's energies and laws have been few and little heeded.

Men have been glad enough to enjoy the fruits of such arts as they possess, and in recent centuries have increasingly devoted themselves to their multiplication. But this effort has been conjoined with a profound distrust of the arts as a method of dealing with the serious perils of life.

Doubt as to the truth of this statement will be dispelled if one considers the disesteem in which the idea of practice has been held. Philosophers have celebrated the method of change in personal ideas, and religious teachers that of change in the affections of the heart. These conversions have been prized on their own account, and only incidentally because of a change in action which would ensue. The latter has been esteemed as an evidence of the change in thought and sentiment, not as a method of transforming the scene of life. The places in which the use of the arts has effected actual objective transformation have been regarded as inferior, if not base, and the activities connected with them as menial. The disparagement attending the idea of the material has seized upon them. The honorable quality associated with the idea of the "spiritual" has been reserved for change in inner attitudes.

The depreciation of action, of doing and making, has been cultivated by philosophers. But while philosophers have perpetuated the derogation by formulating and justifying it, they did not originate it. They glorified their own office without doubt in placing theory so much above practice. But independently of their attitude, many things conspired to the same effect. Work has been onerous, toilsome, associated with a primeval curse. It has been done under compulsion and the pressure of necessity, while intellectual activity is associated with leisure. On account of the unpleasantness of practical activity, as much of it as possible has been put upon slaves and serfs. Thus the social dishonor in which this class was held was extended to the work they do. There is also the age-long association of knowing and thinking with immaterial and spiritual principles, and of the arts, of all practical activity in doing and making, with matter. For work is done with the body, by means of mechanical applicances and is directed upon material things. The disrepute which has attended the thought of material things in comparison with immaterial thought has been transferred to everything associated with practice.

One might continue in this strain. The natural history of conceptions about work and the arts if it were traced through a succession of peoples and cultures would be instructive. But all that is needed for our purpose is to raise the question: Why this invidious discrimination? A very little reflection shows that the suggestions which have been offered by way of explanation themselves need to be explained. Ideas derived from social castes and emotional revulsions are hardly reasons to be offered in justification of a belief, although they may have a bearing on its causation. Contempt for matter and bodies and glorification of the immaterial are affairs which are not self-explanatory. And, as we shall be at some pains to show later in the discussion, the idea which connects thinking and knowing with some principle or force that is wholly separate from connection with physical things will not stand examination, especially since the whole-hearted adoption of experimental method in the natural sciences.

The questions suggested have far-reaching issues. What is the cause and the import of the sharp division between theory and practice? Why should the latter be disesteemed along with matter and the body? What has been the effect upon the various modes in which action is manifested: industry, politics, the fine arts, and upon morals conceived of as overt activity having consequences, instead of as mere inner personal attitude? How has the separation of intellect from action affected the theory of knowledge? What has been in particular the effect upon the conception and course of philosophy? What forces are at work to break down the division? What would the effect be if the divorce were annulled, and knowing and doing were brought into intrinsic connection with one another? What revisions of the traditional theory of mind, thought and knowing would be required, and what change in the idea of the office of philosophy would be demanded? What modifications would ensue in the disciplines which are concerned with the various phases of human activity?

These questions form the theme of this book, and indicate the nature of the problems to be discussed. In this opening chapter we shall consider especially some historic grounds for the elevation of knowledge above making and doing. This phase of the discussion will disclose that exaltation of pure intellect and its activity above practical affairs is fundamentally connected with the quest for a certainty which shall be absolute and unshakeable. The distinctive characteristic of practical activity, one which is so inherent that it cannot be eliminated, is the uncertainty which attends it. Of it we are compelled to say: Act, but act at your peril. Judgment and belief regarding actions to be performed can never attain more than a precarious probability. Through thought, however, it has seemed that men might escape from the perils of uncertainty.

Practical activity deals with individualized and unique situations which are never exactly duplicable and about which, accordingly, no complete assurance is possible. All activity, moreover, involves change. The intellect, however, according to the traditional doctrine, may grasp universal Being, and Being which is universal is fixed and immutable. Wherever there is practical activity we human beings are involved as partakers in the issue. All the fear, disesteem and lack of confidence which gather about the thought of ourselves, cluster also about the thought of the actions in which we are partners. Man's distrust of himself has caused him to desire to get beyond and above himself; in pure knowledge he has thought he could attain this self-transcendence.

There is no need to expatiate upon the risk which attends overt action. The burden of proverbs and wise saws is that the best laid plans of men as of mice gang agley. Fortune rather than our own intent and act determines eventual success and failure. The pathos of unfulfilled expectation, the tragedy of defeated purpose and ideals, the catastrophes of accident, are the commonplaces of all comment on the human scene. We survey conditions, make the wisest choice we can; we act, and we must trust the rest to fate, fortune or providence. Moralists tell us to look to the end when we act and then inform us that the end is always uncertain. Judging, planning, choice, no matter how thoroughly conducted, and action no matter how prudently executed, never are the sole determinants of any outcome. Alien and indifferent natural forces, unforeseeable conditions enter in and have a decisive voice. The more important the issue, the greater is their say as to the ulterior event.

Hence men have longed to find a realm in which there is an activity which is not overt and which has no external consequences. "Safety first" has played a large rôle in effecting a preference for knowing over doing and making. With those to whom the process of pure thinking is congenial and who have the leisure and the aptitude to pursue their preference, the happiness attending knowing is unalloyed; it is not entangled in the risks which overt action cannot escape. Thought has been alleged to be a purely inner activity, intrinsic to mind alone; and according to traditional classic doctrine, "mind" is complete and self-sufficient in itself. Overt action may follow upon its operations but in an external way, a way not intrinsic to its completion. Since rational activity is complete within itself it needs no external manifestation. Failure and frustration are attributed to the accidents of an alien, intractable and inferior realm of existence. The outer lot of thought is cast in a world external to it, but one which in no way injures the supremacy and completeness of thought and knowledge in their intrinsic natures.

Thus the arts by which man attains such practical security as is possible of achievement are looked down upon. The security they provide is relative, ever incomplete, at the risk of untoward circumstance. The multiplication of arts may even be bemoaned as a source of new dangers. Each of them demands its own measures of protection. Each one in its operation brings with it new and unexpected consequences having perils for which we are not prepared. The quest for certainty is a quest for a peace which is assured, an object which is unqualified by risk and the shadow of fear which action casts. For it is not uncertainty *per se* which men dislike, but the fact that uncertainty involves us in peril of evils. Uncertainty that affected only the detail of consequences to be experienced provided they had a warrant of being enjoyable would have no sting. It would bring the zest of adventure and the spice of variety. Quest for complete certainty can be fulfilled in pure knowing alone. Such is the verdict of our most enduring philosophic tradition.

While the tradition has, as we shall see later, found its way into all themes and subjects, and determines the form of current problems and conclusions regarding mind and knowledge, it may be doubted whether if we were suddenly released from the burden of tradition, we should, on the basis of present experience take the disparaging view of practice and the exalted view of knowledge apart from action which tradition dictates. For man, in spite of the new perils in which the machinery of his new arts of production and transportation have involved him, has learned to play with sources of danger. He even seeks them out, weary of the routine of a too sheltered life. The enormous change taking place in the position of women is itself, for example, a commentary on a change of attitude toward the value of protection as an end in itself. We have attained, at least subconsciously, a certain feeling of confidence; a feeling that control of the main conditions of fortune is to an appreciable degree passing into our own hands. We live surrounded with the protection of thousands of arts and we have devised schemes of insurance which mitigate and distribute the evils which accrue. Barring the fears which war leaves in its train, it is perhaps a safe speculation that if contemporary western man were completely deprived of all the old beliefs about knowledge and actions he would assume, with a fair degree of confidence, that it lies within his power to achieve a reasonable degree of security in life.

This suggestion is speculative. Acceptance of it is not needed by the argument. It has its value as an indication of the earlier conditions in which a felt need for assurance was the dominant emotion. For primitive men had none of the elaborate arts of protection and use which we now enjoy and no confidence in his own powers when they were reinforced by appliances of art. He lived under conditions in which he was extraordinarily exposed to peril, and at the same time he was without the means of defense which are to-day matters of course. Most of our simplest tools and utensils did not exist; there was no accurate foresight; men faced the forces of nature in a state of nakedness which was more than physical; save under unusually benign conditions he was beset with dangers that knew no remission. In consequence, mystery attended experiences of good and evil; they could not be traced to their natural causes and they seemed to be the dispensations, the gifts and the inflictions, of powers beyond possibility of control. The precarious crises of birth, puberty, illness, death, war, famine, plague, the uncertainties of the hunt, the vicissitudes of climate and the great seasonal changes, kept imagination occupied with the uncertain. Any scene or object that was implicated in any conspicuous tragedy or triumph, in no matter how accidental a way, got a peculiar significance. It was seized upon as a harbinger of good or as an omen of evil. Accordingly, some things were cherished as means of encompassing safety just as a good artisan to-day looks after his tools; others were feared and shunned because of their potencies for harm.

As a drowning man is said to grasp at a straw, so men who lacked the instruments and skills developed in later days, snatched at whatever, by any stretch of imagination, could be regarded as a source of help in time of trouble. The attention, interest and care which now go to acquiring skill in the use of appliances and to the invention of means for better service of ends, were devoted to noting omens, making irrelevant prognostications, performing ritualistic ceremonies and manipulating objects possessed of magical power over natural events. In such an atmosphere primitive religion was born and fostered. Rather this atmosphere *was* the religious disposition.

Search for alliance with means which might promote prosperity and which would afford defense against hostile powers was constant. While this attitude was most marked in connection with the recurrent crises of life, yet the boundary line between these crucial affairs with their extraordinary risks and everyday acts was shadowy. The acts that related to commonplace things and everyday occupations were usually accompanied, for good measure of security, by ritual acts. The making of a weapon, the molding of a bowl, the weaving of a mat, the sowing of seed, the reaping of a harvest, required acts different in kind to the technical skills employed. These other acts had a special solemnity and were thought necessary in order to ensure the success of the practical operations used.

While it is difficult to avoid the use of the word supernatural, we must avoid the meaning the word has for us. As long as there was no defined area of the *natural*, that which is over and beyond the natural can have no significance. The distinction, as anthropological students have pointed out, was between ordinary and extraordinary; between the prosaic, usual run of events and the crucial incident or irruption which determined the direction which the average and expected course of events took. But the two realms were in no way sharply demarcated from each other. There was a no-man's land, a vague territory, in which they overlapped. At any moment the extraordinary might invade the commonplace and either wreck it or clothe it with some surprising glory. The use of ordinary things under critical conditions was fraught with inexplicable potentialities of good and evil.

The two dominant conceptions, cultural categories one might call them, which grew and flourished under such circumstances were those of the holy and the fortunate, with their opposites, the profane and the unlucky. As with the idea of the supernatural, meanings are not to be assigned on the basis of present usage. Everything which was charged with some extraordinary potency for benefit or injury was holy; holiness meant necessity for being approached with ceremonial scruples. The holy thing, whether place, object, person or ritual appliance, has its sinister face; "to be handled with care" is written upon it. From it there issues the command: *Noli me tangere*. Tabus, a whole set of prohibitions and injunctions, gather about it. It is capable of transmitting its mysterious potency to other things. To secure the favor of the holy is to be on the road to success, while any conspicuous success is proof of the favor of some overshadowing power—a fact which politicians of all ages have known how to utilize. Because of its surcharge of power, ambivalent in quality, the holy has to be approached not only with scruples but in an attitude of subjection. There are rites of purification, humiliation, fasting and prayer which are preconditions of securing its favor.

The holy is the bearer of blessing or fortune. But a difference early developed between the ideas of the holy and the lucky, because of the different dispositions in which each was to be approached. A lucky object is something to be used. It is to be manipulated rather than approached with awe. It calls for incantations, spells, divinations rather than for supplication and humiliation. Moreover, the lucky thing tends to be a concrete and tangible object, while the holy one is not usually definitely localized; it is the more potent in the degree in which its habitation and form are vague. The lucky object is subject to pressure, at a pinch to coercion, to scolding and punishment. It might be discarded if it failed to bring luck. There developed a certain element of mastery in its use, in distinction from the dependence and subjection which remained the proper attitude toward the holy. Thus there was a kind of rhythm of domination and submission, of imprecation and supplication, of utilization and communion.

Such statements give, of course, a one-sided picture. Men at all times have gone about many things in a matter-of-fact way and have had their daily enjoyments. Even in the ceremonies of which we have spoken there entered the ordinary love of the dramatic as well as the desire for repetition, once routine is established. Primitive man early developed some tools and some modes of skill. With them went prosaic knowledge of the properties of ordinary things. But these beliefs were surrounded by others of an imaginative and emotional type, and were more or less submerged in the latter. Moreover, prestige attached to the latter. Just because some beliefs were matter-of-fact they did not have the weight and authority that belong to those about the extraordinary and unaccountable. We find the same phenomenon repeated to-day wherever religious beliefs have marked vitality.

Prosaic beliefs about verifiable facts, beliefs backed up by evidence of the senses and by useful fruits, had little glamour and prestige compared with the vogue of objects of rite and ceremony. Hence the things forming their subject-matter were felt to be lower in rank. Familiarity breeds a sense of equality if not of contempt. We deem ourselves on a par with things we daily administer. It is a truism to say that objects regarded with awe have perforce a superior status. Herein is the source of the fundamental dualism of human attention and regard. The distinction between the two attitudes of everyday control and dependence on something superior was finally generalized intellectually. It took effect in the conception of two distinct realms. The inferior was that in which man could foresee and in which he had instruments and arts by which he might expect a reasonable degree of control. The superior was that of occurrences so uncontrollable that they testified to the presence and operation of powers beyond the scope of everyday and mundane things.

The philosophical tradition regarding knowledge and practice, the immaterial or spiritual and the material, was not original and primitive. It had for its background the state of culture which has been sketched. It developed in a social atmosphere in which the division of the ordinary and extraordinary was domesticated. Philosophy reflected upon it and gave it a rational formulation and justification. The bodies of information that corresponded to the everyday arts, the store of matter-of-fact knowledge, were things men knew because of what they did. They were products and promises of utilities. They shared in the relatively low esteem belonging to such things in comparison with the extraordinary and divine. Philosophy inherited the realm with which religion had been concerned. Its mode of knowing was different from that accompanying the empirical arts, just because it dealt with a realm of higher Being. It breathed an air purer than that in which exist the making and doing that relate to livelihood, just as the activities which took the form of rites and ceremonies were nobler and nearer the divine than those spent in toil.

The change from religion to philosophy was so great in form that their identity as to content is easily lost from view. The form ceases to be that of the story told in imaginative and emotional style, and becomes that of rational discourse observing the canons of logic. It is well known that that portion of Aristotle's system which later generations have called metaphysics he called First Philosophy. It is possible to quote from him sentences descriptive of "First Philosophy" which make it seem that the philosophic enterprise is a coldly rational one, objective and analytic. Thus he says it is the most comprehensive of all branches of knowledge because it has for its subject-matter definition of the traits which belong to all forms of Being whatsoever, however much they may differ from one another in detail.

But when these passages are placed in the context they had in Aristotle's own mind, it is clear that the comprehensiveness and universality of first philosophy are not of a strictly analytic sort. They mark a distinction with respect to grade of value and title to reverence. For he explicitly identifies his first philosophy—or metaphysics—with theology; he says it is higher than other sciences. For these deal with generation and production, while its subject-matter permits of demonstrative, that is necessary, truth; and its objects are divine and such as are meet for God to occupy himself with. Again, he says that the objects of philosophy are such as are the causes of as much of the divine as is manifest to us, and that if the divine is anywhere present, it is present in things of the sort with which philosophy deals. The supremacy of worth and dignity of these objects are also made clear in the statement that the Being with which philosophy is occupied is primary, eternal and self-sufficient, because its nature is the Good, so that the Good is among the first principles which are philosophy's subject-matter:—yet not, it must be understood, the good in the sense in which it has meaning and standing in human life but the inherently and eternally perfect, that which is complete and self-sufficient.

Aristotle tells us that from remote antiquity tradition has handed down the idea, in story form, that the heavenly bodies are gods, and that the divine encompasses the entire natural world. This core of truth, he goes on to say in effect, was embroidered with myths for the benefit of the masses, for reasons of expediency, namely, the preservation of social institutions. The negative work of philosophy was then to strip away these imaginative accretions. From the standpoint of popular belief this was its chief work, and it was a destructive one. The masses only felt that their religion was attacked. But the enduring contribution was positive. The belief that the divine encompasses the world was detached from its mythical context and made the basis of philosophy, and it became also the foundation of physical science—as is suggested by the remark that the heavenly bodies are gods. Telling the story of the universe in the form of rational discourse instead of emotionalized imagination signified the discovery of logic as a rational science. Conformity on the part of supreme reality to the requirements of logic conferred upon its constitutive objects necessary and immutable characteristics. Pure contemplation of these forms was man's highest and most divine bliss, a communion with unchangeable truth.

The geometry of Euclid doubtless gave the clew to logic as the instrument of translation of what was sound in opinion into the forms of rational discourse. Geometry seemed to reveal the possibility of a science which owed nothing to observation and sense beyond mere exemplification in figures or diagrams. It seemed to disclose a world of ideal (or non-sensible) forms which were connected with one another by eternal and necessary relations which reason alone could trace. This discovery was generalized by philosophy into the doctrine of a realm of fixed Being which, when grasped by thought, formed a complete system of immutable and necessary truth.

If one looks at the foundations of the philosophies of Plato and Aristotle as an anthropologist looks at his material, that is, as cultural subject-matter, it is clear that these philosophies were systematizations in rational form of the content of Greek religious and artistic beliefs. The systematization involved a purification. Logic provided the patterns to which ultimately real objects had to conform, while physical science was possible in the degree in which the natural world, even in its mutabilities, exhibited exemplification of ultimate immutable rational objects. Thus, along with the elimination of myths and grosser superstitions, there were set up the ideals of science and of a life of reason. Ends which could justify themselves to reason were to take the place of custom as the guide of conduct. These two ideals form a permanent contribution to western civilization.

But with all our gratitude for these enduring gifts, we cannot forget the conditions which attended them. For they brought with them the idea of a higher realm of fixed reality of which alone true science is possible and of an inferior world of changing things with which experience and practical matters are concerned. They glorified the invariant at the expense of change, it being evident that all practical activity falls within the realm of change. It bequeathed the notion, which has ruled philosophy ever since the time of the Greeks, that the office of knowledge is to uncover the antecedently real, rather than, as is the case with our practical judgments, to gain the kind of understanding which is necessary to deal with problems as they arise.

In fixing this conception of knowledge it established also, as far as philosophies of the classic type are concerned, the special task of philosophic inquiry. As a form of knowledge it is concerned with the disclosure of the Real in itself, of Being in and of itself. It is differentiated from other modes of knowing by its preoccupation with a higher and more ultimate form of Being than that with which the sciences of nature are concerned. As far as it occupied itself at all with human conduct, it was to superimpose upon acts ends said to flow from the nature of reason. It thus diverted thought from inquiring into the purposes which experience of actual conditions suggest and from concrete means of their actualization. It translated into a rational form the doctrine of escape from the vicissitudes of existence by means of measures which do not demand an active coping with conditions. For deliverance by means of rites and cults, it substituted deliverance through reason. This deliverance was an intellectual, a theoretical affair, constituted by a knowledge to be attained apart from practical activity.

The realms of knowledge and action were each divided into two regions. It is not to be inferred that Greek philosophy separated activity from knowing. It connected them. But it distinguished activity from action— that is, from making and doing. Rational and necessary knowledge was treated, as in the celebrations of it by Aristotle, as an ultimate, self-sufficient and self-enclosed form of self-originated and self-conducted activity. It was ideal and eternal, independent of change and hence of the world in which men act and live, the world we experience perceptibly and practically. "Pure activity" was sharply marked off from practical action. The latter, whether in the industrial or the fine arts, in morals or in politics, was concerned with an inferior region of Being in which change rules, and which accordingly has Being only by courtesy, for it manifests deficiency of sure footing in Being by the very fact of change. It is infected with *non*-being.

On the side of knowledge, the division carried with it a difference between knowledge, in its full sense, and belief. The former is demonstrative, necessary—that is, sure. Belief on the contrary is only opinion; in its uncertainty and mere probability, it relates to the world of change as knowledge corresponds to the realm of true reality. This fact brings the discussion around once more to our special theme as far as it affects the conception of the office and nature of philosophy. That man has two modes, two dimensions, of belief, cannot be doubted. He has beliefs about actual existences and the course of events, and he has beliefs about ends to be striven for, policies to be adopted, goods to be attained and evils to be averted. The most urgent of all practical problems concerns the connection the subject-matter of these two kinds of beliefs sustain to each other. How shall our most authentic and dependable cognitive beliefs be used to regulate our practical beliefs? How shall the latter serve to organize and integrate our intellectual beliefs?

There is a genuine possibility that the true problem of philosophy is connected with precisely this type of question. Man has beliefs which scientific inquiry vouchsafes, beliefs about the actual structure and processes of things; and he also has beliefs about the values which should regulate his conduct. The question of how these two ways of believing may most effectively and fruitfully interact with one another is the most general and significant of all the problems which life presents to us. Some reasoned discipline, one obviously other than any science, should deal with this issue. Thus there is supplied one way of conceiving of the function of philosophy. But from this mode of defining philosophy we are estopped by the chief philosophical tradition. For according to it the realms of knowledge and of practical action have no inherent connection with each other. Here then is the focus to which the various elements in our discussion converge. We may then profitably recapitulate. The realm of the practical is the region of change, and change is always contingent; it has in it an element of chance that cannot be eliminated. If a thing changes, its alteration is convincing evidence of its lack of true or complete Being. What *is*, in the full and pregnant sense of the world, is always, eternally. It is self-contradictory for that which *is* to alter. If it had no defect or imperfection in it how could it change? That which becomes merely *comes* to be, never truly is. It is infected with non-being; with privation of Being in the perfect sense. The world of generation is the world of decay and destruction. Wherever one thing comes into being something else passes out of being.

Thus the depreciation of practice was given a philosophic, an ontological, justification. Practical action, as distinct from self-revolving rational self-activity, belongs in the realm of generation and decay, a realm inferior in value as in Being. In form, the quest for absolute certainty has reached its goal. Because ultimate Being or reality is fixed, permanent, admitting of no change or variation, it may be grasped by rational intuition and set forth in rational, that is, universal and necessary, demonstration. I do not doubt that there was a feeling before the rise of philosophy that the unalterably fixed and the absolutely certain are one, or that change is the source from which comes all our uncertainties and woes. But in philosophy this inchoate feeling was definitely formulated. It was asserted on grounds held to be as demonstrably necessary as are the conclusions of geometry and logic. Thus the predisposition of philosophy toward the universal, invariant and eternal was fixed. It remains the common possession of the entire classic philosophic tradition.

All parts of the scheme hang together. True Being or Reality is complete; in being complete, it is perfect, divine, immutable, the "unmoved mover." Then there are things that change, that come and go, that are generated and perish, because of lack of the stability which participation in ultimate Being alone confers. These changes, however, have form and character and are knowable in the degree in which they tend toward an end which is the fulfillment and completion of the changes in question. Their instability is not absolute but is marked by aspiration toward a goal.

The perfect and complete is rational thought, the ultimate "end" or terminus of all natural movement. That which changes, which becomes and passes away, *is* material; change *defines* the physical. At most and best, it is a potentiality of reaching a stable and fixed end. To these two realms belong two sorts of knowledge. One of them is alone knowledge in the full sense, *science*. This has a rational, necessary and unchanging form. It is *certain*. The other, dealing with change, is belief or opinion; empirical and particular; it is contingent, a matter of probability, not of certainty. The most it can assert is that things are so and so "upon the whole," usually. Corresponding to the division in Being and in knowledge is that in activities. Pure activity is rational; it is theoretical, in the sense in which theory is apart from practical action. Then there is action in doing and making, occupied with the needs and defects of the lower realm of change in which, in his physical nature, man is implicated.

Although this Greek formulation was made long ago and much of it is now strange in its specific terms, certain features of it are as relevant to present thought as they were significant in their original formulation. For in spite of the great, the enormous changes in the subject-matter and method of the sciences and the tremendous expansion of practical activities by means of arts and technologies, the main tradition of western culture has retained intact this framework of ideas. Perfect certainty is what man wants. It cannot be found by practical doing or making; these take effect in an uncertain future, and involve peril, the risk of misadventure, frustration and failure. Knowledge, on the other hand, is thought to be concerned with a region of being which is fixed in itself. Being eternal and unalterable, human knowing is not to make any difference in it. It can be approached through the medium of the apprehensions and demonstrations of thought, or by some other organ of mind, which does nothing to the real, except just to know it.

There is involved in these doctrines a whole system of philosophical conclusions. The first and foremost is that there is complete correspondence between knowledge in its true meaning and what is real. What is known, what is true for cognition, is what is real in being. The objects of knowledge form the standards of measures of the reality of all other objects of experience. Are the objects of the affections, of desire, effort, choice, that is to say everything to which we attach value, real? Yes, if they can be warranted by knowledge; if we can *know objects* having these value properties, we are justified in thinking them real. But as objects of desire and purpose they have no sure place in Being until they are approached and validated through knowledge. The idea is so familiar that we overlook the unexpressed premise upon which it rests, namely that only the completely fixed and unchanging can be real. The quest for certitude has determined our basic metaphysics.

Secondly, the theory of knowledge has its basic premises fixed by the same doctrine. For knowledge to be certain must relate to that which has antecedent existence or essential being. There are certain things which are alone inherently the proper objects of knowledge and science. Things in the production of which we participate we cannot know in the true sense of the word, for such things succeed instead of preceding our action. What concerns action forms the realm of mere guesswork and probability, as distinct from the warrant of rational assurance which is the ideal of true knowledge. We are so accustomed to the separation of knowledge from doing and making that we fail to recognize how it controls our conceptions of mind, of consciousness and of reflective inquiry. For as relates to genuine knowledge, these must all be defined, on the basis of the premise, so as not to admit of the presence of any overt action that modifies conditions having prior and independent existence.

Special theories of knowledge differ enormously from one another. Their quarrels with one another fill the air. The din thus created makes us deaf to the way in which they say one thing in common. The controversies are familiar. Some theories ascribe the ultimate test of knowledge to impressions passively received, forced upon us whether we will or no. Others ascribe the guarantee of knowledge to synthetic activity of the intellect. Idealistic theories hold that mind and the object known are ultimately one; realistic doctrines reduce knowledge to awareness of what exists independently, and so on. But they all make one common assumption. They all hold that the operation of inquiry excludes any element of practical activity that enters into the construction of the object known. Strangely enough this is as true of idealism as of realism, of theories of synthetic activity as of those of passive receptivity. For according to them "mind" constructs the known object not in any observable way, or by means of practical overt acts having a temporal quality, but by some occult internal operation.

The common essence of all these theories, in short, is that what is known is antecedent to the mental act of observation and inquiry, and is totally unaffected by these acts; otherwise it would not be fixed and unchangeable. This negative condition, that the processes of search, investigation, reflection, involved in knowledge relate to something having prior being, fixes once for all the main characters attributed to mind, and to the organs of knowing. They *must* be outside what is known, so as not to interact in any way with the object to be known. If the word "interaction" be used, it cannot denote that overt production of change it signifies in its ordinary and practical use.

The theory of knowing is modeled after what was supposed to take place in the act of vision. The object refracts light to the eye and is seen; it makes a difference to the eye and to the person having an optical apparatus, but none to the thing seen. The real object is the object so fixed in its regal aloofness that it is a king to any beholding mind that may gaze upon it. A spectator theory of knowledge is the inevitable outcome. There have been theories which hold that mental activity intervenes, but they have retained the old premise. They have therefore concluded that it is impossible to know reality. Since mind intervenes, we know, according to them, only some modified semblance of the real object, some "appearance." It would be hard to find a more thoroughgoing confirmation than this conclusion provides of the complete hold possessed by the belief that the object of knowledge is a reality fixed and complete in itself, in isolation from an act of inquiry which has in it any element of production of change.

All of these notions about certainty and the fixed, about the nature of the real world, about the nature of the mind and its organs of knowing, are completely bound up with one another, and their consequences ramify into practically all important ideas entertained upon any philosophic question. They all flow—such is my basic thesis—from the separation (set up in the interest of the quest for absolute certainty) between theory and practice, knowledge and action. Consequently the lat-

ter problem cannot be attacked in isolation, by itself. It is too
thoroughly entangled with fundamental beliefs and ideas in all sorts of
fields.

In later chapters the theme will, therefore, be approached in relation
to each of the above-mentioned points. We shall first take up the effect
of the traditional separation upon the conception of the nature of
philosophy, especially in connection with the question of the secure
place of values in existence. We shall then pass on to an account of the
way in which modern philosophies have been dominated by the problem
of reconciling the conclusions of natural science with the objective
validity of the values by which men live and regulate their conduct:—a
problem which would have no existence were it not for the prior uncritical acceptance of the traditional notion that knowledge has a
monopolistic claim to access to reality. The discussion will then take up
various phases of the development of actual knowing as exemplified in
scientific procedure, so as to show, by an analysis of experimental inquiry in its various phases, how completely the traditional assumptions,
mentioned above, have been abandoned in concrete scientific procedure. For science in becoming experimental has itself become a mode
of directed practical doing. There will then follow a brief statement of
the effect of the destruction of the barriers which have divided theory
and practice upon reconstruction of the basic ideas about mind and
thought, and upon the solution of a number of long-standing problems
as to the theory of knowledge. The consequences of substituting search
for security by practical means for quest of absolute certainty by
cognitive means will then be considered in its bearing upon the problem
of our judgments regarding the values which control conduct, especially
its social phases.

22. Philosophy's Search for the Immutable*

In this selection, the second chapter of *The Quest for Certainty*, Dewey is more specific about the contribution of
philosophy to the age-old depreciation of the "practical" and
the "useful" in the history of Western culture. He contends
that "the whole classic tradition down to our day has continued

* From John Dewey, *The Quest for Certainty* (New York, Capricorn Books,
1960) (1929), pp. 26-48. Reprinted by permission of G. P. Putnam's Sons.

to hold a slighting view of experience as such, and to hold up as the proper goal and ideal of fine knowledge realities which even if they are located in empirical things cannot be known by experimental methods.'' This denigration of experience has led to two unfortunate results: first, an overassessment of the power of philosophical reason to divine the meaning of reality, and second, an underassessment, if not an ignorance, of the cognitive implications of day-to-day experiencing in human life. Dewey believes that the separation of reflection from concrete experience generates a cultural crisis in which the activities of men lack reflective direction and philosophy becomes irrelevant.

In the previous chapter, we noted incidentally the distinction made in the classic tradition between knowledge and belief, or, as Locke put it, between knowledge and judgment. According to this distinction the certain and knowledge are co-extensive. Disputes exist, but they are whether sensation or reason affords the basis of certainty; or whether existence or essence is its object. In contrast with this identification, the very word ''belief'' is eloquent on the topic of certainty. We *believe* in the absence of knowledge or complete assurance. Hence the quest for certainty has always been an effort to transcend belief. Now since, as we have already noted, all matters of practical action involve an element of uncertainty, we can ascend from belief to knowledge only by isolating the latter from practical doing and making.

In this chapter we are especially concerned with the effect of the ideal of certainty as something superior to belief upon the conception of the nature and function of philosophy. Greek thinkers saw clearly—and logically—that experience cannot furnish us, as respects cognition of existence, with anything more than contingent probability. Experience cannot deliver to us necessary truths; truths completely demonstrated by reason. Its conclusions are particular, not universal. Not being ''exact'' they come short of ''science.'' Thus there arose the distinction between rational truths or, in modern terminology, truths relating to the relation of ideas, and ''truths'' about matters of existence, empirically ascertained. Thus not merely the arts of practice, industrial and social, were stamped matters of belief rather than of knowledge, but also all those sciences which are matters of inductive inference from observation.

One might indulge in the reflection that they are none the worse for all that, especially since the natural sciences have developed a technique for achieving a high degree of probability and for measuring, within assignable limits, the amount of probability which attaches in particular cases to conclusions. But historically the matter is not so simple as to permit of this retort. For empirical or observational sciences were placed in invidious contrast to rational sciences which dealt with eternal and universal objects and which therefore were possessed of necessary truth. Consequently all observational sciences as far as their material could not be subsumed under forms and principles supplied by rational science shared in the depreciatory view held about practical affairs. They are relatively low, secular and profane compared with the perfect realities of rational science.

And here is a justification for going back to something as remote in time as Greek philosophy. The whole classic tradition down to our day has continued to hold a slighting view of experience as such, and to hold up as the proper goal and ideal of true knowledge realities which even if they are located in empirical things cannot be known by experimental methods. The logical consequence for philosophy itself is evident. Upon the side of method, it has been compelled to claim for itself the possession of a method issuing from reason itself, and having the warrant of reason, independently of experience. As long as the view obtained that nature itself is truly known by the same rational method, the consequences—at least those which were evident—were not serious. There was no break between philosophy and genuine science—or what was conceived to be such. In fact, there was not even a distinction; there were simply various branches of philosophy, metaphysical, logical, natural, moral, etc., in a descending scale of demonstrative certainty. Since, according to the theory, the subject-matter of the lower sciences was inherently of a different character from that of true knowledge, there was no ground for rational dissatisfaction with the lower degree of knowledge called belief. Inferior knowledge or belief corresponded to the inferior state of subject-matter.

The scientific revolution of the seventeenth century effected a great modification. Science itself through the aid of mathematics carried the scheme of demonstrative knowledge over to natural objects. The "laws" of the natural world had that fixed character which in the older scheme had belonged only to rational and ideal forms. A mathematical science of nature couched in mechanistic terms claimed to be the only sound natural philosophy. Hence the older philosophies lost alliance with natural knowledge and the support that had been given to philosophy by them. Philosophy in maintaining its claim to be a superior form of knowledge was compelled to take an invidious and so to say malicious attitude toward the conclusions of natural science. The framework of the old tradition had in the meantime become embedded in Christian theology, and through religious teaching was made a part of the inherited culture of those innocent of any technical philosophy. Consequently, the rivalry between philosophy and the new science, with respect to the claim to know reality, was converted in effect into a rivalry between the spiritual values guaranteed by the older philosophic tradition and the conclusions of natural knowledge. The more science advanced the more it seemed to encroach upon the special province of the territory over which philosophy had claimed jurisdiction. Thus philosophy in its classic form became a species of apologetic justification for belief in an ultimate reality in which the values which should regulate life and control conduct are securely enstated.

There are undoubted disadvantages in the historic manner of approach to the problem which has been followed. It may readily be thought either that the Greek formulation which has been emphasized has no especial pertinency with respect to modern thought and especially to contemporary philosophy; or that no philosophical statement is of any great importance for the mass of non-philosophic persons. Those interested in philosophy may object that the criticisms passed are directed if not at a man of straw at least to positions that have long since lost their actuality. Those not friendly to any form of philosophy may inquire what import they have for any except professed philosophers.

The first type of objection will be dealt with somewhat *in extenso* in the succeeding chapter, in which I shall try to show how modern philosophies, in spite of their great diversity, have been concerned with problems of adjustment of the conclusions of modern science to the chief religious and moral tradition of the western world; together with the way in which these problems are connected with retention of the conception of the relation of knowledge to reality formulated in Greek thought. At the point in the discussion now reached, it suffices to point out that, in spite of great changes in detail, the notion of a separation between knowledge and action, theory and practice, has been perpetuated, and that the beliefs connected with action are taken to be uncertain and inferior to value compared with those inherently connected with objects of knowledge, so that the former are securely established only as they derived from the latter. Not the specific content of Greek thought is pertinent to present problems, but its insistence that security is measured by certainty of knowledge, while the latter is measured by adhesion to fixed and immutable objects, which therefore are independent of what men do in practical activity.

The other objection is of a different sort. It comes from those who feel that not merely Greek philosophy but philosophy in any form is remote from all significant human concern. It is willing to admit or rather assert that it is presumptuous for philosophy to lay claim to knowledge of a higher order than that given by natural science, but it also holds that this is no great matter in any case except for professional philosophers.

There would be force in this latter objection were it not that those who make it hold for the most part the same philosophy of certainty and its proper object that is held by philosophers, save in an inchoate form. They are not interested in the notion that philosophic thought is a special means of attaining this object and the certainty it affords, but they are far from holding, either explicitly or implicitly, that the arts of intelligently directed action are the means by which security of values are to be attained. With respect to certain ends and goods they accept this idea. But in thinking of these ends and values as material, as related to health, wealth, control of conditions for the sake of an inferior order of consequences, they retain the same division between a higher reality and a lower that is formulated in classic philosophy. They may be innocent of the vocabulary that speaks of reason, necessary truth, the universal, things in themselves and appearances. But they incline to believe that there is some other road than that of action, directed by knowledge, to achieve ultimate security of higher ideals and purposes. They think of practical action as necessary for practical utilities, but they mark off practical utilities from spiritual and ideal values. Philosophy did not originate the underlying division. It only gave intellectual formulation and justification to ideas that were operative in men's minds generally. And the elements of these ideas are as active in present culture as they ever were in the past. Indeed, through the diffusion of religious doctrines, the idea that ultimate values are a matter of special revelation and are to be embodied in life by special means radically different from the arts of action that deal with lower and lesser ends has been accentuated in the popular mind.

Here is the point which is of general human import instead of concern merely to professional philosophers. What about the security of values, of the things which are admirable, honorable, to be approved of and striven for? It is probably in consequence of the derogatory view held of practice that the question of the secure place of values in human experience is so seldom raised in connection with the problem of the relation of knowledge and practice. But upon any view concerning the status of action, the scope of the latter cannot be restricted to self-seeking acts, nor to those of a prudential aspect, nor in general to things of expediency and what are often termed "utilitarian" affairs. The maintenance and diffusion of intellectual values, of moral excellencies, the esthetically admirable, as well as the maintenance of order and decorum in human relations are dependent upon what men do.

Whether because of the emphasis of traditional religion upon salvation of the personal soul or for some other reason, there is a tendency to restrict the ultimate scope of morals to the reflex effect of conduct on one's self. Even utilitarianism, with all its seeming independence of traditional theology and its emphasis upon the general good as the criterion for judging conduct, insisted in its hedonistic psychology upon private pleasure as the motive for action. The idea that the stable and expanding institution of all things that make life worth while throughout all human relationships is the real object of *all* intelligent conduct is depressed from view by the current conception of morals as a special kind of action chiefly concerned with either the virtues or the enjoyments of individuals in their personal capacities. In changed form, we still retain the notion of a division of activity into two kinds having very different worths. The result is the depreciated meaning that has come to be attached to the very meaning of the "practical" and the useful. Instead of being extended to cover all forms of action by means of which all the values of life are extended and rendered more secure, including the diffusion of the fine arts and the cultivation of taste, the processes of education and all activities which are concerned with rendering human relationships more significant and worthy, the meaning of "practical" is limited to matters of ease, comfort, riches, bodily security and police order, possibly health, etc., things which in their isolation from other goods can only lay claim to restricted and narrow value. In consequence, these subjects are handed over to technical sciences and arts; they are no concern of "higher" interests which feel that no matter what happens to inferior goods in the vicissitudes of natural existence, the highest values are immutable characters of the ultimately real.

Our depreciatory attitude toward "practice" would be modified if we habitually thought of it in its most liberal sense, and if we surrendered our customary dualism between two separate kinds of value, one intrinsically higher and one inherently lower. We should regard practice as the only means (other than accident) by which whatever is judged to be honorable, admirable, approvable can be kept in concrete experienceable existence. In this connection the entire import of "morals" would be transformed. How much of the tendency to ignore permanent objective consequences in differences made in natural and social relations;

and how much of the emphasis upon personal and internal motives and dispositions irrespective of what they objectively produce and sustain are products of the habitual depreciation of the worth of action in comparision with forms of mental processes, of thought and sentiment, which make no objective difference in things themselves?

It would be possible to argue (and, I think, with much justice) that failure to make action central in the search for such security as is humanly possible is a survival of the impotency of men in those stages of civilization when he had few means of regulating and utilizing the conditions upon which the occurrence of consequences depend. As long as man was unable by means of the arts of practice to direct the course of events, it was natural for him to seek an emotional substitute; in the absence of actual certainty in the midst of a precarious and hazardous world, men cultivated all sorts of things that would give them the *feeling* of certainty. And it is possible that, when not carried to an illusory point, the cultivation of the feeling gave man courage and confidence and enabled him to carry the burdens of life more successfully. But one could hardly seriously contend that this fact, if it be such, is one upon which to found a reasoned philosophy.

It is to the conception of philosophy that we come back. No mode of action can, as we have insisted, give anything approaching absolute certitude; it provides insurance but no assurance. Doing is always subject to peril, to the danger of frustration. When men began to reflect philosophically it seemed to them altogether too risky to leave the place of values at the mercy of acts the results of which are never sure. This precariousness might hold as far as empirical existence, existence in the sensible and phenomenal world, is concerned; but this very uncertainty seemed to render it the more needful that ideal goods should be shown to have, by means of knowledge of the most assured type, an indefeasible and inexpugnable position in the realm of the ultimately real. So at least we may imagine men to have reasoned. And to-day many persons find a peculiar consolation in the face of the unstable and dubious presence of values in actual experience by projecting a perfect form of good into a realm of essence, if not into a heaven beyond the earthly skies, wherein their authority, if not their existence, is wholly unshakeable.

Instead of asking how far this process is of that compensatory kind with which recent psychology has made us familiar, we are inquiring into the effect upon philosophy. It will not be denied, I suppose, that the chief aim of those philosophies which I have called classical, has been to show that the realities which are the objects of the highest and most necessary knowledge are also endowed with the values which correspond to our best aspirations, admirations and approvals. That, one may say, is the very heart of all traditional philosophic idealisms. There is a pathos, having its own nobility, in philosophies which think it their proper office to give an intellectual or cognitive certification to the ontological reality of the highest values. It is difficult for men to see desire and choice set earnestly upon the good and yet being frustrated, without their imagining a realm in which the good has come completely to its own, and is identified with a Reality in which resides all ultimate power. The failure and frustration of actual life is then attributed to the fact that this world is finite and phenomenal, sensible rather than real, or to the weakness of our finite apprehension, which cannot see that the discrepancy between existence and value is merely seeming, and that a fuller vision would behold partial evil an element in complete good. Thus the office of philosophy is to project by dialectic, resting supposedly upon self-evident premises, a realm in which the object of completest cognitive certitude is also one with the object of the heart's best aspiration. The fusion of the good and the true with unity and plenitude of Being thus becomes the goal of classic philosophy.

The situation would strike us as a curious one were it not so familiar. Practical activity is dismissed to a world of low grade reality. Desire is found only where something is lacking and hence its existence is a sign of imperfection of Being. Hence one must go to passionless reason to find perfect reality and complete certitude. But nevertheless the chief philosophic interest is to prove that the essential properties of the reality that is the object of pure knowledge are precisely those characteristics which have meaning in connection with affection, desire and choice. After degrading practical affairs in order to exalt knowledge, the chief task of knowledge turns out to be to demonstrate the absolutely assured and permanent reality of the values with which practical activity is concerned! Can we fail to see the irony in a situation wherein desire and emotion are relegated to a position inferior in every way to that of knowledge, while at the same time the chief problem of that which is termed the highest and most perfect knowledge is taken to be the existence of evil—that is, of desires errant and frustrated?

The contradiction involved, however, is much more than a purely intellectual one—which if purely theoretical would be innocuously lacking in practical consequences. The thing which concerns all of us as human beings is precisely the greatest attainable security of values in concrete existence. The thought that the values which are unstable and wavering in the world in which we live are eternally secure in a higher realm (which reason demonstrates but which we cannot experience), that all the goods which are defeated here are triumphant there, may give consolation to the depressed. But it does not change the existential situation in the least. The separation that has been instituted between theory and practice, with its consequent substitution of cognitive quest for absolute assurance for practical endeavor to make the existence of good more secure in experience, has had the effect of distracting attention and diverting energy from a task whose performance would yield definite results.

The chief consideration in achieving concrete security of values lies in the perfecting of *methods* of action. More activity, blind striving, gets nothing forward. Regulation of conditions upon which results depend is possible only by doing, yet only by doing which has intelligent direction, which takes cognizance of conditions, observes relations of sequence, and which plans and executes in the light of this knowledge. The notion that thought, apart from action, can warrant complete certitude as to the status of supreme good, makes no contribution to the central problem of development of intelligent methods of regulation. It rather depresses and deadens effort in that direction. That is the chief indictment to be brought against the classic philosophic tradition. Its import raises the question of the relation which action sustains to knowledge in fact, and whether the quest for certainty by other means than those of intelligent action does not mark a baneful diversion of thought from its proper office. It raises the question whether mankind has not now achieved a sufficient degree of control of methods of knowing and of the arts of practical action so that a radical change in our conceptions of knowledge and practice is rendered both possible and necessary.

That knowing, as judged from the actual procedures of scientific inquiry, has completely abandoned in fact that traditional separation of knowing and doing, that the experimental procedure is one that installs doing as the heart of knowing, is a theme that will occupy our attention in later chapters. What would happen to philosophy if it wholeheartedly made a similar surrender? What would be its office if it ceased to deal with the problem of reality and knowledge at large? In effect, its function would be to facilitate the fruitful interaction of our cognitive beliefs, our beliefs resting upon the most dependable methods of inquiry, with our practical beliefs about the values, the ends and purposes, that should control human action in the things of large and liberal human import.

Such a view renounces the traditional notion that action is inherently inferior to knowledge and preference for the fixed over the changing; it involves the conviction that security attained by active control is to be more prized than certainty in theory. But it does not imply that action is higher and better than knowledge, and practice inherently superior to thought. Constant and effective interaction of knowledge and practice is something quite different from an exaltation of activity for its own sake. Action, when directed by knowledge, is method and means, not an end. The aim and end is the securer, freer and more widely shared embodiment of values in experience by means of that active control of objects which knowledge alone makes possible.[1]

From this point of view, the problem of philosophy concerns the *interaction* of our judgments about ends to be sought with knowledge of the means for achieving them. Just as in science the question of the advance of knowledge is the question of *what to do*, what experiments to perform, what apparatus to invent and use, what calculations to engage in, what branches of mathematics to employ or to perfect, so *the* problem of practice is what do we need to *know*, how shall we obtain that knowledge and how shall we apply it?

It is an easy and altogether too common a habit to confuse a personal division of labor with an isolation of function and meaning. Human beings as individuals tend to devote themselves either to the practice of knowing or to the practice of a professional, business, social or esthetic art. Each takes the other half of the circle for granted. Theorists and practitioners, however, often indulge in unseemly wrangles as to the importance of their respective tasks. Then the personal difference of callings is hypostatized and made into an intrinsic difference between knowledge and practice.

If one looks at the history of knowledge, it is plain that at the beginning men tried to know because they had to do so in order to live. In the absence of that organic guidance given by their structure to other animals, man had to find out what he was about, and he could find out only by studying the environment which constituted the means, obstacles and results of his behavior. The desire for intellectual or cognitive understanding had no meaning except as a means of obtaining greater security as to the issues of action. Moreover, even when after the coming of leisure some men were enabled to adopt knowing as their

---

[1] In reaction against the age-long depreciation of practice in behalf of contemplative knowledge, there is a temptation simply to turn things upside down. But the essence of pragmatic instrumentalism is to conceive of *both* knowledge and practice as means of making goods—excellencies of all kinds—secure in experienced existence.

special calling or profession, *merely* theoretical uncertainty continues to have no meaning.

This statement will arouse protest. But the reaction against the statement will turn out when examined to be due to the fact that it is so difficult to find a case of purely intellectual uncertainty, that is one upon which nothing hangs. Perhaps as near to it as we can come is in the familiar story of the Oriental potentate who declined to attend a horse race on the ground that it was already well known to him that one horse could run faster than another. His uncertainty as to which of several horses could outspeed the others may be said to have been purely intellectual. But also in the story nothing depended from it; no curiosity was aroused; no effort was put forth to satisfy the uncertainty. In other words, he did not care; it made no difference. And it is a strict truism that no one would care about *any* exclusively theoretical uncertainty or certainty. For by definition in being *exclusively* theoretical it is one which makes no difference anywhere.

Revulsion against this proposition is a tribute to the fact that actually the intellectual and the practical are so closely bound together. Hence when we imagine we are thinking of an exclusively theoretical doubt, we smuggle in unconsciously some consequence which hangs upon it. We think of uncertainty arising in the course of an inquiry; in this case, uncertainty until it is resolved blocks the progress of the inquiry—a distinctly practical affair, since it involves conclusions and the means of producing them. If we had no desires and no purposes, then, as sheer truism, one state of things would be as good as any other. Those who have set such store by the demonstration that Absolute Being already contains in eternal safety within itself all values, have had as their interest the fact that while the demonstration would make no difference in the concrete existence of these values—unless perhaps to weaken effort to generate and sustain them—it would make a difference in their own personal attitudes—in a feeling of comfort or of release from responsibility, the consciousness of a "moral holiday" in which some philosophers have found the distinction between morals and religion.

Such considerations point to the conclusion that the ultimate ground of the quest for cognitive certainty is the need for security in the results of action. Men readily persuade themselves that they are devoted to intellectual certainty for its own sake. Actually they want it because of its bearing on safeguarding what they desire and esteem. The need for protection and prosperity in action created the need for warranting the validity of intellectual beliefs.

After a distinctively intellectual class had arisen, a class having leisure and in a large degree protected against the more serious perils which afflict the mass of humanity, its members proceeded to glorify their own office. Since no amount of pains and care in action can ensure complete certainty, certainty in knowledge was worshipped as a substitute. In minor matters, those that are relatively technical, professional, "utilitarian," men continued to resort to improving their methods of operation in order to be surer of results. But in affairs of momentous value the requisite knowledge is hard to come by and the bettering of methods is a slow process to be realized only by the coöperative endeavor of many persons. The arts to be formed and developed are social arts; an individual by himself can do little to regulate the conditions which will render important values more secure, though with shrewdness and special knowledge he can do much to further his own peculiar aims—given a fair share of luck. So because of impatience and because, as Aristotle was given to pointing out, an individual is self-sufficient in that kind of thinking which involves no action, the ideal of a cognitive certainty and truth having no connection with practice, and prized because of its lack of connection, developed. The doctrine worked out practically so as to strengthen dependence upon authority and dogma in the things of highest value, while increase of specialized knowledge was relied upon in everyday, especially economic, affairs. Just as belief that a magical ceremony will regulate the growth of seeds to full harvest stifles the tendency to investigate natural causes and their workings, so acceptance of dogmatic rules as bases of conduct in education, morals and social matters, lessens the impetus to find out about the conditions which are involved in forming intelligent plans.

It is more or less of a commonplace to speak of the crisis which has been caused by the progress of the natural sciences in the last few centuries. The crisis is due, it is asserted, to the incompatibility between the conclusions of natural science about the world in which we live and the realm of higher values, of ideal and spiritual qualities, which get no support from natural science. The new science, it is said, has stripped the world of the qualities which made it beautiful and congenial to men; has deprived nature of all aspiration towards ends, all preference for accomplishing the good, and presented nature to us as a scene of indifferent physical particles acting according to mathematical and mechanical laws.

This effect of modern science has, it is notorious, set the main problems for modern philosophy. How is science to be accepted and yet the realm of values to be conserved? This question forms the philosophic version of the popular conflict of science and religion. Instead of being troubled about the inconsistency of astronomy with the older religious beliefs about heaven and the ascension of Christ, or the differences between the geological record and the account of creation in Genesis, philosophers have been troubled by the gap in kind which exists between the fundamental principles of the natural world and the reality of the values according to which mankind is to regulate its life.

Philosophers, therefore, set to work to mediate, to find some harmony behind the apparent discord. Everybody knows that the trend of modern philosophy has been to arrive at theories regarding the nature of the universe by means of theories regarding the nature of knowledge—a procedure which reverses the apparently more judicious method of the ancients in basing their conclusions about knowledge on the nature of the universe in which knowledge occurs. The "crisis" of which we have just been speaking accounts for the reversal.

Since science has made the trouble, the cure ought to be found in an examination of the nature of knowledge, of the conditions which make science possible. If the conditions of the possibility of knowledge can be shown to be of an ideal and rational character, then, so it has been thought, the loss of an idealistic cosmology in physics can be readily borne. The physical world can be surrendered to matter and mechanism, since we are assured that matter and mechanism have their foundation in immaterial mind. Such has been the characteristic course of modern spiritualistic philosophies since the time of Kant; indeed, since that of Descartes, who first felt the poignancy of the problem involved in reconciling the conclusions of science with traditional religious and moral beliefs.

It would presumably be taken as a sign of extreme naïveté, if not of callous insensitiveness, if one were to ask why all this ardor to reconcile the findings of natural science with the validity of values? Why should any increase of knowledge seem like a threat to what we prize, admire and approve? Why should we not proceed to employ our gains in science to improve our judgments about values, and to regulate our actions so as to make values more secure and more widely shared in existence?

I am willing to run the risk of charge of naïveté for the sake of making manifest the difference upon which we have been dwelling. If men had associated their ideas about values with practical activity instead of with cognition of antecedent Being, they would *not* have been troubled by the findings of science. They would have welcomed the latter. For anything ascertained about the structure of actually existing conditions would be a definite aid in making judgments about things to be prized and striven for more adequate, and would instruct us as to the means to be employed in realizing them. But according to the religious and philosophic tradition of Europe, the valid status of all the highest values, the good, true and beautiful, was bound up with their being properties of ultimate and supreme Being, namely, God. All went well as long as what passed for natural science gave no offence to this conception. Trouble began when science ceased to disclose in the objects of knowledge the possession of any such properties. Then some roundabout method had to be devised for substantiating them.

The point of the seemingly crass question which was asked is thus to elicit the radical difference made when the problem of values is seen to be connected with the problem of intelligent action. If the validity of beliefs and judgments about values is dependent upon the consequences of action undertaken in their behalf, if the assumed association of values with knowledge capable of being demonstrated apart from activity, is abandoned, then the problem of the intrinsic relation of science to value is wholly artificial. It is replaced by a group of practical problems: How shall we employ what we know to direct the formation of our beliefs about value and how shall we direct our practical behavior so as to test these beliefs and make possible better ones? The question is seen to be just what it has always been empirically: What shall we *do* to make objects having value more secure in existence? And we approach the answer to the problem with all the advantages given us by increase of knowledge of the conditions and relations under which this doing must proceed.

But for over two thousand years the weight of the most influential and authoritatively orthodox tradition of thought has been thrown into the opposite scale. It has been devoted to the problem of a purely cognitive certification (perhaps by revelation, perhaps by intuition, perhaps by reason) of the antecedent immutable reality of truth, beauty and goodness. As against such a doctrine, the conclusions of natural science constitute the materials of a serious problem. The appeal has been made to the Court of Knowledge and the verdict has been adverse. There are two rival systems that must have their respective claims adjusted. The crisis in contemporary culture, the confusions and conflicts in it, arise from a division of authority. Scientific inquiry seems to tell one thing, and traditional beliefs about ends and ideals that have authority over conduct tell us something quite different. The problem of reconciliation arises and persists for one reason only. As long as the notions persist that knowledge is a disclosure of reality, of reality prior to and independent of knowing, and that knowing is independent of a purpose to control the quality of experienced objects, the failure of natural science to disclose significant values in its objects will come as a shock. Those seriously concerned with the validity and authority of value will have a problem on their hands. As long as the notion persists that values are authentic and valid only on condition that they are properties of Being independent of human action, as long as it is supposed that their right to regulate action is dependent upon their being independent of action, so long there will be needed schemes to prove that values are, in spite of the findings of science, genuine and known qualifications of reality in itself. For men will not easily surrender all regulative guidance in action. If they are forbidden to find standards in the course of experience they will seek them somewhere else, if not in revelation, then in the deliverance of a reason that is above experience.

This then is the fundamental issue for present philosophy. Is the doctrine justified that knowledge is valid in the degree in which it is a revelation of antecedent existences or Being? Is the doctrine justified that regulative ends and purposes have validity only when they can be shown to be properties belonging to things, whether as existences or as essences, apart from human action? It is proposed to make another start. Desires, affections, preferences, needs and interests at least exist in human experience; they are characteristics of it. Knowledge about nature also exists. What does this knowledge imply and entail with respect to the guidance of our emotional and volitional life? How shall the latter lay hold of what is known in order to make it of service?

These latter questions do not seem to many thinkers to have the dignity that is attached to the traditional problems of philosophy. They are proximate questions, not ultimate. They do not concern Being and Knowledge "in themselves" and at large, but the state of existence at specified times and places and the state of affection, plans and purposes under concrete circumstances. They are not concerned with framing a general theory of reality, knowledge and value once for all, but with finding how authentic beliefs about existence as they currently exist can operate fruitfully and efficaciously in connection with the practical problems that are urgent in actual life.

In restricted and technical fields, men now proceed unhesitatingly along these lines. In technology and the arts of engineering and medicine, men do not think of operating in any other way. Increased knowledge of nature and its conditions does not raise the problem of validity of the value of health or of communication in general, although it may well make dubious the validity of certain conceptions men in the past have entertained about the nature of health and communication and the best ways of attaining these goods in fact.

In such matters, science has placed in our hands the means by which we can better judge our wants, and has aided in forming the instruments and operations by which to satisfy them. That the same sort of thing has not happened in the moral and distinctly humane arts is evident. Here is a problem which might well trouble philosophers.

Why have not the arts which deal with the wider, more generous, more distinctly humane values enjoyed the release and expansion which have accrued to the technical arts? Can it be seriously urged that it is because natural science has disclosed to us the kind of world which it has disclosed? It is easy to see that these disclosures are hostile to some beliefs about values which have been widely accepted, which have prestige, which have become deeply impregnated with sentiment, and which authoritative institutions as well as the emotion and inertia of men are slow to surrender. But this admission, which practically enforces itself, is far from excluding the formation of new beliefs about things to be honored and prized by men in their supreme loyalties of action. The difficulty in the road is a practical one, a social one, connected with institutions and the methods and aims of education, not with science nor with value. Under such circumstances the first problem for philosophy would seem to be to clear itself of further responsibility for the doctrine that the supreme issue is whether values have antecedent Being, while its further office is to make clear the revisions and reconstructions that have to be made in traditional judgments about values. Having done this, it would be in a position to undertake the more positive task of projecting ideas about values which might be the basis of a new integration of human conduct.

We come back to the fact that the genuine issue is not whether certain values, associated with traditions and institutions, have Being already (whether that of existence or of essence), but what concrete judgments we are to form about ends and means in the regulation of practical behavior. The emphasis which has been put upon the former question, the creation of dogmas about the way in which values are already real independently of what we do, dogmas which have appealed not in vain to philosophy for support, have naturally bred, in the face of the changed character of science, confusion, irresolution and numbness of will. If the men had been educated to think about broader humane values as they have now learned to think about matters which fall within the scope of technical arts, our whole present situation would be very different. The attention which has gone to achieving a purely theoretical certainty with respect to them would have been devoted to perfecting the arts by which they are to be judged and striven for.

Indulge for a moment in an imaginative flight. Suppose that men had been systematically educated in the belief that the existence of values can cease to be accidental, narrow and precarious only by human activity directed by the best available knowledge. Suppose also men had been systematically educated to believe that the important thing is not to get themselves personally "right" in relation to the antecedent author and guarantor of these values, but to form their judgments and carry on their activity on the basis of public, objective and shared consequences. Imagine these things and then imagine what the present situation might be.

The suppositions are speculative. But they serve to indicate the significance of the one point to which this chapter is devoted. The method and conclusions of science have without doubt invaded many cherished beliefs about the things held most dear. The resulting clash constitutes a genuine cultural crisis. But it is a crisis in culture, a social crisis, historical and temporal in character. It is not a problem in the adjustment of properties of reality to one another. And yet modern philosophy has chosen for the most part to treat it as a question of how the realities assumed to be the object of science can have the mathematical and mechanistic properties assigned to them in natural science, while nevertheless the realm of ultimate reality can be characterized by qualities termed ideal and spiritual. The cultural problem is one of definite criticisms to be made and of readjustments to be accomplished. Philosophy which is willing to abandon its supposed task of knowing ultimate reality and to devote itself to a proximate human office might be of great help in such a task. It may be doubted whether it can indefinitely pursue the task of trying to show that the results of science when they are *properly* interpreted do not mean what they seem to say, or of proving, by means of an examination of possibilities and limits of knowledge, that after all they rest upon a foundation congruous with traditional beliefs about values.

Since the root of the traditional conception of philosophy is the separation that has been made between knowledge and action, between theory and practice, it is to the problem of this separation that we are to give attention. Our main attempt will be to show how the actual procedures of knowledge, interpreted after the pattern formed by experimental inquiry, cancel the isolation of knowledge from overt action. Before engaging in this attempt, we shall in the next chapter show the extent to which modern philosophy has been dominated by effort to adjust to each other two systems of belief, one relating to the objects of knowledge and the other to objects of ideal value.

23. Science and Society*

Written at the outset of the Depression, this essay finds Dewey perplexed at the inability of Western culture to apply the resources of modern technology to social problems. There are some confusions in Dewey's presentation, such as an inadequate distinction between science and machine technology and his belief that "science is strictly impersonal," a position which runs counter to his contextualist theory of knowledge.

This essay, however, is valuable for a number of reasons: first, due to its strong polemic against the smugness which results from an overblown sense of scientific progress; second, because Dewey applies to science a critique he long reserved for philosophy—namely, the condemnation of sheerly intellectual breakthroughs when not accompanied by a sense of social responsibility and by a program of social amelioration; and finally, he reminds us that "the intellectual function of trouble is to lead men to think."

The significant outward forms of the civilization of the western world are the product of the machine and its technology. Indirectly, they are the product of the scientific revolution which took place in the seventeenth century. In its effect upon men's external habits, dominant interests, the conditions under which they work and associate, whether in the family, the factory, the state, or internationally, science is by far the most potent social factor in the modern world. It operates, however, through its undesigned effects rather than as a transforming influence of men's thoughts and purposes. This contrast between outer and inner operation is the great contradiction in our lives. Habits of thought and desire remain in substance what they were before the rise of science,

* From John Dewey, *Philosophy and Civilization* (New York, Capricorn Books, 1963) (1931), pp. 318-30. Reprinted by permission of G. P. Putnam's Sons.

while the conditions under which they take effect have been radically altered by science.

When we look at the external social consequences of science, we find it impossible to apprehend the extent or gauge the rapidity of their occurrence. Alfred North Whitehead has recently called attention to the progressive shortening of the time-span of social change. That due to basic conditions seems to be of the order of half a million years; that due to lesser physical conditions, like alterations in climate, to be of the order of five thousand years. Until almost our own day the time-span of sporadic technological changes was of the order of five hundred years; according to him, no great technological changes took place between, say, 100 A.D. and 1400 A.D. With the introduction of steam-power, the fifty years from 1780 to 1830 were marked by more changes than are found in any previous thousand years. The advance of chemical techniques and in use of electricity and radio-energy in the last forty years makes even this last change seem slow and awkward.

Domestic life, political institutions, international relations and personal contacts are shifting with kaleidoscopic rapidity before our eyes. We cannot appreciate and weigh the changes; they occur too swiftly. We do not have time to take them in. No sooner do we begin to understand the meaning of one such change than another comes and displaces the former. Our minds are dulled by the sudden and repeated impacts. Externally, science through its applications is manufacturing the conditions of our institutions at such a speed that we are too bewildered to know what sort of civilization is in process of making.

Because of this confusion, we cannot even draw up a ledger account of social gains and losses due to the operation of science. But at least we know that the earlier optimism which thought that the advance of natural science was to dispel superstition, ignorance, and oppression, by placing reason on the throne, was unjustified. Some superstitions have given way, but the mechanical devices due to science have made it possible to spread new kinds of error and delusion among a larger multitude. The fact is that it is foolish to try to draw up a debit and credit account for science. To do so is to mythologize; it is to personify science and impute to it a will and an energy on its own account. In truth science is strictly impersonal; a method and a body of knowledge. It owes its operation and its consequences to the human beings who use it. It adapts itself passively to the purposes and desires which animate these human beings. It lends itself with equal impartiality to the kindly offices of medicine and hygiene and the destructive deeds of war. It elevates some through opening new horizons; it depresses others by making them slaves of machines operated for the pecuniary gain of owners.

The neutrality of science to the uses made of it renders it silly to talk about its bankruptcy, or to worship it as the usherer in of a new age. In the degree in which we realize this fact, we shall devote our attention to the human purposes and motives which control its application. Science is an instrument, a method, a body of technique. While it is an end for those inquirers who are engaged in its pursuit, in the large human sense it is a means, a tool. For what ends shall it be used? Shall it be used deliberately, systematically, for the promotion of social well-being, or shall it be employed primarily for private aggrandizement, leaving its larger social results to chance? Shall the scientific attitude be used to create new mental and moral attitudes, or shall it continue to be subordinated to service of desires, purposes and institutions which were formed before science came into existence? Can the attitudes which control the use of science be themselves so influenced by scientific technique that they will harmonize with its spirit?

The beginning of wisdom is, I repeat, the realization that science itself is an instrument which is indifferent to the external uses to which it is put. Steam and electricity remain natural forces when they operate through mechanisms; the only problem is the purposes for which men set the mechanisms to work. The essential technique of gunpowder is the same whether it be used to blast rocks from the quarry to build better human habitations, or to hurl death upon men at war with one another. The airplane binds men at a distance in closer bonds of intercourse and understanding, or it rains missiles of death upon hapless populations. We are forced to consider the relation of human ideas and ideals to the social consequences which are produced by science as an instrument.

The problem involved is the greatest which civilization has ever had to face. It is, without exaggeration, the most serious issue of contemporary life. Here is the instrumentality, the most powerful, for good and evil, the world has ever known. What are we going to do with it? Shall we leave our underlying aims unaffected by it, treating it merely as a means by which unco-operative individuals may advance their own fortunes? Shall we try to improve the hearts of men without regard to the new methods which science puts at our disposal? There are those, men in high position in church and state, who urge this course. They trust to a transforming influence of a morals and religion which have not been affected by science to change human desire and purpose, so that they will employ science and machine technology for beneficent social ends. The recent Encyclical of the Pope is a classic document in expression of a point of view which would rely wholly upon inner regeneration to protect society from the injurious uses to which science may be put. Quite apart from any ecclesiastical connection, there are many "intellectuals" who appeal to inner "spiritual" concepts, totally divorced from scientific intelligence, to effect the needed work. But there is another alternative: to take the method of science home into our own controlling attitudes and dispositions, to employ the new techniques as means of directing our thoughts and efforts to a planned control of social forces.

Science and machine technology are young from the standpoint of human history. Though vast in stature, they are infants in age. Three hundred years are but a moment in comparison with thousands of centuries man has lived on the earth. In view of the inertia of institutions and of the mental habits they breed, it is not surprising that the new technique of apparatus and calculation, which is the essence of science, has made so little impression on underlying human attitudes. The momentum of traditions and purposes that preceded its rise took possession of the new instrument and turned it to their ends. Moreover, science had to struggle for existence. It had powerful enemies in church and state. It needed friends and it welcomed alliance with the rising capitalism which it so effectively promoted. If it tended to foster secularism and to create predominantly material interests, it could still be argued that it was in essential harmony with traditional morals and religion. But there were lacking the conditions which are indispensable to the serious application of scientific method in reconstruction of fundamental beliefs and attitudes. In addition, the development of the new science was attended with so many internal difficulties that energy had to go to perfecting the instrument just as an instrument. Because of all these circumstances the fact that science was used in behalf of old interests is nothing to be wondered at.

The conditions have now changed, radically so. The claims of natural science in the physical field are undisputed. Indeed, its prestige is so great that an almost superstitious aura gathers about its name and work. Its progress is no longer dependent upon the adventurous inquiry of a few untrammeled souls. Not only are universities organized to promote scientific research and learning, but one may almost imagine the university laboratories abolished and still feel confident of the continued advance of science. The development of industry has compelled the inclusion of scientific inquiry within the processes of production and distribution. We find in the public prints as many demonstrations of the benefits of science from a business point of view as there are proofs of its harmony with religion.

It is not possible that, under such conditions, the subordination of scientific techniques to purposes and institutions that flourished before its rise can indefinitely continue. In all affairs there comes a time when a cycle of growth reaches maturity. When this stage is reached, the period of protective nursing comes to an end. The problem of securing proper use succeeds to that of securing conditions of growth. Now that science has established itself and has created a new social environment, it has (if I may for the moment personify it) to face the issue of its social responsibilities. Speaking without personification, we who have a powerful and perfected instrument in our hands, one which is determining the quality of social changes, must ask what changes we want to see achieved and what we want to see averted. We must, in short, plan its social effects with the same care with which in the past we have planned its physical operation and consequences. Till now we have employed science absent-mindedly as far as its effects upon human beings are concerned. The present situation with its extraordinary control of natural energies and its totally unplanned and haphazard social economy is a dire demonstration of the folly of continuing this course.

The social effects of the application of science have been accidental, even though they are intrinsic to the private and unorganized motives which we have permitted to control that application. It would be hard to find a better proof that such is the fact than the vogue of the theory that such unregulated use of science is in accord with "natural law," and that all effort at planned control of its social effects is an interference with nature. The use which has been made of a peculiar idea of personal liberty to justify the dominion of accident in social affairs is another convincing proof. The doctrine that the most potent instrument of widespread, enduring, and objective social changes must be left at the mercy of purely private desires for purely personal gain is a doctrine of anarchy. Our present insecurity of life is the fruit of the adoption in practice of this anarchic doctrine.

The technologies of industry have flowed from the intrinsic nature of science. For that is itself essentially a technology of apparatus, materials and numbers. But the pecuniary aims which have decided the social results of the use of these technologies have not flowed from the inherent nature of science. They have been derived from institutions and attendant mental and moral habits which were entrenched before there was any such thing as science and the machine. In consequence, science has operated as a means for extending the influence of the institution of private property and connected legal relations far beyond their former limits. It has operated as a device to carry an enormous load of stocks and bonds and to make the reward of investment in the way of profit and power one out of all proportion to that accruing from actual work and service.

Here lies the heart of our present social problem. Science has hardly been used to modify men's fundamental acts and attitudes in social matters. It has been used to extend enormously the scope and power of interests and values which anteceded its rise. Here is the contradiction in our civilization. The potentiality of science as the most powerful instrument of control which has ever existed puts to mankind its one outstanding present challenge.

There is one field in which science has been somewhat systematically employed as an agent of social control. Condorcet, writing during the French Revolution in the prison from which he went to the guillotine, hailed the invention of the calculus of probabilities as the opening of a new era. He saw in this new mathematical technique the promise of methods of insurance which should distribute evenly and widely the impact of the disasters to which humanity is subject. Insurance against death, fire, hurricanes and so on have in a measure confirmed his prediction. Nevertheless, in large and important social areas, we have only made the merest beginning of the method of insurance against the hazards of life and death. Insurance against the risks of maternity, of sickness, old age, unemployment, is still rudimentary; its idea is fought by all reactionary forces. Witness the obstacles against which social insurance with respect to accidents incurred in industrial employment had to contend. The anarchy called natural law and personal liberty still operates with success against a planned social use of the resources of scientific knowledge.

Yet insurance against perils and hazards is the place where the application of science has gone the furthest, not the least, distance in present society. The fact that motor cars kill and maim more persons yearly than all factories, shops, and farms is a fair symbol of how backward we are in that province where we have done most. Here, however, is one field in which at least the idea of planned use of scientific knowledge for social welfare has received recognition. We no longer regard plagues, famine and disease as visitations of necessary "natural law" or of a power beyond nature. By preventive means of medicine and public hygiene as well as by various remedial measures we have in idea, if not in fact, placed technique in the stead of magic and chance and uncontrollable necessity in this one area of life. And yet, as

I have said, here is where the socially planned use of science has made the most, not least, progress. Were it not for the youth of science and the historically demonstrated slowness of all basic mental and moral change, we could hardly find language to express astonishment at the situation in which we have an extensive and precise control of physical energies and conditions, and in which we leave the social consequences of their operation to chance, *laissez-faire*, privileged pecuniary status, and the inertia of tradition and old institutions.

Condorcet thought and worked in the Baconian strain. But the Baconian ideal of the systematic organization of all knowledge, the planned control of discovery and invention, for the relief and advancement of the human estate, remains almost as purely an ideal as when Francis Bacon put it forward centuries ago. And this is true in spite of the fact that the physical and mathematical technique upon which a planned control of social results depends has made in the meantime incalculable progress. The conclusion is inevitable. The outer arena of life has been transformed by science. The effectively working mind and character of man have hardly been touched.

Consider that phase of social action where science might theoretically be supposed to have taken effect most rapidly, namely, education. In dealing with the young, it would seem as if scienctific methods might at once take effect in transformation of mental attitudes, without meeting the obstacles which have to be overcome in dealing with adults. In higher education, in universities and technical schools, a great amount of research is done and much scientific knowledge is imparted. But it is a principle of modern psychology that the basic attitudes of mind are formed in the earlier years. And I venture the assertion that for the most part the formation of intellectual habits in elementary education, in the home and school, is hardly affected by scientific method. Even in our so-called progressive schools, science is usually treated as a side line, an ornamental extra, not as the chief means of developing the right mental attitudes. It is treated generally as one more body of ready-made information to be acquired by traditional methods, or else as an occasional diversion. That it is the method of all effective mental approach and attack in all subjects has not gained even a foothold. Yet if scientific method is not something esoteric but is a realization of the most effective operation of intelligence, it should be axiomatic that the development of scientific attitudes of thought, observation, and inquiry is the chief business of study and learning.

Two phases of the contradiction inhering in our civilization may be especially mentioned. We have long been committed in theory and words to the principle of democracy. But criticism of democracy, assertions that it is failing to work and even to exist are everywhere rife. In the last few months we have become accustomed to similar assertions regarding our economic and industrial system. Mr. Ivy Lee, for example, in a recent commencement address, entitled *This Hour of Bewilderment*, quoted from a representative clergyman, a railway president, and a publicist, to the effect that our capitalistic system is on trial. And yet the statements had to do with only one feature of that system: the prevalence of unemployment and attendant insecurity. It is not necessary for me to invade the territory of economics and politics. The essential fact is that if both democracy and capitalism are on trial, it is in reality our collective intelligence which is on trial. We have displayed enough intelligence in the physical field to create the new and powerful instrument of science and technology. We have not as yet had enough intelligence to use this instrument deliberately and systematically to control its social operations and consequences.

The first lesson which the use of scientific method teaches is that control is co-ordinate with knowledge and understanding. Where there is technique there is the possibility of administering forces and conditions in the region where the technique applies. Our lack of control in the sphere of human relations, national, domestic, international, requires no emphasis of notice. It is proof that we have not begun to operate scientifically in such matters. The public press is full of discussion of the five-year plan and the ten-year plan in Russia. But the fact that the plan is being tried by a country which has a dictatorship foreign to all our beliefs tends to divert attention from the fundamental consideration. The point for us is not this political setting nor its communistic context. It is that by the use of all available resources of knowledge and experts an attempt is being made at organized social planning and control. Were we to forget for the moment the special Russian political setting, we should see here an effort to use co-ordinated knowledge and technical skill to direct economic resources toward social order and stability.

To hold that such organized planning is possible only in a communistic society is to surrender the case to communism. Upon any other basis, the effort of Russia is a challenge and a warning to those who live under another political and economic regime. It is a call to use our more advanced knowledge and technology in scientific thinking about our own needs, problems, evils, and possibilities so as to achieve some degree of control of the social consequences which the application of science is, willy-nilly, bringing about. What stands in the way is a lot of outworn traditions, moth-eaten slogans and catchwords, that do substitute duty for thought, as well as our entrenched predatory self-interest. We shall only make a real beginning in intelligent thought when we cease mouthing platitudes; stop confining our idea to antitheses of individualism and socialism, capitalism and communism, and realize that the issue is between chaos and order, chance and control: the haphazard use and the planned use of scientific techniques.

Thus the statement with which we began, namely, that we are living in a world of change extraordinary in range and speed, is only half true. It holds of the outward applications of science. It does not hold of our intellectual and moral attitudes. About physical conditions and energies we think scientifically; at least, some men do, and the results of their thinking enter into the experiences of all of us. But the entrenched and stubborn institutions of the past stand in the way of our thinking scientifically about human relations and social issues. Our mental habits in these respects are dominated by institutions of family, state, church, and business that were formed long before men had an effective technique of inquiry and validation. It is this contradiction from which we suffer to-day.

Disaster follows in its wake. It is impossible to overstate the mental confusion and the practical disorder which are bound to result when external and physical effects are planned and regulated, while the attitudes of mind upon which the direction of external results depends are left to the medley of chance, tradition, and dogma. It is a common saying that our physical science has far outrun our social knowledge; that our physical skill has become exact and comprehensive while our humane arts are vague, opinionated, and narrow. The fundamental trouble, however, is not lack of sufficient information about social facts, but unwillingness to adopt the scientific attitude in what we do know. Men floundered in a morass of opinion about physical matters for thousands of years. It was when they began to use their ideas experimentally and to create a technique or direction of experimentation that physical science advanced with system and surety. No amount of mere fact-finding develops science nor the scientific attitude in either physics or social affairs. Facts merely amassed and piled up are dead; a burden which only adds to confusion. When ideas, hypotheses, begin to play upon facts, when they are methods for experimental use in action, then light dawns; then it becomes possible to discriminate significant from trivial facts, and relations take the place of isolated scraps. Just as soon as we begin to use the knowledge and skills we have to control social consequences in the interest of shared abundant and secured life, we shall cease to complain of the backwardness of our social knowledge.

We shall take the road which leads to the assured building up of social science just as men built up physical science when they actively used the techniques of tools and numbers in physical experimentation.

In spite, then, of all the record of the past, the great scientific revolution is still to come. It will ensue when men collectively and co-operatively organize their knowledge for application to achieve and make secure social values; when they systematically use scientific procedures for the control of human relationships and the direction of the social effects of our vast technological machinery. Great as have been the social changes of the last century, they are not to be compared with those which will emerge when our faith in scientific method is made manifest in social works. We are living in a period of depression. The intellectual function of trouble is to lead men to think. The depression is a small price to pay if it induces us to think about the cause of the disorder, confusion, and insecurity which are the outstanding traits of our social life. If we do not go back to their cause, namely our half-way and accidental use of science, mankind will pass through depressions, for they are the graphic record of our unplanned social life. The story of the achievement of science in physical control is evidence of the possibility of control in social affairs. It is our human intelligence and human courage which are on trial; it is incredible that men who have brought the technique of physical discovery, invention, and use to such a pitch of perfection will abdicate in the face of the infinitely more important human problem.

24. Social Inquiry*

This selection is the penultimate chapter in Dewey's *Logic*, and as such it provides something of a review of positions stated throughout that work. After restating those positions, Dewey then proceeds to indicate their significance for social inquiry when considered as a science in the wide sense—that is, as an experimental mode of inquiry. Dewey details a number of obstacles to the development of fruitful social inquiry, the most obvious one being the adoption of an *a priori* stance

* From John Dewey, *Logic: The Theory of Inquiry*, pp. 487-512. Copyright 1938 by Holt, Rinehart and Winston, Inc. Copyright © 1966 by Roberta L. Dewey. Reprinted by permission of Holt, Rinehart and Winston, Inc.

about the nature of the "ends" or "goals" to be reached and a concomitant manipulation of data for that purpose. To that attitude, regarded by Dewey as widespread, he contrasts the following . position: "Only recognition in both theory and practice that ends to be attained (ends-in-view) are of the nature of hypotheses and that hypotheses have to be formed and tested in strict correlativity with existential conditions as means, can alter current habits of dealing with social issues."

In addition to Dewey's attempt to reformulate the means-end continuum, this selection is also characterized by a strong statement on the necessity of dealing with the cultural matrix of all inquiry, including that of natural science. And, of course, he repeats his long-standing judgment that science, both social and natural, has to develop an increased sense of social responsibility.

The subject-matter of social problems is existential. In the broad sense of "natural," social sciences are, therefore, branches of natural science. Social inquiry is, however, relatively so backward in comparison with physical and biological inquiry as to suggest need for special discussion. The question is not whether the subject-matter of human relations is or can ever become a science in the sense in which physics is now a science, but whether it is such as to permit of the development of methods which, as far as they go, satisfy the logical conditions that have to be satisfied in other branches of inquiry. That there are serious difficulties in the way is evidenced by the backward state of social inquiry. One obvious source of the difficulty lies in the fact that the subject-matter of the latter is so "complex" and so intricately interwoven that the difficulty of instituting a relatively closed system (a difficulty which exists in physical science) is intensified. The very backwardness of social inquiry may serve, then, to test the general logical conceptions that have been reached. For the results of discussion of the topic may show that failure to act in accord with the logical conditions which have been pointed out throws light on its retarded state.

I. *Introduction.* Certain conclusions already arrived at form an introduction to the discussion.

1. All inquiry proceeds within a cultural matrix which is ultimately determined by the nature of social relations. The subject-matter of physical inquiry at any time falls within a larger social field. The techniques available at a given time depend upon the state of material and intellectual culture. When we look back at earlier periods, it is evident that

certain problems could not have arisen in the context of institutions, customs, occupations and interests that then existed, and that even if, *per impossibile*, they had been capable of detection and formulation, there were no means available for solving them. If we do not see that this conditioning, both negative and positive, exists at present, the failure to see it is due to an illusion of perspective. For since conceptions standardized in previous culture provide the ideational means by which problems are formulated and dealt with, even if certain problems were felt at a particular period (past or present), the hypotheses required to suggest and guide methods of their solution would be absent. "There is an inalienable and ineradicable framework of conceptions which is not of our own making, but given to us ready-made by society—a whole apparatus of concepts and categories, within which and by which individual thinking, however daring and original, is compelled to move."[1]

a. The impact of cultural conditions upon social inquiry is obvious. Prejudices of race, nationality, class and sect play such an important role that their influence is seen by any observer of the field. We have only to recall the story of astronomy and of more recent incidents in the doctrine of evolution to be aware that in the past institutional vested interests have told upon the development of physical and biological science. If they do not do so at present to anything like the same extent, it is in large measure because physics has now developed specialized subject-matters and techniques. The result is that to many persons the "physical" seems not only relatively independent of social issues (which it is) but inherently set apart from all social context. The appearance of absence of conflict is to some extent a function of this isolation. What has actually happened, however, is that the influence of cultural conditions has become indirect. The general type of physical problems that are uppermost determines the order of conceptions that are still dominant. Social tendencies and the problems attending them evoke special emphasis upon certain orders of physical problems rather than upon others. It is not possible, for example, to separate nineteenth century devotion to

---

[1] Cornford, *From Religion to Philosophy*, p. 45, quoted by Stebbing, *A Modern Introduction to Logic*, p. 16n. The latter author adds: "No thinker, not even the physicist, is wholly independent of the context of experience provided for him by the society within which he works." While this is especially true of the relation of a given physicist to the smaller society of scientific workers within which he works, it is also true that the activities of this group as a whole are determined in their main features by the "context of experience provided" by the wider contemporaneous community.

exclusively mechanical conceptions from the needs of industry in that period. "Evolutionary" ideas were active, on the other hand, in dealing with cultural-social material before they were applied in biology. The notion of the complete separation of science from the social environment is a fallacy which encourages irresponsibility, on the part of scientists, regarding the social consequences of their work.

b. That physical science and its conclusions do as a matter of fact exercise an enormous influence upon social conditions need not be argued. Technological developments are the direct result of application of physical science. These technological applications have profound and extensive consequences upon human relations. Change in methods of production, distribution, and communication is the chief determining condition of social relationships and, to a large extent, of actual cultural values in every advanced industrial people, while they have reacted intensively into the lives of all "backward" peoples. Moreover, only an arbitrary, or else purely conventional point of view (itself a cultural heritage from earlier periods), can rule out such consequences as these from the scope of science itself. The convention in question posits a complete separation between "pure" and "applied" science.[2] The ultimate ground of every valid proposition and warranted judgment consists in some existential reconstruction ultimately effected. When the logician or philosopher is faced by the reconstructions resulting from physical discoveries, it is not possible for him to say, like Canute to the tide, "thus far shalt thou go and no further."

2. One of the points discussed in an earlier chapter concerned the experiential continuum and the continuity of inquiry. This expressed the principle of the "long run" phase of knowledge connected with the self-developing and self-correcting nature of scientific inquiry. Just as the validity of a proposition in discourse, or of conceptual material generally, cannot be determined short of the consequences to which its functional use gives rise, so the sufficient warrant of a judgment as a

---

[2] "The only valid distinction between pure and applied research in natural science lies between inquiries concerned with issues which *may eventually* and issues which *already do* arise in the social practice of mankind." Hogben, *Retreat from Reason*, p. 8. The following passage from the same author is pertinent to the earlier remark concerning the tendency toward intellectual irresponsibility bred by isolation of the field of physical inquiry from the needs and possibilities inhering in the "social practice of mankind." "The education of the scientist and technician leaves him indifferent to the social consequences of his own activities." (*Ibid*, p. 3)

claimant to knowledge (in its eulogistic sense) cannot be determined apart from connection with a widening circle of consequences. An inquirer in a given special field appeals to the experiences of the community of his fellow workers for confirmation and correction of his results. Until agreement upon consequences is reached by those who reinstate the conditions set forth, the conclusions that are announced by an individual inquirer have the status of an hypothesis, especially if the findings fail to agree with the general trend of already accepted results.[3] While agreement among the activities and their consequences that are brought about in the wider (technically non-scientific) public stands upon a different plane, nevertheless such agreement is an integral part of a *complete* test of physical conclusions wherever their public bearings are relevant.[4] The point involved comes out clearly when the social consequences of scientific conclusions invoke intensification of social conflicts. For these conflicts provide presumptive evidence of the insufficiency, or partiality, and incompleteness of conclusions as they stand.

3. The conclusion that agreement of activities and their consequences is a test and a moving force in scientific advance is in harmony with the position that the ultimate end and test of all inquiry is the transformation of a problematic situation (which involves confusion and conflict) into a unified one. That it is much more difficult to accomplish this end in social inquiry than in the restricted field of physical inquiry is a fact. But it is not a fact which constitutes an inherent logical or theoretical difference between the two kinds of inquiry. On the contrary, the

---

[3] C. S. Peirce is notable among writers on logical theory for his explicit recognition of the necessity of the social factor in the determination of evidence and its probative force. The following representative passage is cited: "The next most vital factor of the method of modern science is that it has been made social. On the one hand, what a scientific man recognizes as a fact of science must be something open to anybody to observe, provided he fulfills the necessary conditions, external and internal. As long as only one man has been able to see a marking upon the planet Venus, it is not an established fact. . . . On the other hand, the method of modern science is social in respect to the solidarity of its efforts. The scientific world is like a colony of insects, in that the individual strives to produce that which he himself cannot hope to enjoy."—*Dictionary of Philosophy and Psychology*, Vol. 2, p. 502.

[4] The "agreement" in question is agreement in activities, not intellectual acceptance of the same set of propositions. A proposition does not gain validity because of the number of persons who accept it. Moreover, continuity of inquiry as a going concern must be taken into account rather than the exact state of belief at a given moment.

presence of *practical* difficulties should operate, as within physical inquiry itself, as an intellectual stimulus and challenge to further application.

4. That social inquiry must satisfy the conjoint conditions of observational ascertainment of fact and of appropriate operational conceptions may seem too evident to require explicit statement. For they are obviously conditions of all scientific achievement with respect to existential subject-matter. But the failure to satisfy the requirement of institution of factual and conceptual subject-matter in conjugate correspondence with each other is such a marked characteristic of the present estate of the social disciplines (as is shown in some detail later) that it is necessary to make the point explicitly. On the positive side, the necessity of this conjugate relation indicates the most important way in which physical science serves as a model for social inquiry. For if there is one lesson more than any other taught by the methods of the physical sciences, it is the strict correlativity of fact and ideas. Until social inquiry succeeds in establishing methods of observing, discriminating and arranging data that evoke and test correlated ideas, and until, on the other side, ideas formed and used are (1) employed as *hypotheses*, and are (2) of a form to direct and prescribe operations of analytic-synthetic determination of facts, social inquiry has no chance of satisfying the logical conditions for attainment of scientific status.

5. One further point will be mentioned before we come to discussion of social inquiry in its own terms. The wide field and intricate constitution of social phenomena, as compared with physical phenomena, is more than a source of practical difficulties in their scientific treatment. It has a definite theoretical import. For the existential conditions which form the physical environment enter at every point into the constitution of socio-cultural phenomena. No individual person and no group *does* anything except in interaction with physical conditions. There are no consequences taking place, there are no social events that can be referred to the human factor exclusively. Let desires, skills, purposes, beliefs be what they will, what happens is the product of the interacting intervention of physical conditions like soil, sea, mountains, climate, tools and machines, in all their vast variety, with the human factor.[5] The theoretical bearing of this consideration is that social phenomena cannot be understood except as there is prior understanding of physical conditions and the laws of their interactions. Social phenomena cannot be at-

---

[5] This consideration is fatal to the view that social sciences are exclusively, or even dominantly, psychological.

tacked, *qua* social, directly. Inquiry into them, with respect both to data that are significant and to their relations or proper ordering, is conditioned upon extensive prior knowledge of physical phenomena and their laws. This fact accounts in part for the retarded and immature state of social subjects. Only recently has there been sufficient understanding of physical relations (including the biological under this caption) to provide the necessary intellectual instrumentalities for effective intellectual attack upon social phenomena. Without physical knowledge there are no means of analytic resolution of complex and grossly macroscopic social phenomena into simpler forms. We now come to discussion of the bearing of logical principles of inquiry upon distinctive social subject-matter.

II. *Social Inquiry and Judgments of Practice.* It was shown in the course of earlier discussions that there are judgments which are formed with *express* reference to entering integrally into the reconstitution of the very existential material which they are ultimately about, or concern. It was also shown that the judgments in which this phase is explicit—namely, judgments of practice and historical judgments,—are special instances of the reconstructive transformation of antecedent problematic subject-matter which is the end-in-view and the objective consequence of all inquiry. These considerations have a peculiar bearing upon social inquiry in its present condition. For the idea commonly prevails that such inquiry is genuinely scientific only as it deliberately and systematically abstains from all concern with matters of social practice. The special lesson which the logic of the methods of physical inquiry has to teach to social inquiry is, accordingly, that social inquiry, *as inquiry*, involves the necessity of operations which existentially modify actual conditions that, as they exist, are the occasions of genuine inquiry and that provide its subject-matter. For, as we have seen, this lesson is the logical import of the experimental method.

Physical inquiry to a considerable extent and mathematics to an even greater extent have now reached the point where problems are mainly set by subject-matter already prepared by the results of prior inquiries, so that further inquiries have a store of scientific data, conceptions and methods already at hand. This is not the case with the material of social inquiry. This material exists chiefly in a crude qualitative state. The problem of institution of methods by which the material of existential situations may be converted into the prepared materials which facilitate and control inquiry is, therefore, the primary and urgent problem of social inquiry. It is then to this phase of the logic of social inquiry that further discussion will be particularly directed.

1. Most current social inquiry is marked, as analytic examination will disclose, by the dominance of one or the other of two modes of procedure, which, in their contrast with one another, illustrate the separation of practice and theory. On the practical side, or among persons directly occupied with management of practical affairs, it is commonly assumed that the problems which exist are already definite in their main features. When this assumption is made, it follows that the business of inquiry is but to ascertain the best method of solving them. The consequence of this assumption is that the work of analytic discrimination, which is necessary to convert a problematic situation into a set of conditions forming a definite problem, is largely foregone. The inevitable result is that methods for resolving problematic situations are proposed without any clear conception of the material in which projects and plans are to be applied and to take effect. The further result is that often difficulties are intensified. For additional obstructions to intelligent action are created; or else, in alleviating some symptoms, new troubles are generated. Survey of political problems and the methods by which they are dealt with, in both domestic and international fields, will disclose any number of pertinent illustrations.

The contrast at this point with methods in physical inquiry is striking. For, in the latter, a large part of the techniques employed have to do with determination of the nature of the problem by means of methods that procure a wide range of data, that determine their pertinency as evidential, that ensure their accuracy by devices of measurement, and that arrange them in the order which past inquiry has shown to be most likely to indicate appropriate modes of procedure. Controlled *analytic* observation, involving systematic comparison-contrast, is accordingly a matter of course in the subjects that have achieved scientific status. The futility of attempting to solve a problem whose conditions have not been determined is taken for granted.

The analogy between social practice and medical practice as it was conducted before the rise of techniques of clinical observation and record, is close enough to be instructive. In both, there is the assumption that gross observation suffices to ascertain the nature of the trouble. Except in unusually obscure cases, symptoms sufficiently large and coarse to be readily observable sufficed in medical practice to supply the data that were used as means of diagnosis. It is now recognized that choice of remedial measures looking to restoration of health is haphazard until the conditions which constitute the trouble or disease have been determined as completely and accurately as possible. The primary problem is, then, to institute the techniques of observation and record that provide the data taken to be evidential and testing. The lesson, as far as method of social inquiry is concerned, is the prime necessity for development of techniques of analytic observation and comparison, so that problematic social situations may be resolved into definitely formulated problems.

One of the many obstructions in the way of satisfying the logical conditions of scientific method should receive special notice. Serious social troubles tend to be interpreted in *moral* terms. That the situations themselves are profoundly moral in their causes and consequences, in the genuine sense of moral, need not be denied. But conversion of the situations investigated into definite problems, that can be intelligently dealt with, demands objective *intellectual* formulation of conditions; and such a formulation demands in turn complete abstraction from the qualities of sin and righteousness, of vicious and virtuous motives, that are so readily attributed to individuals, groups, classes, nations. There was a time when desirable and obnoxious physical phenomena were attributed to the benevolence and malevolence of overruling powers. There was a time when diseases were attributed to the machinations of personal enemies. Spinoza's contention that the occurrence of moral evils should be treated upon the same basis and plane as the occurrence of thunderstorms is justifiable on the ground of the requirements of scientific method, independently of its context in his own philosophic system. For such procedure is the only way in which they can be formulated objectively or in terms of selected and ordered conditions. And such formulation is the sole mode of approach through which plans of remedial procedure can be projected in objective terms. Approach to human problems in terms of moral blame and moral approbation, of wickedness or righteousness, is probably the greatest single obstacle now existing to development of competent methods in the field of social subject-matter.

2. When we turn from consideration of the methods of inquiry currently employed in political and many administrative matters, to the methods that are adopted in the professed name of social science, we find quite an opposite state of affairs. We come upon an assumption which if it were made explicit or formulated would take some such shape as "The facts are out there and only need to be observed, assembled and arranged to give rise to suitable and grounded generalizations." Investigators of physical phenomena often speak and write in similar fashion. But analysis of what they *do* as distinct from what they *say* yields a very different result. Before, however, considering this point I shall discuss a closely connected assumption, namely the

assumption that in order to base conclusions upon the facts and only the facts, all *evaluative* procedures must be strictly ruled out.

This assumption on the part of those engaged, in the name of science, in social investigation derives in the minds of those who entertain it from a sound principle. It springs, at least in large measure, from realization of the harm that has been wrought by forming social judgments on the ground of moral preconceptions, conceptions of what is right and wrong, vicious and virtuous. As has just been stated, this procedure inevitably prejudices the institution of relevant significant data, the statement of the problems that are to be solved, and the methods by which they may be solved. The soundness of the principle that moral condemnation and approbation should be excluded from the operations of obtaining and weighing material data and from the operations by which conceptions for dealing with the data are instituted, is, however, often converted into the notion that all evaluations should be excluded. This conversion is, however, effected only through the intermediary of a thoroughly fallacious notion; the notion, namely, that the moral blames and approvals in question *are* evaluative and that they exhaust the field of evaluation. For they are *not* evaluative in any logical sense of evaluation. They are not even judgments in the logical sense of judgment. For they rest upon some preconception of *ends* that *should* or *ought* to be attained. This preconception excludes ends (consequences) from the field of inquiry and reduces inquiry at its very best to the truncated and distorted business of finding out means for realizing objectives already settled upon. Judgment which is actually judgment (that satisfies the logical conditions of judgment) institutes means-consequences (ends) in *strict conjugate relation* to each other. Ends have to be adjudged (evaluated) on the basis of the available means by which they can be attained just as much as existential materials have to be adjudged (evaluated) with respect to their function as material means of effecting a resolved situation. For an end-in-view is itself a means, namely, a procedural means.

The idea that "the end justifies the means" is in as bad repute in moral theory as its adoption is a commonplace of political practice. The doctrine may be given a strictly logical formulation, and when so formulated its inherent defect becomes evident. From the logical standpoint, it rests upon the postulate that some end is already so fixedly given that it is outside the scope of inquiry, so that the only problem for inquiry is to ascertain and manipulate the materials by which the end may be attained. The hypothetical and directive function of ends-in-view as procedural means is thus ignored and a fundamental logical condition of inquiry is violated. Only an end-in-view that is treated as a *hypothesis* (by which discrimination and ordering of existential material is operatively effected) can by any logical possibility determine the existential materials that are means. In all fields but the social, the notion that the correct solution is already given and that it only remains to find the facts that prove it is so thoroughly discredited that those who act upon it are regarded as pretenders, or as cranks who are trying to impose some pet notion upon facts. But in social matters, those who claim that they are in possession of the one sure solution of social problems often set themselves up as being peculiarly scientific while others are floundering around in an "empirical" morass. Only recognition in both theory and practice that ends to be attained (ends-in-view) are of the nature of hypotheses and that hypotheses have to be formed and tested in strict correlativity with existential conditions as means, can alter current habits of dealing with social issues.

What has been said indicates the valid meaning of evaluation in inquiry in general and also shows the necessity of evaluative judgments in social inquiry. The need for selective discrimination of certain existential or factual material to be data proves that an evaluative estimate is operating. The notion that evaluation is concerned only with *ends* and that, with the ruling out of moral ends, evaluative judgments are ruled out rests, then, upon a profound misconception of the nature of the logical conditions and constituents of all scientific inquiry. All competent and authentic inquiry demands that out of the complex welter of existential and potentially observable and recordable material, certain material be selected and weighed *as* data or the "facts of the case." This process is one of adjudgment, of appraisal or evaluation. On the other end, there is, as has been just stated, no evaluation when ends are taken to be already given. An idea of an end *to be* reached, an end-*in-view*, is logically indispensable in discrimination of existential material as the evidential and testing facts of the case. Without it, there is no guide for observation; without it, one can have no conception of what one should look for or even *is* looking for. One "fact" would be just as good as another—that is, good for nothing in control of inquiry and in formation and settlement of a problem.

3. What has been said has direct bearing upon another assumption which underlies a considerable part of allegedly scientific social inquiry; the idea, namely, that facts are just there and need only to be observed accurately and be assembled in sufficient number to warrant generalizations. A *generalization* in the form of a *hypothesis* is a *prerequisite* condition of selection and ordering of material *as* facts. A generalization is

quite as much an *antecedent* of observation and assemblage of facts as it is a consequence of observing and assembling them. Or, more correctly stated, no generalization can emerge as a warranted conclusion unless a generalization in the form of a hypothesis has previously exercised control of the operations of discriminative selection and (synthetic) ordering of material to form the facts of and for a problem. To return to the point suggested earlier: What scientific inquirers *do*, as distinct from what they say, is to execute certain operations of experimentation—which are operations of doing and making—that modify antecedently given existential conditions so that the results of the transformation are facts which are relevant and weighty in solution of a given problem. Operations of experimentation are cases of blind trial and error which at best only succeed in *suggesting* a hypothesis to be later tried except as they are themselves directed by a hypothesis about a solution.

The assumption that social inquiry is scientific if proper techniques of observation and record (preferably statistical) are employed (the standard of propriety being set by borrowing from *techniques* used in physical science), thus fails to observe the logical conditions which in physical science give the techniques of observing and measuring their standing and force. This point will be developed by considering the idea, which is current, that social inquiry is scientific only when complete renunciation of any reference to *practical* affairs is made its precondition. Discussion of this fallacy (fallacious from the strictly logical point of view) will start from a consideration of the nature of the *problems* of social inquiry.

III. *Institution of Problems.* A genuine problem is one set by existential problematic *situations*. In social inquiry, genuine problems are set only by actual social situations which are themselves conflicting and confused. Social conflicts and confusions exist in fact before problems for inquiry exist. The latter are intellectualizations in inquiry of these "practical" troubles and difficulties. The intellectual determinations can be tested and warranted only by doing something about the problematic existential situations out of which they arise, so as to transform it in the direction of an ordered situation. The connection of social inquiry, as to social data and as to conceptual generalizations, with practice is intrinsic not external. Any problem of scientific inquiry that does not grow out of actual (or "practical") social conditions is factitious; it is arbitrarily set by the inquirer instead of being objectively produced and controlled. All the techniques of observation employed in the advanced sciences may be conformed to, including the use of the best statistical methods to calculate probable errors, etc., and yet the material ascertained be scientifically "dead," i.e., irrelevant to a genuine issue, so that concern with it is hardly more than a form of intellectual busy work. That which is observed, no matter how carefully and no matter how accurate the record, is capable of being *understood* only in terms of projected consequences of activities. In fine, problems with which inquiry into social subject-matter is concerned must, if they satisfy the conditions of scientific method, (1) grow out of actual social tensions, needs, "troubles"; (2) have their subject-matter determined by the conditions that are material means of bringing about a unified situation, and (3) be related to some hypothesis, which is a plan and policy for existential resolution of the conflicting social situation.

IV. *Determination of Facts in Social Inquiry.* This topic has, of necessity, been anticipated in the foregoing discussion which has shown that facts are such in a logical sense only as they serve to delimit a problem in a way that affords indication and test of proposed solutions. Two involved considerations will, however, be explicitly dealt with.

1. Since transformation of a problematic situation (a confused situation whose constituents conflict with one another) is effected by interaction of specially discriminated existential conditions, facts have to be determined in their dual function as obstacles and as resources; that is, with reference to operations of negation (elimination) and affirmation, the latter being determination of materials as positively agreeing with or reinforcing one another. No existing situation can be modified without counteracting obstructive and deflecting forces that render a given situation confused and conflicting. Operations of elimination are indispensable. Nor can an objectively unified situation be instituted except as the *positive* factors of existing conditions are released and ordered so as to move in the direction of the objective consequence desired. Otherwise, ends-in-view are utopian and "idealistic," in the sentimental sense of the latter word.

Realistic social thinking is precisely the mode of observation which discriminates adverse and favorable conditions in an existing situation, "adverse" and "favorable" being understood in connection with the end proposed. "Realism" does *not* mean apprehension of the existing situation *in toto*, but selective discrimination of conditions as obstructive and as resources; i.e., as negative and positive. When it is said "We must take conditions as they are" the statement is either a logical truism or a fallacy which then operates as an excuse for inaction. It is a truism if it is understood to mean that existing conditions are the material, and the only material, of analytic observation. But if it is taken to mean that "conditions as they are" are *final* for judgment as to what can or should be done, there results complete abnegation of intelligent direction of both observation and action. For conditions in any doubtful and undesirable situation are never all of a piece—otherwise there would be no conflict or confusion involved—and, moreover, they are never so fixed that no change in them can be effected. In actual fact, they are themselves changing anyhow in *some* direction, so that the problem is to institute modes of interaction among them which will produce changes in the direction that leads to the proposed objective consequence.

2. That conditions are never completely fixed means that they are in process—that, in any case, they are moving toward the production of a state of affairs which is going to be different in *some* respect. The purpose of the operations of observation which differentiate conditions into obstructive factors and positive resources is precisely to indicate the intervening activities which will give the movement (and hence its consequences) a different form from what it would take if it were left to itself; that is, movement toward a proposed unified existential situation.

The result of taking facts as finished and over with is more serious in inquiry into social phenomena than it is with respect to physical objects. For the former phenomena are inherently historical. But in physics, although universal conceptions are defined and kinds are described in reference to some final existential application, they are free from the necessity of any immediate application. Every social phenomenon, however, is itself a sequential course of changes, and hence a fact isolated from the history of which it is a moving constituent loses the qualities that make it distinctively social. Generic propositions are indispensable in order to determine the unique sequence of events, but as far as the latter is interpreted wholly in terms of general and universal propositions, it loses that unique individuality in virtue of which it is a historic and social fact. A physical fact may be treated as a "case." Any account of, say, the assassination of Julius Caesar assuredly involves the generic conceptions of assassination, conspiracy, political ambition, human beings, of which it is an exemplifying case and it cannot be reported and accounted for without the use of such general conceptions. But treatment of it as just and merely a case eliminates its qualities that make it a social fact. The conceptions are indispensable but they are indispensable as *means* for determining a non-recurring temporal sequence. Even in physics "laws" are in their logical import ultimately means of selecting and linking together events which form an individual temporal sequence.

It was just affirmed that social phenomena are historical, or of the nature of individual temporal sequences. Argument in support of this assumption is superfluous if "history" is understood to include the present. No one would dream of questioning that the social phenomena which constitute the rise of the papacy, the industrial revolution, the rise of cultural and political nationalism, are historical. It cannot be denied that what is now going on in the countries of the world, in their domestic institutions and foreign relations, will be the material of history in the future. It is absurd to suppose that history includes events that happened up to yesterday but does not take in those occurring today. As there are no temporal gaps in a historically determined sequence, so there are none in social phenomena that are determined by inquiry for the latter constitute a developing course of events. Hence, although observation and assemblage of materials in isolation from their movement into an eventual consequence may yield "facts" of some sort, the latter will not be facts in any social sense of that word, since they will be non-historical.

This consideration reinforces the conclusion already drawn: Inquiry into social phenomena involves judgments of evaluation, for they can be understood only in terms of eventuations to which they are capable of moving. Hence, there are as many possible interpretations in the abstract as there are possible kinds of consequences. This statement does not entail carrying over into social phenomena a teleology that has been outmoded in the case of physical phenomena. It does not imply that there is some purpose ruling social events or that they are moving to a predetermined goal. The meaning is that any problematic situation, *when it is analyzed*, presents, in connection with the idea of operations to be performed, *alternative* possible ends in the sense of terminating consequences. Even in physical inquiry, what the inquirer observes and the conceptions he entertains are controlled by an objective purpose— that of attaining a resolved situation. The difference between physical and social inquiry does not reside in the presence or absence of an end-in-view, formulated in terms of possible consequences. It consists in the respective *subject-matters* of the purposes. This difference makes a great practical difference in the conduct of inquiry: a difference in the kind of operations to be performed in instituting the subject-matters that in their interactions will resolve a situation. In the case of social inquiry, *associated* activities are directly involved in the operations to be performed; these associated activities enter into the *idea* of any proposed solution. The practical difficulties in the way of securing the agreements in actual association that are necessary for the required activity are great. In physical matters, the inquirer may reach the outcome in his laboratory or observatory. Utilization of the conclusions of others is indispensable, and others must be able to attain similar conclusions by use of materials and methods similar to those employed by the individual investigator. His activity is socially conditioned in its beginning and close. But in physical inquiry the conditioning social factors are relatively indirect, while in solution of social problems they are directly involved. Any hypothesis as to a social end must include as part of itself the idea of organized association among those who are to execute the operations it formulates and directs.

Evaluative judgments, judgments of better and worse about the means to be employed, material and procedural, are required. The evils in current social judgments of ends and policies arise, as has been said, from importations of judgments of value from outside of inquiry. The evils spring from the fact that the values employed are not determined in and by the process of inquiry: for it is assumed that certain ends have an inherent value so unquestionable that they regulate and validate the means employed, instead of ends being determined on the basis of existing conditions as obstacles-resources. Social inquiry, in order to satisfy the conditions of scientific method, must judge certain objective consequences to be the end which is *worth* attaining under the given conditions. But, to repeat, this statement does not mean what it is often said to mean: Namely, that ends and values can be assumed outside of scientific inquiry so that the latter is then confined to determination of the means best calculated to arrive at the realization of such values. On the contrary, it means that ends in their capacity of values can be validly determined only on the basis of the tensions, obstructions and positive potentialities that are found, by controlled observation, to exist in the actual situation.

V. *Conceptual Subject-matter in Social Inquiry.* This theme was necessarily touched upon in the consideration of the first point, the nature of problems. It was also treated in the foregoing section regarding "fact-findings" that are carried on in isolation from conceptions of an end to be attained. For it was pointed out that such conceptions, while they need to be tested and revised in terms of observed facts, are required to control the selection, arrangement and interpretation of facts. Consideration of the present theme will, accordingly, be confined for the most part, to pointing out the logical mistake of those methods that treat conceptual subject-matter as if it consisted of first and ultimate, self-validating truths, principles, norms. As so often happens with contrary one-sided views, the defects of the factual, so called "positivistic" school and of the conceptual school, provide arguments by which each evokes and supports the views of the other. It cannot be said that the conceptual or "rationalistic" school pays no attention whatever to facts. But it can be stated that it places its entire emphasis upon conceptions, so that facts are subsumed directly under "principles," the latter being regarded as fixed norms that decide the legitimacy or illegitimacy of existing phenomena and that prescribe the ends towards which endeavor should be directed.

There can be no doubt that in some form or other the past history of social thought has been dominated by the conceptual approach. There have existed (to mention merely some outstanding phases) first, the conception, in classical, moral and political theory of ends-in-themselves that are fixed in and by Nature (and hence ontological and cosmological); secondly, the doctrine of "Natural Laws," which itself assumed a variety of forms in successive epochs; thirdly, the theory of intuitions of *a priori* necessary truths, and, finally, as in contemporary thought, the doctrine of an intrinsic hierarchy of fixed values. It is no part of the present task to examine these various historical manifestations of identification of ends having objective status with *a priori* conceptual material. An illustration, exemplary as to the logic involved although not exemplary as to its material, will be given.

Classical political economy, with respect to its logical form, claimed to be a science in virtue, first, of certain ultimate first truths, and, secondly, in virtue of the possibility of rigorous "deduction" of actual economic phenomena from these truths. From these "premises," it followed, in the third place, that the first truths provided the norms of practical activity in the field of economic phenomena; or that actual measures were right or wrong, and actual economic phenomena normal or abnormal, in the degree of their correspondence with deductions made from the system of conceptions forming the premises. The members of this school, from Adam Smith to the Mills and their contemporary followers, differed of course from the traditional *rationalistic* school. For they held that first principles were themselves derived inductively, instead of being established by *a priori* intuition. But once arrived at, they were regarded as unquestionable truths, or as axioms with respect to any further truths, since the latter should be deductively derived from them. The actual content of the fixed premises was taken to be certain truths regarding human nature, such as the universal desire of each individual to better his condition; the desire to do so with the least effort (since effort constituted cost in the sense of pain to be minimized); the impulse to exchange of goods and services in maximum satisfaction of wants at least cost, etc.

We are not concerned with the question of the validity or invalidity of the content of these premises. The point at issue concerns the import of the logic of the method involved. The net consequence of the procedure of classic economics was reinstatement of the older conception of "natural laws" by means of a reinterpretation of their content. For it was concluded that the "laws" of human activity in the economic field, which were theoretically deducible, were the *norms* of proper or right human activity in that field. The laws were supposed to "govern" the phenomena in the sense that all phenomena which failed to conform to them were abnormal or "unnatural"—were a vicious attempt to suspend the working of natural laws or to escape from their inevitable consequences. Any attempt to regulate economic phenomena by control of the social conditions under which production and distribution of goods and services occur was thereby judged to be a violation of natural laws, an "interference" with the normal order, so that ensuing consequences were bound to be as disastrous as are the consequences of an attempt to suspend or interfere with the working of any physical law, say, the law of gravitation.

Discussion of this position is concerned only with its inherent logic, not with the fact that its practical product was a system of *laissez-faire* "individualism" and a denial of the validity of attempts at social control of economic phenomena. From the standpoint of logical method, the conceptions involved were not regarded as *hypotheses* to be employed in observation and ordering of phenomena, and hence to be tested by the consequences produced by acting upon them. They were regarded as *truths* already established and therefore unquestionable. Furthermore, it is evident that the conceptions were not framed with reference to the needs and tensions existing at a particular *time* and *place*, or as methods of resolving ills *then* and *there* existing, but as universal principles applicable anywhere and everywhere. A strong case might be made out for the position that if they had been framed and interpreted on the ground of applicability to conditions existing under specified spatio-temporal conditions, say, in the first half of the nineteenth century in Great Britain, they were to a considerable extent directive operational hypotheses relevant to those historical conditions. But the method that was employed forbade an interpretation in specified spatio-temporal terms.

In consequence, the three indispensable logical conditions of conceptual subject-matter in scientific method were ignored; namely, (1) the status of theoretical conceptions as hypotheses which (2) have a directive function in control of observation and ultimate practical transformation of antecedent phenomena, and which (3) are tested and continually revised on the ground of the consequences they produce in existential application.

A further illustration of the demands of logical method may be found in other current theories about social phenomena, such as the supposed issue of "individualism" versus "collectivism" or "socialism," or the theory that all social phenomena are to be envisaged in terms of the class-conflict of the bourgeoisie and the proletariat. From the standpoint of method, such conceptual generalizations, no matter which one of the opposed conceptions is adopted, *pre*judge the characteristic traits and the kinds of actual phenomena that the proposed plans of action are to deal with. Hence the work of *analytic* observations by which actual phenomena will be reduced to terms of definite problems that may be dealt with by means of determinate specified operations is intrinsically compromised from the start. The "generalizations" are of the nature of all-or-none contradictory "truths." Like all such sweeping universals, they do not delimit the field so as to determine problems that may be attacked one by one, but are of such a nature that, from the standpoint of theory, one theory must be accepted and the other rejected *in toto*.

One of the simplest ways of grasping the logical difference between social inquiry that rests upon fixed conceptual principles and physical inquiry, is to note that in the latter the theoretical controversies which exist concern the *efficacy* of different conceptions *of procedure*, while in the former they are about the question of an alleged intrinsic truth or falsity. This attitude is generative of conflict in opinion, and clash in action, instead of promoting inquiries into observable and verifiable facts. If one looks at the early stage of what is now the body of facts and ideas that constitute physics, chemistry, biology and medicine, one finds that at some earlier period controversy in those fields was also mainly about the intrinsic truth and falsity of certain conceptions. As these sciences have advanced in genuine scientific quality, doubt and inquiry have centered upon the efficacy of different *methods* of procedure. The result has been that instead of a state of rigid alternatives of which one must be accepted and the other rejected, a plurality of hypotheses is positively welcome. For the plurality of alternatives is the effective means of rendering inquiry more extensive (sufficient) and more flexible, more capable of taking cognizance of all facts that are discovered.

* * *

In fine, fact-finding procedures are necessary for (1) determination of *problems* and for (2) provision of data that indicate and test hypotheses; while formulation of conceptual structures and frames of reference is necessary to guide observation in discriminating and ordering data. The immature state of social inquiry may thus be measured by the extent to which these two operations of fact-finding and of setting up theoretical ends are carried on independently of each other, with the consequence that factual propositions on one side and conceptual or theoretical structures on the other are regarded each as final and complete in itself by one or another school. With reference to the conceptual framework, some additional considerations are appended.

1. Directing conceptions tend to be taken for granted after they have once come into general currency. In consequence they either remain implicit or unstated, or else are propositionally formulated in a way which is static instead of functional. Failure to examine the conceptual structures and frames of reference which are unconsciously implicated in even the seemingly most innocent factual inquiries is the greatest single defect that can be found in any field of inquiry. Even in physical matters, after a certain conceptual frame of reference has once become habitual, it tends to become finally obstructive with reference to new lines of investigation. In biology and in the social disciplines, law, politics, economics and morals, the danger is more acute and more disastrous. Failure to encourage fertility and flexibility in formation of hypotheses as frames of reference is closer to a death warrant of a science than any other one thing.

2. With respect to social subject-matter in particular, failure to translate influential conceptions into *formulated* propositions is especially harmful. For only explicit formulation stimulates examination of their meanings in terms of the consequences to which they lead and promotes critical comparison of alternative hypotheses. Without systematic formulation of ruling ideas, inquiry is kept in the domain of opinion and action in the realm of conflict. For ultimately the only logical alternative to open and aboveboard propositional formulation of conceptual alternatives (as many as possible) is formation of controlling ideas on the ground of either custom and tradition or some special interest. The result is dichotomization of a social field into conservatives and progressives, "reactionaries" and "radicals," etc.

3. One of the chief practical obstacles to the development of social inquiry is the existing division of social phenomena into a number of

compartmentalized and supposedly independent non-interacting fields, as in the different provinces assigned, for example to economics, politics, jurisprudence, morals, anthropology, etc. It is no part of a general logical theory to indicate special methods and devices by which existing barriers may be broken down. That task is the business of inquirers in the several fields. But a survey from the logical point of view of the historical development of the social disciplines instructively discloses the causes of splitting up social phenomena into a number of relatively closed compartments and the injurious effects of the division. It is legitimate to suggest that there is an urgent need for breaking down these conceptual barriers so as to promote cross-fertilization of ideas, and greater scope, variety and flexibility of hypotheses.

4. The practical difficulties in the way of experimental method in the case of social phenomena as compared with physical investigations do not need elaborate exposition. Nevertheless, every measure of policy put into operation is, *logically*, and *should* be actually, of the nature of an experiment. For (1) it represents the adoption of one out of a number of alternative conceptions as possible plans of action, and (2) its execution is followed by consequences which, while not as capable of definite or exclusive differentiation as in the case of physical experimentation, are none the less observable within limits, so they may serve as tests of the validity of the conception acted upon. The idea that because social phenomena do not permit the controlled variation of sets of conditions in a one-by-one series of operations, therefore the experimental method has no application at all, stands in the way of taking advantage of the experimental method to the extent that is practicable. Suppose, for example, it is a question of the introduction of some legislative policy. Recognition of its experimental character would demand, on the side of its contents, that they be rendered as definite as possible in terms of a number of well thought out alternatives, or as members of a disjunctive system. That is, failure to recognize its experimental character encourages treatment of a policy as an isolated independent measure. This relative isolation puts a premium upon formation of policies in a comparatively improvised way, influenced by immediate conditions and pressures rather than by surveys of conditions and consequences. On the other side, failure to take into account the experimental nature of policies undertaken, encourages laxity and discontinuity in *discriminative* observation of the consequences that result from its adoption. The result is merely that it works or it does not work as a gross whole, and some other policy is then improvised. Lack of careful, selec-

tive, continued observation of conditions promotes indefiniteness in formation of policies, and this indefiniteness reacts in turn to obstruct
definiteness of the observations relevant to its test and revision.

Finally, it may be pointed out that the present state of social inquiry
provides a test of the adequacy of general logical theory, and in this
respect furnishes confirmation of the validity of the general theory
which has been developed. To consider in detail its value as a test of
logical theories held regarding facts and conception and their relation to
each other would be to repeat what has already been said. A word may
be added about its value as a test of formalistic logical theories. A logic
of forms in isolation from matter is confined in social inquiry to the
function of forms in locating formal fallacies in discourse, especially in
giving warning against the confusion of words having emotional immediate practical effect, (so called "expressive sentences") with those having objective meaning. This purging of reasoning from formal fallacies
is a valuable service. But it rarely requires any elaborate formal scheme
to enable them to be detected. The important fallacies are the material
ones. They spring from lack of proper methods of observation on one
hand, and, on the other, from lack of methods for forming and testing
hypotheses. With respect to these material concerns, formalistic logic is
necessarily silent. The silence is sometimes defended on the ground that
propositions about social matters and about what is to be done with
respect to them involve valuations (which is correct), and then holding
that propositions about values are pseudo-propositions, expressing
merely resolutions to act in certain ways. That an element of practical
resolution exists need not be denied; it is found also in every conception
as to how to operate in physical science. The point which is important is
that formalistic logic provides no possible ground for deciding upon one
practical policy rather than another, and none for following out the consequences of a policy when put into operation as a test of its validity.
The net effect is to throw the very field in which intelligent control is of
the utmost importance wholly outside the scope of scientific method.
There are those to whom this result will present itself as a *reductio ad
absurdum* of the theory in question. In any case, the formalistic position
is very likely to provoke a reaction that contributes to strengthening the
theory of fixed *a priori* schemes of value, known by direct rational intuition. For any denial of the possibility of application of a scientific
method is bound to encourage resort, in a matter of such importance, to
use of non-scientific and even anti-scientific procedures.

I conclude discussion of the topic of the logic of social inquiry by referring again to the point which is fundamental in the foregoing discussion—its intrinsic reference to practice. This reference has been shown to be involved in determination of genuine problems, in discriminating, weighing and ordering facts as evidential, and in formation and test of the hypotheses that are entertained. I add a few words upon the special topic of *understanding* facts. Understanding or interpretation is a matter of the *ordering* of those materials that are ascertained to be facts; that is, determination of their *relations*. In any given subject-matter there exist many relations of many kinds. That particular set of relations which is relevant to the problem in hand has to be determined. Relevant *theoretical* conceptions come into play only as the problem in hand is clear and definite; that is, theory alone cannot decide what set of relations is to be instituted, or how a given body of facts is to be understood. A mechanic, for example, understands the various parts of a machine, say an automobile, when and only when he knows how the parts *work together;* it is the way in which they work together that provides the principle of order upon and by which they are related to one another. The conception of "working together" involves the conception of consequences: the *significance* of things resides in the consequences they produce when they interact with other specified things. The heart of the experimental method is determination of the significance of observed things by means of deliberate institution of modes of interaction.

It follows that in social inquiry "facts" may be carefully ascertained and assembled without being understood. They are capable of being ordered or related in the way that constitutes understanding of them only when their *bearing* is seen, and "bearing" is a matter of connection with consequences. Social phenomena are so interwoven with one another that it is impossible to assign special consequences (and hence bearing and significance) to any given body of facts unless the special consequences are of the latter *differentially* determined. This differential determination can be effected only by active or "practical" operations conducted according to an idea which is a plan. Social phenomena are not unique in being complexly interwoven with another. All existential events, as existential, are in a similar state. But methods of experimentation and their directive conceptions are now so well established in the case of physical phenomena that vast bodies of facts seem to carry their significance with them almost on their face as soon as they are ascertained. For prior experimental operations have shown what their probable consequences will be under specified conditions to a high degree of accuracy. No such state of affairs exists with reference to social phenomena and facts. A like state of affairs can be brought into existence, even approximately, only as social facts are related together and hence understood, on the basis of their connection with differential consequences that are effected by definite plans of dealing practically with the phenomena:—the plans, once more, being hypotheses directive of practical operations, not truths or dogmas.

VI
Experience Is Pedagogical

Never has a philosopher devoted himself so practically, so assiduously, and yet so reflectively to the problems of education as John Dewey. Starting with his experience as a young teacher in a South Oil City, Pennsylvania, classroom, and on through his sponsorship of a laboratory school at the University of Chicago and his work at Teachers College, Columbia University, Dewey's involvement in education was both philosophical and program oriented. Dewey's philosophy of experience was a pedagogy and his pedagogy was a philosophy of experience. Readers of Dewey and practitioners of his philosophy who separate these lifelong strands in his work understand little if anything of either concern.

25. Interest in Relation to Training of the Will*

In this essay, written more than seventy-five years ago, Dewey confronts a problem of great moment to educators of the present. In our idiom, the problem of interest is articulated under the rubric of relevance, but the fundamental difficulty remains the same, the tension between the often onerous burden of mastering subject matter and the pedagogical concern for the joy of learning.

Dewey's position is that sheer effort, especially under authoritarian duress, does not generate either learning or moral fiber. Rather, such an approach results in either narrowness or obstinacy, or a "character dull, mechanical, unalert." Nor, on the other hand, does he approve of turning education into patterns of "amusement and distraction," characterized by a pandering to the self-indulgent.

* From *Second Supplement to the Herbart Year Book for 1895* (Bloomington, Ill., National Herbart Society, 1896), pp. 209-46.

Dewey's own position is a function of confidence that a genuine interaction of interest and effort is generated when the person confronts experience in problematic terms. The personal need to resolve problems, both intellectual and practical, takes precedence for Dewey over artificial inducements or regimens of discipline. Dewey's approach seems ideal, but as he is to write at a later time, the school environment and the expectations of the community often militate against its implementation.

There is much the same difficulty in isolating any educational topic for discussion that there is in the case of philosophy. The issues are so interdependent that any one of them can be selected only at the risk of ignoring important considerations, or else of begging the question by bringing in the problem under discussion under cover of some other subject. Yet limits of time and space require that some one field be entered and occupied by itself. Under such circumstances about all one can do is to pursue a method which shall at least call attention to the problems involved, and to indicate the main relations of the matters discussed to relevant topics. The difficulty is particularly great in the discussion of interest. Interest is in the closest relation to the emotional life, on one side; and, through its close relation, if not identity with attention, to the intellectual life, on the other side. Any adequate explanation of it, therefore, would require the development of the complete psychology both of feeling and of knowledge, and of their relations to each other, and the discussion of their connection or lack of connection with volition.

Accordingly, I can only hope to bring out what seem to me to be the salient points, and if my results do not command agreement, to help at least define the problem for further discussion.

While it would be sanguine to anticipate agreement upon any important educational doctrine, there is perhaps more hope of reaching a working consensus by beginning with the educational side. If we can lay down some general principle regarding the place and function of Interest in the school, we shall have a more or less sure basis on which to proceed to the psychological analysis of interest in its relation to the other factors and aspects of volition. At all events, we shall have limited the field and fixed the boundaries within which the psychological discussion may proceed. After this we may with more promise of success proceed to the discussion of some of the chief attitudes assumed toward the problem of interest in historic and current investigations.

Finally, we may return with the results reached by this psychological and critical consideration to the educational matter. We may restate and reinterpret the part played by interest in instruction with deeper insight and more definite emphasis upon the question of moral training.

I

At first sight the hope of gaining a working consensus regarding interest on the educational side seems futile. The first thing that strikes us is the profound contradiction sometimes expressed, more often latent, in current educational ideas and standards regarding precisely this matter of interest. On the one hand, we have the school which insists that interest is the keynote both of instruction and of moral training, that the essential problem of the teacher is to make the material presented so interesting that it shall command and retain attention. On the other hand, we have the assertion that the putting forth of effort from within is alone truly educative; that to rely upon the principle of interest is to distract the child intellectually and to weaken him morally.

In this educational law-suit of interest versus effort let us consider the respective briefs of plaintiff and defendant. In behalf of interest it is claimed that it is the sole guarantee of attention; that, if we can secure interest in a given set of facts or ideas, we may be perfectly sure that the pupil will direct his energies towards mastering them; that if we can secure interest in a certain moral train or line of conduct, we are equally safe in assuming that the child's activities are responding in that direction; that if we have not secured interest we have no safeguard as to what will be done in any given case. As matter of fact the doctrine of discipline has not succeeded. It is absurd to suppose that a child gets more intellectual or mental discipline when he goes at a matter unwillingly than when he goes at it with complete interest and out of the fullness of his heart. The theory of effort simply says that unwilling attention (doing something which is disagreeable and because it is disagreeable) should take precedence over spontaneous attention.

Practically the theory of effort amounts to nothing. When a child feels that his work is a task it is only under compulsion that he gives himself to it. At the least let-up of external pressure we find his attention at once directed to what interests him. The child brought up on the basis of the theory of effort simply acquires marvelous skill in appearing to be occupied with an uninteresting subject, while the real heart and core of his energies are otherwise engaged. Indeed, the theory contradicts itself. It is psychologically impossible to call forth any activity without some interest. The theory of effort simply substitutes one interest for another. It substitutes the impure interest of fear of the teacher or hope of future reward for pure interest in the material presented. The type of character induced is that illustrated by Emerson at the beginning of his essay on Compensation, where he holds up the current doctrine of compensation as virtually implying that if you only sacrifice yourself enough now, you will be permitted to indulge yourself a great deal more in the future; or that if you are only good now (goodness consisting in attention to what is uninteresting) you will have a great many more pleasing interests at some future time;—that is, may then be bad.

While the theory of effort is always holding up to us a strong, vigorous character as the outcome of its method of education, practically we do not get this character. We get either the narrow, bigoted man who is obstinate and irresponsible save in the line of his own preconceived aims and beliefs; or else we get a character dull, mechanical, unalert, because the vital juice of the principle of spontaneous interest has been squeezed out of it.

We may now hear the defendant's case. Life, says the other theory, is full of things not interesting, but which have to be faced none the less. Demands are continually made, situations have to be dealt with which present no features of interest. Unless the individual has had previous training in devoting himself to uninteresting work, unless habits have been formed of attending to matters simply because they have to be attended to, irrespective of the personal satisfaction gotten out of them, character will either break down, or avoid the issue, when confronted with the more serious matters of life. Life is too serious to be degraded to a merely pleasant affair, or reduced to the continual satisfaction of personal interests. The concerns of future life, therefore, imperatively demand such continual exercise of effort in the performance of tasks as to form the habit of recognizing the real labors of life. Anything else eats out the fiber of character and reduces the person to a wishy washy, colorless being; or else to a state of moral dependence, with over-reliance upon others and with continual demand for amusement and distraction.

Apart from the question of the future, continually to appeal in childhood days even to the principle of interest is eternally to excite, that is distract the child. Continuity of activity is destroyed. Everything is made play, amusement. This means over-stimulation; it means dissipation of energy. Will is never called into action at all. The reliance is upon external attractions and amusements. Everything is sugar-coated for the child, and he soon learns to turn from everything which is not artificially surrounded with diverting circumstances. The spoiled child who does only what he likes is the inevitable outcome of the theory of interest in education.

The theory is intellectually as well as morally harmful. Attention is never directed to the essential and important facts. It is directed simply to the wrappings of attraction with which the facts are surrounded. If a fact is repulsive or uninteresting, it has to be faced in its own naked character sooner or later. Putting a fringe of fictitious interest around it does not bring the child any nearer to it than he was at the outset. The fact that two and two make four is a naked fact which has to be mastered in and of itself. The child gets no greater hold upon the fact by having attached to it amusing stories of birds or dandelions than he would if the simple naked fact were presented to him. It is self-deception to suppose that the child is being interested in the numerical relation. His attention is going out to and taking in only the amusing images associated with this relation. The theory thus defeats its own end. It would be more direct and straightforward to recognize at the outset that certain facts have to be learned which have little or no interest, and that the only way to deal with these facts is through the power of effort, the internal power of putting forth activity wholly independent of any external inducement. Moreover, in this way the discipline, the habit of responding to serious matters, is formed which is necessary to equip the child for the life that lies ahead of him.

I have attempted to set forth the respective claims of each side as we find them, not only in current discussions but in the old controversy, as old as Plato and Aristotle. A little reflection will convince one that the strong point in each argument is not so much what it says in its own behalf, as in its attacks on the weak places of the opposite theory. Each theory is strong in its negations rather than in its position. It is a common, though somewhat surprising, fact that there is generally a common principle unconsciously assumed at the basis of two theories which to all outward appearances are the extreme opposites of each other. Such a common principle is presupposed by the theories of effort and interest in the one-sided forms in which they have already been stated.

This identical assumption is the externality of the object or idea to be mastered, the end to be reached, the act to be performed, to the self. It is because the object or end is assumed to be outside self that it has to be *made* interesting, that it has to be surrounded with artificial stimuli and with fictitious inducements to attention. It is equally because the object lies outside the sphere of self that the sheer power of "will," the putting forth of effort without interest, has to be appealed to. The genuine principle of interest is the principle of the recognized identity of the fact or proposed line of action with the self; that it lies in the direction of the agent's own self-expression and is therefore, imperiously demanded, if the agent is to be himself. Let this condition of identification once be secured, and we neither have to appeal to sheer strength of will nor do we have to occupy ourselves with making things interesting to the child.

The theory of effort, as already stated, means a virtual division of attention and the corresponding disintegration of character, intellectually and morally. The great fallacy of the so-called effort theory is that it identifies the exercise and training of will with certain external activities and certain external results. It is supposed that because a child is occupied at some outward task and because he succeeds in exhibiting the required product, that he is really putting forth will, and that definite intellectual and moral habits are in process of formation. But as a matter of fact, the moral exercise of the will is not found in the external assumption of any posture, and the formation of moral habits can not be identified with the ability to show up results at the demand of another. The exercise of the will is manifest in the direction of attention, and depends upon the spirit, the motive, the disposition in which work is carried on.

A child may be externally entirely occupied with mastering the multiplication table, and be able to reproduce that table when asked to do so by his teacher. The teacher may congratulate himself that the child has been so exercising his will power as to be forming right intellectual and moral habits. Not so, unless moral habit be identified with this ability to show certain results when required. The question of moral training has not been touched until we know what the child has been internally occupied with, what the predominating direction of his attention, his feelings, his disposition has been while engaged upon this task. If the task has appealed to him merely as a task, it is as certain, psychologically, as the law of action and reaction is, physically, that the child is simply engaged in acquiring the habit of divided attention; that he is getting the ability to direct eye and ear, lips and mouth, to what is present before him in such a way as to impress those things upon his memory, while at the same time getting his mental imagery free to work upon matters of real interest to him.

No account of the actual moral training secured is adequate unless it recognizes this division of attention into which the child is being educated, and faces the question of what the moral worth of such a division may be. External mechanical attention to a task conceived as a task is the inevitable correlate of an internal random mind-wandering along the lines of the pleasurable.

The spontaneous power of the child, his demand for self-expression, can not by any possibility be suppressed. If the external conditions are such that the child cannot put his spontaneous activity into the work to be done, if he finds that he cannot express himself in that, he learns in a most miraculous way the exact amount of attention that has to be given to this external material to satisfy the requirements of the teacher, while saving up the rest of his mental powers for following out lines of imagery that appeal to him. I do not say that there is absolutely no moral training involved in forming these habits of external attention, but I do say that there is a question of moral import involved in the formation of the habits of internal inattention.

While we are congratulating ourselves upon the well disciplined habits which the pupil is acquiring, judged by his ability to reproduce a lesson when called upon, we forget to commiserate ourselves because the deeper intellectual and moral nature of the child has secured absolutely no discipline at all, but has been left to follow its own caprices, the disordered suggestions of the moment, or of past experience. I do not see how anyone can deny that the training of this internal imagery is at least equally important with the development of certain outward habits of action. For myself, when it comes to the mere moral question and not a question of practical convenience, I think it is infinitely more important. Nor do I see how anyone at all familiar with the great mass of existing school work can deny that the greater part of the pupils are gradually forming habits of divided attention. If the teacher is skillful and wide-awake, if she is what is termed a good disciplinarian, the child will indeed learn to keep his senses intent in certain ways, but he will also learn to direct the fruitful imagery, which constitutes the value of what is before his senses, in totally other directions. I do not think it would be well for us to have to face the actual psychological condition of the majority of the pupils that leave our schools. We should find this division of attention and the resulting disintegration so great that we might be discouraged from all future endeavor. None the less, it is well for us to recognize that this state of things exists, and that it is the inevitable outcome of those conditions which require the simulation of attention without requiring its essence.

The principle of making objects and ideas interesting implies the same divorce between object and self as does the theory of "effort."

When things have to be *made* interesting it is because interest itself is wanting. Moreover, the phrase is a misnomer. The thing, the object is no more interesting than it was before. The appeal is simply made to the child's love of pleasure. He is excited in a given direction with the hope that somehow or rather during this excitation he will assimilate something otherwise repulsive. There are two types of pleasure. One is the accompaniment of activity. It is found wherever there is self-expression. It is simply the internal realization of the outgoing energy. This sort of pleasure is always absorbed in the activity itself. It has no separate existence in consciousness. This is the type of pleasure found in legitimate interest. Its stimulus is found in the needs of the organism. The other sort of pleasure arises from contact. It marks receptivity. Its stimuli are external. We take interest; we get pleasure. The type of pleasure which arises from external stimulation is isolated. It exists by itself in consciousness as a pleasure, not as the pleasure of activity.

When objects are made interesting it is this latter type of pleasure that comes into play. Advantage is taken of the fact that a certain amount of excitation of any organ is pleasurable. The pleasure arising is employed to cover the gap between self and some fact not in itself arousing interest.

The result here also is division of energies. In the case of disagreeable effort the division is simultaneous. In this case it is successive. Instead of having a mechanical external activity and a random internal activity at the same time there is oscillation of excitement and apathy. The child alternates between periods of over-stimulation and of inertness. It is a condition realized in some so-called kindergartens. Moreover, this excitation of any particular organ, as eye or ear by itself, creates an abiding demand for such stimulation. It is as possible to create an appetite on the part of the eye or the ear for pleasurable stimulation as it is on the part of the taste. Some kindergarten children are as dependent upon the recurrent presence of bright colors or agreeable sounds as the drunkard is upon his dram. It is this which accounts for the distraction and dissipation of energy so characteristic of such children, and for their dependence upon external suggestion.

Before attempting a more specific psychological analysis, the discussion up to this point may be summarized as follows: Genuine interest in education is the accompaniment of the identification, through action, of the self with some object or idea, because of the necessity of that object or idea for the maintenance of self-expression. Effort, in the sense in which it may be opposed to interest, implies a separation between the self and the fact to be mastered or task to be performed, and sets up an habitual division of activities. Externally, we have mechanical habits with no psychical end or value. Internally, we have random energy or mind-wandering, a sequence of ideas with no end at all because not brought to a focus in action. Interest, in the sense in which it is opposed to effort, means simply an excitation of the sense organ to give pleasure, resulting in strain on one side and listlessness on the other.

Self-expression in which the psychical energy assimilates material because of the recognized value of this material in aiding the self to reach its end, does not find it necessary to oppose interest to effort. Effort is the result of interest, and indicates the persistent outgo of activities in attaining an end felt as valuable; while interest is the consciousness of the value of this end, and of the means necessary to realize it.

II

We come now to our second main topic, the psychology of interest. It should be obvious from the preceding educational discussion that the points upon which we particularly need enlightenment are its relation to desire and pleasure on one side, to ideas and effort on the other.

I begin with a brief descriptive account of interest. Interest is first active, projective, or propulsive. We take interest. To be interested in any matter is to be actively concerned with it. The mere feeling regarding a subject may be static or inert, but interest is dynamic. Second, it is objective. We say a man has many interests to care for or look after. We talk about the range of a man's interests, his business interests, local interests, etc. We identify interests with concerns or affairs. Interest does not end simply in itself as bare feelings may, but always has some object, end, or aim to which it attaches itself. Third, interest is subjective; it signifies an *internal* realization, or feeling, of worth. It has its emotional, as well as its active and objective sides. Wherever there is interest there is response in the way of feeling.

These are the various meanings in which common sense employs the term interest. The root idea of the term seems to be that of being engaged, engrossed, or entirely taken up with some activity because of its recognized worth. The etymology of the term inter-esse, "to be between," points in the same direction. Interest marks the annihilation of the distance between subject and object; it is the instrument which effects their organic union.

It is true that the term interest is also used in a definitely disparaging sense. We speak of interest as opposed to principle, of self-interest as a motive to action which regards only one's personal advantage; but these are neither the only nor the controlling senses in which the term is used. It may fairly be questioned whether this is anything but a narrowing or degrading of the legitimate sense of the term. However that may be, it appears to me certain that much of the controversy regarding the moral use of interest arises because one party is using the term in the larger objective sense of recognized value or engrossing activity, while the other is using it as equivalent to selfish motive.

We have now to deal more in detail with each of the three phases mentioned. (1) First, the active or propulsive phase of interest takes us back to the consideration of impulse and the spontaneous urgencies or tendencies of activity. There is no such thing as absolutely diffuse, impartial impulse. Impulse is always differentiated along some more or less specific channel. Impulse has its own special lines of discharge. The old puzzle about the ass between two bundles of hay is only too familiar, but the recognition of its fundamental fallacy is not so common. If the self were purely passive or purely indifferent, waiting upon stimulation from without, then the self illustrated in this supposed example would remain forever helpless, starving to death, because of its equipoise between two sources of food. The error is in the supposition of this balanced internal condition. The self is always already doing something, intent on something urgent. And this ongoing activity always gives it a bent in one direction rather than another. The ass, in other words, is always already moving toward one bundle rather than the other. No amount of physical cross-eyedness could induce such psychical cross-eyedness that the animal would be in a condition of equal stimulation from both sides.

In this primitive condition of spontaneous impulsive activity, we have the basis for natural interest. Interest is no more passively waiting around to be excited from the outside than is impulse. In the selective or preferential quality of impulse we have the basis of the fact that at any given time, if we are psychically awake at all, we are always interested in one direction rather than another. The condition of total lack of interest, or of absolutely impartially distributed interest, is as mythical as the story of the ass in scholastic ethics.

An equally great fallacy is the oft-made assumption of some chasm between impulse and the self. Impulse is spoken of as if it were a force swaying the self in this direction or that; as if the self were an indifferent, passive something waiting to be moved by the pressure of impulse; in reality, impulse is simply the impetus or outgoing of the self in one direction or other. This point is mentioned now because the connection of impulse and interest is so close that any assumption, at this point, of impulse as external to self is sure to manifest itself later on in the assumption that interest is of the nature of an external inducement or attraction to self, instead of being an absorption of the activities of the self in the object that allows these activities to function.

(2) Second, the objective side of interest. Every interest, as already said, attaches itself to an object. The artist is interested in his brushes, in his colors, in his technique. The business man is interested in the play of supply and demand, in the movement of markets, etc. Take whatever instance of interest we choose and we shall find that, if we cut out the factor of the object about which interest clusters, interest itself disappears, relapsing into mere subjective feeling.

The question of psychological import is the relationship existing between activity and idea or object. The object arises as the definition or interpretation of the impulsive activity. The objects exhibit the bringing to consciousness of the quality of the impulsive activity.

Error begins in supposing the object already there, and then calling the activity into being. Canvas, brushes, and paints interest the artist, for example, only because they help him find his existing artistic capacity. There is nothing in a wheel and a piece of string to arouse a child's activity save as they set before him, in objective shape, some capacity which he already possesses and of whose mode of translation into action he is thereby made conscious. The object, in other words, transfers the impulsive activity into intellectual terms. The impulse itself is blind. This only means that it does not know what it wants, what it is after. But as it finds outlet and expression, it reveals itself. The object of interest is that which gives the spontaneous activity filling or content. The object which supplies means and ends to an impulse brings it to consciousness and thus transforms it into an abiding interest.

(3) We now come to the emotional phase. Value is not only objective but subjective. That is, there is not only the thing which is projected as valuable or worth while, but there is also the feeling of its worth. It is, of course, impossible to define feeling. We can only say that it is the purely individual consciousness of worth and recognize that wherever we have interest there we have internal realization of value.

The gist of the psychology of interest may, accordingly, be stated as follows: An interest is primarily a form of self-expressive activity. If we examine this activity on the side of the content of expression, of what is done, we get its objective features, the ideas, objects, etc., to which the interest is attached, about which it clusters. If we take into account that it is self-expression, that self finds itself, is reflected back to itself, in

this content, we get its emotional or feeling side. Any account of genuine interest must, therefore, grasp it as outgoing activity holding within its grasp an intellectual content, and reflecting itself in felt value.

At this point, it is necessary to distinguish two typical phases into
which the one activity of self-expression, at the basis of all interest, differentiates itself, as this differentiation gives us also two types of interest. These two types of self-expression arise according as the end and
means of expression do, or do not, coincide in time. In the former case
we have immediate interest, in the latter mediate. It is all-important to
carry our analysis over into an examination of these points, because it is
in the matter of mediate interest that the one-sided theories arise,
which, on one side (isolating the emotional phase), identify pleasure
with interest; or, on the other (isolating the intellectual or ideal phase),
deny interest and identify volition with effort.

There are cases where self-expression is direct and immediate. It puts
itself forth with no thought of anything beyond. The present activity is
the only ultimate in consciousness. It satisfies in and of itself. The end *is*
the present activity, and so there is no gap in space nor time between
means and end. All play is of this immediate character. All purely aesthetic appreciation approximates this type. The existing experience
holds us for its own sake and we do not demand of it that it take us into
something beyond itself. With the child and his ball, the amateur and
the hearing of a symphony, the immediate engrosses. Its value is there,
and is there in what is directly present.

We may, if we choose, say that the interest is in the object present to
the senses, but we must beware how we interpret this saying. The object
has no conscious existence, at the time, save *in* the activity. The ball to
the child is his game, his game is his ball. The music has no existence
save in the rapt hearing of the music—so long as the interest is immediate or aesthetic. It is frequently said to be the object which attracts attention, which calls forth interest to itself by its own inherent qualities.
But this is a psychological impossibility. The bright color, the sweet
sound, that interest the child are themselves phases of his organic activity. To say the child attends to the color does not mean that he gives
himself up to an external object, but rather that he continues the activity
which results in the presence of the color. His own activity so engrosses
him that he endeavors to maintain it. But when the object or end exists
in idea or symbol, then the end, the object to be reached and the means,
the energies at command for reaching it, fall apart. A period of adjustment is required. We do things in which we would not be interested if

they were ultimates; in which we are interested because they are conceived as necessary to an end.

It is a mistake, however, to suppose that we regard these intermediates *merely* as means;—as *lacking* in interest. In a case of sheer drudgery we feel that we have to go through things merely in order to reach a final end. But these intermediate steps are not recognized as in any sense *really* means; and hence interest in the end is never transferred over into them. If we felt they were in reality means to the end, we should feel them so organically bound up with the end as to share in its value. The fact that they are repulsive indicates that we do not consider them intrinsically connected with the desired end. They are necessary evils, accidentally and externally attached to something we want, so that we can't get one without the other. They are not regarded as in the same process of self-expression as is the end. If we take the example of a man doing a day's work utterly repulsive to him simply for the sake of getting his wage, it is obvious that the day's task is to him only incidentally, accidentally, not intrinsically, a means to the end. The wage is an end simply in the sense that it comes last or afterwards; it is a physical, not a psychical, end. So the day's work is a means simply in the sense that it must precede getting pay, not in the sense that it organically aids in realizing the end.

The all-important point then in the consideration of mediate interest or voluntary attention is the kind of relationship which exists between the putting forth of energy considered as means, and the idea or object to be reached considered as end. If the two fall apart, if the means are not identified with the end, interest is not really mediated. The intervening steps are regarded simply as necessary evils to be gotten over with as soon as possible for the sake of the final outcome.

Here self-contradiction emerges. If the interest is wholly in the end and not at all in the means, there is nothing to insure attention being kept upon the means, and hence no way to guarantee the reaching of the end. The mind is not really on the work. The agent is not taken up with what he is doing. He is not psychically, but only externally, engaged. Hence, so far as he is concerned, it is a mere accident whether or not the end be reached. The break in interest between means and end marks, in other words, a break in the self.

On the other hand, if the means are recognized truly as means, if they are felt to be simply the way in which the end presents itself at the particular moment, then the full interest in the end is at once transferred to the so-called means. For the time being that becomes the end. As we illustrated the other case by an instance of drudgery, we may illustrate this by one of artistic construction. The sculptor has his end, his ideal, in view. To realize that end he must go through a series of intervening steps which are not, on the face of it, equivalent to the end. He must model and mould and chisel in a series of particular acts, no one of which is the beautiful form he has in mind, and every one of which represents the putting forth of personal energy on his own part. But because these are to him necessary means for the end, the ideal, the finished form is completely transferred over into these special acts. Each moulding of the clay, each stroke of the chisel, is for him at the time the whole end in process of realization. Whatever interest or value attaches to the end attaches to each of these steps. He is as much absorbed in one as in the other. Any failure in this complete identification means an inartistic product, means that he is not really interested in his ideal. A genuine interest in the ideal indicates of necessity an equal interest in all the conditions of its expression.

We are now in position to deal with the question of the relation of interest to desire and to effort. Desire and effort in their legitimate meaning are both of them phases of this mediated interest. They are correlatives, not opposites. Both effort and desire exist only when the end is somewhat remote. When energy is put forth purely for its own sake, there is no question of effort and equally no question of desire. Effort and desire both imply a state of tension. There is a certain amount of opposition existing between the ideal in view and the present actual state of things. We call it effort when we are thinking of the necessity of a decided transformation of the actual state of things in order to make it conform to the ideal—when we are thinking of the process from the side of the idea and interested in the question how to get it realized. We call it desire when we think of the tendency of the existing energies to push themselves forward so as to secure this transformation, or change the idea into a fact—when we think of the process from the side of the means at hand. But in either case, obstacles delaying us, and the continued persistence of activity against them, are implied. The only sure evidence of desire as against mere vague wishing, is effort, and desire is aroused only when the exercise of effort is required.

In discussing the condition of mediate interest we may emphasize either the end in view, the idea, or we may start with the consideration of the present means, the active side urgent for expression. The former is the intellectual side, the latter the emotional. The tendency of the end to realize itself through the process of mediation, overcoming resistance, is effort. The tendency of the present powers to continue a struggle for complete expression in an end remote in time is desire.

According to the previous account, there is absolutely one and the same psychical process at the basis of both desire and effort. The distinction is not in the facts themselves, but simply in the attitude which the psychologist or observer takes toward the facts. Both desire and effort are phases of self-expression arising whenever it becomes so complex that the end, the self to be expressed, and the powers at hand, the means of expression, do not directly coincide with each other. The errors previously discussed on the educational side arise from abstracting either desire or effort from the active process of self-expression. Separated from activity, one may be set over against the other. For the sake of dealing with these educational errors at their root, it becomes necessary, accordingly, to discuss both desire and effort somewhat more in detail.

We often speak of appetite as blind and lawless. We conceive it as insisting upon its own satisfaction, irrespective of circumstances or of the good to the self. This means that the appetite is only felt; it is not known. It is not considered from the standpoint of its bearings or relationships. It is not translated over into terms of its results. Consequently, it is not made intelligent. It is not rationalized. As a result energy is wasted. In any strong appetite there is an immense amount of power, physical and psychical, stirred up; but where the agent does not anticipate the ends corresponding to this power it is undirected. The energy expends itself in chance channels or according to some accidental stimulus. The organism is exhausted, and nothing positive or objective is accomplished. The disturbance or agitation is out of proportion to any ends reached. All there is to show for such a vast excitation of energy is the momentary satisfaction felt in its stimulation and expenditure.

Even as regards this blind appetite, there is, however, a decided difference of type between the lower animals and man. In the animals, while the appetite is not conscious of its own end, it none the less seeks that end by a sort of harmony pre-established in the animal structure. Fear serves the animal as a stimulus to flight or to seeking cover. Anger serves it for purposes of attack and defence. It is a very unusual occurrence when the feeling gets the better of the animal and causes it to waste its powers uselessly. But of the blind feelings in the human being, it is to be said that most of them require adjustment before they are of any regular permanent service. There is no doubt that fear or anger may be rendered useful to the man as they are to the animal. But in the former case they have to be trained to this use; in the latter they originally possess it. The ultimate function of anger is undoubtedly to do away with obstacles hindering the process of self-expression, but in a child the exhibition of anger is almost sure to leave the object, the obstacle, untouched and to exhaust the child. The blind feeling needs to be rationalized. The agent has to become conscious of the end or object and control his aroused powers by conscious reference to it.

For the process of self-expression to be effective and mechanical, there must, in other words, be a consciousness of both end and means. Whenever there is difficulty in effecting adjustment of means and ends the agent is thrown into a condition of emotion. Whenever we have on one side the idea corresponding to some end or object, and whenever we have on the other side a stirring up of the active impulses and habits, together with a tendency of the latter to focus themselves at once upon the former, there we have a disturbance or agitation, known on its psychical side as emotion. It is a common-place that as fast as habit gets definitely formed in relation to its own special end the feeling element drops out. But now let the usual end to which the habit is adapted be taken away and a sudden demand be made for the old habit to become a means towards a new end, and emotional stress at once becomes urgent. The active side is all stirred up, but neither discharges itself at once, without any end, nor yet directs itself towards any accustomed end. The result is tension between habit and aim, between impulse and idea, between means and end. This tension is the essential feature of emotion.

It is obvious from this account that the function of emotion is to secure a sufficient arousing of energy in critical periods of the life of the agent. When the end is new or unusual and there is great difficulty in attending to it, the natural tendency would be to let it go or turn away from it. But the very newness of the end often represents the importance of the demand that is being made. To neglect the end would be a serious, if not fatal, matter for the agent. The very difficulty in effecting the adjustment sends out successive waves of stimuli, which call into play more impulses and habits, thus reinforcing the powers, resources at the agent's command. The function of emotion is thus to brace or reinforce the agent in coping with the novel element in unexpected and immediate situations.

The normal moral outcome is found in a balance between the excitation and the ideal. If the former is too weak or diffused, the agent lacks in motor power. If it is relatively too strong, the agent is not able to handle the powers which have been stirred up. He is more or less beside himself. He is carried away by the extent of his own agitation. He relapses, in other words, into the phase of blind feeling.

Desire is a phase of this excitation or disturbance in the adjustment of active impulses or habits as means to an object considered as end or ideal. Desire cannot be identified with mere impulse or with blind feeling. Desire differs from the appetite of the animal in that it is always conscious, at least dimly, of its own end. When the agent is in the condition known as desire, he is conscious of some object ahead of him, and the consciousness of this object serves to reinforce his active tendencies. The thought of the desired object serves, in a word, to stimulate the means necessary to its attainment. While desire is thus not a purely impulsive state, neither, of course, is it a purely intellectual one. The object may be present in consciousness, but it is simply contemplated as an object; if it does not serve as stimulus to activity, it occupies a purely aesthetic or theoretic place. At most, it will arouse only a pious wish or a vague sentimental longing, not an active desire.

The true moral function of desire is thus identical with that of emotion, of which, indeed, it is only one special phase. Its place in the moral life is to arouse energy, to stimulate the means necessary to accomplish the realization of ends otherwise purely theoretic or aesthetic. Our desires in a given direction simply measure the hold which certain ends or ideals have upon us. They *exhibit* the force of character, the *Drang* in that direction. They *test* the sincerity of character. A produced end which does not awaken desire is a mere pretension. It indicates a growing division of character, a threatening hypocrisy.

The moral treatment of desire, like that of emotion, involves securing a balance. Desire tends continually to overdo itself. It marks energy stirred up to serve as means; but the energy once stirred up tends to express itself on its own account independently of the end. Desire is greedy, lends itself to overhastiness, and unless watched makes the agent overhasty. It runs away with him. It is not enough that the contemplation of the end stir up the impulses and habits; the consciousness of the end must also abide, after they are excited, to direct the energy called into being.

The question, in other words, is whether the desire is made to contribute to the realization of the end, whether it has held strictly to its function as instrument, or whether the end gets subordinated to the desire. In the latter case we have self-indulgence. The end is thought of in order to get the impulses into play; but the moment this is secured the end is dropped or pushed out of sight, and the satisfaction got out of the excitation is substituted for it. The object, end, in other words, is prostituted to be an instrument of excitation only. Its claim to direct the powers which it has stimulated is ignored or willfully denied. Hence, the contradiction involved in the immoral use of emotion and desire. The end, the ideal, cannot be entirely absent from consciousness, as it is in the case of purely brute appetite. The end or aim has to be in consciousness to stir up or reinforce the active tendencies. It must be admitted, therefore, as end, but no sooner has it done the work of stimulation than it is denied to be an end and is reduced purely to the place of means.

We thus get a criterion for the normal position of pleasure in relation to desire. There can be no doubt that desire is always more or less pleasurable. It is pleasurable in so far as the end of self-expression is present in consciousness. For the end defines satisfaction, and any conception of it awakens, therefore, an image of satisfaction, which, so far as it goes, is itself pleasurable. The use of this pleasure is to give the end such a hold upon the agent that it may pass over from its ideal condition into one of actualization. Normal pleasure has a strictly instrumental place. It is *due* to the thought of the end on one side, and it *contributes* to the practical efficiency of the end on the other. In the case of self-indulgence the end is used simply to excite the pleasurable state of consciousness, and having done this, is thereafter denied. Pleasure, instead of serving to hold the mind to the end, is now made itself the end.

What, it may be asked, is the connection of this with the question of interest? Precisely this. In the analysis of desire we are brought back exactly to the question of mediate interest. Normal desire is simply a case of properly mediated interest. The problem of attaining the proper balance between the impulses on one side and an ideal or end on the other is just the question of getting enough interest in the end to prevent a too sudden expenditure of the waste energy—to direct this excited energy so that it shall be tributary to realizing the end. Here the interest in the end is taken over into the means. Interest, in other words, marks the fact that the emotional force aroused is functioning. This is our definition of interest; it is impulse functioning with reference to an idea of self-expression.

Interest in the end indicates that desire is both calmed and steadied. Over-greedy desire, like over-anxious aversion, defeats itself. The youthful hunter is so anxious to kill his game, he is so stimulated by the thought of reaching his end, that he cannot control himself sufficiently to take steady aim. He shoots wild. The successful hunter is not the one who has lost interest in his end, in killing the game, but the one who is able to translate this interest completely over into the means necessary to accomplish his purpose. It is no longer the killing of the game that occupies his consciousness by itself, but the thought of the steps he has to perform. The means, once more, have been identified with the end; the desire has become mediate interest. The ideal dies as bare ideal to live again in instrumental powers.

We are thus able to see the error in those theories which hold that pleasure is the end of desire. As is well known, these theories divide themselves into two types. On one hand, one school of moralists holds that since pleasure is the object of desire it is the ideal and standard of conduct. The other school, accepting the same theory of the relation of pleasure and desire, holds that, on this very account, desire must be eliminated from the moral will; that the presence of desire in the motivation of conduct indicates a purely selfish or pleasure-seeking factor. Once recognized, however, that pleasure marks the satisfaction taken in the ideal of self-expression, and we see the falsity of both these theories. The real object of desire is not pleasure, but self-expression. The presence of desire marks simply the tension in the stage of self-expression reached. The pleasure felt is simply the reflex of the satisfaction which the self is anticipating in its own expression.

The fundamental mistake, in other words, lies in considering desire as a process prior to or outside of volition. It marks one stage in the development of volition—that stage in which the end, the purpose, the ideal, is sufficiently present to arouse and reinforce active impulses, and when there is still enough conflict within the self, as ideal on one side and as actual on the other, to make it a problem whether the end will succeed in directing the active powers as well as in exciting them. The development of desire into interest marks the happy solution of this problem.

So far we have been discussing the process of mediated self-expression from the standpoint of the means. We have now to consider the same process, throwing the emphasis of intellectual analysis on the side of the end. Because of the length of the foregoing discussion we may here briefly consider the end or ideal, on the sides, respectively, of its origin and its function.

First, its origin. The ideal is normally a projection of the active powers. It is not generated in a vacuum nor introduced into the mind from outside impulses and habits actually striving for expression. It is simply these active powers getting off and looking at themselves to see what they are like; to see what they are upon the whole, permanently, in their final bearings, and not simply as they are at the moment and in their relative isolation. The ideal, in other words, is the self-consciousness of the impulse. It is its self-interpretation; its value in terms of objective self-expression.

Second, hence its function. If the ideal had its genesis independent of the active powers, it is impossible to see how it could ever get to work. The psychical machinery by which it should cease to be barely an ideal, and become an actuality, would be wanting. But just because the ideal is normally the projection of the active powers into intellectual terms the ideal inevitably possesses active quality. This dynamic factor is present to stay. Its appearance as motive is not anything different in kind from its appearance as ideal. Motivation is just the realization of the active value originally attaching to it.

In other words, when the ideal has the function of motive (a power inducing to activity), we have precisely the same fact, viewed from the standpoint of the end, that we have just now considered as the passing over of desire into mediate interest when viewing it from the side of the means. So long as the ideal does not become a motive it indicates that the ideal itself is not yet definitely formed. There is conflict of ideals. The agent has two possible ends before him, one corresponding to one set of his active powers and another to another set of impulses or habits. Thought, reflection, is not focused, accordingly, in any single direction. The self has not yet found itself. It does not know what it really wants. It is in process of tentative self-expression, first trying on one self and then another to see how they fit. The attainment of a single purpose or the defining of one final ideal indicates the self has found its unity of expression. At this exact point the ideal, having no longer any opposition to hold it back, begins to show itself in overt action. The ideal has become a motive. The interest in the end is now taken over into the impulses and habits, and they become the present ends. Motive is the interest in the ideal mediated into impulse and habit.

Normal effort is precisely this self-realizing tendency of the ideal—its struggle to pass over into motive. The empty or formal ideal is the end which is not suggested by, or does not grow out of, the agent's active powers. Lacking any dynamic qualities, it does not assert itself; it does not become a motor, a motive. But whenever the ideal is really a projection or translation of self-expression, it must strive to assert itself. It must persist through obstacles, and endeavor to transform obstacles into means of its own realization. The degree of its persistency simply marks the extent to which it is in reality and not simply in name a true ideal or conceived form of self-expression.

The matter of good intentions or "meaning well" affords a good illustration of this principle. When a person who has outwardly failed in his duty offers his good intentions as a justification or palliation of conduct, what determines whether or no his excuse shall be accepted? Is it not precisely whether he can or not show effort on the part of his intention, his ideal, to realize itself, and can show obstacles intervening from without which have prevented its expression up to the point of overt realization? If he cannot show such overwhelming interference from without, we have a right to conclude either that the agent is attempting to deceive us or else is self-deceived—that his so-called good intention was in reality but a vague sentimental wish or else a second-handed reference to some conventional ideal which had no real hold upon him. We always use the persistence of an end against obstacles as a test of its vitality, its genuineness.

On the other hand, effort in the sense of strain because of lack in interest is evidence of the abnormal use of effort. The necessity of effort in this sense indicates that the end nominally held up is not recognized as a form of self-expression—that it is external to the self and hence fails in interest. The *conscious* stirring up of effort marks simply the unreal strain necessarily involved in any attempt to reach an end which is not part and parcel of the self's own process. The strain is always artificial; it requires external stimulation of some sort or other to keep it going and always leads to exhaustion. Not only does effort in its true sense play no part in moral training, but it plays a distinctly immoral part. The externality of the end as witnessed in its failure to arouse the active impulses and to persist towards its own realization makes it impossible that any strain to attain this end should have any other than a relatively immoral motive. Only selfish fear, the dread of some external power, or else purely mechanical habit, or else the hope of some external reward, some more or less subtle form of bribery, can be really a motive in any such instance.

We thus see how the theories of pleasure as a motive and artificial effort as a motive have the same practical outcome. The theory of strain always involves some reference to either pleasure or pain as the real controlling motive. And the theory of pleasure, because of its lack of an intrinsic end which holds and directs the powers, has continually to fall back upon some external inducement to excite the flagging powers. It is a common-place in morals that no one puts forth more effort with less avail than the habitual seeker after pleasure.

The outcome of our psychological analysis is thus identical with the results reached by consideration of the practical educational side. There we found that the appeal to making things interesting, to stirring up pleasure in things not of themselves interesting, leads as a matter of common experience to alternation of over-stimulation and dull apathy. Here we find that the desire for pleasure as an end leads necessarily to the stirring up of energies uselessly on one side, and the undirected wasteful expenditure of energies on the other.

On the educational side we saw that the appeal to the sheer force of "will," so-called, apart from any interest in the object, means the formation of habits of divided attention—the mechanical doing of certain things in a purely external way on the one side and the riotous uncontrolled play of imagery on the other. On the psychological side we find that interest in an end or object simply means that the self is finding its own expression in a certain direction; that, therefore, the effort to realize an end where such interest is wanting means necessarily a division of the self. On one side, its natural tendency to self-expression cannot be got rid of by being ignored. On the other, external circumstances force it to utilize some of its energies in ways which to it are valueless.

On the educational side we were led to assume that normal interest and effort are identical with the process of self-expression. We have now through the process of mediated self-expression secured a fairly adequate psychological justification for that practical postulate of education.

26. My Pedagogic Creed*

Although written comparatively early in Dewey's career, "My Pedagogic Creed" contains, in seminal form, most of his subsequent judgments about matters educational. His stress on the individual as social, the school as a community, and the necessity of integrating discipline with the needs and potentialities of the children constitute major themes in *Democracy and Education, Schools of Tomorrow*, and *Experience and Education*.

Dewey also attempts to sketch the necessary relationship between feeling, thought, and action, while opposing both dull academic formalism and sentimentalism. Perhaps the most trenchant remark in his "Creed" is Dewey's comment that "education must be conceived as a continuing reconstruction of experience; that the process and the goal of

* From *School Journal*, LIV (January, 1897), pp. 77-80.

education are one and the same thing.'' Learning for Dewey is not an epiphenomenon, tacked onto a regimen of mental flagellation. Rather it is a process, yielding its rewards enroute and from time to time consummating in an insight, a breakthrough, or even a mastery of a discipline or an area of study. Attention to detail and rigor of method are not separated in Dewey's purview from the joy and celebration that accompanies the process of learning.

ARTICLE I—*What Education Is*

I Believe that

—all education proceeds by the participation of the individual in the social consciousness of the race. This process begins unconsciously almost at birth, and is continually shaping the individual's powers, saturating his consciousness, forming his habits, training his ideas, and arousing his feelings and emotions. Through this unconscious education the individual gradually comes to share in the intellectual and moral resources which humanity has succeeded in getting together. He becomes an inheritor of the funded capital of civilization. The most formal and technical education in the world cannot safely depart from this general process. It can only organize it or differentiate it in some particular direction.

—the only true education comes through the stimulation of the child's powers by the demands of the social situations in which he finds himself. Through these demands he is stimulated to act as a member of a unity, to emerge from his original narrowness of action and feeling, and to conceive of himself from the standpoint of the welfare of the group to which he belongs. Through the responses which others make to his own activities he comes to know what these mean in social terms. The value which they have is reflected back into them. For instance, through the response which is made to the child's instinctive babblings the child comes to know what those babblings mean; they are transformed into articulate language, and thus the child is introduced into the consolidated wealth of ideas and emotions which are now summed up in language.

—this educational process has two sides—one psychological and one sociological—and that neither can be subordinated to the other, or neglected, without evil results following. Of these two sides, the psychological is the basis. The child's own instincts and powers furnish the material and give the starting-point for all education. Save as the efforts of the educator connect with some activity which the child is carrying on of his own initiative independent of the educator, education becomes reduced to a pressure from without. It may, indeed, give certain external results, but cannot truly be called educative. Without insight into the psychological structure and activities of the individual, the educative process will, therefore, be haphazard and arbitrary. If it chances to coincide with the child's activity it will get a leverage; if it does not, it will result in friction, or disintegration, or arrest of the child nature.

—knowledge of social conditions, of the present state of civilization, is necessary in order properly to interpret the child's powers. The child has his own instincts and tendencies, but we do not know what these mean until we can translate them into their social equivalents. We must be able to carry them back into a social past and see them as the inheritance of previous race activities. We must also be able to project them into the future to see what their outcome and end will be. In the illustration just used, it is the ability to see in the child's babblings the promise and potency of a future social intercourse and conversation which enables one to deal in the proper way with that instinct.

—the psychological and social sides are organically related, and that education cannot be regarded as a compromise between the two, or a superimposition of one upon the other. We are told that the psychological definition of education is barren and formal—that it gives us only the idea of a development of all the mental powers without giving us any idea of the use to which these powers are put. On the other hand, it is urged that the social definition of education, as getting adjusted to civilization, makes of it a forced and external process, and results in subordinating the freedom of the individual to a preconceived social and political status.

—each of these objections is true when urged against one side isolated from the other. In order to know what a power really is we must know what its end, use, or function is, and this we cannot know save as we conceive of the individual as active in social relationships. But, on the other hand, the only possible adjustment which we can give to the child under existing conditions is that which arises through putting him in complete possession of all his powers. With the advent of democracy and modern industrial conditions, it is impossible to foretell definitely just what civilization will be twenty years from now. Hence it is impossible to prepare the child for any precise set of conditions. To prepare him for the future life means to give him command of himself; it means so to train him that he will have the full and ready use of all his capacities; that his eye and ear and hand may be tools ready to command, that his judgment may be capable of grasping the conditions under which it has to work, and the executive forces be trained to act economically and efficiently. It is impossible to reach this sort of adjustment save as constant regard is had to the individual's own powers, tastes, and interests—that is, as education is continually converted into psychological terms.

In sum, I believe that the individual who is to be educated is a social individual, and that society is an organic union of individuals. If we eliminate the social factor from the child we are left only with an abstraction; if we eliminate the individual factor from society, we are left only with an inert and lifeless mass. Education, therefore, must begin with a psychological insight into the child's capacities, interests, and habits. It must be controlled at every point by reference to these same considerations. These powers, interests, and habits must be continually interpreted—we must know what they mean. They must be translated into terms of their social equivalents—into terms of what they are capable of in the way of social service.

ARTICLE II—*What the School Is*

I Believe that

—the school is primarily a social institution. Education being a social process, the school is simply that form of community life in which all those agencies are concentrated that will be most effective in bringing the child to share in the inherited resources of the race, and to use his own powers for social ends.

—education, therefore, is a process of living and not a preparation for future living.

—the school must represent present life—life as real and vital to the child as that which he carries on in the home, in the neighborhood, or on the playground.

—that education which does not occur through forms of life, forms that are worth living for their own sake, is always a poor substitute for the genuine reality, and tends to cramp and to deaden.

—the school, as an institution, should simplify existing social life; should reduce it, as it were, to an embryonic form. Existing life is so complex that the child cannot be brought into contact with it without either confusion or distraction; he is either overwhelmed by the multiplicity of activities which are going on, so that he loses his own power of orderly reaction, or he is so stimulated by these various activities that his powers are prematurely called into play and he becomes either unduly specialized or else disintegrated.

—as such simplified social life, the school life should grow gradually out of the home life; that it should take up and continue the activities with which the child is already familiar in the home.

—it should exhibit these activities to the child, and reproduce them in such ways that the child will gradually learn the meaning of them, and be capable of playing his own part in relation to them.

—this is a psychological necessity, because it is the only way of securing continuity in the child's growth, the only way of giving a background of past experience to the new ideas given in school.

—it is also a social necessity because the home is the form of social life in which the child has been nurtured and in connection with which he has had his moral training. It is the business of the school to deepen and extend his sense of the values bound up in his home life.

—much of present education fails because it neglects this fundamental principle of the school as a form of community life. It conceives the school as a place where certain information is to be given, where certain lessons are to be learned, or where certain habits are to be formed. The value of these is conceived as lying largely in the remote future; the child must do these things for the sake of something else he is to do;

they are mere preparations. As a result they do not become a part of the life experience of the child and so are not truly educative.

—the moral education centers upon this conception of the school as a mode of social life, that the best and deepest moral training is precisely that which one gets through having to enter into proper relations with others in a unity of work and thought. The present educational systems, so far as they destroy or neglect this unity, render it difficult or impossible to get any genuine, regular moral training.

—the child should be stimulated and controlled in his work through the life of the community.

—under existing conditions far too much of the stimulus and control proceeds from the teacher, because of neglect of the idea of the school as a form of social life.

—the teacher's place and work in the school is to be interpreted from this same basis. The teacher is not in the school to impose certain ideas or to form certain habits in the child, but is there as a member of the community to select the influences which shall affect the child and to assist him in properly responding to these influences.

—the discipline of the school should proceed from the life of the school as a whole and not directly from the teacher.

—the teacher's business is simply to determine, on the basis of larger experience and riper wisdom, how the discipline of life shall come to the child.

—all questions of the grading of the child and his promotion should be determined by reference to the same standard. Examinations are of use only so far as they test the child's fitness for social life and reveal the place in which he can be of the most service and where he can receive the most help.

ARTICLE III—*The Subject-Matter of Education*

I Believe that

—the social life of the child is the basis of concentration, or correlation, in all his training or growth. The social life gives the unconscious unity and the background of all his efforts and of all his attainments.

—the subject-matter of the school curriculum should mark a gradual differentiation out of the primitive unconscious unity of social life.

—we violate the child's nature and render difficult the best ethical results by introducing the child too abruptly to a number of special studies, of reading, writing, geography, etc., out of relation to this social life.

—the true center of correlation on thc school subjects is not science, nor literature, nor history, nor geography, but the child's own social activities.

—education cannot be unified in the study of science, or so-called nature study, because apart from human activity, nature itself is not a unity; nature in itself is a number of diverse objects in space and time, and to attempt to make it the center of work by itself is to introduce a principle of radiation rather than one of concentration.

—literature is the reflex expression and interpretation of social experience; that hence it must follow upon and not precede such experience. It, therefore, cannot be made the basis, although it may be made the summary of unification.

—once more that history is of educative value in so far as it presents phases of social life and growth. It must be controlled by reference to social life. When taken simply as history it is thrown into the distant past and becomes dead and inert. Taken as the record of man's social life and progress it becomes full of meaning. I believe, however, that it cannot be so taken excepting as the child is also introduced directly into social life.

—the primary basis of education is in the child's powers at work along the same general constructive lines as those which have brought civilization into being.

—the only way to make the child conscious of his social heritage is to enable him to perform those fundamental types of activity which make civilization what it is.

—in the so-called expressive or constructive activities as the center of correlation.

—this gives the standard for the place of cooking, sewing, manual training, etc., in the school.

—they are not special studies which are to be introduced over and above a lot of others in the way of relaxation or relief, or as additional accomplishments. I believe rather that they represent, as types, fundamental forms of social activity; and that it is possible and desirable that the child's introduction into the more formal subjects of the curriculum be through the medium of these activities.

—the study of science is educational in so far as it brings out the materials and processes which make social life what it is.

—one of the greatest difficulties in the present teaching of science is that the material is presented in purely objective form, or is treated as a new peculiar kind of experience which the child can add to that which he has already had. In reality, science is of value because it gives the ability to interpret and control the experience already had. It should be introduced, not as so much new subject-matter, but as showing the factors already involved in previous experience and as furnishing tools by which that experience can be more easily and effectively regulated.

—at present we lose much of the value of literature and language studies because of our elimination of the social element. Language is almost always treated in the books of pedagogy simply as the expression of thought. It is true that language is a logical instrument, but it is fundamentally and primarily a social instrument. Language is the device for communication; it is the tool through which one individual comes to share the ideas and feelings of others. When treated simply as a way of getting individual information, or as a means of showing off what one has learned, it loses its social motive and end.

—there is, therefore, no succession of studies in the ideal school curriculum. If education is life, all life has, from the outset, a scientific aspect, an aspect of art and culture, and an aspect of communication. It cannot, therefore, be true that the proper studies for one grade are mere reading and writing, and that at a later grade, reading, or literature, or science, may be introduced. The progress is not in the succession of studies, but in the development of new attitudes towards, and new interests in, experience.

—education must be conceived as a continuing reconstruction of experience; that the process and the goal of education are one and the same thing.

—to set up any end outside of education, as furnishing its goal and standard, is to deprive the educational process of much of its meaning, and tends to make us rely upon false and external stimuli in dealing with the child.

ARTICLE IV—*The Nature of Method*

I Believe that

—the question of method is ultimately reducible to the question of the order of development of the child's powers and interests. The law for presenting and treating material is the law implicit within the child's own nature. Because this is so I believe the following statements are of supreme importance as determining the spirit in which education is carried on:

—the active side precedes the passive in the development of the child-nature; that expression comes before conscious impression; that the muscular development precedes the sensory; that movements come before conscious sensations; I believe that consciousness is essentially motor or impulsive; that conscious states tend to project themselves in action.

—the neglect of this principle is the cause of a large part of the waste of time and strength in school work. The child is thrown into a passive, receptive, or absorbing attitude. The conditions are such that he is not permitted to follow the law of his nature; the result is friction and waste.

—ideas (intellectual and rational processes) also result from action and devolve for the sake of the better control of action. What we term reason is primarily the law of orderly or effective action. To attempt to develop the reasoning powers, the powers of judgment, without reference to the selection and arrangement of means in action, is the fundamental fallacy in our present methods of dealing with this matter. As a result we present the child with arbitrary symbols. Symbols are a necessity in mental development, but they have their place as tools for economizing effort; presented by themselves they are a mass of meaningless and arbitrary ideas imposed from without.

—the image is the great instrument of instruction. What a child gets out of any subject presented to him is simply the images which he himself forms with regard to it.

—if nine-tenths of the energy at present directed towards making the child learn certain things were spent in seeing to it that the child was forming proper images, the work of instruction would be indefinitely facilitated.

—much of the time and attention now given to the preparation and presentation of lessons might be more wisely and profitably expended in training the child's power of imagery and in seeing to it that he was continually forming definite, vivid, and growing images of the various subjects with which he comes in contact in his experience.

—interests are the signs and symptoms of growing power. I believe that they represent dawning capacities. Accordingly the constant and careful observation of interests is of the utmost importance for the educator.

—these interests are to be observed as showing the state of development which the child has reached.

—they prophesy the stage upon which he is about to enter.

—only through the continual and sympathetic observation of child-hood's interests can the adult enter into the child's life and see what it is ready for, and upon what material it could work most readily and fruitfully.

—these interests are neither to be humored nor repressed. To repress interest is to substitute the adult for the child, and so to weaken intellectual curiosity and alertness, to suppress initiative, and to deaden interest. To humor the interests is to substitute the transient for the permanent. The interest is always the sign of some power below; the important thing is to discover this power. To humor the interest is to fail to penetrate below the surface, and its sure result is to substitute caprice and whim for genuine interest.

—the emotions are the reflex of actions.

—to endeavor to stimulate or arouse the emotions apart from their corresponding activities is to introduce an unhealthy and morbid state of mind.

—if we can only secure right habits of action and thought, with reference to the good, the true, and the beautiful, the emotions will for the most part take care of themselves.

—next to deadness and dullness, formalism and routine, our education is threatened with no greater evil than sentimentalism.

—this sentimentalism is the necessary result of the attempt to divorce feeling from action.

ARTICLE V—*The School and Social Progress*

I Believe that

—education is the fundamental method of social progress and reform.

—all reforms which rest simply upon the enactment of law, or the threatening of certain penalties, or upon changes in mechanical or outward arrangements, are transitory and futile.

—education is a regulation of the process of coming to share in the social consciousness; and that the adjustment of individual activity on the basis of this social consciousness is the only sure method of social reconstruction.

—this conception has due regard for both the individualistic and socialistic ideals. It is duly individual because it recognizes the formation of a certain character as the only genuine basis of right living. It is socialistic because it recognizes that this right character is not to be formed by merely individual precept, example, or exhortation, but rather by the influence of a certain form of institutional or community life upon the individual, and that the social organism through the school, as its organ, may determine ethical results.

—in the ideal school we have the reconciliation of the individualistic and the institutional ideals.

—the community's duty to education is, therefore, its paramount moral duty. By law and punishment, by social agitation and discussion, society can regulate and form itself in a more or less haphazard and chance way. But through education society can formulate its own purposes, can organize its own means and resources, and thus shape itself with definiteness and economy in the direction in which it wishes to move.

—when society once recognizes the possibilities in this direction, and the obligations which these possibilities impose, it is impossible to conceive of the resources of time, attention, and money which will be put at the disposal of the educator.

—it is the business of every one interested in education to insist upon the school as the primary and most effective interest of social progress and reform in order that society may be awakened to realize what the school stands for, and aroused to the necessity of endowing the educator with sufficient equipment properly to perform his task.

—education thus conceived marks the most perfect and intimate union of science and art conceivable in human experience.

—the art of thus giving shape to human powers and adapting them to social service is the supreme art; one calling into its service the best of artists; that no insight, sympathy, tact, executive power, is too great for such service.

—with the growth of psychological service, giving added insight into individual structure and laws of growth; and with growth of social science, adding to our knowledge of the right organization of individuals, all scientific resources can be utilized for the purposes of education.

—when science and art thus join hands the most commanding motive for human action will be reached, the most genuine springs of human conduct aroused, and the best service that human nature is capable of guaranteed.

—the teacher is engaged, not simply in the training of individuals, but in the formation of the proper social life.

—every teacher should realize the dignity of his calling; that he is a social servant set apart for the maintenance of proper social order and the securing of the right social growth.

—in this way the teacher always is the prophet of the true God and the usherer in of the true kingdom of God.

27. The School and Social Progress*

This selection constitutes the first chapter of Dewey's book *School and Society*. Although brief, it is extraordinarily rich in suggestion and stands the test of time remarkably well. Departing from the experience of what used to be called manual training, Dewey actually details the use of the project method in learning situations. In addition to the pedagogical significance of this method, Dewey also has in mind the social responsibility of the school to provide children with realistic

---

* From John Dewey, *The School and Society* (Chicago, University of Chicago Press, 1943) (1899), Rev. ed., pp. 6-29. Reprinted by permission of the University of Chicago Press © 1900, 1943.

programs, enabling them to live fruitful lives in the new industrial society then emerging.

A striking note of contemporaneity appears in the opening paragraph. Dewey acknowledges how strong a concern exists for individual children on the part of parents. But he warns that this concern when exercised on behalf of our own children alone is apt to misfire, for it is often narrow in goal and unrealistic about the difficulties confronting those children whose parents are not as motivated. Dewey tells us that we must widen our outlook, for "what the best and wisest parent wants for his own child, that must the community want for all of its children. Any other ideal for our schools is narrow and unlovely; acted upon, it destroys our democracy."

We are apt to look at the school from an individualistic standpoint, as something between teacher and pupil, or between teacher and parent. That which interests us most is naturally the progress made by the individual child of our acquaintance, his normal physical development, his advance in ability to read, write, and figure, his growth in the knowledge of geography and history, improvement in manners, habits of promptness, order, and industry—it is from such standards as these that we judge the work of the school. And rightly so. Yet the range of the outlook needs to be enlarged. What the best and wisest parent wants for his own child, that must the community want for all of its children. Any other ideal for our schools is narrow and unlovely; acted upon, it destroys our democracy. All that society has accomplished for itself is put, through the agency of the school, at the disposal of its future members. All its better thoughts of itself it hopes to realize through the new possibilities thus opened to its future self. Here individualism and socialism are at one. Only by being true to the full growth of all the individuals who make it up, can society by any chance be true to itself. And in the self-direction thus given, nothing counts as much as the school, for, as Horace Mann said, "Where anything is growing, one former is worth a thousand re-formers."

Whenever we have in mind the discussion of a new movement in education, it is especially necessary to take the broader, or social, view. Otherwise, changes in the school institution and tradition will be looked at as the arbitrary inventions of particular teachers, at the worst transitory fads, and at the best merely improvements in certain details—and this is the plane upon which it is too customary to consider school changes. It is as rational to conceive of the locomotive or the telegraph as personal devices. The modification going on in the method and curriculum of education is as much a product of the changed social situation, and as much an effort to meet the needs of the new society that is forming, as are changes in modes of industry and commerce.

It is to this, then, that I especially ask your attention: the effort to conceive what roughly may be termed the "New Education" in the light of larger changes in society. Can we connect this "New Education" with the general march of events? If we can, it will lose its isolated character; it will cease to be an affair which proceeds only from the over-ingenious minds of pedagogues dealing with particular pupils. It will appear as part and parcel of the whole social evolution, and, in its more general features at least, as inevitable. Let us then ask after the main aspects of the social movement; and afterward turn to the school to find what witness it gives of effort to put itself in line. And since it is quite impossible to cover the whole ground, I shall for the most part confine myself in this chapter to one typical thing in the modern school movement—that which passes under the name of manual training —hoping, if the relation of that to changed social conditions appears, we shall be ready to concede the point as well regarding other educational innovations.

I make no apology for not dwelling at length upon the social changes in question. Those I shall mention are writ so large that he who runs may read. The change that comes first to mind, the one that overshadows and even controls all others, is the industrial one—the application of science resulting in the great inventions that have utilized the forces of nature on a vast and inexpensive scale: the growth of a world-wide market as the object of production, of vast manufacturing centers to supply this market, of cheap and rapid means of communication and distribution between all its parts. Even as to its feebler beginnings, this change is not much more than a century old; in many of its most important aspects it falls within the short span of those now living. One can hardly believe there has been a revolution in all history so rapid, so extensive, so complete. Through it the face of the earth is making over, even as to its physical forms; political boundaries are wiped out and moved about, as if they were indeed only lines on a paper map; population is hurriedly gathered into cities from the ends of the earth; habits of living are altered with startling abruptness and thoroughness; the search for the truths of nature is infinitely stimulated and facilitated, and their application to life made not only practicable, but commercially necessary. Even our moral and religious ideas and interests, the most conservative because the deepest-lying things in our nature, are profoundly affected. That this revolution should not affect education in some other than a formal and superficial fashion is inconceivable.

Back of the factory system lies the household and neighborhood system. Those of us who are here today need go back only one, two, or at most three generations, to find a time when the household was practically the center in which were carried on, or about which were clustered, all the typical forms of industrial occupation. The clothing worn was for the most part made in the house; the members of the household were usually familiar also with the shearing of the sheep, the carding and spinning of the wool, and the plying of the loom. Instead of pressing a button and flooding the house with electric light, the whole process of getting illumination was followed in its toilsome length from the killing of the animal and the trying of fat to the making of wicks and dipping of candles. The supply of flour, of lumber, of foods, of building materials, of household furniture, even of metal ware, of nails, hinges, hammers, etc., was produced in the immediate neighborhood, in shops which were constantly open to inspection and often centers of neighborhood congregation. The entire industrial process stood revealed, from the production on the farm of the raw materials till the finished article was actually put to use. Not only this, but practically every member of the household had his own share in the work. The children, as they gained in strength and capacity, were gradually initiated into the mysteries of the several processes. It was a matter of immediate and personal concern, even to the point of actual participation.

We cannot overlook the factors of discipline and of character-building involved in this kind of life: training in habits of order and of industry, and in the idea of responsibility, of obligation to do something, to produce something, in the world. There was always something which really needed to be done, and a real necessity that each member of the household should do his own part faithfully and in co-operation with others. Personalities which became effective in action were bred and tested in the medium of action. Again, we cannot overlook the importance for educational purposes of the close and intimate acquaintance got with nature at first hand, with real things and materials, with the actual processes of their manipulation, and the knowledge of their social necessities and uses. In all this there was continual training of observation, of ingenuity, constructive imagination, of logical thought, and of the sense of reality acquired through first-hand contact with actualities. The educative forces of the domestic spinning and weaving, of the sawmill, the gristmill, the cooper shop, and the blacksmith forge, were continuously operative.

No number of object-lessons, got up as object-lessons for the sake of giving information, can afford even the shadow of a substitute for acquaintance with the plants and animals of the farm and garden acquired through actual living among them and caring for them. No training of sense-organs in school, introduced for the sake of training, can begin to compete with the alertness and fulness of sense-life that comes through daily intimacy and interest in familiar occupations. Verbal memory can be trained in committing tasks, a certain discipline of the reasoning powers can be acquired through lessons in science and mathematics; but, after all, this is somewhat remote and shadowy compared with the training of attention and of judgment that is acquired in having to do things with a real motive behind and a real outcome ahead. At present, concentration of industry and division of labor have practically eliminated household and neighborhood occupations—at least for educational purposes. But it is useless to bemoan the departure of the good old days of children's modesty, reverence, and implicit obedience, if we expect merely by bemoaning and by exhortation to bring them back. It is radical conditions which have changed, and only an equally radical change in education suffices. We must recognize our compensations—the increase in toleration, in breadth of social judgment, the larger acquaintance with human nature, the sharpened alertness in reading signs of character and interpreting social situations, greater accuracy of adaptation to differing personalities, contact with greater commercial activities. These considerations mean much to the city-bred child of today. Yet there is a real problem: how shall we retain these advantages, and yet introduce into the school something representing the other side of life—occupations which exact personal responsibilities and which train the child in relation to the physical realities of life?

When we turn to the school, we find that one of the most striking tendencies at present is toward the introduction of so-called manual training, shopwork, and the household arts—sewing and cooking.

This has not been done "on purpose," with a full consciousness that the school must now supply that factor of training formerly taken care of in the home, but rather by instinct, by experimenting and finding that such work takes a vital hold of pupils and gives them something which was not to be got in any other way. Consciousness of its real import is still so weak that the work is often done in a half-hearted, confused, and unrelated way. The reasons assigned to justify it are painfully inadequate or sometimes even positively wrong.

If we were to cross-examine even those who are most favorably disposed to the introduction of this work into our school system, we should, I imagine, generally find the main reasons to be that such work engages the full spontaneous interest and attention of the children. It keeps them alert and active, instead of passive and receptive; it makes them more useful, more capable, and hence more inclined to be helpful at home; it prepares them to some extent for the practical duties of later life—the girls to be more efficient house managers, if not actually cooks and seamstresses; the boys (were our educational system only adequately rounded out into trade schools) for their future vocations. I do not underestimate the worth of these reasons. Of those indicated by the changed attitude of the children I shall indeed have something to say in the next chapter, when speaking directly of the relationship of the school to the child. But the point of view is, upon the whole, unnecessarily narrow. We must conceive of work in wood and metal, of weaving, sewing, and cooking, as methods of living and learning, not as distinct studies.

We must conceive of them in their social significance, as types of the processes by which society keeps itself going, as agencies for bringing home to the child some of the primal necessities of community life, and as ways in which these needs have been met by the growing insight and ingenuity of man; in short, as instrumentalities through which the school itself shall be made a genuine form of active community life, instead of a place set apart in which to learn lessons.

A society is a number of people held together because they are working along common lines, in a common spirit, and with reference to common aims. The common needs and aims demand a growing interchange of thought and growing unity of sympathetic feeling. The radical reason that the present school cannot organize itself as a natural social unit is because just this element of common and productive activity is absent. Upon the playground, in game and sport, social organization takes place spontaneously and inevitably. There is something to do, some activity to be carried on, requiring natural divisions of labor, selection of leaders and followers, mutual co-operation and emulation. In the school-room the motive and the cement of social organization are alike wanting. Upon the ethical side, the tragic weakness of the present school is that it endeavors to prepare future members of the social order in a medium in which the conditions of the social spirit are eminently wanting.

The difference that appears when occupations are made the articulating centers of school life is not easy to describe in words; it is a difference in motive, of spirit and atmosphere. As one enters a busy kitchen in which a group of children are actively engaged in the preparation of food, the psychological difference, the change from more or less passive and inert recipiency and restraint to one of buoyant outgoing energy, is so obvious as fairly to strike one in the face. Indeed, to those whose image of the school is rigidly set the change is sure to give a shock. But the change in the social attitude is equally marked. The mere absorbing of facts and truths is so exclusively individual an affair that it tends very naturally to pass into selfishness. There is no obvious social motive for the acquirement of mere learning, there is no clear social gain in success thereat. Indeed, almost the only measure for success is a competitive one, in the bad sense of that term—a comparison of results in the recitation or in the examination to see which child has succeeded in getting ahead of others in storing up, in accumulating, the maximum of information. So thoroughly is this the prevailing atmosphere that for one child to help another in his task has become a school crime. Where the school work consists in simply learning lessons, mutual assistance, instead of being the most natural form of co-operation and association, becomes a clandestine effort to relieve one's neighbor of his proper duties. Where active work is going on, all this is changed. Helping others, instead of being a form of charity which impoverishes the recipient, is simply an aid in setting free the powers and furthering the impulse of the one helped. A spirit of free communication, of interchange of ideas, suggestions, results, both successes and failures of previous experiences, becomes the dominating note of the recitation. So far as emulation enters in, it is in the comparison of individuals, not with regard to the quantity of information personally absorbed, but with reference to the quality of work done—the genuine community standard of value. In an informal but all the more pervasive way, the school life organizes itself on a social basis.

Within this organization is found the principle of school discipline or order. Of course, order is simply a thing which is relative to an end. If you have the end in view of forty or fifty children learning certain set lessons, to be recited to a teacher, your discipline must be devoted to securing that result. But if the end in view is the development of a spirit of social co-operation and community life, discipline must grow out of and be relative to such an aim. There is little of one sort of order where things are in process of construction; there is a certain disorder in any busy workshop; there is not silence; persons are not engaged in maintaining certain fixed physical postures; their arms are not folded; they are not holding their books thus and so. They are doing a variety of things, and there is the confusion, the bustle, that results from activity. But out of the occupation, out of doing things that are to produce results, and out of doing these in a social and co-operative way, there is born a discipline of its own kind and type. Our whole conception of school discipline changes when we get this point of view. In critical moments we all realize that the only discipline that stands by us, the only training that becomes intuition, is that got through life itself. That we learn from experience, and from books or the sayings of others *only* as they are related to experience, are not mere phrases. But the school has been so set apart, so isolated from the ordinary conditions and motives of life, that the place where children are sent for discipline is the one place in the world where it is most difficult to get experience—the mother of all discipline worth the name. It is only when a narrow and fixed image of traditional school discipline dominates that one is in any danger of overlooking that deeper and infinitely wider discipline that comes from having a part to do in constructive work, in contributing to a result which, social in spirit, is none the less obvious and tangible in form—and hence in a form with reference to which responsibility may be exacted and accurate judgment passed.

The great thing to keep in mind, then, regarding the introduction into the school of various forms of active occupation, is that through them the entire spirit of the school is renewed. It has a chance to affiliate itself with life, to become the child's habitat, where he learns through directed living, instead of being only a place to learn lessons having an abstract and remote reference to some possible living to be done in the future. It gets a chance to be a miniature community, an embryonic society. This is the fundamental fact, and from this arise continuous and orderly streams of instruction. Under the industrial régime described, the child, after all, shared in the work, not for the sake of the sharing, but for the sake of the product. The educational results secured were real, yet incidental and dependent. But in the school the typical occupations followed are freed from all economic stress. The aim is not the economic value of the products, but the development of social power and insight. It is this liberation from narrow utilities, this openness to the possibilities of the human spirit, that makes these practical activities in the school allies of art and centers of science and history.

The unity of all the sciences is found in geography. The significance of geography is that it presents the earth as the enduring home of the occupations of man. The world without its relationship to human activity is less than a world. Human industry and achievement, apart from their roots in the earth, are not even a sentiment, hardly a name. The earth is the final source of all man's food. It is his continual shelter and protection, the raw material of all his activities, and the home to whose humanizing and idealizing all his achievement returns. It is the great field, the great mine, the great source of the energies of heat, light, and electricity; the great scene of ocean, stream, mountain, and plain, of which all our agriculture and mining and lumbering, all our manufacturing and distributing agencies, are but the partial elements and factors. It is through occupations determined by this environment that mankind has made its historical and political progress. It is through these occupations that the intellectual and emotional interpretation of nature has been developed. It is through what we do in and with the world that we read its meaning and measure its value.

In educational terms, this means that these occupations in the school shall not be mere practical devices or modes of routine employment, the gaining of better technical skill as cooks, seamstresses, or carpenters, but active centers of scientific insight into natural materials and processes, points of departure whence children shall be led out into a realization of the historic development of man. The actual significance of this can be told better through one illustration taken from actual school work than by general discourse.

There is nothing which strikes more oddly upon the average intelligent visitor than to see boys as well as girls of ten, twelve, and thirteen years of age engaged in sewing and weaving. If we look at this from the standpoint of preparation of the boys for sewing on buttons and making patches, we get a narrow and utilitarian conception—a basis that hardly justifies giving prominence to this sort of work in the school. But if we look at it from another side, we find that this work gives the point of departure from which the child can trace and follow the progress of mankind in history, getting an insight also into the materials used and the mechanical principles involved. In connection with these occupations the historic development of man is recapitulated. For example, the children are first given the raw material—the flax, the cotton plant, the wool as it comes from the back of the sheep (if we could take them to the place where the sheep are sheared, so much the better). Then a study is made of these materials from the standpoint of their adaptation to the uses to which they may be put. For instance, a comparison of the cotton fiber with wool fiber is made. I did not know, until the children told me, that the reason for the late development of the cotton industry as compared with the woolen is that the cotton fiber is so very difficult to free by hand from the seeds. The children in one group worked thirty minutes freeing cotton fibers from the boll and seeds, and succeeded in getting out less than one ounce. They could easily believe that one person could gin only one pound a day by hand, and could understand why their ancestors wore woolen instead of cotton clothing. Among other things discovered as affecting their relative utilities was the shortness of the cotton fiber as compared with that of wool, the former averaging, say, one-third of an inch in length, while the latter run to three inches in length; also that the fibers of cotton are smooth and do not cling together, while the wool has a certain roughness which makes the fibers stick, thus assisting the spinning. The children worked this out for themselves with the actual material, aided by questions and suggestions from the teacher.

They then followed the processes necessary for working the fibers up into cloth. They reinvented the first frame for carding the wool—a couple of boards with sharp pins in them for scratching it out. They redevised the simplest process for spinning the wool—a pierced stone or some other weight through which the wool is passed, and which as it is twirled draws out the fiber; next the top, which was spun on the floor, while the children kept the wool in their hands until it was gradually drawn out and wound upon it. Then the children are introduced to the invention next in historic order, working it out experimentally, thus seeing its necessity, and tracing its effects, not only upon that particular industry, but upon modes of social life—in this way passing in review the entire process up to the present complete loom, and all that goes with the application of science in the use of our present available powers. I need not speak of the science involved in this—the study of the fibers, of geographical features, the conditions under which raw materials are grown, the great centers of manufacture and distribution, the physics involved in the machinery of production; nor, again, of the historical side—the influence which these inventions have had upon humanity. You can concentrate the history of all mankind into the evolution of the flax, cotton, and wool fibers into clothing. I do not mean that this is the only, or the best, center. But it is true that certain very real and important avenues to the consideration of the history of the race are thus opened—that the mind is introduced to much more fundamental and controlling influences than appear in the political and chronological records that usually pass for history.

Now, what is true of this one instance of fibers used in fabrics (and, of course, I have only spoken of one or two elementary phases of that) is true in its measure of every material used in every occupation, and of the processes employed. The occupation supplies the child with a genuine motive; it gives him experience at first hand; it brings him into contact with realities. It does all this, but in addition it is liberalized throughout by translation into its historic and social values and scientific equivalencies. With the growth of the child's mind in power and knowledge it ceases to be a pleasant occupation merely and becomes more and more a medium, an instrument, an organ of understanding—and is thereby transformed.

This, in turn, has its bearing upon the teaching of science. Under present conditions, all activity, to be successful, has to be directed somewhere and somehow by the scientific expert—it is a case of applied science. This connection should determine its place in education. It is not only that the occupations, the so-called manual or industrial work in the school, give the opportunity for the introduction of science which illuminates them, which makes them material, freighted with meaning, instead of being mere devices of hand and eye; but that the scientific insight thus gained becomes an indispensable instrument of free and active participation in modern social life. Plato somewhere speaks of the slave as one who in his actions does not express his own ideas, but those of some other man. It is our social problem now, even more urgent than in the time of Plato, that method, purpose, understanding, shall exist in the consciousness of the one who does the work, that his activity shall have meaning to himself.

When occupations in the school are conceived in this broad and generous way, I can only stand lost in wonder at the objections so often heard, that such occupations are out of place in the school because they are materialistic, utilitarian, or even menial in their tendency. It sometimes seems to me that those who make these objections must live in quite another world. The world in which most of us live is a world in which everyone has a calling and occupation, something to do. Some are managers and others are subordinates. But the great thing for one as for the other is that each shall have had the education which enables him to see within his daily work all there is in it of large and human significance. How many of the employed are today mere appendages to the machines which they operate! This may be due in part to the machine itself or the régime which lays so much stress upon the products of the machine; but it is certainly due in large part to the fact that the worker has had no opportunity to develop his imagination and his sympathetic insight as to the social and scientific values found in his work. At present, the impulses which lie at the basis of the industrial system are either practically neglected or positively distorted during the school period. Until the instincts of construction and production are systematically laid hold of in the years of childhood and youth, until they are trained in social directions, enriched by historical interpretation, controlled and illuminated by scientific methods, we certainly are in no position even to locate the source of our economic evils, much less to deal with them effectively.

If we go back a few centuries, we find a practical monopoly of learning. The term *possession* of learning is, indeed, a happy one. Learning was a class matter. This was a necessary result of social conditions. There were not in existence any means by which the multitude could possibly have access to intellectual resources. These were stored up and hidden away in manuscripts. Of these there were at best only a few, and it required long and toilsome preparation to be able to do anything with them. A high-priesthood of learning, which guarded the treasury of truth and which doled it out to the masses under severe restrictions, was the inevitable expression of these conditions. But, as a direct result of the industrial revolution of which we have been speaking, this has been changed. Printing was invented; it was made commercial. Books, magazines, papers were multiplied and cheapened. As a result of the locomotive and telegraph, frequent, rapid, and cheap intercommunication by mails and electricity was called into being. Travel has been rendered easy; freedom of movement, with its accompanying exchange of ideas, indefinitely facilitated. The result has been an intellectual revolution. Learning has been put into circulation. While there still is, and probably always will be, a particular class having the special business of inquiry in hand, a distinctively learned class is henceforth out of the question. It is an anachronism. Knowledge is no longer an immobile solid; it has been liquefied. It is actively moving in all the currents of society itself.

It is easy to see that this revolution, as regards the materials of knowledge, carries with it a marked change in the attitude of the individual. Stimuli of an intellectual sort pour in upon us in all kinds of ways. The merely intellectual life, the life of scholarship and of learning, thus gets a very altered value. Academic and scholastic, instead of being titles of honor, are becoming terms of reproach.

But all this means a necessary change in the attitude of the school, one of which we are as yet far from realizing the full force. Our school methods, and to a very considerable extent our curriculum, are inherited from the period when learning and command of certain symbols, affording as they did the only access to learning, were all-important. The ideals of this period are still largely in control, even where the outward methods and studies have been changed. We sometimes hear the introduction of manual training, art, and science into the elementary, and even the secondary, schools deprecated on the ground that they tend toward the production of specialists—that they detract from our present scheme of generous, liberal culture. The point of this objection would be ludicrous if it were not often so effective as to make it tragic. It is our present education which is highly specialized, one-sided, and narrow. It is an education dominated almost entirely by the mediaeval conception of learning. It is something which appeals for the most part simply to the intellectual aspect of our natures, our desire to learn, to accumulate information, and to get control of the symbols of learning; not to our impulses and tendencies to make, to do, to create, to produce, whether in the form of utility or of art. The very fact that manual training, art, and science are objected to as technical, as tending toward mere specialism, is of itself as good testimony as could be offered to the specialized aim which controls current education. Unless education had been virtually identified with the exclusively intellectual pursuits, with learning as such, all these materials and methods would be welcome, would be greeted with the utmost hospitality.

While training for the profession of learning is regarded as the type of culture, or a liberal education, the training of a mechanic, a musician, a lawyer, a doctor, a farmer, a merchant, or a railroad manager is regarded as purely technical and professional. The result is that which we see about us everywhere—the division into "cultured" people and "workers," the separation of theory and practice. Hardly 1 per cent of the entire school population ever attains to what we call higher education; only 5 per cent to the grade of our high school; while much more than half leave on or before the completion of the fifth year of the elementary grade. The simple facts of the case are that in the great majority of human beings the distinctively intellectual interest is not dominant. They have the so-called practical impulse and disposition. In many of those in whom by nature intellectual interest is strong, social conditions prevent its adequate realization. Consequently by far the larger number of pupils leave school as soon as they have acquired the rudiments of learning, as soon as they have enough of the symbols of reading, writing, and calculating to be of practical use to them in getting a living. While our educational leaders are talking of culture, the development of personality, etc., as the end and aim of education, the great majority of those who pass under the tuition of the school regard it only as a narrowly practical tool with which to get bread and butter enough to eke out a restricted life. If we were to conceive our educational end and aim in a less exclusive way, if we were to introduce into educational processes the activities which appeal to those whose dominant interest is to do and to make, we should find the hold of the school upon its members to be more vital, more prolonged, containing more of culture.

But why should I make this labored presentation? The obvious fact is that our social life has undergone a thorough and radical change. If our education is to have any meaning for life, it must pass through an equally complete transformation. This transformation is not something to appear suddenly, to be executed in a day by conscious purpose. It is already in progress. Those modifications of our school system which often appear (even to those most actively concerned with them, to say nothing of their spectators) to be mere changes of detail, mere improvement within the school mechanism, are in reality signs and evidences of evolution. The introduction of active occupations, of nature-study, of elementary science, of art, of history; the relegation of the merely symbolic and formal to a secondary position; the change in the moral school atmosphere, in the relation of pupils and teachers—of discipline; the introduction of more active, expressive, and self-directing factors—all these are not mere accidents, they are necessities of the larger social evolution. It remains but to organize all these factors, to appreciate them in their fulness of meaning, and to put the ideas and ideals involved into complete, uncompromising possession of our school system. To do this means to make each one of our schools an embryonic community life, active with types of occupations that reflect the life of the larger society and permeated throughout with the spirit of art, history, and science. When the school introduces and trains each child of society into membership within such a little community, saturating him with the spirit of service, and providing him with the instruments of effective self-direction, we shall have the deepest and best guaranty of a larger society which is worthy, lovely, and harmonious.

28. The Child and the Curriculum*

One decade before the work of Maria Montessori and several before that of Martin Buber, John Dewey wrote about the experience of the child in a classroom setting and in relationship to a teacher. As always, Dewey strives to structure a

* From John Dewey, *The Child and the Curriculum* (Chicago, University of Chicago Press, 1902), 40 pp.

situation optimum for human living, while not being seduced by shortcuts or the latest nostrum. Dewey is well aware that much subject matter is often difficult to teach and to learn. And he admits that "unguided spontaneity" will not result in a satisfactory educational experience.

He is equally opposed, however, to the belief that a curriculum teaches itself or is learned because of its ostensible but unrevealed importance. Nor does he believe that genuine learning takes place under duress. The path to a solution, Dewey believes, is in the area of the nature of a child. If we were to have a deeper insight to the actual ways that children learn and couple that with a knowledge of both their needs and potentialities, the curriculum would then take on a significance heretofore closed off from the child.

Contrary to the oft-held view, Dewey's position is not that of a child-centered classroom, if that means learning is subordinate to the whim of the child. He does hold, however, that it is the child who learns, and any efforts to teach a curriculum in which the qualities of the lives of children and the differences among them are not grasped is doomed to failure.

Profound differences in theory are never gratuitous or invented. They grow out of conflicting elements in a genuine problem—a problem which is genuine just because the elements, taken as they stand, are conflicting. Any significant problem involves conditions that for the moment contradict each other. Solution comes only by getting away from the meaning of terms that is already fixed upon and coming to see the conditions from another point of view, and hence in a fresh light. But this reconstruction means travail of thought. Easier than thinking with surrender of already formed ideas and detachment from facts already learned is just to stick by what is already said, looking about for something with which to buttress it against attack.

Thus sects arise: schools of opinion. Each selects that set of conditions that appeals to it; and then erects them into a complete and independent truth, instead of treating them as a factor in a problem, needing adjustment.

The fundamental factors in the educative process are an immature, undeveloped being; and certain social aims, meanings, values incarnate in the matured experience of the adult. The educative process is the due interaction of these forces. Such a conception of each in relation to the other as facilitates completest and freest interaction is the essence of educational theory.

But here comes the effort of thought. It is easier to see the conditions in their separateness, to insist upon one at the expense of the other, to make antagonists of them, than to discover a reality to which each belongs. The easy thing is to seize upon something in the nature of the child, or upon something in the developed consciousness of the adult, and insist upon *that* as the key to the whole problem. When this happens a really serious practical problem—that of interaction—is transformed into an unreal, and hence insoluble, theoretic problem. Instead of seeing the educative steadily and as a whole, we see conflicting terms. We get the case of the child *vs.* the curriculum; of the individual nature *vs.* social culture. Below all other divisions in pedagogic opinion lies this opposition.

The child lives in a somewhat narrow world of personal contacts. Things hardly come within his experience unless they touch, intimately and obviously, his own well-being, or that of his family and friends. His world is a world of persons with their personal interests, rather than a realm of facts and laws. Not truth, in the sense of conformity to external fact, but affection and sympathy, is its keynote. As against this, the course of study met in the school presents material stretching back indefinitely in time, and extending outward indefinitely into space. The child is taken out of his familiar physical environment, hardly more than a square mile or so in area, into the wide world—yes, and even to the bounds of the solar system. His little span of personal memory and tradition is overlaid with the long centuries of the history of all peoples.

Again, the child's life is an integral, a total one. He passes quickly and readily from one topic to another, as from one spot to another, but is not conscious of transition or break. There is no conscious isolation, hardly conscious distinction. The things that occupy him are held together by the unity of the personal and social interests which his life carries along. Whatever is uppermost in his mind constitutes to him, for the time being, the whole universe. That universe is fluid and fluent; its contents dissolve and re-form with amazing rapidity. But, after all, it is the child's own world. It has the unity and completeness of his own life. He goes to school, and various studies divide and fractionize the world for him. Georgraphy selects, it abstracts and analyzes one set of facts, and from one particular point of view. Arithmetic is another division, grammar another department, and so on indefinitely.

Again, in school each of these subjects is classified. Facts are torn away from their original place in experience and rearranged with reference to some general principle. Classification is not a matter of child experience; things do not come to the individual pigeonholed. The vital ties of affection, the connecting bonds of activity, hold together the variety of his personal experiences. The adult mind is so familiar with the notion of logically ordered facts that it does not recognize—it cannot realize—the amount of separating and reformulating which the facts of direct experience have to undergo before they can appear as a "study," or branch of learning. A principle, for the intellect, has had to be distinguished and defined; facts have had to be interpreted in relation to this principle, not as they are in themselves. They have had to be regathered about a new center which is wholly abstract and ideal. All this means a development of a special intellectual interest. It means ability to view facts impartially and objectively; that is, without reference to their place and meaning in one's own experience. It means capacity to analyze and to synthesize. It means highly matured intellectual habits and the command of a definite technique and apparatus of scientific inquiry. The studies as classified are the product, in a word, of the science of the ages, not of the experience of the child.

These apparent deviations and differences between child and curriculum might be almost indefinitely widened. But we have here sufficiently fundamental divergences: first, the narrow but personal world of the child against the impersonal but infinitely extended world of space and time; second, the unity, the single wholeheartedness of the child's life, and the specializations and divisions of the curriculum; third, an abstract principle of logical classification and arrangement, and the practical and emotional bonds of child life.

From these elements of conflict grow up different educational sects. One school fixes its attention upon the importance of the subject-matter of the curriculum as compared with the contents of the child's own experience. It is as if they said: Is life petty, narrow, and crude? Then studies reveal the great, wide universe with all its fulness and complexity of meaning. Is the life of the child egoistic, self-centered, impulsive? Then in these studies is found an objective universe of truth, law, and order. Is his experience confused, vague, uncertain, at the mercy of the moment's caprice and circumstance? Then studies introduce a world arranged on the basis of eternal and general truth; a world where all is measured and defined. Hence the moral: ignore and minimize the child's individual peculiarities, whims, and experiences. They are what we need to get away from. They are to be obscured or eliminated. As educators our work is precisely to substitute for these superficial and casual affairs stable and well-ordered realities; and these are found in studies and lessons.

Subdivide each topic into studies; each study into lessons; each lesson into specific facts and formulae. Let the child proceed step by step to master each one of these separate parts, and at last he will have covered the entire ground. The road which looks so long when viewed in its entirety is easily traveled, considered as a series of particular steps. Thus emphasis is put upon the logical subdivisions and consecutions of the subject-matter. Problems of instruction are problems of procuring texts giving logical parts and sequences, and of presenting these portions in class in a similar definite and graded way. Subject-matter furnishes the end, and it determines method. The child is simply the immature being who is to be matured; he is the superficial being who is to be deepened; his is narrow experience which is to be widened. It is his to receive, to accept. His part is fulfilled when he is ductile and docile.

Not so, says the other sect. The child is the starting-point, the center, and the end. His development, his growth, is the ideal. It alone furnishes the standard. To the growth of the child all studies are subservient; they are instruments valued as they serve the needs of growth. Personality, character, is more than subject-matter. Not knowledge or information, but self-realization, is the goal. To possess all the world of knowledge and lose one's own self is as awful a fate in education as in religion. Moreover, subject-matter never can be got into the child from without. Learning is active. It involves reaching out of the mind. It involves organic assimilation starting from within. Literally, we must take our stand with the child and our departure from him. It is he and not the subject-matter which determines both quality and quantity of learning.

The only significant method is the method of the mind as it reaches out and assimilates. Subject-matter is but spiritual food, possible nutritive material. It cannot digest itself; it cannot of its own accord turn into bone and muscle and blood. The source of whatever is dead, mechanical, and formal in schools is found precisely in the subordination of the life and experience of the child to the curriculum. It is because of this that "study" has become a synonym for what is irksome, and a lesson identical with a task.

This fundamental opposition of child and curriculum set up by these two modes of doctrine can be duplicated in a series of other terms. "Discipline" is the watchword of those who magnify the course of study; "interest" that of those who blazon "The Child" upon their banner. The standpoint of the former is logical; that of the latter psychological. The first emphasizes the necessity of adequate training and scholarship on the part of the teacher; the latter that of need of sympathy with the child, and knowledge of his natural instincts. "Guidance and control" are the catchwords of one school; "freedom and initiative" of the other. Law is asserted here; spontaneity proclaimed there. The old, the conservation of what has been achieved in the pain and toil of the ages, is dear to the one; the new, change, progress, wins the affection of the other. Inertness and routine, chaos and anarchism, are accusations bandied back and forth. Neglect of the sacred authority of duty is charged by one side, only to be met by counter-charges of suppression of individuality through tyrannical despotism.

Such oppositions are rarely carried to their logical conclusion. Common-sense recoils at the extreme character of these results. They are left to theorists, while common-sense vibrates back and forward in a maze of inconsistent compromise. The need of getting theory and practical common-sense into closer connection suggests a return to our original thesis: that we have here conditions which are necessarily related to each other in the educative process, since this is precisely one of interaction and adjustment.

What, then, is the problem? It is just to get rid of the prejudicial notion that there is some gap in kind (as distinct from degree) between the child's experience and the various forms of subject-matter that make up the course of study. From the side of the child, it is a question of seeing how his experience already contains within itself elements—facts and truths—of just the same sort as those entering into the formulated study; and, what is of more importance, of how it contains within itself the attitudes, the motives, and the interests which have operated in developing and organizing the subject-matter to the plane which it now occupies. From the side of the studies, it is a question of interpreting them as outgrowths of forces operating in the child's life, and of discovering the steps that intervene between the child's present experience and their richer maturity.

Abandon the notion of subject-matter as something fixed and ready-made in itself, outside the child's experience; cease thinking of the child's experience as also something hard and fast; see it as something fluent, embryonic, vital; and we realize that the child and the curriculum are simply two limits which define a single process. Just as two points define a straight line, so the present standpoint of the child and the facts and truths of studies define instruction. It is continuous reconstruction, moving from the child's present experience out into that represented by the organized bodies of truth that we call studies.

On the face of it, the various studies, arithmetic, geography, language, botany, etc., are themselves experience—they are that of the race. They embody the cumulative outcome of the efforts, the strivings, and the successes of the human generation after generation. They present this, not as a mere accumulation, not as a miscellaneous heap of separate bits of experience, but in some organized and systematized way—that is, as reflectively formulated.

Hence, the facts and truths that enter into the child's present experience, and those contained in the subject-matter of studies, are the initial and final terms of one reality. To oppose one to the other is to oppose the infancy and maturity of the same growing life; it is to set the moving tendency and the final result of the same process over against each other; it is to hold that the nature and the destiny of the child war with each other.

If such be the case, the problem of the relation of the child and the curriculum presents itself in this guise: Of what use, educationally speaking, is it to be able to see the end in the beginning? How does it assist us in dealing with the early stages of growth to be able to anticipate its later phases? The studies, as we have agreed, represent the possibilities of development inherent in the child's immediate crude experience. But, after all, they are not parts of that present and immediate life. Why, then, or how, make account of them?

Asking such a question suggests its own answer. To see the outcome is to know in what direction the present experience is moving, provided it move normally and soundly. The far-away point, which is of no significance to us simply as far away, becomes of huge importance the moment we take it as defining a present direction of movement. Taken in this way it is no remote and distant result to be achieved, but a guiding method in dealing with the present. The systematized and defined experience of the adult mind, in other words, is of value to us in interpreting the child's life as it immediately shows itself, and in passing on to guidance or direction.

Let us look for a moment at these two ideas: interpretation and guidance. The child's present experience is in no way self-explanatory. It is not final, but transitional. It is nothing complete in itself, but just a sign or index of certain growth-tendencies. As long as we confine our gaze to what the child here and now puts forth, we are confused and misled. We cannot read its meaning. Extreme depreciations of the child morally and intellectually, and sentimental idealizations of him, have their root in a common fallacy. Both spring from taking stages of a growth or movement as something cut off and fixed. The first fails to see the promise contained in feelings and deeds which, taken by themselves, are uncompromising and repellent; the second fails to see that even the most pleasing and beautiful exhibitions are but signs, and that they begin to spoil and rot the moment they are treated as achievements.

What we need is something which will enable us to interpret, to appraise, the elements in the child's present puttings forth and fallings away, his exhibitions of power and weakness, in the light of some larger growth-process in which they have their place. Only in this way can we discriminate. If we isolate the child's present inclinations, purposes, and experiences from the place they occupy and the part they have to perform in a developing experience, all stand upon the same level; all alike are equally good and equally bad. But in the movement of life different elements stand upon different planes of value. Some of the child's deeds are symptoms of a waning tendency; they are survivals in functioning of an organ which has done its part and is passing out of vital use. To give positive attention to such qualities is to arrest development upon a lower level. It is systematically to maintain a rudimentary phase of growth. Other activities are signs of a culminating power and interest; to them applies the maxim of striking while the iron is hot. As regards them, it is perhaps a matter of now or never. Selected, utilized, emphasized, they may mark a turning-point for good in the child's whole career; neglected, an opportunity goes, never to be recalled. Other acts and feelings are prophetic; they represent the dawning of flickering light that will shine steadily only in the far future. As regards them there is little at present to do but give them fair and full chance, waiting for the future for definite direction.

Just as, upon the whole, it was the weakness of the "old education" that it made invidious comparisons between the immaturity of the child and the maturity of the adult, regarding the former as something to be got away from as soon as possible and as much as possible; so it is the danger of the "new education" that it regard the child's present powers and interests as something finally significant in themselves. In truth, his learnings and achievements are fluid and moving. They change from day to day and from hour to hour.

It will do harm if child-study leave in the popular mind the impression that a child of a given age has a positive equipment of purposes and interests to be cultivated just as they stand. Interests in reality are but attitudes toward possible experiences; they are not achievements; their worth is in the leverage they afford, not in the accomplishment they represent. To take the phenomena presented at a given age as in any way self-explanatory or self-contained is inevitably to result in indulgence and spoiling. Any power, whether of child or adult, is indulged when it is taken on its given and present level in consciousness. Its genuine meaning is in the propulsion it affords toward a higher level. It is just something to do with. Appealing to the interest upon the present plane means excitation; it means playing with a power so as continually to stir it up without directing it toward definite achievement. Continuous initiation, continuous starting of activities that do not arrive, is, for all practical purposes, as bad as the continual repression of initiative in conformity with supposed interests of some more perfect thought or will. It is as if the child were forever tasting and never eating; always having his palate tickled upon the emotional side, but never getting the organic satisfaction that comes only with digestion of food and transformation of it into working power.

As against such a view, the subject-matter of science and history and art serves to reveal the real child to us. We do not know the meaning either of his tendencies or of his performances excepting as we take them as germinating seed, or opening bud, of some fruit to be borne. The whole world of visual nature is all too small an answer to the problem of the meaning of the child's instinct for light and form. The entire science of physics is none too much to interpret adequately to us what is involved in some simple demand of the child for explanation of some casual change that has attracted his attention. The art of Raphael or of Corot is none too much to enable us to value the impulses stirring in the child when he draws and daubs.

So much for the use of the subject-matter in interpretation. Its further employment in direction or guidance is but an expansion of the same thought. To interpret the fact is to see it in its vital movement, to see it in its relation to growth. But to view it as a part of a normal growth is to secure the basis for guiding it. Guidance is not external imposition. *It is freeing the life-process for its own most adequate fulfilment.* What was said about disregard of the child's present experience because of its remoteness from mature experience; and of the sentimental idealization of the child's naïve caprices and performances, may be repeated here with slightly altered phrase. There are those who see no alternative between forcing the child from without, or leaving him entirely alone. Seeing no alternative, some choose one mode, some another. Both fall into the same fundamental error. Both fail to see that development is a definite process, having its own law which can be fulfilled only when adequate and normal conditions are provided. Really to interpret the child's present crude impulses in counting, measuring, and arranging things in rhythmic series involves mathematical scholarship—a knowledge of the mathematical formulae and relations which have, in the history of the race, grown out of just such crude beginnings. To see the whole history of development which intervenes between these two terms is simply to see what step the child needs to take just here and now; to what use he needs to put his blind impulse in order that it may get clarity and gain force.

If, once more, the "old education" tended to ignore the dynamic quality, the developing force inherent in the child's present experience, and therefore to assume that direction and control were just matters of arbitrarily putting the child in a given path and compelling him to walk there, the "new education" is in danger of taking the idea of development in altogether too formal and empty a way. The child is expected to "develop" this or that fact or truth out of his own mind. He is told to think things out, or work things out for himself, without being supplied any of the environing conditions which are requisite to start and guide thought. Nothing can be developed from nothing; nothing but the crude can be developed out of the crude—and this is what surely happens when we throw the child back upon his achieved self as a finality, and invite him to spin new truths of nature or of conduct out of that. It is certainly as futile to expect a child to evolve a universe out of his own mere mind as it is for a philosopher to attempt that task. Development does not mean just getting something out of the mind. It is a development of experience and into experience that is really wanted. And this is impossible save as just that educative medium is provided which will enable the powers and interests that have been selected as valuable to function. They must operate, and how they operate will depend almost entirely upon the stimuli which surround them and the material upon which they exercise themselves. The problem of direction is thus the problem of selecting appropriate stimuli for instincts and impulses which it is desired to employ in the gaining of new experience. What new experiences are desirable, and thus what stimuli are needed, it is impossible to tell except as there is some comprehension of the development which is aimed at; except, in a word, as the adult knowledge is drawn upon as revealing the possible career open to the child.

It may be of use to distinguish and to relate to each other the logical and the psychological aspects of experience—the former standing for subject-matter in itself, the latter for it in relation to the child. A psychological statement of experience follows its actual growth; it is historic; it notes steps actually taken, the uncertain and tortuous, as well as the efficient and successful. The logical point of view, on the other hand, assumes that the development has reached a certain stage of fulfilment. It neglects the process and considers the outcome. It summarizes and arranges, and thus separates the achieved results from the actual steps by which they were forthcoming in the first instance. We may compare the difference between the logical and the psychological to the difference between the notes which an explorer makes in a new country, blazing a trail and finding his way along as best he may, and the finished map that is constructed after the country has been thoroughly explored. The two are mutually dependent. Without the more or less accidental and devious paths traced by the explorer there would be no facts which could be utilized in the making of the complete and related chart. But no one would get the benefit of the explorer's trip if it was not compared and checked up with similar wanderings undertaken by others; unless the new geographical facts learned, the streams crossed, the mountains climbed, etc., were viewed, not as mere incidents in the journey of the particular traveler, but (quite apart from the individual explorer's life) in relation to other similar facts already known. The map orders individual experiences, connecting them with one another irrespective of the local and temporal circumstances and accidents of their original discovery.

Of what use is this formulated statement of experience? Of what use is the map?

Well, we may first tell what the map is not. The map is not a substitute for a personal experience. The map does not take the place of an actual journey. The logically formulated material of a science or branch of learning, of a study, is no substitute for the having of individual experiences. The mathematical formula for a falling body does not take the place of personal contact and immediate individual experience with the falling thing. But the map, a summary, an arranged and orderly view of previous experiences, serves as a guide to future experience; it gives direction; it facilitates control; it economizes effort, preventing useless wandering, and pointing out the paths which lead most quickly and most certainly to a desired result. Through the map every new traveler may get for his own journey the benefits of the results of others' explorations without the waste of energy and loss of time involved in their wanderings—wanderings which he himself would be obliged to repeat were it not for just the assistance of the objective and generalized record of their performances. That which we call a science or study puts the net product of past experience in the form which makes it most available for the future. It represents a capitalization which may at once be turned to interest. It economizes the workings of the mind in every way. Memory is less taxed because the facts are grouped together about some common principle, instead of being connected solely with the varying incidents of their original discovery. Observation is assisted; we know what to look for and where to look. It is the difference between looking for a needle in a haystack, and searching for a given paper in a well-arranged cabinet. Reasoning is directed, because there is a certain general path or line laid out along which ideas naturally march, instead of moving from one chance association to another.

There is, then, nothing final about a logical rendering of experience. Its value is not contained in itself; its significance is that of standpoint, outlook, method. It intervenes between the more casual, tentative, and roundabout experiences of the past, and more controlled and orderly experiences of the future. It gives past experience in that net form which renders it most available and most significant, most fecund for future experience. The abstractions, generalizations, and classifications which it introduces all have prospective meaning.

The formulated result is then not to be opposed to the process of growth. The logical is not set over against the psychological. The surveyed and arranged result occupies a critical position in the process of growth. It marks a turning-point. It shows how we may get the benefit of past effort in controlling future endeavor. In the largest sense the logical standpoint is itself psychological; it has its meaning as a point in the development of experience, and its justification is in its functioning in the future growth which it insures.

Hence the need of reinstating into experience the subject-matter of the studies, or branches of learning. It must be restored to the experience from which it has been abstracted. It needs to be *psychologized*; turned over, translated into the immediate and individual experiencing within which it has its origin and significance.

Every study or subject thus has two aspects: one for the scientist as a scientist; the other for the teacher as a teacher. These two aspects are in no sense opposed or conflicting. But neither are they immediately identical. For the scientist, the subject-matter represents simply a given body of truth to be employed in locating new problems, instituting new researches, and carrying them through to a verified outcome. To him the subject-matter of the science is self-contained. He refers various portions of it to each other; he connects new facts with it. He is not, as a scientist, called upon to travel outside its particular bounds; if he does, it is only to get more facts of the same general sort. The problem of the teacher is a different one. As a teacher he is not concerned with adding new facts to the science he teaches; in propounding new hypotheses or in verifying them. He is concerned with the subject-matter of the science as *representing a given stage and phase of the development of experience*. His problem is that of inducing a vital and personal experiencing. Hence, what concerns him, as teacher, is the ways in which that subject may become a part of experience; what there is in the child's present that is usable with reference to it; how such elements are to be used; how his own knowledge of the subject-matter may assist in interpreting the child's needs and doings, and determine the medium in which the child should be placed in order that his growth may be properly directed. He is concerned, not with the subject-matter as such, but with the subject-matter as a related factor in a total and growing experience. Thus to see it is to psychologize it.

It is the failure to keep in mind the double aspect of subject-matter which causes the curriculum and child to be set over against each other as described in our early pages. The subject-matter, just as it is for the scientist, has no direct relationship to the child's present experience. It stands outside of it. The danger here is not a merely theoretical one. We are practically threatened on all sides. Textbook and teacher vie with each other in presenting to the child the subject-matter as it stands to the specialist. Such modification and revision as it undergoes are a mere elimination of certain scientific difficulties, and the general reduction to a lower intellectual level. The material is not translated into life-terms, but is directly offered as a substitute for, or an external annex to, the child's present life.

Three typical evils result: In the first place, the lack of any organic connection with what the child has already seen and felt and loved makes the material purely formal and symbolic. There is a sense in which it is impossible to value too highly the formal and the symbolic. The genuine form, the real symbol, serve as methods in the holding and discovery of truth. They are tools by which the individual pushes out most surely and widely into unexplored areas. They are means by which he brings to bear whatever of reality he has succeeded in gaining in past searchings. But this happens only when the symbol really symbolizes—when it stands for and sums up in shorthand actual experiences which the individual has already gone through. A symbol which is induced from without, which has not been led up to in preliminary activities, is, as we say, a *bare* or *mere* symbol; it is dead and barren. Now, any fact, whether of arithmetic, or geography, or grammar, which is not led up to and into out of something which has previously occupied a significant position in the child's life for its own sake, is forced into this position. It is not a reality, but just the sign of a reality which *might* be experienced if certain conditions were fulfilled.

But the abrupt presentation of the fact as something known by others, and requiring only to be studied and learned by the child, rules out such conditions of fulfilment. It condemns the fact to be a hieroglyph: it would mean something if one only had the key. The clue being lacking, it remains an idle curiosity, to fret and obstruct the mind, a dead weight to burden it.

The second evil in this external presentation is lack of motivation. There are not only no facts or truths which have been previously felt as such with which to appropriate and assimilate the new, but there is no craving, no need, no demand. When the subject-matter has been psychologized, that is, viewed as an outgrowth of present tendencies and activities, it is easy to locate in the present some obstacle, intellectual, practical, or ethical, which can be handled more adequately if the truth in question be mastered. This need supplies motive for the learning. An end which is the child's own carries him on to possess the means of its accomplishment. But when material is directly supplied in the form of a lesson to be learned as a lesson, the connecting links of need and aim are conspicuous for their absence. What we mean by the mechanical and dead in instruction is a result of this lack of motivation. The organic and vital mean interaction—they mean play of mental demand and material supply.

The third evil is that even the most scientific matter, arranged in most logical fashion, loses this quality, when presented in external, ready-made fashion, by the time it gets to the child. It has to undergo some modification in order to shut out some phases too hard to grasp, and to reduce some of the attendant difficulties. What happens? Those things which are most significant to the scientific man, and most valuable in the logic of actual inquiry and classification, drop out. The really thought-provoking character is obscured, and the organizing function disappears. Or, as we commonly say, the child's reasoning powers, the faculty of abstraction and generalization, are not adequately developed. So the subject-matter is evacuated of its logical value, and, though it is what it is only from the logical standpoint, is presented as stuff only for "memory." This is the contradiction: the child gets the advantage neither of the adult logical formulation, nor of his own native competencies of apprehension and response. Hence the logic of the child is hampered and mortified, and we are almost fortunate if he does not get actual non-science, flat and commonplace residua of what was gaining scientific vitality a generation or two ago—degenerate reminiscence of what someone else once formulated on the basis of the experience that some further person had, once upon a time, experienced.

The train of evils does not cease. It is all too common for opposed erroneous theories to play straight into each other's hands. Psychological
considerations may be slurred or shoved one side; they cannot be
crowded out. Put out of the door, they come back through the window.
Somehow and somewhere motive must be appealed to, connection must
be established between the mind and its material. There is no question
of getting along without this bond of connection; the only question is
whether it be such as grows out of the material itself in relation to the
mind, or be imported and hitched on from some outside source. If the
subject-matter of the lessons be such as to have an appropriate place
within the expanding consciousness of the child, if it grows into application in further achievements and receptivities, then no device or trick of
method has to be resorted to in order to enlist "interest." The psychologized *is* of interest—that is, it is placed in the whole of conscious
life so that it shares the worth of that life. But the externally presented
material, conceived and generated in standpoints and attitudes remote
from the child, and developed in motives alien to him, has no such place
of its own. Hence the recourse to adventitious leverage to push it in, to
factitious drill to drive it in, to artificial bribe to lure it in.

Three aspects of this recourse to outside ways for giving the subject-
matter some psychological meaning may be worth mentioning.
Familiarity breeds contempt, but it also breeds something like affection.
We get used to the chains we wear, and we miss them when removed.
'Tis an old story that through custom we finally embrace what at first
wore a hideous mien. Unpleasant, because meaningless, activities may
get agreeable if long enough persisted in. *It is possible for the mind to
develop interest in a routine or mechanical procedure if conditions are
continually supplied which demand that mode of operation and preclude any other sort.* I frequently hear dulling devices and empty exercises defended and extolled because "the children take such an 'interest'
in them." Yes, that is the worst of it; the mind, shut out from worthy
employ and missing the taste of adequate performance, comes down to
the level of that which is left to it to know and do, and perforce takes an
interest in a cabined and cramped experience. To find satisfaction in its
own exercise is the normal law of mind, and if large and meaningful
business for the mind be denied, it tries to content itself with the formal
movements that remain to it—and too often succeeds, save in those
cases of more intense activity which cannot accommodate themselves,
and that make up the unruly and *déclassé* of our school product. An
interest in the formal apprehension of symbols and in their memorized
reproduction becomes in many pupils a substitute for the original and

vital interest in reality; and all because, the subject-matter of the course of study being out of relation to the concrete mind of the individual, some substitute bond to hold it in some kind of working relation to the mind must be discovered and elaborated.

The second substitute for living motivation in the subject-matter is that of contrast-effects; the material of the lesson is rendered interesting, if not in itself, at least in contrast with some alternative experience. To learn the lesson is more interesting than to take a scolding, be held up to general ridicule, stay after school, receive degradingly low marks, or fail to be promoted. And very much of what goes by the name of "discipline," and prides itself upon opposing the doctrines of a soft pedagogy and upon upholding the banner of effort and duty, is nothing more or less than just this appeal to "interest" in its obverse aspect—to fear, to dislike of various kinds of physical, social, and personal pain. The subject-matter does not appeal; it cannot appeal; it lacks origin and bearing in a growing experience. So the appeal is to the thousand and one outside and irrelevant agencies which may serve to throw, by sheer rebuff and rebound, the mind back upon the material from which it is constantly wandering.

Human nature being what it is, however, it tends to seek its motivation in the agreeable rather than in the disagreeable, in direct pleasure rather than in alternative pain. And so has come up the modern theory and practice of the "interesting," in the false sense of that term. The material is still left; so far as its own characteristics are concerned, just material externally selected and formulated. It is still just so much geography and arithmetic and grammar study; not so much potentiality of child-experience with regard to language, earth, and numbered and measured reality. Hence the difficulty of bringing the mind to bear upon it; hence its repulsiveness; the tendency for attention to wander; for other acts and images to crowd in and expel the lesson. The legitimate way out is to transform the material; to psychologize it—that is, once more, to take it and to develop it within the range and scope of the child's life. But it is easier and simpler to leave it as it is, and then by trick of method to *arouse* interest, to *make* it *interesting;* to cover it with sugar-coating; to conceal its barrenness by intermediate and unrelated material; and finally, as it were, to get the child to swallow and digest the unpalatable morsel while he is enjoying tasting something quite different. But alas for the analogy! Mental assimilation is a matter of consciousness; and if the attention has not been playing upon the actual material, that has not been apprehended, nor worked into faculty.

How, then, stands the case of Child *vs.* Curriculum? What shall the verdict be? The radical fallacy in the original pleadings with which we set out is the supposition that we have no choice save either to leave the child to his own unguided spontaneity or to inspire direction upon him from without. Action is response; it is adaptation, adjustment. There is no such thing as sheer self-activity possible—because all activity takes place in a medium, in a situation, and with reference to its conditions. But, again, no such thing as imposition of truth from without, as insertion of truth from without, is possible. All depends upon the activity which the mind itself undergoes in responding to what is presented from without. Now, the value of the formulated wealth of knowledge that makes up the course of study is that it may enable the educator *to determine the environment of the child*, and thus by indirection to direct. Its primary value, its primary indication, is for the teacher, not for the child. It says to the teacher: Such and such are the capacities, the fulfilments, in truth and beauty and behavior, open to these children. Now see to it that day by day the conditions are such that *their own activities* move inevitably in this direction, toward such culmination of themselves. Let the child's nature fulfil its own destiny, revealed to you in whatever of science and art and industry the world now holds as its own.

The case is of Child. It is his present powers which are to assert themselves; his present capacities which are to be exercised; his present attitudes which are to be realized. But save as the teacher knows, knows wisely and thoroughly, the race-expression which is embodied in that thing we call the Curriculum, the teacher knows neither what the present power, capacity, or attitude is, nor yet how it is to be asserted, exercised, and realized.

29. Education as Growth*

This chapter from *Democracy and Education* contains one of Dewey's most controversial and misunderstood statements. He writes that "since in reality there is nothing to which growth is relative save more growth, there is nothing to which education is subordinate save more education." The com-

* From John Dewey, *Democracy and Education* (New York, Macmillan Co., 1961) (1916), pp. 41-53. Reprinted by permission of the Macmillan Co., Copyright 1916 by the Macmillan Co., renewed 1944 by John Dewey.

monplace interpretation of this remark is that Dewey, in his
desire to reject absolute and fixed goals, advocates an aimless
wandering and playing as characteristic of education.

Dewey, of course, has something quite different in mind.
Growth is not a linear notion but rather signifies the interaction with nature as problematic and the ability to resolve, to
overcome, and to recover from loss. Growth is an "on the
way" fruit of experiencing and is not solely dependent on
habitual responses or on reaching preconceived goals. He
writes that "the inclination to learn from life itself and to
make the conditions of life such that all will learn in the process of living is the finest product of schooling."

1. *The Conditions of Growth*. In directing the activities of the young,
society determines its own future in determining that of the young. Since
the young at a given time will at some later date compose the society of
that period, the latter's nature will largely turn upon the direction children's activities were given at an earlier period. This cumulative movement of action toward a later result is what is meant by growth.

The primary condition of growth is immaturity. This may seem to be
a mere truism—saying that a being can develop only in some point in
which he is undeveloped. But the prefix "im" of the word immaturity
means something positive, not a mere void or lack. It is noteworthy that
the terms "capacity" and "potentiality" have a double meaning, one
sense being negative, the other positive. Capacity may denote mere
receptivity, like the capacity of a quart measure. We may mean by
potentiality a merely dormant or quiescent state—a capacity to become
something different under external influences. But we also mean by
capacity an ability, a power; and by potentiality potency, force. Now
when we say that immaturity means the possibility of growth, we are
not referring to absence of powers which may exist at a later time; we
express a force positively present—the *ability* to develop.

Our tendency to take immaturity as mere lack, and growth as something which fills up the gap between the immature and the mature is due
to regarding childhood *comparatively*, instead of intrinsically. We treat
it simply as a privation because we are measuring it by adulthood as a
fixed standard. This fixes attention upon what the child has not, and
will not have till he becomes a man. This comparative standpoint is
legitimate enough for some purposes, but if we make it final, the question arises whether we are not guilty of an overweening presumption.
Children, if they could express themselves articulately and sincerely,

would tell a different tale; and there is excellent adult authority for the conviction that for certain moral and intellectual purposes adults must become as little children.

The seriousness of the assumption of the negative quality of the possibilities of immaturity is apparent when we reflect that it sets up as an ideal and standard a static end. The fulfillment of growing is taken to mean an *accomplished* growth: that is to say, an Ungrowth, something which is no longer growing. The futility of the assumption is seen in the fact that every adult resents the imputation of having no further possibilities of growth; and so far as he finds that they are closed to him mourns the fact as evidence of loss, instead of falling back on the achieved as adequate manifestation of power. Why an unequal measure for child and man?

Taken absolutely, instead of comparatively, immaturity designates a positive force or ability,—the *power* to grow. We do not have to draw out or educe positive activities from a child, as some educational doctrines would have it. Where there is life, there are already eager and impassioned activities. Growth is not something done to them; it is something they do. The positive and constructive aspect of possibility gives the key to understanding the two chief traits of immaturity, dependence and plasticity. (1) It sounds absurd to hear dependence spoken of as something positive, still more absurd as a power. Yet if helplessness were all there were in dependence, no development could ever take place. A merely impotent being has to be carried, forever, by others. The fact that dependence is accompanied by growth in ability, not by an ever-increasing lapse into parasitism, suggests that it is already something constructive. Being merely sheltered by others would not promote growth. For (2) it would only build a wall around impotence. With reference to the physical world, the child is helpless. He lacks at birth and for a long time thereafter power to make his way physically, to make his own living. If he had to do that by himself, he would hardly survive an hour. On this side his helplessness is almost complete. The young of the brutes are immeasurably his superiors. He is physically weak and not able to turn the strength which he possesses to coping with the physical environment.

1. The thoroughgoing character of this helplessness suggests, however, some compensating power. The relative ability of the young of brute animals to adapt themselves fairly well to physical conditions from an early period suggests the fact that their life is not intimately bound up with the life of those about them. They are compelled, so to speak, to have physical gifts because they are lacking in social gifts.

Human infants, on the other hand, can get along with physical incapacity just because of their social capacity. We sometimes talk and think as if they simply happened to be *physically* in a social environment; as if social forces exclusively existed in the adults who take care of them, they being passive recipients. If it were said that children are themselves marvelously endowed with *power* to enlist the coöperative attention of others, this would be thought to be a backhanded way of saying that others are marvelously attentive to the needs of children. But observation shows that children are gifted with an equipment of the first order for social intercourse. Few grown-up persons retain all of the flexible and sensitive ability of children to vibrate sympathetically with the attitudes and doings of those about them. Inattention to physical things (going with incapacity to control them) is accompanied by a corresponding intensification of interest and attention as to the doings of people. The native mechanism of the child and his impulses all tend to facile social responsiveness. The statement that children, before adolescence, are egotistically self-centered, even if it were true, would not contradict the truth of this statement. It would simply indicate that their social responsiveness is employed on their own behalf, not that it does not exist. But the statement is not true as matter of fact. The facts which are cited in support of the alleged pure egoism of children really show the intensity and directness with which they go to their mark. If the ends which form the mark seem narrow and selfish to adults, it is only because adults (by means of a similar engrossment in their day) have mastered these ends, which have consequently ceased to interest them. Most of the remainder of children's alleged native egoism is simply an egoism which runs counter to an adult's egoism. To a grown-up person who is too absorbed in his own affairs to take an interest in children's affairs, children doubtless seem unreasonably engrossed in *their* own affairs.

From a social standpoint, dependence denotes a power rather than a weakness; it involves interdependence. There is always a danger that increased personal independence will decrease the social capacity of an individual. In making him more self-reliant, it may make him more self-sufficient; it may lead to aloofness and indifference. It often makes an individual so insensitive in his relations to others as to develop an illusion of being really able to stand and act alone—an unnamed form of insanity which is responsible for a large part of the remediable suffering of the world.

2. The specific adaptability of an immature creature for growth con-

stitutes his *plasticity*. This is something quite different from the plasticity of putty or wax. It is not a capacity to take on change of form in accord with external pressure. It lies near the pliable elasticity by which some persons take on the color of their surroundings while retaining their own bent. But it is something deeper than this. It is essentially the ability to learn from experience; the power to retain from one experience something which is of avail in coping with the difficulties of a later situation. This means power to modify actions on the basis of the results of prior experiences, the power to *develop dispositions*. Without it, the acquisition of habits is impossible.

It is a familiar fact that the young of the higher animals, and especially the human young, have to *learn* to utilize their instinctive reactions. The human being is born with a greater number of instinctive tendencies than other animals. But the instincts of the lower animals perfect themselves for appropriate action at an early period after birth, while most of those of the human infant are of little account just as they stand. An original specialized power of adjustment secures immediate efficiency, but, like a railway ticket, it is good for one route only. A being who, in order to use his eyes, ears, hands, and legs, has to experiment in making varied combinations of their reactions, achieves a control that is flexible and varied. A chick, for example, pecks accurately at a bit of food in a few hours after hatching. This means that definite coördinations of activities of the eyes in seeing and of the body and head in striking are perfected in a few trials. An infant requires about six months to be able to gauge with approximate accuracy the action in reaching which will coordinate with his visual activities; to be able, that is, to tell whether he can reach a seen object and just how to execute the reaching. As a result, the chick is limited by the relative perfection of its original endowment. The infant has the advantage of the *multitude* of instinctive tentative reactions and of the experiences that accompany them, even though he is at a temporary disadvantage because they cross one another. In learning an action, instead of having it given readymade, one of necessity learns to vary its factors, to make varied combinations of them, according to change of circumstances. A possibility of continuing progress is opened up by the fact that in learning one act, methods are developed good for use in other situations. Still more important is the fact that the human being acquires a habit of learning. He learns to learn.

The importance for human life of the two facts of dependence and variable control has been summed up in the doctrine of the significance of prolonged infancy.[1] This prolongation is significant from the stand-point of the adult members of the group as well as from that of the young. The presence of dependent and learning beings is a stimulus to nurture and affection. The need for constant continued care was prob-ably a chief means in transforming temporary cohabitations into per-manent unions. It certainly was a chief influence in forming habits of af-fectionate and sympathetic watchfulness; that constructive interest in the well-being of others which is essential to associated life. Intellec-tually, this moral development meant the introduction of many new ob-jects of attention; it stimulated foresight and planning for the future. Thus there is a reciprocal influence. Increasing complexity of social life requires a longer period of infancy in which to acquire the needed powers; this prolongation of dependence means prolongation of plasticity, or power of acquiring variable and novel modes of control. Hence it provides a further push to social progress.

2. *Habits as Expressions of Growth*. We have already noted that plasticity is the capacity to retain and carry over from prior experience factors which modify subsequent activities. This signifies the capacity to acquire habits, or develop definite dispositions. We have now to con-sider the salient features of habits. In the first place, a habit is a form of executive skill, of efficiency in doing. A habit means an ability to use natural conditions as means to ends. It is an active control of the en-vironment through control of the organs of action. We are perhaps apt to emphasize the control of the body at the expense of control of the en-vironment. We think of walking, talking, playing the piano, the spe-cialized skills characteristic of the etcher, the surgeon, the bridge-builder, as if they were simply ease, deftness, and accuracy on the part of the organism. They are that, of course; but the measure of the value of these qualities lies in the economical and effective control of the en-vironment which they secure. To be able to walk is to have certain properties of nature at our disposal—and so with all other habits.

Education is not infrequently defined as consisting in the acquisition of those habits that effect an adjustment of an individual and his en-vironment. The definition expresses an essential phase of growth. But it is essential that adjustment be understood in its active sense of *control* of means for achieving ends. If we think of a habit simply as a change wrought in the organism, ignoring the fact that this change consists in

---

[1] Intimations of its significance are found in a number of writers, but John Fiske, in his *Excursions of an Evolutionist*, is accredited with its first systematic exposition.

ability to effect subsequent changes in the environment, we shall be led to think of "adjustment" as a conformity to environment as wax conforms to the seal which impresses it. The environment is thought of as something fixed, providing in its fixity the end and standard of changes taking place in the organism; adjustment is just fitting ourselves to this fixity of external conditions.[2] Habit as *habituation* is indeed something *relatively* passive; we get used to our surroundings—to our clothing, our shoes, and gloves; to the atmosphere as long as it is fairly equable; to our daily associates, etc. Conformity to the environment, a change wrought in the organism without reference to ability to modify surroundings, is a marked trait of such habituations. Aside from the fact that we are not entitled to carry over the traits of such adjustments (which might well be called *accommodations*, to mark them off from active adjustments) into habits of active use of our surroundings, two features of habituations are worth notice. In the first place, we get used to things by *first* using them.

Consider getting used to a strange city. At first, there is excessive stimulation and excessive and ill-adapted response. Gradually certain stimuli are selected because of their relevancy, and others are degraded. We can say either that we do not respond to them any longer, or more truly that we have effected a persistent response to them—an equilibrium of adjustment. This means, in the second place, that this enduring adjustment supplies the background upon which are made specific adjustments, as occasion arises. We are never interested in changing the *whole* environment; there is much that we take for granted and accept just as it already is. Upon this background our activities focus at certain points in an endeavor to introduce needed changes. Habituation is thus our adjustment to an environment which at the time we are not concerned with modifying, and which supplies a leverage to our active habits.

Adaptation, in fine, is quite as much adaptation *of* the environment to our own activities as of our activities *to* the environment. A savage tribe manages to live on a desert plain. It adapts itself. But its adaptation involves a maximum of accepting, tolerating, putting up with things as they are, a maximum of passive acquiescence, and a minimum of active control, of subjection to use. A civilized people enters upon the scene. It also adapts itself. It introduces irrigation; it searches the world

---

[2] This conception is, of course, a logical correlate of the conceptions of the external relation of stimulus and response, considered in the last chapter, and of the negative conceptions of immaturity and plasticity noted in this chapter.

for plants and animals that will flourish under such conditions; it improves, by careful selection, those which are growing there. As a consequence, the wilderness blossoms as a rose. The savage is merely habituated; the civilized man has habits which transform the environment.

The significance of habit is not exhausted, however, in its executive and motor phase. It means formation of intellectual and emotional disposition as well as an increase in ease. economy, and efficiency of action. Any habit marks an *inclination*—an active preference and choice for the conditions involved in its exercise. A habit does not wait, Micawber-like, for a stimulus to turn up so that it may get busy; it actively seeks for occasions to pass into full operation. If its expression is unduly blocked, inclination shows itself in uneasiness and intense craving. A habit also marks an intellectual disposition. Where there is a habit, there is acquaintance with the materials and equipment to which action is applied. There is a definite way of understanding the situations in which the habit operates. Modes of thought, of observation and reflection, enter as forms of skill and of desire into the habits that make a man an engineer, an architect, a physician, or a merchant. In unskilled forms of labor, the intellectual factors are at minimum precisely because the habits involved are not of a high grade. But there are habits of judging and reasoning as truly as of handling a tool, painting a picture, or conducting an experiment.

Such statements are, however, understatements. The habits of mind involved in habits of the eye and hand supply the latter with their significance. Above all, the intellectual element in a habit fixes the relation of the habit to varied and elastic use, and hence to continued growth. We speak of *fixed* habits. Well, the phrase may mean powers so well established that their possessor always has them as resources when needed. But the phrase is also used to mean ruts, routine ways, with loss of freshness, openmindedness, and originality. Fixity of habit may mean that something has a fixed hold upon us, instead of our having a free hold upon things. This fact explains two points in a common notion about habits: their identification with mechanical and external modes of action to the neglect of mental and moral attitudes, and the tendency to give them a bad meaning, an identification with "bad habits." Many a person would feel surprised to have his aptitude in his chosen profession called a habit, and would naturally think of his use of tobacco, liquor, or profane language as typical of the meaning of habit. A habit is to him something which has a hold on him, something not easily thrown off even though judgment condemn it.

Habits reduce themselves to routine ways of acting, or degenerate into ways of action to which we are enslaved just in the degree in which intelligence is disconnected from them. Routine habits are unthinking habits: "bad" habits are habits so severed from reason that they are opposed to the conclusions of conscious deliberation and decision. As we have seen, the acquiring of habits is due to an original plasticity of our natures: to our ability to vary responses till we find an appropriate and efficient way of acting. Routine habits, and habits that possess us instead of our possessing them, are habits which put an end to plasticity. They mark the close of power to vary. There can be no doubt of the tendency of organic plasticity, of the physiological basis, to lessen with growing years. The instinctively mobile and eagerly varying action of childhood, the love of new stimuli and new developments, too easily passes into a "settling down," which means aversion to change and a resting on past achievements. Only an environment which secures the full use of intelligence in the process of forming habits can counteract this tendency. Of course, the same hardening of the organic conditions affects the physiological structures which are involved in thinking. But this fact only indicates the need of persistent care to see to it that the function of intelligence is invoked to its maximum possibility. The short-sighted method which falls back on mechanical routine and repetition to secure external efficiency of habit, motor skill without accompanying thought, marks a deliberate closing in of surroundings upon growth.

3. *The Educational Bearings of the Conception of Development.* We have had so far but little to say in this chapter about education. We have been occupied with the conditions and implications of growth. If our conclusions are justified, they carry with them, however, definite educational consequences. When it is said that education is development, everything depends upon *how* development is conceived. Our net conclusion is that life is development, and that developing, growing, is life. Translated into its educational equivalents, that means (*i*) that the educational process has no end beyond itself; it is its own end; and that (*ii*) the educational process is one of continual reorganizing, reconstructing, transforming.

1. Development when it is interpreted in *comparative* terms, that is, with respect to the special traits of child and adult life, means the direction of power into special channels: the formation of habits involving executive skill, definiteness of interest, and specific objects of observation and thought. But the comparative view is not final. The child has specific powers; to ignore that fact is to stunt or distort the organs upon which his growth depends. The adult uses his powers to transform his

environment, thereby occasioning new stimuli which redirect his powers and keep them developing. Ignoring this fact means arrested development, a passive accommodation. Normal child and normal adult alike, in other words, are engaged in growing. The difference between them is not the difference between growth and no growth, but between the modes of growth appropriate to different conditions. With respect to the development of powers devoted to coping with specific scientific and economic problems we may say the child should be growing in manhood. With respect to sympathetic curiosity, unbiased responsiveness, and openness of mind, we may say that the adult should be growing in childlikeness. One statement is as true as the other.

Three ideas which have been criticized, namely, the merely privative nature of immaturity, static adjustment to a fixed environment, and rigidity of habit, are all connected with a false idea of growth or development,—that it is a movement toward a fixed goal. Growth is regarded as *having* an end, instead of *being* an end. The educational counterparts of the three fallacious ideas are first, failure to take account of the instinctive or native powers of the young; secondly, failure to develop initiative in coping with novel situations; thirdly, an undue emphasis upon drill and other devices which secure automatic skill at the expense of personal perception. In all cases, the adult environment is accepted as a standard for the child. He is to be brought up *to* it.

Natural instincts are either disregarded or treated as nuisances—as obnoxious traits to be suppressed, or at all events to be brought into conformity with external standards. Since conformity is the aim, what is distinctively individual in a young person is brushed aside, or regarded as a source of mischief or anarchy. Conformity is made equivalent to uniformity. Consequently, there are induced lack of interest in the novel, aversion to progress, and dread of the uncertain and the unknown. Since the end of growth is outside of and beyond the process of growing, external agents have to be resorted to to induce movement toward it. Whenever a method of education is stigmatized as mechanical, we may be sure that external pressure is brought to bear to reach an external end.

2. Since in reality there is nothing to which growth is relative save more growth, there is nothing to which education is subordinate save more education. It is a commonplace to say that education should not cease when one leaves school. The point of this commonplace is that the purpose of school education is to insure the continuance of education by organizing the powers that insure growth. The inclination to learn

from life itself and to make the conditions of life such that all will learn in the process of living is the finest product of schooling.

When we abandon the attempt to define immaturity by means of fixed comparison with adult accomplishments, we are compelled to give up thinking of it as denoting lack of desired traits. Abandoning this notion, we are also forced to surrender our habit of thinking of instruction as a method of supplying this lack by pouring knowledge into a mental and moral hole which awaits filling. Since life means growth, a living creature lives as truly and positively at one stage as at another, with the same intrinsic fullness and the same absolute claims. Hence education means the enterprise of supplying the conditions which insure growth, or adequacy of life, irrespective of age. We first look with impatience upon immaturity, regarding it as something to be got over as rapidly as possible. Then the adult formed by such educative methods looks back with impatient regret upon childhood and youth as a scene of lost opportunities and wasted powers. This ironical situation will endure till it is recognized that living has its own intrinsic quality and that the business of education is with that quality.

Realization that life is growth protects us from that so-called idealizing of childhood which in effect is nothing but lazy indulgence. Life is not to be identified with every superficial act and interest. Even though it is not always easy to tell whether what appears to be mere surface fooling is a sign of some nascent as yet untrained power, we must remember that manifestations are not to be accepted as ends in themselves. They are signs of possible growth. They are to be turned into means of development, of carrying power forward, not indulged or cultivated for their own sake. Excessive attention to surface phenomena (even in the way of rebuke as well as of encouragement) may lead to their fixation and thus to arrested development. What impulses are moving toward, not what they have been, is the important thing for parent and teacher. The true principle of respect for immaturity cannot be better put than in the words of Emerson: "Respect the child. Be not too much his parent. Trespass not on his solitude. But I hear the outcry which replies to this suggestion: Would you verily throw up the reins of public and private discipline; would you leave the young child to the mad career of his own passions and whimsies, and call this anarchy a respect for the child's nature? I answer,—Respect the child, respect him to the end, but also respect yourself. . . . The two points in a boy's training are, to keep his *naturel* and train off all but that; to keep his *naturel*, but stop off his uproar, fooling, and horseplay; keep his nature *and arm it with knowledge in the very direction in which it points."* And as Emerson goes on to show, this reverence for childhood and youth instead of opening up an easy and easy-going path to the instructors, "involves at once, immense claims on the time, the thought, on the life of the teacher. It requires time, use, insight, event, all the great lessons and assistances of God; and only to think of using it implies character and profoundness."

Summary. Power to grow depends upon need for others and plasticity. Both of these conditions are at their height in childhood and youth. Plasticity or the power to learn from experience means the formation of habits. Habits give control over the environment, power to utilize it for human purposes. Habits take the form both of habituation, or a general and persistent balance of organic activities with the surroundings, and of active capacities to readjust activity to meet new conditions. The former furnishes the background of growth; the latter constitute growing. Active habits involve thought, invention, and initiative in applying capacities to new aims. They are opposed to routine which marks an arrest of growth. Since growth is the characteristic of life, education is all one with growing; it has no end beyond itself. The criterion of the value of school education is the extent in which it creates a desire for continued growth and supplies means for making the desire effective in fact.

30. Experience and Thinking*

Two themes stand out in this chapter from *Democracy and Education*: first, the profound importance of experience to the activity of thinking, and second, "the discernment of relations" as the genuinely intellectual or educative matter. In general terms, Dewey states the context of his position by writing that "an experience, a very humble experience, is capable of generating and carrying any amount of theory (or intellectual content), but a theory apart from an experience cannot be definitely grasped even as a theory."

From this it follows that the task of thinking—that is, of a reflective experience—is not only to discern relationships but

* From John Dewey, *Democracy and Education* (New York, Macmillan Co., 1961) (1916), pp. 139-51. Reprinted by permission of the Macmillan Co., Copyright 1916 by the Macmillan Co., renewed 1944 by John Dewey.

to "institute connections between what is done and its consequences," as well as to detail these connections. Although difficult to describe, it would seem that Dewey believes that when we think, we are undergoing experience in a reflective way—that is, we are not severing mind from our "undergoing," as though looking at a thing or an object "out there." It is the making and articulating of relationships that constitutes thinking as an experience.

1. *The Nature of Experience.* The nature of experience can be understood only by noting that it includes an active and a passive element peculiarly combined. On the active hand, experience is *trying*—a meaning which is made explicit in the connected term experiment. On the passive, it is *undergoing*. When we experience something we act upon it, we do something with it; then we suffer or undergo the consequences. We do something to the thing and then it does something to us in return: such is the peculiar combination. The connection of these two phases of experience measures the fruitfulness or value of the experience. Mere activity does not constitute experience. It is dispersive, centrifugal, dissipating. Experience as trying involves change, but change is meaningless transition unless it is consciously connected with the return wave of consequences which flow from it. When an activity is continued *into* the undergoing of consequences, when the change made by action is reflected back into a change made in us, the mere flux is loaded with significance. We learn something. It is not experience when a child merely sticks his finger into a flame; it is experience when the movement is connected with the pain which he undergoes in consequence. Henceforth the sticking of the finger into flame *means* a burn. Being burned is a mere physical change, like the burning of a stick of wood, if it is not perceived as a consequence of some other action.

Blind and capricious impulses hurry us on heedlessly from one thing to another. So far as this happens, everything is writ in water. There is none of that cumulative growth which makes an experience in any vital sense of that term. On the other hand, many things happen to us in the way of pleasure and pain which we do not connect with any prior activity of our own. They are mere accidents so far as we are concerned. There is no before or after to such experience; no retrospect nor outlook, and consequently no meaning. We get nothing which may be carried over to foresee what is likely to happen next, and no gain in ability to adjust ourselves to what is coming—no added control. Only by courtesy can such an experience be called experience. To "learn from experience" is to make a backward and forward connection between what we do to things and what we enjoy or suffer from things in consequence. Under such conditions, doing becomes a trying; an experiment with the world to find out what it is like; the undergoing becomes instruction—discovery of the connection of things.

Two conclusions important for education follow. (1) Experience is primarily an active-passive affair; it is not primarily cognitive. But (2) the *measure of the value* of an experience lies in the perception of relationships or continuities to which it leads up. It includes cognition in the degree in which it is cumulative or amounts to something, or has meaning. In schools, those under instruction are too customarily looked upon as acquiring knowledge as theoretical spectators, minds which appropriate knowledge by direct energy of intellect. The very word pupil has almost come to mean one who is engaged not in having fruitful experiences but in absorbing knowledge directly. Something which is called mind or consciousness is severed from the physical organs of activity. The former is then thought to be purely intellectual and cognitive; the latter to be an irrelevant and intruding physical factor. The intimate union of activity and undergoing its consequences which leads to recognition of meaning is broken; instead we have two fragments: mere bodily action on one side, and meaning directly grasped by "spiritual" activity on the other.

It would be impossible to state adequately the evil results which have flowed from this dualism of mind and body, much less to exaggerate them. Some of the more striking effects, may, however, be enumerated. (*a*) In part bodily activity becomes an intruder. Having nothing, so it is thought, to do with mental activity, it becomes a distraction, an evil to be contended with. For the pupil has a body, and brings it to school along with his mind. And the body is, of necessity, a wellspring of energy; it has to do something. But its activities, not being utilized in occupation with things which yield significant results, have to be frowned upon. They lead the pupil away from the lesson with which his "mind" ought to be occupied; they are sources of mischief. The chief source of the "problem of discipline" in schools is that the teacher has often to spend the larger part of the time in suppressing the bodily activities which take the mind away from its material. A premium is put on physical quietude; on silence, on rigid uniformity of posture and movement; upon a machine-like simulation of the attitudes of intelligent interest. The teachers' business is to hold the pupils up to these requirements and to punish the inevitable deviations which occur.

The nervous strain and fatigue which result with both teacher and pupil are a necessary consequence of the abnormality of the situation in which bodily activity is divorced from the perception of meaning. Callous indifference and explosions from strain alternate. The neglected body, having no organized fruitful channels of activity, breaks forth, without knowing why or how, into meaningless boisterousness, or settles into equally meaningless fooling—both very different from the normal play of children. Physically active children become restless and unruly; the more quiescent, so-called conscientious ones spend what energy they have in the negative task of keeping their instincts and active tendencies suppressed, instead of in a positive one of constructive planning and execution; they are thus educated not into responsibility for the significant and graceful use of bodily powers, but into an enforced duty not to give them free play. It may be seriously asserted that a chief cause for the remarkable achievements of Greek education was that it was never misled by false notions into an attempted separation of mind and body.

(b) Even, however, with respect to the lessons which have to be learned by the application of "mind," some bodily activities have to be used. The senses—especially the eye and ear—have to be employed to take in what the book, the map, the blackboard, and the teacher say. The lips and vocal organs, and the hands, have to be used to reproduce in speech and writing what has been stowed away. The senses are then regarded as a kind of mysterious conduit through which information is conducted from the external world into the mind; they are spoken of as gateways and avenues of knowledge. To keep the eyes on the book and the ears open to the teacher's words is a mysterious source of intellectual grace. Moreover, reading, writing, and figuring—important school arts—demand muscular or motor training. The muscles of eye, hand, and vocal organs accordingly have to be trained to act as pipes for carrying knowledge back out of the mind into external action. For it happens that using the muscles repeatedly in the same way fixes in them an automatic tendency to repeat.

The obvious result is a mechanical use of the bodily activities which (in spite of the generally obtrusive and interfering character of the body in mental action) have to be employed more or less. For the senses and muscles are used not as organic participants in having an instructive experience, but as external inlets and outlets of mind. Before the child goes to school, he learns with his hand, eye, and ear, because they are organs of the process of doing something from which meaning results. The boy flying a kite has to keep his eye on the kite, and has to note the various pressures of the string on his hand. His senses are avenues of knowledge not because external facts are somehow "conveyed" to the brain, but because they are *used* in doing something with a purpose. The qualities of seen and touched things have a bearing on what is done, and are alertly perceived; they have a meaning. But when pupils are expected to use their eyes to note the form of words, irrespective of their meaning, in order to reproduce them in spelling or reading, the resulting training is simply of isolated sense organs and muscles. It is such isolation of an act from a purpose which makes it mechanical. It is customary for teachers to urge children to read with expression, so as to bring out the meaning. But if they originally learned the sensory-motor technique of reading—the ability to identify forms and to reproduce the sounds they stand for—by methods which did not call for attention to meaning, a mechanical habit was established which makes it difficult to read subsequently with intelligence. The vocal organs have been trained to go their own way automatically in isolation; and meaning cannot be tied on at will. Drawing, singing, and writing may be taught in the same mechanical way; for, we repeat, any way *is* mechanical which narrows down the bodily activity so that a separation of body from mind—that is, from recognition of meaning—is set up. Mathematics, even in its higher branches, when undue emphasis is put upon the technique of calculation, and science, when laboratory exercises are given for their own sake, suffer from the same evil.

(c) On the intellectual side, the separation of "mind" from direct occupation with things throws emphasis on *things* at the expense of *relations* or connections. It is altogether too common to separate perceptions and even ideas from judgments. The latter are thought to come after the former in order to compare them. It is alleged that the mind perceives things apart from relations; that it forms ideas of them in isolation from their connections—with what goes before and comes after. Then judgment or thought is called upon to combine the separated items of "knowledge" so that their resemblance or causal connection shall be brought out. As matter of fact, every perception and every idea is a sense of the bearings, use, and cause, of a thing. We do not really know a chair or have an idea of it by inventorying and enumerating its various isolated qualities, but only by bringing these qualities into connection with something else—the purpose which makes it a chair and not a table; or its difference from the kind of chair we are accustomed to, or the "period" which it represents, and so on. A wagon is not perceived when all its parts are summed up; it is the characteristic connection of the parts which makes it a wagon. And these connections are not those of mere physical juxtaposition; they involve connection with the animals that draw it, the things that are carried on it, and so on. Judgment is employed in the perception; otherwise the perception is mere sensory excitation or else a recognition of the result of a prior judgment, as in the case of familiar objects.

Words, the counters for ideals, are, however, easily taken for ideas. And in just the degree in which mental activity is separated from active concern with the world, from doing something and connecting the doing with what is undergone, words, symbols, come to take the place of ideas. The substitution is the more subtle because *some* meaning is recognized. But we are very easily trained to be content with a minimum of meaning, and to fail to note how restricted is our perception of the relations which confer significance. We get so thoroughly used to a kind of pseudo-idea, a half perception, that we are not aware how half-dead our mental action is, and how much keener and more extensive our observations and ideas would be if we formed them under conditions of a vital experience which required us to use judgment: to hunt for the connections of the thing dealt with.

There is no difference of opinion as to the theory of the matter. All authorities agree that that discernment of relationships is the genuinely intellectual matter; hence, the educative matter. The failure arises in supposing that relationships can become perceptible without *experience* —without that conjoint trying and undergoing of which we have spoken. It is assumed that "mind" can grasp them if it will only give attention, and that this attention may be given at will irrespective of the situation. Hence the deluge of half-observations, of verbal ideas, and unassimilated "knowledge" which afflicts the world. An ounce of experience is better than a ton of theory simply because it is only in experience that any theory has vital and verifiable significance. An experience, a very humble experience, is capable of generating and carrying any amount of theory (or intellectual content), but a theory apart from an experience cannot be definitely grasped even as theory. It tends to become a mere verbal formula, a set of catchwords used to render thinking, or genuine theorizing, unnecessary and impossible. Because of our education we use words, thinking they are ideas, to dispose of questions, the disposal being in reality simply such an obscuring of perception as prevents us from seeing any longer the difficulty.

2. *Reflection in Experience.* Thought or reflection, as we have already seen virtually if not explicitly, is the discernment of the relation between what we try to do and what happens in consequence. No experience having a meaning is possible without some element of thought. But we may contrast two types of experience according to the propor-

tion of reflection found in them. All our experiences have a phase of "cut and try" in them—what psychologists call the method of trial and error. We simply do something, and when it fails, we do something else, and keep on trying till we hit upon something which works, and then we adopt that method as a rule of thumb measure in subsequent procedure. Some experiences have very little else in them than this hit and miss or succeed process. We see *that* a certain way of acting and a certain consequence are connected, but we do not see *how* they are. We do not see the details of the connection; the links are missing. Our discernment is very gross. In other cases we push our observation farther. We analyze to see just what lies between so as to bind together cause and effect, activity and consequence. This extension of our insight makes foresight more accurate and comprehensive. The action which rests simply upon the trial and error method is at the mercy of circumstances; they may change so that the act performed does not operate in the way it was expected to. But if we know in detail upon what the result depends, we can look to see whether the required conditions are there. The method extends our practical control. For if some of the conditions are missing, we may, if we know what the needed antecedents for an effect are, set to work to supply them; or, if they are such as to produce undesirable effects as well, we may eliminate some of the superfluous causes and economize effort.

In discovery of the detailed connections of our activities and what happens in consequence, the thought implied in cut and dry experience is made explicit. Its quantity increases so that its proportionate value is very different. Hence the quality of the experience changes; the change is so significant that we may call this type of experience reflective—that is, reflective *par excellence*. The deliberate cultivation of this phase of thought constitutes thinking as a distinctive experience. Thinking, in other words, is the intentional endeavor to discover specific connections between something which we do and the consequences which result, so that the two become continuous. Their isolation, and consequently their purely arbitrary going together, is cancelled; a unified developing situation takes its place. The occurrence is now understood; it is explained; it is reasonable, as we say, that the thing should happen as it does.

Thinking is thus equivalent to an explicit rendering of the intelligent element in our experience. It makes it possible to act with an end in view. It is the condition of our having aims. As soon as an infant begins to *expect* he begins to use something which is now going on as a sign of something to follow; he is, in however simple a fashion, judging. For he takes one thing as *evidence* of something else, and so recognizes a relationship. Any future development, however elaborate it may be, is only an extending and a refining of this simple act of inference. All that the wisest man can do is to observe what is going on more widely and more minutely and then select more carefully from what is noted just those factors which point to something to happen. The opposites, once more, to thoughtful action are routine and capricious behavior. The former accepts what has been customary as a full measure of possibility and omits to take into account the connections of the particular things done. The latter makes the momentary act a measure of value, and ignores the connections of our personal action with the energies of the environment. It says, virtually, "things are to be just as I happen to like them at this instant," as routine says in effect "let things continue just as I have found them in the past." Both refuse to acknowledge responsibility for the future consequences which flow from present action. Reflection is the acceptance of such responsibility.

The starting point of any process of thinking is something going on, something which just as it stands is incomplete or unfulfilled. Its point, its meaning lies literally in what it is going to be, in how it is going to turn out. As this is written, the world is filled with the clang of contending armies. For an active participant in the war, it is clear that the momentous thing is the issue, the future consequences, of this and that happening. He is identified, for the time at least, with the issue; *his* fate hangs upon the course things are taking. But even for an onlooker in a neutral country, the significance of every move made, of every advance here and retreat there, lies in what it portends. To *think* upon the news as it comes to us is to attempt to see what is indicated as probable or possible regarding an outcome. To fill our heads, like a scrapbook, with this and that item as a finished and done-for thing, is not to think. It is to turn ourselves into a piece of registering apparatus. To consider the *bearing* of the occurrence upon what may be, but is not yet, is to think. Nor will the reflective experience be different in kind if we substitute distance in time for separation in space. Imagine the war done with, and a future historian giving an account of it. The episode is, by assumption, past. But he cannot give a thoughtful account of the war save as he preserves the time sequence; the meaning of each occurrence, as he deals with it, lies in what was future for *it*, though not for the historian. To take it by itself as a complete existence is to take it unreflectively.

Reflection also implies concern with the issue—a certain sympathetic identification of our own destiny, if only dramatic, with the outcome of the course of events. For the general in the war, or a common soldier, or a citizen of one of the contending nations, the stimulus to thinking is direct and urgent. For neutrals, it is indirect and dependent upon imagination. But the flagrant partisanship of human nature is evidence of the intensity of the tendency to identify ourselves with one possible course of events, and to reject the other as foreign. If we cannot take sides in overt action, and throw in our little weight to help determine the final balance, we take sides emotionally and imaginatively. We desire this or that outcome. One wholly indifferent to the outcome does not follow or think about what is happening at all. From this dependence of the act of thinking upon a sense of sharing in the consequences of what goes on, flows one of the chief paradoxes of thought. Born in partiality, in order to accomplish its tasks it must achieve a certain detached impartiality. The general who allows his hopes and desires to affect his observations and interpretations of the existing situation will surely make a mistake in calculation. While hopes and fears may be the chief motive for a thoughtful following of the war on the part of an onlooker in a neutral country, he too will think ineffectively in the degree in which his preferences modify the stuff of his observations and reasonings. There is, however, no incompatibility between the fact that the occasion of reflection lies in a personal sharing in what is going on and the fact that the value of the reflection lies upon keeping one's self out of the data. The almost insurmountable difficulty of achieving this detachment is evidence that thinking originates in situations where the course of thinking is an actual part of the course of events and is designed to influence the result. Only gradually and with a widening of the area of vision through a growth of social sympathies does thinking develop to include what lies beyond our *direct* interests: a fact of great significance for education.

To say that thinking occurs with reference to situations which are still going on, and incomplete, is to say that thinking occurs when things are uncertain or doubtful or problematic. Only what is finished, completed, is wholly assured. Where there is reflection there is suspense. The object of thinking is to help *reach* a conclusion, to project a possible termination of the basis of what is already given. Certain other facts about thinking accompany this feature. Since the situation in which thinking occurs is a doubtful one, thinking is a process of inquiry, of looking into things, of investigating. *Ac*quiring is always secondary, and instrumental to the act of *in*quiring. It is seeking, a quest, for something that is not at hand. We sometimes talk as if "original research" were a peculiar prerogative of scientists or at least of advanced students. But all thinking is research, and all research is native, original, with him who carries it on, even if everybody else in the world already is sure of what he is still looking for.

It also follows that all thinking involves a risk. Certainty cannot be guaranteed in advance. The invasion of the unknown is of the nature of an adventure; we cannot be sure in advance. The conclusions of thinking, till confirmed by the event, are, accordingly, more or less tentative or hypothetical. Their dogmatic assertion as final is unwarranted, short of the issue, in fact. The Greeks acutely raised the question: How can we learn? For either we know already what we are after, or else we do not know. In neither case is learning possible; on the first alternative because we know already; on the second, because we do not know what to look for, nor if, by chance, we find it can we tell that it is what we were after. The dilemma makes no provision for *coming* to know, for learning; it assumes either complete knowledge or complete ignorance. Nevertheless the twilight zone of inquiry, of thinking, exists. The possibility of *hypothetical* conclusions, of *tentative* results, is the fact which the Greek dilemma overlooked. The perplexities of the situation suggest certain ways out. We try these ways, and either push our way out, in which case we know we have found what we were looking for, or the situation gets darker and more confused—in which case, we know we are still ignorant. Tentative means trying out, feeling one's way along provisionally. Taken by itself, the Greek argument is a nice piece of formal logic. But it is also true that as long as men kept a sharp disjunction between knowledge and ignorance, science made only slow and accidental advance. Systematic advance in invention and discovery began when men recognized that they could utilize doubt for purposes of inquiry by forming conjectures to guide action in tentative explorations, whose development would confirm, refute, or modify the guiding conjecture. While the Greeks made knowledge more than learning, modern science makes conserved knowledge only a means to learning, to discovery.

To recur to our illustration. A commanding general cannot base his actions upon either absolute certainty or absolute ignorance. He has a certain amount of information at hand which is, we will assume, reasonably trustworthy. He then *infers* certain prospective movements, thus assigning meaning to the bare facts of the given situation. His inference is more or less dubious and hypothetical. But he acts upon it. He develops a plan of procedure, a method of dealing with the situation. The consequences which directly follow from his acting this way rather than that test and reveal the worth of his reflections. What he already knows functions and has value in what he learns. But will this account apply in the case of the one in a neutral country who is thoughtfully following as best he can the progress of events? In form, yes, though not of course in content. It is self-evident that his guesses about the future indicated by present facts, guesses by which he attempts to supply meaning to a multitude of disconnected data, cannot be the basis of a method which shall take effect in the campaign. *That* is not *his* problem. But in the degree in which he is actively thinking, and not merely passively following the course of events, his tentative inferences will take effect in *a* method of procedure appropriate to *his* situation. He will anticipate certain future moves, and will be on the alert to see whether they happen or not. In the degree in which he is intellectually concerned, or thoughtful, he will be *actively* on the lookout; he will take steps which although they do not affect the campaign, modify in some degree *his* subsequent actions. Otherwise his later "I told you so" has no intellectual quality at all; it does not mark any testing or verification of prior thinking, but only a coincidence that yields emotional satisfaction—and includes a large factor of self-deception.

The case is comparable to that of an astronomer who from given data has been led to foresee (infer) a future eclipse. No matter how great the mathematical probability, the inference is hypothetical—a matter of probability.[1] The hypothesis as to the date and position of the anticipated eclipse becomes the material of forming a method of future conduct. Apparatus is arranged; possibly an expedition is made to some far part of the globe. In any case, some active steps are taken which actually change *some* physical conditions. And apart from such steps and the consequent modification of the situation, there is no completion of the act of thinking. It remains suspended. Knowledge, already attained knowledge, controls thinking and makes it fruitful.

So much for the general features of a reflective experience. They are (i) perplexity, confusion, doubt, due to the fact that one is implicated in an incomplete situation whose full character is not yet determined; (ii) a conjectural anticipation—a tentative interpretation of the given elements, attributing to them a tendency to effect certain consequences; (iii) a careful survey (examination, inspection, exploration, analysis) of all attainable consideration which will define and clarify the problem in hand; (iv) a consequent elaboration of the tentative hypothesis to make

---

[1] It is most important for the practice of science that men in many cases can calculate the degree of probability and the amount of probable error involved, but that does not alter the features of the situation as described. It refines them.

it more precise and more consistent, because squaring with a wider range of facts; (v) taking one stand upon the projected hypothesis as a plan of action which is applied to the existing state of affairs: doing something overtly to bring about the anticipated result, and thereby testing the hypothesis. It is the extent and accuracy of steps three and four which mark off a distinctive reflective experience from one on the trial and error plane. They make *thinking* itself into an experience. Nevertheless, we never get wholly beyond the trial and error situation. Our most elaborate and rationally consistent thought has to be tried in the world and thereby tried out. And since it can never take into account all the connections, it can never cover with perfect accuracy all the consequences. Yet a thoughtful survey of conditions is so careful, and the guessing at results so controlled, that we have a right to mark off the reflective experience from the grosser trial and error forms of action.

Summary. In determining the place of thinking in experience we first noted that experience involves a connection of doing or trying with something which is undergone in consequence. A separation of the active doing phase from the passive undergoing phase destroys the vital meaning of an experience. Thinking is the accurate and deliberate instituting of connections between what is done and its consequences. It notes not only that they are connected, but the details of the connection. It makes connecting links explicit in the form of relationships. The stimulus to thinking is found when we wish to determine the significance of some act, performed or to be performed. Then we anticipate consequences. This implies that the situation as it stands is, either in fact or to us, incomplete and hence indeterminate. The projection of consequences means a proposed or tentative solution. To perfect this hypothesis, existing conditions have to be carefully scrutinized and the implications of the hypothesis developed—an operation called reasoning. Then the suggested solution—the idea or theory—has to be tested by acting upon it. If it brings about certain consequences, certain determinate changes, in the world, it is accepted as valid. Otherwise it is modified, and another trial made. Thinking includes all of these steps,—the sense of a problem, the observation of conditions, the formation and rational elaboration of a suggested conclusion, and the active experimental testing. While all thinking results in knowledge, ultimately the value of knowledge is subordinate to its use in thinking. For we live not in a settled and finished world, but in one which is going on, and where our main task is prospective, and where retrospect—and all knowledge as distinct from thought is retrospect—is of value in the solidity, security, and fertility it affords our dealings with the future.

31. The Need of a Theory of Experience*

In 1938, John Dewey published his Kappa Delta Pi lectures, *Experience and Education*, in an attempt to clarify his relationship to progressive education, then so strongly identified with his name. Dewey affirms that in itself "departure from the old solves no problems." He also contends that the central role of experience in education does not imply experience and education can be directly equated one to the other. There are, after all, innumerable miseducative experiences, which have the effect of engendering "callousness," or lack of sensitivity and responsiveness.

Fundamentally, Dewey holds that educative experiences are those that do not arrest or distort the growth of further experience—that is, they open the person to relationships and possibilities of enhanced human living. He warns the proponents of progressive education that "it is not enough to insist upon the necessity of experience, nor even of activity in experience. Everything depends on the *quality* of the experience which is had." Finally, Dewey laments that progressive education has failed to organize adequate school and classroom structures sufficient to do justice to the wisdom of their own viewpoint. He sees this inadequacy as unnecessary to the values of progressive education and as playing into the hands of reactionary forces who gain support on this ancillary issue. Once again, Dewey's terrain is familiar to students of contemporary education.

In short, the point I am making is that rejection of the philosophy and practice of traditional education sets a new type of difficult educational problem for those who believe in the new type of education. We shall

* From John Dewey, *Experience and Education* (New York, Macmillan Co., 1965) (1938), pp. 12-22. Used by permission of Kappa Delta Pi, An Honor Society in Education, Owners of the Copyright.

operate blindly and in confusion until we recognize this fact; until we thoroughly appreciate that departure from the old solves no problems. What is said in the following pages is, accordingly, intended to indicate some of the main problems with which the newer education is confronted and to suggest the main lines along which their solution is to be sought. I assume that amid all uncertainties there is one permanent frame of reference: namely, the organic connection between education and personal experience; or, that the new philosophy of education is committed to some kind of empirical and experimental philosophy. But experience and experiment are not self-explanatory ideas. Rather, their meaning is part of the problem to be explored. To know the meaning of empiricism we need to understand what experience is.

The belief that all genuine education comes about through experience does not mean that all experiences are genuinely or equally educative. Experience and education cannot be directly equated to each other. For some experiences are mis-educative. Any experience is mis-educative that has the effect of arresting or distorting the growth of further experience. An experience may be such as to engender callousness; it may produce lack of sensitivity and of responsiveness. Then the possibilities of having richer experience in the future are restricted. Again, a given experience may increase a person's automatic skill in a particular direction and yet tend to land him in a groove or rut; the effect again is to narrow the field of further experience. An experience may be immediately enjoyable and yet promote the formation of a slack and careless attitude; this attitude then operates to modify the quality of subsequent experiences so as to prevent a person from getting out of them what they have to give. Again, experiences may be so disconnected from one another that, while each is agreeable or even exciting in itself, they are not linked cumulatively to one another. Energy is then dissipated and a person becomes scatter-brained. Each experience may be lively, vivid, and "interesting," and yet their disconnectedness may artificially generate dispersive, disintegrated, centrifugal habits. The consequence of formation of such habits is inability to control future experiences. They are then taken, either by way of enjoyment or of discontent and revolt, just as they come. Under such circumstances, it is idle to talk of self-control.

Traditional education offers a plethora of examples of experiences of the kinds just mentioned. It is a great mistake to suppose, even tacitly, that the traditional schoolroom was not a place in which pupils had experiences. Yet this is tacitly assumed when progressive education as a

508 THE PHILOSOPHY OF JOHN DEWEY

plan of learning by experience is placed in sharp opposition to the old. The proper line of attack is that the experiences which were had, by pupils and teachers alike, were largely of a wrong kind. How many students, for example, were rendered callous to ideas, and how many lost the impetus to learn because of the way in which learning was experienced by them? How many acquired special skills by means of automatic drill so that their power of judgment and capacity to act intelligently in new situations was limited? How many came to associate the learning process with ennui and boredom? How many found what they did learn so foreign to the situations of life outside the school as to give them no power of control over the latter? How many came to associate books with dull drudgery, so that they were "conditioned" to all but flashy reading matter?

If I ask these questions, it is not for the sake of wholesale condemnation of the old education. It is for quite another purpose. It is to emphasize the fact, first, that young people in traditional schools do have experiences; and, secondly, that the trouble is not the absence of experiences, but their defective and wrong character—wrong and defective from the standpoint of connection with further experience. The positive side of this point is even more important in connection with progressive education. It is not enough to insist upon the necessity of experience, nor even of activity in experience. Everything depends upon the *quality* of the experience which is had. The quality of any experience has two aspects. There is an immediate aspect of agreeableness or disagreeableness, and there is its influence upon later experiences. The first is obvious and easy to judge. The *effect* of an experience is not borne on its face. It sets a problem to the educator. It is his business to arrange for the kind of experiences which, while they do not repel the student, but rather engage his activities are, nevertheless, more than immediately enjoyable since they promote having desirable future experiences. Just as no man lives or dies to himself, so no experience lives and dies to itself. Wholly independent of desire or intent, every experience lives on in further experiences. Hence the central problem of an education based upon experience is to select the kind of present experiences that live fruitfully and creatively in subsequent experiences.

Later, I shall discuss in more detail the principle of the continuity of experience of what may be called the experiential continuum. Here I wish simply to emphasize the importance of this principle for the philosophy of educative experience. A philosophy of education, like any theory, has to be stated in words, in symbols. But so far as it is more than verbal it is a plan for conducting education. Like any plan, it must be framed with reference to what is to be done and how it is to be done. The more definitely and sincerely it is held that education is a development within, by, and for experience, the more important it is that there shall be clear conceptions of what experience is. Unless experience is so conceived that the result is a plan for deciding upon subject-matter, upon methods of instruction and discipline, and upon material equipment and social organization of the school, it is wholly in the air. It is reduced to a form of words which may be emotionally stirring but for which any other set of words might equally well be substituted unless they indicate operations to be initiated and executed. Just because traditional education was a matter of routine in which the plans and programs were handed down from the past, it does not follow that progressive education is a matter of planless improvisation.

The traditional school could get along without any consistently developed philosophy of education. About all it required in that line was a set of abstract words like culture, discipline, our great cultural heritage, etc., actual guidance being derived not from them but from custom and established routines. Just because progressive schools cannot rely upon established traditions and institutional habits, they must either proceed more or less haphazardly or be directed by ideas which, when they are made articulate and coherent, form a philosophy of education. Revolt against the kind of organization characteristic of the traditional school constitutes a demand for a kind of organization based upon ideas. I think that only slight acquaintance with the history of education is needed to prove that educational reformers and innovators alone have felt the need for a philosophy of education. Those who adhered to the established system needed merely a few fine-sounding words to justify existing practices. The real work was done by habits which were so fixed as to be institutional. The lesson for progressive education is that it requires in an urgent degree, a degree more pressing than was incumbent upon former innovators, a philosophy of education based upon a philosophy of experience.

I remarked incidentally that the philosophy in question is, to paraphrase the saying of Lincoln about democracy, one of education of, by, and for experience. No one of these words, *of, by,* or *for*, names anything which is self-evident. Each of them is a challenge to discover and put into operation a principle of order and organization which follows from understanding what educative experience signifies.

It is, accordingly, a much more difficult task to work out the kinds of materials, of methods, and of social relationships that are appropriate to the new education than is the case with traditional education. I think

many of the difficulties experienced in the conduct of progressive
schools and many of the criticisms leveled against them arise from this
source. The difficulties are aggravated and the criticisms are increased
when it is supposed that the new education is somehow easier than the
old. This belief is, I imagine, more or less current. Perhaps it illustrates
again the *Either-Or* philosophy, springing from the idea that about all
which is required is *not* to do what is done in traditional schools.

I admit gladly that the new education is *simpler* in principle than the
old. It is in harmony with principles of growth, while there is very much
which is artificial in the old selection and arrangement of subjects and
methods, and artificiality always leads to unnecessary complexity. But
the easy and the simple are not identical. To discover what is really
simple and to act upon the discovery is an exceedingly difficult task. After the artificial and complex is once institutionally established and
ingrained in custom and routine, it is easier to walk in the paths that
have been beaten than it is, after taking a new point of view, to work out
what is practically involved in the new point of view. The old Ptolemaic
astronomical system was more complicated with its cycles and epicycles
than the Copernican system. But until organization of actual astronomical phenomena on the ground of the latter principle had been effected the easiest course was to follow the line of least resistance provided by the old intellectual habit. So we come back to the idea that a
coherent *theory* of experience, affording positive direction to selection
and organization of appropriate educational methods and materials, is
required by the attempt to give new direction to the work of the schools.
The process is a slow and arduous one. It is a matter of growth, and
there are many obstacles which tend to obstruct growth and to deflect it
into wrong lines.

I shall have something to say later about organization. All that is
needed, perhaps, at this point is to say that we must escape from the
tendency to think of organization in terms of the *kind* of organization,
whether of content (or subject-matter), or of methods and social relations, that mark traditional education. I think that a good deal of the
current opposition to the idea of organization is due to the fact that it is
so hard to get away from the picture of the studies of the old school.
The moment "organization" is mentioned imagination goes almost
automatically to the kind of organization that is familiar, and in revolt-
ing against that we are led to shrink from the very idea of any organization. On the other hand, educational reactionaries, who are now gathering force, use the absence of adequate intellectual and moral organization in the newer type of school as proof not only of the need of

organization, but to identify any and every kind of organization with that instituted before the rise of experimental science. Failure to develop a conception of organization upon the empirical and experimental basis gives reactionaries a too easy victory. But the fact that the empirical sciences now offer the best type of intellectual organization which can be found in any field shows that there is no reason why we, who call ourselves empiricists, should be "push-overs" in the matter of order and organization.

32. Criteria of Experience*

This selection, also from *Experience and Education*, is a more developed presentation of Dewey's notion of the "experience-continuum" and its significance for education. In the main, Dewey offers a principle of accountability as essential to evaluating the educational significances of varying experiences. The teacher is disloyal to the principle of experience if either the objective or internal conditions of an educational situation are not met. By this Dewey refers to the importance of knowing the child in the actuality of his or her participation in the learning situation. In Buber's phrase, the teacher must experience from the standpoint of the other, the child. On the other hand, the teacher must master the material to be presented and, above all, have a grasp of the implications and relationships engendered by the introduction of this educational matter.

For Dewey, "continuity and interaction in their active union with each other provide the measure of the educative significance and value of an experience." It is important to realize that these twin burdens placed upon the teacher, extreme sensitivity to the child and a grasp of the material in terms of relevancy to the life of the child, constitute a major challenge to the personal and intellectual quality of the teacher. If Dewey's attempt to reform education has been less than successful, it is due not to the softness or naïveté of the

---

* From John Dewey, *Experience and Education* (New York, Macmillan Co., 1965) (1938), pp. 23-52. Used by permission of Kappa Delta Pi, An Honor Society in Education, Owners of the Copyright.

approach as claimed but rather to the heightened demand for quality placed upon teachers utilizing his approach.

If there is any truth in what has been said about the need of forming a theory of experience in order that education may be intelligently conducted upon the basis of experience, it is clear that the next thing in order in this discussion is to present the principles that are most significant in framing this theory. I shall not, therefore, apologize for engaging in a certain amount of philosophical analysis, which otherwise might be out of place. I may, however, reassure you to some degree by saying that this analysis is not an end in itself but is engaged in for the sake of obtaining criteria to be applied later in discussion of a number of concrete and, to most persons, more interesting issues.

I have already mentioned what I called the category of continuity, or the experiential continuum. This principle is involved, as I pointed out, in every attempt to discriminate between experiences that are worth while educationally and those that are not. It may seem superfluous to argue that this discrimination is necessary not only in criticizing the traditional type of education but also in initiating and conducting a different type. Nevertheless, it is advisable to pursue for a little while the idea that it is necessary. One may safely assume, I suppose, that one thing which has recommended the progressive movement is that it seems more in accord with the democratic ideal to which our people is committed than do the procedures of the traditional school, since the latter have so much of the autocratic about them. Another thing which has contributed to its favorable reception is that its methods are humane in comparison with the harshness so often attending the policies of the traditional school.

The question I would raise concerns why we prefer democratic and humane arrangements to those which are autocratic and harsh. And by "why," I mean the *reason* for preferring them, not just the *causes* which lead us to the preference. One *cause* may be that we have been taught not only in the schools but by the press, the pulpit, the platform, and our laws and law-making bodies that democracy is the best of all social institutions. We may have so assimilated this idea from our surroundings that it has become an habitual part of our mental and moral make-up. But similar causes have led other persons in different surroundings to widely varying conclusions—to prefer fascism, for example. The cause for our preference is not the same thing as the reason why we *should* prefer it.

It is not my purpose here to go in detail into the reason. But I would ask a single question: Can we find any reason that does not ultimately come down to the belief that democratic social arrangements promote a better quality of human experience, one which is more widely accessible and enjoyed, than do non-democratic and anti-democratic forms of social life? Does not the principle of regard for individual freedom and for decency and kindliness of human relations come back in the end to the conviction that these things are tributary to a higher quality of experience on the part of a greater number than are methods of repression and coercion or force? Is it not the reason for our preference that we believe that mutual consultation and convictions reached through persuasion, make possible a better quality of experience than can otherwise be provided on any wide scale?

If the answer to these questions is in the affirmative (and personally I do not see how we can justify our preference for democracy and humanity on any other ground), the ultimate reason for hospitality to progressive education, because of its reliance upon and use of humane methods and its kinship to democracy, goes back to the fact that discrimination is made between the inherent values of different experiences. So I come back to the principle of continuity of experience as a criterion of discrimination.

At bottom, this principle rests upon the fact of habit, when *habit* is interpreted biologically. The basic characteristic of habit is that every experience enacted and undergone modifies the one who acts and undergoes, while this modification affects, whether we wish it or not, the quality of subsequent experiences. For it is a somewhat different person who enters into them. The principle of habit so understood obviously goes deeper than the ordinary conception of *a* habit as a more or less fixed way of doing things, although it includes the latter as one of its special cases. It covers the formation of attitudes, attitudes that are emotional and intellectual; it covers our basic sensitivities and ways of meeting and responding to all the conditions which we meet in living. From this point of view, the principle of continuity of experience means that every experience both takes up something from those which have gone before and modifies in some way the quality of those which come after. As the poet states it,

> ". . . all experience is an arch wherethro'
> Gleams that untraveled world, whose margin fades
> For ever and for ever when I move."

So far, however, we have no ground for discrimination among experiences. For the principle is of universal application. There is *some* kind of continuity in every case. It is when we note the different forms in which continuity of experience operates that we get the basis of discriminating among experiences. I may illustrate what is meant by an objection which has been brought against an idea which I once put forth —namely, that the educative process can be identified with growth when that is understood in terms of the active participle, *growing*.

Growth, or growing as developing, not only physically but intellectually and morally, is one exemplification of the principle of continuity. The objection made is that growth might take many different directions: a man, for example, who starts out on a career of burglary may grow in that direction, and by practice may grow into a highly expert burglar. Hence it is argued that "growth" is not enough; we must also specify the direction in which growth takes place, the end towards which it tends. Before, however, we decide that the objection is conclusive we must analyze the case a little further.

That a man may grow in efficiency as a burglar, as a gangster, or as a corrupt politician, cannot be doubted. But from the standpoint of growth as education and education as growth the question is whether growth in this direction promotes or retards growth in general. Does this form of growth create conditions for further growth, or does it set up conditions that shut off the person who has grown in this particular direction from the occasions, stimuli, and opportunities for continuing growth in new directions? What is the effect of growth in a special direction upon the attitudes and habits which alone open up avenues for development in other lines? I shall leave you to answer these questions, saying simply that when and *only* when development in a particular line conduces to continuing growth does it answer to the criterion of education as growing. For the conception is one that must find universal and not specialized limited application.

I return now to the question of continuity as a criterion by which to discriminate between experiences which are educative and those which are mis-educative. As we have seen, there is some kind of continuity in any case since every experience affects for better or worse the attitudes which help decide the quality of further experiences, by setting up certain preference and aversion, and making it easier or harder to act for this or that end. Moreover, every experience influences in some degree the objective conditions under which further experiences are had. For example, a child who learns to speak has a new facility and new desire. But he has also widened the external conditions of subsequent learning. When he learns to read, he similarly opens up a new environment. If a person decides to become a teacher, lawyer, physician, or stockbroker, when he executes his intention he thereby necessarily determines to some extent the environment in which he will act in the future. He has rendered himself more sensitive and responsive to certain conditions, and relatively immune to those things about him that would have been stimuli if he had made another choice.

But, while the principle of continuity applies in some way in every case, the quality of the present experience influences the *way* in which the principle applies. We speak of spoiling a child and of the spoilt child. The effect of over-indulging a child is a continuing one. It sets up an attitude which operates as an automatic demand that persons and objects cater to his desires and caprices in the future. It makes him seek the kind of situation that will enable him to do what he feels like doing at the time. It renders him averse to and comparatively incompetent in situations which require effort and perseverance in overcoming obstacles. There is no paradox in the fact that the principle of the continuity of experience may operate so as to leave a person arrested on a low plane of development, in a way which limits later capacity for growth.

On the other hand, if an experience arouses curiosity, strengthens initiative, and sets up desires and purposes that are sufficiently intense to carry a person over dead places in the future, continuity works in a very different way. Every experience is a moving force. Its value can be judged only on the ground of what it moves toward and into. The greater maturity of experience which should belong to the adult as educator puts him in a position to evaluate each experience of the young in a way in which the one having the less mature experience cannot do. It is then the business of the educator to see in what direction an experience is heading. There is no point in his being more mature if, instead of using his greater insight to help organize the conditions of the experience of the immature, he throws away his insight. Failure to take the moving force of an experience into account so as to judge and direct it on the ground of what it is moving into means disloyalty to the principle of experience itself. The disloyalty operates in two directions. The educator is false to the understanding that he should have obtained from his own past experience. He is also unfaithful to the fact that all human experience is ultimately social: that it involves contact and communication. The mature person, to put it in moral terms, has no right to withhold from the young on given occasions whatever capacity for sympathetic understanding his own experience has given him.

No sooner, however, are such things said than there is a tendency to react to the other extreme and take what has been said as a plea for some sort of disguised imposition from outside. It is worth while, accordingly, to say something about the way in which the adult can exercise the wisdom his own wider experience gives him without imposing a merely external control. On one side, it is his business to be on the alert to see what attitudes and habitual tendencies are being created. In this direction he must, if he is an educator, be able to judge what attitudes are actually conducive to continued growth and what are detrimental. He must, in addition, have that sympathetic understanding of individuals as individuals which gives him an idea of what is actually going on in the minds of those who are learning. It is, among other things, the need for these abilities on the part of the parent and teacher which makes a system of education based upon living experience a more difficult affair to conduct successfully than it is to follow the patterns of traditional education.

But there is another aspect of the matter. Experience does not go on simply inside a person. It does go on there, for it influences the formation of attitudes of desire and purpose. But this is not the whole of the story. Every genuine experience has an active side which changes in some degree the objective conditions under which experiences are had. The difference between civilization and savagery, to take an example on a large scale, is found in the degree in which previous experiences have changed the objective conditions under which subsequent experiences take place. The existence of roads, of means of rapid movement and transportation, tools, implements, furniture, electric light and power, are illustrations. Destroy the external conditions of present civilized experience, and for a time our experience would relapse into that of barbaric peoples.

In a word, we live from birth to death in a world of persons and things which in large measure is what it is because of what has been done and transmitted from previous human activities. When this fact is ignored, experience is treated as if it were something which goes on exclusively inside an individual's body and mind. It ought not to be necessary to say that experience does not occur in a vacuum. There are sources outside an individual which give rise to experience. It is constantly fed from these springs. No one would question that a child in a slum tenement has a different experience from that of a child in a cultured home; that the country lad has a different kind of experience from the city boy, or a boy on the seashore one different from the lad who is brought up on inland prairies. Ordinarily we take such facts for granted as too commonplace to record. But when their educational import is recognized, they indicate the second way in which the educator can direct the experience of the young without engaging in imposition. A primary responsibility of educators is that they not only be aware of the general principle of the shaping of actual experience by environing conditions, but that they also recognize in the concrete what surroundings are conducive to having experiences that lead to growth. Above all, they should know how to utilize the surroundings, physical and social, that exist so as to extract from them all that they have to contribute to building up experiences that are worth while.

Traditional education did not have to face this problem; it could systematically dodge this responsibility. The school environment of desks, blackboards, a small school yard, was supposed to suffice. There was no demand that the teacher should become intimately acquainted with the conditions of the local community, physical, historical, economic, occupational, etc., in order to utilize them as educational resources. A system of education based upon the necessary connection of education with experience must, on the contrary, if faithful to its principle, take these things constantly into account. This tax upon the educator is another reason why progressive education is more difficult to carry on than was ever the traditional system.

It is possible to frame schemes of education that pretty systematically subordinate objective conditions to those which reside in the individuals being educated. This happens whenever the place and function of the teacher, of books, of apparatus and equipment, of everything which represents the products of the more mature experience of elders, is systematically subordinated to the immediate inclinations and feelings of the young. Every theory which assumes that importance can be attached to these objective factors only at the expense of imposing external control and of limiting the freedom of individuals rests finally upon the notion that experience is truly experience only when objective conditions are subordinated to what goes on within the individuals having the experience.

I do not mean that it is supposed that objective conditions can be shut out. It is recognized that they must enter in: so much concession is made to the inescapable fact that we live in a world of things and persons. But I think that observation of what goes on in some families and some schools would disclose that some parents and some teachers are acting upon the idea of *subordinating* objective conditions to internal ones. In that case, it is assumed not only that the latter are primary, which in one sense they are, but that just as they temporarily exist they fix the whole educational process.

Let me illustrate from the case of an infant. The needs of a baby for food, rest, and activity are certainly primary and decisive in one respect. Nourishment must be provided; provision must be made for comfortable sleep, and so on. But these facts do not mean that a parent shall feed the baby at any time when the baby is cross or irritable, that there shall not be a program of regular hours of feeding and sleeping, etc. The wise mother takes account of the needs of the infant but not in a way which dispenses with her own responsibility for regulating the objective conditions under which the needs are satisfied. And if she is a wise mother in this respect, she draws upon past experiences of experts as well as her own for the light that these shed upon what experiences are in general most conducive to the normal development of infants. Instead of these conditions being subordinated to the immediate internal condition of the baby, they are definitely ordered so that a particular kind of *interaction* with these immediate internal states may be brought about.

The word "interaction," which has just been used, expresses the second chief principle for interpreting an experience in its educational function and force. It assigns equal rights to both factors in experience —objective and internal conditions. Any normal experience is an interplay of these two sets of conditions. Taken together, or in their interaction, they form what we call a *situation*. The trouble with traditional education was not that it emphasized the external conditions that enter into the control of the experiences but that it paid so little attention to the internal factors which also decide what kind of experience is had. It violated the principle of interaction from one side. But this violation is no reason why the new education should violate the principle from the other side—except upon the basis of the extreme *Either-Or* educational philosophy which has been mentioned.

The illustration drawn from the need for regulation of the objective conditions of a baby's development indicates, first, that the parent has responsibility for arranging the conditions under which an infant's experience of food, sleep, etc., occurs, and, secondly, that the responsibility is fulfilled by utilizing the funded experience of the past, as this is represented, say, by the advice of competent physicians and others who have made a special study of normal physical growth. Does it limit the freedom of the mother when she uses the body of knowledge thus provided to regulate the objective conditions of nourishment and sleep? Or does the enlargment of her intelligence in fulfilling her parental function widen her freedom? Doubtless if a fetish were made of the advice and directions so that they came to be inflexible dictates to be followed under every possible condition, then restriction of freedom of both parent and child would occur. But this restriction would also be a limitation of the intelligence that is exercised in personal judgment.

In what respect does regulation of objective conditions limit the freedom of the baby? Some limitation is certainly placed upon its immediate movements and inclinations when it is put in its crib, at a time when it wants to continue playing, or does not get food at the moment it would like it, or when it isn't picked up and dandled when it cries for attention. Restriction also occurs when mother or nurse snatches a child away from an open fire into which it is about to fall. I shall have more to say later about freedom. Here it is enough to ask whether freedom is to be thought of and adjudged on the basis of relatively momentary incidents or whether its meaning is found in the continuity of developing experience.

The statement that individuals live in a world means, in the concrete, that they live in a series of situations. And when it is said that they live *in* these situations, the meaning of the word "in" is different from its meaning when it is said that pennies are "in" a pocket or paint is "in" a can. It means, once more, that interaction is going on between an individual and objects and other persons. The conceptions of *situation* and of *interaction* are inseparable from each other. An experience is always what it is because of a transaction taking place between an individual and what, at the time, constitutes his environment, whether the latter consists of persons with whom he is talking about some topic or event, the subject talked about being also a part of the situation; or the toys with which he is playing; the book he is reading (in which his environing conditions at the time may be England or ancient Greece or an imaginary region); or the materials of an experiment he is performing. The environment, in other words, is whatever conditions interact with personal needs, desires, purposes, and capacities to create the experience which is had. Even when a person builds a castle in the air he is interacting with the objects which he constructs in fancy.

The two principles of continuity and interaction are not separate from each other. They intercept and unite. They are, so to speak, the longitudinal and lateral aspects of experience. Different situations succeed one another. But because of the principle of continuity something is carried over from the earlier to the later ones. As an individual passes from one situation to another, his world, his environment, expands or contracts. He does not find himself living in another world but in a different part or aspect of one and the same world. What he has learned in the way of knowledge and skill in one situation becomes an instrument of understanding and dealing effectively with the situations which follow. The process goes on as long as life and learning continue. Otherwise the course of experience is disorderly, since the individual factor that enters into making an experience is split. A divided world, a world whose parts and aspects do not hang together, is at once a sign and a cause of a divided personality. When the splitting-up reaches a certain point we call the person insane. A fully integrated personality, on the other hand, exists only when successive experiences are integrated with one another. It can be built up only as a world of related objects is constructed.

Continuity and interaction in their active union with each other provide the measure of the educative significance and value of an experience. The immediate and direct concern of an educator is then with the situations in which interaction takes place. The individual, who enters as a factor into it, is what he is at a given time. It is the other factor, that of objective conditions, which lies to some extent within the possibility of regulation by the educator. As has already been noted, the phrase "objective conditions" covers a wide range. It includes what is done by the educator and the way in which it is done, not only words spoken but the tone of voice in which they are spoken. It includes equipment, books, apparatus, toys, games played. It includes the materials with which an individual interacts, and, most important of all, the total *social* set-up of the situations in which a person is engaged.

When it is said that the objective conditions are those which are within the power of the educator to regulate, it is meant, of course, that his ability to influence directly the experience of others and thereby the education they obtain places upon him the duty of determining that environment which will interact with the existing capacities and needs of those taught to create a worth-while experience. The trouble with traditional education was not that educators took upon themselves the responsibility for providing an environment. The trouble was that they did not consider the other factor in creating an experience; namely, the powers and purposes of those taught. It was assumed that a certain set of conditions was intrinsically desirable, apart from its ability to evoke a certain quality of response in individuals. This lack of mutual adaptation made the process of teaching and learning accidental. Those to whom the provided conditions were suitable managed to learn. Others got on as best they could. Responsibility for selecting objective conditions carries with it, then, the responsibility for understanding the needs and capacities of the individuals who are learning at a given time. It is not enough that certain materials and methods have proved effective

with other individuals at other times. There must be a reason for thinking that they will function in generating an experience that has
educative quality with particular individuals at a particular time.

It is no reflection upon the nutritive quality of beefsteak that it is not
fed to infants. It is not an invidious reflection upon trigonometry that
we do not teach it in the first or fifth grade of school. It is not the subject *per se* that is educative or that is conducive to growth. There is no
subject that is in and of itself, or without regard to the stage of growth
attained by the learner, such that inherent educational value can be attributed to it. Failure to take into account adaptation to the needs and
capacities of individuals was the source of the idea that certain subjects
and certain methods are intrinsically cultural or intrinsically good for
mental discipline. There is no such thing as educational value in the
abstract. The notion that some subjects and methods and that acquaintance with certain facts and truths possess educational value in and of
themselves is the reason why traditional education reduced the material
of education so largely to a diet of predigested materials. According to
this notion, it was enough to regulate the quantity and difficulty of the
material provided, in a scheme of quantitative grading, from month to
month and from year to year. Otherwise a pupil was expected to take it
in the doses that were prescribed from without. If the pupil left it instead of taking it, if he engaged in physical truancy, or in the mental
truancy of mind-wandering and finally built up an emotional revulsion
against the subject, he was held to be at fault. No question was raised as
to whether the trouble might not lie in the subject-matter or in the way
in which it was offered. The principle of interaction makes it clear that
failure of adaptation of material to needs and capacities of individuals
may cause an experience to be non-educative quite as much as failure of
an individual to adapt himself to the material.

The principle of continuity in its educational application means,
nevertheless, that the future has to be taken into account at every stage
of the educational process. This idea is easily misunderstood and is
badly distorted in traditional education. Its assumption is, that by acquiring certain skills and by learning certain subjects which would be
needed later (perhaps in college or perhaps in adult life) pupils are as a
matter of course made ready for the needs and circumstances of the
future. Now "preparation" is a treacherous idea. In a certain sense
every experience should do something to prepare a person for later experiences of a deeper and more expansive quality. That is the very
meaning of growth, continuity, reconstruction of experience. But it is a
mistake to suppose that the mere acquisition of a certain amount of

arithmetic, geography, history, etc., which is taught and studied because it may be useful at some time in the future, has this effect, and it is a mistake to suppose that acquisition of skills in reading and figuring will automatically constitute preparation for their right and effective use under conditions very unlike those in which they were acquired.

Almost everyone has had occasion to look back upon his school days and wonder what has become of the knowledge he was supposed to have amassed during his years of schooling, and why it is that the technical skills he acquired have to be learned over again in changed form in order to stand him in good stead. Indeed, he is lucky who does not find that in order to make progress, in order to go ahead intellectually, he does not have to unlearn much of what he learned in school. These questions cannot be disposed of by saying that the subjects were not actually learned, for they were learned at least sufficiently to enable a pupil to pass examinations in them. One trouble is that the subject-matter in question was learned in isolation; it was put, as it were, in a water-tight compartment. When the question is asked, then, what has become of it, where has it gone to, the right answer is that it is still there in the special compartment in which it was originally stowed away. If exactly the same conditions recurred as those under which it was acquired, it would also recur and be available. But it was segregated when it was acquired and hence is so disconnected from the rest of experience that it is not available under the actual conditions of life. It is contrary to the laws of experience that learning of this kind, no matter how thoroughly engrained at the time, should give genuine preparation.

Nor does failure in preparation end at this point. Perhaps the greatest of all pedagogical fallacies is the notion that a person learns only the particular thing he is studying at the time. Collateral learning in the way of formation of enduring attitudes, of likes and dislikes, may be and often is much more important than the spelling lesson or lesson in geography or history that is learned. For these attitudes are fundamentally what count in the future. The most important attitude that can be formed is that of desire to go on learning. If impetus in this direction is weakened instead of being intensified, something much more than mere lack of preparation takes place. The pupil is actually robbed of native capacities which otherwise would enable him to cope with the circumstances that he meets in the course of his life. We often see persons who have had little schooling and in whose case the absence of set schooling proves to be a positive asset. They have at least retained their native common sense and power of judgment, and its exercise in the actual conditions of living has given them the precious gift of ability to learn from the experiences they have. What avail is it to win prescribed amounts of information about geography and history, to win ability to read and write, if in the process the individual loses his own soul: loses his appreciation of things worth while, of the values to which these things are relative; if he loses desire to apply what he has learned and, above all, loses the ability to extract meaning from his future experiences as they occur?

What, then, is the true meaning of preparation in the educational scheme? In the first place, it means that a person, young or old, gets out of his present experience all that there is in it for him at the time in which he has it. When preparation is made the controlling end, then the potentialities of the present are sacrificed to a supposititious future. When this happens, the actual preparation for the future is missed or distorted. The ideal of using the present simply to get ready for the future contradicts itself. It omits, and even shuts out, the very conditions by which a person can be prepared for his future. We always live at the time we live and not at some other time, and only by extracting at each present time the full meaning of each present experience are we prepared for doing the same thing in the future. This is the only preparation which in the long run amounts to anything.

All this means that attentive care must be devoted to the conditions which give each present experience a worth-while meaning. Instead of inferring that it doesn't make much difference what the present experience is as long as it is enjoyed, the conclusion is the exact opposite. Here is another matter where it is easy to react from one extreme to the other. Because traditional schools tended to sacrifice the present to a remote and more or less unknown future, therefore it comes to be believed that the educator has little responsibility for the kind of present experiences the young undergo. But the relation of the present and the future is not an *Either-Or* affair. The present affects the future anyway. The persons who should have some idea of the connection between the two are those who have achieved maturity. Accordingly, upon them devolves the responsibility for instituting the conditions for the kind of present experience which has a favorable effect upon the future. Education as growth or maturity should be an ever-present process.

VII
Experience as Aesthetic

John Dewey's philosophy of experience was always associated with his writings on education, methodology of the social sciences, and judgments about culture. Much less so was it associated with the arts. In part, this opinion was traceable to the comparative paucity of Dewey's writing about art prior to *Experience and Nature*. Once his aesthetics are understood, however, it becomes apparent that Dewey's philosophy from very early on was characterized by a deep recognition of aesthetic transactions in human living, although articulated in a different way.

In the judgment of the present editor, the following three chapters from *Art As Experience* when joined with selection 19, "Experience, Nature and Art," constitute the dramatic center of Dewey's philosophy. Seminal in thought and profound in implication these selections are also graced by Dewey's finest prose.

33. The Live Creature*

Art as Experience is not as much about art as it is about the potentially incessant drama of everyday experience. Thus

the significance of the title of this selection, "The Live Creature." As a matter of fact, Dewey attacks the role of art in Western culture, contending that it has become honorific, thereby cutting us off from both its experiential origins and from the qualities of our own experiencing. The task of one writing about the fine arts is stated by Dewey as follows: "This task is to restore continuity that are works of art and the everyday events, doings and sufferings that are universally recognized to constitute experience."

It is in this selection that Dewey becomes most explicit

* From John Dewey, *Art as Experience* (New York, Capricorn Books, 1958) (1934), pp. 3-19. Reprinted by permission of G. P. Putnam's Sons.

about the aesthetics of ordinary experience, holding that works of art are "celebrations, recognized as such, of the things of ordinary experience." In an anticipation of much of contemporary art, such as ready-mades and found art, Dewey writes that "even a crude experience, if authentically an experience, is more fit to give a clue to the intrinsic nature of aesthetic experience than is an object already set apart from any other mode of experience." Dewey then works out the relationship between the rhythm of experience ordinarily undergone and the achievement of the enhancements and consummations which characterize human living at its peak.

By one of the ironic perversities that often attend the course of affairs, the existence of the works of art upon which formation of an esthetic theory depends has become an obstruction to theory about them. For one reason, these works are products that exist externally and physically. In common conception, the work of art is often identified with the building, book, painting, or statue in its existence apart from human experience. Since the actual work of art is what the product does with and in experience, the result is not favorable to understanding. In addition, the very perfection of some of these products, the prestige they possess because of a long history of unquestioned admiration, creates conventions that get in the way of fresh insight. When an art product once attains classic status, it somehow becomes isolated from the human conditions under which it was brought into being and from the human consequences it engenders in actual life-experience.

When artistic objects are separated from both conditions of origin and operation in experience, a wall is built around them that renders almost opaque their general significance, with which esthetic theory deals. Art is remitted to a separate realm, where it is cut off from that association with the materials and aims of every other form of human effort, undergoing, and achievement. A primary task is thus imposed upon one who undertakes to write upon the philosophy of the fine arts. This task is to restore continuity between the refined and intensified forms of experience that are works of art and the everyday events, doings, and sufferings that are universally recognized to constitute experience. Mountain peaks do not float unsupported; they do not even just rest upon the earth. They *are* the earth in one of its manifest operations. It is the business of those who are concerned with the theory of the earth, geographers and geologists, to make this fact evident in its various implications. The theorist who would deal philosophically with fine art has a like task to accomplish.

If one is willing to grant this position, even if only by way of temporary experiment, he will see that there follows a conclusion at first sight surprising. In order to understand the meaning of artistic products, we have to forget them for a time, to turn aside from them and have recourse to the ordinary forces and conditions of experience that we do not usually regard as esthetic. We must arrive at the theory of art by means of a detour. For theory is concerned with understanding, insight, not without exclamations of admiration, and stimulation of that emotional outburst often called appreciation. It is quite possible to enjoy flowers in their colored form and delicate fragrance without knowing anything about plants theoretically. But if one sets out to *understand* the flowering of plants, he is committed to finding out something about the interactions of soil, air, water and sunlight that condition the growth of plants.

By common consent, the Parthenon is a great work of art. Yet it has esthetic standing only as the work becomes an experience for a human being. And, if one is to go beyond personal enjoyment into the formation of a theory about that large republic of art of which the building is one member, one has to be willing at some point in his reflections to turn from it to the bustling, arguing, acutely sensitive Athenian citizens, with civic sense identified with a civic religion, of whose experience the temple was an expression, and who built it not as a work of art but as a civic commemoration. The turning to them is as human beings who had needs that were a demand for the building and that were carried to fulfillment in it; it is not an examination such as might be carried on by a sociologist in search for material relevant to his purpose. The one who sets out to theorize about the esthetic experience embodied in the Parthenon must realize in thought what the people into whose lives it entered had in common, as creators and as those who were satisfied with it, with people in our own homes and on our own streets.

In order to *understand* the esthetic in its ultimate and approved forms, one must begin with it in the raw; in the events and scenes that hold the attentive eye and ear of man, arousing his interest and affording him enjoyment as he looks and listens: the sights that hold the crowd—the fire-engine rushing by; the machines excavating enormous holes in the earth; the human-fly climbing the steeple-side; the men perched high in air on girders, throwing and catching red-hot bolts. The sources of art in human experience will be learned by him who sees how the tense grace of the ball-player infects the onlooking crowd; who notes the delight of the housewife in tending her plants, and the intent interest of her goodman in tending the patch of green in front of the house; the zest of the spectator in poking the wood burning on the hearth and in watching the darting flames and crumbling coals. These people, if questioned as to the reason for their actions, would doubtless return reasonable answers. The man who poked the sticks of burning wood would say he did it to make the fire burn better; but he is none the less fascinated by the colorful drama of change enacted before his eyes and imaginatively partakes in it. He does not remain a cold spectator. What Coleridge said of the reader of poetry is true in its way of all who are happily absorbed in their activities of mind and body: "The reader should be carried forward, not merely or chiefly by the mechanical impulse of curiosity, not by a restless desire to arrive at the final solution, but by the pleasurable activity of the journey itself."

The intelligent mechanic engaged in his job, interested in doing well and finding satisfaction in his handiwork, caring for his materials and tools with genuine affection, is artistically engaged. The difference between such a worker and the inept and careless bungler is as great in the shop as it is in the studio. Oftentimes the product may not appeal to the esthetic sense of those who use the product. The fault, however, is oftentimes not so much with the worker as with the conditions of the market for which his product is designed. Were conditions and opportunities different, things as significant to the eye as those produced by earlier craftsmen would be made.

So extensive and subtly pervasive are the ideas that set Art upon a remote pedestal, that many a person would be repelled rather than pleased if told that he enjoyed his casual recreations, in part at least, because of their esthetic quality. The arts which today have most vitality for the average person are things he does not take to be arts: for instance, the movie, jazzed music, the comic strip, and, too frequently, newspaper accounts of love-nests, murders, and exploits of bandits. For, when what he knows as art is relegated to the museum and gallery, the unconquerable impulse towards experiences enjoyable in themselves finds such outlet as the daily environment provides. Many a person who protests against the museum conception of art, still shares the fallacy from which that conception springs. For the popular notion comes from a separation of art from the objects and scenes of ordinary experience that many theorists and critics pride themselves upon holding and even elaborating. The times when select and distinguished objects are closely connected with the products of usual vocations are the times when appreciation of the former is most rife and most keen. When, because of their remoteness, the objects acknowledged by the cultivated to be works of fine art seem anemic to the mass of people, esthetic hunger is likely to seek the cheap and the vulgar.

The factors that have glorified fine art by setting it upon a far-off pedestal did not arise within the realm of art nor is their influence confined to the arts. For many persons an aura of mingled awe and unreality encompasses the "spiritual" and the "ideal" while "matter" has become by contrast a term of depreciation, something to be explained away or apologized for. The forces at work are those that have removed religion as well as fine art from the scope of the common or community life. The forces have historically produced so many of the dislocations and divisions of modern life and thought that art could not escape their influence. We do not have to travel to the ends of the earth nor return many millennia in time to find peoples for whom everything that intensifies the sense of immediate living is an object of intense admiration. Bodily scarification, waving feathers, gaudy robes, shining ornaments of gold and silver, of emerald and jade, formed the contents of esthetic arts, and, presumably, without the vulgarity of class exhibitionism that attends their analogues today. Domestic utensils, furnishings of tent and house, rugs, mats, jars, pots, bows, spears, were wrought with such delighted care that today we hunt them out and give them places of honor in our art museums. Yet in their own time and place, such things were enhancements of the processes of everyday life. Instead of being elevated to a niche apart, they belonged to display of prowess, the manifestation of group and clan membership, worship of gods, feasting and fasting, fighting, hunting, and all the rhythmic crises that punctuate the stream of living.

Dancing and pantomime, the sources of the art of the theater, flourished as part of religious rites and celebrations. Musical art abounded in the fingering of the stretched string, the beating of the taut skin, the blowing with reeds. Even in the caves, human habitations were adorned with colored pictures that kept alive to the senses experiences with the animals that were so closely bound with the lives of humans. Structures that housed their gods and the instrumentalities that facilitated commerce with the higher powers were wrought with especial fineness. But the arts of the drama, music, painting, and architecture thus exemplified had no peculiar connection with theaters, galleries, museums. They were part of the significant life of an organized community.

The collective life that was manifested in war, worship, the forum, knew no division between what was characteristic of these places and operations, and the arts that brought color, grace, and dignity, into them. Painting and sculpture were organically one with architecture, as that was one with the social purpose that buildings served. Music and song were intimate parts of the rites and ceremonies in which the meaning of group life was consummated. Drama was a vital reënactment of the legends and history of group life. Not even in Athens can such arts be torn loose from this setting in direct experience and yet retain their significant character. Athletic sports, as well as drama, celebrated and enforced traditions of race and group, instructing the people, commemorating glories, and strengthening their civic pride.

Under such conditions, it is not surprising that the Athenian Greeks, when they came to reflect upon art, formed the idea that it is an act of reproduction, or imitation. There are many objections to this conception. But the vogue of the theory is testimony to the close connection of the fine arts with daily life; the idea would not have occurred to any one had art been remote from the interests of life. For the doctrine did not signify that art was a literal copying of objects, but that it reflected the emotions and ideas that are associated with the chief institutions of social life. Plato felt this connection so strongly that it led him to his idea of the necessity of censorship of poets, dramatists, and musicians. Perhaps he exaggerated when he said that a change from the Doric to the Lydian mode in music would be the sure precursor of civic degeneration. But no contemporary would have doubted that music was an integral part of the ethos and the institutions of the community. The idea of "art for art's sake" would not have been even understood.

There must then be historic reasons for the rise of the compartmental conception of fine art. Our present museums and galleries to which works of fine art are removed and stored illustrate some of the causes that have operated to segregate art instead of finding it an attendant of temple, forum, and other forms of associated life. An instructive history of modern art could be written in terms of the formation of the distinctively modern institutions of museum and exhibition gallery. I may point to a few outstanding facts. Most European museums are, among other things, memorials of the rise of nationalism and imperialism. Every capital must have its own museum of painting, sculpture, etc., devoted in part to exhibiting the greatness of its artistic past, and, in other part, to exhibiting the loot gathered by its monarchs in conquest of other nations; for instance, the accumulations of the spoils of Napoleon that are in the Louvre. They testify to the connection between the modern segregation of art and nationalism and militarism. Doubtless this connection has served at times a useful purpose, as in the case of Japan, who, when she was in the process of westernization, saved much of her art treasures by nationalizing the temples that contained them.

The growth of capitalism has been a powerful influence in the development of the museum as the proper home for works of art, and in the promotion of the idea that they are apart from the common life. The *nouveaux riches,* who are an important by-product of the capitalist system, have felt especially bound to surround themselves with works of fine art which, being rare, are also costly. Generally speaking, the typical collector is the typical capitalist. For evidence of good standing in the realm of higher culture, he amasses paintings, statuary, and artistic *bijoux,* as his stocks and bonds certify to his standing in the economic world.

Not merely individuals, but communities and nations, put their cultural good taste in evidence by building opera houses, galleries, and museums. These show that a community is not wholly absorbed in material wealth, because it is willing to spend its gains in patronage of art. It erects these buildings and collects their contents as it now builds a cathedral. These things reflect and establish superior cultural status, while their segregation from the common life reflects the fact that they are not part of a native and spontaneous culture. They are a kind of counterpart of a holier-than-thou attitude, exhibited not toward persons as such but toward the interests and occupations that absorb most of the community's time and energy.

Modern industry and commerce have an international scope. The contents of galleries and museums testify to the growth of economic cosmopolitanism. The mobility of trade and of populations, due to the economic system, has weakened or destroyed the connection between works of art and the *genius loci* of which they were once the natural expression. As works of art have lost their indigenous status, they have acquired a new one—that of being specimens of fine art and nothing else. Moreover, works of art are now produced, like other articles, for sale in the market. Economic patronage by wealthy and powerful individuals has at many times played a part in the encouragement of artistic production. Probably many a savage tribe had its Maecenas. But now even that much of intimate social connection is lost in the impersonality of a world market. Objects that were in the past valid and significant because of their place in the life of a community now function in isolation from the conditions of their origin. By that fact they are also set apart from common experience, and serve as insignia of taste and certificates of special culture.

Because of changes in industrial conditions the artist has been pushed to one side from the main streams of active interest. Industry has been mechanized and an artist cannot work mechanically for mass production. He is less integrated than formerly in the normal flow of social services. A peculiar esthetic "individualism" results. Artists find it incumbent upon them to betake themselves to their work as an isolated means of "self-expression." In order not to cater to the trend of economic forces, they often feel obliged to exaggerate their separateness to the point of eccentricity. Consequently artistic products take on to a still greater degree the air of something independent and esoteric.

Put the action of all such forces together, and the conditions that create the gulf which exists generally between producer and consumer in modern society operate to create also a chasm between ordinary and esthetic experience. Finally we have, as the record of this chasm, accepted as if it were normal, the philosophies of art that locate it in a region inhabited by no other creature, and that emphasize beyond all reason the merely contemplative character of the esthetic. Confusion of values enters in to accentuate the separation. Adventitious matters, like the pleasure of collecting, of exhibiting, of ownership and display, simulate esthetic values. Criticism is affected. There is much applause for the wonders of appreciation and the glories of the transcendent beauty of art indulged in without much regard to capacity for esthetic perception in the concrete.

My purpose, however, is not to engage in an economic interpretation of the history of the arts, much less to argue that economic conditions are either invariably or directly relevant to perception and enjoyment, or even to interpretation of individual works of art. It is to indicate that *theories* which isolate art and its appreciation by placing them in a realm of their own, disconnected from other modes of experiencing, are not inherent in the subject-matter but arise because of specifiable extraneous conditions. Embedded as they are in institutions and in habits of life, these conditions operate effectively because they work so unconsciously. Then the theorist assumes they are embedded in the nature of things. Nevertheless, the influence of these conditions is not confined to theory. As I have already indicated, it deeply affects the practice of living, driving away esthetic perceptions that are necessary ingredients of happiness, or reducing them to the level of compensating transient pleasurable excitations.

Even to readers who are adversely inclined to what has been said, the implications of the statements that have been made may be useful in defining the nature of the problem: that of recovering the continuity of esthetic experience with normal processes of living. The understanding of art and of its rôle in civilization is not furthered by setting out with eulogies of it nor by occupying ourselves exclusively at the outset with great works of art recognized as such. The comprehension which theory essays will be arrived at by a detour; by going back to experience of the common or mill run of things to discover the esthetic quality such experience possesses. Theory can start with and from acknowledged works of art only when the esthetic is already compartmentalized, or only when works of art are set in a niche apart instead of being celebrations, recognized as such, of the things of ordinary experience. Even a crude experience, if authentically an experience, is more fit to give a clue to the intrinsic nature of esthetic experience than is an object already set apart from any other mode of experience. Following this clue we can discover how the work of art develops and accentuates what is characteristically valuable in things of everyday enjoyment. The art product will then be seen to issue from the latter, when the full meaning of ordinary experience is expressed, as dyes come out of coal tar products when they receive special treatment.

Many theories about art already exist. If there is justification for proposing yet another philosophy of the esthetic, it must be found in a new mode of approach. Combinations and permutations among existing theories can easily be brought forth by those so inclined. But, to my mind, the trouble with existing theories is that they start from a ready-made compartmentalization, or from a conception of art that "spiritualizes" it out of connection with the objects of concrete experience. The alternative, however, to such spiritualization is not a degrading and Philistinish materialization of works of fine art, but a conception that discloses the way in which these works idealize qualities found in common experience. Were works of art placed in a directly human context in popular esteem, they would have a much wider appeal than they can have when pigeon-hole theories of art win general acceptance.

A conception of fine art that sets out from its connection with discovered qualities of ordinary experience will be able to indicate the factors and forces that favor the normal development of common human activities into matters of artistic value. It will also be able to point out those conditions that arrest its normal growth. Writers on esthetic theory often raise the question of whether esthetic philosophy can aid in cultivation of esthetic appreciation. The question is a branch of the general theory of criticism, which, it seems to me, fails to accomplish its full office if it does not indicate what to look for and what to find in concrete esthetic objects. But, in any case, it is safe to say that a philosophy of art is sterilized unless it makes us aware of the function of art in relation to other modes of experience, and unless it indicates why this function is so inadequately realized, and unless it suggests the conditions under which the office would be successfully performed.

The comparison of the emergence of works of art out of ordinary experiences to the refining of raw materials into valuable products may seem to some unworthy, if not an actual attempt to reduce works of art to the status of articles manufactured for commercial purposes. The point, however, is that no amount of ecstatic eulogy of finished works can of itself assist the understanding or the generation of such works. Flowers can be enjoyed without knowing about the interactions of soil, air, moisture, and seeds of which they are the result. But they cannot be *understood* without taking just these interactions into account—and theory is a matter of understanding. Theory is concerned with discovering the nature of the production of works of art and of their enjoyment in perception. How is it that the everyday making of things grows into that form of making which is genuinely artistic? How is it that our everyday enjoyment of scenes and situations develops into the peculiar satisfaction that attends the experience which is emphatically esthetic? These are the questions theory must answer. The answers cannot be found, unless we are willing to find the germs and roots in matters of experience that we do not currently regard as esthetic. Having discovered these active seeds, we may follow the course of their growth into the highest forms of finished and refined art.

It is a commonplace that we cannot direct, save accidentally, the growth and flowering of plants, however lovely and enjoyed, without understanding their causal conditions. It should be just a commonplace that esthetic understanding—as distinct from sheer personal enjoyment—must start with the soil, air, and light out of which things esthetically admirable arise. And these conditions are the conditions and factors that make an ordinary experience complete. The more we recognize this fact, the more we shall find ourselves faced with a problem rather than with a final solution. *If* artistic and esthetic quality is implicit in every normal experience, how shall we explain how and why it so generally fails to become explicit? Why is it that to multitudes art seems to be an importation into experience from a foreign country and the esthetic to be a synonym for something artificial?

We cannot answer these questions any more than we can trace the development of art out of everyday experience, unless we have a clear and coherent idea of what is meant when we say "normal experience." Fortunately, the road to arriving at such an idea is open and well marked. The nature of experience is determined by the essential conditions of life. While man is other than bird and beast, he shares basic vital functions with them and has to make the same basal adjustments if he is to continue the process of living. Having the same vital needs, man derives the means by which he breathes, moves, looks and listens, the very brain with which he coördinates his senses and his movements, from his animal forbears. The organs with which he maintains himself in being are not of himself alone, but by the grace of struggles and achievements of a long line of animal ancestry.

Fortunately a theory of the place of the esthetic in experience does not have to lose itself in minute details when it starts with experience in its elemental form. Broad outlines suffice. The first great consideration is that life goes on in an environment; not merely *in* it but because of it, through interaction with it. No creature lives merely under its skin; its subcutaneous organs are means of connection with what lies beyond its bodily frame, and to which, in order to live, it must adjust itself, by accommodation and defense but also by conquest. At every moment, the living creature is exposed to dangers from its surroundings, and at every moment, it must draw upon something in its surroundings to satisfy its needs. The career and destiny of a living being are bound up with its interchanges with its environment, not externally but in the most intimate way.

The growl of a dog crouching over his food, his howl in time of loss and loneliness, the wagging of his tail at the return of his human friend are expressions of the implication of a living in a natural medium which includes man along with the animal he has domesticated. Every need, say hunger for fresh air or food, is a lack that denotes at least a temporary absence of adequate adjustment with surroundings. But it is also a demand, a reaching out into the environment to make good the lack and to restore adjustment by building at least a temporary equilibrium. Life itself consists of phases in which the organism falls out of step with the march of surrounding things and then recovers unison with it—either through effort or by some happy chance. And, in a growing life, the recovery is never mere return to a prior state, for it is enriched by the state of disparity and resistance through which it has successfully passed. If the gap between organism and environment is too wide, the creature dies. If its activity is not enhanced by the temporary alienation, it merely subsists. Life grows when a temporary falling out is a transition to a more extensive balance of the energies of the organism with those of the conditions under which it lives.

These biological commonplaces are something more than that; they reach to the roots of the esthetic in experience. The world is full of things that are indifferent and even hostile to life; the very processes by which life is maintained tend to throw it out of gear with its surroundings. Nevertheless, if life continues and if in continuing it expands, there is an overcoming of factors of opposition and conflict; there is a transformation of them into differentiated aspects of a higher powered and more significant life. The marvel of organic, of vital, adaptation through expansion (instead of by contraction and passive accommodaion) actually takes place. Here in germ are balance and harmony attained through rhythm. Equilibrium comes about not mechanically and inertly but out of, and because of, tension.

There is in nature, even below the level of life, something more than mere flux and change. Form is arrived at whenever a stable, even though moving, equilibrium is reached. Changes interlock and sustain one another. Wherever there is this coherence there is endurance. Order is not imposed from without but is made out of the relations of harmonious interactions that energies bear to one another. Because it is active (not anything static because foreign to what goes on) order itself develops. It comes to include within its balanced movement a greater variety of changes.

Order cannot but be admirable in a world constantly threatened with disorder—in a world where living creatures can go on living only by taking advantage of whatever order exists about them, incorporating it into themselves. In a world like ours, every living creature that attains sensibility welcomes order with a response of harmonious feeling whenever it finds a congruous order about it.

For only when an organism shares in the ordered relations of its environment does it secure the stability essential to living. And when the participation comes after a phase of disruption and conflict, it bears within itself the germs of a consummation akin to the esthetic.

The rhythm of loss of integration with environment and recovery of union not only persists in man but becomes conscious with him; its conditions are material out of which he forms purposes. Emotion is the conscious sign of a break, actual or impending. The discord is the occasion that induces reflection. Desire for restoration of the union converts mere emotion into interest in objects as conditions of realization of harmony. With the realization, material of reflection is incorporated into objects as their meaning. Since the artist cares in a peculiar way for the phase of experience in which union is achieved, he does not shun moments of resistance and tension. He rather cultivates them, not for their own sake but because of their potentialities, bringing to living consciousness an experience that is unified and total. In contrast with the person whose purpose is esthetic, the scientific man is interested in problems, in situations wherein tension between the matter of observation and of thought is marked. Of course he cares for their resolution. But he does not rest in it; he passes on to another problem using an attained solution only as a stepping stone from which to set on foot further inquiries.

The difference between the esthetic and the intellectual is thus one of the place where emphasis falls in the constant rhythm that marks the interaction of the live creature with his surroundings. The ultimate matter of both emphases in experience is the same, as is also their general form. The odd notion that an artist does not think and a scientific inquirer does nothing else is the result of converting a difference of tempo and emphasis into a difference in kind. The thinker has his esthetic moment when his ideas cease to be mere ideas and become the corporate meanings of objects. The artist has his problems and thinks as he works. But his thought is more immediately embodied in the object. Because of the comparative remoteness of his end, the scientific worker operates with symbols, words and mathematical signs. The artist does his thinking in the very qualitative media he works in, and the terms lie so close to the object that he is producing that they merge directly into it.

The live animal does not have to project emotions into the objects experienced. Nature is kind and hateful, bland and morose, irritating and comforting, long before she is mathematically qualified or even a congeries of "secondary" qualities like colors and their shapes. Even such words as long and short, solid and hollow, still carry to all, but those who are intellectually specialized, a moral and emotional connotation. The dictionary will inform any one who consults it that the early use of words like sweet and bitter was not to denote qualities of sense as such but to discriminate things as favorable and hostile. How could it be otherwise? Direct experience comes from nature and man interacting with each other. In this interaction, human energy gathers, is released, dammed up, frustrated and victorious. There are rhythmic beats of want and fulfillment, pulses of doing and being withheld from doing.

All interactions that effect stability and order in the whirling flux of change are rhythms. There is ebb and flow, systole and diastole: ordered change. The latter moves within bounds. To overpass the limits that are set is destruction and death, out of which, however, new rhythms are built up. The proportionate interception of changes establishes an order that is spatially, not merely temporally patterned: like the waves of the sea, the ripples of sand where waves have flowed back and forth, the fleecy and the black-bottomed cloud. Contrast of lack and fullness, of struggle and achievement, of adjustment after consummated irregularity, form the drama in which action, feeling, and meaning are one. The outcome is balance and counterbalance. These are not static nor mechanical. They express power that is intense because measured through overcoming resistance. Environing objects avail and counteravail.

There are two sorts of possible worlds in which esthetic experience would not occur. In a world of mere flux, change would not be cumulative; it would not move toward a close. Stability and rest would have no being. Equally is it true, however, that a world that is finished, ended, would have no traits of suspense and crisis, and would offer no opportunity for resolution. Where everything is already complete, there is no fulfillment. We envisage with pleasure Nirvana and a uniform heavenly bliss only because they are projected upon the background of our present world of stress and conflict. Because the actual world, that in which we live, is a combination of movement and culmination, of breaks and re-unions, the experience of a living creature is capable of esthetic quality. The live being recurrently loses and reëstablishes equilibrium with his surroundings. The moment of passage from disturbance into harmony is that of intensest life. In a finished world, sleep and waking could not be distinguished. In one wholly perturbed, conditions could not even be struggled with. In a world made after the pattern of ours, moments of fulfillment punctuate experience with rhythmically enjoyed intervals.

Inner harmony is attained only when, by some means, terms are made with the environment. When it occurs on any other than an "objective" basis, it is illusory—in extreme cases to the point of insanity. Fortunately for variety in experience, terms are made in many ways— ways ultimately decided by selective interest. Pleasures may come about through chance contact and stimulation; such pleasures are not to be despised in a world full of pain. But happiness and delight are a different sort of thing. They come to be through a fulfillment that reaches to the depths of our being—one that is an adjustment of our whole being with the conditions of existence. In the process of living, attainment of a period of equilibrium is at the same time the initiation of a new relation to the environment, one that brings with it potency of new adjustments to be made through struggle. The time of consummation is also one of beginning anew. Any attempt to perpetuate beyond its term the enjoyment attending the time of fulfillment and harmony constitutes withdrawal from the world. Hence it marks the lowering and loss of vitality. But, through the phases of perturbation and conflict, there abides the deep-seated memory of an underlying harmony, the sense of which haunts life like the sense of being founded on a rock.

Most mortals are conscious that a split often occurs between their present living and their past and future. Then the past hangs upon them as a burden; it invades the present with a sense of regret, of opportunities not used, and of consequences we wish undone. It rests upon the present as an oppression, instead of being a storehouse of resources by which to move confidently forward. But the live creature adopts its past; it can make friends with even its stupidities, using them as warnings that increase present wariness. Instead of trying to live upon whatever may have been achieved in the past, it uses past successes to inform the present. Every living experience owes its richness to what Santayana well calls "hushed reverberations."[1]

To the being fully alive, the future is not ominous but a promise; it surrounds the present as a halo. It consists of possibilities that are felt as a possession of what is now and here. In life that is truly life, everything overlaps and merges. But all too often we exist in apprehensions of what the future may bring, and are divided within ourselves. Even when not overanxious, we do not enjoy the present because we subordinate it to that which is absent. Because of the frequency of this abandonment of the present to the past and future, the happy periods of an experience that is now complete because it absorbs into itself memories of the past and anticipations of the future, come to constitute an esthetic ideal. Only when the past ceases to trouble and anticipations of the future are not perturbing is a being wholly united with his environment and therefore fully alive. Art celebrates with peculiar intensity the moments in which the past reënforces the present and in which the future is a quickening of what now is.

To grasp the sources of esthetic experience it is, therefore, necessary to have recourse to animal life below the human scale. The activities of the fox, the dog, and the thrush may at least stand as reminders and

---

[1] "These familiar flowers, these well-remembered bird notes, this sky with its fitful brightness, these furrowed and grassy fields, each with a sort of personality given to it by the capricious hedge, such things as these are the mother tongue of our imagination, the language that is laden with all the subtle inextricable associations the fleeting hours of our childhood left behind them. Our delight in the sunshine on the deep-bladed grass today might be no more than the faint perception of wearied souls, if it were not for the sunshine and grass of far-off years, which still live in us and transform our perception into love." George Eliot in *The Mill on the Floss*.

symbols of that unity of experience which we so fractionize when work is labor, and thought withdraws us from the world. The live animal is fully present, all there, in all of its actions: in its wary glances, its sharp sniffings, its abrupt cocking of ears. All senses are equally on the *qui vive*. As you watch, you see motion merging into sense and sense into motion—constituting that animal grace so hard for man to rival. What the live creature retains from the past and what it expects from the future operate as directions in the present. The dog is never pedantic nor academic; for these things arise only when the past is severed in consciousness from the present and is set up as a model to copy or a storehouse upon which to draw. The past absorbed into the present carries on; it presses forward.

There is much in the life of the savage that is sodden. But, when the savage is most alive, he is most observant of the world about him and most taut with energy. As he watches what stirs about him, he, too, is stirred. His observation is both action in preparation and foresight of the future. He is as active through his whole being when he looks and listens as when he stalks his quarry or stealthily retreats from a foe. His senses are sentinels of immediate thought and outposts of action, and not, as they so often are with us, mere pathways along which material is gathered to be stored away for a delayed and remote possibility.

It is mere ignorance that leads then to the supposition that connection of art and esthetic perception with experience signifies a lowering of their significance and dignity. Experience in the degree in which it *is* experience is heightened vitality. Instead of signifying being shut up within one's own private feelings and sensations, it signifies active and alert commerce with the world; at its height it signifies complete interpenetration of self and the world of objects and events. Instead of signifying surrender to caprice and disorder, it affords our sole demonstration of a stability that is not stagnation but is rhythmic and developing. Because experience is the fulfillment of an organism in its struggles and achievements in a world of things, it is art in germ. Even in its rudimentary forms, it contains the promise of that delightful perception which is esthetic experience.

34. The Live Creature and
"Etherial Things"*[1]

Continuing the theme of "The Live Creature," Dewey devotes this chapter to illustrations of the depth and wisdom of affective experience. Speaking of the anatomy of experience, Dewey stresses the human ability to forge a unity of sense and reflection. The ethereal does not have its roots outside of man nor does it deprecate distinctively human behavior. "Nothing that a man has ever reached by the highest flight of thought or penetrated by any probing insight is inherently such that it may not become the heart and core of sense." This judgment by Dewey cuts deeper than at first glance, for his rooting of the ethereal in sensibility points also to the finitude of man and his work, as well as to the uncertainty of his quest.

Why is the attempt to connect the higher and ideal things of experience with basic vital roots so often regarded as betrayal of their nature and denial of their value? Why is there repulsion when the high achievements of fine art are brought into connection with common life, the life that we share with all living creatures? Why is life thought of as an affair of low appetite, or at its best a thing of gross sensation, and ready to sink from its best to the level of lust and harsh cruelty? A complete answer to the question would involve the writing of a history of morals that would set forth the conditions that have brought about contempt for the body, fear of the senses, and the opposition of flesh to spirit.

One aspect of this history is so relevant to our problem that it must receive at least passing notice. The institutional life of mankind is marked by disorganization. This disorder is often disguised by the fact that it takes the form of static division into classes, and this static separation is accepted as the very essence of order as long as it is so fixed and so accepted as not to generate open conflict. Life is compartmentalized and the institutionalized compartments are classified as

* From John Dewey, *Art as Experience* (New York, Capricorn Books, 1958) (1939), pp. 20-34. Reprinted by permission of G. P. Putnam's Sons.
[1] The Sun, the Moon, the Earth and its contents, are material to form greater things, that is, etherial things—greater things than the Creator himself made.—JOHN KEATS.

high and as low; their values as profane and spiritual, as material and
ideal. Interests are related to one another externally and mechanically,
through a system of checks and balances. Since religion, morals,
politics, business has each its own compartment, within which it is fitting each should remain, art, too, must have its peculiar and private
realm. Compartmentalization of occupations and interests brings about
separation of that mode of activity commonly called "practice" from insight, of imagination from executive doing, of significant purpose from
work, of emotion from thought and doing. Each of these has, too, its
own place in which it must abide. Those who write the anatomy of experience then suppose that these divisions inhere in the very constitution of human nature.

Of much of our experience as it is actually lived under present
economic and legal institutional conditions, it is only too true that these
separations hold. Only occasionally in the lives of many are the senses
fraught with the sentiment that comes from deep realization of intrinsic
meanings. We undergo sensations as mechanical stimuli or as irritated
stimulations, without having a sense of the reality that is in them and
behind them: in much of our experience our different senses do not
unite to tell a common and enlarged story. We see without feeling; we
hear, but only a second-hand report, second hand because not
reënforced by vision. We touch, but the contact remains tangential because it does not fuse with qualities of senses that go below the surface.
We use the senses to arouse passion but not to fulfill the interest of insight, not because that interest is not potentially present in the exercise
of sense but because we yield to conditions of living that force sense to
remain an excitation on the surface. Prestige goes to those who use their
minds without participation of the body and who act vicariously
through control of the bodies and labor of others.

Under such conditions, sense and flesh get a bad name. The moralist,
however, has a truer sense of the intimate connections of sense with the
rest of our being than has the professional psychologist and
philosopher, although his sense of these connections takes a direction
that reverses the potential facts of our living in relation to the environment. Psychologist and philosopher have in recent times been so
obsessed with the problem of knowledge that they have treated "sensations" as mere elements of knowledge. The moralist knows that sense is
allied with emotion, impulse and appetition. So he denounces the lust of
the eye as part of the surrender of spirit to flesh. He identifies the sensuous with the sensual and the sensual with the lewd. His moral theory
is askew, but at least he is aware that the eye is not an imperfect

telescope designed for intellectual reception of material to bring about knowledge of distant objects.

"Sense" covers a wide range of contents: the sensory, the sensational, the sensitive, the sensible, and the sentimental, along with the sensuous. It includes almost everything from bare physical and emotional shock to sense itself—that is, the meaning of things present in immediate experience. Each term refers to some real phase and aspect of the life of an organic creature as life occurs through sense organs. But sense, as meaning so directly embodied in experience as to be its own illuminated meaning, is the only signification that expresses the function of sense organs when they are carried to full realization. The senses are the organs through which the live creature participates directly in the ongoings of the world about him. In this participation the varied wonder and splendor of this world are made actual for him in the qualities he experiences. This material cannot be opposed to action, for motor apparatus and "will" itself are the means by which this participation is carried on and directed. It cannot be opposed to "intellect," for mind is the means by which participation is rendered fruitful through sense; by which meanings and values are extracted, retained, and put to further service in the intercourse of the live creature with his surroundings.

Experience is the result, the sign, and the reward of that interaction of organism and environment which, when it is carried to the full, is a transformation of interaction into participation and communication. Since sense-organs with their connected motor apparatus are the means of this participation, any and every derogation of them, whether practical or theoretical, is at once effect and cause of a narrowed and dulled life-experience. Oppositions of mind and body, soul and matter, spirit and flesh all have their origin, fundamentally, in fear of what life may bring forth. They are marks of contraction and withdrawal. Full recognition, therefore, of the continuity of the organs, needs and basic impulses of the human creature with his animal forbears, implies no necessary reduction of man to the level of the brutes. On the contrary, it makes possible the drawing of a ground-plan of human experience upon which is erected the superstructure of man's marvelous and distinguishing experience. What is distinctive in man makes it possible for him to sink below the level of the beasts. It also makes it possible for him to carry to new and unprecedented heights that unity of sense and impulse, of brain and eye and ear, that is exemplified in animal life, saturating it with the conscious meanings derived from communication and deliberate expression.

Man excels in complexity and minuteness of differentiations. This very fact constitutes the necessity for many more comprehensive and exact relationships among the constituents of his being. Important as are the distinctions and relations thus made possible, the story does not end here. There are more opportunities for resistance and tension, more drafts upon experimentation and invention, and therefore more novelty in action, greater range and depth of insight and increase of poignancy in feeling. As an organism increases in complexity, the rhythms of struggle and consummation in its relation to its environment are varied and prolonged, and they come to include within themselves an endless variety of sub-rhythms. The designs of living are widened and enriched. Fulfillment is more massive and more subtly shaded.

Space thus becomes something more than a void in which to roam about, dotted here and there with dangerous things and things that satisfy the appetite. It becomes a comprehensive and enclosed scene within which are ordered the multiplicity of doings and undergoings in which man engages. Time ceases to be either the endless and uniform flow or the succession of instantaneous points which some philosophers have asserted it to be. It, too, is the organized and organizing medium of the rhythmic ebb and flow of expectant impulse, forward and retracted movement, resistance and suspense, with fulfillment and consummation. It is an ordering of growth and maturations—as James said, we learn to skate in summer after having commenced in winter. Time as organization in change is growth, and growth signifies that a varied series of change enters upon intervals of pause and rest; of completions that become the initial points of new processes of development. Like the soil, mind is fertilized while it lies fallow, until a new burst of bloom ensues.

When a flash of lightning illumines a dark landscape, there is a momentary recognition of objects. But the recognition is not itself a mere point in time. It is the focal culmination of long, slow processes of maturation. It is the manifestation of the continuity of an ordered temporal experience in a sudden discrete instant of climax. It is as meaningless in isolation as would be the drama of Hamlet were it confined to a single line or word with no context. But the phrase "the rest is silence" is infinitely pregnant as the conclusion of a drama enacted through development in time; so may be the momentary perception of a natural scene. Form, as it is present in the fine arts, is the art of making clear what is involved in the organization of space and time prefigured in every course of a developing life-experience.

Moments and places, despite physical limitation and narrow localization, are charged with accumulations of long-gathering energy. A return to a scene of childhood that was left long years before floods the spot with a release of pent-up memories and hopes. To meet in a strange country one who is a casual acquaintance at home may arouse a satisfaction so acute as to bring a thrill. Mere recognitions occur only when we are occupied with something else than the object or person recognized. It marks either an interruption or else an intent to use what is recognized as a means for something else. To see, to perceive, is more than to recognize. It does not identify something present in terms of a past disconnected from it. The past is carried into the present so as to expand and deepen the content of the latter. There is illustrated the translation of bare continuity of external time into the vital order and organization of experience. Identification nods and passes on. Or it defines a passing moment in isolation, it marks a dead spot in experience that is merely filled in. The extent to which the process of living in any day or hour is reduced to labeling situations, events, and objects as "so-and-so" in mere succession marks the cessation of a life that is a conscious experience. Continuities realized in an individual, discrete, form are the essence of the latter.

Art is thus prefigured in the very processes of living. A bird builds its nest and a beaver its dam when internal organic pressures coöperate with external materials so that the former are fulfilled and the latter are transformed in a satisfying culmination. We may hesitate to apply the word "art," since we doubt the presence of directive intent. But all deliberation, all conscious intent, grows out of things once performed organically through the interplay of natural energies. Were it not so, art would be built on quaking sands, nay, on unstable air. The distinguishing contribution of man is consciousness of the relations found in nature. Through consciousness, he converts the relations of cause and effect that are found in nature into relations of means and consequence. Rather, consciousness itself is the inception of such a transformation. What was mere shock becomes an invitation; resistance becomes something to be used in changing existing arrangements of matter; smooth facilities become agencies for executing an idea. In these operations, an organic stimulation becomes the bearer of meanings, and motor responses are changed into instruments of expression and communication; no longer are they mere means of locomotion and direct reaction. Meanwhile, the organic substratum remains as the quickening and deep foundation. Apart from relations of cause and effect in nature, conception and invention could not be. Apart from the relation of processes of rhythmic conflict and fulfillment in animal life, experience would be without design and pattern. Apart from organs inherited from animal ancestry, idea and purpose would be without a mechanism of realization. The primeval arts of nature and animal life are so much the material, and, in gross outline, so much the model for the intentional achievements of man, that the theologically minded have imputed conscious intent to the structure of nature—as man, sharing many activities with the ape, is wont to think of the latter as imitating his own performances.

The existence of art is the concrete proof of what has just been stated abstractly. It is proof that man uses the materials and energies of nature with intent to expand his own life, and that he does so in accord with the structure of his organism—brain, sense-organs, and muscular system. Art is the living and concrete proof that man is capable of restoring consciously, and thus on the plane of meaning, the union of sense, need, impulse and action characteristic of the live creature. The intervention of consciousness adds regulation, power of selection, and redisposition. Thus it varies the arts in ways without end. But its intervention also leads in time to the *idea* of art as a conscious idea—the greatest intellectual achievement in the history of humanity.

The variety and perfection of the arts in Greece led thinkers to frame a generalized conception of art and to project the ideal of an art of organization of human activities as such—the art of politics and morals as conceived by Socrates and Plato. The ideas of design, plan, order, pattern, purpose emerged in distinction from and relation to the materials employed in their realization. The conception of man as the being that uses art became at once the ground of the distinction of man from the rest of nature and of the bond that ties him to nature. When the conception of art as the distinguishing trait of man was made explicit, there was assurance that, short of complete relapse of humanity below even savagery, the possibility of invention of new arts would remain, along with use of old arts, as the guiding ideal of mankind. Although recognition of the fact still halts, because of traditions established before the power of art was adequately recognized, science itself is but a central art auxiliary to the generation and utilization of other arts.[2]

It is customary, and from some points of view necessary, to make a

---

[2] I have developed this point in *Experience and Nature,* in Chapter Nine, on Experience, Nature and Art. As far as the present point is concerned, the conclusion is contained in the statement that "art, the mode of activity that is charged with meanings capable of immediately enjoyed possession, is the complete culmination of nature, and that science is properly a handmaiden that conducts natural events to this happy issue." (P. 358.)

distinction between fine art and useful or technological art. But the point of view from which it is necessary is one that is extrinsic to the work of art itself. The customary distinction is based simply on acceptance of certain existing social conditions. I suppose the fetiches of the negro sculptor were taken to be useful in the highest degree to his tribal group, more so even than spears and clothing. But now they are fine art, serving in the twentieth century to inspire renovations in arts that had grown conventional. But they are fine art only because the anonymous artist lived and experienced so fully during the process of production. An angler may eat his catch without thereby losing the esthetic satisfaction he experienced in casting and playing. It is this degree of completeness of living in the experience of making and of perceiving that makes the difference between what is fine or esthetic in art and what is not. Whether the thing made is put to use, as are bowls, rugs, garments, weapons, is, *intrinsically* speaking, a matter of indifference. That many, perhaps most, of the articles and utensils made at present for use are not genuinely esthetic happens, unfortunately, to be true. But it is true for reasons that are foreign to the relation of the "beautiful" and "useful" as such. Wherever conditions are such as to prevent the act of production from being an experience in which the whole creature is alive and in which he possesses his living through enjoyment, the product will lack something of being esthetic. No matter how useful it is for special and limited ends, it will not be useful in the ultimate degree—that of contributing directly and liberally to an expanding and enriched life. The story of the severance and final sharp opposition of the useful and the fine is the history of that industrial development through which so much of production has become a form of postponed living and so much of consumption a superimposed enjoyment of the fruits of the labor of others.

Usually there is a hostile reaction to a conception of art that connects it with the activities of a live creature in its environment. The hostility to association of fine art with normal processes of living is a pathetic, even a tragic, commentary on life as it is ordinarily lived. Only because that life is usually so stunted, aborted, slack, or heavy laden, is the idea entertained that there is some inherent antagonism between the process of normal living and creation and enjoyment of works of esthetic art. After all, even though "spiritual" and "material" are separated and set in opposition to one another, there must be conditions through which the ideal is capable of embodiment and realization—and this is all, fundamentally, that "matter" signifies. The very currency which the opposition has acquired testifies, therefore, to a widespread operation of forces that convert what might be means of executing liberal ideas into oppressive burdens and that cause ideals to be loose aspirations in an uncertain and ungrounded atmosphere.

While art itself is the best proof of the existence of a realized and therefore realizable, union of material and ideal, there are general arguments that support the thesis in hand. Wherever continuity is possible, the burden of proof rests upon those who assert opposition and dualism. Nature is the mother and the habitat of man, even if sometimes a stepmother and an unfriendly home. The fact that civilization endures and culture continues—and sometimes advances—is evidence that human hopes and purposes find a basis and support in nature. As the developing growth of an individual from embryo to maturity is the result of interaction of organism with surroundings, so culture is the product not of efforts of men put forth in a void or just upon themselves, but of prolonged and cumulative interaction with environment. The depth of the responses stirred by works of art shows *their* continuity with the operations of this enduring experience. The works and the responses they evoke are continuous with the very processes of living as these are carried to unexpected happy fulfillment.

As to absorption of the esthetic in nature, I cite a case duplicated in some measure in thousands of persons, but notable because expressed by an artist of the first order, W. H. Hudson. "I feel when I am out of sight of living, growing grass, and out of the sound of birds' voices and all rural sounds, that I am not properly alive." He goes on to say, ". . . when I hear people say that they have not found the world and life so agreeable and interesting as to be in love with it, or that they look with equanimity to its end, I am apt to think that they have never been properly alive, nor seen with clear vision the world they think so meanly of or anything in it—not even a blade of grass." The mystic aspect of acute esthetic surrender, that renders it so akin as an experience to what religionists term ecstatic communion, is recalled by Hudson from his boyhood life. He is speaking of the effect the sight of acacia trees had upon him. "The loose feathery foliage on moonlight nights had a peculiar hoary aspect that made this tree seem more intensely alive than others, more conscious of me and of my presence. . . . Similar to a feeling a person would have if visited by a supernatural being if he was perfectly convinced that it was there in his presence, albeit silent and unseen, intently regarding him and divining every thought in his mind." Emerson is often regarded as an austere thinker. But it was Emerson as an adult who said, quite in the spirit of the passage quoted from Hudson: "Crossing a bare common, in snow puddles, at twilight, under a clouded sky, without having in my thought any occurrence of special good fortune, I have enjoyed a perfect exhilaration. I am glad to the brink of fear."

I do not see any way of accounting for the multiplicity of experiences of this kind (something of the same quality being found in every spontaneous and uncoerced esthetic response), except on the basis that there are stirred into activity resonances of dispositions acquired in primitive relationships of the living being to its surroundings, and irrecoverable in distinct or intellectual consciousness. Experiences of the sort mentioned take us to a further consideration that testifies to natural continuity. There is no limit to the capacity of immediate sensuous experience to absorb into itself meanings and values that in and of themselves—that is in the abstract—would be designated "ideal" and "spiritual." The animistic strain of religious experience, embodied in Hudson's memory of his childhood days, is an instance on one level of experience. And the poetical, in whatever medium, is always a close kin of the animistic. And if we turn to an art that in many ways is at the other pole, architecture, we learn how ideas, wrought out at first perhaps in highly technical thought like that of mathematics, are capable of direct incorporation in sensuous form. The sensible surface of things is never merely a surface. One can discriminate rock from flimsy tissue-paper by the surface alone, so completely have the resistances of touch and the solidities due to stresses of the entire muscular system been embodied in vision. The process does not stop with incarnation of other sensory qualities that give depth of meaning to surface. Nothing that a man has ever reached by the highest flight of thought or penetrated by any probing insight is inherently such that it may not become the heart and core of sense.

The same word, "symbol," is used to designate expressions of abstract thought, as in mathematics, and also such things as a flag, crucifix, that embody deep social value and the meaning of historic faith and theological creed. Incense, stained glass, the chiming of unseen bells, embroidered robes accompany the approach to what is regarded as divine. The connection of the origin of many arts with primitive rituals becomes more evident with every excursion of the anthropologist into the past. Only those who are so far removed from the earlier experiences as to miss their sense will conclude that rites and ceremonies were merely technical devices for securing rain, sons, crops, success in battle. Of course they had this magical intent, but they were enduringly enacted, we may be sure, in spite of all practical failures, because they were immediate enhancements of the experience of living. Myths were something other than intellectualistic essays of primitive man in science. Uneasiness before any unfamiliar fact doubtless played its part. But delight in the story, in the growth and rendition of a good yarn, played its dominant part then as it does in the growth of popular mythologies today. Not only does the direct sense element—and emotion is a mode of sense—tend to absorb all ideational matter but, apart from special discipline enforced by physical apparatus, it subdues and digests all that is merely intellectual.

The introduction of the supernatural into belief and the all too human easy reversion to the supernatural is much more an affair of the psychology that generates works of art than of effort at scientific and philosophic explanation. It intensifies emotional thrill and punctuates the interest that belongs to all break in familiar routine. Were the hold of the supernatural on human thought an exclusively—or even mainly—intellectual matter, it would be comparatively insignificant. Theologies and cosmogonies have laid hold of imagination because they have been attended with solemn processions, incense, embroidered robes, music, the radiance of colored lights, with stories that stir wonder and induce hypnotic admiration. That is, they have come to man through a direct appeal to sense and to sensuous imagination. Most religions have identified their sacraments with the highest reaches of art, and the most authoritative beliefs have been clothed in a garb of pomp and pageantry that gives immediate delight to eye and ear and that evokes massive emotions of suspense, wonder, and awe. The flights of physicists and astronomers today answer to the esthetic need for satisfaction of the imagination rather than to any strict demand of unemotional evidence for rational interpretation.

Henry Adams made it clear that the theology of the middle ages is a construction of the same intent as that which wrought the cathedrals. In general this middle age, popularly deemed to express the acme of Christian faith in the western world, is a demonstration of the power of sense to absorb the most highly spiritualized ideas. Music, painting, sculpture, architecture, drama and romance were handmaidens of religion, as much as were science and scholarship. The arts hardly had a being outside of the church, and the rites and ceremonies of the church were arts enacted under conditions that gave them the maximum possible of emotional and imaginative appeal. For I do not know what would give the spectator and auditor of the manifestation of the arts a more poignant surrender than the conviction that they were informed with the necessary means of eternal glory and bliss.

The following words of Pater are worth quoting in this connection.

"The Christianity of the middle ages made its way partly by its esthetic beauty, a thing so profoundly felt by the Latin hymn writers, *who for one moral or spiritual sentiment had a hundred sensuous images*. A passion of which the outlets are sealed begets a tension of nerve in which the sensible world comes to one with a reinforced brilliancy and relief—all redness turned into blood, all water into tears. Hence a wild convulsed sensuousness in all the poetry of the middle ages, in which the things of nature began to play a strange delirious part. Of the things of nature, the medieval mind had a deep sense; but its sense of them was not objective, no real escape to the world without us."

In his autobiographical essay, *The Child in the House*, he generalizes what is implicit in this passage. He says: "In later years he came upon philosophies which occupied him much in the estimate of the proportions of the sensuous and ideal elements in human knowledge, the relative parts they bear in it; and, in his intellectual scheme, was led to assign very little to the abstract thought, and much to its sensible vehicle or occasion." The latter "became the necessary concomitant of any perception of things, real enough to have any weight or reckoning, in his house of thought. . . . He came more and more to be unable to care for, or think of soul but as in an actual body, or of any world but that wherein are water and trees, and where men and women look, so or so, and press actual hands." The elevation of the ideal above and beyond immediate sense has operated not only to make it pallid and bloodless, but it has acted, like a conspirator with the sensual mind, to impoverish and degrade all things of direct experience.

In the title of this chapter I took the liberty of borrowing from Keats the word "ethereal" to designate the meanings and values that many philosophers and some critics suppose are inaccessible to sense, because of their spiritual, eternal and universal characters—thus exemplifying the common dualism of nature and spirit. Let me re-quote his words. The artist may look "upon the Sun, the Moon, the Stars, and the Earth and its contents as material to form greater things, that is ethereal things—greater things than the Creator himself made." In making this use of Keats, I had also in mind the fact that he identified the attitude of the artist with that of the live creature; and did so not merely in the implicit tenor of his poetry but in reflection expressed the idea explicitly in words. As he wrote in a letter to his brother: "The greater part of men make their way with the same instinctiveness, the same unwandering eye from their purposes as the Hawk. The Hawk wants a mate, so does the man—look at them both, they set about and procure one in the same manner. They both want a nest and they both set about it in the same manner—they get their food in the same manner. The noble animal Man for his amusement smokes his pipe—the Hawk balances about in the clouds—this is the only difference of their leisures. This is that which makes the amusement of Life to a speculative mind. I go out among the Fields and catch a glimpse of a Stoat or a field mouse hurrying along—to what? The creature has a purpose and his eyes are bright with it. I go amongst the buildings of a city and see a Man hurrying along—to what? The Creature has a purpose and his eyes are bright with it. . . .

"Even here though I am pursuing the same instinctive course as the veriest human animal I can think of [though] I am, however young, writing at random straining at particles of light in the midst of great darkness, without knowing the bearing of any assertion, of any one opinion. Yet may I not in this be free from sin? May there not be superior beings amused with any graceful, though instinctive, attitude my mind may fall into as I am entertained with the alertness of a Stoat or the anxiety of a Deer? Though a quarrel in the streets is to be hated, the energies displayed in it are fine; the commonest Man has a grace in his quarrel. Seen by a supernatural Being our reasonings may take the same tone—though erroneous, they may be fine. *This is the very thing in which consists poetry.* There may be reasonings, but when they take an instinctive form, like that of animal forms and movements, they are poetry, they are fine; they have grace."

In another letter he speaks of Shakespeare as a man of enormous "Negative Capability"; as one who was "capable of being in uncertainties, mysteries, doubts, without any irritable reaching after fact and reason." He contrasts Shakespeare in this respect with his own contemporary Coleridge, who would let a poetic insight go when it was surrounded with obscurity, because he could not intellectually justify it; could not, in Keats' language, be satisfied with "*half*-knowledge." I think the same idea is contained in what he says, in a letter to Bailey, that he "never yet has been able to perceive how anything can be known for truth by consecutive reasoning. . . . Can it be that even the greatest Philosopher ever arrived at his Goal without putting aside numerous objections": asking, in effect, Does not the reasoner have also to trust to his "intuitions", to what come upon him in his immediate sensuous and emotional experiences, even against objections that reflection presents to him. For he goes on to say "the simple imaginative mind may have its rewards in the repetitions of its own silent workings coming continually on the Spirit with a fine suddenness"—a remark that contains more of the psychology of productive thought than many treatises.

In spite of the elliptical character of Keats' statements two points emerge. One of them is his conviction that "reasonings" have an origin like that of the movements of a wild creature toward its goal, and they may become spontaneous, "instinctive," and when they become instinctive are sensuous and immediate, poetic. The other side of this conviction is his belief that no "reasoning" as reasoning, that is, as excluding imagination and sense, can reach truth. Even "the greatest philosopher" exercises an animal-like preference to guide his thinking to its conclusions. He selects and puts aside as his imaginative sentiments move. "Reason" at its height cannot attain complete grasp and a self-contained assurance. It must fall back upon imagination—upon the embodiment of ideas in emotionally charged sense.

There has been much dispute as to what Keats meant in his famous lines:

> *"Beauty is truth, truth beauty—that is all*
> *Ye know on earth, and all ye need to know,"*

and what he meant in the cognate prose statement—"What imagination seizes as beauty must be truth." Much of the dispute is carried on in ignorance of the particular tradition in which Keats wrote and which gave the term "truth" its meaning. In this tradition, "truth" never signifies correctness of intellectual statements about things, or truth as its meaning is now influenced by science. It denotes the wisdom by which men live, especially "the lore of good and evil." And in Keats' mind it was particularly connected with the question of justifying good and trusting to it in spite of the evil and destruction that abound. "Philosophy" is the attempt to answer this question rationally. Keats' belief that even philosophers cannot deal with the question without depending on imaginative intuitions receives an independent and positive statement in his identification of "beauty" with "truth"—the particular truth that solves for man the baffling problem of destruction and death—which weighed so constantly on Keats—in the very realm where life strives to assert supremacy. Man lives in a world of surmise, of mystery, of uncertainties. "Reasoning" must fail man—this of course is a doctrine long taught by those who have held to the necessity of a divine revelation. Keats did not accept this supplement and substitute for reason. The insight of imagination must suffice. "This is all ye know on earth and all ye need to know." The critical words are "on earth"—that is amid a scene in which "irritable reaching after fact and reason" confuses and distorts instead of bringing us to the light. It was in moments of most intense esthetic perception that Keats found his utmost solace and his deepest convictions. This is the fact recorded at the close of his Ode. Ultimately there are but two philosophies. One of them accepts life and experience in all its uncertainty, mystery, doubt, and half-knowledge and turns that experience upon itself to deepen and intensify its own qualities—to imagination and art. This is the philosophy of Shakespeare and Keats.

35. Having an Experience*

"Having an Experience" was published in 1934, when Dewey was seventy-five years of age. Yet, it can be said that the attitude and perspective articulated therein, especially the distinction between experience as inchoate and as *an* experience, lay behind almost everything that Dewey had written previously. It is also striking that at an age when most people are retrospective and nostalgic, Dewey writes a piece bristling with the future, with anticipation of the future, the cardinal motif.

The word "having" is used by Dewey as in "having" a friend or "having" a good time. It is not used in the sense of "having" as possessing. Dewey creates a delicate relationship between the myriad interactions that make up an ongoing experience and the realizations or consummations that emerge when anticipations are realized and we "have *an* experience." But such consummations are not final or fixed ends, for they shed meaning fore and aft. A consummation "is anticipated throughout and is recurrently savored with special intensity," and when finally undergone or "had," it points the way to a new gathering of possibilities and anticipations.

Deeply indebted to the relational metaphysics of William James, this selection evokes the doing and undergoing, the rhythm of everyday experience and, however inadvertently, casts light on countless contemporary movements in the arts and social psychology.

* From John Dewey, *Art as Experience* (New York, Capricorn Books, 1958) (1939), pp. 35-57. Reprinted by permission of G. P. Putnam's Sons.

* * *

Experience occurs continuously, because the interaction of live creature and environing conditions is involved in the very process of living. Under conditions of resistance and conflict, aspects and elements of the self and the world that are implicated in this interaction qualify experience with emotions and ideas so that conscious intent emerges. Oftentimes, however, the experience had is inchoate. Things are experienced but not in such a way that they are composed into *an* experience. There is distraction and dispersion; what we observe and what we think, what we desire and what we get, are at odds with each other. We put our hands to the plow and turn back; we start and then we stop, not because the experience has reached the end for the sake of which it was initiated but because of extraneous interruptions or of inner lethargy.

In contrast with such experience, we have *an* experience when the material experienced runs its course to fulfillment. Then and then only is it integrated within and demarcated in the general stream of experience from other experiences. A piece of work is finished in a way that is satisfactory; a problem receives its solution; a game is played through; a situation, whether that of eating a meal, playing a game of chess, carrying on a conversation, writing a book, or taking part in a political campaign, is so rounded out that its close is a consummation and not a cessation. Such an experience is a whole and carries with it its own individualizing quality and self-sufficiency. It is *an* experience.

Philosophers, even empirical philosophers, have spoken for the most part of experience at large. Idiomatic speech, however, refers to experiences each of which is singular, having its own beginning and end. For life is no uniform uninterrupted march or flow. It is a thing of histories, each with its own plot, its own inception and movement toward its close, each having its own particular rhythmic movement; each with its own unrepeated quality pervading it throughout. A flight of stairs, mechanical as it is, proceeds by individualized steps, not by undifferentiated progression, and an inclined plane is at least marked off from other things by abrupt discreteness.

Experience in this vital sense is defined by those situations and episodes that we spontaneously refer to as being "real experiences"; those things of which we say in recalling them, "that *was* an experience." It may have been something of tremendous importance—a quarrel with one who was once an intimate, a catastrophe finally averted by a hair's breadth. Or it may have been something that in comparison was slight—and which perhaps because of its very slightness illustrates all the better what is to be an experience. There is that meal in a Paris restaurant of which one says "that *was* an experience." It stands out as an enduring memorial of what food may be. Then there is that storm one went through in crossing the Atlantic—the storm that seemed in its fury, as it was experienced, to sum up in itself all that a storm can be, complete in itself, standing out because marked out from what went before and what came after.

In such experiences, every successive part flows freely, without seam and without unfilled blanks, into what ensues. At the same time there is no sacrifice of the self-identity of the parts. A river, as distinct from a pond, flows. But its flow gives a definiteness and interest to its successive portions greater than exist in the homogenous portions of a pond. In an experience, flow is from something to something. As one part leads into another and as one part carries on what went before, each gains distinctness in itself. The enduring whole is diversified by successive phases that are emphases of its varied colors.

Because of continuous merging, there are no holes, mechanical junctions, and dead centers when we have *an* experience. There are pauses, places of rest, but they punctuate and define the quality of movement. They sum up what has been undergone and prevent its dissipation and idle evaporation. Continued acceleration is breathless and prevents parts from gaining distinction. In a work of art, different acts, episodes, occurrences melt and fuse into unity, and yet do not disappear and lose their own character as they do so—just as in a genial conversation there is a continuous interchange and blending, and yet each speaker not only retains his own character but manifests it more clearly than is his wont.

An experience has a unity that gives it its name, *that* meal, that storm, that rupture of friendship. The existence of this unity is constituted by a single *quality* that pervades the entire experience in spite of the variation of its constituent parts. This unity is neither emotional, practical, nor intellectual, for these terms name distinctions that reflection can make within it. In discourse *about* an experience, we must make use of these adjectives of interpretation. In going over an experience in mind *after* its occurrence, we may find that one property rather than another was sufficiently dominant so that it characterizes the experience as a whole. There are absorbing inquiries and speculations which a scientific man and philosopher will recall as "experiences" in the emphatic sense. In final import they are intellectual. But in their actual occurrence they were emotional as well; they were purposive and volitional. Yet the experience was not a sum of these different characters; they were lost in it as distinctive traits. No thinker can ply his occupation save as he is lured and rewarded by total integral experiences that are intrinsically worth while. Without them he would never know what it is really to think and would be completely at a loss in distinguishing real thought from the spurious article. Thinking goes on in trains of ideas, but the ideas form a train only because they are much more than what an analytic psychology calls ideas. They are phases, emotionally and practically distinguished, of a developing underlying quality; they are its moving variations, not separate and independent like Locke's and Hume's so-called ideas and impressions, but are subtle shadings of a pervading and developing hue.

We say of an experience of thinking that we reach or draw a conclusion. Theoretical formulation of the process is often made in such terms as to conceal effectually the similarity of "conclusion" to the consummating phase of every developing integral experience. These formulations apparently take their cue from the separate propositions that are premisses and the proposition that is the conclusion as they appear on the printed page. The impression is derived that there are first two independent and ready-made entities that are then manipulated so as to give rise to a third. In fact, in an experience of thinking, premisses emerge only as a conclusion becomes manifest. The experience, like that of watching a storm reach its height and gradually subside, is one of continuous movement of subject-matters. Like the ocean in the storm, there are a series of waves; suggestions reaching out and being broken in a clash, or being carried onwards by a coöperative wave. If a conclusion is reached, it is that of a movement of anticipation and cumulation, one that finally comes to completion. A "conclusion" is no separate and independent thing; it is the consummation of a movement.

Hence *an* experience of thinking has its own esthetic quality. It differs from those experiences that are acknowledged to be esthetic, but only in its materials. The material of the fine arts consists of qualities; that of experience having intellectual conclusion are signs or symbols having no intrinsic quality of their own, but standing for things that may in another experience be qualitatively experienced. The difference is enormous. It is one reason why the strictly intellectual art will never be popular as music is popular. Nevertheless, the experience itself has a satisfying emotional quality because it possesses internal integration and fulfillment reached through ordered and organized movement. This artistic structure may be immediately felt. In so far, it is esthetic. What is even more important is that not only is this quality a significant motive in undertaking intellectual inquiry and in keeping it honest, but that no intellectual activity is an integral event (is *an* experience), unless it is rounded out with this quality. Without it, thinking is inconclusive. In short, esthetic cannot be sharply marked off from intellectual experience since the latter must bear an esthetic stamp to be itself complete.

The same statement holds good of a course of action that is dominantly practical, that is, one that consists of overt doings. It is possible to be efficient in action and yet not have a conscious experience. The activity is too automatic to permit of a sense of what it is about and where it is going. It comes to an end but not to a close or consummation in consciousness. Obstacles are overcome by shrewd skill, but they do not feed experience. There are also those who are wavering in action, uncertain, and inconclusive like the shades in classic literature. Between the poles of aimlessness and mechanical efficiency, there lie those courses of action in which through successive deeds there runs a sense of growing meaning conserved and accumulating toward an end that is felt as accomplishment of a process. Successful politicians and generals who turn statesmen like Caesar and Napoleon have something of the showman about them. This of itself is not art, but it is, I think, a sign that interest is not exclusively, perhaps not mainly, held by the result taken by itself (as it is in the case of mere efficiency), but by it as the outcome of a process. There is interest in completing an experience. The experience may be one that is harmful to the world and its consummation undesirable. But it has esthetic quality.

The Greek identification of good conduct with conduct having proportion, grace, and harmony, the *kalon-agathon*, is a more obvious example of distinctive esthetic quality in moral action. One great defect in what passes as morality is its anesthetic quality. Instead of exemplifying wholehearted action, it takes the form of grudging piecemeal concessions to the demands of duty. But illustrations may only obscure the fact that any practical activity will, provided that it is integrated and moves by its own urge to fulfillment, have esthetic quality.

A generalized illustration may be had if we imagine a stone, which is rolling down hill, to have an experience. The activity is surely sufficiently "practical." The stone starts from somewhere, and moves, as consistently as conditions permit, toward a place and state where it will be at rest—toward an end. Let us add, by imagination, to these external facts, the ideas that it looks forward with desire to the final outcome; that it is interested in the things it meets on its way, conditions that accelerate and retard its movement with respect to their bearing on the end; that it acts and feels toward them according to the hindering or helping function it attributes to them; and that the final coming to rest is related to all that went before as the culmination of a continuous movement. Then the stone would have an experience, and one with esthetic quality.

If we turn from this imaginary case to our own experience, we shall find much of it is nearer to what happens to the actual stone than it is to anything that fulfills the conditions fancy just laid down. For in much of our experience we are not concerned with the connection of one incident with what went before and what comes after. There is no interest that controls attentive rejection or selection of what shall be organized into the developing experience. Things happen, but they are neither definitely included nor decisively excluded; we drift. We yield according to external pressure, or evade and compromise. There are beginnings and cessations, but no genuine initiations and concludings. One thing replaces another, but does not absorb it and carry it on. There is experience, but so slack and discursive that it is not *an* experience. Needless to say, such experiences are anesthetic.

Thus the non-esthetic lies within two limits. At one pole is the loose succession that does not begin at any particular place and that ends—in the sense of ceasing—at no particular place. At the other pole is arrest, constriction, proceeding from parts having only a mechanical connection with one another. There exists so much of one and the other of these two kinds of experience that unconsciously they come to be taken as norms of all experience. Then, when the esthetic appears, it so sharply contrasts with the picture that has been formed of experience, that it is impossible to combine its special qualities with the features of the picture and the esthetic is given an outside place and status. The account that has been given of experience dominantly intellectual and practical is intended to show that there is no such contrast involved in having an experience; that, on the contrary, no experience of whatever sort is a unity unless it has esthetic quality.

The enemies of the esthetic are neither the practical nor the intellectual. They are the humdrum; slackness of loose ends; submission to convention in practice and intellectual procedure. Rigid abstinence, coerced submission, tightness on one side and dissipation, incoherence and aimless indulgence on the other, are deviations in opposite directions from the unity of an experience. Some such considerations perhaps induced Aristotle to invoke the "mean proportional" as the proper designation of what is distinctive of both virtue and the esthetic. He was formally correct. "Mean" and "proportion" are, however, not self-explanatory, nor to be taken over in a prior mathematical sense, but are properties belonging to an experience that has a developing movement toward its own consummation.

I have emphasized the fact that every integral experience moves toward a close, an ending, since it ceases only when the energies active in it have done their proper work. This closure of a circuit of energy is the opposite of arrest, of *stasis*. Maturation and fixation are polar opposites. Struggle and conflict may be themselves enjoyed, although they are painful, when they are experienced as means of developing an experience; members in that they carry it forward, not just because they are there. There is, as will appear later, an element of undergoing, of suffering in its large sense, in every experience. Otherwise there would be no taking in of what preceded. For "taking in" in any vital experience is something more than placing something on the top of consciousness over what was previously known. It involves reconstruction which may be painful. Whether the necessary undergoing phase is by itself pleasurable or painful is a matter of particular conditions. It is indifferent to the total esthetic quality, save that there are few intense esthetic experiences that are wholly gleeful. They are certainly not to be characterized as amusing, and as they bear down upon us they involve a suffering that is none the less consistent with, indeed a part of, the complete perception that is enjoyed.

I have spoken of the esthetic quality that rounds out an experience into completeness and unity as emotional. The reference may cause difficulty. We are given to thinking of emotions as things as simple and compact as are the words by which we name them. Joy, sorrow, hope, fear, anger, curiosity, are treated as if each in itself were a sort of entity that enters full-made upon the scene, an entity that may last a long time or a short time, but whose duration, whose growth and career, is irrelevant to its nature. In fact emotions are qualities, when they are significant, of a complex experience that moves and changes. I say, when they are *significant*, for otherwise they are but the outbreaks and eruptions of a disturbed infant. All emotions are qualifications of a drama and they change as the drama develops. Persons are sometimes said to fall in love at first sight. But what they fall into is not a thing of that instant. What would love be were it compressed into a moment in which there is no room for cherishing and for solicitude? The intimate nature of emotion is manifested in the experience of one watching a play on the stage or reading a novel. It attends the development of a plot; and a plot requires a stage, a space, wherein to develop and time in which to unfold.

Experience is emotional but there are no separate things called emotions in it.

By the same token, emotions are attached to events and objects in their movement. They are not, save in pathological instances, private. And even an "objectless" emotion demands something beyond itself to which to attach itself, and thus it soon generates a delusion in lack of something real. Emotion belongs of a certainty to the self. But it belongs to the self that is concerned in the movement of events toward an issue that is desired or disliked. We jump instantaneously when we are scared, as we blush on the instant when we are ashamed. But fright and shamed modesty are not in this case emotional states. Of themselves they are but automatic reflexes. In order to become emotional they must become parts of an inclusive and enduring situation that involves concern for objects and their issues. The jump of fright becomes emotional fear when there is found or thought to exist a threatening object that must be dealt with or escaped from. The blush becomes the emotion of shame when a person connects, in thought, an action he has performed with an unfavorable reaction to himself of some other person.

Physical things from far ends of the earth are physically transported and physically caused to act and react upon one another in the construction of a new object. The miracle of mind is that something similar takes place in experience without physical transport and assembling. Emotion is the moving and cementing force. It selects what is congruous and dyes what is selected with its color, thereby giving qualitative unity to materials externally disparate and dissimilar. It thus provides unity in and through the varied parts of an experience. When the unity is of the sort already described, the experience has esthetic character even though it is not, dominantly, an esthetic experience.

Two men meet; one is the applicant for a position, while the other has the disposition of the matter in his hands. The interview may be mechanical, consisting of set questions, the replies to which perfunctorily settle the matter. There is no experience in which the two men meet, nothing that is not a repetition, by way of acceptance or dismissal, of something which has happened a score of times. The situation is disposed of as if it were an exercise in bookkeeping. But an interplay may take place in which a new experience develops. Where should we look for an account of such an experience? Not to ledger-entries nor yet to a treatise on economics or sociology or personnel-psychology, but to drama or fiction. Its nature and import can be expressed only by art, because there is a unity of experience that can be expressed only as an experience. The *experience* is of material fraught with suspense and moving toward its own consummation through a connected series of varied incidents. The primary emotions on the part of the applicant may be at the beginning hope or despair, and elation or disappointment at the close. These emotions qualify the experience as a unity. But as the interview proceeds, secondary emotions are evolved as variations of the primary underlying one. It is even possible for each attitude and gesture, each sentence, almost every word, to produce more than a fluctuation in the intensity of the basic emotion; to produce, that is, a change of shade and tint in its quality. The employer sees by means of his own emotional reactions the character of the one applying. He projects him imaginatively into the work to be done and judges his fitness by the way in which the elements of the scene assemble and either clash or fit together. The presence and behavior of the applicant either harmonize with his own attitudes and desires or they conflict and jar. Such factors as these, inherently esthetic in quality, are the forces that carry the varied elements of the interview to a decisive issue. They enter into the settlement of every situation, whatever its dominant nature, in which there are uncertainty and suspense.

There are, therefore, common patterns in various experiences, no matter how unlike they are to one another in the details of their subject matter. There are conditions to be met without which an experience cannot come to be. The outline of the common pattern is set by the fact that every experience is the result of interaction between a live creature and some aspect of the world in which he lives. A man does something; he lifts, let us say, a stone. In consequence he undergoes, suffers, something: the weight, strain, texture of the surface of the thing lifted. The properties thus undergone determine further doing. The stone is too heavy or too angular, not solid enough; or else the properties undergone show it is fit for the use for which it is intended. The process continues until a mutual adaptation of the self and the object emerges and that particular experience comes to a close. What is true of this simple instance is true, as to form, of every experience. The creature operating may be a thinker in his study and the environment with which he interacts may consist of ideas instead of a stone. But interaction of the two constitutes the total experience that is had, and the close which completes it is the institution of a felt harmony.

An experience has pattern and structure, because it is not just doing and undergoing in alternation, but consists of them in relationship. To put one's hand in the fire that consumes it is not necessarily to have an experience. The action and its consequence must be joined in perception. This relationship is what gives meaning; to grasp it is the objective of all intelligence. The scope and content of the relations measure the significant content of an experience. A child's experience may be intense, but, because of lack of background from past experience, relations between undergoing and doing are slightly grasped, and the experience does not have great depth or breadth. No one ever arrives at such maturity that he perceives all the connections that are involved. There was once written (by Mr. Hinton) a romance called "The Unlearner." It portrayed the whole endless duration of life after death as a living over of the incidents that happened in a short life on earth, in continued discovery of the relationships involved among them.

Experience is limited by all the causes which interfere with perception of the relations between undergoing and doing. There may be interference because of excess on the side of doing or of excess on the side of receptivity, of undergoing. Unbalance on either side blurs the perception of relations and leaves the experience partial and distorted, with scant or false meaning. Zeal for doing, lust for action, leaves many a person, especially in this hurried and impatient human environment in which we live, with experience of an almost incredible paucity, all on the surface. No one experience has a chance to complete itself because something else is entered upon so speedily. What is called experience becomes so dispersed and miscellaneous as hardly to deserve the name. Resistance is treated as an obstruction to be beaten down, not as an invitation to reflection. An individual comes to seek, unconsciously even more than by deliberate choice, situations in which he can do the most things in the shortest time.

Experiences are also cut short from maturing by excess of receptivity. What is prized is then the mere undergoing of this and that, irrespective of perception of any meaning. The crowding together of as many impressions as possible is thought to be "life," even though no one of them is more than a flitting and a sipping. The sentimentalist and the daydreamer may have more fancies and impressions pass through their consciousness than has the man who is animated by lust for action. But his experience is equally distorted, because nothing takes root in mind when there is no balance between doing and receiving. Some decisive action is needed in order to establish contact with the realities of the world and in order that impressions may be so related to facts that their value is tested and organized.

Because perception of relationship between what is done and what is undergone constitutes the work of intelligence, and because the artist is controlled in the process of his work by his grasp of the connection between what he has already done and what he is to do next, the idea that the artist does not think as intently and penetratingly as a scientific inquirer is absurd. A painter must consciously undergo the effect of his every brush stroke or he will not be aware of what he is doing and where his work is going. Moreover, he has to see each particular connection of doing and undergoing in relation to the whole that he desires to produce. To apprehend such relations is to think, and is one of the most exacting modes of thought. The difference between the pictures of different painters is due quite as much to differences of capacity to carry on this thought as it is to differences of sensitivity to bare color and to differences in dexterity of execution. As respects the basic quality of pictures, difference depends, indeed, more upon the quality of intelligence brought to bear upon perception of relations than upon anything else—though of course intelligence cannot be separated from direct sensitivity and is connected, though in a more external manner, with skill.

Any idea that ignores the necessary rôle of intelligence in production of works of art is based upon identification of thinking with use of one special kind of material, verbal signs and words. To think effectively in terms of relations of qualities is as severe a demand upon thought as to think in terms of symbols, verbal and mathematical. Indeed, since words are easily manipulated in mechanical ways, the production of a work of genuine art probably demands more intelligence than does most of the so-called thinking that goes on among those who pride themselves on being "intellectuals."

I have tried to show in these chapters that the esthetic is no intruder in experience from without, whether by way of idle luxury or transcendent ideality, but that it is the clarified and intensified development of traits that belong to every normally complete experience. This fact I take to be the only secure basis upon which esthetic theory can build. It remains to suggest some of the implications of the underlying fact.

We have no word in the English language that unambiguously includes what is signified by the two words "artistic" and "esthetic." Since "artistic" refers primarily to the act of production and "esthetic" to that of perception and enjoyment, the absence of a term designating the two processes taken together is unfortunate. Sometimes, the effect is to separate the two from each other, to regard art as something superimposed upon esthetic material, or, upon the other side, to an assumption that, since art is a process of creation, perception and enjoyment of it have nothing in common with the creative act. In any case, there is a certain verbal awkwardness in that we are compelled sometimes to use the term "esthetic" to cover the entire field and sometimes to limit it to the receiving perceptual aspect of the whole operation. I refer to these obvious facts as preliminary to an attempt to show how the conception of conscious experience as a perceived relation between doing and undergoing enables us to understand the connection that art as production and perception and appreciation as enjoyment sustain to each other.

Art denotes a process of doing or making. This is as true of fine as of technological art. Art involves molding of clay, chipping of marble, casting of bronze, laying on of pigments, construction of buildings, singing of songs, playing of instruments, enacting rôles on the stage, going through rhythmic movements in the dance. Every art does something with some physical material, the body or something outside the body, with or without the use of intervening tools, and with a view to production of something visible, audible, or tangible. So marked is the active or "doing" phase of art, that the dictionaries usually define it in terms of skilled action, ability in execution. The Oxford Dictionary illustrates by a quotation from John Stuart Mill: "Art is an endeavor after perfection in execution" while Matthew Arnold calls it "pure and flawless workmanship."

The word "esthetic" refers, as we have already noted, to experience as appreciative, perceiving, and enjoying. It denotes the consumer's rather than the producer's standpoint. It is Gusto, taste; and, as with cooking, overt skillful action is on the side of the cook who prepares, while taste is on the side of the consumer, as in gardening there is a distinction between the gardener who plants and tills and the householder who enjoys the finished product.

These very illustrations, however, as well as the relation that exists in having an experience between doing and undergoing, indicate that the distinction between esthetic and artistic cannot be pressed so far as to become a separation. Perfection in execution cannot be measured or defined in terms of execution; it implies those who perceive and enjoy the product that is executed. The cook prepares food for the consumer and the measure of the value of what is prepared is found in consumption. Mere perfection in execution, judged in its own terms in isolation, can probably be attained better by a machine than by human art. By itself, it is at most technique, and there are great artists who are not in the first ranks as technicians (witness Cézanne), just as there are great performers on the piano who are not great esthetically, and as Sargent is not a great painter.

Craftsmanship to be artistic in the final sense must be "loving"; it must care deeply for the subject matter upon which skill is exercised. A sculptor comes to mind whose busts are marvelously exact. It might be difficult to tell in the presence of a photograph of one of them and of a photograph of the original which was of the person himself. For virtuosity they are remarkable. But one doubts whether the maker of the busts had an experience of his own that he was concerned to have those share who look at his products. To be truly artistic, a work must also be esthetic—that is, framed for enjoyed receptive perception. Constant observation is, of course, necessary for the maker while he is producing. But if his perception is not also esthetic in nature, it is a colorless and cold recognition of what has been done, used as a stimulus to the next step in a process that is essentially mechanical.

In short, art, in its form, unites the very same relation of doing and undergoing, outgoing and incoming energy, that makes an experience to be an experience. Because of elimination of all that does not contribute to mutual organization of the factors of both action and reception into one another, and because of selection of just the aspects and traits that contribute to their interpenetration of each other, the product is a work of esthetic art. Man whittles, carves, sings, dances, gestures, molds, draws and paints. The doing or making is artistic when the perceived result is of such a nature that *its* qualities *as perceived* have controlled the question of production. The act of producing that is directed by intent to produce something that is enjoyed in the immediate experience of perceiving has qualities that a spontaneous or uncontrolled activity does not have. The artist embodies in himself the attitude of the perceiver while he works.

Suppose, for the sake of illustration, that a finely wrought object, one whose texture and proportions are highly pleasing in perception, has been believed to be a product of some primitive people. Then there is discovered evidence that proves it to be an accidental natural product. As an external thing, it is now precisely what it was before. Yet at once it ceases to be a work of art and becomes a natural "curiosity." It now belongs in a museum of natural history, not in a museum of art. And the extraordinary thing is that the difference that is thus made is not one of just intellectual classification. A difference is made in appreciative perception and in a direct way. The esthetic experience—in its limited sense

—is thus seen to be inherently connected with the experience of making.

The sensory satisfaction of eye and ear, when esthetic, is so because it does not stand by itself but is linked to the activity of which it is the consequence. Even the pleasures of the palate are different in quality to an epicure than in one who merely "likes" his food as he eats it. The difference is not of mere intensity. The epicure is conscious of much more than the taste of the food. Rather, there enter into the taste, as directly experienced, qualities that depend upon reference to its source and its manner of production in connection with criteria of excellence. As production must absorb into itself qualities of the product as perceived and be regulated by them, so, on the other side, seeing, hearing, tasting, become esthetic when relation to a distinct manner of activity qualifies what is perceived.

There is an element of passion in all esthetic perception. Yet when we are overwhelmed by passion, as in extreme rage, fear, jealousy, the experience is definitely non-esthetic. There is no relationship felt to the qualities of the activity that has generated the passion. Consequently, the material of the experience lacks elements of balance and proportion. For these can be present only when, as in the conduct that has grace or dignity, the act is controlled by an exquisite sense of the relations which the act sustains—its fitness to the occasion and to the situation.

The process of art in production is related to the esthetic in perception organically—as the Lord God in creation surveyed his work and found it good. Until the artist is satisfied in perception with what he is doing, he continues shaping and reshaping. The making comes to an end when its result is experienced as good—and that experience comes not by mere intellectual and outside judgment but in direct perception. An artist, in comparison with his fellows, is one who is not only especially gifted in powers of execution but in unusual sensitivity to the qualities of things. This sensitivity also directs his doings and makings.

As we manipulate, we touch and feel, as we look, we see; as we listen, we hear. The hand moves with etching needle or with brush. The eye attends and reports the consequence of what is done. Because of this intimate connection, subsequent doing is cumulative and not a matter of caprice nor yet of routine. In an emphatic artistic-esthetic experience, the relation is so close that it controls simultaneously both the doing and the perception. Such vital intimacy of connection cannot be had if only hand and eye are engaged. When they do not, both of them, act as organs of the whole being, there is but a mechanical sequence of sense and movement, as in walking that is automatic. Hand and eye, when the experience is esthetic, are but instruments through which the entire live creature, moved and active throughout, operates. Hence the expression is emotional and guided by purpose.

Because of the relation between what is done and what is undergone, there is an immediate sense of things in perception as belonging together or as jarring; as reënforcing or as interfering. The consequences of the act of making as reported in sense show whether what is done carries forward the idea being executed or marks a deviation and break. In as far as the development of an experience is *controlled* through reference to these immediately felt relations of order and fulfillment, that experience becomes dominantly esthetic in nature. The urge to action becomes an urge to that kind of action which will result in an object satisfying in direct perception. The potter shapes his clay to make a bowl useful for holding grain; but he makes it in a way so regulated by the series of perceptions that sum up the serial acts of making, that the bowl is marked by enduring grace and charm. The general situation remains the same in painting a picture or molding a bust. Moreover, at each stage there is anticipation of what is to come. This anticipation is the connecting link between the next doing and its outcome for sense. What is done and what is undergone are thus reciprocally, cumulatively, and continuously instrumental to each other.

The doing may be energetic, and the undergoing may be acute and intense. But unless they are related to each other to form a whole in perception, the thing done is not fully esthetic. The making for example may be a display of technical virtuosity, and the undergoing a gush of sentiment or a revery. If the artist does not perfect a new vision in his process of doing, he acts mechanically and repeats some old model fixed like a blue print in his mind. An incredible amount of observation and of the kind of intelligence that is exercised in perception of qualitative relations characterizes creative work in art. The relations must be noted not only with respect to one another, two by two, but in connection with the whole under construction; they are exercised in imagination as well as in observation. Irrelevancies arise that are tempting distractions; digressions suggest themselves in the guise of enrichments. There are occasions when the grasp of the dominant idea grows faint, and then the artist is moved unconsciously to fill in until his thought grows strong again. The real work of an artist is to build up an experience that is coherent in perception while moving with constant change in its development.

When an author puts on paper ideas that are already clearly con-

ceived and consistently ordered, the real work has been previously
done. Or, he may depend upon the greater perceptibility induced by the
activity and its sensible report to direct his completion of the work. The
mere act of transcription is esthetically irrelevant save as it enters integrally into the formation of an experience moving to completeness.
Even the composition conceived in the head and, therefore, physically
private, is public in its significant content, since it is conceived with
reference to execution in a product that is perceptible and hence belongs
to the common world. Otherwise it would be an aberration or a passing
dream. The urge to express through painting the perceived qualities of a
landscape is continuous with demand for pencil or brush. Without external embodiment, an experience remains incomplete; physiologically
and functionally, sense organs are motor organs and are connected, by
means of distribution of energies in the human body and not merely
anatomically, with other motor organs. It is no linguistic accident that
"building," "construction," "work," designate both a process and its
finished product. Without the meaning of the verb that of the noun remains blank.

Writer, composer of music, sculptor, or painter can retrace, during
the process of production, what they have previously done. When it is
not satisfactory in the undergoing or perceptual phase of experience,
they can to some degree start afresh. This retracing is not readily accomplished in the case of architecture—which is perhaps one reason
why there are so many ugly buildings. Architects are obliged to complete their idea before its translation into a complete object of perception takes place. Inability to build up simultaneously the idea and its
objective embodiment imposes a handicap. Nevertheless, they too are
obliged to think out their ideas in terms of the medium of embodiment
and the object of ultimate perception unless they work mechanically
and by rote. Probably the esthetic quality of medieval cathedrals is due
in some measure to the fact that their constructions were not so much
controlled by plans and specifications made in advance as is now the
case. Plans grew as the building grew. But even a Minerva-like product,
if it is artistic, presupposes a prior period of gestation in which doings
and perceptions projected in imagination interact and mutually modify
one another. Every work of art follows the plan of, and pattern of, a
complete experience, rendering it more intensely and concentratedly
felt.

It is not so easy in the case of the perceiver and appreciator to understand the intimate union of doing and undergoing as it is in the case
of the maker. We are given to supposing that the former merely takes in

what is there in finished form, instead of realizing that this taking in involves activities that are comparable to those of the creator. But receptivity is not passivity. It, too, is a process consisting of a series of responsive acts that accumulate toward objective fulfillment. Otherwise, there is not perception but recognition. The difference between the two is immense. Recognition is perception arrested before it has a chance to develop freely. In recognition there is a beginning of an act of perception. But this beginning is not allowed to serve the development of a full perception of the thing recognized. It is arrested at the point where it will serve some *other* purpose, as we recognize a man on the street in order to greet or to avoid him, not so as to see him for the sake of seeing what is there.

In recognition we fall back, as upon a stereotype, upon some previously formed scheme. Some detail or arrangement of details serves as cue for bare identification. It suffices in recognition to apply this bare outline as a stencil to the present object. Sometimes in contact with a human being we are struck with traits, perhaps of only physical characteristics, of which we were not previously aware. We realize that we never knew the person before; we had not seen him in any pregnant sense. We now begin to study and to "take in." Perception replaces bare recognition. There is an act of reconstructive doing, and consciousness becomes fresh and alive. *This* act of seeing involves the coöperation of motor elements even though they remain implicit and do not become overt, as well as coöperation of all funded ideas that may serve to complete the new picture that is forming. Recognition is too easy to arouse vivid consciousness. There is not enough resistance between new and old to secure consciousness of the experience that is had. Even a dog that barks and wags his tail joyously on seeing his master return is more fully alive in his reception of his friend than is a human being who is content with mere recognition.

Bare recognition is satisfied when a proper tag or label is attached, "proper" signifying one that serves a purpose outside the act of recognition—as a salesman identifies wares by a sample. It involves no stir of the organism, no inner commotion. But an act of perception proceeds by waves that extend serially throughout the entire organism. There is, therefore, no such thing in perception as seeing or hearing *plus* emotion. The perceived object or scene is emotionally pervaded throughout. When an aroused emotion does not permeate the material that is perceived or thought of, it is either preliminary or pathological.

The esthetic or undergoing phase of experience is receptive. It involves surrender. But adequate yielding of the self is possibly only through a controlled activity that may well be intense. In much of our intercourse with our surroundings we withdraw; sometimes from fear, if only of expending unduly our store of energy; sometimes from preoccupation with other matters, as in the case of recognition. Perception is an act of the going-out of energy in order to receive, not a withholding of energy. To steep ourselves in a subject-matter we have first to plunge into it. When we are only passive to a scene, it overwhelms us and, for lack of answering activity, we do not perceive that which bears us down. We must summon energy and pitch it at a responsive key in order to *take* in.

Every one knows that it requires apprenticeship to see through a microscope or telescope, and to see a landscape as the geologist sees it. The idea that esthetic perception is an affair for odd moments is one reason for the backwardness of the arts among us. The eye and the visual apparatus may be intact; the object may be physically there, the cathedral of Notre Dame, or Rembrandt's portait of Hendrik Stoeffel. In some bald sense, the latter may be "seen." They may be looked at, possibly recognized, and have their correct names attached. But for lack of continuous interaction between the total organism and the objects, they are not perceived, certainly not esthetically. A crowd of visitors steered through a picture-gallery by a guide, with attention called here and there to some high point, does not perceive; only by accident is there even interest in seeing a picture for the sake of subject matter vividly realized.

For to perceive, a beholder must *create* his own experience. And his creation must include relations comparable to those which the original producer underwent. They are not the same in any literal sense. But with the perceiver, as with the artist, there must be an ordering of the elements of the whole that is in form, although not in details, the same as the process of organization the creator of the work consciously experienced. Without an act of recreation the object is not perceived as a work of art. The artist selected, simplified, clarified, abridged and condensed according to his interest. The beholder must go through these operations according to his point of view and interest. In both, an act of abstraction, that is of extraction of what is significant, takes place. In both, there is comprehension in its literal signification—that is, a gathering together of details and particulars physically scattered into an experienced whole. There is work done on the part of the percipient as there is on the part of the artist. The one who is too lazy, idle, or indurated in convention to perform this work will not see or hear. His "appreciation" will be a mixture of scraps of learning with conformity to norms of conventional admiration and with a confused, even if gen-uine, emotional excitation.

The considerations that have been presented imply both the com-munity and the unlikeness, because of specific emphasis, of *an* ex-perience, in its pregnant sense, and esthetic experience. The former has esthetic quality; otherwise its materials would not be rounded out into a single coherent experience. It is not possible to divide in a vital ex-perience the practical, emotional, and intellectual from one another and to set the properties of one over against the characteristics of the others. The emotional phase binds parts together into a single whole; "intellec-tual" simply names the fact that the experience has meaning; "prac-tical" indicates that the organism is interacting with events and objects which surround it. The most elaborate philosophic or scientific inquiry and the most ambitious industrial or political enterprise has, when its different ingredients constitute an integral experience, esthetic quality. For then its varied parts are linked to one another, and do not merely succeed one another. And the parts through their experienced linkage move toward a consummation and close, not merely to cessation in time. This consummation, moreover, does not wait in consciousness for the whole undertaking to be finished. It is anticipated throughout and is recurrently savored with special intensity.

Nevertheless, the experiences in question are dominantly intellectual or practical, rather than *distinctively* esthetic, because of the interest and purpose that initiate and control them. In an intellectual ex-perience, the conclusion has value on its own account. It can be ex-tracted as a formula or as a "truth," and can be used in its independent entirety as factor and guide in other inquiries. In a work of art there is no such single self-sufficient deposit. The end, the terminus, is signifi-cant not by itself but as the integration of the parts. It has no other ex-istence. A drama or novel is not the final sentence, even if the charac-ters are disposed of as living happily ever after. In a distinctively es-thetic experience, characteristics that are subordinate are con-trolling—namely, the characteristics in virtue of which the experience is an integrated complete experience on its own account.

In every integral experience there is form because there is dynamic organization. I call the organization dynamic because it takes time to complete it, because it is a growth. There is inception, development, ful-fillment. Material is ingested and digested through interaction with that vital organization of the results of prior experience that constitutes the mind of the worker. Incubation goes on until what is conceived is brought forth and is rendered perceptible as part of the common world. An esthetic experience can be crowded into a moment only in the sense that a climax of prior long enduring processes may arrive in an outstanding movement which so sweeps everything else into it that all else is forgotten. That which distinguishes an experience as esthetic is conversion of resistance and tensions, of excitations that in themselves are temptations to diversion, into a movement toward an inclusive and fulfilling close.

Experiencing like breathing is a rhythm of intakings and outgivings. Their succession is punctuated and made a rhythm by the existence of intervals, periods in which one phase is ceasing and the other is inchoate and preparing. William James aptly compared the course of a conscious experience to the alternate flights and perchings of a bird. The flights and perchings are intimately connected with one another; they are not so many unrelated lightings succeeded by a number of equally unrelated hoppings. Each resting place in experience is an undergoing in which is absorbed and taken home the consequences of prior doing, and, unless the doing is that of utter caprice or sheer routine, each doing carries in itself meaning that has been extracted and conserved. As with the advance of an army, all gains from what has been already effected are periodically consolidated, and always with a view to what is to be done next. If we move too rapidly, we get away from the base of supplies—of accrued meanings—and the experience is flustered, thin, and confused. If we dawdle too long after having extracted a net value, experience perishes of inanition.

The *form* of the whole is therefore present in every member. Fulfilling, consummating, are continuous functions, not mere ends, located at one place only. An engraver, painter, or writer is in process of completing at every stage of his work. He must at each point retain and sum up what has gone before as a whole and with reference to a whole to come. Otherwise there is no consistency and no security in his successive acts. The series of doings in the rhythm of experience give variety and movement; they save the work from monotony and useless repetitions. The undergoings are the corresponding elements in the rhythm, and they supply unity; they save the work from the aimlessness of a mere succession of excitations. An object is peculiarly and dominantly esthetic, yielding the enjoyment characteristic of esthetic perception, when the factors that determine anything which can be called *an* experience are lifted high above the threshold of perception and are made manifest for their own sake.

VIII
Experience as Problematic: Ethical, Political, Religious, and Social Dimensions

It would be foreign to Dewey's thought to make a distinction between philosophy and applied philosophy. Nonetheless, even for Dewey there is often a difference of subject matter to be utilized as a source of his philosophical judgments. In addition to his extensive writings on education, Dewey, especially in his later years, wrote essays on ethical, political, religious, and social problems. The following selections provide some instances of these concerns, and they demonstrate as well Dewey's ability to concretize philosophical method in the context of the human situation as lived.

36. The Construction of Good*

Quite often, in the midst of a technical philosophical discussion, Dewey will venture some strong commentary on those operations and structures of society which have direct bearing on the quality of life for the community at large. In this selection, which is devoted to a construction of a viable theory of value, he renews his attack on the bifurcation of reason from experience and points to the ramifications in the area of economics.

Dewey believes in striving for an integration of "beliefs about the world" and "beliefs about the values and purposes" that direct our conduct. We cannot achieve the objectivity of values at the price of isolating them from experience, nor can

* From John Dewey, *The Quest for Certainty* (New York, Capricorn Books, 1960) (1929), pp. 254-86. Reprinted by permission of G. P. Putnam's Sons.

we assert their relevance by identifying them as "mere statements of our own feelings." By contrast with these approaches, Dewey offers an experimental empiricism drawn from
the method of science, "which finds values to be identical
with goods that are the fruit of intelligently directed activity."

We saw at the outset of our discussion that insecurity generates the
quest for certainty. Consequences issue from every experience, and they
are the source of our interest in what is present. Absence of arts of
regulation diverted the search for security into irrelevant modes of practice, into rite and cult; thought was devoted to discovery of omens
rather than of signs of what is to occur. Gradually there was differentiation of two realms, one higher, consisting of the powers which determine human destiny in all important affairs. With this religion was concerned. The other consisted of the prosaic matters in which man relied
upon his own skill and his matter-of-fact insight. Philosophy inherited
the idea of this division. Meanwhile in Greece many of the arts had attained a state of development which raised them above a merely routine
state; there were intimations of measure, order and regularity in
materials dealt with which give intimations of underlying rationality.
Because of the growth of mathematics, there arose also the ideal of a
purely rational knowledge, intrinsically solid and worthy and the means
by which the intimations of rationality within changing phenomena
could be comprehended within science. For the intellectual class the
stay and consolation, the warrant of certainty, provided by religion was
henceforth found in intellectual demonstration of the reality of the objects of an ideal realm.

With the expansion of Christianity, ethico-religious traits came to
dominate the purely rational ones. The ultimate authoritative standards
for regulation of the dispositions and purposes of the human will were
fused with those which satisfied the demands for necessary and universal truth. The authority of ultimate Being was, moreover, represented
on earth by the Church; that which in its nature transcended intellect
was made known by a revelation of which the Church was the interpreter and guardian. The system endured for centuries. While it endured, it provided an integration of belief and conduct for the western
world. Unity of thought and practice extended down to every detail of
the management of life; efficacy of its operation did not depend upon
thought. It was guaranteed by the most powerful and authoritative of all
social institutions.

Its seemingly solid foundation was, however, undermined by the conclusions of modern science. They effected, both in themselves and even more in the new interests and activities they generated, a breach between what man is concerned with here and now and the faith concerning ultimate reality which, in determining his ultimate and eternal destiny, had previously given regulation to his present life. The problem of restoring integration and coöperation between man's beliefs about the world in which he lives and his beliefs about the values and purposes that should direct his conduct is the deepest problem of modern life. It is the problem of any philosophy that is not isolated from that life.

The attention which has been given to the fact that in its experimental procedure science has surrendered the separation between knowing and doing has its source in the fact that there is now provided within a limited, specialized and technical field the possibility and earnest, as far as theory is concerned, of effecting the needed integration in the wider field of collective human experience. Philosophy is called upon to be the theory of the practice, through ideas sufficiently definite to be operative in experimental endeavor, by which the integration may be made secure in actual experience. Its central problem is the relation that exists between the beliefs about the nature of things due to natural science to beliefs about values—using that word to designate whatever is taken to have rightful authority in the direction of conduct. A philosophy which should take up this problem is struck first of all by the fact that beliefs about values are pretty much in the position in which beliefs about nature were before the scientific revolution. There is either a basic distrust of the capacity of experience to develop its own regulative standards, and an appeal to what philosophers call eternal values, in order to ensure regulation of belief and action; or there is acceptance of enjoyments actually experienced irrespective of the method or operation by which they are brought into existence. Complete bifurcation between rationalistic method and an empirical method has its final and most deeply human significance in the ways in which good and bad are thought of and acted for and upon.

As far as technical philosophy reflects this situation, there is division of theories of values into two kinds. On the one hand, goods and evils, in every region of life, as they are concretely experienced, are regarded as characteristic of an inferior order of Being—intrinsically inferior. Just because they are things of human experience, their worth must be estimated by reference to standards and ideals derived from ultimate reality. Their defects and perversion are attributed to the same fact; they are to be corrected and controlled through adoption of methods of conduct derived from loyalty to the requirements of Supreme Being.

This philosophic formulation gets actuality and force from the fact that it is a rendering of the beliefs of men in general as far as they have come under the influence of institutional religion. Just as rational conceptions were once superimposed upon observed and temporal phenomena, so eternal values are superimposed upon experienced goods. In one case as in the other, the alternative is supposed to be confusion and lawlessness. Philosophers suppose these eternal values are known by reason; the mass of persons that they are divinely revealed.

Nevertheless, with the expansion of secular interests, temporal values have enormously multiplied; they absorb more and more attention and energy. The sense of transcendent values has become enfeebled; instead of permeating all things in life, it is more and more restricted to special times and acts. The authority of the church to declare and impose divine will and purpose has narrowed. Whatever men say and profess, their tendency in the presence of actual evils is to resort to natural and empirical means to remedy them. But in formal belief, the old doctrine of the inherently disturbed and unworthy character of the goods and standards of ordinary experience persists. This divergence between what men do and what they nominally profess is closely connected with the confusions and conflicts of modern thought.

It is not meant to assert that no attempts have been made to replace the older theory regarding the authority of immutable and transcendent values by conceptions more congruous with the practices of daily life. The contrary is the case. The utilitarian theory, to take one instance, has had great power. The idealistic school is the only one in contemporary philosophies, with the exception of one form of neo-realism, that makes much of the notion of a reality which is all one with ultimate moral and religious values. But this school is also the one most concerned with the conservation of "spiritual" life. Equally significant is the fact that empirical theories retain the notion that thought and judgment are concerned with values that are experienced independently of them. For these theories, emotional satisfactions occupy the same place that sensations hold in traditional empiricism. Values are constituted by liking and enjoyment; to be enjoyed and to be a value are two names for one and the same fact. Since science has extruded values from its objects, these empirical theories do everything possible to emphasize their purely subjective character of value. A psychological theory of desire and liking is supposed to cover the whole ground of the theory of values; in it, immediate feeling is the counterpart of immediate sensation.

I shall not object to this empirical theory as far as it connects the theory of values with concrete experiences of desire and satisfaction.

The idea that there is such a connection is the only way known to me by which the pallid remoteness of the rationalistic theory, and the only too glaring presence of the institutional theory of transcendental values can be escaped. The objection is that the theory in question holds down value to objects *antecedently* enjoyed, apart from reference to the method by which they come into existence; it takes enjoyments which are casual because unregulated by intelligent operations to be values in and of themselves. Operational thinking needs to be applied to the judgment of values just as it has now finally been applied in conceptions of physical objects. Experimental empiricism in the field of ideas of good and bad is demanded to meet the conditions of the present situation.

The scientific revolution came about when material of direct and un-controlled experience was taken as problematic; as supplying material to be transformed by reflective operations into known objects. The contrast between experienced and known objects was found to be a temporal one; namely, one between empirical subject-matters which were had or "given" prior to the acts of experimental variation and redisposition and those which succeeded these acts and issued from them. The notion of an act whether of sense or thought which supplied a valid measure of thought in immediate knowledge was discredited. Consequences of operations became the important thing. The suggestion almost imperatively follows that escape from the defects of transcendental absolutism is not to be had by setting up as values enjoyments that happen anyhow, but in defining value by enjoyments which are the consequences of intelligent action. Without the intervention of thought, enjoyments are not values but problematic goods, becoming values when they re-issue in a changed form from intelligent behavior. The fundamental trouble with the current empirical theory of values is that it merely formulates and justifies the socially prevailing habit of regarding enjoyments as they are actually experienced as values in and of themselves. It completely side-steps the question of regulation of these enjoyments. This issue involves nothing less than the problem of the directed reconstruction of economic, political and religious institutions.

There was seemingly a paradox involved in the notion that if we turned our backs upon the immediately perceived qualities of things, we should be enabled to form valid conceptions of objects, and that these conceptions could be used to bring about a more secure and more significant experience of them. But the method terminated in disclosing the connections or interactions upon which perceived objects, viewed as events, depend. Formal analogy suggests that we regard our direct and original experience of things liked and enjoyed as only *possibilities* of values to be achieved; that enjoyment becomes a value when we discover the relations upon which its presence depends. Such a causal and operational definition gives only a conception of a value, not a value itself. But the utilization of the conception in action results in an object having secure and significant value.

The formal statement may be given concrete content by pointing to the difference between the enjoyed and the enjoyable, the desired and the desirable, the satis*fying* and the satis*factory*. To say that something is enjoyed is to make a statement about a fact, something already in existence; it is not to judge the value of that fact. There is no difference between such a proposition and one which says that something is sweet or sour, red or black. It is just correct or incorrect and that is the end of the matter. But to call an object a value is to assert that it satisfies or fulfills certain conditions. Function and status in meeting conditions is a different matter from bare existence. The fact that something is desired only raises the *question* of its desirability; it does not settle it. Only a child in the degree of his immaturity thinks to settle the question of desirability by reiterated proclamation: "I want it, I want it, I want it.' What is objected to in the current empirical theory of values is not connection of them with desire and enjoyment but failure to distinguish between enjoyments of radically different sorts. There are many common expressions in which the difference of the two kinds is clearly recognized. Take for example the difference between the ideas of "satisfying" and "satisfactory." To say that something satisfies is to report something as an isolated finality. To assert that it is satis*factory* is to define it in its connections and interactions. The fact that it pleases or is immediately congenial poses a problem to judgment. How shall the satisfaction be rated? Is it a value or is it not? Is it something to be prized and cherished, *to be* enjoyed? Not stern moralists alone but everyday experience informs us that finding satisfaction in a thing may be a warning, a summons to be on the lookout for consequences. To declare something satis*factory* is to assert that it meets specifiable conditions. It is, in effect, a judgment that the thing "will do." It involves a prediction; it contemplates a future in which the thing will continue to serve; it *will* do. It asserts a consequence the thing will actively institute; it will *do*. That it is satisfying is the content of a proposition of fact; that it is satisfactory is a judgment, an estimate, an appraisal. It denotes an attitude *to be* taken, that of striving to perpetuate and to make secure.

It is worth notice that besides the instances given, there are many other recognitions in ordinary speech of the distinction. The endings "able," "worthy" and "ful" are cases in point. Noted and notable, noteworthy; remarked and remarkable; advised and advisable; wondered at and wonderful; pleasing and beautiful; loved and lovable; blamed and blameable, blameworthy; objected to and objectionable; esteemed and estimable; admired and admirable; shamed and shameful; honored and honorable; approved and approvable, worthy of approbation, etc. The multiplication of words adds nothing to the force of the distinction. But it aids in conveying a sense of the fundamental character of the distinction; of the difference between mere report of an already existent fact and judgment as to the importance and need of bringing a fact into existence; or, if it is already there, of sustaining it in existence. The latter is a genuine practical judgment, and marks the only type of judgment that has to do with the direction of action. Whether or no we reserve the term "value" for the latter, (as seems to me proper) is a minor matter; that the distinction be acknowledged as the key to understanding the relation of values to the direction of conduct is the important thing.

This element of direction by an idea of value applies to science as well as anywhere else. For in every scientific undertaking, there is passed a constant succession of estimates; such as "it is worth treating these facts as data or evidence; it is advisable to try this experiment; to make that observation; to entertain such and such a hypothesis; to perform this calculation," etc.

The word "taste" has perhaps got too completely associated with arbitrary liking to express the nature of judgments of value. But if the word be used in the sense of an appreciation at once cultivated and active, one may say that the formation of taste is the chief matter wherever values enter in, whether intellectual, esthetic or moral. Relatively immediate judgments, which we call fact or to which we give the name of intuition, do not precede reflective inquiry, but are the funded products of much thoughtful experience. Expertness of taste is at once the result and the reward of constant exercise of thinking. Instead of there being no disputing about tastes, they are the one thing worth disputing about, if by "dispute" is signified discussion involving reflective inquiry. Taste, if we use the word in its best sense, is the outcome of experience brought cumulatively to bear on the intelligent appreciation of the real worth of likings and enjoyments. There is nothing in which a person so completely reveals himself as in the things which he judges enjoyable and desirable. Such judgments are the sole alternative to the domination of belief by impulse, chance, blind habit and self-interest. The formation of a cultivated and effectively operative good judgment or taste with respect to what is esthetically admirable, intellectually acceptable and morally approvable is the supreme task set to human beings by the incidents of experience.

Propositions about what is or has been liked are of instrumental value in reaching judgments of value, in as far as the conditions and consequences of the thing liked are thought about. In themselves they make no claims; they put forth no demand upon subsequent attitudes and acts; they profess no authority to direct. If one likes a thing he likes it; that *is* a point about which there can be no dispute:—although it is not so easy to state just *what* is liked as is frequently assumed. A judgment about what is *to be* desired and enjoyed is, on the other hand, a claim on future action; it possesses *de jure* and not merely *de facto* quality. It is a matter of frequent experience that likings and enjoyments are of all kinds, and that many are such as reflective judgments condemn. By way of self-justification and "rationalization," an enjoyment creates a tendency to assert that the thing enjoyed is a value. This assertion of validity adds authority to the fact. It is a decision that the object has a right to exist and hence a claim upon action to further its existence.

The analogy between the status of the theory of values and the theory of ideas about natural objects before the rise of experimental inquiry may be carried further. The sensationalistic theory of the origin and test of thought evoked, by way of reaction, the transcendental theory of *a priori* ideas. For it failed utterly to account for objective connection, order and regularity in objects observed. Similarly, any doctrine that identifies the mere fact of being liked with the value of the object liked so fails to give direction to conduct when direction is needed that it automatically calls forth the assertion that there are values eternally in Being that are the standards of all judgments and the obligatory ends of all action. Without the introduction of operational thinking, we oscillate between a theory that, in order to save the objectivity of judgments of values, isolates them from experience and nature, and a theory that, in order to save their concrete and human significance, reduces them to mere statements about our own feelings.

Not even the most devoted adherents of the notion that enjoyment and value are equivalent facts would venture to assert that because we have once liked a thing we should go on liking it; they are compelled to introduce the idea that *some* tastes are to be cultivated. Logically, there is no ground for introducing the idea of cultivation; liking is liking, and one is as good as another. If enjoyments *are* values, the judgment of value cannot regulate the form which liking takes; it cannot regulate its own conditions. Desire and purpose, and hence action, are left without guidance, although the question of regulation of their formation is the supreme problem of practical life. Values (to sum up) may be connected inherently with liking, and yet not with *every* liking but only with those that judgment has approved, after examination of the relation upon which the object liked depends. A casual liking is one that happens without knowledge of how it occurs nor to what effect. The difference between it and one which is sought because of a judgment that it is worth having and is to be striven for, makes just the difference between enjoyments which are accidental and enjoyments that have value and hence a claim upon our attitude and conduct.

In any case, the alternative rationalistic theory does not afford the guidance for the sake of which eternal and immutable norms are appealed to. The scientist finds no help in determining the probable truth of some proposed theory by comparing it with a standard of absolute truth and immutable being. He has to rely upon definite operations undertaken under definite conditions—upon method. We can hardly imagine an architect getting aid in the construction of a building from an ideal at large, though we can understand his framing an ideal on the basis of knowledge of actual conditions and needs. Nor does the ideal of perfect beauty in antecedent Being give direction to a painter in producing a particular work of art. In morals, absolute perfection does not seem to be more than a generalized hypostatization of the recognition that there is a good to be sought, an obligation to be met—both being concrete matters. Nor is the defect in this respect merely negative. An examination of history would reveal, I am confident, that these general and remote schemes of value actually obtain a content definite enough and near enough to concrete situations as to afford guidance in action only by consecrating some institution or dogma already having social currency. Concreteness is gained, but it is by protecting from inquiry some accepted standard which perhaps is outworn and in need of criticism.

When theories of values do not afford intellectual assistance in framing ideas and beliefs about values that are adequate to direct action, the gap must be filled by other means. If intelligent method is lacking, prejudice, the pressure of immediate circumstance, self-interest and class-interest, traditional customs, institutions of accidental historic origin, are *not* lacking, and they tend to take the place of intelligence. Thus we are led to our main proposition: *Judgments about values are judgments about the conditions and the results of experienced objects; judgments about that which should regulate the formation of our desires, affec-tions and enjoyments.* For whatever decides their formation will deter-mine the main course of our conduct, personal and social.

If it sounds strange to hear that we should frame our judgments as to what has value by considering the connections in existence of what we like and enjoy, the reply is not far to seek. As long as we do not engage in this inquiry enjoyments (values if we choose to apply that term) are casual; they are given by "nature," not constructed by art. Like natural objects in their qualitative existence, they at most only supply material for elaboration in rational discourse. A *feeling* of good or excellence is as far removed from goodness in fact as a feeling that objects are in-tellectually thus and so is removed from their being actually so. To recognize that the truth of natural objects can be reached only by the greatest care in selecting and arranging directed operations, and then to suppose that values can be truly determined by the mere fact of liking seems to leave us in an incredible position. All the serious perplexities of life come back to the genuine difficulty of forming a judgment as to the values of the situation; they come back to a conflict of goods. Only dogmatism can suppose that serious moral conflict is between some-thing clearly bad and something known to be good, and that uncertainty lies wholly in the will of the one choosing. Most conflicts of importance are conflicts between things which are or have been satisfying, not be-tween good and evil. And to suppose that we can make a hierarchical table of values at large once for all, a kind of catalogue in which they are arranged in an order of ascending or descending worth, is to indulge in a gloss on our inability to frame intelligent judgments in the concrete. Or else it is to dignify customary choice and prejudice by a title of honor.

The alternative to definition, classification and systematization of satisfactions just as they happen to occur is judgment of them by means of the relations under which they occur. If we know the conditions un-der which the act of liking, of desire and enjoyment, takes place, we are in a position to know what are the consequences of that act. The dif-ference between the desired and the desirable, admired and the ad-mirable, becomes effective at just this point. Consider the difference between the proposition "That thing has been eaten," and the judgment "That thing is edible." The former statement involves no knowledge of any relation except the one stated; while we are able to judge of the edibility of anything only when we have a knowledge of its interactions with other things sufficient to enable us to foresee its probable effects when it is taken into the organism and produces effects there.

To assume that anything can be known in isolation from its connections with other things is to identify knowing with merely having some object before perception or in feeling, and is thus to lose the key to the traits that distinguish an object as known. It is futile, even silly, to suppose that some quality that is directly present constitutes the whole of the thing presenting the quality. It does not do so when the quality is that of being hot or fluid or heavy, and it does not when the quality is that of giving pleasure, or being enjoyed. Such qualities are, once more, effects, ends in the sense of closing termini of processes involving causal connections. They are something to be investigated, challenges to inquiry and judgment. The more connections and interactions we ascertain, the more we *know* the object in question. Thinking is search for these connections. Heat experienced as a consequence of directed operations has a meaning quite different from the heat that is casually experienced without knowledge of how it came about. The same is true of enjoyments. Enjoyments that issue from conduct directed by insight into relations have a meaning and a validity due to the way in which they are experienced. Such enjoyments are not repented of; they generate no after-taste of bitterness. Even in the midst of direct enjoyment, there is a sense of validity, of authorization, which intensifies the enjoyment. There is solicitude for perpetuation of the *object* having value which is radically different from mere anxiety to perpetuate the *feeling* of enjoyment.

Such statements as we have been making are, therefore, far from implying that there are values apart from things actually enjoyed as good. To find a thing enjoy*able* is, so to say, a *plus* enjoyment. We saw that it was foolish to treat the scientific object as a rival to or substitute for the perceived object, since the former is intermediate between uncertain and settled situations and those experienced under conditions of greater control. In the same way, judgment of the value of an object to be experienced is instrumental to appreciation of it when it is realized. But the notion that every object that happens to satisfy has an equal claim with every other to be a value is like supposing that every object of perception has the same cognitive force as every other. There is no knowledge without perception; but objects perceived are *known* only when they are determined as consequences of connective operations. There is no value except where there is satisfaction, but there have to be certain conditions fulfilled to transform a satisfaction into a value.

The time will come when it will be found passing strange that we of this age should take such pains to control by every means at command the formation of ideas of physical things, even those most remote from human concern, and yet are content with haphazard beliefs about the qualities of objects that regulate our deepest interests; that we are scrupulous as to methods of forming ideas of natural objects, and either dogmatic or else driven by immediate conditions in framing those about values. There is, by implication, if not explicitly, a prevalent notion that values are already well known and that all which is lacking is the will to cultivate them in the order of their worth. In fact the most profound lack is not the will to act upon goods already known but the will to know what they are.

It is not a dream that it is possible to exercise some degree of regulation of the occurrence of enjoyments which are of value. Realization of the possibility is exemplified, for example, in the technologies and arts of industrial life—that is, up to a definite limit. Men desired heat, light, and speed of transit and of communication beyond what nature provides of itself. These things have been attained not by lauding the enjoyment of these things and preaching their desirability, but by study of the conditions of their manifestation. Knowledge of relations having been obtained, ability to produce followed, and enjoyment ensued as a matter of course. It is, however, an old story that enjoyment of these things as goods is no warrant of their bringing only good in their train. As Plato was given to pointing out, the physician knows how to heal and the orator to persuade, but the ulterior knowledge of whether it is better for a man to be healed or to be persuaded to the orator's opinion remains unsettled. Here there appears the split between what are traditionally and conventionally called the values of the baser arts and the higher values of the truly personal and humane arts.

With respect to the former, there is no assumption that they can be had and enjoyed without definite operative knowledge. With respect to them it is also clear that the degree in which we value them is measurable by the pains taken to control the conditions of their occurrence. With respect to the latter, it is assumed that no one who is honest can be in doubt what they are; that by revelation, or conscience, or the instruction of others, or immediate feeling, they are clear beyond question. And instead of action in their behalf being taken to be a measure of the extent to which things *are* values to us, it is assumed that the difficulty is to persuade men to act upon what they already know to be good. Knowledge of conditions and consequences is regarded as wholly indifferent to judging what is of serious value, though it is useful in a prudential way in trying to actualize it. In consequence, the existence of values that are by common consent of a secondary and technical sort are under a fair degree of control, while those denominated supreme and imperative are subject to all the winds of impulse, custom and arbitrary authority.

This distinction between higher and lower types of value is itself something to be looked into. Why should there be a sharp division made between some goods as physical and material and others as ideal and "spiritual"? The question touches the whole dualism of the material and the ideal at its root. To denominate anything "matter" or "material" is not in truth to disparage it. It is, if the designation is correctly applied, a way of indicating that the thing in question is a condition or means of the existence of something else. And disparagement of effective means is practically synonymous with disregard of the things that are termed, in eulogistic fashion, ideal and spiritual. For the latter terms if they have any concrete application at all signify something which is a desirable consummation of conditions, a cherished fulfillment of means. The sharp separation between material and ideal good thus deprives the latter of the underpinning of effective support while it opens the way for treating things which should be employed as means as ends in themselves. For since men cannot after all live without some measure of possession of such matters as health and wealth, the latter things will be viewed as values and ends in isolation unless they are treated as integral constituents of the goods that are deemed supreme and final.

The relations that determine the occurrence of what human beings experience, especially when social connections are taken into account, are indefinitely wider and more complex than those that determine the events termed physical; the latter are the outcome of definite selective operations. This is the reason why we know something about remote objects like the stars better than we know significantly characteristic things about our own bodies and minds. We forget the infinite number of things we do not know about the stars, or rather that what we call a star is itself the product of the elimination, enforced and deliberate, of most of the traits that belong to an actual existence. The amount of knowledge we possess about stars would not seem very great or very important if it were carried over to human beings and exhausted our knowledge of them. It is inevitable that genuine knowledge of man and society should lag far behind physical knowledge.

But this difference is not a ground for making a sharp division between the two, nor does it account for the fact that we make so little use of the experimental method of forming our ideas and beliefs about the concerns of man in his characteristic social relations. For this separation religions and philosophies must admit some responsibility. They have erected a distinction between a narrower scope of relations and a wider and fuller one into a difference of kind, naming one kind material, and the other mental and moral. They have charged themselves gratuitously with the office of diffusing belief in the necessity of the division, and with instilling contempt for the material as something inferior in kind in its intrinsic nature and worth. Formal philosophies undergo evaporation of their technical solid contents; in a thinner and more viable form they find their way into the minds of those who know nothing of their original forms. When these diffuse and, so to say, airy emanations re-crystallize in the popular mind they form a hard deposit of opinion that alters slowly and with great difficulty.

What difference would it actually make in the arts of conduct, personal and social, if the experimental theory were adopted not as a mere theory, but as a part of the working equipment of habitual attitudes on the part of everyone? It would be impossible, even were time given, to answer the question in adequate detail, just as men could not foretell in advance the consequences for knowledge of adopting the experimental method. It is the nature of the method that it has to be tried. But there are generic lines of difference which, within the limits of time at disposal, may be sketched.

Change from forming ideas and judgments of value on the basis of conformity to antecedent objects, to constructing enjoyable objects directed by knowledge of consequences, is a change from looking to the past to looking to the future. I do not for a moment suppose that the experiences of the past, personal and social, are of no importance. For without them we should not be able to frame any ideas whatever of the conditions under which objects are enjoyed nor any estimate of the consequences of esteeming and liking them. But past experiences are significant in giving us intellectual instrumentalities of judging just these points. They are tools, not finalities. Reflection upon what we have liked and have enjoyed is a necessity. But it tells us nothing about the *value* of these things until enjoyments are themselves reflectively controlled, or, until, as they are recalled, we form the best judgment possible about what led us to like this sort of thing and what has issued from the fact that we liked it.

We are not, then, to get away from enjoyments experienced in the past and from recall of them, but from the notion that they are the arbiters of things to be further enjoyed. At present, the arbiter is found in the past, although there are many ways of interpreting what in the past is authoritative. Nominally, the most influential conception doubtless is that of a revelation once had or a perfect life once lived. Reliance upon precedent, upon institutions created in the past, especially in law, upon rules of morals that have come to us through unexamined customs, upon uncriticized tradition, are other forms of dependence. It is not for a moment suggested that we can get away from customs and established institutions. A mere break would doubtless result simply in chaos. But there is no danger of such a break. Mankind is too inertly conservative both by constitution and by education to give the idea of this danger actuality. What there is genuine danger of is that the force of new conditions will produce disruption externally and mechanically: this is an ever present danger. The prospect is increased, not mitigated, by that conservatism which insists upon the adequacy of old standards to meet new conditions. What is needed is intelligent examination of the consequences that are actually effected by inherited institutions and customs, in order that there may be intelligent consideration of the ways in which they are to be intentionally modified in behalf of generation of different consequences.

This is the significant meaning of transfer of experimental method from the technical field of physical experience to the wider field of human life. We trust the method in forming our beliefs about things not directly connected with human life. In effect, we distrust it in moral, political and economic affairs. In the fine arts, there are many signs of a change. In the past, such a change has often been an omen and precursor of changes in other human attitudes. But, generally speaking, the idea of actively adopting experimental method in social affairs, in the matters deemed of most enduring and ultimate worth, strikes most persons as a surrender of all standards and regulative authority. But in principle, experimental method does not signify random and aimless action; it implies direction by ideas and knowledge. The question at issue is a practical one. Are there in existence the ideas and the knowledge that permit experimental method to be effectively used in social interests and affairs?

Where will regulation come from if we surrender familiar and traditionally prized values as our directive standards? Very largely from the findings of the natural sciences. For one of the effects of the separation drawn between knowledge and action is to deprive scientific knowledge of its proper service as a guide of conduct—except once more in those technological fields which have been degraded to an inferior rank. Of course, the complexity of the conditions upon which objects of human and liberal value depend is a great obstacle, and it would be too optimistic to say that we have as yet enough knowledge of the scientific type to enable us to regulate our judgments of value very extensively. But we have more knowledge than we try to put to use, and until we try more systematically we shall not know what are the important gaps in our sciences judged from the point of view of their moral and humane use.

For moralists usually draw a sharp line between the field of the natural sciences and the conduct that is regarded as moral. But a moral that frames its judgments of value on the basis of consequences must depend in a most intimate manner upon the conclusions of science. For the knowledge of the relations between changes which enable us to connect things as antecedents and consequences *is* science. The narrow scope which moralists often give to morals, their isolation of some conduct as virtuous and vicious from other large ranges of conduct, those having to do with health and vigor, business, education, with all the affairs in which desires and affection are implicated, is perpetuated by this habit of exclusion of the subject-matter of natural science from a rôle in formation of moral standards and ideals. The same attitude operates in the other direction to keep natural science a technical specialty, and it works unconsciously to encourage its use exclusively in regions where it can be turned to personal and class advantage, as in war and trade.

Another great difference to be made by carrying the experimental habit into all matter of practice is that it cuts the roots of what is often called subjectivism, but which is better termed egoism. The subjective attitude is much more wisespread than would be inferred from the philosophies which have that label attached. It is as rampant in realistic philosophies as in any others, sometimes even more so, although disguised from those who hold these philosophies under the cover of reverence for and enjoyment of ultimate values. For the implication of placing the standard of thought and knowledge in antecedent existence is that our thought makes no difference in what is significantly real. It then affects only our own attitude toward it.

This constant throwing of emphasis back upon a change made in ourselves instead of one made in the world in which we live seems to me the essence of what is objectionable in "subjectivism." Its taint hangs about even Platonic realism with its insistent evangelical dwelling upon the change made within the mind by contemplation of the realm of essence, and its depreciation of action as transient and all but sordid—a concession to the necessities of organic existence. All the theories which put conversion "of the eye of the soul" in the place of a conversion of natural and social objects that modifies goods actually experienced, is a retreat and escape from existence—and this retraction into self is, once more, the heart of subjective egoisms. The typical example is perhaps the other-worldliness found in religions whose chief concern is with the salvation of the personal soul. But other-worldliness is found as well in estheticism and in all seclusion within ivory towers.

It is not in the least implied that change in personal attitudes, in the disposition of the "subject," is not of great importance. Such change, on the contrary, is involved in any attempt to modify the conditions of the environment. But there is a radical difference between a change in the self that is cultivated and valued as an end, and one that is a means to alteration, through action, of objective conditions. The Aristotelian-medieval conviction that highest bliss is found in contemplative possession of ultimate Being presents an ideal attractive to some types of mind; it sets forth a refined sort of enjoyment. It is a doctrine congenial to minds that despair of the effort involved in creation of a better world of daily experience. It is, apart from theological attachments, a doctrine sure to recur when social conditions are so troubled as to make actual endeavor seem hopeless. But the subjectivism so externally marked in modern thought as compared with ancient is either a development of the old doctrine under new conditions or is of merely technical import. The medieval version of the doctrine at least had the active support of a great social institution by means of which man could be brought into the state of mind that prepared him for ultimate enjoyment of eternal Being. It had a certain solidity and depth which is lacking in modern theories that would attain the result by merely emotional or speculative procedures, or by any means not demanding a change in objective existence so as to render objects of value more empirically secure.

The nature in detail of the revolution that would be wrought by carrying into the region of values the principle now embodied in scientific practice cannot be told; to attempt it would violate the fundamental idea that we know only after we have acted and in consequences of the outcome of action. But it would surely effect a transfer of attention and energy from the subjective to the objective. Men would think of themselves as agents not as ends; ends would be found in experienced enjoyment of the fruits of a transforming activity. In as far as the subjectivity of modern thought represents a discovery of the part played by personal responses, organic and acquired, in the causal production of the qualities and values of objects, it marks the possibility of a decisive gain. It puts us in possession of some of the conditions that control the occurrence of experienced objects, and thereby it supplies us with an instrument of regulation. There is something querulous in the sweeping denial that things as experienced, as perceived and enjoyed, in any way depend upon interaction with human selves. The error of doctrines that have exploited the part played by personal and subjective reactions in determining what is perceived and enjoyed lies either in exaggerating this factor of constitution into the sole condition—as happens in subjective idealism—or else in treating it as a finality instead of, as with all knowledge, an instrument in direction of further action.

A third significant change that would issue from carrying over experimental method from physics to man concerns the import of standards, principles, rules. With the transfer, these, and all tenets and creeds about good and goods, would be recognized to be hypotheses. Instead of being rigidly fixed, they would be treated as intellectual instruments to be tested and confirmed—and altered—through consequences effected by acting upon them. They would lose all pretence of finality—the ulterior source of dogmatism. It is both astonishing and depressing that so much of the energy of mankind has gone into fighting for (with weapons of the flesh as well as of the spirit) the truth of creeds, religious, moral and political, as distinct from what has gone into effort to try creeds by putting them to the test of acting upon them. The change would do away with the intolerance and fanaticism that attend the notion that beliefs and judgments are capable of inherent truth and authority; inherent in the sense of being independent of what they lead to when used as directive principles. The transformation does not imply merely that men are responsible for acting upon what they profess to believe; that is an old doctrine. It goes much further. Any belief as such is tentative, hypothetical; it is not just to be acted upon, but is to be *framed* with reference to its office as a guide to action. Consequently, it should be the last thing in the world to be picked up casually and then clung to rigidly. When it is apprehended as a tool and only a tool, an instrumentality of direction, the same scrupulous attention will go to its formation as now goes into the making of instruments of precision in technical fields. Men, instead of being proud of accepting and asserting beliefs and "principles" on the ground of loyalty, will be as ashamed of that procedure as they would now be to confess their assent to a scientific theory out of reverence for Newton or Helmholz or whomever, without regard to evidence.

If one stops to consider the matter, is there not something strange in the fact that men should consider loyalty to "laws," principles, standards, ideals to be an inherent virtue, accounted unto them for righteousness? It is as if they were making up for some secret sense of weakness by rigidity and intensity of insistent attachment. A moral law, like a law in physics, is not something to swear by and stick to at all hazards; it is a formula of the way to respond when specified conditions present themselves. Its soundness and pertinence are tested by what happens when it is acted upon. Its claim or authority rests finally upon the imperativeness of the situation that has to be dealt with, not upon its own intrinsic nature—as any tool achieves dignity in the measure of needs served by it. The idea that adherence to standards external to experienced objects is the only alternative to confusion and lawlessness was once held in science. But knowledge became steadily progressive when it was abandoned, and clews and tests found within concrete acts and objects were employed. The test of consequences is more exacting than that afforded by fixed general rules. In addition, it secures constant development, for when new acts are tried new results are experienced, while the lauded immutability of eternal ideals and norms is in itself a denial of the possibility of development and improvement.

The various modifications that would result from adoption in social and humane subjects of the experimental way of thinking are perhaps summed up in saying that it would place *method and means* upon the level of importance that has, in the past, been imputed exclusively to ends. Means have been regarded as menial, and the useful as the servile. Means have been treated as poor relations to be endured, but not inherently welcome. The very meaning of the word "ideals" is significant of the divorce which has obtained between means and ends. "Ideals" are thought to be remote and inaccessible of attainment; they are too high and fine to be sullied by realization. They serve vaguely to arouse "aspiration," but they do not evoke and direct strivings for embodiment in actual existence. They hover in an indefinite way over the actual scene; they are expiring ghosts of a once significant kingdom of divine reality whose rule penetrated to every detail of life.

It is impossible to form a just estimate of the paralysis of effort that has been produced by indifference to means. Logically, it is truistic that lack of consideration for means signifies that so-called ends are not taken seriously. It is as if one professed devotion to painting pictures conjoined with contempt for canvas, brush and paints; or love of music on condition that no instruments, whether the voice or something external, be used to make sounds. The good workman in the arts is known by his respect for his tools and by his interest in perfecting his technique. The glorification in the arts of ends at the expense of means would be taken to be a sign of complete insincerity or even insanity. Ends separated from means are either sentimental indulgences or if they happen to exist are merely accidental. The ineffectiveness in action of

594 THE PHILOSOPHY OF JOHN DEWEY

"ideals" is due precisely to the supposition that means and ends are not on exactly the same level with respect to the attention and care they demand.

It is, however, much easier to point out the formal contradiction implied in ideals that are professed without equal regard for the instruments and techniques of their realization, than it is to appreciate the concrete ways in which belief in their separation has found its way into life and borne corrupt and poisonous fruits. The separation marks the form in which the traditional divorce of theory and practice has expressed itself in actual life. It accounts for the relative impotency of arts concerned with enduring human welfare. Sentimental attachment and subjective eulogy take the place of action. For there is no art without tools and instrumental agencies. But it also explains the fact that in actual behavior, energies devoted to matters nominally thought to be inferior, material and sordid, engross attention and interest. After a polite and pious deference has been paid to "ideals," men feel free to devote themselves to matters which are more immediate and pressing.

It is usual to condemn the amount of attention paid by people in general to material ease, comfort, wealth, and success gained by competition, on the ground that they give to mere means the attention that ought to be given to ends, or that they have taken for ends things which in reality are only means. Criticisms of the place which economic interest and action occupy in present life are full of complaints that men allow lower aims to usurp the place that belongs to higher and ideal values. The final source of the trouble is, however, that moral and spiritual "leaders" have propagated the notion that ideal ends may be cultivated in isolation from "material" means, as if means and material were not synonymous. While they condemn men for giving to means the thought and energy that ought to go to ends, the condemnation should go to them. For they have not taught their followers to think of material and economic activities as *really* means. They have been unwilling to frame their conception of the values that should be regulative of human conduct on the basis of the actual conditions and operations by which alone values can be actualized.

Practical needs are imminent; with the mass of mankind they are imperative. Moreover, speaking generally, men are formed to act rather than to theorize. Since the ideal ends are so remotely and accidentally connected with immediate and urgent conditions that need attention, after lip service is given to them, men naturally devote themselves to the latter. If a bird in the hand is worth two in a neighboring bush, an actuality in hand is worth, for the direction of conduct, many ideals that are so remote as to be invisible and inaccessible. Men hoist the banner of the ideal, and then march in the direction that concrete conditions suggest and reward.

Deliberate insincerity and hypocrisy are rare. But the notion that action and sentiment are inherently unified in the constitution of human nature has nothing to justify it. Integration is something to be achieved. Division of attitudes and responses, compartmentalizing of interests, is easily acquired. It goes deep just because the acquisition is unconscious, a matter of habitual adaptation to conditions. Theory separated from concrete doing and making is empty and futile; practice then becomes an immediate seizure of opportunities and enjoyments which conditions afford without the direction which theory—knowledge and ideas—has power to supply. The problem of the relation of theory and practice is not a problem of theory alone; it is that, but it is also the most practical problem of life. For it is the question of how intelligence may inform action, and how action may bear the fruit of increased insight into meaning: a clear view of the values that are worth while and of the means by which they are to be made secure in experienced objects. Construction of ideals in general and their sentimental glorification are easy; the responsibilities both of studious thought and of action are shirked. Persons having the advantage of positions of leisure and who find pleasure in abstract theorizing—a most delightful indulgence to those to whom it appeals—have a large measure of liability for a cultivated diffusion of ideals and aims that are separated from the conditions which are the means of actualization. Then other persons who find themselves in positions of social power and authority readily claim to be the bearers and defenders of ideal ends in church and state. They then use the prestige and authority their representative capacity as guardians of the highest ends confers on them to cover actions taken in behalf of the harshest and narrowest of material ends.

The present state of industrial life seems to give a fair index of the existing separation of means and ends. Isolation of economics from ideal ends, whether of morals or of organized social life, was proclaimed by Aristotle. Certain things, he said, are conditions of a worthy life, personal and social, but are not constituents of it. The economic life of man, concerned with satisfaction of wants, is of this nature. Men have wants and they must be satisfied. But they are only prerequisites of a good life, not intrinsic elements in it. Most philosophers have not been so frank nor perhaps so logical. But upon the whole, economics has been treated as on a lower level than either morals or politics. Yet the life which men, women and children actually lead, the opportunities open to them, the values they are capable of enjoying, their education, their share in all the things of art and science, are mainly determined by economic conditions. Hence we can hardly expect a moral system which ignores economic conditions to be other than remote and empty.

Industrial life is correspondingly brutalized by failure to equate it as the means by which social and cultural values are realized. That the economic life, thus exiled from the pale of higher values, takes revenge by declaring that it is the only social reality, and by means of the doctrine of materialistic determination of institutions and conduct in all fields, denies to deliberate morals and politics any share of causal regulation, is not surprising.

When economists were told that their subject-matter was merely material, they naturally thought they could be "scientific" only by excluding all reference to distinctively human values. Material wants, efforts to satisfy them, even the scientifically regulated technologies highly developed in industrial activity, are then taken to form a complete and closed field. If any reference to social ends and values is introduced it is by way of an external addition, mainly hortatory. That economic life largely determines the conditions under which mankind has access to concrete values may be recognized or it may not be. In either case, the notion that it is the means to be utilized in order to secure significant values as the common and shared possession of mankind is alien and inoperative. To many persons, the idea that the ends professed by morals are impotent save as they are connected with the working machinery of economic life seems like deflowering the purity of moral values and obligations.

The social and moral effects of the separation of theory and practice have been merely hinted at. They are so manifold and so pervasive that an adequate consideration of them would involve nothing less than a survey of the whole field of morals, economics and politics. It cannot be justly stated that these effects are in fact direct consequences of the quest for certainty by thought and knowledge isolated from action. For, as we have seen, this quest was itself a reflex product of actual conditions. But it may be truly asserted that this quest, undertaken in religion and philosophy, has had results which have reinforced the conditions which originally brought it about. Moreover, search for safety and consolation amid the perils of life by means other than intelligent action, by feeling and thought alone, began when actual means of control were lacking, when arts were undeveloped. It had then a relative historic justification that is now lacking. The primary problem for thinking which lays claim to be philosophic in its breadth and depth is to assist in bringing about a reconstruction of all beliefs rooted in a basic separation of knowledge and action; to develop a system of operative ideas congruous with present knowledge and with present facilities of control over natural events and energies.

We have noted more than once how modern philosophy has been absorbed in the problem of affecting an adjustment between the conclusions of natural science and the beliefs and values that have authority in the direction of life. The genuine and poignant issue does not reside where philosophers for the most part have placed it. It does not consist in accommodation to each other of two realms, one physical and the other ideal and spiritual, nor in the reconciliation of the "categories" of theoretical and practical reason. It is found in that isolation of executive means and ideal interests which has grown up under the influence of the separation of theory and practice. For this, by nature, involves the separation of the material and the spiritual. Its solution, therefore, can be found only in action wherein the phenomena of material and economic life are equated with the purposes that command the loyalties of affection and purpose, and in which ends and ideals are framed in terms of the possibilities of actually experienced situations. But while the solution cannot be found in "thought" alone, it can be furthered by thinking which is operative—which frames and defines ideas in terms of what may be done, and which uses the conclusions of science as instrumentalities. William James was well within the bounds of moderation when he said that looking forward instead of backward, looking to what the world and life might become instead of to what they have been, is an alteration in the "seat of authority."

It was incidentally remarked earlier in our discussion that the serious defect in the current empirical philosophy of values, the one which identifies them with things actually enjoyed irrespective of the conditions upon which they depend, is that it formulates and in so far consecrates the conditions of our present social experience. Throughout these chapters, primary attention has perforce been given to the methods and statements of philosophic theories. But these statements are technical and specialized in formulation only. In origin, content and import they are reflections of some condition or some phase of concrete human experience. Just as the theory of the separation of theory and practice has a practical origin and a momentous practical consequence, so the empirical theory that values are identical with whatever men actually enjoy, no matter how or what, formulates an aspect, and an undesirable one, of the present social situation.

For while our discussion has given more attention to the other type of philosophical doctrine, that which holds that regulative and authoritative standards are found in transcendent eternal values, it has not passed in silence over the fact that actually the greater part of the activities of the greater number of human beings is spent in effort to seize upon and hold onto such enjoyments as the actual scene permits. Their energies and their enjoyments are controlled in fact, but they are controlled by external conditions rather than by intelligent judgment and endeavor. If philosophies have any influence over the thoughts and acts of men, it is a serious matter that the most widely held empirical theory should in effect justify this state of things by identifying values with the objects of any interest as such. As long as the only theories of value placed before us for intellectual assent alternate between sending us to a realm of eternal and fixed values and sending us to enjoyments such as actually obtain, the formulation, even as only a theory, of an experimental empiricism which finds values to be identical with goods that are the fruit of intelligently directed activity has its measure of practical significance.

37. The Lost Individual*

Although it was written in 1930, the following commentary by John Dewey has a descriptive accuracy worthy of today. "It would be difficult to find in history an epoch as lacking in solid and assured objects of belief and approved ends of action as is the present. . . . Individuals vibrate between a past that is intellectually too empty to give stability and a present that is too diversely crowded and chaotic to afford balance or direction to ideas and emotion."

Throughout this selection, Dewey shows a compassion for the hordes of people who have become isolated in their lives, despite their living in crowded surroundings and hectic circumstances. He realizes that isolation is not simply a spatial affair but proceeds as well from the breakdown of those social and economic structures which encourage and sustain a humane and free life. And when faced with such a crisis, he warns against abandoning realistic possibilities for social

* From John Dewey, *Individualism Old and New* (New York, Capricorn Books, 1962) (1930), pp. 51-73. Reprinted by permission of G. P. Putnam's Sons.

change for the temptations of "esoteric occultism or private estheticism." Dewey's strategy for change is transformative rather than revolutionary, but he makes it clear that "only by economic revision can the sound element in the older individualism—equality of opportunity—be made a reality."

The development of a civilization that is outwardly corporate—or rapidly becoming so—has been accompanied by a submergence of the individual. Just how far this is true of the individual's opportunities in action, how far initiative and choice in what an individual does are restricted by the economic forces that make for consolidation, I shall not attempt to say. It is arguable that there has been a diminution of the range of decision and activity for the many along with exaggeration of opportunity of personal expression for the few. It may be contended that no one class in the past has the power now possessed by an industrial oligarchy. On the other hand, it may be held that this power of the few is, with respect to genuine individuality, specious; that those outwardly in control are in reality as much carried by forces external to themselves as are the many; that in fact these forces impel them into a common mold to such an extent that individuality is suppressed.

What is here meant by "the lost individual" is, however, so irrelevant to this question that it is not necessary to decide between the two views. For by it is meant a moral and intellectual fact which is independent of any manifestation of power in action. The significant thing is that the loyalties which once held individuals, which gave them support, direction, and unity of outlook on life, have well-nigh disappeared. In consequence, individuals are confused and bewildered. It would be difficult to find in history an epoch as lacking in solid and assured objects of belief and approved ends of action as is the present. Stability of individuality is dependent upon stable objects to which allegiance firmly attaches itself. There are, of course, those who are still militantly fundamentalist in religious and social creed. But their very clamor is evidence that the tide is set against them. For the others, traditional objects of loyalty have become hollow or are openly repudiated, and they drift without sure anchorage. Individuals vibrate between a past that is intellectually too empty to give stability and a present that is too diversely crowded and chaotic to afford balance or direction to ideas and emotion.

Assured and integrated individuality is the product of definite social relationships and publicly acknowledged functions. Judged by this standard, even those who seem to be in control, and to carry the expression of their special individual abilities to a high pitch, are submerged. They may be captains of finance and industry, but until there is some consensus of belief as to the meaning of finance and industry in civilization as a whole, they cannot be captains of their own souls—their beliefs and aims. They exercise leadership surreptitiously and, as it were, absentmindedly. They lead, but it is under cover of impersonal and socially undirected economic forces. Their reward is found not in what they do, in their social office and function, but in a deflection of social consequences to private gain. They receive the acclaim and command the envy and admiration of the crowd, but the crowd is also composed of private individuals who are equally lost to a sense of social bearings and uses.

The explanation is found in the fact that while the actions promote corporate and collective results, these results are outside their intent and irrelevant to that reward of satisfaction which comes from a sense of social fulfillment. To themselves and to others, their business is private and its outcome is private profit. No complete satisfaction is possible where such a split exists. Hence the absence of a sense of social value is made up for by an exacerbated acceleration of the activities that increase private advantage and power. One cannot look into the inner consciousness of his fellows; but if there is any general degree of inner contentment on the part of those who form our pecuniary oligarchy, the evidence is sadly lacking. As for the many, they are impelled hither and yon by forces beyond their control.

The most marked trait of present life, economically speaking, is insecurity. It is tragic that millions of men desirous of working should be recurrently out of employment; aside from cyclical depressions there is a standing army at all times who have no regular work. We have not any adequate information as to the number of these persons. But the ignorance even as to numbers is slight compared with our inability to grasp the psychological and moral consequences of the precarious condition in which vast multitudes live. Insecurity cuts deeper and extends more widely than bare unemployment. Fear of loss of work, dread of the oncoming of old age, create anxiety and eat into self-respect in a way that impairs personal dignity. Where fears abound, courageous and robust individuality is undermined. The vast development of technological resources that might bring security in its train has actually brought a new mode of insecurity, as mechanization displaces labor. The mergers and consolidations that mark a corporate age are beginning to bring uncertainty into the economic lives of the higher salaried class, and that tendency is only just in its early stage. Realization that honest and industrious pursuit of a calling or business will not guarantee any stable level of life lessens respect for work and stirs large numbers to take a chance of some adventitious way of getting the wealth that will make security possible: witness the orgies of the stock-market in recent days.

The unrest, impatience, irritation and hurry that are so marked in American life are inevitable accompaniments of a situation in which individuals do not find support and contentment in the fact that they are sustaining and sustained members of a social whole. They are evidence, psychologically, of abnormality, and it is as idle to seek for their explanation within the deliberate intent of individuals as it is futile to think that they can be got rid of by hortatory moral appeal. Only an acute maladjustment between individuals and the social conditions under which they live can account for such widespread pathological phenomena. Feverish love of anything as long as it is a change which is distracting, impatience, unsettlement, nervous discontentment, and desire for excitement, are not native to human nature. They are so abnormal as to demand explanation in some deep-seated cause.

I should explain a seeming hypocrisy on the same ground. We are not consciously insincere in our professions of devotion to ideals of "service"; they mean something. Neither the Rotarian nor the big business enterprise uses the term merely as a cloak for "putting something over" which makes for pecuniary gain. But the lady doth protest too much. The wide currency of such professions testifies to a sense of a social function of business which is expressed in words because it is so lacking in fact, and yet which is felt to be rightfully there. If our external combinations in industrial activity were reflected in organic integrations of the desires, purposes and satisfactions of individuals, the verbal protestations would disappear, because social utility would be a matter of course.

Some persons hold that a genuine mental counterpart of the outward social scheme is actually forming. Our prevailing mentality, our "ideology," is said to be that of the "business mind" which has become so deplorably pervasive. Are not the prevailing standards of value those derived from pecuniary success and economic prosperity? Were the answer unqualifiedly in the affirmative, we should have to admit that our outer civilization is attaining an inner culture which corresponds to it, however much we might disesteem the quality of that culture. The objection that such a condition is impossible, since man cannot live by bread, by material prosperity, alone, is tempting, but it may be said to beg the question. The conclusive answer is that the business mind is not itself unified. It is divided within itself and must remain so as long as the results of industry as the determining force in life are corporate and collective while its animating motives and compensations are so unmitigatedly private. A unified mind, even of the business type, can come into being only when conscious intent and consummation are in harmony with consequences actually effected. This statement expresses conditions so psychologically assured that it may be termed a law of mental integrity. Proof of the existence of the split is found in the fact that while there is much planning of future development with a view to dividends within large business corporations, there is no corresponding coördinated planning of social development.

The growth of corporateness is arbitrarily restricted. Hence it operates to limit individuality, to put burdens on it, to confuse and submerge it. It crowds more out than it incorporates in an ordered and secure life. It has made rural districts stagnant while bringing excess and restless movement to the city. The restriction of corporateness lies in the fact that it remains on the cash level. Men are brought together on the one side by investment in the same joint stock company, and on the other hand by the fact that the machine compels mass production in order that investors may get their profits. The results affect all society in all its phases. But they are as inorganic as the ultimate human motives that operate are private and egoistic. An economic individualism of motives and aims underlies our present corporate mechanisms, and undoes the individual.

The loss of individuality is conspicuous in the economic region because our civilization is so predominantly a business civilization. But the fact is even more obvious when we turn to the political scene. It would be a waste of words to expatiate on the meaninglessness of present political platforms, parties and issues. The old-time slogans are still reiterated, and to a few these words still seem to have a real meaning. But it is too evident to need argument that on the whole our politics, as far as they are not covertly manipulated in behalf of the pecuniary advantage of groups, are in a state of confusion; issues are improvised from week to week with a constant shift of allegiance. It is impossible for individuals to find themselves politically with surety and efficiency under such conditions. Political apathy broken by recurrent sensations and spasms is the natural outcome.

The lack of secure objects of allegiance, without which individuals are lost, is especially striking in the case of the liberal. The liberalism of the past was characterized by the possession of a definite intellectual creed and program; that was its distinction from conservative parties which needed no formulated outlook beyond defense of things as they were. In contrast, liberals operated on the basis of a thought-out social philosophy, a theory of politics sufficiently definite and coherent to be easily translated into a program of policies to be pursued. Liberalism to-day is hardly more than a temper of mind, vaguely called forward-looking, but quite uncertain as to where to look and what to look forward to. For many individuals, as well as in its social results, this fact is hardly less than a tragedy. The tragedy may be unconscious for the mass, but they show its reality in their aimless drift, while the more thoughtful are consciously disturbed. For human nature is self-possessed only as it has objects to which it can attach itself.

I do not think it is fantastic to connect our excited and rapacious nationalism with the situation in which corporateness has gone so far as to detach individuals from their old local ties and allegiances but not far enough to give them a new center and order of life. The most militaristic of nations secures the loyalty of its subjects not by physical force but through the power of ideas and emotions. It cultivates ideals of loyalty, of solidarity, and common devotion to a common cause. Modern industry, technology and commerce have created modern nations in their external form. Armies and navies exist to protect commerce, to make secure the control of raw materials, and to command markets. Men would not sacrifice their lives for the purpose of securing economic gain for a few if the conditions presented themselves to their minds in this bald fashion. But the balked demand for genuine coöperativeness and reciprocal solidarity in daily life finds an outlet in nationalistic sentiment. Men have a pathetic instinct toward the adventure of living and struggling together; if the daily community does not feed this impulse, the romantic imagination pictures a grandiose nation in which all are one. If the simple duties of peace do not establish a common life, the emotions are mobilized in the service of a war that will supply its temporary simulation.

I have thus far made no reference to what many persons would consider the most serious and the most overtly evident of all the modes of loss of secure objects of loyalty—religion. It is probably easy to exaggerate the extent of the decadence of religion in an outward sense, church membership, church-going and so on. But it is hardly possible to overstate its decline as a vitally integrative and directive force in men's thought and sentiments. Whether even in the ages of the past that are called religious, religion was itself the actively central force that it is sometimes said to have been may be doubted. But it cannot be doubted that it was the symbol of the existence of conditions and forces that gave unity and a center to men's views of life. It at least gathered together in weighty and shared symbols a sense of the objects to which men were so attached as to have support and stay in their outlook on life.

Religion does not now effect this result. The divorce of church and state has been followed by that of religion and society. Wherever religion has not become a merely private indulgence, it has become at best a matter of sects and denominations divided from one another by doctrinal differences, and united internally by tenets that have a merely historical origin, and a purely metaphysical or else ritualistic meaning. There is no such bond of social unity as once united Greeks, Romans, Hebrews, and Catholic medieval Europe. There are those who realize what is portended by the loss of religion as an integrating bond. Many of them despair of its recovery through the development of social values to which the imagination and sentiments of individuals can attach themselves with intensity. They wish to reverse the operation and to form the social bond of unity and of allegiance by regeneration of the isolated individual soul.

Aside from the fact that there is no consensus as to what a new religious attitude is to center itself about, the injunction puts the cart before the horse. Religion is not so much a root of unity as it is its flower or fruit. The very attempt to secure integration for the individual, and through him for society, by means of a deliberate and conscious cultivation of religion, is itself proof of how far the individual has become lost through detachment from acknowledged social values. It is no wonder that when the appeal does not take the form of dogmatic fundamentalism, it tends to terminate in either some form of esoteric occultism or private estheticism. The sense of wholeness which is urged as the essence of religion can be built up and sustained only through membership in a society which has attained a degree of unity. The attempt to cultivate it first in individuals and then extend it to form an organically unified society is fantasy. Indulgence in this fantasy infects such interpretations of American life as are found, to take one signal example, in Waldo Frank's[1] "The Rediscovery of America." It marks a manner of yearning and not a principle of construction.

---

[1] After a brilliant exposition of the dissolution of the European synthesis, he goes on to say "man's need of order and his making of order are his science, his art, his religion; and these are all to be referred to the initial sense of order called the self," quite oblivious of the fact that this doctrine of the primacy of the self is precisely a reaction of the romantic and subjective age to the dissolution he has depicted, having its meaning only in that dissolution.

For the idea that the outward scene is chaotic because of the machine, which is a principle of chaos, and that it will remain so until individuals reinstitute wholeness within themselves, simply reverses the true state of things. The outward scene, if not fully organized, is relatively so in the corporateness which the machine and its technology have produced; the inner man is the jungle which can be subdued to order only as the forces of organization at work in externals are reflected in corresponding patterns of thought, imagination and emotion. The sick cannot heal themselves by means of their disease, and disintegrated individuals can achieve unity only as the dominant energies of community life are incorporated to form their minds. If these energies were, in reality, mere strivings for private pecuniary gain, the case would indeed be hopeless. But they are constituted by a collective art of technology, which individuals merely deflect to their private ends. There are the beginnings of an objective order through which individuals may get their bearings.

Conspicuous signs of the disintegration of individuality due to failure to reconstruct the self so as to meet the realities of present social life have not been mentioned. In a census that was taken among leaders of opinion concerning the urgency of present social problems, the state of law, the courts, lawlessness and criminality stood at the head of the list, and by a considerable distance. We are even more emphatically than when Kipling wrote the words, the people that make "the laws they flout, and flout the laws they make." We combine an ardor unparalleled in history for "passing" laws with a casual and deliberate disregard for them when they are on the statute books. We believe—to judge by our legislative actions—that we can create morals by law (witness the prohibition amendment for an instance on a large scale) and neglect the fact that all laws except those which regulate technical procedures are registrations of existing social customs and their attendant moral habits and purposes. I can, however, only think of this phenomenon as a symptom, not as a cause. It is a natural expression of a period in which changes in the structure of society have dissolved old bonds and allegiances. We attempt to make good this social relaxation and dissolution by legal enactments, while the actual disintegration discloses itself in the lawlessness which reveals the artificial character of this method of securing social integrity.

Volumes could be formed by collecting articles and editorials written about relaxation of traditional moral codes. A movement has caught public attention, which, having for some obscure reason assumed the name "humanism," proposes restraint and moderation, exercised in and by the higher volition of individuals, as the solution of our ills. It finds that naturalism as practiced by artists and mechanism as taught by philosophers who take their clew from natural science, have broken down the inner laws and imperatives which can alone bring order and loyalty. I should be glad to be able to believe that artists and intellectuals have any such power in their hands; if they had, after using it to bring evil to society, they might change face and bring healing to it. But a sense of fact, together with a sense of humor, forbids the acceptance of any such belief. Literary persons and academic thinkers are now, more than ever, effects, not causes. They reflect and voice the disintegration which new modes of living, produced by new forms of industry and commerce, have introduced. They give witness to the unreality that has overtaken traditional codes in the face of the impact of new forces; indirectly, they proclaim the need of some new synthesis. But this synthesis can be humanistic only as the new conditions are themselves taken into account and are converted into the instrumentalities of a free and humane life. I see no way to "restrain" or turn back the industrial revolution and its consequences. In the absence of such a restraint (which would be efficacious if only it could occur), the urging of some inner restraint through the exercise of the higher personal will, whatever that may be, is itself only a futile echo of just the old individualism that has so completely broken down.

There are many phases of life which illustrate to anyone who chooses to think in terms of realities instead of words the utter irrelevance of the proposed remedy to actual conditions. One might take the present estate of amusements, of the movies, the radio, and organized vicarious sport, and ask just how this powerful eruption in which the resources of technology are employed for economic profit is to be met by the application of the inner *frein* or brake. Perhaps the most striking instance is found in the disintegration due to changes in family life and sex morale. It was not deliberate human intention that undermined the traditional household as the center of industry and education and as the focus of moral training; that sapped the older institution of enduring marriage. To ask the individuals who suffer the consequences of the general undermining and sapping to put an end to the consequences by acts of personal volition is merely to profess faith in moral magic. Recovery of individuals capable of stable and effective self-control can be had only as there is first a humbler exercise of will to observe existing social realities and to direct them according to their own potentialities.

* * *

Instances of the flux in which individuals are loosened from the ties that once gave order and support to their lives are glaring. They are indeed so glaring that they blind our eyes to the causes which produce them. Individuals are groping their way through situations which they do not direct and which do not give them direction. The beliefs and ideals that are uppermost in their consciousness are not relevant to the society in which they outwardly act and which constantly reacts upon them. Their conscious ideas and standards are inherited from an age that has passed away; their minds, as far as consciously entertained principles and methods of interpretation are concerned, are at odds with actual conditions. This profound split is the cause of distraction and bewilderment.

Individuals will refind themselves only as their ideas and ideals are brought into harmony with the realities of the age in which they act. The task of attaining this harmony is not an easy one. But it is more negative than it seems. If we could inhibit the principles and standards that are merely traditional, if we could slough off the opinions that have no living relationship to the situations in which we live, the unavowed forces that now work upon us unconsciously but unremittingly would have a chance to build minds after their own pattern, and individuals might, in consequence, find themselves in possession of objects to which imagination and emotion would stably attach themselves.

I do not mean, however, that the process of rebuilding can go on automatically. Discrimination is required in order to detect the beliefs and institutions that dominate merely because of custom and inertia, and in order to discover the moving realities of the present. Intelligence must distinguish, for example, the tendencies of the technology which produce the new corporateness from those inheritances proceeding out of the individualism of an earlier epoch which arrest and divide the operation of the new dynamics. It is difficult for us to conceive of individualism except in terms of stereotypes derived from former centuries. Individualism has been identified with ideas of initiative and invention that are bound up with private and exclusive economic gain. As long as this conception possesses our minds, the ideal of harmonizing our thought and desire with the realities of present social conditions will be interpreted to mean accommodation and surrender. It will even be understood to signify rationalization of the evils of existing society. A stable recovery of individuality waits upon an elimination of the older economic and political individualism, an elimination which will liberate imagination and endeavor for the task of making corporate society contribute to the free culture of its members. Only by economic revision

can the sound element in the older individualism—equality of op- ^
portunity—be made a reality.

It is the part of wisdom to note the double meaning of such ideas as
"acceptance." There is an acceptance that is of the intellect; it signifies
facing facts for what they are. There is another acceptance that is of the
emotions and will; that involves commitment of desire and effort. So far
are the two from being identical that acceptance in the first sense is the
precondition of all intelligent refusal of acceptance in the second sense.
There is a prophetic aspect to all observation; we can perceive the
meaning of what exists only as we forecast the consequences it entails.
When a situation is as confused and divided within itself as is the present social estate, choice is implicated in observation. As one perceives
different tendencies and different possible consequences, preference
inevitably goes out to one or the other. Because acknowledgment in
thought brings with it intelligent discrimination and choice, it is the first
step out of confusion, the first step in forming those objects of significant allegiance out of which stable and efficacious individuality may
grow. It might even perform the miracle of rendering conservatism relevant and thoughtful. It certainly is the prerequisite of an anchored
liberalism.

38. Toward a New Individualism*

In this selection Dewey attacks the older "rugged individualism," so long identified with America, as being no longer
viable. Dewey points out that the spatial options made possible by a wilderness and by a frontier ethos had been
obliterated by the rise of new technology. In turn,
dramatically new social conditions had come to the fore and
in turn created profoundly different sets of social relations.
Obviously, then, the meaning of the "individual" had also undergone distinctive transformation.

In such a context, Dewey laments the clinging to a
nostalgic view of the "individual," as though a return to
pioneer energy could solve the social problems of Americans.

* From John Dewey, *Individualism Old and New* (New York, Capricorn
Books, 1962) (1930), pp. 74-100. Reprinted by permission of G. P. Putnam's
Sons.

He writes that "I see little social unrest which is the straining of energy for outlet in action; I find rather the protest against a weakening of vigor and sapping of energy that emanate from the absence of constructive opportunity; and I see a confusion that is an expression of the inability to find a secure and morally rewarding place in a troubled and tangled economic scene." Written just on the beginning edge of our Great Depression, this perceptive judgment can be regarded only as an understatement.

Our material culture, as anthropologists would call it, is verging upon the collective and corporate. Our moral culture, along with our ideology, is, on the other hand, still saturated with ideal and values of an individualism derived from the prescientific, pretechnological age. Its spiritual roots are found in medieval religion, which asserted the ultimate nature of the individual soul and centered the drama of life about the destiny of that soul. Its institutional and legal concepts were framed in the feudal period.

This moral and philosophical individualism anteceded the rise of modern industry and the era of the machine. It was the context in which the latter operated. The apparent subordination of the individual to established institutions often conceals from recognition the vital existence of a deep-seated individualism. But the fact that the controlling institution was the Church should remind us that in ultimate intent it existed to secure the salvation of the individual. That this individual was conceived as a soul, and that the end served by the institution was deferred to another and everlasting life conceal from contemporary realization the underlying individualism. In its own time, its substance consisted in just this eternal spiritual character of the personal soul; the power of the established institutions proceeded from their being the necessary means of accomplishing the supreme end of the individual.

The early phase of the industrial revolution wrought a great transformation. It gave a secular and worldly turn to the career of the individual, and it liquefied the static property concepts of feudalism by the shift of emphasis from agriculture to manufacturing. Still, the idea persisted that property and reward were intrinsically individual. There were, it is true, incompatible elements in the earlier and later versions of individualism. But a fusion of individual capitalism, of natural rights, and of morals founded in strictly individual traits and values remained, under the influence of Protestantism, the dominant intellectual synthesis.

The basis of this synthesis was destroyed, however, by the later development of the industrial system, which brought about the merging of personal capacity, effort and work into collective wholes. Meanwhile, the control of natural energies eliminated time and distance, so that action once adapted to local conditions was swallowed up in complex undertakings of indefinite extent. Yet the older mental equipment remained after its causes and foundations had disappeared. This, fundamentally, is the inner division out of which spring our present confusion and insincerities.

The earlier economic individualism had a definite creed and function. It sought to release from legal restrictions man's wants and his efforts to satisfy those wants. It believed that such emancipation would stimulate latent energy into action, would automatically assign individual ability to the work for which it was suited, would cause it to perform that work under stimulus of the advantage to be gained, and would secure for capacity and enterprise the reward and position to which they were entitled. At the same time, individual energy and savings would be serving the needs of others, and thus promoting the general welfare and effecting a general harmony of interests.

We have gone a long way since this philosophy was formulated. Today, the most stalwart defenders of this type of individualism do not venture to repeat its optimistic assertions. At most, they are content to proclaim its consistency with unchanging human nature—which is said to be moved to effort only by the hope of personal gain—and to paint dire pictures of the inevitable consequences of change to any other régime. They ascribe all the material benefits of our present civilization to this individualism—as if machines were made by the desire for money profit, not by impersonal science; and as if they were driven by money alone, and not by electricity and steam under the direction of a collective technology.

In America, the older individualism assumed a romantic form. It was hardly necessary to elaborate a theory which equated personal gain with social advance. The demands of the practical situation called for the initiative, enterprise and vigor of individuals in all immediate work that urgently asked for doing, and their operation furthered the national life. The spirit of the time is expressed by Dr. Crothers, whose words Mr. Sims has appropriately taken for part of the text of his "Adventurous America":

"If you would understand the driving power of America,

> you must understand 'the divers discontented and impatient young men' who in each generation have found an outlet for their energy. . . . The noises which disturb you are not the cries of an angry proletariat, but are the shouts of eager young people who are finding new opportunities. . . . They represent to-day the enthusiasm of a new generation. They represent the Oregons and Californias toward which sturdy pioneers are moving undisturbed by obstacles. This is what the social unrest means in America.''

If that is not an echo of the echo of a voice of long ago, I do not know what it is. I do not, indeed, hear the noises of an angry proletariat; but I should suppose the sounds heard are the murmurs of lost opportunities, along with the din of machinery, motor cars and speakeasies, by which the murmurs of discontent are drowned, rather than shouts of eagerness for adventurous opportunity.

The European version of the older individualism had its value and temporal justification because the new technology needed liberation from vexatious legal restrictions. Machine industry was itself in a pioneer condition, and those who carried it forward against obstacles of lethargy, skepticism and political obstruction were deserving of special reward. Moreover, accumulation of capital was thought of in terms of enterprises that to-day would be petty; there was no dream of the time when it would reach such a mass that it would determine the legal and political order. Poverty had previously been accepted as a dispensation of nature that was inevitable. The new industry promised a way out, at least to those possessed of energy and will to save and accumulate. But there was no anticipation of a time when the development of machine technology would afford the material basis for reasonable ease and comfort and of extensive leisure for all.

The shift that makes the older individualism a dying echo is more marked as well as more rapid in this country. Where is the wilderness which now beckons creative energy and affords untold opportunity to initiative and vigor? Where is the pioneer who goes forth rejoicing, even in the midst of privation, to its conquest? The wilderness exists in the movie and the novel; and the children of the pioneers, who live in the midst of surroundings artificially made over by the machine, enjoy pioneer life idly in the vicarious film. I see little social unrest which is the straining of energy for outlet in action; I find rather the protest against a weakening of vigor and a sapping of energy that emanate from the absence of constructive opportunity; and I see a confusion that is an expression of the inability to find a secure and morally rewarding place in a troubled and tangled economic scene.

Because of the bankruptcy of the older individualism, those who are aware of the breakdown often speak and argue as if individualism were itself done and over with. I do not suppose that those who regard socialism and individualism as antithetical really mean that individuality is going to die out or that it is not something intrinsically precious. But in speaking as if the only individualism were the local episode of the last two centuries, they play into the hands of those who would keep it alive in order to serve their own ends, and they slur over the chief problem— that of remaking society to serve the growth of a new type of individual. There are many who believe that socialism of some form is needed to realize individual initiative and security on a wide scale. They are concerned about the restriction of power and freedom to a few in the present régime, and they think that collective social control is necessary, at least for a time, in order to achieve its advantages for all. But they too often seem to assume that the result will be merely an extension of the earlier individualism to the many.

Such thinking treats individualism as if it were something static, having a uniform content. It ignores the fact that the mental and moral structure of individuals, the pattern of their desires and purposes, change with every great change in social constitution. Individuals who are not bound together in associations, whether domestic, economic, religious, political, artistic or educational, are monstrosities. It is absurd to suppose that the ties which hold them together are merely external and do not react into mentality and character, producing the framework of personal disposition.

The tragedy of the "lost individual" is due to the fact that while individuals are now caught up into a vast complex of associations, there is no harmonious and coherent reflection of the import of these connections into the imaginative and emotional outlook on life. This fact is of course due in turn to the absence of harmony within the state of society. There is an undoubted circle. But it is a vicious circle only as far as men decline to accept—in the intellectual, observing and inquiring spirit defined in the previous chapter—the realities of the social estate, and because of this refusal either surrender to the division or seek to save their individuality by escape or sheer emotional revolt. The habit of opposing the corporate and collective to the individual tends to the persistent continuation of the confusion and uncertainty. It distracts attention from the crucial issue: How shall the individual refind himself in an un-precedentedly new social situation, and what qualities will the new in-dividualism exhibit?

That the problem is not merely one of extending to all individuals the traits of economic initiative, opportunity and enterprise; that it is one of forming a new psychological and moral type, is suggested by the great pressure now brought to bear to effect conformity and standardization of American opinion. Why should regimentation, the erection of an average struck from the opinions of large masses into regulative norms, and in general the domination of quantity over quality, be so charac-teristic of present American life? I see but one fundamental explana-tion. The individual cannot remain intellectually a vacuum. If his ideas and beliefs are not the spontaneous function of a communal life in which he shares, a seeming consensus will be secured as a substitute by artificial and mechanical means. In the absence of mentality that is con-gruous with the new social corporateness that is coming into being, there is a desperate effort to fill the void by external agencies which ob-tain a factitious agreement.

In consequence, our uniformity of thought is much more superficial than it seems to be. The standardization is deplorable, but one might al-most say that one of the reasons it is deplorable is because it does not go deep. It goes far enough to effect suppression of original quality of thought, but not far enough to achieve enduring unity. Its superficial character is evident in its instability. All agreement of thought obtained by external means, by repression and intimidation, however subtle, and by calculated propaganda and publicity, is of necessity superficial; and whatever is superficial is in continual flux. The methods employed pro-duce mass credulity, and this jumps from one thing to another ac-cording to the dominant suggestions of the day. We think and feel alike—but only for a month or a season. Then comes some other sensa-tional event or personage to exercise a hypnotizing uniformity of response. At a given time, taken in cross-section, conformity is the rule. In a time span, taken longitudinally, instability and flux dominate. . . . I suppose there are others who have a feeling of irritation at such terms as "radio-conscious" and "air-minded," now so frequently forced upon us. I do not think the irritation is wholly due to linguistic causes. It testifies to a half-conscious sense of the external ways in which our minds are formed and swayed and of the superficiality and inconsistency of the result.

There are, I suppose, those who fancy that the emphasis which I put upon the corporateness of existing society in the United States is in effect, even if not in the writer's conscious intent, a plea for greater conformity than now exists. Nothing could be further from the truth. Identification of society with a level, whatever it be, high as well as low, of uniformity is just another evidence of that distraction because of which the individual is lost. Society is of course but the relations of individuals to one another in this form and that. And all relations are interactions, not fixed molds. The particular interactions that compose a human society include the give and take of participation, of a sharing that increases, that expands and deepens, the capacity and significance of the interacting factors. Conformity is a name for the absence of vital interplay; the arrest and benumbing of communication. As I have been trying to say, it is the artificial substitute used to hold men together in lack of associations that are incorporated into inner dispositions of thought and desire. I often wonder what meaning is given to the term "society" by those who oppose it to the intimacies of personal intercourse, such as those of friendship. Presumably they have in their minds a picture of rigid institutions or some set and external organization. But an institution that is other than the structure of human contact and intercourse is a fossil of some past society; organization, as in any living organism, is the coöperative consensus of multitudes of cells, each living in exchange with others.

I should suppose that the more intelligent of those who wield the publicity agencies which produce conformity would be disturbed at beholding their own success. I can easily understand that they should have a cynical sense of their ability to obtain the results they want at a given time; but I should think they would fear that like-mindedness might, at a critical juncture, veer in an unexpected direction and turn with equal unanimity against the things and interests it has been manipulated to support. Crowd psychology is dangerous in its instability. To rely upon it for permanent support is playing with a fire that may get out of control. Conformity is enduringly effective when it is a spontaneous and largely unconscious manifestation of the agreements that spring from genuine communal life. An artificially induced uniformity of thought and sentiment is a sympton of an inner void. Not all of it that now exists is intentionally produced; it is not the result of deliberate manipulation. But it is, on the other hand, the result of causes so external as to be accidental and precarious.

The "joining" habit of the average American, and his excessive sociability, may well have an explanation like that of conformity. They, too, testify to nature's abhorrence of that vacuum which the passing of the older individualism has produced. We should not be so averse to solitude if we had, when we were alone, the companionship of communal thought built into our mental habits. In the absence of this communion, there is the need for reinforcement by external contact. Our sociability is largely an effort to find substitutes for that normal consciousness of connection and union that proceeds from being a sustained and sustaining member of a social whole.

Just as the new individualism cannot be achieved by extending the benefits of the older economic individualism to more persons, so it cannot be obtained by a further development of generosity, good will and altruism. Such traits are desirable, but they are also more or less constant expressions of human nature. There is much in the present situation that stimulates them to active operation. They are probably more marked features of American life than of that of any other civilization at any time. Our charity and philanthropy are partly the manifestation of an uneasy conscience. As such a manifestation, they testify to a realization that a régime of industry carried on for private gain does not satisfy the full human nature of even those who profit by it. The impulse and need which the existing economic régime chokes, through preventing its articulated expression, find outlet in actions that acknowledge a social responsibility which the system as a system denies. Hence the development of philanthropic measures is not only compensatory to a stifling of human nature undergone in business, but it is in a way prophetic. Construction is better than relief; prevention than cure. Activities by way of relief of poverty and its attendant mental strains and physical ills—and our philanthropic activities including even the endowment of educational institutions have their ultimate causes in the existence of economic insecurity and distress—suggest, in dim forecast, a society in which daily occupations and relationships will give independence and substantial living to all normal individuals who share in its ongoings, reserving relief for extraordinary emergencies. One does not need to reflect upon the personal motives of great philanthropists to see in what they do an emphatic record of the breakdown of our existing economic organization.

For the chief obstacle to the creation of a type of individual whose pattern of thought and desire is enduringly marked by consensus with others, and in whom sociability is one with coöperation in all regular human associations, is the persistence of that feature of the earlier individualism which defines industry and commerce by ideas of private pecuniary profit. Why, once more, is there such zeal for standardized likeness? It is not, I imagine, because conformity for its own sake appears to be a great boon. It is rather because a certain kind of conformity gives defense and protection to the pecuniary features of our present régime. The foreground may be filled with depiction of the horror of change, and with clamor for law and order and the support of the Constitution. But behind there is desire for perpetuation of that régime which defines individual initiative and ability by success in conducting business so as to make money.

It is not too much to say that the whole significance of the older individualism has now shrunk to a pecuniary scale and measure. The virtues that are supposed to attend rugged individualism may be vocally proclaimed, but it takes no great insight to see that what is cherished is measured by its connection with those activities that make for success in business conducted for personal gain. Hence, the irony of the gospel of "individualism" in business conjoined with suppression of individuality in thought and speech. One cannot imagine a bitterer comment on any professed individualism than that it subordinates the only creative individuality—that of mind—to the maintenance of a régime which gives the few an opportunity for being shrewd in the management of monetary business.

It is claimed, of course, that the individualism of economic self-seeking, even if it has not produced the adjustment of ability and reward and the harmony of interests earlier predicted, has given us the advantage of material prosperity. It is not needful to raise here the question of how far that material prosperity extends. For it is not true that its moving cause is pecuniary individualism. That has been the cause of some great fortunes, but not of national wealth; it counts in the process of distribution, but not in ultimate creation. Scientific insight taking effect in machine technology has been the great productive force. For the most part, economic individualism interpreted as energy and enterprise devoted to private profit, has been an adjunct, often a parasitical one, to the movement of technical and scientific forces.

The scene in which individuality is created has been transformed. The pioneer, such as is depicted in the quotation from Crothers, had no great need for any ideas beyond those that sprang up in the immediate tasks in which he was engaged. His intellectual problems grew out of struggle with the forces of physical nature. The wilderness was a reality and it had to be subdued. The type of character that evolved was strong and hardy, often picturesque, and sometimes heroic. Individuality was a reality because it corresponded to conditions. Irrelevant traditional ideas in religion and morals were carried along, but they were reduced to a size where they did no harm; indeed, they could easily be interpreted in such a way as to be a reinforcement to the sturdy and a consolation to the weak and failing.

But it is no longer a physical wilderness that has to be wrestled with. Our problems grow out of social conditions: they concern human relations rather than man's direct relationship to physical nature. The adventure of the individual, if there is to be any venturing of individuality and not a relapse into the deadness of complacency or of despairing discontent, is an unsubdued social frontier. The issues cannot be met with ideas improvised for the occasion. The problems to be solved are general, not local. They concern complex forces that are at work throughout the whole country, not those limited to an immediate and almost face-to-face environment. Traditional ideas are more than irrelevant. They are an encumbrance; they are the chief obstacle to the formation of a new individuality integrated within itself and with a liberated function in the society wherein it exists. A new individualism can be achieved only through the controlled use of all the resources of the science and technology that have mastered the physical forces of nature.

They are not controlled now in any fundamental sense. Rather do they control us. They are indeed physically controlled. Every factory, power-house and railway system testifies to the fact that we have attained this measure of control. But control of power through the machine is not control of the machine itself. Control of the energies of nature by science is not controlled use of science. We are not even approaching a climax of control; we are hardly at its feeble beginnings. For control is relative to consequences, ends, values; and we do not manage, we hardly have commenced to dream of managing, physical power for the sake of projected purposes and prospective goods. The machine took us unawares and unprepared. Instead of forming new purposes commensurate with its potentialities, we accordingly tried to make it the servant of aims that were the expression of an age when mastery of natural energies on any large scale was the fantasy of magic. As Clarence Ayres has said: "Our industrial revolution began, as some historians say, with half a dozen technical improvements in the textile industry; and it took us a century to realize that anything of moment had happened to us beyond the obvious improvement of spinning and weaving."

I do not say that the aims and values of the earlier day were petty in themselves. But they are almost inconceivably petty in comparison with the means now at our command—if we had an imagination large enough to encompass their potential uses. They are worse than petty; they are confusing and distracting when men are confronted with the physical instrumentalities and agencies which, in the lack of comprehensive purpose and concerted planning, work blindly and carry us drifting hither and yon. I cannot obtain intellectual, moral or esthetic satisfaction from the professed philosophy which animates Bolshevik Russia. But I am sure that the future historian of our times will combine admiration of those who had the imagination first to see that the resources of technology might be directed by organized planning to serve chosen ends with astonishment at the intellectual and moral hebetude of other peoples who were technically so much further advanced.

There is no greater sign of the paralysis of the imagination which custom and involvement in immediate detail can induce than the belief, sedulously propagated by some who pride themselves on superior taste, that the machine is itself the source of our troubles. Of course immense potential resources impose responsibility, and it has yet to be demonstrated whether human capacity can rise to utilization of the opportunities which the machine and technology have opened to us. But it is hard to think of anything more childish than the animism that puts the blame on machinery. For machinery means an undreamed-of reservoir of power. If we have harnessed this power to the dollar rather than to the liberation and enrichment of human life, it is because we have been content to stay within the bounds of traditional aims and values although we are in possession of a revolutionary transforming instrument. Repetition of the older credo of individualism is but the evidence of contentment within these bonds. I for one think it is incredible that this particular form of confession of inferiority will endure very much longer. When we begin to ask what can be done with the machine for the creation and fulfillment of values corresponding to its potency and begin organized planning to effect these goods, a new individual correlative to the realities of the age in which we live will also begin to take form.

Revolt against the machine as the author of social evils usually has an esthetic origin. A more intellectual and quasi-philosophic reaction finds natural science to be their source; or if not science itself (which is allowed to be all very well if it keeps its appropriate humble place) then the attitude of those who depend upon science as an organ of vision and light. Contempt for nature is understandable, at least historically; even though it seems both intellectually petty and morally ungracious to feel contempt for the matrix of our being and the inescapable condition of our lives. But that men should fear and dislike the method of approach to nature I do not find understandable. The eye sees many foul things and the arm and hand do many cruel things. Yet the fanatic who would pluck out the eye and cut off the arm is recognized for what he is. Science, one may say, is but the extension of our natural organs of approach to nature. And I do not mean merely an extension in quantitative range and penetration, as a microscope multiplies the capacity of the unaided eye, but an extension of insight and understanding through bringing relationships and interactions into view. Since we must in any case approach nature in some fashion and by some path—if only that of death—I confess my total inability to understand those who object to an intelligently controlled approach—for that is what science is.

The only way in which I can obtain any sympathetic realization of their attitude is by recalling that there have been those who have professed adoration of science—writing it with a capital S—; those who have thought of it not as a method of approach but as a kind of self-enclosed entity and end in itself, a new theology of self-sufficient authoritatively revealed inherent and absolute Truth. It would, however, seem simpler to correct their misapprehension than first to share it and then to reverse their worship into condemnation. The opposite of intelligent method is no method at all or blind and stupid method. It is a curious state of mind which finds pleasure in setting forth the "limits of science." For the intrinsic limit of knowledge is simply ignorance; and the point in extolling ignorance is not clear except when expressed by those who profit by keeping others in ignorance. There is of course an extrinsic limit of science. But that limitation lies in the ineptitude of those who put it to use; its removal lies in rectification of its use, not in abuse of the thing used.

This reference to science and technology is relevant because they are the forces of present life which are finally significant. It is through employing them with understanding of their possible import that a new individualism, consonant with the realities of the present age, may be brought into operative being. There are many levels and many elements in both the individual and his relations. Neither can be comprehended nor dealt with in mass. Discriminative sensitivity, selection, is imperative. Art is the fruit of such selection when it is given objective effect. The art which our time needs in order to create a new type of individuality is the art which, being sensitive to the technology and science that are the moving forces of our time, will envisage the expansive, the social, culture which they may be made to serve. I am not anxious to depict the form which this emergent individualism will assume. Indeed, I do not see how it can be described until more progress has been made in its production. But such progress will not be initiated until we cease opposing the socially corporate to the individual, and until we develop a constructively imaginative observation of the rôle of science and technology in actual society. The greatest obstacle to that vision is, I repeat, the perpetuation of the older individualism now reduced, as I have said, to the utilization of science and technology for ends of private pecuniary gain. I sometimes wonder if those who are conscious of present ills but who direct their blows of criticism at everything except this obstacle are not stirred by motives which they unconsciously prefer to keep below consciousness.

39. Search for the Great Community*

It is unfortunate that John Dewey did not acknowledge the thought of Josiah Royce in this chapter from *The Public and Its Problems*. Royce wrote eloquently about the "Great Community" in his last major work on *The Problem of Christianity*, and he shared Dewey's view that it was a searching, an interpreting which was necessary if we were to move from static and isolated roles to the experience of genuine community.

In keeping with his relational philosophy, Dewey believes that "only continuous inquiry, continuous in the sense of being connected as well as persistent, can provide the material of enduring opinion about public matters." In effect, Dewey is calling for articulation of our shared experiences, especially those regarded as ordinary, for it is by such communication that we learn to dwell together as persons and to fend off the mock unity foisted upon us by the organs of bureaucracy, advertising, and controlled public opinion. Dewey cites Walt Whitman as the seer of a genuine democracy and contends that his vision will be realized when "free social inquiry is indissolubly wedded to the act of full and moving communication."

We have had occasion to refer in passing to the distinction between

* From John Dewey, *The Public and Its Problems* (New York, Henry Holt and Company, 1927), pp. 143-84. Copyright 1946 by John Dewey.

democracy as a social idea and political democracy as a system of government. The two are, of course, connected. The idea remains barren and empty save as it is incarnated in human relationships. Yet in discussion they must be distinguished. The idea of democracy is a wider and fuller idea than can be exemplified in the state even at its best. To be realized it must affect all modes of human association, the family, the school, industry, religion. And even as far as political arrangements are concerned, governmental institutions are but a mechanism for securing to an idea channels of effective operation. It will hardly do to say that criticisms of the political machinery leave the believer in the idea untouched. For, as far as they are justified—and no candid believer can deny that many of them are only too well grounded—they arouse him to bestir himself in order that the idea may find a more adequate machinery through which to work. What the faithful insist upon, however, is that the idea and its external organs and structures are not to be identified. We object to the common supposition of the foes of existing democratic government that the accusations against it touch the social and moral aspirations and ideas which underlie the political forms. The old saying that the cure for the ills of democracy is more democracy is not apt if it means that the evils may be remedied by introducing more machinery of the same kind as that which already exists, or by refining and perfecting that machinery. But the phrase may also indicate the need of returning to the idea itself, of clarifying and deepening our apprehension of it, and of employing our sense of its meaning to criticize and re-make its political manifestations.

Confining ourselves, for the moment, to political democracy, we must, in any case, renew our protest against the assumption that the idea has itself produced the governmental practices which obtain in democratic states: General suffrage, elected representatives, majority rule, and so on. The idea has influenced the concrete political movement, but it has not caused it. The transition from family and dynastic government supported by the loyalties of tradition to popular government was the outcome primarily of technological discoveries and inventions working a change in the customs by which men had been bound together. It was not due to the doctrines of doctrinaires. The forms to which we are accustomed in democratic governments represent the cumulative effect of a multitude of events, unpremeditated as far as political effects were concerned and having unpredictable consequences. There is no sanctity in universal suffrage, frequent elections, majority rule, congressional and cabinet government. These things are devices evolved in the direction in which the current was moving, each wave of which involved at the time of its impulsion a minimum of departure from antecedent custom and law. The devices served a purpose; but the purpose was rather that of meeting existing needs which had become too intense to be ignored, than that of forwarding the democratic idea. In spite of all defects, they served their own purpose well.

Looking back, with the aid which *ex posto facto* experience can give, it would be hard for the wisest to devise schemes which, under the circumstances, would have met the needs better. In this retrospective glance, it is possible, however, to see how the doctrinal formulations which accompanied them were inadequate, one-sided and positively erroneous. In fact they were hardly more than political war-cries adopted to help in carrying on some immediate agitation or in justifying some particular practical polity struggling for recognition, even though they were asserted to be absolute truths of human nature or of morals. The doctrines served a particular local pragmatic need. But often their very adaptation to immediate circumstances unfitted them, pragmatically, to meet more enduring and more extensive needs. They lived to cumber the political ground, obstructing progress, all the more so because they were uttered and held not as hypotheses with which to direct social experimentation but as final truths, dogmas. No wonder they call urgently for revision and displacement.

Nevertheless the current has set steadily in one direction: toward democratic forms. That government exists to serve its community, and that this purpose cannot be achieved unless the community itself shares in selecting its governors and determining their policies, are a deposit of fact left, as far as we can see, permanently in the wake of doctrines and forms, however transitory the latter. They are not the whole of the democratic idea, but they express it in its political phase. Belief in this political aspect is not a mystic faith as if in some overruling providence that cares for children, drunkards and others unable to help themselves. It marks a well-attested conclusion from historic facts. We have every reason to think that whatever changes may take place in existing democratic machinery, they will be of a sort to make the interest of the public a more supreme guide and criterion of governmental activity, and to enable the public to form and manifest its purposes still more authoritatively. In this sense the cure for the ailments of democracy is more democracy. The prime difficulty, as we have seen, is that of discovering the means by which a scattered, mobile and manifold public may so recognize itself as to define and express its interests. This discovery is necessarily precedent to any fundamental change in the machinery. We are not concerned therefore to set forth counsels as to advisable improvements in the political forms of democracy. Many have been suggested. It is no derogation of their relative worth to say that consideration of these changes is not at present an affair of primary importance. The problem lies deeper; it is in the first instance an intellectual problem: the search for conditions under which the Great Society may become the Great Community. When these conditions are brought into being they will make their own forms. Until they have come about, it is somewhat futile to consider what political machinery will suit them.

In a search for the conditions under which the inchoate public now extant may function democratically, we may proceed from a statement of the nature of the democratic idea in its generic social sense.[1] From the standpoint of the individual, it consists in having a responsible share according to capacity in forming and directing the activities of the groups to which one belongs and in participating according to need in the values which the groups sustain. From the standpoint of the groups, it demands liberation of the potentialities of members of a group in harmony with the interests and goods which are common. Since every individual is a member of many groups, this specification cannot be fulfilled except when different groups interact flexibly and fully in connection with other groups. A member of a robber band may express his powers in a way consonant with belonging to that group and be directed by the interest common to its members. But he does so only at the cost of repression of those of his potentialities which can be realized only through membership in other groups. The robber band cannot interact flexibly with other groups; it can act only through isolating itself. It must prevent the operation of all interests save those which circumscribe it in its separateness. But a good citizen finds his conduct as a member of a political group enriching and enriched by his participation in family life, industry, scientific and artistic associations. There is a free give-and-take: fullness of integrated personality is therefore possible of achievement, since the pulls and responses of different groups reënforce one another and their values accord.

Regarded as an idea, democracy is not an alternative to other principles of associated life. It is the idea of community life itself. It is an ideal in the only intelligible sense of an ideal: namely, the tendency and movement of some thing which exists carried to its final limit, viewed as completed, perfected. Since things do not attain such fulfillment but are

[1] The most adequate discussion of this ideal with which I am acquainted is T. V. Smith's *The Democratic Way of Life*.

in actuality distracted and interfered with, democracy in this sense is not a fact and never will be. But neither in this sense is there or has there ever been anything which is a community in its full measure, a community unalloyed by alien elements. The idea or ideal of a community presents, however, actual phases of associated life as they are freed from restrictive and disturbing elements, and are contemplated as having attained their limit of development. Wherever there is conjoint activity whose consequences are appreciated as good by all singular persons who take part in it, and where the realization of the good is such as to effect an energetic desire and effort to sustain it in being just because it is a good shared by all, there is in so far a community. The clear consciousness of a communal life, in all its implications, constitutes the idea of democracy.

Only when we start from a community as a fact, grasp the fact in thought so as to clarify and enhance its constituent elements, can we reach an idea of democracy which is not utopian. The conceptions and shibboleths which are traditionally associated with the idea of democracy take on a veridical and directive meaning only when they are construed as marks and traits of an association which realizes the defining characteristics of a community. Fraternity, liberty and equality isolated from communal life are hopeless abstractions. Their separate assertion leads to mushy sentimentalism or else to extravagant and fanatical violence which in the end defeats its own aims. Equality then becomes a creed of mechanical identity which is false to facts and impossible of realization. Effort to attain it is divisive of the vital bonds which hold men together; as far as it puts forth issue, the outcome is a mediocrity in which good is common only in the sense of being average and vulgar. Liberty is then thought of as independence of social ties, and ends in dissolution and anarchy. It is more difficult to sever the idea of brotherhood from that of a community, and hence it is either practically ignored in the movements which identify democracy with Individualism, or else it is a sentimentally appended tag. In its just connection with communal experience, fraternity is another name for the consciously appreciated goods which accrue from an association in which all share, and which give direction to the conduct of each. Liberty is that secure release and fulfillment of personal potentialities which take place only in rich and manifold association with others: the power to be an individualized self making a distinctive contribution and enjoying in its own way the fruits of association. Equality denotes the unhampered share which each individual member of the community has in the consequences of associated action. It is equitable because it is measured only by need and capacity to utilize, not by extraneous factors which deprive one in order that another may take and have. A baby in the family is equal with others, not because of some antecedent and structural quality which is the same as that of others, but in so far as his needs for care and development are attended to without being sacrificed to the superior strength, possessions and matured abilities of others. Equality does not signify that kind of mathematical or physical equivalence in virtue of which any one element may be substituted for another. It denotes effective regard for whatever is distinctive and unique in each, irrespective of physical and psychological inequalities. It is not a natural possession but is a fruit of the community when its action is directed by its character as a community.

Associated or joint activity is a condition of the creation of a community. But association itself is physical and organic, while communal life is moral, that is emotionally, intellectually, consciously sustained. Human beings combine in behavior as directly and unconsciously as do atoms, stellar masses and cells; as directly and unknowingly as they divide and repel. They do so in virtue of their own structure, as man and woman unite, as the baby seeks the breast and the breast is there to supply its need. They do so from external circumstances, pressure from without, as atoms combine or separate in presence of an electric charge, or as sheep huddle together from the cold. Associated activity needs no explanation; things are made that way. But no amount of aggregated collective action of itself constitutes a community. For beings who observe and think, and whose ideas are absorbed by impulses and become sentiments and interests, "we" is as inevitable as "I." But "we" and "our" exist only when the consequences of combined action are perceived and become an object of desire and effort, just as "I" and "mine" appear on the scene only when a distinctive share in mutual action is consciously asserted or claimed. Human associations may be ever so organic in origin and firm in operation, but they develop into societies in a human sense only as their consequences, being known, are esteemed and sought for. Even if "society" were as much an organism as some writers have held, it would not on that account be society. Interactions, transactions, occur *de facto* and the results of interdependence follow. But participation in activities and sharing in results are additive concerns. They demand *communication* as a prerequisite.

Combined activity happens among human beings; but when nothing else happens it passes as inevitably into some other mode of interconnected activity as does the interplay of iron and the oxygen of water. What takes place is wholly describable in terms of energy, or, as we say in the case of human interactions, of force. Only when there exist *signs* or *symbols* of activities and of their outcome can the flux be viewed as from without, be arrested for consideration and esteem, and be regulated. Lightning strikes and rives a tree or rock, and the resulting fragments take up and continue the process of interaction, and so on and on. But when phases of the process are represented by signs, a new medium is interposed. As symbols are related to one another, the important relations of a course of events are recorded and are preserved as meanings. Recollection and foresight are possible; the new medium facilitates calculation, planning, and a new kind of action which intervenes in what happens to direct its course in the interest of what is foreseen and desired.

Symbols in turn depend upon and promote communication. The results of conjoint experience are considered and transmitted. Events cannot be passed from one to another, but meanings may be shared by means of signs. Wants and impulses are then attached to common meanings. They are thereby transformed into desires and purposes, which, since they implicate a common or mutually understood meaning, present new ties, converting a conjoint activity into a community of interest and endeavor. Thus there is generated what, metaphorically, may be termed a general will and social consciousness: desire and choice on the part of individuals in behalf of activities that, by means of symbols, are communicable and shared by all concerned. A community thus presents an order of energies transmuted into one of meanings which are appreciated and mutually referred by each to every other on the part of those engaged in combined action. "Force" is not eliminated but is transformed in use and direction by ideas and sentiments made possible by means of symbols.

The work of conversion of the physical and organic phase of associated behavior into a community of action saturated and regulated by mutual interest in shared meanings, consequences which are translated into ideas and desired objects by means of symbols, does not occur all at once nor completely. At any given time, it sets a problem rather than marks a settled achievement. We are born organic beings associated with others, but we are not born members of a community. The young have to be brought within the traditions, outlook and interests which characterize a community by means of education: by unremitting instruction and by learning in connection with the phenomena of overt association. Everything which is distinctively human is learned, not native, even though it could not be learned without native structures which mark man off from other animals. To learn in a human way and to human effect is not just to acquire added skill through refinement of original capacities.

To learn to be human is to develop through the give-and-take of communication an effective sense of being an individually distinctive member of a community; one who understands and appreciates its beliefs, desires and methods, and who contributes to a further conversion of organic powers into human resources and values. But this translation is never finished. The old Adam, the unregenerate element in human nature, persists. It shows itself wherever the method obtains of attaining results by use of force instead of by the method of communication and enlightenment. It manifests itself more subtly, pervasively and effectually when knowledge and the instrumentalities of skill which are the product of communal life are employed in the service of wants and impulses which have not themselves been modified by reference to a shared interest. To the doctrine of "natural" economy which held that commercial exchange would bring about such an interdependence that harmony would automatically result, Rousseau gave an adequate answer in advance. He pointed out that interdependence provides just the situation which makes it possible and worth while for the stronger and abler to exploit others for their own ends, to keep others in a state of subjection where they can be utilized as animated tools. The remedy he suggested, a return to a condition of independence based on isolation, was hardly seriously meant. But its desperateness is evidence of the urgency of the problem. Its negative character was equivalent to surrender of any hope of solution. By contrast it indicates the nature of the only possible solution: the perfecting of the means and ways of communication of meanings so that genuinely shared interest in the consequences of interdependent activities may inform desire and effort and thereby direct action.

This is the meaning of the statement that the problem is a moral one dependent upon intelligence and education. We have in our prior account sufficiently emphasized the rôle of technological and industrial factors in creating the Great Society. What was said may even have seemed to imply acceptance of the deterministic version of an economic interpretation of history and institutions. It is silly and futile to ignore and deny economic facts. They do not cease to operate because we refuse to note them, or because we smear them over with sentimental idealizations. As we have also noted, they generate as their result overt and external conditions of action and these are known with various degrees of adequacy. What actually happens in consequence of industrial forces is dependent upon the presence or absence of perception and communication of consequences, upon foresight and its effect upon desire and endeavor. Economic agencies produce one result when they are left to work themselves out on the merely physical level, or on that level modified only as the knowledge, skill and technique which the community has accumulated are transmitted to its members unequally and by chance. They have a different outcome in the degree in which knowledge of consequences is equitably distributed, and action is animated by an informed and lively sense of a shared interest. The doctrine of economic interpretation as usually stated ignores the transformation which meanings may effect; it passes over the new medium which communication may interpose between industry and its eventual consequences. It is obsessed by the illusion which vitiated the "natural economy": an illusion due to failure to note the difference made in action by perception and publication of its consequences, actual and possible. It thinks in terms of antecedents, not of the eventual; of origins, not fruits.

We have returned, through this apparent excursion, to the question in which our earlier discussion culminated: What are the conditions under which it is possible for the Great Society to approach more closely and vitally the status of a Great Community, and thus take form in genuinely democratic societies and state? What are the conditions under which we may reasonably picture the Public emerging from its eclipse?

The study will be an intellectual or hypothetical one. There will be no attempt to state how the required conditions might come into existence, nor to prophesy that they will occur. The object of the analysis will be to show that *unless* ascertained specifications are realized, the Community cannot be organized as a democratically effective Public. It is not claimed that the conditions which will be noted will suffice, but only that at least they are indispensable. In other words, we shall endeavor to frame a hypothesis regarding the democratic state to stand in contrast with the earlier doctrine which has been nullified by the course of events.

Two essential constituents in that older theory, as will be recalled, were the notions that each individual is of himself equipped with the intelligence needed, under the operation of self-interest, to engage in political affairs; and that general suffrage, frequent elections of officials and majority rule are sufficient to ensure the responsibility of elected rulers to the desires and interests of the public. As we shall see, the second conception is logically bound up with the first and stands or falls with it. At the basis of the scheme lies what Lippmann has well called the idea of the "omnicompetent" individual: competent to know in all situations demanding political action what is for his own good, and competent to enforce his idea of good and the will to effect it against contrary forces. Subsequent history has proved that the assumption involved illusion. Had it not been for the misleading influence of a false psychology, the illusion might have been detected in advance. But current philosophy held that ideas and knowledge were functions of a mind or consciousness which originated in individuals by means of isolated contact with objects. But in fact, knowledge is a function of association and communication; it depends upon tradition, upon tools and methods socially transmitted, developed and sanctioned. Faculties of effectual observation, reflection and desire are habits acquired under the influence of the culture and institutions of society, not ready-made inherent powers. The fact that man acts from crudely intelligized emotion and from habit rather than from rational consideration, is now so familiar that it is not easy to appreciate that the other idea was taken seriously as the basis of economic and political philosophy. The measure of truth which it contains was derived from observation of a relatively small group of shrewd business men who regulated their enterprises by calculation and accounting, and of citizens of small and stable local communities who were so intimately acquainted with the persons and affairs of their locality that they could pass competent judgment upon the bearing of proposed measures upon their own concerns.

Habit is the mainspring of human action, and habits are formed for the most part under the influence of the customs of a group. The organic structure of man entails the formation of habit, for, whether we wish it or not, whether we are aware of it or not, every act effects a modification of attitude and set which directs future behavior. The dependence of habit-forming upon those habits of a group which constitute customs and institutions is a natural consequence of the helplessness of infancy. The social consequences of habit have been stated once for all by James: "Habit is the enormous fly-wheel of society, its most precious conservative influence. It alone is what keeps us within the bounds of ordinance, and saves the children of fortune from the uprisings of the poor. It alone prevents the hardest and most repulsive walks of life from being deserted by those brought up to tread therein. It keeps the fisherman and the deck-hand at sea through the winter; it holds the miner in his darkness, and nails the country-man to his log cabin and his lonely farm through all the months of snow; it protects us from invasion by the natives of the desert and the frozen zone. It dooms us all to fight out the battle of life upon the lines of our nurture or our early choice, and to make the best of a pursuit that disagrees, because there is no other for which we are fitted and it is too late to begin again. It keeps different social strata from mixing.''

The influence of habit is decisive because all distinctively human action has to be learned, and the very heart, blood and sinews of learning is creation of habitudes. Habits bind us to orderly and established ways of action because they generate ease, skill and interest in things to which we have grown used and because they instigate fear to walk in different ways, and because they leave us incapacitated for the trial of them. Habit does not preclude the use of thought, but it determines the channels within which it operates. Thinking is secreted in the interstices of habits. The sailor, miner, fisherman and farmer think, but their thoughts fall within the framework of accustomed occupations and relationships. We dream beyond the limits of use and wont, but only rarely does revery become a source of acts which break bounds; so rarely that we name those in whom it happens demonic geniuses and marvel at the spectacle. Thinking itself becomes habitual along certain lines; a specialized occupation. Scientific men, philosophers, literary persons, are not men and women who have so broken the bonds of habits that pure reason and emotion undefiled by use and wont speak through them. They are persons of a specialized infrequent habit. Hence the idea that men are moved by an intelligent and calculated regard for their own good is pure mythology. Even if the principle of self-love actuated behavior, it would still be true that the *objects* in which men find their love manifested, the objects which they take as constituting their peculiar interests, are set by habits reflecting social customs.

These facts explain why the social doctrinaires of the new industrial movement had so little prescience of what was to follow in consequence of it. These facts explain why the more things changed, the more they were the same; they account, that is, for the fact that instead of the sweeping revolution which was expected to result from democratic political machinery, there was in the main but a transfer of vested power from one class to another. A few men, whether or not they were good judges of their own true interest and good, were competent judges of the conduct of business for pecuniary profit, and of how the new governmental machinery could be made to serve their ends. It would have taken a new race of human beings to escape, in the use made of political forms, from the influence of deeply engrained habits, of old institutions and customary social status, with their inwrought limitations of expectation, desire and demand. And such a race, unless of disembodied angelic constitution, would simply have taken up the task where human beings assumed it upon emergence from the condition of anthropoid apes. In spite of sudden and catastrophic revolutions, the essential continuity of history is doubly guaranteed. Not only are personal desire and belief functions of habit and custom, but the objective conditions which provide the resources and tools of action, together with its limitations, obstructions and traps, are precipitates of the past, perpetuating, willy-nilly, its hold and power. The creation of a *tabula rasa* in order to permit the creation of a new order is so impossible as to set at naught both the hope of buoyant revolutionaries and the timidity of scared conservatives.

Nevertheless, changes take place and are cumulative in character. Observation of them in the light of their recognized consequences arouses reflection, discovery, invention, experimentation. When a certain state of accumulated knowledge, of techniques and instrumentalities is attained, the process of change is so accelerated, that, as to-day, it appears externally to be the dominant trait. But there is a marked lag in any corresponding change of ideas and desires. Habits of opinion are the toughest of all habits; when they have become second nature, and are supposedly thrown out of the door, they creep in again as stealthily and surely as does first nature. And as they are modified, the alteration first shows itself negatively, in the disintegration of old beliefs, to be replaced by floating, volatile and accidentally snatched up opinions. Of course there has been an enormous increase in the amount of knowledge possessed by mankind, but it does not equal, probably, the increase in the amount of errors and half-truths which have got into circulation. In social and human matters, especially, the development of a critical sense and methods of discriminating judgment has not kept pace with the growth of careless reports and of motives for positive misrepresentation.

What is more important, however, is that so much of knowledge is not knowledge in the ordinary sense of the word, but is "science." The quotation marks are not used disrespectfully, but to suggest the technical character of scientific material. The layman takes certain conclusions which get into circulation to be science. But the scientific inquirer knows that they constitute science only in connection with the methods by which they are reached. Even when true, they are not science in virtue of their correctness, but by reason of the apparatus which is employed in reaching them. This apparatus is so highly specialized that it requires more labor to acquire ability to use and understand it than to get skill in any other instrumentalities possessed by man. Science, in other words, is a highly specialized language, more difficult to learn than any natural language. It is an artificial language, not in the sense of being factitious, but in that of being a work of intricate art, devoted to a particular purpose and not capable of being acquired nor understood in the way in which the mother tongue is learned. It is, indeed, conceivable that sometime methods of instruction will be devised which will enable laymen to read and hear scientific material with comprehension, even when they do not themselves use the apparatus which is science. The latter may then become for large numbers what students of language call a passive, if not an active, vocabulary. But that time is in the future.

For most men, save the scientific workers, science is a mystery in the hands of initiates, who have become adepts in virtue of following ritualistic ceremonies from which the profane herd is excluded. They are fortunate who get as far as a sympathetic appreciation of the methods which give pattern to the complicated apparatus: methods of analytic, experimental observation, mathematical formulation and deduction, constant and elaborate check and test. For most persons, the reality of the apparatus is found only in its embodiments in practical affairs, in mechanical devices and in techniques which touch life as it is lived. For them, electricity is *known* by means of the telephones, bells and lights they use, by the generators and magnetos in the automobiles they drive, by the trolley cars in which they ride. The physiology and biology they are acquainted with is that they have learned in taking precautions against germs and from the physicians they depend upon for health. The science of what might be supposed to be closest to them, of human nature, was for them an esoteric mystery until it was applied in advertising, salesmanship and personnel selection and management, and until, through psychiatry, it spilled over into life and popular consciousness, through its bearings upon "nerves," the morbidities and common forms of crankiness which make it difficult for persons to get along with one another and with themselves. Even now, popular psychology is a mass of cant, of slush and of superstition worthy of the most flourishing days of the medicine man.

Meanwhile the technological application of the complex apparatus which is science has revolutionized the conditions under which associated life goes on. This may be known as a fact which is stated in a proposition and assented to. But it is not known in the sense that men understand it. They do not know it as they know some machine which they operate, or as they know electric light and steam locomotives. They do not understand *how* the change has gone on nor *how* it affects their conduct. Not understanding its "how," they cannot use and control its manifestations. They undergo the consequences, they are affected by them. They cannot manage them, though some are fortunate enough—what is commonly called good fortune—to be able to exploit some phase of the process for their own personal profit. But even the most shrewd and successful man does not in any analytic and systematic way—in a way worthy to compare with the knowledge which he has won in lesser affairs by means of the stress of experience—know the system within which he operates. Skill and ability work within a framework which we have not created and do not comprehend. Some occupy strategic positions which give them advance information of forces that affect the market; and by training and an innate turn that way they have acquired a special technique which enables them to use the vast impersonal tide to turn their own wheels. They can dam the current here and release it there. The current itself is as much beyond them as was ever the river by the side of which some ingenious mechanic, employing a knowledge which was transmitted to him, erected his saw-mill to make boards of trees which he had not grown. That within limits those successful in affairs have knowledge and skill is not to be doubted. But such knowledge goes relatively but little further than that of the competent skilled operator who manages a machine. It suffices to employ the conditions which are before him. Skill enables him to turn the flux of events this way or that in his own neighborhood. It gives him no control of the flux.

Why should the public and its officers, even if the latter are termed statesmen, be wiser and more effective? The prime condition of a democratically organized public is a kind of knowledge and insight which does not yet exist. In its absence, it would be the height of absurdity to try to tell what it would be like if it existed. But some of the conditions which must be fulfilled if it is to exist can be indicated. We can borrow that much from the spirit and method of science even if we are ignorant of it as a specialized apparatus. An obvious requirement is freedom of social inquiry and of distribution of its conclusions. The notion that men may be free in their thought even when they are not in its expression and dissemination has been sedulously propagated. It had its origin in the idea of a mind complete in itself, apart from action and from objects. Such a consciousness presents in fact the spectacle of mind deprived of its normal functioning, because it is baffled by the actualities in connection with which alone it is truly mind, and is driven back into secluded and impotent revery.

There can be no public without full publicity in respect to all consequences which concern it. Whatever obstructs and restricts publicity, limits and distorts public opinion and checks and distorts thinking on social affairs. Without freedom of expression, not even methods of social inquiry can be developed. For tools can be evolved and perfected only in operation; in application to observing, reporting and organizing actual subject-matter; and this application cannot occur save through free and systematic communication. The early history of physical knowledge, of Greek conceptions of natural phenomena, proves how inept become the conceptions of the best endowed minds when those ideas are elaborated apart from the closest contact with the events which they purport to state and explain. The ruling ideas and methods of the human sciences are in much the same condition to-day. They are also evolved on the basis of past gross observations, remote from constant use in regulation of the material of new observations.

The belief that thought and its communication are now free simply because legal restrictions which once obtained have been done away with is absurd. Its currency perpetuates the infantile state of social knowledge. For it blurs recognition of our central need to possess conceptions which are used as tools of directed inquiry and which are tested, rectified and caused to grow in actual use. No man and no mind was ever emancipated merely by being left alone. Removal of formal limitations is but a negative condition; positive freedom is not a state but an act which involves methods and instrumentalities for control of conditions. Experience shows that sometimes the sense of external oppression, as by censorship, acts as a challenge and arouses intellectual energy and excites courage. But a belief in intellectual freedom where it does not exist contributes only to complacency in virtual enslavement, to sloppiness, superficiality and recourse to sensations as a substitute for ideas: marked traits of our present estate with respect to social knowledge. On one hand, thinking deprived of its normal course takes refuge in academic specialism, comparable in its way to what is called scholasticism. On the other hand, the physical agencies of publicity which exist in such abundance are utilized in ways which constitute a large part of the present meaning of publicity: advertising, propaganda, invasion of private life, the "featuring" of passing incidents in a way which violates all the moving logic of continuity, and which leaves us with those isolated intrusions and shocks which are the essence of "sensations."

It would be a mistake to identify the conditions which limit free communication and circulation of facts and ideas, and which thereby arrest and pervert social thought or inquiry, merely with overt forces which are obstructive. It is true that those who have ability to manipulate social relations for their own advantage have to be reckoned with. They have an uncanny instinct for detecting whatever intellectual tendencies even remotely threaten to encroach upon their control. They have developed an extraordinary facility in enlisting upon their side the inertia, prejudices and emotional partisanship of the masses by use of a technique which impedes free inquiry and expression. We seem to be approaching a state of government by hired promoters of opinion called publicity agents. But the more serious enemy is deeply concealed in hidden entrenchments.

Emotional habituations and intellectual habitudes on the part of the mass of men create the conditions of which the exploiters of sentiment and opinion only take advantage. Men have got used to an experimental method in physical and technical matters. They are still afraid of it in human concerns. The fear is the more efficacious because like all deep-lying fears it is covered up and disguised by all kinds of rationalizations. One of its commonest forms is a truly religious idealization of, and reverence for, established institutions; for example in our own politics, the Constitution, the Supreme Court, private property, free contract and so on. The words "sacred" and "sanctity" come readily to our lips when such things come under discussion. They testify to the religious aureole which protects the institutions. If "holy" means that which is not to be approached nor touched, save with ceremonial precautions and by specially anointed officials, then such things are holy in contemporary political life. As supernatural matters have progressively been left high and dry upon a secluded beach, the actuality of religious taboos has more and more gathered about secular institutions, especially those connected with the nationalistic state.[2] Psychiatrists have discovered that one of the commonest causes of mental disturbance is an underlying fear of which the subject is not aware, but which leads to withdrawal from reality and to unwillingness to think things through. There is a social pathology which works powerfully against effective inquiry into social institutions and conditions. It manifests itself in a thousand ways; in querulousness, in impotent drifting, in uneasy snatching at distractions, in idealization of the long established, in a facile optimism assumed as a cloak, in riotous glorification of things "as they are," in intimidation of all dissenters—ways which depress and dissipate thought all the more effectually because they operate with subtle and unconscious pervasiveness.

The backwardness of social knowledge is marked in its division into

---

[2] The religious character of nationalism has been forcibly brought out by Carleton Hayes, in his *Essays on Nationalism*, especially Chap. IV.

independent and insulated branches of learning. Anthropology, history, sociology, morals, economics, political science, go their own ways without constant and systematized fruitful interaction. Only in appearance is there a similar division in physical knowledge. There is continuous cross-fertilization between astronomy, physics, chemistry and the biological sciences. Discoveries and improved methods are so recorded and organized that constant exchange and intercommunication take place. The isolation of the humane subjects from one another is connected with their aloofness from physical knowledge. The mind still draws a sharp separation between the world in which man lives and the life of man in and by that world, a cleft reflected in the separation of man himself into a body and a mind, which, it is currently supposed, can be known and dealt with apart. That for the past three centuries energy should have gone chiefly into physical inquiry, beginning with the things most remote from man such as heavenly bodies, was to have been expected. The history of the physical sciences reveals a certain order in which they developed. Mathematical tools had to be employed before a new astronomy could be constructed. Physics advanced when ideas worked out in connection with the solar system were used to describe happenings on the earth. Chemistry waited on the advance of physics; the sciences of living things required the material and methods of physics and chemistry in order to make headway. Human psychology ceased to be chiefly speculative opinion only when biological and physiological conclusions were available. All this is natural and seemingly inevitable. Things which had the most outlying and indirect connection with human interests had to be mastered in some degree before inquiries could competently converge upon man himself.

Nevertheless the course of development has left us of this age in a plight. When we say that a subject of science is technically specialized, or that it is highly "abstract," what we practically mean is that it is not conceived in terms of its bearing upon human life. All *merely* physical knowledge is technical, couched in a technical vocabulary communicable only to the few. Even physical knowledge which does affect human conduct, which does modify what we do and undergo, is also technical and remote in the degree in which its bearings are not understood and used. The sunlight, rain, air and soil have always entered in visible ways into human experience; atoms and molecules and cells and most other things with which the sciences are occupied affect us, but not visibly. Because they enter life and modify experience in imperceptible ways, and their consequences are not realized, speech about them is technical; communication is by means of peculiar symbols. One would think, then, that a fundamental and ever-operating aim would be to translate knowledge of the subject-matter of physical conditions into terms which are generally understood, into signs denoting human consequences of services and disservices rendered. For ultimately all consequences which enter human life depend upon physical conditions; they can be understood and mastered only as the latter are taken into account. One would think, then, that any state of affairs which tends to render the things of the environment unknown and incommunicable by human beings in terms of their own activities and sufferings would be deplored as a disaster; that it would be felt to be intolerable, and to be put up with only as far as it is, at any given time, inevitable.

But the facts are to the contrary. Matter and the material are words which in the minds of many convey a note of disparagement. They are taken to be foes of whatever is of ideal value in life, instead of as conditions of its manifestation and sustained being. In consequence of this division, they do become in fact enemies, for whatever is consistently kept apart from human values depresses thought and renders values sparse and precarious in fact. There are even some who regard the materialism and dominance of commercialism of modern life as fruits of undue devotion to physical science, not seeing that the split between man and nature, artificially made by a tradition which originated before there was understanding of the physical conditions that are the medium of human activities, is the benumbing factor. The most influential form of the divorce is separation between pure and applied science. Since "application" signifies recognized bearing upon human experience and well-being, honor of what is "pure" and contempt for what is "applied" has for its outcome a science which is remote and technical, communicable only to specialists, and a conduct of human affairs which is haphazard, biased, unfair in distribution of values. What is applied and employed as the alternative to knowledge in regulation of society is ignorance, prejudice, class-interest and accident. Science is converted into knowledge in its honorable and emphatic sense *only* in application. Otherwise it is truncated, blind, distorted. When it is then applied, it is in ways which explain the unfavorable sense so often attached to "application" and the "utilitarian": namely, use for pecuniary ends to the profit of a few.

At present, the application of physical science is rather *to* human concerns than *in* them. That is, it is external, made in the interests of its consequences for a possessing and acquisitive class. Application *in* life would signify that science was absorbed and distributed; that it was the instrumentality of that common understanding and thorough communication which is the precondition of the existence of a genuine and effective public. The use of science to regulate industry and trade has gone on steadily. The scientific revolution of the seventeenth century was the precursor of the industrial revolution of the eighteenth and nineteenth. In consequence, man has suffered the impact of an enormously enlarged control of physical energies without any corresponding ability to control himself and his own affairs. Knowledge divided against itself, a science to whose incompleteness is added an artificial split, has played its part in generating enslavement of men, women and children in factories in which they are animated machines to tend inanimate machines. It has maintained sordid slums, flurried and discontented careers, grinding poverty and luxurious wealth, brutal exploitation of nature and man in times of peace and high explosives and noxious gases in times of war. Man, a child in understanding of himself, has placed in his hands physical tools of incalculable power. He plays with them like a child, and whether they work harm or good is largely a matter of accident. The instrumentality becomes a master and works fatally as if possessed of a will of its own—not because it has a will but because man has not.

The glorification of "pure" science under such conditions is a rationalization of an escape; it marks a construction of an asylum of refuge, a shirking of responsibility. The true purity of knowledge exists not when it is uncontaminated by contact with use and service. It is wholly a moral matter, an affair of honesty, impartiality and generous breadth of intent in search and communication. The adulteration of knowledge is due not to its use, but to vested bias and prejudice, to one-sidedness of outlook, to vanity, to conceit of possession and authority, to contempt or disregard of human concern in its use. Humanity is not, as was once thought, the end for which all things were formed; it is but a slight and feeble thing, perhaps an episodic one, in the vast stretch of the universe. But for man, man is the center of interest and the measure of importance. The magnifying of the physical realm at the cost of man is but an abdication and a flight. To make physical science a rival of human interests is bad enough, for it forms a diversion of energy which can ill be afforded. But the evil does not stop there. The ultimate harm is that the understanding by man of his own affairs and his ability to direct them are sapped at their root when knowledge of nature is disconnected from its human function.

It has been implied throughout that knowledge is communication as well as understanding. I well remember the saying of a man, uneducated from the standpoint of the schools, in speaking of certain matters: "Sometime they will be found out and not only found out, but they will be known." The schools may suppose that a thing is known when it is found out. My old friend was aware that a thing is fully known only when it is published, shared, socially accessible. Record and communication are indispensable to knowledge. Knowledge cooped up in a private consciousness is a myth, and knowledge of social phenomena is peculiarly dependent upon dissemination, for only by distribution can such knowledge be either obtained or tested. A fact of community life which is not spread abroad so as to be a common possession is a contradiction in terms. Dissemination is something other than scattering at large. Seeds are sown, not by virtue of being thrown out at random, but by being so distributed as to take root and have a chance of growth. Communication of the results of social inquiry is the same thing as the formation of public opinion. This marks one of the first ideas framed in the growth of political democracy as it will be one of the last to be fulfilled. For public opinion is judgment which is formed and entertained by those who constitute the public and is about public affairs. Each of the two phases imposes for its realization conditions hard to meet.

Opinions and beliefs concerning the public presuppose effective and organized inquiry. Unless there are methods for detecting the energies which are at work and tracing them through an intricate network of interactions to their consequences, what passes as public opinion will be "opinion" in its derogatory sense rather than truly public, no matter how widespread the opinion is. The number who share error as to fact and who partake of a false belief measures power for harm. Opinion casually formed and formed under the direction of those who have something at stake in having a lie believed can be *public* opinion only in name. Calling it by this name, acceptance of the name as a kind of warrant, magnifies its capacity to lead action estray. The more who share it, the more injurious its influence. Public opinion, even if it happens to be correct, is intermittent when it is not the product of methods of investigation and reporting constantly at work. It appears only in crises. Hence its "rightness" concerns only an immediate emergency. Its lack of continuity makes it wrong from the standpoint of the course of events. It is as if a physician were able to deal for the moment with an emergency in disease but could not adapt his treatment of it to the underlying conditions which brought it about. He may then "cure" the disease—that is, cause its present alarming symptoms to subside—but he does not modify its causes; his treatment may even affect them for the worse. Only continuous inquiry, continuous in the sense of being connected as well as persistent, can provide the material of enduring opinion about public matters.

There is a sense in which "opinion" rather than knowledge, even under the most favorable circumstances, is the proper term to use—namely, in the sense of judgment, estimate. For in its strict sense, knowledge can refer only to what *has* happened and been done. What is still *to be* done involves a forecast of a future still contingent, and cannot escape the liability to error in judgment involved in all anticipation of probabilities. There may well be honest divergence as to policies to be pursued, even when plans spring from knowledge of the same facts. But genuinely public policy cannot be generated unless it be informed by knowledge, and this knowledge does not exist except when there is systematic, thorough, and well-equipped search and record.

Moreover, inquiry must be as nearly contemporaneous as possible; otherwise it is only of antiquarian interest. Knowledge of history is evidently necessary for connectedness of knowledge. But history which is not brought down close to the actual scene of events leaves a gap and exercises influence upon the formation of judgments about the public interest only by guess-work about intervening events. Here, only too conspicuously, is a limitation of the existing social sciences. Their material comes too late, too far after the event, to enter effectively into the formation of public opinion about the immediate public concern and what is to be done about it.

A glance at the situation shows that the physical and external means of collecting information in regard to what is happening in the world have far outrun the intellectual phase of inquiry and organization of its results. Telegraph, telephone, and now the radio, cheap and quick mails, the printing press, capable of swift reduplication of material at low cost, have attained a remarkable development. But when we ask what sort of material is recorded and how it is organized, when we ask about the intellectual form in which the material is presented, the tale to be told is very different. "News" signifies something which has just happened, and which is new just because it deviates from the old and regular. But its *meaning* depends upon relation to what it imports, to what its social consequences are. This import cannot be determined unless the new is placed in relation to the old, to what has happened and been integrated into the course of events. Without coördination and consecutiveness, events are not events, but mere occurrences, intrusions; an event implies that out of which a happening proceeds. Hence even if we discount the influence of private interests in procuring suppression, secrecy and misrepresentation, we have here an explanation of the triviality and "sensational" quality of so much of what passes as news. The catastrophic, namely, crime, accident, family rows, personal clashes and conflicts, are the most obvious forms of breaches of continuity; they supply the element of shock which is the strictest meaning of sensation; they are the *new* par excellence, even though only the date of the newspaper could inform us whether they happened last year or this, so completely are they isolated from their connections.

So accustomed are we to this method of collecting, recording and presenting social changes, that it may well sound ridiculous to say that a genuine social science would manifest its reality in the daily press, while learned books and articles supply and polish tools of inquiry. But the inquiry which alone can furnish knowledge as a precondition of public judgments must be contemporary and quotidian. Even if social sciences as a specialized apparatus of inquiry were more advanced than they are, they would be comparatively impotent in the office of directing opinion on matters of concern to the public as long as they are remote from application in the daily and unremitting assembly and interpretation of "news." On the other hand, the tools of social inquiry will be clumsy as long as they are forged in places and under conditions remote from contemporary events.

What has been said about the formation of ideas and judgments concerning the public apply as well to the distribution of the knowledge which makes it an effective possession of the members of the public. Any separation between the two sides of the problem is artificial. The discussion of propaganda and propagandism would alone, however, demand a volume, and could be written only by one much more experienced than the present writer. Propaganda can accordingly only be mentioned, with the remark that the present situation is one unprecedented in history. The political forms of democracy and quasi-democratic habits of thought on social matters have compelled a certain amount of public discussion and at least the simulation of general consultation in arriving at political decisions. Representative government must at least seem to be founded on public interests as they are revealed to public belief. The days are past when government can be carried on without any pretense of ascertaining the wishes of the governed. In theory, their assent must be secured. Under the older forms, there was no need to muddy the sources of opinion on political matters. No current of energy flowed from them. To-day the judgments popularly formed on political matters are so important, in spite of all factors to the contrary, that there is an enormous premium upon all methods which affect their formation.

The smoothest road to control of political conduct is by control of opinion. As long as interests of pecuniary profit are powerful, and a public has not located and identified itself, those who have this interest will have an unresisted motive for tampering with the springs of political action in all that affects them. Just as in the conduct of industry and exchange generally the technological factor is obscured, deflected and defeated by "business," so specifically in the management of publicity. The gathering and sale of subject-matter having a public import is part of the existing pecuniary system. Just as industry conducted by engineers on a factual technological basis would be a very different thing from what it actually is, so the assembling and reporting of news would be a very different thing if the genuine interests of reporters were permitted to work freely.

One aspect of the matter concerns particularly the side of dissemination. It is often said, and with a great appearance of truth, that the freeing and perfecting of inquiry would not have any especial effect. For, it is argued, the mass of the reading public is not interested in learning and assimilating the results of accurate investigation. Unless these are read, they cannot seriously affect the thought and action of members of the public; they remain in secluded library alcoves, and are studied and understood only by a few intellectuals. The objection is well taken save as the potency of art is taken into account. A technical high-brow presentation would appeal only to those technically high-brow; it would not be news to the masses. Presentation is fundamentally important, and presentation is a question of art. A newspaper which was only a daily edition of a quarterly journal of sociology or political science would undoubtedly possess a limited circulation and a narrow influence. Even at that, however, the mere existence and accessibility of such material would have some regulative effect. But we can look much further than that. The material would have such an enormous and widespread human bearing that its bare existence would be an irresistible invitation to a presentation of it which would have a direct popular appeal. The freeing of the artist in literary presentation, in other words, is as much a precondition of the desirable creation of adequate opinion on public matters as is the freeing of social inquiry. Men's conscious life of opinion and judgment often proceeds on a superficial and trivial plane. But their lives reach a deeper level. The function of art has always been to break through the crust of conventionalized and routine consciousness. Common things, a flower, a gleam of moonlight, the song of a bird, not things rare and remote, are means with which the deeper levels of life are touched so that they spring up as desire and thought. This process is art. Poetry, the drama, the novel, are proofs that the problem of presentation is not insoluble. Artists have always been the real purveyors of news, for it is not the outward happening in itself which is new, but the kindling by it of emotion, perception and appreciation.

We have but touched lightly and in passing upon the conditions which must be fulfilled if the Great Society is to become a Great Community; a society in which the ever-expanding and intricately ramifying consequences of associated activities shall be known in the full sense of that word, so that an organized, articulate Public comes into being. The highest and most difficult kind of inquiry and a subtle, delicate, vivid and responsive art of communication must take possession of the physical machinery of transmission and circulation and breathe life into it. When the machine age has thus perfected its machinery it will be a means of life and not its despotic master. Democracy will come into its own, for democracy is a name for a life of free and enriching communion. It had its seer in Walt Whitman. It will have its consummation when free social inquiry is indissolubly wedded to the art of full and moving communication.

40. Renascent Liberalism*

In "Renascent Liberalism" Dewey calls for an application of the experimental method to social and political problems. He rejects the use of violence as a necessary prerequisite to social change but admits that too often the alternative has been a posture of criticism combined with a *de facto laissez faire* policy with regard to instituting social change. Dewey is not naïve about a fundamental weakness in our society—namely, the inability to anticipate serious difficulties and the panic which accompanies strident voices in favor of overdue reforms. He asks, "Why is it, apart from our tradition of violence, that liberty of expression is tolerated and even lauded when social affairs seem to be going in a quiet fashion, and yet is so readily destroyed whenever matters grow critical?"

* From John Dewey, *Liberalism and Social Action* (New York, Capricorn Books, 1963) (1935), pp. 56-93. Reprinted by permission of G. P. Putnam's Sons.

For Dewey, social change does not spring *ab ovo* from the head of a charismatic reformer, for flux is always present. It is the direction that is in question. And this direction cannot be plotted by some grand scheme, either reminiscent of the past or indicative of the future, for both approaches "overlook the fact that history in being a process of change generates change not only in details but also in the method of directing social change." This fact of history, Dewey holds, necessitates that the proponents of social change apply the method of intelligence experimentally, so as to relate to the realities of the situation rather than to a rhetorical version.

Nothing is blinder than the supposition that we live in a society and world so static that either nothing new will happen or else it will happen because of the use of violence. Social change is here as a fact, a fact having multifarious forms and marked in intensity. Changes that are revolutionary in effect are in process in every phase of life. Transformations in the family, the church, the school, in science and art, in economic and political relations, are occurring so swiftly that imagination is baffled in attempt to lay hold of them. Flux does not have to be created. But it does have to be directed. It has to be so controlled that it will move to some end in accordance with the principles of life, since life itself is development. Liberalism is committed to an end that is at once enduring and flexible: the liberation of individuals so that realization of their capacities may be the law of their life. It is committed to the use of freed intelligence as the method of directing change. In any case civilization is faced with the problem of uniting the changes that are going on into a coherent pattern of social organization. The liberal spirit is marked by its own picture of the pattern that is required: a social organization that will make possible effective liberty and opportunity for personal growth in mind and spirit in all individuals. Its present need is recognition that established material security is a prerequisite of the ends which it cherishes, so that, the basis of life being secure, individuals may actively share in the wealth of cultural resources that now exist and may contribute, each in his own way, to their further enrichment.

The fact of change has been so continual and so intense that it overwhelms our minds. We are bewildered by the spectacle of its rapidity, scope and intensity. It is not surprising that men have protected themselves from the impact of such vast change by resorting to what psychoanalysis has taught us to call rationalizations, in other words, protective fantasies. The Victorian idea that change is a part of an evolution that necessarily leads through successive stages to some preordained divine far-off event is one rationalization. The conception of a sudden, complete, almost catastrophic, transformation, to be brought about by the victory of the proletariat over the class now dominant, is a similar rationalization. But men have met the impact of change in the realm of actuality, mostly by drift and by temporary, usually incoherent, improvisations. Liberalism, like every other theory of life, has suffered from the state of confused uncertainty that is the lot of a world suffering from rapid and varied change for which there is no intellectual and moral preparation.

Because of this lack of mental and moral preparation the impact of swiftly moving changes produced, as I have just said, confusion, uncertainty and drift. Change in patterns of belief, desire and purpose has lagged behind the modification of the external conditions under which men associate. Industrial habits have changed most rapidly; there has followed at considerable distance, change in political relations; alterations in legal relations and methods have lagged even more, while changes in the institutions that deal most directly with patterns of thought and belief have taken place to the least extent. This fact defines the primary, though not by any means the ultimate, responsibility of a liberalism that intends to be a vital force. Its work is first of all education, in the broadest sense of that term. Schooling is a part of the work of education, but education in its full meaning includes all the influences that go to form the attitudes and dispositions (of desire as well as of belief), which constitute dominant habits of mind and character.

Let me mention three changes that have taken place in one of the institutions in which immense shifts have occurred, but that are still relatively external—external in the sense that the pattern of intelligent purpose and emotion has not been correspondingly modified. Civilization existed for most of human history in a state of scarcity in the material basis for a humane life. Our ways of thinking, planning and working have been attuned to this fact. Thanks to science and technology we now live in an age of potential plenty. The immediate effect of the emergence of the new possibility was simply to stimulate, to a point of incredible exaggeration, the striving for the material resources, called wealth, opened to men in the new vista. It is a characteristic of all development, physiological and mental, that when a new force and factor appears, it is first pushed to an extreme. Only when its possibilities have been exhausted (at least relatively) does it take its place in the life perspective. The economic-material phase of life, which belongs in the basal ganglia of society, has usurped for more than a century the cortex of the social body. The habits of desire and effort that were bred in the age of scarcity do not readily subordinate themselves and take the place of the matter-of-course routine that becomes appropriate to them when machines and impersonal power have the capacity to liberate man from bondage to the strivings that were once needed to make secure his physical basis. Even now when there is a vision of an age of abundance and when the vision is supported by hard fact, it is material security as an end that appeals to most rather than the way of living which this security makes possible. Men's minds are still pathetically held in the clutch of old habits and haunted by old memories.

For, in the second place, insecurity is the natural child and the foster child, too, of scarcity. Early liberalism emphasized the importance of insecurity as a fundamentally necessary economic motive, holding that without this goad men would not work, abstain or accumulate. Formulation of this conception was new. But the fact that was formulated was nothing new. It was deeply rooted in the habits that were formed in the long struggle against material scarcity. The system that goes by the name of capitalism is a systematic manifestation of desires and purposes built up in an age of ever threatening want and now carried over into a time of ever increasing potential plenty. The conditions that generate insecurity for the many no longer spring from nature. They are found in institutions and arrangements that are within deliberate human control. Surely this change marks one of the greatest revolutions that has taken place in all human history. Because of it, insecurity is not now the motive to work and sacrifice but to despair. It is not an instigation to put forth energy but to an impotency that can be converted from death into endurance only by charity. But the habits of mind and action that modify institutions to make potential abundance an actuality are still so inchoate that most of us discuss labels like individualism, socialism and communism instead of even perceiving the possibility, much less the necessity for realizing what can and should be.

In the third place, the patterns of belief and purpose that still dominate economic institutions were formed when individuals produced with their hands, alone or in small groups. The notion that society in general is served by the unplanned coincidence of the consequences of a vast multitude of efforts put forth by isolated individuals without reference to any social end, was also something new as a formulation. But it also formulated the working principle of an epoch which the advent of new forces of production was to bring to an end. It demands no great power of intelligence to see that under present conditions the isolated individual is well-nigh helpless. Concentration and corporate organization are the rule. But the concentration and corporate organization are still controlled in their operation by ideas that were institutionalized in eons of separate individual effort. The attempts at coöperation for mutual benefit that are put forth are precious as experimental moves. But that society itself should see to it that a coöperative industrial order be instituted, one that is consonant with the realities of production enforced by an era of machinery and power, is so novel an idea to the general mind that its mere suggestion is hailed with abusive epithets—sometimes with imprisonment.

When, then, I say that the first object of a renascent liberalism is education, I mean that its task is to aid in producing the habits of mind and character, the intellectual and moral patterns, that are somewhere near even with the actual movements of events. It is, I repeat, the split between the latter as they have externally occurred and the ways of desiring, thinking, and of putting emotion and purpose into execution that is the basic cause of present confusion in mind and paralysis in action. The educational task cannot be accomplished merely by working upon men's minds, without action that effects actual change in institutions. The idea that dispositions and attitudes can be altered by merely "moral" means conceived of as something that goes on wholly inside of persons is itself one of the old patterns that has to be changed. Thought, desire and purpose exist in a constant give and take of interaction with environing conditions. But resolute thought is the first step in that change of action that will itself carry further the needed change in patterns of mind and character.

In short, liberalism must now become radical, meaning by "radical" perception of the necessity of thorough-going changes in the set-up of institutions and corresponding activity to bring the changes to pass. For the gulf between what the actual situation makes possible and the actual state itself is so great that it cannot be bridged by piecemeal policies undertaken *ad hoc*. The process of producing the changes will be, in any case, a gradual one. But "reforms" that deal now with this abuse and now with that without having a social goal based upon an inclusive plan, differ entirely from effort at re-forming, in its literal sense, the institutional scheme of things. The liberals of more than a century ago were denounced in their time as subversive radicals, and only when the new economic order was established did they become apologists for the *status quo* or else content with social patchwork. If radicalism be defined as perception of need for radical change, then today any liberalism which is not also radicalism is irrelevant and doomed.

But radicalism also means, in the minds of many, both supporters and opponents, dependence upon use of violence as the main method of effecting drastic changes. Here the liberal parts company. For he is committed to the organization of intelligent action as the chief method. Any frank discussion of the issue must recognize the extent to which those who decry the use of any violence are themselves willing to resort to violence and are ready to put their will into operation. Their fundamental objection is to change in the economic institution that now exists, and for its maintenance they resort to the use of the force that is placed in their hands by this very institution. They do not need to advocate the use of force; their only need is to employ it. Force, rather than intelligence, is built into the procedures of the existing social system, regularly as coercion, in times of crisis as overt violence. The legal system, conspicuously in its penal aspect, more subtly in civil practice, rests upon coercion. Wars are the methods recurrently used in settlement of disputes between nations. One school of radicals dwells upon the fact that in the past the transfer of power in one society has either been accomplished by or attended with violence. But what we need to realize is that physical force is used, at least in the form of coercion, in the very set-up of our society. That the competitive system, which was thought of by early liberals as the means by which the latent abilities of individuals were to be evoked and directed into socially useful channels, is now in fact a state of scarcely disguised battle hardly needs to be dwelt upon. That the control of the means of production by the few in legal possession operates as a standing agency of coercion of the many, may need emphasis in statement, but is surely evident to one who is willing to observe and honestly report the existing scene. It is foolish to regard the political state as the only agency now endowed with coercive power. Its exercise of this power is pale in contrast with that exercised by concentrated and organized property interests.

It is not surprising in view of our standing dependence upon the use of coercive force that at every time of crisis coercion breaks out into open violence. In this country, with its tradition of violence fostered by frontier conditions and by the conditions under which immigration went on during the greater part of our history, resort to violence is especially recurrent on the part of those who are in power. In times of imminent change, our verbal and sentimental worship of the Constitution, with its guarantees of civil liberties of expression, publication and assemblage, readily goes overboard. Often the officials of the law are the worst offenders, acting as agents of some power that rules the economic life of a community. What is said about the value of free speech as a safety valve is then forgotten with the utmost of ease: a comment, perhaps, upon the weakness of the defense of freedom of expression that values it simply as a means of blowing-off steam.

It is not pleasant to face the extent to which, as matter of fact, coercive and violent force is relied upon in the present social system as a means of social control. It is much more agreeable to evade the fact. But unless the fact is acknowledged as a fact in its full depth and breadth, the meaning of dependence upon intelligence as the alternative method of social direction will not be grasped. Failure in acknowledgment signifies, among other things, failure to realize that those who propagate the dogma of dependence upon force have the sanction of much that is already entrenched in the existing system. They would but turn the use of it to opposite ends. The assumption that the method of intelligence already rules and that those who urge the use of violence are introducing a new element into the social picture may not be hypocritical but it is unintelligently unaware of what is actually involved in intelligence as an alternative method of social action.

I begin with an example of what is really involved in the issue. Why is it, apart from our tradition of violence, that liberty of expression is tolerated and even lauded when social affairs seem to be going in a quiet fashion, and yet is so readily destroyed whenever matters grow critical? The general answer, of course, is that at bottom social institutions have habituated us to the use of force in some veiled form. But a part of the answer is found in our ingrained habit of regarding intelligence as an individual possession and its exercise as an individual right. It is false that freedom of inquiry and of expression are not modes of action. They are exceedingly potent modes of action. The reactionary grasps this fact, in practice if not in express idea, more quickly than the liberal, who is too much given to holding that this freedom is innocent of consequences, as well as being a merely individual right. The result is that this liberty is tolerated as long as it does not seem to menace in any way the *status quo* of society. When it does, every effort is put forth to identify the established order with the public good. When this identification is established, it follows that any merely individual right must yield to the general welfare. As long as freedom of thought and speech is claimed as a merely individual right, it will give way, as do other merely personal claims, when it is, or is successfully represented to be, in opposition to the general welfare.

I would not in the least disparage the noble fight waged by early liberals in behalf of individual freedom of thought and expression. We owe more to them than it is possible to record in words. No more eloquent words have ever come from any one than those of Justice Brandeis in the case of a legislative act that in fact restrained freedom of political expression. He said: "Those who won our independence believed that the final end of the State was to make men free to develop their faculties, and that in its government the deliberative faculties should prevail over the arbitrary. They valued liberty both as an end and as a means. They believed liberty to be the secret of happiness and courage to be the secret of liberty. They believed that freedom to think as you will and to speak as you think are means indispensable to the discovery and spread of political truth; that without free speech and assembly discussion would be futile; that with them, discussion affords ordinarily adequate protection against the dissemination of noxious doctrines; that the greatest menace to freedom is an inert people; that public discussion is a political duty; and that this should be a fundamental principle of the American government." This is the creed of a fighting liberalism. But the issue I am raising is connected with the fact that these words are found in a dissenting, a minority opinion of the Supreme Court of the United States. The public function of free individual thought and speech is clearly recognized in the words quoted. But the reception of the truth of the words is met by an obstacle: the old habit of defending liberty of thought and expression as something inhering in individuals apart from and even in opposition to social claims.

Liberalism has to assume the responsibility for making it clear that intelligence is a social asset and is clothed with a function as public as is its origin, in the concrete, in social coöperation. It was Comte who, in reaction against the purely individualistic ideas that seemed to him to underlie the French Revolution, said that in mathematics, physics and astronomy there is no right of private conscience. If we remove the statement from the context of actual scientific procedure, it is dangerous because it is false. The individual inquirer has not only the right but the duty to criticize the ideas, theories and "laws" that are current in science. But if we take the statement in the context of scientific method, it indicates that he carries on this criticism in virtue of a socially generated body of knowledge and by means of methods that are not of private origin and possession. He uses a method that retains public validity even when innovations are introduced in its use and application.

Henry George, speaking of ships that ply the ocean with a velocity of five or six hundred miles a day, remarked, "There is nothing whatever to show that the men who today build and navigate and use such ships are one whit superior in any physical or mental quality to their ancestors, whose best vessel was a coracle of wicker and hide. The enormous improvement which these ships show is not an improvement of human nature; it is an improvement of society—it is due to a wider and fuller union of individual efforts in accomplishment of common ends." This single instance, duly pondered, gives a better idea of the nature of intelligence and its social office than would a volume of abstract dissertation. Consider merely two of the factors that enter in and their social consequences. Consider what is involved in the production of steel, from the first use of fire and then the crude smelting of ore, to the processes that now effect the mass production of steel. Consider also the development of the power of guiding ships across trackless wastes from the day when they hugged the shore, steering by visible sun and stars, to the appliances that now enable a sure course to be taken. It would require a heavy tome to describe the advances in science, in mathematics, astronomy, physics, chemistry, that have made these two things possible. The record would be an account of a vast multitude of coöperative efforts, in which one individual uses the results provided for him by a countless number of other individuals, and uses them so as to add to the common and public store. A survey of such facts brings home the actual social character of intelligence as it actually develops and makes its way. Survey of the consequences upon the ways of living of individuals and upon the terms on which men associate together, due to the new method of transportation would take us to the wheat farmer of the prairies, the cattle raiser of the plains, the cotton grower of the South; into a multitude of mills and factories, and to the counting-room of banks, and what would be seen in this country would be repeated in every country of the globe.

It is to such things as these, rather than to abstract and formal psychology that we must go if we would learn the nature of intelligence: in itself, in its origin and development, and its uses and consequences. At this point, I should like to recur to an idea put forward in the preceding chapter. I then referred to the contempt often expressed for reliance upon intelligence as a social method, and I said this scorn is due to the identification of intelligence with native endowments of individuals. In contrast to this notion, I spoke of the power of individuals to appropriate and respond to the intelligence, the knowledge, ideas and purposes that have been integrated in the medium in which individuals live. Each of us knows, for example, some mechanic of ordinary native capacity who is intelligent within the matters of his calling. He has lived in an environment in which the cumulative intelligence of a multitude of coöperating individuals is embodied, and by the use of his native capacities he makes some phase of this intelligence his own. Given a social medium in whose institutions the available knowledge, ideas and art of humanity were incarnate, and the average individual would rise to undreamed heights of social and political intelligence.

The rub, the problem is found in the proviso. Can the intelligence actually existent and potentially available be embodied in that institutional medium in which an individual thinks, desires and acts? Before dealing directly with this question, I wish to say something about the operation of intelligence in our present political institutions, as exemplified by current practices of democratic government. I would not minimize the advance scored in substitution of methods of discussion and conference for the method of arbitrary rule. But the better is too often the enemy of the still better. Discussion, as the manifestation of intelligence in political life, stimulates publicity; by its means sore spots are brought to light that would otherwise remain hidden. It affords opportunity for promulgation of new ideas. Compared with despotic rule, it is an invitation to individuals to concern themselves with public affairs. But discussion and dialectic, however indispensable they are to the elaboration of ideas and policies after ideas are once put forth, are weak reeds to depend upon for systematic origination of comprehensive plans, the plans that are required if the problem of social organization is to be met. There was a time when discussion, the comparison of ideas already current so as to purify and clarify them, was thought to be sufficient in discovery of the structure and laws of physical nature. In the latter field, the method was displaced by that of experimental observation guided by comprehensive working hypotheses, and using all the resources made available by mathematics.

But we still depend upon the method of discussion, with only incidental scientific control, in politics. Our system of popular suffrage, immensely valuable as it is in comparison with what preceded it, exhibits the idea that intelligence is an individualistic possession, at best enlarged by public discussion. Existing political practice, with its complete ignoring of occupational groups and the organized knowledge and purposes that are involved in the existence of such groups, manifests a dependence upon a summation of individuals quantitatively, similar to Bentham's purely quantitative formula of the greatest sum of pleasures of the greatest possible number. The formation of parties or, as the eighteenth-century writers called them, factions, and the system of party government is the practically necessary counterweight to a numerical and atomistic individualism. The idea that the conflict of parties will, by means of public discussion, bring out necessary public truths is a kind of political watered-down version of the Hegelian dialectic, with its synthesis arrived at by a union of antithetical conceptions. The method has nothing in common with the procedure of organized coöperative inquiry which has won the triumphs of science in the field of physical nature.

Intelligence in politics when it is identified with discussion means reliance upon symbols. The invention of language is probably the greatest single invention achieved by humanity. The development of political forms that promote the use of symbols in place of arbitrary power was another great invention. The nineteenth-century establishment of parliamentary institutions, written constitutions and the suffrage as means of political rule, is a tribute to the power of symbols. But symbols are significant only in connection with realities behind them. No intelligent observer can deny, I think, that they are often used in party politics as a substitute for realities instead of as means of contact with them. Popular literacy, in connection with the telegraph, cheap postage and the printing press, has enormously multiplied the number of those influenced. That which we term education has done a good deal to generate habits that put symbols in the place of realities. The forms of popular government make necessary the elaborate use of words to influence political action. "Propaganda" is the inevitable consequence of the combination of these influences and it extends to every area of life. Words not only take the place of realities but are themselves debauched. Decline in the prestige of suffrage and of parliamentary government are intimately associated with the belief, manifest in practice even if not expressed in words, that intelligence is an individual possession to be reached by means of verbal persuasion.

This fact suggests, by way of contrast, the genuine meaning of intelligence in connection with public opinion, sentiment and action. The crisis in democracy demands the substitution of the intelligence that is exemplified in scientific procedure for the kind of intelligence that is now accepted. The need for this change is not exhausted in the demand for greater honesty and impartiality, even though these qualities be now corrupted by discussion carried on mainly for purposes of party supremacy and for imposition of some special but concealed interest. These qualities need to be restored. But the need goes further. The social use of intelligence would remain deficient even if these moral traits were exalted, and yet intelligence continued to be identified simply with discussion and persuasion, necessary as are these things. Approximation to use of scientific method in investigation and of the engineering mind in the invention and projection of far-reaching social plans is demanded. The habit of considering social realities in terms of cause and effect and social policies in terms of means and consequences is still inchoate. The contrast between the state of intelligence in politics and in the physical control of nature is to be taken literally. What has happened in this latter is the outstanding demonstration of the meaning of organized intelligence. The combined effect of science and technology has released more productive energies in a bare hundred years than stands to the credit of prior human history in its entirety. Productively it has multiplied nine million times in the last generation alone. The prophetic vision of Francis Bacon of subjugation of the energies of nature through change in methods of inquiry has well-nigh been realized. The stationary engine, the locomotive, the dynamo, the motor car, turbine, telegraph, telephone, radio and moving picture are not the products of either isolated individual minds nor of the particular economic régime called capitalism. They are the fruit of methods that first penetrated to the working causalities of nature and then utilized the resulting knowledge in bold imaginative ventures of invention and construction.

We hear a great deal in these days about class conflict. The past history of man is held up to us as almost exclusively a record of struggles between classes, ending in the victory of a class that had been oppressed and the transfer of power to it. It is difficult to avoid reading the past in terms of the contemporary scene. Indeed, fundamentally it is impossible to avoid this course. With a certain proviso, it is highly important that we are compelled to follow this path. For the past as past is gone, save for esthetic enjoyment and refreshment, while the present is with us. Knowledge of the past is significant only as it deepens and extends our understanding of the present. Yet there is a proviso. We must grasp the things that are most important in the present when we turn to the past and not allow ourselves to be misled by secondary phenomena no matter how intense and immediately urgent they are. Viewed from this standpoint, the rise of scientific method and of technology based upon it is the genuinely active force in producing the vast complex of changes the world is now undergoing, not the class struggle whose spirit and method are opposed to science. If we lay hold upon the causal force exercised by this embodiment of intelligence we shall know where to turn for the means of directing further change.

When I say that scientific method and technology have been the active force in producing the revolutionary transformations society is undergoing, I do not imply no other forces have been at work to arrest, deflect and corrupt their operation. Rather this fact is positively implied. At this point, indeed, is located the conflict that underlies the confusions and uncertainties of the present scene. The conflict is between institutions and habits originating in the pre-scientific and pre-technological age and the new forces generated by science and technology. The application of science, to a considerable degree, even its own growth, has been conditioned by the system to which the name of capitalism is given, a rough designation of a complex of political and legal arrangements centering about a particular mode of economic relations. Because of the conditioning of science and technology by this setting, the second and humanly most important part of Bacon's prediction has so far largely missed realization. The conquest of natural energies has not accrued to the betterment of the common human estate in anything like the degree he anticipated.

Because of conditions that were set by the legal institutions and the moral ideas existing when the scientific and industrial revolutions came into being, the chief usufruct of the latter has been appropriated by a relatively small class. Industrial entrepreneurs have reaped out of all proportion to what they sowed. By obtaining private ownership of the means of production and exchange they deflected a considerable share of the results of increased productivity to their private pockets. This appropriation was not the fruit of criminal conspiracy or of sinister intent. It was sanctioned not only by legal institutions of age-long standing but by the entire prevailing moral code. The institution of private property long antedated feudal times. It is the institution with which men have lived, with few exceptions, since the dawn of civilization. Its existence has deeply impressed itself upon mankind's moral conceptions. Moreover, the new industrial forces tended to break down many of the rigid class barriers that had been in force, and to give to millions a new outlook and inspire a new hope;—especially in this country with no feudal background and no fixed class system.

Since the legal institutions and the patterns of mind characteristic of ages of civilization still endure, there exists the conflict that brings confusion into every phase of present life. The problem of bringing into being a new social orientation and organization is, when reduced to its ultimates, the problem of using the new resources of production, made possible by the advance of physical science, for social ends, for what Bentham called the greatest good of the greatest number. Institutional relationships fixed in the pre-scientific age stand in the way of accomplishing this great transformation. Lag in mental and moral patterns provides the bulwark of the older institutions; in expressing the past they still express present beliefs, outlooks and purposes. Here is the place where the problem of liberalism centers today.

The argument drawn from past history that radical change must be effected by means of class struggle, culminating in open war, fails to discriminate between the two forces, one active, the other resistant and deflecting, that have produced the social scene in which we live. The active force is, as I have said, scientific method and technological application. The opposite force is that of older institutions and the habits that have grown up around them. Instead of discrimination between forces and distribution of their consequences, we find the two things lumped together. The compound is labeled the capitalistic or the bourgeois class, and to this class as a class is imputed all the important features of present industrialized society—much as the defenders of the régime of economic liberty exercised for private property are accustomed to attribute every improvement made in the last century and a half to the same capitalistic régime. Thus in orthodox communist literature, from the Communist Manifesto of 1848 to the present day, we are told that the bourgeoisie, the name for a distinctive class, has done this and that. It has, so it is said, given a cosmopolitan character to production and consumption; has destroyed the national basis of industry; has agglomerated population in urban centers; has transferred power from the country to the city, in the process of creating colossal productive force, its chief achievement. In addition, it has created crises of ever renewed intensity; has created imperialism of a new type in frantic effort to control raw materials and markets. Finally, it has created a new class, the proletariat, and has created it as a class having a common interest opposed to that of the bourgeoisie, and is giving an irresistible stimulus to its organization, first as a class and then as a political power. According to the economic version of the Hegelian dialectic, the bourgeois class is thus creating its own complete and polar opposite, and this in time will end the old power and rule. The class struggle of veiled civil war will finally burst into open revolution and the result will be either the common ruin of the contending parties or a revolutionary reconstitution of society at large through a transfer of power from one class to another.

The position thus sketched unites vast sweep with great simplicity. I am concerned with it here only as far as it emphasizes the idea of a struggle between classes, culminating in open and violent warfare as being the method for production of radical social change. For, be it noted, the issue is not whether some amount of violence will accompany the effectuation of radical change of institutions. The question is whether force or intelligence is to be the method upon which we consistently rely and to whose promotion we devote our energies. Insistence that the use of violent force is *inevitable* limits the use of available intelligence, for wherever the inevitable reigns intelligence cannot be used. Commitment to inevitability is always the fruit of dogma; intelligence does not pretend to *know* save as a result of experimentation, the opposite of preconceived dogma. Moreover, acceptance in advance of the inevitability of violence tends to produce the use of violence in cases where peaceful methods might otherwise avail. The curious fact is that while it is generally admitted that this and that particular social problem, say of the family, or railroads or banking, must be solved, if at all, by the method of intelligence, yet there is supposed to be some one all-inclusive social problem which can be solved only by the use of violence. This fact would be inexplicable were it not a conclusion from dogma as its premise.

It is frequently asserted that the method of experimental intelligence can be applied to physical facts because physical nature does not present conflicts of class interests, while it is inapplicable to society because the latter is so deeply marked by incompatible interests. It is then assumed that the "experimentalist" is one who has chosen to ignore the uncomfortable fact of conflicting interests. Of course, there *are* conflicting interests; otherwise there would be no social problems. The problem under discussion is precisely *how* conflicting claims are to be settled in the interest of the widest possible contribution to the interests of all—or at least of the great majority. The method of democracy—inasfar as it is that of organized intelligence—is to bring these conflicts out into the open where their special claims can be seen and appraised, where they can be discussed and judged in the light of more inclusive interests than are represented by either of them separately. There is, for example, a clash of interests between munition manufacturers and most of the rest of the population. The more the respective claims of the two are publicly and scientifically weighed, the more likely it is that the public interest will be disclosed and be made effective. There is an undoubted objective clash of interests between finance-capitalism that controls the means of production and whose profit is served by maintaining relative scarcity, and idle workers and hungry consumers. But what generates violent strife is failure to bring the conflict into the light of intelligence where the conflicting interests can be adjudicated in behalf of the interest of the great majority. Those most committed to the dogma of inevitable force recognize the need for intelligently discovering and expressing the dominant social interest up to a certain point and then draw back. The "experimentalist" is one who would see to it that the method depended upon by all in some degree in every democratic community be followed through to completion.

In spite of the existence of class conflicts, amounting at times to veiled civil war, any one habituated to the use of the method of science will view with considerable suspicion the erection of actual human beings into fixed entities called classes, having no overlapping interests and so internally unified and externally separated that they are made the protagonists of history—itself hypothetical. Such an idea of classes is a survival of a rigid logic that once prevailed in the sciences of nature, but that no longer has any place there. This conversion of abstractions into entities smells more of a dialectic of concepts than of a realistic examination of facts, even though it makes more of an emotional appeal to many than do the results of the latter. To say that all past historic social progress has been the result of coöperation and not of conflict would be also an exaggeration. But exaggeration against exaggeration, it is the more reasonable of the two. And it is no exaggeration to say that the measure of civilization is the degree in which the method of coöperative intelligence replaces the method of brute conflict.

But the point I am especially concerned with just here is the indiscriminate lumping together as a single force of two different things—the results of scientific technology and of a legal system of property relations. It is science and technology that have had the revolutionary social effect while the legal system has been the relatively static element. According to the Marxians themselves, the economic foundations of society consist of two things, the forces of production on one side and, on the other side, the social relations of production, that is, the legal property system under which the former operates. The latter lags behind, and "revolutions" are produced by the power of the forces of production to change the system of institutional relations. But what are the modern forces of production save those of scientific technology? And what is scientific technology save a large-scale demonstration of organized intelligence in action?

It is quite true that what is happening socially is the result of the combination of the two factors, one dynamic, the other relatively static. If we choose to call the combination by the name of capitalism, then it is true, or a truism, that capitalism is the "cause" of all the important social changes that have occurred—an argument that the representatives of capitalism are eager to put forward whenever the increase of productivity is in question. But if we want to *understand*, and not just to paste labels, unfavorable or favorable as the case may be, we shall certainly begin and end with discrimination. Colossal increase in productivity, the bringing of men together in cities and large factories, the elimination of distance, the accumulation of capital, fixed and liquid—these things would have come about, at a certain stage, no matter what the established institutional system. They are the consequence of the new means of technological production. Certain other things have happened because of inherited institutions and the habits of belief and character that accompany and support them. If we begin at this point, we shall see that the release of productivity is the product of coöperatively organized intelligence, and shall also see that the institutional framework is precisely that which is not subjected as yet, in any considerable measure, to the impact of inventive and constructive intelligence. That coercion and oppression on a large scale exist, no honest person can deny. But these things are not the product of science and technology but of the perpetuation of old institutions and patterns untouched by scientific method. The inference to be drawn is clear.

The argument, drawn from history, that great social changes have been effected only by violent means, needs considerable qualification, in view of the vast scope of changes that are taking place without the use of violence. But even if it be admitted to hold of the past, the conclusion that violence is the method now to be depended upon does not follow—unless one is committed to a dogmatic philosophy of history. The radical who insists that the future method of change must be like that of the past has much in common with the hide-bound reactionary who holds to the past as an ultimate fact. Both overlook the *fact that history in being a process of change generates change not only in details but also in the method of directing social change.* I recur to what I said at the beginning of this chapter. It is true that the social order is largely conditioned by the use of coercive force, bursting at times into open violence. But what is also true is that mankind now has in its possession a new method, that of coöperative and experimental science which expresses the method of intelligence. I should be meeting dogmatism with dogmatism if I asserted that the existence of this historically new factor completely invalidates all arguments drawn from the effect of force in the past. But it is within the bounds of reason to assert that the presence of this social factor demands that the present situation be analyzed on its own terms, and not be rigidly subsumed under fixed conceptions drawn from the past.

Any analysis made in terms of the present situation will not fail to note one fact that militates powerfully against arguments drawn from past use of violence. Modern warfare is destructive beyond anything known in older times. This increased destructiveness is due primarily, of course, to the fact that science has raised to a new pitch of destructive power all the agencies of armed hostility. But it is also due to the much greater interdependence of all the elements of society. The bonds that hold modern communities and states together are as delicate as they are numerous. The self-sufficiency and independence of a local community, characteristic of more primitive societies, have disappeared in every highly industrialized country. The gulf that once separated the civilian population from the military has virtually gone. War involves paralysis of all normal social activities, and not merely the meeting of armed forces in the field. The Communist Manifesto presented two alternatives: *either* the revolutionary change and transfer of power to the proletariat, *or* the common ruin of the contending parties. Today, the civil war that would be adequate to effect transfer of power and a reconstitution of society at large, as understood by official Communists, would seem to present but one possible consequence: the ruin of all parties and the destruction of civilized life. This fact alone is enough to lead us to consider the potentialities of the method of intelligence.

The argument for putting chief dependence upon violence as the method of effecting radical change is, moreover, usually put in a way that proves altogether too much for its own case. It is said that the dominant economic class has all the agencies of power in its hands, directly the army, militia and police; indirectly, the courts, schools, press and radio. I shall not stop to analyze this statement. But if one admits it to be valid, the conclusion to be drawn is surely the folly of resorting to a use of force against force that is so well intrenched. The positive conclusion that emerges is that conditions that would promise success in the case of use of force are such as to make possible great change without any great recourse to such a method.[1]

Those who uphold the necessity of dependence upon violence usually much oversimplify the case by setting up a disjunction they regard as self-evident. They say that the sole alternative is putting our trust in parliamentary procedures as they now exist. This isolation of law-making from other social forces and agencies that are constantly operative is wholly unrealistic. Legislatures and congresses do not exist in a vacuum—not even the judges on the bench live in completely secluded sound-proof chambers. The assumption that it is possible for

---

[1] It should be noted that Marx himself was not completely committed to the dogma of the inevitability of force as the means of effecting revolutionary changes in the system of "social relations." For at one time he contemplated that the change might occur in Great Britain and the United States, and possibly in Holland, by peaceful means.

the constitution and activities of law-making bodies to persist unchanged while society itself is undergoing great change is an exercise in verbal formal logic.

It is true that in this country, because of the interpretations made by courts of a written constitution, our political institutions are unusually inflexible. It is also true, as well as even more important (because it is a factor in causing this rigidity) that our institutions, democratic in form, tend to favor in substance a privileged plutocracy. Nevertheless, it is sheer defeatism to assume in advance of actual trial that democratic political institutions are incapable either of further development or of constructive social application. Even as they now exist, the forms of representative government are potentially capable of expressing the public will when that assumes anything like unification. And there is nothing inherent in them that forbids their supplementation by political agencies that represent definitely economic social interests, like those of producers and consumers.

The final argument in behalf of the use of intelligence is that as are the means used so are the actual ends achieved—that is, the consequences. I know of no greater fallacy than the claim of those who hold to the dogma of the necessity of brute force that this use will be the method of calling genuine democracy into existence—of which they profess themselves the simon-pure adherents. It requires an unusually credulous faith in the Hegelian dialectic of opposites to think that all of a sudden the use of force by a class will be transmuted into a democratic classless society. Force breeds counter-force; the Newtonian law of action and reaction still holds in physics, and violence is physical. To profess democracy as an ultimate ideal and the suppression of democracy as a means to the ideal may be possible in a country that has never known even rudimentary democracy, but when professed in a country that has anything of a genuine democratic spirit in its traditions, it signifies desire for possession and retention of power by a class, whether that class be called Fascist or Proletarian. In the light of what happens in non-democratic countries, it is pertinent to ask whether the rule of a class signifies the dictatorship of the majority, or dictatorship over the chosen class by a minority party; whether dissenters are allowed even within the class the party claims to represent; and whether the development of literature and the other arts proceeds according to a formula prescribed by a party in conformity with a doctrinaire dogma of history and of infallible leadership, or whether artists are free from regimentation? Until these questions are satisfactorily answered, it is permissible to look with considerable suspicion upon those who assert that suppression of democracy is the road to the adequate establishment of genuine democracy. The one exception—and that apparent rather than real—to dependence upon organized intelligence as the method for directing social change is found when society through an authorized majority has entered upon the path of social experimentation leading to great social change, and a minority refuses by force to permit the method of intelligent action to go into effect. Then force may be intelligently employed to subdue and disarm the recalcitrant minority.

There may be some who think I am unduly dignifying a position held by a comparatively small group by taking their arguments as seriously as I have done. But their position serves to bring into strong relief the alternatives before us. It makes clear the meaning of renascent liberalism. The alternatives are continuation of drift with attendant improvisations to meet special emergencies; dependence upon violence; dependence upon socially organized intelligence. The first two alternatives, however, are not mutually exclusive, for if things are allowed to drift the result may be some sort of social change effected by the use of force, whether so planned or not. Upon the whole, the recent policy of liberalism has been to further "social legislation"; that is, measures which add performance of social services to the older functions of government. The value of this addition is not to be despised. It marks a decided move away from *laissez faire* liberalism, and has considerable importance in educating the public mind to a realization of the possibilities of organized social control. It has helped to develop some of the techniques that in any case will be needed in a socialized economy. But the cause of liberalism will be lost for a considerable period if it is not prepared to go further and socialize the forces of production, now at hand, so that the liberty of individuals will be supported by the very structure of economic organization.

The ultimate place of economic organization in human life is to assure the secure basis for an ordered expression of individual capacity and for the satisfaction of the needs of man in non-economic directions. The effort of mankind in connection with material production belongs, as I said earlier, among interests and activities that are, relatively speaking, routine in character, "routine" being defined as that which, without absorbing attention and energy, provides a constant basis for liberation of the values of intellectual, esthetic and companionship life. Every significant religious and moral teacher and prophet has asserted that the material is instrumental to the good life. Nominally at least, this idea is accepted by every civilized community. The transfer of the burden of material production from human muscles and brain to steam, electricity and chemical processes now makes possible the effective actualization of this ideal. Needs, wants and desires are always the moving force in generating creative action. When these wants are compelled by force of conditions to be directed for the most part, among the mass of mankind, into obtaining the means of subsistence, what should be a means becomes perforce an end in itself. Up to the present the new mechanical forces of production, which are the means of emancipation from this state of affairs, have been employed to intensify and exaggerate the reversal of the true relation between means and ends. Humanly speaking, I do not see how it would have been possible to avoid an epoch having this character. But its perpetuation is the cause of the continually growing social chaos and strife. Its termination cannot be effected by preaching to individuals that they should place spiritual ends above material means. It can be brought about by organized social reconstruction that puts the results of the mechanism of abundance at the free disposal of individuals. The actual corrosive "materialism" of our times does not proceed from science. It springs from the notion, sedulously cultivated by the class in power, that the creative capacities of individuals can be evoked and developed only in a struggle for material possessions and material gain. We either should surrender our professed belief in the supremacy of ideal and spiritual values and accommodate our beliefs to the predominant material orientation, or we should through organized endeavor institute the socialized economy of material security and plenty that will release human energy for pursuit of higher values.

Since liberation of the capacities of individuals for free, self-initiated expression is an essential part of the creed of liberalism, liberalism that is sincere must will the means that condition the achieving of its ends. Regimentation of material and mechanical forces is the only way by which the mass of individuals can be released from regimentation and consequent suppression of their cultural possibilities. The eclipse of liberalism is due to the fact that it has not faced the alternatives and adopted the means upon which realization of its professed aims depends. Liberalism can be true to its ideals only as it takes the course that leads to their attainment. The notion that organized social control of economic forces lies outside the historic path of liberalism shows that liberalism is still impeded by remnants of its earlier *laissez faire* phase, with its opposition of society and the individual. The thing which now dampens liberal ardor and paralyzes its efforts is the conception that liberty and development of individuality as ends exclude the use of organized social effort as means. Earlier liberalism regarded the separate and competing economic action of individuals as the means to social well-being as the end. We must reverse the perspective and see that socialized economy is the means of free individual development as the end.

That liberals are divided in outlook and endeavor while reactionaries are held together by community of interests and the ties of custom is well-nigh a commonplace. Organization of standpoint and belief among liberals can be achieved only in and by unity of endeavor. Organized unity of action attended by consensus of beliefs will come about in the degree in which social control of economic forces is made the goal of liberal action. The greatest educational power, the greatest force in shaping the dispositions and attitudes of individuals, is the social medium in which they live. The medium that now lies closest to us is that of unified action for the inclusive end of a socialized economy. The attainment of a state of society in which a basis of material security will release the powers of individuals for cultural expression is not the work of a day. But by concentrating upon the task of securing a socialized economy as the ground and medium for release of the impulses and capacities men agree to call ideal, the now scattered and often conflicting activities of liberals can be brought to effective unity.

It is no part of my task to outline in detail a program for renascent liberalism. But the question of "what is to be done" cannot be ignored. Ideas must be organized, and this organization implies an organization of individuals who hold these ideas and whose faith is ready to translate itself into action. Translation into action signifies that the general creed of liberalism be formulated as a concrete program of action. It is in organization for action that liberals are weak, and without this organization there is danger that democratic ideals may go by default. Democracy has been a fighting faith. When its ideals are reënforced by those of scientific method and experimental intelligence, it cannot be that it is incapable of evoking discipline, ardor and organization. To narrow the issue for the future to a struggle between Fascism and Communism is to invite a catastrophe that may carry civilization down in the struggle. Vital and courageous democratic liberalism is the one force that can surely avoid such a disastrous narrowing of the issue. I for one do not believe that Americans living in the tradition of Jefferson and Lincoln will weaken and give up without a whole-hearted effort to make democracy a living reality. This, I repeat, involves organization.

The question cannot be answered by argument. Experimental method means experiment, and the question can be answered only by trying, by organized effort. The reasons for making the trial are not abstract or recondite. They are found in the confusion, uncertainty and conflict that mark the modern world. The reasons for thinking that the effort if made will be successful are also not abstract and remote. They lie in what the method of experimental and coöperative intelligence has already accomplished in subduing to potential human use the energies of physical nature. In material production, the method of intelligence is now the established rule; to abandon it would be to revert to savagery. The task is to go on, and not backward, until the method of intelligence and experimental control is the rule in social relations and social direction. Either we take this road or we admit that the problem of social organization in behalf of human liberty and the flowering of human capacities is insoluble.

It would be fantastic folly to ignore or to belittle the obstacles that stand in the way. But what has taken place, also against great odds, in the scientific and industrial revolutions, is an accomplished fact; the way is marked out. It may be that the way will remain untrodden. If so, the future holds the menace of confusion moving into chaos, a chaos that will be externally masked for a time by an organization of force, coercive and violent, in which the liberties of men will all but disappear. Even so, the cause of the liberty of the human spirit, the cause of opportunity of human beings for full development of their powers, the cause for which liberalism enduringly stands, is too precious and too ingrained in the human constitution to be forever obscured. Intelligence after millions of years of errancy has found itself as a method, and it will not be lost forever in the blackness of night. The business of liberalism is to bend every energy and exhibit every courage so that these precious goods may not even be temporarily lost but be intensified and expanded here and now.

41. The Problem of Freedom*

Under the influence of recent work in anthropology, Dewey focuses on "culture" as the locus for an understanding of a series of social and political problems. He comments that "it is at least as true that the state of culture determines the order and arrangement of native tendencies as that human

* From John Dewey, *Freedom and Culture* (New York, Capricorn Books, 1963) (1939), pp. 3-23. Reprinted by permission of G. P. Putnam's Sons.

nature produces any particular set or system of social phenomena so as to obtain satisfaction for itself."

With this judgment in mind, Dewey analyzes the difficulties facing those who wish to write about the problem of freedom. If the meaning of freedom, as of other significant concerns, is inseparable from the anticipations, rejections, and projections of an individual culture, then nothing less than a full-scale cultural anthropology will be adequate as a backdrop to the inquiry. The Greeks referred to this cultural context as *paideia*, interpreted here simply as the way in which people came to a shared consciousness. Although a reading of the full text of *Freedom and Culture*, as well as other works by Dewey, is necessary to grasp his version of an American *paideia*, this selection and the one following provide some methodological suggestions as to his procedure.

What is freedom and why is it prized? Is desire for freedom inherent in human nature or is it a product of special circumstances? Is it wanted as an end or as a means of getting other things? Does its possession entail responsibilities, and are these responsibilities so onerous that the mass of men will readily surrender liberty for the sake of greater ease? Is the struggle for liberty so arduous that most men are easily distracted from the endeavor to achieve and maintain it? Does freedom in itself and in the things it brings with it seem as important as security of livelihood; as food, shelter, clothing, or even as having a good time? Did man ever care as much for it as we in this country have been taught to believe? Is there any truth in the old notion that the driving force in political history has been the effort of the common man to achieve freedom? Was our own struggle for political independence in any genuine sense animated by desire for freedom, or were there a number of discomforts that our ancestors wanted to get rid of, things having nothing in common save that they were felt to be troublesome?

Is love of liberty ever anything more than a desire to be liberated from some special restriction? And when it is got rid of does the desire for liberty die down until something else feels intolerable? Again, how does the desire for freedom compare in intensity with the desire to feel equal with others, especially with those who have previously been called superiors? How do the fruits of liberty compare with the enjoyments that spring from a feeling of union, of solidarity, with others? Will men surrender their liberties if they believe that by so doing they will obtain the satisfaction that comes from a sense of fusion with others and that respect by others which is the product of the strength furnished by solidarity?

The present state of the world is putting questions like these to citizens of all democratic countries. It is putting them with special force to us in a country where democratic institutions have been bound up with a certain tradition, the "ideology" of which the Declaration of Independence is the classic expression. This tradition has taught us that attainment of freedom is the goal of political history; that self-government is the inherent right of free men and is that which, when it is achieved, men prize above all else. Yet as we look at the world we see supposedly free institutions in many countries not so much overthrown as abandoned willingly, apparently with enthusiasm. We may infer that what has happened is proof they never existed in reality but only in name. Or we may console ourselves with a belief that unusual conditions, such as national frustration and humiliation, have led men to welcome any kind of government that promised to restore national self-respect. But conditions in our country as well as the eclipse of democracy in other countries compel us to ask questions about the career and fate of free societies, even our own.

There perhaps was a time when the questions asked would have seemed to be mainly or exclusively political. Now we know better. For we know that a large part of the causes which have produced the conditions that are expressed in the questions is the dependence of politics upon other forces, notably the economic. The problem of the constitution of human nature is involved, since it is part of our tradition that love of freedom is inherent in its make-up. Is the popular psychology of democracy a myth? The old doctrine about human nature was also tied up with the ethical belief that political democracy is a moral right and that the laws upon which it is based are fundamental moral laws which every form of social organization should obey. If belief in natural rights and natural laws as the foundation of free government is surrendered, does the latter have any other moral basis? For while it would be foolish to believe that the American colonies fought the battles that secured their independence and that they built their government consciously and deliberately upon a foundation of psychological and moral theories, yet the democratic tradition, call it dream or call it penetrating vision, was so closely allied with beliefs about human nature and about the moral ends which political institutions should serve, that a rude shock occurs when these affiliations break down. Is there anything to take their place, anything that will give the kind of support they once gave?

The problems behind the questions asked, the forces which give the questions their urgency, go beyond the particular beliefs which formed the early psychological and moral foundation of democracy. After retiring from public office, Thomas Jefferson in his old age carried on a friendly philosophical correspondence with John Adams. In one of his letters he made a statement about existing American conditions and expressed a hope about their future estate: "The advance of liberalism encourages a hope that the human mind will some day get back to the freedom it enjoyed two thousand years ago. This country, which has given to the world the example of physical liberty, owes to it that of moral emancipation also, for as yet it is but nominal with us. The inquisition of public opinion overwhelms in practice the freedom asserted by the laws in theory." The situation that has developed since his time may well lead us to reverse the ideas he expressed, and inquire whether political freedom can be maintained without that freedom of culture which he expected to be the final result of political freedom. It is no longer easy to entertain the hope that given political freedom as the one thing necessary all other things will in time be added to it—and so to us. For we now know that the relations which exist between persons, outside of political institutions, relations of industry, of communication, of science, art and religion, affect daily associations, and thereby deeply affect the attitudes and habits expressed in government and rules of law. If it is true that the political and legal react to shape the other things, it is even more true that political institutions are an effect, not a cause.

It is this knowledge that sets the theme to be discussed. For this complex of conditions which taxes the terms upon which human beings associate and live together is summed up in the word *Culture*. The problem is to know what kind of culture is so free in itself that it conceives and begets political freedom as its accompaniment and consequence. What about the state of science and knowledge; of the arts, fine and technological; of friendships and family life; of business and finance; of the attitudes and dispositions created in the give and take of ordinary day by day associations? No matter what is the native make-up of human nature, its working activities, those which respond to institutions and rules and which finally shape the pattern of the latter, are created by the whole body of occupations, interests, skills, beliefs that constitute a given culture. As the latter changes, especially as it grows complex and intricate in the way in which American life has changed since our political organization took shape, new problems take the place of those governing the earlier formation and distribution of political powers. The view that love of freedom is so inherent in man that, if it only has a chance given it by abolition of oppressions exercised by church and state, it will produce and maintain free institutions is no longer adequate. The idea naturally arose when settlers in a new country felt that the distance they had put between themselves and the forces that oppressed them effectively symbolized everything that stood between them and permanent achievement of freedom. We are now forced to see that positive conditions, forming the prevailing state of culture, are required. Release from oppressions and repressions which previously existed marked a necessary transition, but transitions are but bridges to something different.

Early republicans were obliged even in their own time to note that general conditions, such as are summed up under the name of culture, had a good deal to do with political institutions. For they held that oppressions of state and church had exercised a corrupting influence upon human nature, so that the original impulse to liberty had either been lost or warped out of shape. This was a virtual admission that surrounding conditions may be stronger than native tendencies. It proved a degree of plasticity in human nature that required exercise of continual solicitude—expressed in the saying that eternal vigilance is the price of liberty. The Founding Fathers were aware that love of power is a trait of human nature, so strong a one that definite barriers had to be erected to keep persons who get into positions of official authority from encroachments that undermine free institutions. Admission that men may be brought by long habit to hug their chains implies a belief that second or acquired nature is stronger than original nature.

Jefferson at least went further than this. For his fear of the growth of manufacturing and trade and his preference for agrarian pursuits amounted to acceptance of the idea that interests bred by certain pursuits may fundamentally alter original human nature and the institutions that are congenial to it. That the development Jefferson dreaded has come about and to a much greater degree than he could have anticipated is an obvious fact. We face today the consequences of the fact that an agricultural and rural people has become an urban industrial population.

Proof is decisive that economic factors are an intrinsic part of the culture that determines the actual turn taken by political measures and rules, no matter what verbal beliefs are held. Although it later became the fashion to blur the connection which exists between economics and politics, and even to reprove those who called attention to it, Madison as well as Jefferson was quite aware of the connection and of its bearing upon democracy. Knowledge that the connection demanded a general distribution of property and the prevention of rise of the extremely poor and the extremely rich, was however different from explicit recognition of a relation between culture and nature so intimate that the former may shape the patterns of thought and action.

Economic relations and habits cannot be set apart in isolation any more than political institutions can be. The state of knowledge of nature, that is, of physical science, is a phase of culture upon which industry and commerce, the production and distribution of goods and the regulation of services directly depend. Unless we take into account the rise of the new science of nature in the seventeenth century and its growth to its present state, our economic agencies of production and distribution and ultimately of consumption cannot be understood. The connection of the events of the industrial revolution with those of the advancing scientific revolution is an incontrovertible witness.

It has not been customary to include the arts, the fine arts, as an important part of the social conditions that bear upon democratic institutions and personal freedom. Even after the influence of the state of industry and of natural science has been admitted, we still tend to draw the line at the idea that literature, music, painting, the drama, architecture, have any intimate connection with the cultural bases of democracy. Even those who call themselves good democrats are often content to look upon the fruits of these arts as adornments of culture rather than as things in whose enjoyment all should partake, if democracy is to be a reality. The state of things in totalitarian countries may induce us to revise this opinion. For it proves that no matter what may be the case with the impulses and powers that lead the creative artist to do his work, works of art once brought into existence are the most compelling of the means of communication by which emotions are stirred and opinions formed. The theater, the movie and music hall, even the picture gallery, eloquence, popular parades, common sports and recreative agencies, have all been brought under regulation as part of the propaganda agencies by which dictatorship is kept in power without being regarded by the masses as oppressive. We are beginning to realize that emotions and imagination are more potent in shaping public sentiment and opinion than information and reason.

Indeed, long before the present crisis came into being there was a saying that if one could control the songs of a nation, one need not care who made its laws. And historical study shows that primitive religions owe their power in determining belief and action to their ability to reach emotions and imagination by rites and ceremonies, by legend and folklore, all clothed with the traits that mark works of art. The Church that has had by far the greatest influence in the modern world took over their agencies of esthetic appeal and incorporated them into its own structure, after adapting them to its own purpose, in winning and holding the allegiance of the masses.

A totalitarian regime is committed to control of the whole life of all its subjects by its hold over feelings, desires, emotions, as well as opinions. This indeed is a mere truism, since a totalitarian state has to be total. But save as we take it into account we shall not appreciate the intensity of the revival of the warfare between state and church that exists in Germany and Russia. The conflict is not the expression of the whim of a leader. It is inherent in any regime that demands the *total* allegiance of all its subjects. It must first of all, and most enduringly of all, if it is to be permanent, command the imagination, with all the impulses and motives we have been accustomed to call *inner*. Religious organizations are those which rule by use of these means, and for that reason are an inherent competitor with any political state that sets out on the totalitarian road. Thus it is that the very things that seem to us in democratic countries the most obnoxious features of the totalitarian state are the very things for which its advocates recommend it. They are the things for whose absence they denounce democratic countries. For they say that failure to enlist the whole make-up of citizens, emotional as well as ideological, condemns democratic states to employ merely external and mechanical devices to hold the loyal support of its citizens. We may regard all this as a symptom of a collective hallucination, such as at times seems to have captured whole populations. But even so, we must recognize the influence of this factor if we are ourselves to escape collective delusion—that totalitarianism rests upon external coercion alone.

Finally, the moral factor is an intrinsic part of the complex of social forces called culture. For no matter whether or not one shares the view, now held on different grounds by different groups, that there is no scientific ground or warrant for moral conviction and judgments—it is certain that human beings hold some things dearer than they do others, and that they struggle for the things they prize, spending time and energy in their behalf: doing so indeed to such an extent that the best measure we have of what is valued is the effort spent in its behalf. Not only so, but for a number of persons to form anything that can be called a community in its pregnant sense there must be values prized in common. Without them, any so-called social group, class, people, nation, tends to fall apart into molecules having but mechanically enforced connections with one another. For the present at least we do not have to ask whether values are moral, having a kind of life and potency of their own, or are but by-products of the working of other conditions, biological, economic or whatever.

The qualification will indeed seem quite superfluous to most, so habituated have most persons become to believing, at least nominally, that moral forces are the ultimate determinants of the rise and fall of all human societies—while religion has taught many to believe that cosmic as well as social forces are regulated in behalf of moral ends. The qualification is introduced, nevertheless, because of the existence of a school of philosophy holding that opinions about the values which move conduct are lacking in any scientific standing, since (according to them) the only things that can be *known* are physical events. The denial that values have any influence in the long run course of events is also characteristic of the Marxist belief that forces of production ultimately control every human relationship. The idea of the impossibility of intellectual regulation of ideas and judgments about values is shared by a number of intellectuals who have been dazzled by the success of mathematical and physical science. These last remarks suggest that there is at least one other factor in culture which needs some attention:—namely, the existence of schools of social philosophy, of competing ideologies.

The intent of the previous discussion should be obvious. The problem of freedom and of democratic institutions is tied up with the question of what kind of culture exists; with the necessity of free culture for free political institutions. The import of this conclusion extends far beyond its contrast with the simpler faith of those who formulated the democratic tradition. The question of human psychology, of the make-up of human nature in its original state, is involved. It is involved not just in a general way but with respect to its special constituents and their significance in their relations to one another. For every social and political philosophy currently professed will be found upon examination to involve a certain view about the constitution of human nature: in itself and in its relation to physical nature. What is true of this factor is true of every factor in culture, so that they need not here be listed again, although it is necessary to bear them all in mind if we are to appreciate the variety of factors involved in the problem of human freedom.

Running through the problem of the relation of this and that constituent of culture to social institutions in general and political democracy in particular is a question rarely asked. Yet it so underlies any critical consideration of the principles of each of them that some conclusion on the matter ultimately decides the position taken on each special issue. The question is whether any one of the factors is so predominant that it is *the* causal force, so that other factors are secondary and derived effects. Some kind of answer in what philosophers call a *monistic* direction has been usually given. The most obvious present example is the belief that economic conditions are ultimately the controlling forces in human relationships. It is perhaps significant that this view is comparatively recent. At the height of the eighteenth century, Enlightenment, the prevailing view, gave final supremacy to reason, to the advance of science and to education. Even during the last century, a view was held which is expressed in the motto of a certain school of historians: "History is past politics and politics is present history."

Because of the present fashion of economic explanation, this political view may now seem to have been the crotchet of a particular set of historical scholars. But, after all, it only formulated an idea consistently acted upon during the period of the formation of national states. It is possible to regard the present emphasis upon economic factors as a sort of intellectual revenge taken upon its earlier all but total neglect. The very word "political economy" suggests how completely economic considerations were once subordinated to political. The book that was influential in putting an end to this subjection, Adam Smith's *Wealth of Nations*, continued in its title, though not its contents, the older tradition. In the Greek period, we find that Aristotle makes the political factor so controlling that all normal economic activities are relegated to the household, so that all morally justifiable economic practice is literally domestic economy. And in spite of the recent vogue of the Marxist theory, Oppenheim has produced a considerable body of evidence in support of the thesis that political states are the result of military conquests in which defeated people have become subjects of their conquerors, who, by assuming rule over the conquered, begot the first political states.

The rise of totalitarian states cannot, because of the bare fact of their totalitarianism, be regarded as mere reversions to the earlier theory of supremacy of the political institutional factor. Yet as compared with theories that had subordinated the political to the economic, whether in the Marxist form or in that of the British classical school, it marks reversion to ideas and still more to practices which it was supposed had disappeared forever from the conduct of any modern state. And the practices have been revived and extended with the benefit of scientific technique of control of industry, finance and commerce in ways which show the earlier governmental officials who adopted "mercantile" economics in the interest of government were the veriest bunglers at their professed job.

The idea that morals ought to be, even if it is not, the supreme regulator of social affairs is not so widely entertained as it once was, and there are circumstances which support the conclusion that when moral forces were as influential as they were supposed to be it was because morals were identical with customs which happened in fact to regulate the relations of human beings with one another. However, the idea is still advanced by sermons from the pulpit and editorials from the press that adoption of say the Golden Rule would speedily do away with all social discord and trouble; and as I write the newspapers report the progress of a campaign for something called "moral re-armament." Upon a deeper level, the point made about the alleged identity of ethics with established customs raises the question whether the effect of the disintegration of customs that for a long time held men together in social groups can be overcome save by development of new generally accepted traditions and customs. This development, upon this view, would be equivalent to the creation of a new ethics.

However, such questions are here brought up for the sake of the emphasis they place upon the question already raised: Is there any one factor or phase of culture which is dominant, or which tends to produce and regulate others, or are economics, morals, art, science, and so on only so many aspects of the interaction of a number of factors, each of which acts upon and is acted upon by the others? In the professional language of philosophy: shall our point of view be monistic or pluralistic? The same question recurs moreover about each one of the factors listed:—about economics, about politics, about science, about art. I shall here illustrate the point by reference not to any of these things but to theories that have at various times been influential about the make-up of human nature. For these psychological theories have been marked by serious attempts to make some one constituent of human nature *the* source of motivation of action; or at least to reduce all conduct to the action of a small number of alleged native "forces." A comparatively recent example was the adoption by the classic school of economic theory of self-interest as the main motivating force of human behavior; an idea linked up on its technical side with the notion that pleasure and pain are the causes and the ends-in-view of all conscious human conduct, in desire to obtain one and avoid the other. Then there was a view that self-interest and sympathy are the two components of human nature, as opposed and balanced centrifugal and centripetal tendencies are the moving forces of celestial nature.

Just now the favorite ideological psychological candidate for control of human activity is love of power. Reasons for its selection are not far to seek. Success of search for economic profit turned out to be largely conditioned in fact upon possession of superior power while success reacted to increase power. Then the rise of national states has been attended by such vast and flagrant organization of military and naval force that politics have become more and more markedly power-politics, leading to the conclusion that there is not any other kind, although in the past the power-element has been more decently and decorously covered up. One interpretation of the Darwinian struggle for existence and survival of the fittest was used as ideological support; and some writers, notably Nietzsche (though not in the crude form often alleged), proposed an ethics of power in opposition to the supposed Christian ethics of sacrifice.

Because human nature is the factor which in one way or another is always interacting with environing conditions in production of culture, the theme receives special attention later. But the shift that has occurred from time to time in theories that have gained currency about the "ruling motive" in human nature suggests a question which is seldom asked. It is the question whether these psychologies have not in fact taken the cart to be the horse. Have they not gathered their notion as to the ruling element in human nature from observation of tendencies that are marked in contemporary collective life, and then bunched these tendencies together in some alleged psychological "force" as their cause? It is significant that human nature was taken to be strongly moved by an inherent love of freedom at the time when there was a struggle for representative government; that the motive of self-interest appeared when conditions in England enlarged the role of money, because of new methods of industrial production; that the growth of organized philanthropic activities brought sympathy into the psychological picture, and that events today are readily converted into love of power as the mainspring of human action.

In any case, the idea of culture that has been made familiar by the work of anthropological students points to the conclusion that whatever are the native constituents of human nature, the culture of a period and group is the determining influence in their arrangement; it is that which determines the patterns of behavior that mark out the activities of any group, family, clan, people, sect, faction, class. It is at least as true that the state of culture determines the order and arrangement of native tendencies as that human nature produces any particular set or system of social phenomena so as to obtain satisfaction for itself. The problem is to find out the way in which the elements of a culture interact with each other and the way in which the elements of human nature are caused to interact with one another under conditions set by their interaction with the existing environment. For example, if our American culture is largely a pecuniary culture, it is not because the original or innate structure of human nature tends of itself to obtaining pecuniary profit. It is rather that a certain complex culture stimulates, promotes and consolidates native tendencies so as to produce a certain pattern of desires and purposes. If we take all the communities, peoples, classes, tribes and nations that ever existed, we may be sure that since human nature in its native constitution is the relative constant, it cannot be appealed to, in isolation, to account for the multitude of diversities presented by different forms of association.

Primitive peoples for reasons that are now pretty evident attribute magical qualities to blood. Popular beliefs about race and inherent race differences have virtually perpetuated the older superstitions. Anthropologists are practically all agreed that the differences we find in different "races" are not due to anything in inherent physiological structure but to the effects exercised upon members of various groups by the cultural conditions under which they are reared; conditions that act upon raw or original human nature unremittingly from the very moment of birth. It has always been known that infants, born without ability in any language, come to speak the language, whatever it may be, of the community in which they were born. Like most uniform phenomena the fact aroused no curiosity and led to no generalization about the influence of cultural conditions. It was taken for granted; as a matter of course it was so "natural" as to appear inevitable. Only since the rise of systematic inquiries carried on by anthropological students has it been noted that the conditions of culture which bring about the common language of a given group produce other traits they have in common;—traits which like the mother tongue differentiate one group or society from others.

Culture as a complex body of customs tends to maintain itself. It can reproduce itself only through effecting certain differential changes in the original or native constitutions of its members. Each culture has its own pattern, its own characteristic arrangement of its constituent energies. By the mere force of its existence as well as by deliberately adopted methods systematically pursued, it perpetuates itself through transformation of the raw or original human nature of those born immature.

These statements do not signify that biological heredity and native individual differences are of no importance. They signify that as they operate within a given social form, they are shaped and take effect *within* that particular form. They are not indigenous traits that mark off one people, one group, one class, from another, but mark differences in every group. Whatever the "white man's burden," it was not imposed by heredity.

We have traveled a seemingly long way from the questions with which we set out, so that it may appear that they had been forgotten on the journey. But the journey was undertaken for the sake of finding out something about the nature of the problem that is expressed in the questions asked. The maintenance of democratic institutions is not such a simple matter as was supposed by some of the Founding Fathers—although the wiser among them realized how immensely the new political experiment was favored by external circumstances—like the ocean that separated settlers from the governments that had an interest in using the colonists for their own purposes; the fact that feudal institutions had been left behind; that so many of the settlers had come here to escape restrictions upon religious beliefs and form of worship; and especially the existence of a vast territory with free land and immense unappropriated natural resources.

The function of culture in determining what elements of human nature are dominant and their pattern or arrangement in connection with one another goes beyond any special point to which attention is called. It affects the very idea of individuality. The idea that human nature is inherently and exclusively individual is itself a product of a cultural individualistic movement. The idea that mind and consciousness are intrinsically individual did not even occur to any one for much the greater part of human history. It would have been rejected as the inevitable source of disorder and chaos if it had occurred to anyone to suggest it:—not that their ideas of human nature on that account were any better than later ones but that they also were functions of culture. All that we can safely say is that human nature, like other forms of life, tends to differentiation, and this moves in the direction of the distinctively individual, and that it also tends toward combination, association. In the lower animals, physical-biological factors determine which tendency is dominant in a given animal or plant species and the ratio existing between the two factors—whether, for example, insects are what students call "solitary" or "social." With human beings, cultural conditions replace strictly physical ones. In the earlier periods of human history they acted almost like physiological conditions as far as deliberate intention was concerned. They were taken to be "natural" and change in them to be unnatural. At a later period the cultural conditions were seen to be subject in some degree to deliberate formation.

For a time radicals then identified their policies with the belief that if only artificial social conditions could be got rid of human nature would produce almost automatically a certain kind of social arrangements, those which would give it free scope in its supposed exclusively individual character.

Tendencies toward sociality, such as sympathy, were admitted. But they were taken to be traits of an individual isolated by nature, quite as much as, say, a tendency to combine with others in order to get protection against something threatening one's own private self. Whether complete identification of human nature with individuality would be desirable or undesirable if it existed is an idle academic question. For it does not exist. Some cultural conditions develop the psychological constituents that lead toward differentiation; others stimulate those which lead in the direction of the solidarity of the beehive or anthill. The human problem is that of securing the development of each constituent so that it serves to release and mature the other. Cooperation—called fraternity in the classic French formula—is as much a part of the democratic ideal as is personal initiative. That cultural conditions were allowed to develop (markedly so in the economic phase) which subordinated cooperativeness to liberty and equality serves to explain the decline in the two latter. Indirectly, this decline is responsible for the present tendency to give a bad name to the very word *individualism* and to make *sociality* a term of moral honor beyond criticism. But that association of nullities on even the largest scale would constitute a realization of human nature is as absurd as to suppose that the latter can take place in beings whose only relations to one another are those entered into in behalf of exclusive private advantage.

The problem of freedom of cooperative individualities is then a problem to be viewed in the context of culture. The state of culture is a state of interaction of many factors, the chief of which are law and politics, industry and commerce, science and technology, the arts of expression and communication, and of morals, or the values men prize and the ways in which they evaluate them; and finally, though indirectly, the system of general ideas used by men to justify and to criticize the fundamental conditions under which they live, their social philosophy. We are concerned with the problem of freedom rather than with solutions: in the conviction that solutions are idle until the problem has been placed in the context of the elements that constitute culture as they interact with elements of native human nature. The fundamental postulate of the discussion is that isolation of any one factor, no matter how strong its workings at a given time, is fatal to understanding and to intelligent action. Isolations have abounded, both on the side of taking some one thing in human nature to be a supreme "motive" and in taking some one form of social activity to be supreme. Since the problem is here thought of as that of the ways in which a great number of factors within and without human nature interact, our next task is to ask concerning the reciprocal connections raw human nature and culture bear to one another.

42. Culture and Human Nature*

One of the difficulties with taking contemporary culture as the context for philosophical judgments is the "dating" of the illustrative material. Some antiquated commentary and some quaint descriptions characterize this selection, but remarkably, Dewey's interpretation of those events has deep and immediate relevance. Was it 1939 or only yesterday that Dewey wrote: "Common observation, especially of the young, shows that nothing is more exasperating and more resented than stirring up certain impulses and tendencies and then checking their manifestation."

Throughout this chapter, Dewey expresses deep reservations about the external signs of progress, whether of material or intellectual accomplishments. He contends that they mask, in superficial ways, the deep disconnection that most people experience in their lives. The real war, he believes, goes on inside our lives and inside our institutions. The self-congratulatory notices of technological and organizational breakthroughs provide only momentary and specious relief from dealing with more fundamental human problems. In an eloquent passage, significant for a number of recent periods in American history, Dewey writes: "Schooling in literacy is no substitute for the dispositions which were formerly provided by direct experiences of an educative quality. The void created by lack of relevant personal experiences combines with the confusion produced by impact of multitudes of unrelated incidents to create attitudes which are responsive to

* From John Dewey, *Freedom and Culture* (New York, Capricorn Books, 1963) (1939), pp. 24-49. Reprinted by permission of G. P. Putnam's Sons.

organized propaganda, hammering in day after day the few
and relatively simple beliefs asseverated to be 'truths' essential to national welfare.''

In the American as in the English liberal tradition, the idea of
freedom has been connected with the idea of individuality, of *the* individual. The connection has been so close and so often reiterated that it
has come to seem inherent. Many persons will be surprised if they hear
that freedom has ever been supposed to have another source and foundation than the very nature of individuality. Yet in the continental
European tradition the affiliation of the idea of freedom is with the idea
of rationality. Those are free who govern themselves by the dictates of
reason; those who follow the promptings of appetite and sense are so
ruled by them as to be unfree. Thus it was that Hegel at the very time he
was glorifying the State wrote a philosophy of history according to
which the movement of historical events was from the despotic state of
the Oriental World in which only one was free to the era dawning in
Germany in the Western World in which *all* are free. The same difference in contexts that give freedom its meaning is found when representatives of totalitarian Germany at the present time claim their
regime is giving the subjects of their state a "higher" freedom than can
be found in democratic states, individuals in the latter being unfree because their lives are chaotic and undisciplined. The aroma of the continental tradition hangs about the sayings of those who settle so many
social problems to their own satisfaction by invoking a distinction between liberty and license, identifying the former with "liberty under
law"—for in the classic tradition law and reason are related as child
and parent. So far as the saying assigns to law an origin and authority
having nothing to do with freedom, so far, that is, as it affirms the impossibility of free conditions determining their own law, it points
directly, even if unintentionally, to the totalitarian state.

We do not, however, have to go as far abroad as the European continent to note that freedom has had its practical significance fixed in different ways in different cultural contexts. For in the early nineteenth
century there was a great practical difference between the English and
the American theories, although both associated freedom with qualities
that cause human beings to be *individuals* in the distinctive sense of that
word. The contrast is so flat that it would be amusing if it were not so
instructive. Jefferson, who was the original and systematic promulgator
of the doctrine of free, self-governing institutions, found that the properties of individuals with which these institutions were most closely

associated were traits found in the farming class. In his more pessimistic moments he even went so far as to anticipate that the development of manufacturing and commerce would produce a state of affairs in which persons in this country "would eat one another" as they did in Europe. In England, on the other hand, landed proprietors were the great enemy of the new freedom, which was connected in its social and political manifestations with the activities and aims of the manufacturing class.

It is not, of course, the bare fact of contrast which is instructive but the causes for its existence. They are not far to seek. Landed proprietors formed the aristocracy in Great Britain. The hold landed interests had over law-making bodies due to feudalism was hostile to the development of manufacturing and commerce. In the United States traces of feudalism were so faint that laws against primogeniture were about all that was needed to erase them. It was easy in this country to idealize the farmers as the sturdy yeomanry who embodied all the virtues associated with the original Anglo-Saxon love of liberty, the Magna Charta, and the struggle against the despotism of the Stuarts. Farmers were the independent self-supporting class that had no favors to ask from anybody, since they were not dependent for their livelihood nor their ideas upon others, owning and managing their own farms. It is a history that again would be amusing, were it not instructive, to find that as this country changed from an agrarian one to an urban industrial one, the qualities of initiative, invention, vigor and intrinsic contribution to progress which British *laissez-faire* liberalism had associated with manufacturing pursuits were transferred by American Courts and by the political representatives of business and finance from Jeffersonian individuals and given to the entrepreneurs who were individuals in the British sense.

In such considerations as these—which would be reinforced by an extensive survey of the history of the meaning given to freedom under different conditions—we have one instance and an important one of the relation of culture to the whole problem of freedom. The facts fall directly in line with the conclusion of the previous chapter:—a conclusion summed up in saying that the idea of Culture, which has become a central idea of anthropology, has such a wide sociological application that it puts a new face upon the old, old problem of the relation of the individual and the social. The idea of culture even outlaws the very terms in which the problem has been conceived, independently of its effect upon solutions proposed. For most statements of the problem have been posed as if there were some inherent difference amounting to opposition between what is called the individual and the social. As a consequence there was a tendency for those who were interested in theory to line up in two parties, which at the poles were so far apart that one denied whatever the other asserted. One party held that social conventions, traditions, institutions, rules are maintained only by some form of coercion, overt or covert, which encroaches upon the natural freedom of individuals; while the other school held that individuals are such by nature that the one standing social problem is the agencies by which recalcitrant individuals are brought under social control or "socialized." The term of honor of one school has been that of reproach of the other. The two extremes serve to define the terms in which the problem was put. Most persons occupy an intermediate and compromise position, one whose classic expression is that the basic problem of law and politics is to find the line which separates legitimate liberty from the proper exercise of law and political authority, so that each can maintain its own province under its own jurisdiction; law operating only when liberty oversteps its proper bounds, an operation supposed, during the heights of *laissez-faire* liberalism, to be legitimate only when police action was required to keep the peace.

Few persons today hold the extreme view of Hobbes, according to which human nature is so inherently anti-social that only experiences of the evil consequences of the war of all against all, reigning when human nature has free play, leads men, in connection with the motive of fear, to submit to authority—human nature even then remaining so intractable that the only assurance of safety against its marauding instincts is subjection to sovereignty. But in reading books on sociology it is still not uncommon to find the basic problem stated as if it were to list and analyze agencies by which individuals are tamed or "socialized." The chief difference of these writers from Hobbes consists in the fact that much less emphasis is laid upon merely political pressure, while it is recognized that there are tendencies in original human nature which render it amenable to social rules and regulations. As a result of the successful struggle of the new industrial class in England against the restrictions which existed even after the disappearance of feudalism in its grosser obvious forms, the favorite formula weighted the scales on the side of liberty, holding that each person was free as long as his actions did not restrict the freedom of others. The latter question, moreover, was never decided by going into the concrete consequences produced by the action of one person upon other persons. It was settled by a formal legal principle such as the equal right of every sane individual of a certain age to enter into contractual relations with others—no matter whether actual conditions gave equally free scope of action on both sides or made "free" contract a jug-handled affair.

However, the purpose is not to thrash over the old straw of these issues or similar issues on the moral side such as the respective parts of altruistic and egoistic tendencies in human nature. The point concerns the situation in which the problems were envisaged; the context of ideas in which as problems they were placed irrespective of the solution reached. With the intellectual resources now available, we can see that such opinions about the inherent make-up of human nature neglected the fundamental question of how its constituents are stimulated and inhibited, intensified and weakened; how their pattern is determined by interaction with cultural conditions. In consequence of this failure the views held regarding human nature were those appropriate to the purposes and policies a given group wanted to carry through. Those who wished to justify the exercise of authority over others took a pessimistic view of the constitution of human nature; those who wanted relief from something oppressive discovered qualities of great promise in its native make-up. There is here a field which has hardly been entered by intellectual explorers:—the story of the way in which ideas put forth about the make-up of human nature, ideas supposed to be the results of psychological inquiry, have been in fact only reflections of practical measures that different groups, classes, factions wished to see continued in existence or newly adopted, so that what passed as psychology was a branch of political doctrine.

We are thus brought back to the earlier statement of principle. The primary trouble has been that issues have been formulated as if they were matters of the structure of human beings on one side and of the very nature of social rules and authority on the other side, when in reality the underlying issue is that of the relation of the "natural" and the "cultural." Rousseau's attack upon the arts and sciences (as well as upon existing law and government) shocked his eighteenth century contemporaries, since the things he claimed to be operating to corrupt human nature, by creating inequality, were the very things they relied upon to generate unending human progress. Nevertheless, he stated, in a way, the problem of culture versus nature; putting, himself, all emphasis upon and giving all advantage to human nature; since to him, in spite of its raw unrefined condition, it retained its natural goodness as long as loss of original equality had not produced conditions that corrupted it. Kant and his German successors took up the challenge presented in the unpopular paradoxes of Rousseau. They tried to reverse his position; they interpreted all history as the continuing process of culture by which the original animal nature of man becomes refined and is transformed from the animal into the distinctively human.

But Rousseau and his opponents carried over into their discussion of the problem in its new form many of the elements derived from the traditional way of putting it. In German philosophy, the issue was further complicated by the rise of Nationalism which followed the encroachments of Napoleon. Though the Germans were defeated in war, in culture they were to be superior—an idea that still persists in the use of *Kultur* in German nationalistic propaganda, since superiority in culture gives the kind of rightful authority over peoples of less culture that the human has over the animal. The French Revolution, as well as the writings of Rousseau, had the effect, in addition, of identifying in the minds of German thinkers the cause of culture with that of law and authority. The individual freedom, which was the "natural right" of mankind according to the philosophers of the Revolution, was to the German philosophers of the reaction but the freedom of primitive sensuous animality. A period of subjection to universal law, expressing the higher non-natural essence of humanity, was required to bring about a condition of "higher" and true freedom. Events in Germany, including the rise of totalitarianism, since the time this view was formulated, have borne the stamp of this idea. Anticipation of the existence of some ultimate and a final social state, different from original "natural" freedom and from present subordination, has played a role in all social philosophies—like the Marxist—framed under German intellectual influences. It has had the function once exercised by the idea of the Second Coming.

In no case, however, could the problem have taken its new form without the material made available by anthropological research. For what has been disclosed about the immense variety of cultures shows that the problem of the relation of individuals and their freedom to social convention, custom, tradition and rules has been stated in a wholesale form, and hence not capable of intelligent and scientific attack. Judged by the methods of the natural sciences, the procedure in the social field has been pre-scientific and anti-scientific. For science has developed by analytic observation, and by interpretations of observed facts on the basis of their relations to one another. Social theory has operated on the basis of general "forces," whether those of inherent natural "motives" or those alleged to be social.

Were it not for the inertia of habit (which applies to opinion as well as to overt acts) it would be astonishing to find today writers who are well acquainted with the procedure of physical science and yet appeal to "forces" in explanation of human and social phenomena. For in the former case, they are aware that electricity, heat, light, etc., are names for ways in which definite observable concrete phenomena behave in relation to one another, and that all description and explanation have to be made in terms of verifiable relations of observed singular events. They know that reference to electricity or heat, etc., is but a shorthand reference to relations between events which have been established by investigation of actual occurrences. But in the field of social phenomena they do not hesitate to explain concrete phenomena by reference to motives as forces (such as love of power), although these so-called forces are but reduplication, in the medium of abstract words, of the very phenomena to be explained.

Statement in terms of the relations of culture and nature to one another takes us away from vague abstractions and glittering generalities. Approach in its terms compels attention to go to the variety of cultures that exist and to the variety of constituents of human nature, including native differences between one human being and another—differences which are not just differences in quantity. The business of inquiry is with the ways in which specified constituents of human nature, native or already modified, *interact* with specified definite constituents of a given culture; conflicts and agreements between human nature on one side and social customs and rules on the other being *products* of specifiable modes of interaction. In a given community some individuals are in practical agreement with its existing institutions and others are in revolt—varying from a condition of moderate irritation and discontent to one of violent rebellion. The resulting differences when they are sufficiently marked to be labelled are the sources of the names conservative and radical, forward-looking or progressive and reactionary, etc. They cut across economic classes. For even revolutionaries have to admit that part of their problem is to create in an oppressed class consciousness of their servitude so as to arouse active protest.

This fact, so patent to even superficial observation, is sufficient disproof of the notion that the problem can be stated as one of the relation of *the* individual and *the* social, as if these names stood for any actual existences. It indicates that *ways of interaction* between human nature and cultural conditions are the first and the fundamental thing to be examined, and that the problem is to ascertain the effects of interactions between different components of different human beings and different customs, rules, traditions, institutions—the things called "social." A fallacy has controlled the traditional statement of the problem.

It took results, good or bad—or both—of specific interactions as if they were original causes, on one side or the other, of what existed or else of what should exist.

It is just as certain, for example, that slaves have at times been contented with their estate of servitude as that a slave class has existed. It is certain that persons who have personally experienced no discomfort—except that commonly called moral—from existing conditions of oppression and injustice have been leaders in campaigns for equality and freedom. It is just as certain that inherent so-called social "instincts" have led men to form criminal gangs marked by certain mutual loyalties as that they have led men to cooperative activities. Now analytic observation of actual interactions to determine the elements operative on each side and their consequences is not easy in any case to execute. But recognition of its necessity is the condition of adequate judgment of actual events. Estimate of the value of any proposed policy is held back by taking the problem as if it were one of individual "forces" on one side and of social forces on the other, the nature of the forces being known in advance. We must start from another set of premises if we are to put the problem of freedom in the context where it belongs.

The questions which are asked at the beginning of the last chapter are genuine questions. But they are not questions in the abstract and cannot be discussed in a wholesale way. They are questions that demand discussion of cultural conditions, conditions of science, art, morals, religion, education and industry, so as to discover which of them in actuality promote and which retard the development of the native constituents of human nature. If we want individuals to be free we must see to it that suitable conditions exist:—a truism which at least indicates the direction in which to look and move.

It tells us among other things to get rid of the ideas that lead us to believe that democratic conditions automatically maintain themselves, or that they can be identified with fulfillment of prescriptions laid down in a constitution. Beliefs of this sort merely divert attention from what is going on, just as the patter of the prestidigitator enables him to do things that are not noticed by those whom he is engaged in fooling. For what is actually going on may be the formation of conditions that are hostile to any kind of democratic liberties. This would be too trite to repeat were it not that so many persons in the high places of business talk as if they believed or could get others to believe that the observance of formulae that have become ritualistic are effective safeguards of our democratic heritage. The same principle warns us to beware of supposing that totalitarian states are brought about by factors so foreign to us that "It can't happen here";—to beware especially of the belief that these states rest only upon unmitigated coercion and intimidation. For in spite of the wide use of purges, executions, concentration camps, deprivation of property and of means of livelihood, no regime can endure long in a country where a scientific spirit has once existed unless it has the support of so-called idealistic elements in the human constitution. There is a tendency in some quarters to treat remarks of this sort as if they were a sort of apology or justification of dictatorships and totalitarian states. This way of reacting to an attempt to find out what it is that commends, at least for a time, totalitarian conditions to persons otherwise intelligent and honorable, is dangerous. It puts hate in place of attempt at understanding; hate once aroused can be directed by skillful manipulation against other objects than those which first aroused it. It also leads us to think that we are immune from the disease to which others have given way so long as the evil things we see in totalitarianism are not known to be developing among us. The belief that only such things operate to harm democracy keeps us from being on our guard against the causes that may be at work undermining the values we nominally prize. It even leads us to ignore beams in our own eyes such as our own racial prejudices.

It is extremely difficult at a distance to judge just what are the appeals made to better elements in human nature by, say, such policies as form the Nazi faith. We may believe that aside from appeal to fear; from desire to escape responsibilities imposed by free citizenship; from impulses to submission strengthened by habits of obedience bred in the past; from desire for compensation for past humiliations, and from the action of nationalistic sentiments growing in intensity for over a century (and not in Germany alone), there is also love for novelty which in this particular case has taken the form of idealistic faith, among the youth in particular, of being engaged in creating a pattern for new institutions which the whole world will in time adopt. For one of the elements of human nature that is often discounted in both idea and practice is the satisfaction derived from a sense of sharing in creative activities; the satisfaction increasing in direct ratio to the scope of the constructive work engaged in.

Other causes may be mentioned, though with the admission that it is quite possible in good faith to doubt or deny their operation. There is the satisfaction that comes from a sense of union with others, a feeling capable of being intensified till it becomes a mystical sense of fusion with others and being mistaken for love on a high level of manifestation.

The satisfaction obtained by the sentiment of communion with others, of the breaking down of barriers, will be intense in the degree in which it has previously been denied opportunity to manifest itself. The comparative ease with which provincial loyalties, which in Germany had been at least as intense and as influential as state-rights sentiments ever were in this country, were broken down; the similar ease, though less in degree, with which habitual religious beliefs and practices were subordinated to a feeling of racial and social union, would seem to testify that underneath there was yearning for emotional fusion. Something of this kind showed itself in most countries when they were engaged in the World War. For the time being it seemed as if barriers that separated individuals from one another had been swept away. Submission to abolition of political parties and to abolition of labor unions which had had great power would hardly have come about so readily had there not been some kind of a void which the new regime promised to fill. Just how far the fact of uniformity is accompanied by a sense of equality in a nation where class distinctions had been rigid, one can only guess at. But there is considerable ground for believing that it has been a strong factor in reconciling "humbler" folk to enforced deprivation of material benefits, so that, at least for a time, a sense of honorable equality more than compensates for less to eat, harder and longer hours of work—since it is psychologically true that man does not live by bread alone.

It might seem as if belief in operation of "idealistic" factors was contradicted by the cruel persecutions that have taken place, things indicative of a reign of sadism rather than of desire for union with others irrespective of birth and locale. But history shows that more than once social unity has been promoted by the presence, real or alleged, of some hostile group. It has long been a part of the technique of politicians who wish to maintain themselves in power to foster the idea that the alternative is the danger of being conquered by an enemy. Nor does what has been suggested slur over in any way the effect of powerful and unremitting propaganda. For the intention has been to indicate some of the conditions whose interaction produces the social spectacle. Other powerful factors in the interaction are those technologies produced by modern science which have multiplied the means of modifying the dispositions of the mass of the populations; and which, in conjunction with economic centralization, have enabled mass opinion to become like physical goods a matter of mass production. Here also is both a warning and a suggestion to those concerned with cultural conditions which will maintain democratic freedom. The warning is obvious as to the role of propaganda, which now operates with us in channels less direct and less official. The suggestion is that the printing press and radio have made the problem of the intelligent and honest use of means of communication in behalf of openly declared public ends a matter of fundamental concern.

What has been said is stated by way of illustration, and it may, if any one desires, be treated as hypothetical. For even so, the suggestions serve to enforce the point that a social regime can come into enduring existence only as it satisfies some elements of human nature not previously afforded expression. On the other hand getting relief from saturation of elements that have become stale makes almost anything welcome if only it is different. The general principle holds even if the elements that are provided a new outlet are the baser things in human nature: fear, suspicion, jealousy, inferiority complexes; factors that were excited by earlier conditions but that are now given channels of fuller expression. Common observation, especially of the young, shows that nothing is more exasperating and more resented than stirring up certain impulses and tendencies and then checking their manifestation. We should also note that a period of uncertainty and insecurity, accompanied as it is by more or less unsettlement and disturbance, creates a feeling that anything would be better than what exists, together with desire for order and stability upon almost any terms—the latter being a reason why revolutions are so regularly followed by reaction, and explain the fact that Lenin expressed by saying revolutions are authoritative, though not for the reason he gave.

Just which of these factors are involved in our own maintenance of democratic conditions or whether any of them are so involved is, at this juncture, not so pertinent as is the principle they illustrate. Negatively speaking, we have to get away from the influence of belief in bald single forces, whether they are thought of as intrinsically psychological or sociological. This includes getting away from mere hatred of abominable things, and it also means refusing to fall back on such a generalized statement as that Fascist institutions are expressions of the sort of thing to be expected in a stage of contracting capitalism, since they are a kind of final spasm of protest against approaching dissolution. We cannot reject out of hand any cause assigned; it may have some truth. But the primary need is to escape from wholesale reasons, as totalitarian as are the states ruled by dictators. We have to analyze conditions by observations, which are as discriminating as they are extensive, until we discover specific interactions that are taking place, and learn to think in terms of interactions instead of force. We are led to search even for the conditions which have given the interacting factors the power they possess.

The lesson is far from being entirely new. The founders of American political democracy were not so naïvely devoted to pure theory that they were unaware of the necessity of cultural conditions for the successful working of democratic forms. I could easily fill pages from Thomas Jefferson in which he insists upon the necessity of a free press, general schooling and local neighborhood groups carrying on, through intimate meetings and discussions, the management of their own affairs, if political democracy was to be made secure. These sayings could be backed up by almost equally numerous expressions of his fears for the success of republican institutions in South American countries that had thrown off the Spanish yoke.

He expressly set forth his fear that their traditions were such that domestic military despotisms would be substituted for foreign subjugations. A background of "ignorance, bigotry and superstition" was not a good omen. On one occasion he even went so far as to suggest that the best thing that could happen would be for the South American states to remain under the nominal supremacy of Spain, under the collective guarantee of France, Russia, Holland and the United States, until experience in self-government prepared them for complete independence.

The real source of the weakness that has developed later in the position of our democratic progenitors is not that they isolated the problem of freedom from the positive conditions that would nourish it, but that they did not—and in their time could not—carry their analysis far enough. The outstanding examples of this inability are their faith in the public press and in schooling. They certainly were not wrong in emphasizing the need of a free press and of common public schools to provide conditions favorable to democracy. But to them the enemy of freedom of the press was official governmental censorship and control; they did not foresee the non-political causes that might restrict its freedom, nor the economic factors that would put a heavy premium on centralization. And they failed to see how education in literacy could become a weapon in the hands of an oppressive government, nor that the chief cause for promotion of elementary education in Europe would be increase of military power.

The inefficacy of education in general, that is, apart from constant attention to all the elements of its constitution, is illustrated in Germany itself. Its schools were so efficient that the country had the lowest rate of illiteracy in the world, the scholarship and scientific researches of its universities were known throughout the civilized globe. In fact it was not so many years ago that a distinguished American educator held them up as models to be followed in this country if the weaknesses of our higher institutions were to be remedied. Nevertheless German lower schools furnished the intellectual fodder for totalitarian propaganda, and the higher schools were the centers of reaction against the German Republic.

The illustrations are simple, and perhaps too familiar to carry much force. Nevertheless they proclaim that while free institutions over a wide territory are not possible without a mechanism, like the press, for quick and extensive communication of ideas and information, and without general literacy to take advantage of the mechanism, yet these very factors create a problem for a democracy instead of providing a final solution. Aside from the fact that the press may distract with trivialities or be an agent of a faction, or be an instrument of inculcating ideas in support of the hidden interest of a group or class (all in the name of public interest), the wide-world present scene is such that individuals are overwhelmed and emotionally confused by publicized reverberation of isolated events. And after a century of belief that the Common School system was bound by the very nature of its work to be what its earlier apostles called a "pillar of the republic," we are learning that everything about the public schools, its official agencies of control, organization and administration, the status of teachers, the subjects taught and methods of teaching them, the prevailing modes of discipline, set *problems*; and that the problems have been largely ignored as far as the relation of schools to democratic institutions is concerned. In fact the attention these things have received from various technical standpoints has been one reason why the central question has been obscured.

After many centuries of struggle and following of false gods, the natural sciences now possess methods by which particular facts and general ideas are brought into effective cooperation with one another. But with respect to means for understanding social events, we are still living in the pre-scientific epoch, although the events to be understood are the consequences of application of scientific knowledge to a degree unprecedented in history. With respect to information and understanding of social events, our state is that on one side of an immense number of undigested and unrelated facts, reported in isolation (and hence easily colored by some twist of interest) and large untested generalizations on the other side.

The generalizations are so general in the sense of remoteness from the events to which they are supposed to apply that they are matters of opinion, and frequently the rallying cries and slogans of factions and classes. They are often expressions of partisan desire clothed in the language of intellect. As matters of opinion, they are batted hither and yon in controversy and are subject to changes of popular fashion. They differ at practically every point from scientific generalizations, since the latter express the relations of facts to one another and, as they are employed to bring together more facts, are tested by the material to which they are applied.

If a glance at an editorial page of a newspaper shows what is meant by untested opinions put forth in the garb of the general principles of sound judgment, the items of the news columns illustrate what is meant by a multitude of diverse unrelated facts. The popular idea of "sensational," as it is derived from the daily press, is more instructive as to meaning of *sensations* than is the treatment accorded that subject in books on psychology. Events are sensational in the degree in which they make a strong impact in isolation from the relations to other events that give them their significance. They appeal to those who like things raw. Ordinary reports of murders, love nests, etc., are of this sort, with an artificial intensity supplied by unusual size or color of type. To say that a response is intellectual, not sensational, in the degree in which its significance is supplied by relations to other things is to state a truism. They are two sets of words used to describe the same thing.

One effect of literacy under existing conditions has been to create in a large number of persons an appetite for the momentary "thrills" caused by impacts that stimulate nerve endings but whose connections with cerebral functions are broken. Then stimulation and excitation are not so ordered that intelligence is produced. At the same time the habit of using judgment is weakened by the habit of depending on external stimuli. Upon the whole it is probably a tribute to the powers of endurance of human nature that the consequences are not more serious than they are.

The new mechanisms resulting from application of scientific discoveries have, of course, immensely extended the range and variety of particular events, or "news items" which are brought to bear upon the senses and the emotions connected with them. The telegraph, telephone, and radio report events going on over the whole face of the globe. They are for the most part events about which the individuals who are told of them can do nothing, except to react with a passing emotional excitation. For, because of lack of relation and organization in reference to one another, no imaginative reproduction of the situation is possible, such as might make up for the absence of personal response. Before we engage in too much pity for the inhabitants of our rural regions before the days of invention of modern devices for circulation of information, we should recall that they knew more about the things that affected their own lives than the city dweller of today is likely to know about the causes of his affairs. They did not possess nearly as many separate items of information, but they were compelled to know, in the sense of *understanding*, the conditions that bore upon the conduct of their own affairs. Today the influences that affect the actions performed by individuals are so remote as to be unknown. We are at the mercy of events acting upon us in unexpected, abrupt, and violent ways.

The bearing of these considerations upon the cultural conditions involved in maintenance of freedom is not far to seek. It is very directly connected with what now seems to us the over-simplification of the democratic idea indulged in by the authors of our republican government. They had in mind persons whose daily occupations stimulated initiative and vigor, and who possessed information which even if narrow in scope, bore pretty directly upon what they had to do, while its sources were pretty much within their control. Their judgment was exercised upon things within the range of their activities and their contacts. The press, the telegraph, the telephone and radio have broadened indefinitely the range of information at the disposal of the average person. It would be foolish to deny that a certain quickening of sluggish minds has resulted. But quite aside from having opened avenues through which organized propaganda may operate continuously to stir emotion and to leave behind a deposit of opinion, there is much information about which judgment is not called upon to respond, and where even if it wanted to, it cannot act effectively so dispersive is the material about which it is called upon to exert itself. The average person is surrounded today by readymade intellectual goods as he is by readymade foods, articles, and all kinds of gadgets. He has not the personal share in making either intellectual or material goods that his pioneer ancestors had. Consequently they knew better what they themselves were about, though they knew infinitely less concerning what the world at large was doing.

Self-government of the town-meeting type is adequate for management of local affairs, such as school buildings, district revenues, school local roads and local taxation. Participation in these forms of self-government was a good preparation for self-government on a larger scale. But such matters as roads and schools under existing conditions have more than local import even in country districts; and while participation in town meetings is good as far as it arouses public spirit, it cannot provide the information that enables a citizen to be an intelligent judge of national affairs—now also affected by world conditions. Schooling in literacy is no substitute for the dispositions which were formerly provided by direct experiences of an educative quality. The void created by lack of relevant personal experiences combines with the confusion produced by impact of multitudes of unrelated incidents to create attitudes which are responsive to organized propaganda, hammering in day after day the same few and relatively simple beliefs asseverated to be "truths" essential to national welfare. In short, we have to take into account the attitudes of human nature that have been created by the immense development in mechanical instrumentalities if we are to understand the present power of organized propaganda.

The effect of the increase in number and diversity of unrelated facts that now play pretty continuously upon the average person is more easily grasped than is the influence of popular generalities, not checked by observed facts, over the interpretation put upon practical events, one that provokes acquiescence rather than critical inquiry. One chief reason for underestimation of the influence of generalities or "principles" is that they are so embodied in habits that those actuated by them are hardly aware of their existence. Or, if they are aware of them, they take them to be self-evident truths of common sense. When habits are so ingrained as to be second nature, they seem to have all of the inevitability that belongs to the movement of the fixed stars. The "principles" and standards which are stated in words and which circulate widely at a given time are usually only formulations of things which men do not so much believe in the intellectual sense of belief as live by unconsciously. Then when men who have lived under different conditions and have formed different life habits put forth different "principles," the latter are rejected as sources of some contagion introduced by foreigners hostile to our institutions.

Opinions are at once the most superficial and the most steel-plated of all human affairs. This difference between them is due to connection or lack of connection with habits that operate all but unconsciously. Verbal habits also exist and have power. Men continue to give assent to formulae after they have ceased to be more than linguistic rituals. Even lip-service has practical effect, that of creating intellectual and emotional divisions. The latter may not be deliberate hypocrisy. But they constitute that kind of insincerity, that incompatibility of actions with professions, which startles us in those cases in which it is clear that a person "believes" what he says in the sense that he is not even aware of its inconsistency with what he does. These gaps, these insincerities, become deeper and wider in times like the present when great change in events and practical affairs is attended with marked cultural lags in verbal formulations. And the persons who have first deceived themselves are most effective in misleading others. One of the most perplexing of human phenomena is the case of persons who do "in good faith" the sort of things which logical demonstration can easily prove to be incompatible with good faith.

Insincerities of this sort are much more frequent than deliberate hypocrisies and more injurious. They exist on a wide scale when there has been a period of rapid change in environment accompanied by change in what men do in response and by a change in overt habits, but without corresponding readjustment of the basic emotional and moral attitudes formed in the period prior to change of environment. This "cultural lag" is everywhere in evidence at the present time. The rate of change in conditions has been so much greater than anything the world has known before that it is estimated that the last century has seen more changes in the conditions under which people live and associate than occurred in thousands of previous years. The pace has been so swift that it was practically impossible for underlying traditions and beliefs to keep step. Not merely individuals here and there but large numbers of people habitually respond to conditions about them by means of actions having no connection with their familiar verbal responses. And yet the latter express dispositions saturated with emotions that find an outlet in words but not in acts.

No estimate of the effects of culture upon the elements that now make up freedom begins to be adequate that does not take into account the moral and religious splits that are found in our very make-up as persons. The problem of creation of genuine democracy cannot be successfully dealt with in theory or in practice save as we create intellectual and moral integration out of present disordered conditions. Splits, divisions, between attitudes emotionally and congenially attuned to the past and habits that are forced into existence because of the necessity of dealing with present conditions are a chief cause of continued profession of devotion to democracy by those who do not think nor act day by day in accord with the moral demands of the profession. The consequence is a further weakening of the environing conditions upon which genuine democracy occurs, whether the division is found in business men, in clergymen, in educators or in politicians. The serious threat to our democracy is not the existence of foreign totalitarian states. It is the existence within our own personal attitudes and within our own institutions of conditions similar to those which have given a victory to exter-

nal authority, discipline, uniformity and dependence upon The Leader
in foreign countries. The battlefield is also accordingly here—within
ourselves and our institutions.

43. The Human Abode of the

Religious Function*

When set into the full body of his work, it can be said that
John Dewey did not write extensively on religion as such. Also, after early abandonment of his Vermont Congrega-
tionalism, Dewey had little sympathy for the institutions of
organized religion and in subsequent years made them the
subject of some of his most telling criticism. Even so, the
critique of religion found in *A Common Faith* would be
regarded today as tame.

What is of more interest is Dewey's awareness of the
human needs fulfilled by traditional religious faith and his effort to account for that need within the province of the activities of the community. Dewey had a deep although unor-
thodox religious sensibility, best expressed perhaps in *Art as
Experience*. Indeed, his concern for the affairs of ordinary experience touched upon both suffering and celebrating, and he
can be said to have anticipated what is now called a secular
liturgy. In this selection, Dewey probes the possibilities of
genuine religious feeling and conviction becoming operative in
"The Human Abode."

In discussing the intellectual content of religion before considering
religion in its social connections, I did not follow the usual temporal order. Upon the whole, collective modes of practice either come first or
are of greater importance. The core of religions has generally been
found in rites and ceremonies. Legends and myths grow up in part as

* From John Dewey, *A Common Faith* (New Haven, Yale University Press,
1960) (1934), pp. 59-87. Reprinted by permission, copyright © 1934 by Yale
University Press.

decorative dressings, in response to the irrepressible human tendency toward story-telling, and in part as attempts to explain ritual practices. Then as culture advances, stories are consolidated, and theogonies and cosmogonies are formed—as with the Babylonians, Egyptians, Hebrews and Greeks. In the case of the Greeks, the stories of creation and accounts of the constitution of the world were mainly poetic and literary, and philosophies ultimately developed from them. In most cases, legends along with rites and ceremonies came under the guardianship of a special body, the priesthood, and were subject to the special arts which it possessed. A special group was set aside as the responsible owners, protectors, and promulgators of the corpus of beliefs.

But the formation of a special social group having a peculiar relation to both the practices and the beliefs of religion is but part of the story. In the widest perspective, it is the less important part. The more significant point as regards the social import of religion is that the priesthoods were official representatives of some community, tribe, city-state or empire. Whether there was a priesthood or not, individuals who were members of a community were born into a religious community as they were into social and political organization. Each social group had its own divine beings who were its founders and protectors. Its rites of sacrifice, purification, and communion were manifestations of organized civic life. The temple was a public institution, the focus of the worship of the community; the influence of its practices extended to all the customs of the community, domestic, economic, and political. Even wars between groups were usually conflicts of their respective deities.

An individual did not join a church. He was born and reared in a community whose social unity, organization and traditions were symbolized and celebrated in the rites, cults and beliefs of a collective religion. Education was the induction of the young into community activities that were interwoven at every point with customs, legends and ceremonies intimately connected with and sanctioned by a religion. There are a few persons, especially those brought up in Jewish communities in Russia, who can understand without the use of imagination what a religion means socially when it permeates all the customs and activities of group life. To most of us in the United States such a situation is only a remote historic episode.

The change that has taken place in conditions once universal and now infrequent is in my opinion the greatest change that has occurred in religion in all history. The intellectual conflict of scientific and theological beliefs has attracted much more attention. It is still near the focus of attention. But the change in the social center of gravity of religion has gone on so steadily and is now so generally accomplished that it has faded from the thought of most persons, save perhaps the historians, and even they are especially aware of it only in its political aspect. For the conflict between state and church still continues in some countries.

There are even now persons who are born into a particular church, that of their parents, and who take membership in it almost as a matter of course; indeed, the fact of such membership may be an important, even a determining, factor in an individual's whole career. But the thing new in history, the thing once unheard of, is that the organization in question is a *special* institution within a secular community. Even where there are established churches, they are constituted by the state and may be unmade by the state. Not only the national state but other forms of organization among groups have grown in power and influence at the expense of organizations built upon and about a religion. The correlate of this fact is that membership in associations of the latter type is more and more a matter of the voluntary choice of individuals, who may tend to accept responsibilities imposed by the church but who accept them of their own volition. If they do accept them, the organization they join is, in many nations, chartered under a general corporation law of the political and secular entity.

The shift in what I have called the social center of gravity accompanies the enormous expansion of associations formed for educational, political, economic, philanthropic and scientific purposes, which has occurred independently of any religion. These social modes have grown so much that they exercise the greater hold upon the thought and interest of most persons, even of those holding membership in churches. This positive extension of interests which, from the standpoint of a religion, are non-religious, is so great that in comparison with it the direct effect of science upon the creeds of religion seems to me of secondary importance.

I say, the *direct* effect; for the indirect effect of science in stimulating the growth of competing organizations is enormous. Changes that are purely intellectual affect at most but a small number of specialists. They are secondary to consequences brought about through impact upon the *conditions* under which human beings associate with one another. Invention and technology, in alliance with industry and commerce, have, needless to say, profoundly affected these underlying conditions of association. Every political and social problem of the present day reflects this indirect influence, from unemployment to banking, from municipal administration to the great migration of peoples made possible by new modes of transportation, from birth control to foreign commerce and war. The social changes that have come about through application of the new knowledge affect everyone, whether he is aware or not of the source of the forces that play upon him. The effect is the deeper, indeed, because so largely unconscious. For, to repeat what I have said, the *conditions* under which people meet and act together have been modified.

The fundamentalist in religion is one whose beliefs in intellectual content have hardly been touched by scientific developments. His notions about heaven and earth and man, as far as their bearing on religion is concerned, are hardly more affected by the work of Copernicus, Newton, and Darwin than they are by that of Einstein. But his actual life, in what he does day by day and in the contacts that are set up, has been radically changed by political and economic changes that have followed from applications of science. As far as strictly intellectual changes are concerned, creeds display great power of accommodation; their articles undergo insensible change of perspective; emphases are altered, and new meanings creep in. The Catholic Church, particularly, has shown leniency in dealing with intellectual deviations as long as they do not touch discipline, rites, and sacraments.

Among the laity only a small number, the more highly educated section, is directly affected by changes in scientific beliefs. Certain ideas recede more or less into the background but are not seriously challenged; nominally they are accepted. Probably most educated people thought the conception of biological evolution had been accepted as a commonplace until legislation in Tennessee and the Scopes trial brought about an acute crisis that revealed how far that was from being the case. Within an ecclesiastic organization, on the other hand, the class of professionals does not sense the change in perspective and emphasis of values in the general mind until some acute situation reveals it. Then they vigorously deny the validity of the new interests that have arisen. But since they are working against interests rather than merely against ideas, their desperate efforts are not convincing except for those already convinced.

Changes in practice that affect collective life go deep and extend far. They have been operating ever since the time we call the Middle Ages. The Renaissance was essentially a new birth of secularism. The development of the idea of "natural religion," characteristic of the eighteenth century, was a protest against control by ecclesiastic bodies—a movement foreshadowed in this respect by the growth of "independent" religious societies in the preceding century. But natural religion no more denied the intellectual validity of supernatural ideas than did the growth of independent congregations. It attempted rather to justify theism and immortality on the basis of the natural reason of the individual. The transcendentalism of the nineteenth century was a further move in the same general direction, a movement in which "reason" took on a more romantic, more colorful, and more collective form. It asserted the diffusion of the supernatural through secular life.

These movements and others not mentioned are the intellectual reflex of the greatest revolution that has taken place in religions during the thousands of years that man has been upon earth. For, as I have said, this change has to do with the *social* place and function of religion. Even the hold of the supernatural upon the general mind has become more and more disassociated from the power of ecclesiastic organization—that is, of any particular form of communal organization. Thus the very idea that was central in religions has more and more oozed away, so to speak, from the guardianship and care of any particular social institution. Even more important is the fact that a steady encroachment upon ecclesiastic institutions of forms of association once regarded as secular has altered the way in which men spend their time in work, recreation, citizenship, and political action. The essential point is not just that secular organizations and actions are legally or externally severed from the control of the church, but that interests and values unrelated to the offices of any church now so largely sway the desires and aims of even believers.

The individual believer may indeed carry the disposition and motivation he has acquired through affiliation with a religious organization into his political action, into his connection with schools, even into his business and amusements. But there remain two facts that constitute a revolution. In the first place, conditions are such that this action is a matter of personal choice and resolution on the part of individuals, not of the very nature of social organization. In the second place, the very fact that an individual imports or carries his personal attitude into affairs that are inherently secular, that are outside the scope of religion, constitutes an enormous change, in spite of the belief that secular matters *should* be permeated by the spirit of religion. Even if it be asserted, as it is by some religionists, that all the new movements and interests of any value grew up under the auspices of a church and received their impetus from the same source, it must be admitted that once the vessels have been launched, they are sailing on strange seas to far lands.

Here, it seems to me, is the issue to be faced. Here is the place where the distinction that I have drawn between a religion and the religious function is peculiarly applicable. It is of the nature of a religion based on the supernatural to draw a line between the religious and the secular and profane, even when it asserts the rightful authority of the Church and its religion to dominate these other interests. The conception that "religious" signifies a certain attitude and outlook, independent of the supernatural, necessitates no such division. It does not shut religious values up within a particular compartment, nor assume that a particular form of association bears a unique relation to it. Upon the social side the future of the religious function seems preëminently bound up with its emancipation from religions and a particular religion. Many persons feel perplexed because of the multiplicity of churches and the conflict of their claims. But the fundamental difficulty goes deeper.

In what has been said I have not ignored the interpretation put, by representatives of religious organizations, upon the historic change that has occurred. The oldest organization, the Roman Catholic church, judges the secularization of life, the growing independence of social interests and values from control by the church, as but one evidence the more of the apostasy of the natural man from God: the corruption inherent in the will of mankind has resulted in defiance of the authority that God has delegated to his designated representatives on earth. This church points to the fact that secularization has proceeded *pari passu* with the extension of Protestantism as evidence of the wilful heresy of the latter in its appeal to private conscience and choice. The remedy is simple. Submission to the will of God, as continuously expressed through the organization that is his established viceregent on earth, is the sole means by which social relations and values can again become coextensive with religion.

Protestant churches, on the contrary, have emphasized the fact that the relation of man to God is primarily an individual matter, a matter of personal choice and responsibility. From this point of view, one aspect of the change outlined marks an advance that is religious as well as moral. For according to it, the beliefs and rites that tend to make relation of man to God a collective and institutional affair erect barriers between the human soul and the divine spirit. Communion with God must be initiated by the individual's heart and will through direct divine assistance. Hence the change that has occurred in the social status of organized religion is nothing to deplore. What has been lost was at best specious and external. What has been gained is that religion has been placed upon its only real and solid foundation: direct relationship of conscience and will to God. Although there is much that is non-Christian and anti-Christian in existing economic and political institutions, it is better that change be accomplished by the sum total of efforts of men and women who are imbued with personal faith, than that they be effected by any wholesale institutional effort that subordinates the individual to an external and ultimately a worldly authority.

Were the question involved in these two opposed views taken up in detail, there are some specific considerations that might be urged. It might be urged that the progressive secularization of the interests of life has not been attended by the increasing degeneration that the argument of the first group implies. There are many who, as historical students, independent of affiliation with any religion, would regard reversal of the process of secularization and return to conditions in which the Church was the final authority as a menace to things held most precious. With reference to the position of Protestantism, it may be urged that in fact such social advances as have taken place are not the product of voluntary religious associations; that, on the contrary, the forces that have worked to humanize human relations, that have resulted in intellectual and aesthetic development, have come from influences that are independent of the churches. A case could be made out for the position that the churches have lagged behind in most important social movements and that they have turned their chief attention in social affairs to moral *symptoms*, to vices and abuses, like drunkenness, sale of intoxicants, divorce, rather than to the causes of war and of the long list of economic and political injustices and oppressions. Protest against the latter has been mainly left to secular movements.

In earlier times, what we now call the supernatural hardly meant anything more definite than the extraordinary, that which was striking and emotionally impressive because of its out-of-the-way character. Probably even today the commonest conception of the natural is that which is usual, customary and familiar. When there is no insight into the cause of unusual events, belief in the supernatural is itself "natural"—in this sense of natural. Supernaturalism was, therefore, a genuinely social religion as long as men's minds were attuned to the supernatural. It gave an "explanation" of extraordinary occurrences while it provided techniques for utilizing supernatural forces to secure advantages and to protect the members of the community against them when they were adverse.

The growth of natural science brought extraordinary things into line with events for which there is a "natural" explanation. At the same time, the development of positive social interests crowded heaven—and its opposite, hell—into the background. The function and offices of churches became more and more specialized; concerns and values that had been regarded, in an earlier contrast, as profane and secular grew in bulk and in importance. At the same time, the notion that basic and ultimate spiritual and ideal values are associated with the supernatural has persisted as a kind of vague background and aura. A kind of polite deference to the notion remains along with a concrete transfer of interest. The general mind is thus left in a confused and divided state. The movement that has been going on for the last few centuries will continue to breed doubleness of mind until religious meanings and values are definitely integrated into normal social relations.

The issue may be more definitely stated. The extreme position on one side is that apart from relation to the supernatural, man is morally on a level with the brutes. The other position is that all significant ends and all securities for stability and peace have grown up in the matrix of human relations, and that the values given a supernatural locus are in fact products of an idealizing imagination that has laid hold of natural goods. There ensues a second contrast. On the one hand, it is held that relation to the supernatural is the only finally dependable source of motive power; that directly and indirectly it has animated every serious effort for the guidance and rectification of man's life on earth. The other position is that goods actually experienced in the concrete relations of family, neighborhood, citizenship, pursuit of art and science, are what men actually depend upon for guidance and support, and that their reference to a supernatural and other-worldly locus has obscured their real nature and has weakened their force.

The contrasts outlined define the religious problem of the present and the future. What would be the consequences upon the values of human association if intrinsic and immanent satisfactions and opportunities were clearly held to and cultivated with the ardor and the devotion that have at times marked historic religions? The contention of an increasing number of persons is that depreciation of natural social values has resulted, both in principle and in actual fact, from reference of their origin and significance to supernatural sources. Natural relations, of husband and wife, of parent and child, friend and friend, neighbor and neighbor, of fellow workers in industry, science, and art, are neglected, passed over, not developed for all that is in them. They are, moreover, not merely depreciated. They have been regarded as dangerous rivals of higher values; as offering temptations to be resisted; as usurpations by flesh of the authority of the spirit; as revolts of the human against the divine.

The doctrine of original sin and total depravity, of the corruption of nature, external and internal, is not especially current in liberal religious circles at present. Rather, there prevails the idea that there are two separate systems of values—an idea similar to that referred to in the previous chapter about a revelation of two kinds of truth. The values found in natural and supernatural relationships are now, in liberal circles, said to be complementary, just as the truths of revelation and of science are the two sides, mutually sustaining, of the same ultimate truth.

I cannot but think that this position represents a great advance upon the traditional one. While it is open logically to the objections that hold against the idea of the dual revelation of truth, practically it indicates a development of a humane point of view. But if it be once admitted that human relations are charged with values that are religious in function, why not rest the case upon what is verifiable and concentrate thought and energy upon its full realization?

History seems to exhibit three stages of growth. In the first stage, human relationships were thought to be so infected with the evils of corrupt human nature as to require redemption from external and supernatural sources. In the next stage, what is significant in these relations is found to be akin to values esteemed distinctively religious. This is the point now reached by liberal theologians. The third stage would realize that in fact the values prized in those religions that have ideal elements are idealizations of things characteristic of natural association, which have then been projected into a supernatural realm for safe-keeping and sanction. Note the rôle of such terms as Father, Son, Bride, Fellowship and Communion in the vocabulary of Christianity, and note also the tendency, even if a somewhat inchoate one, of terms that express the more intimate phases of association to displace those of legal, political origin: King, Judge, and Lord of Hosts.

Unless there is a movement into what I have called the third stage, fundamental dualism and a division in life continue. The idea of a double and parallel manifestation of the divine, in which the latter has superior status and authority, brings about a condition of unstable equilibrium. It operates to distract energy, through dividing the objects to which it is directed. It also imperatively raises the question as to why having gone far in recognition of religious values in normal community life, we should not go further. The values of natural human intercourse and mutual dependence are open and public, capable of verification by the methods through which all natural facts are established. By means of the same experimental method, they are capable of expansion. Why not concentrate upon nurturing and extending them? Unless we take this step, the idea of two realms of spiritual values is only a softened version of the old dualism between the secular and the spiritual, the profane and the religious.

The condition of unstable equilibrium is indeed so evident to the thoughtful mind that there are attempts just now to revert to the earlier stage of belief. It is not difficult to make a severe indictment of existing social relations. It is enough to point to the war, jealousy, and fear that dominate the relations of national states to one another; to the growing demoralization of the older ties of domestic life; to the staggering evidence of corruption and futility in politics, and to the egoism, brutality, and oppression that characterize economic activities. By piling up material of this sort, one may, if one chooses, arrive at the triumphant conclusion that social relations are so debased that the only recourse is to supernatural aid. The general disorder of the Great War and succeeding decades has led to a revival of the theology of corruption, sin, and need for supernatural redemption.

The conclusion does not follow, however, from the data. It ignores, in the first place, that all the positive values which are prized, and in aid of which supernatural power is appealed to, have, after all, emerged from the very scene of human associations of which it is possible to paint so black a picture. Something in the facts has been left out of the picture. I shall not bring forward again at this place what was earlier said as to the effect upon actual conditions of diversion of the thought and action of those who are peculiarly sensitive to ideal considerations into supernatural channels. I shall raise a more directly practical issue. Society is convicted of being "immoral" by evoking all the evils of institutions as they now exist, and the unexpressed premise is that the institutions as they exist are normal expressions of social relations in their own nature.

Were this premise stated, the enormous gap between it and the conclusion set forth would be apparent. The problem of the relation between social relations and institutions that are dominant at a particular time is the most intricate problem presented to social inquiry. The idea that the latter are a direct reflex of the former ignores the multiplicity of factors that historically have entered into the shaping of institutions. Historically speaking, many of these factors are accidental with respect to the institutional form that has been given to social relations. One of my favorite quotations is a statement of Clarence Ayers that "our industrial revolution began, as some historians say, with half a dozen technical improvements in the textile industry; and it took us a century to realize that anything of moment had happened to us, beyond the obvious improvement of spinning and weaving." This statement must serve in lieu of long argument to suggest what I mean by the "accidental" relation of institutional developments to the primary facts of human association. The relation is accidental because institutional consequences that have resulted were not foreseen or intended. To say this, is to say that social intelligence in the sense in which there is intelligence about physical relations is in so far nonexistent.

Here is the negative fact that renders argument for the necessity of supernatural intervention to effect significant betterment only just another instance of the old, old inference to the supernatural from the basis of ignorance. We lack, for example, knowledge of the relation of life to inanimate matter. Therefore supernatural intervention is assumed to have effected the transition from brute to man. We do not know the relation of the organism—the brain and nervous system—to the occurrence of thought. Therefore, it is argued, there is a supernatural link. We do not know the relation of causes to results in social matters, and consequently we lack means of control. Therefore, it is inferred, we must resort to supernatural control. Of course, I make no claim to knowing how far intelligence may and will develop in respect to social relations. But one thing I think I do know. The needed understanding will not develop unless we strive for it. The assumption that only supernatural agencies can give control is a sure method of retarding this effort. It is as sure to be a hindering force now with respect to social intelligence, as the similar appeal was earlier an obstruction in the development of physical knowledge.

Even immediately, without awaiting the development of greater intelligence in relation to social affairs, a great difference would be made by use of natural means and methods. It is even now possible to examine complex social phenomena sufficiently to put the finger on things that are wrong. It is possible to trace to some extent these evils to their causes, and to causes that are something very different from abstract moral forces. It is possible to work out and work upon remedies for some of the sore spots. The outcome will not be a gospel of salvation but it will be in line with that pursued, for example, in matters of disease and health. The method if used would not only accomplish something toward social health but it would accomplish a greater thing; it would forward the development of social intelligence so that it could act with greater hardihood and on a larger scale.

Vested interests, interests vested with power, are powerfully on the side of the *status quo*, and therefore they are especially powerful in hindering the growth and application of the method of natural intelligence. Just because these interests are so powerful, it is the more necessary to fight for recognition of the method of intelligence in action. But one of the greatest obstacles in conducting this combat is the tendency to dispose of social evils in terms of general moral causes. The sinfulness of man, the corruption of his heart, his self-love and love of power, when referred to as causes are precisely of the same nature as was the appeal to abstract powers (which in fact only reduplicated under a general name a multitude of particular effects) that once prevailed in physical "science," and that operated as a chief obstacle to the generation and growth of the latter. Demons were once appealed to in order to explain bodily disease and no such thing as a strictly natural death was supposed to happen. The importation of general moral causes to explain present *social* phenomena is on the same intellectual level. Reinforced by the prestige of traditional religions, and backed by the emotional force of beliefs in the supernatural, it stifles the growth of that social intelligence by means of which direction of social change could be taken out of the region of accident, as accident has been defined. Accident in this broad sense and the idea of the supernatural are twins. Interest in the supernatural therefore reinforces other vested interests to prolong the social reign of accident.

There is a strong reaction in some religious circles today against the idea of mere individual salvation of individual souls. There is also a reaction in politics and economics against the idea of *laissez faire*. Both of these movements reflect a common tendency. Both of them are signs of the growing awareness of the emptiness of individuality in isolation. But the fundamental root of the *laissez faire* idea is denial (more often implicit than express) of the possibility of radical intervention of intelligence in the conduct of human life. Now appeal for supernatural intervention in improvement of social matters is also the expression of a deep-seated *laissez-faireism*; it is the acknowledgment of the desperate situation into which we are driven by the idea of the irrelevance and futility of human intervention in social events and interests. Those contemporary theologians who are interested in social change and who at the same time depreciate human intelligence and effort in behalf of the supernatural, are riding two horses that are going in opposite directions. The old-fashioned ideas of doing something to make the will of God prevail in the world, and of assuming the responsibility of doing the job ourselves, have more to be said for them, logically and practically.

The emphasis that has been put upon intelligence as a method should not mislead anyone. Intelligence, as distinct from the older conception of reason, is inherently involved in action. Moreover, there is no opposition between it and emotion. There is such a thing as passionate intelligence, as ardor in behalf of light shining into the murky places of social existence, and as zeal for its refreshing and purifying effect. The whole story of man shows that there are no objects that may not deeply stir engrossing emotion. One of the few experiments in the attachment of emotion to ends that mankind has not tried is that of devotion, so intense as to be religious, to intelligence as a force in social action.

But this is only part of the scene. No matter how much evidence may be piled up against social institutions as they exist, affection and passionate desire for justice and security are realities in human nature. So are the emotions that arise from living in conditions of inequity, oppression, and insecurity. Combination of the two kinds of emotion has more than once produced those changes that go by the name of revolution. To say that emotions which are not fused with intelligence are blind is tautology. Intense emotion may utter itself in action that destroys institutions. But the only assurance of birth of better ones is the marriage of emotion with intelligence.

Criticism of the commitment of religion to the supernatural is thus positive in import. All modes of human association are "affected with a public interest," and full realization of this interest is equivalent to a sense of a significance that is religious in its function. The objection to supernaturalism is that it stands in the way of an effective realization of the sweep and depth of the implications of natural human relations. It stands in the way of using the means that are in our power to make radical changes in these relations. It is certainly true that great material changes might be made with no corresponding improvement of a spiritual or ideal nature. But development in the latter direction cannot be introduced from without; it cannot be brought about by dressing up material and economic changes with decorations derived from the supernatural. It can come only from more intense realization of values that inhere in the actual connections of human beings with one another. The attempt to segregate the implicit public interest and social value of all institutions and social arrangements in a particular organization is a fatal diversion.

Were men and women actuated throughout the length and breadth of human relations with the faith and ardor that have at times marked historic religions the consequences would be incalculable. To achieve this faith and *élan* is no easy task. But religions have attempted something similar, directed moreover toward a less promising object—the supernatural. It does not become those who hold that faith may move mountains to deny in advance the possibility of its manifestation on the basis of verifiable realities. There already exists, though in a rudimentary form, the capacity to relate social conditions and events to their causes, and the ability will grow with exercise. There is the technical skill with which to initiate a campaign for social health and sanity analogous to that made in behalf of physical public health. Human beings have impulses toward affection, compassion and justice, equality and freedom. It remains to weld all these things together. It is of no use merely to assert that the intrenched foes of class interest and power in high places are hostile to the realization of such a union. As I have already said, if this enemy did not exist, there would be little sense in urging *any* policy of change. The point to be grasped is that, unless one gives up the whole struggle as hopeless, one has to choose between alternatives. One alternative is dependence upon the supernatural; the other, the use of natural agencies.

There is then no sense, logical or practical, in pointing out the difficulties that stand in the way of the latter course, until the question of the alternative is faced. If it is faced, it will also be realized that one factor in the choice is dependence upon enlisting only those committed to the supernatural and alliance with all men and women who feel the stir of social emotion, including the large number of those who, consciously or unconsciously, have turned their backs upon the supernatural. Those who face the alternatives will also have to choose between a continued and even more systematic *laissez faire* depreciation of intelligence and the resources of natural knowledge and understanding, and conscious and organized effort to turn the use of these means from narrow ends, personal and class, to larger human purposes. They will have to ask, as far as they nominally believe in the need for radical social change, whether what they accomplish when they point with one hand to the seriousness of present evils is not undone when the other hand points away from man and nature for their remedy.

The transfer of idealizing imagination, thought and emotion to natural human relations would not signify the destruction of churches that now exist. It would rather offer the means for a recovery of vitality. The fund of human values that are prized and that need to be cherished, values that are satisfied and rectified by *all* human concerns and arrangements, could be celebrated and reinforced, in different ways and with differing symbols, by the churches. In that way the churches would indeed become catholic. The demand that churches show a more active interest in social affairs, that they take a definite stand upon such questions as war, economic injustice, political corruption, that they stimulate action for a divine kingdom on earth, is one of the signs of the times. But as long as social values are related to a supernatural for which the churches stand in some peculiar way, there is an inherent inconsistency between the demand and efforts to execute it. On the one hand, it is urged that the churches are going outside their special province when they involve themselves in economic and political issues. On the other hand, the very fact that they claim if not a monopoly of supreme values and motivating forces, yet a unique relation to them, makes it impossible for the churches to participate in promotion of social ends on a natural and equal human basis. The surrender of claims to an exclusive and authoritative position is a *sine qua non* for doing away with the dilemma in which churches now find themselves in respect to their sphere of social action.

At the outset, I referred to an outstanding historic fact. The coincidence of the realm of social interests and activities with a tribal or civic community has vanished. Secular interests and activities have grown up outside of organized religions and are independent of their authority. The hold of these interests upon the thoughts and desires of men has crowded the social importance of organized religions into a corner and the area of this corner is decreasing. This change either marks a terrible decline in everything that can justly be termed religious in value, in traditional religions, or it provides the opportunity for expansion of these qualities on a new basis and with a new outlook. It is impossible to ignore the fact that historic Christianity has been committed to a separation of sheep and goats; the saved and the lost; the elect and the mass. Spiritual aristocracy as well as *laissez faire* with respect to natural and human intervention, is deeply embedded in its traditions. Lip service—often more than lip service—has been given to the idea of the common brotherhood of all men. But those outside the fold of the church and those who do not rely upon belief in the supernatural have been regarded as only potential brothers, still requiring adoption into the family. I cannot understand how any realization of the democratic ideal as a vital moral and spiritual ideal in human affairs is possible without surrender of the conception of the basic division to which supernatural Christianity is committed. Whether or no we are, save in some metaphorical sense, all brothers, we are at least all in the same boat traversing the same turbulent ocean. The potential religious significance of this fact is infinite.

In the opening chapter I made a distinction between religion and the religious. I pointed out that religion—or religions—is charged with beliefs, practices and modes of organization that have accrued to and been loaded upon the religious element in experience by the state of culture in which religions have developed. I urged that conditions are now ripe for emancipation of the religious quality from accretions that have grown up about it and that limit the credibility and the influence of religion. In the second chapter, I developed this idea with respect to the faith in ideals that is immanent in the religious value of experience, and asserted that the power of this faith would be enhanced were belief freed from the conception that the significance and validity of the ideal are bound up with intellectual assent to the proposition that the ideal is already embodied in some supernatural or metaphysical sense in the very framework of existence.

The matter touched upon in the present chapter includes within itself all that has been previously set forth. It does so upon both its negative and positive sides. The community of causes and consequences in which we, together with those not born, are enmeshed is the widest and deepest symbol of the mysterious totality of being the imagination calls the universe. It is the embodiment for sense and thought of that encompassing scope of existence the intellect cannot grasp. It is the matrix within which our ideal aspirations are born and bred. It is the source of the values that the moral imagination projects as directive criteria and as shaping purposes.

The continuing life of this comprehensive community of beings includes all the significant achievement of men in science and art and all the kindly offices of intercourse and communication. It holds within its content all the material that gives verifiable intellectual support to our ideal faiths. A "creed" founded on this material will change and grow, but it cannot be shaken. What it surrenders it gives up gladly because of new light and not as a reluctant concession. What it adds, it adds because new knowledge gives further insight into the conditions that bear upon the formation and execution of our life purposes. A one-sided psychology, a reflex of eighteenth-century "individualism," treated knowledge as an accomplishment of a lonely mind. We should now be aware that it is a product of the cooperative and communicative operations of human beings living together. Its communal origin is an indication of its rightful communal use. The unification of what is known at any given time, not upon an impossible eternal and abstract basis but upon that of its bearing upon the unification of human desire and purpose, furnishes a sufficient creed for human acceptance, one that would provide a religious release and reinforcement of knowledge.

"Agnosticism" is a shadow cast by the eclipse of the supernatural. Of course, acknowledgment that we do not know what we do not know is a necessity of all intellectual integrity. But generalized agnosticism is only a halfway elimination of the supernatural. Its meaning departs when the intellectual outlook is directed wholly to the natural world. When it is so directed, there are plenty of particular matters regarding which we must say we do not know; we only inquire and form hypotheses which future inquiry will confirm or reject. But such doubts are an incident of faith in the method of intelligence. They are signs of faith, not of a pale and impotent skepticism. We doubt in order that we may find out, not because some inaccessible supernatural lurks behind whatever we can know. The substantial background of practical faith in ideal ends is positive and out-reaching.

The considerations put forward in the present chapter may be summed up in what they imply. The ideal ends to which we attach our faith are not shadowy and wavering. They assume concrete form in our understanding of our relations to one another and the values contained in these relations. We who now live are parts of a humanity that extends into the remote past, a humanity that has interacted with nature. The things in civilization we most prize are not of ourselves. They exist by grace of the doings and sufferings of the continuous human community in which we are a link. Ours is the responsibility of conserving, transmitting, rectifying and expanding the heritage of values we have received that those who come after us may receive it more solid and secure, more widely accessible and more generously shared than we have received it. Here are all the elements for a religious faith that shall not be confined to sect, class, or race. Such a faith has always been implicitly the common faith of mankind. It remains to make it explicit and militant.

44. Morality Is Social*

It is fitting that the last selection in these volumes finds Dewey again exploring the themes of intelligence and moral judgment within the context of social experience. This selection was the concluding chapter to *Human Nature and Conduct*, modestly subtitled *An Introduction to Social Psychology*. Actually it was the capstone of a movement in America, originating with Charles Horton Cooley, James

* From John Dewey, *Human Nature and Conduct: An Introduction to Social Psychology* (New York, Modern Library, 1930) (1922), pp. 314-32. Copyright 1922 by Holt, Rinehart and Winston, Inc. Copyright 1950 by John Dewey. Reprinted by permission of Holt, Rinehart and Winston, Inc.

Mark Baldwin, and Lester Ward, to develop a genetic psychology in social terms. Deeply influenced by his former colleague and friend George Herbert Mead, Dewey set out the principles and problems of this comparatively new approach to human behavior.

This selection, "Morality Is Social," is vintage Dewey, raising more problems than it resolves, prodding us to further work in a different and important area. The conclusion to this chapter, however, is crystal clear and serves to end these volumes with Dewey at his most poetic. Of course, we should realize that for Dewey a conclusion, no matter how fulfilling, is also a beginning:

Within the flickering inconsequential acts of separate selves dwells a sense of the whole which claims and dignifies them. In its presence we put off mortality and live in the universal. The life of the community in which we live and have our being is the fit symbol of this relationship. The acts in which we express our perception of the ties which bind us to others are its only rites and ceremonies.

Intelligence becomes ours in the degree in which we use it and accept responsibility for consequences. It is not ours originally or by production. "It thinks" is a truer psychological statement than "I think." Thoughts sprout and vegetate; ideas proliferate. They come from deep unconscious sources. "I think" is a statement about voluntary action. Some suggestion surges from the unknown. Our active body of habits appropriates it. The suggestion then becomes an assertion. It no longer merely comes to us. It is accepted and uttered by us. We act upon it and thereby assume, by implication, its consequences. The stuff of belief and proposition is not originated by us. It comes to us from others, by education, tradition and the suggestion of the environment. Our intelligence is bound up, so far as its materials are concerned, with the community life of which we are a part. We know what it communicates to us, and know according to the habits it forms in us. Science is an affair of civilization not of individual intellect.

So with conscience. When a child acts, those about him re-act. They shower encouragement upon him, visit him with approval, or they bestow frowns and rebuke. What others do to us when we act is as natural a consequence of our action as what the fire does to us when we plunge our hands in it. The social environment may be as artificial as you please. But its action in response to ours is natural not artificial. In language and imagination we rehearse the responses of others just as we dramatically enact other consequences. We foreknow how others will act, and the foreknowledge is the beginning of judgment passed on action. We know *with* them; there is conscience. An assembly is formed within our breast which discusses and appraises proposed and performed acts. The community without becomes a forum and tribunal within, a judgment-seat of charges, assessments and exculpations. Our thoughts of our own actions are saturated with the ideas that others entertain about them, ideas which have been expressed not only in explicit instruction but still more effectively in reaction to our acts.

Liability is the beginning of responsibility. We are held accountable by others for the consequences of our acts. They visit their like and dislike of these consequences upon us. In vain do we claim that these are not ours; that they are products of ignorance not design, or are incidents in the execution of a most laudable scheme. Their authorship is imputed to us. We are disapproved, and disapproval is not an inner state of mind but a most definite act. Others say to us by their deeds we do not care a fig whether you did this deliberately or not. We intend that you *shall* deliberate before you do it again, and that if possible your deliberation shall prevent a repetition of this act we object to. The reference in blame and every unfavorable judgment is prospective, not retrospective. Theories about responsibility may become confused, but in practice no one is stupid enough to try to change the past. Approbation and disapprobation are ways of influencing the formation of habits and aims; that is, of influencing future acts. The individual is *held* accountable for what he *has* done in order that he may be responsive in what he is *going* to do. Gradually persons learn by dramatic imitation to hold themselves accountable, and liability becomes a voluntary deliberate acknowledgment that deeds are our own, that their consequences come from us.

These two facts, that moral judgment and moral responsibility are the work wrought in us by the social environment, signify that all morality is social; not because we *ought* to take into account the effect of our acts upon the welfare of others, but because of facts. Others *do* take account of what we do, and they respond accordingly to our acts. Their responses actually *do* affect the meaning of what we do. The significance thus contributed is as inevitable as is the effect of interaction with the physical environment. In fact as civilization advances the physical environment gets itself more and more humanized, for the meaning of physical energies and events becomes involved with the part they play in human activities. Our conduct *is* socially conditioned whether we perceive the fact or not.

The effect of custom on habit, and of habit upon thought is enough to prove this statement. When we begin to forecast consequences, the consequences that most stand out are those which will proceed from other people. The resistance and the cooperation of others is the central fact in the furtherance or failure of our schemes. Connections with our fellows furnish both the opportunities for action and the instrumentalities by which we take advantage of opportunity. All of the actions of an individual bear the stamp of his community as assuredly as does the language he speaks. Difficulty in reading the stamp is due to variety of impressions in consequence of membership in many groups. This social saturation is, I repeat, a matter of fact, not of what should be, not of what is desirable or undesirable. It does not guarantee the rightness or goodness of an act; there is no excuse for thinking of evil action as individualistic and right action as social. Deliberate unscrupulous pursuit of self-interest is as much conditioned upon social opportunities, training and assistance as is the course of action prompted by a beaming benevolence. The difference lies in the quality and degree of the perception of ties and interdependencies; in the use to which they are put. Consider the form commonly assumed today by self-seeking; namely command of money and economic power. Money is a social institution; property is a legal custom; economic opportunities are dependent upon the state of society; the objects aimed at, the rewards sought for, are what they are because of social admiration, prestige, competition and power. If money-making is morally obnoxious it is because of the way these social facts are handled, not because a money-making man has withdrawn from society into an isolated selfhood or turned his back upon society. His "individualism" is not found in his original nature but in his habits acquired under social influences. It is found in his concrete aims, and these are reflexes of social conditions. Well-grounded moral objection to a mode of conduct rests upon the kind of social connections that figure, not upon lack of social aim. A man may attempt to utilize social relationships for his own advantage in an inequitable way; he may intentionally or unconsciously try to make them feed one of his own appetites. Then he is denounced as egoistic. But both his course of action and the disapproval he is subject to are facts *within* society. They are social phenomena. He pursues his unjust advantage as a social asset.

Explicit recognition of this fact is a prerequisite of improvement in moral education and of an intelligent understanding of the chief ideas or "categories" of morals. Morals is as much a matter of interaction of a person with his social environment as walking is an interaction of legs with a physical environment. The character of walking depends upon the strength and competency of legs. But it also depends upon whether a man is walking in a bog or on a paved street, upon whether there is a safeguarded path set aside or whether he has to walk amid dangerous vehicles. If the standard of morals is low it is because the education given by the interaction of the individual with his social environment is defective. Of what avail is it to preach unassuming simplicity and contentment of life when communal admiration goes to the man who "succeeds"—who makes himself conspicuous and envied because of command of money and other forms of power? If a child gets on by peevishness or intrigue, then others are his accomplices who assist in the habits which are built up. The notion that an abstract ready-made conscience exists in individuals and that it is only necessary to make an occasional appeal to it and to indulge in occasional crude rebukes and punishments, is associated with the causes of lack of definitive and orderly moral advance. For it is associated with lack of attention to social forces.

There is a peculiar inconsistency in the current idea that morals *ought* to be social. The introduction of the moral "ought" into the idea contains an implicit assertion that morals depend upon something apart from social relations. Morals *are* social. The question of ought, should be, is a question of better and worse *in* social affairs. The extent to which the weight of theories has been thrown against the perception of the place of social ties and connections in moral activity is a fair measure of the extent to which social forces work blindly and develop an accidental morality. The chief obstacle for example to recognizing the truth of a proposition frequently set forth in these pages to the effect that all conduct is potential, if not actual, matter of moral judgment is the habit of identifying moral judgment with praise and blame. So great is the influence of this habit that it is safe to say that every professed moralist when he leaves the pages of theory and faces some actual item of his own or others' behavior, first or "instinctively" thinks of acts as moral or non-moral in the degree in which they are exposed to condemnation or approval. Now this kind of judgment is certainly not one which could profitably be dispensed with. Its influence is much needed. But the tendency to equate it with all moral judgment is largely responsible for the current idea that there is a sharp line between moral conduct and a larger region of non-moral conduct which is a matter of expediency, shrewdness, success or manners.

Moreover this tendency is a chief reason why the social forces effective in shaping actual morality work blindly and unsatisfactorily. Judgment in which the emphasis falls upon blame and approbation has more heat than light. It is more emotional than intellectual. It is guided by custom, personal convenience and resentment rather than by insight into causes and consequences. It makes toward reducing moral instruction, the educative influence of social opinion, to an immediate personal matter, that is to say, to an adjustment of personal likes and dislikes. Fault-finding creates resentment in the one blamed, and approval, complacency, rather than a habit of scrutinizing conduct objectively. It puts those who are sensitive to the judgments of others in a standing defensive attitude, creating an apologetic, self-accusing and self-exculpating habit of mind when what is needed is an impersonal impartial habit of observation. "Moral" persons get so occupied with defending their conduct from real and imagined criticism that they have little time left to see what their acts really amount to, and the habit of self-blame inevitably extends to include others since it is a habit.

Now it is a wholesome thing for any one to be made aware that thoughtless, self-centered action on his part exposes him to the indignation and dislike of others. There is no one who can be safely trusted to be exempt from immediate reactions of criticism, and there are few who do not need to be braced by occasional expressions of approval. But these influences are immensely overdone in comparison with the assistance that might be given by the influence of social judgments which operate without accompaniments of praise and blame; which enable an individual to see for himself what he is doing, and which put him in command of a method of analyzing the obscure and usually unavowed forces which move him to act. We need a permeation of judgments on conduct by the method and materials of a science of human nature. Without such enlightenment even the best-intentioned attempts at the moral guidance and improvement of others often eventuate in tragedies of misunderstanding and division, as is so often seen in the relations of parents and children.

The development therefore of a more adequate science of human nature is a matter of first-rate importance. The present revolt against the notion that psychology is a science of consciousness may well turn out in the future to be the beginning of a definitive turn in thought and action. Historically there are good reasons for the isolation and exaggeration of the conscious phase of human action, an isolation which forgot that "conscious" is an adjective of some acts and which erected the resulting abstraction, "consciousness," into a noun, an existence separate and complete. These reasons are interesting not only to the student of technical philosophy but also to the student of the history of culture and even of politics. They have to do with the attempt to drag realities out of occult essences and hidden forces and get them into the light of day. They were part of the general movement called phenomenalism, and of the growing importance of individual life and private voluntary concerns. But the effect was to isolate the individual from his connections both with his fellows and with nature, and thus to create an artificial human nature, one not capable of being understood and effectively directed on the basis of analytic understanding. It shut out from view, not to say from scientific examination, the forces which really move human nature. It took a few surface phenomena for the whole story of significant human motive-forces and acts.

As a consequence physical science and its technological applications were highly developed while the science of man, moral science, is backward. I believe that it is not possible to estimate how much of the difficulties of the present world situation are due to the disproportion and unbalance thus introduced into affairs. It would have seemed absurd to say in the seventeenth century that in the end the alteration in methods of physical investigation which was then beginning would prove more important than the religious wars of that century. Yet the wars marked the end of one era; the dawn of physical science the beginning of a new one. And a trained imagination may discover that the nationalistic and economic wars which are the chief outward mark of the present are in the end to be less significant than the development of a science of human nature now inchoate.

It sounds academic to say that substantial bettering of social relations waits upon the growth of a scientific social psychology. For the term suggests something specialized and remote. But the formation of habits of belief, desire and judgment is going on at every instant under the influence of the conditions set by men's contact, intercourse and associations with one another. This is the fundamental fact in social life and in personal character. It is the fact about which traditional human science gives no enlightenment—a fact which this traditional science blurs and virtually denies. The enormous rôle played in popular morals by appeal to the supernatural and quasi-magical is in effect a desperate admission of the futility of our science. Consequently the whole matter of the formation of the predispositions which effectively control human relationships is left to accident, to custom and imme-diate personal likings, resentments and ambitions. It is a commonplace that modern industry and commerce are conditioned upon a control of physical energies due to proper methods of physical inquiry and analysis. We have no social arts which are comparable because we have so nearly nothing in the way of psychological science. Yet through the development of physical science, and especially of chemistry, biology, physiology, medicine and anthropology we now have the basis for the development of such a science of man. Signs of its coming into existence are present in the movements in clinical, behavioristic and social (in its narrower sense) psychology.

At present we not only have no assured means of forming character except crude devices of blame, praise, exhortation and punishment, but the very meaning of the general notions of moral inquiry is matter of doubt and dispute. The reason is that these notions are discussed in isolation from the concrete facts of the interactions of human beings with one another—an abstraction as fatal as was the old discussion of phlogiston, gravity and vital force apart from concrete correlations of changing events with one another. Take for example such a basic con-ception as that of Right involving the nature of authority in conduct. There is no need here to rehearse the multitude of contending views which give evidence that discussion of this matter is still in the realm of opinion. We content ourselves with pointing out that this notion is the last resort of the anti-empirical school in morals and that it proves the effect of neglect of social conditions.

In effect its adherents argue as follows: "Let us concede that concrete ideas about right and wrong and particular notions of what is obligatory have grown up within experience. But we cannot admit this about the idea of Right, of Obligation itself. Why does moral authority exist at all? Why is the claim of the Right recognized in conscience even by those who violate it in deed? Our opponents say that such and such a course is wise, expedient, better. But *why* act for the wise, or good, or better? Why not follow our own immediate devices if we are so inclined? There is only one answer: We have a moral nature, a con-science, call it what you will. And this nature responds directly in ac-knowledgment of the supreme authority of the Right over all claims of inclination and habit. We may not act in accordance with this acknowl-edgment, but we still know that the authority of the moral law, al-though not its power, is unquestionable. Men may differ indefinitely ac-cording to what their experience has been as to just *what* is Right, what its contents are. But they all spontaneously agree in recognizing the supremacy of the claims of whatever is thought of as Right. Otherwise there would be no such thing as morality, but merely calculations of how to satisfy desire.

Grant the foregoing argument, and all the apparatus of abstract moralism follows in its wake. A remote goal of perfection, ideals that are contrary in a wholesale way to what is actual, a free will of arbitrary choice; all of these conceptions band themselves together with that of a non-empirical authority of Right and a non-empirical conscience which acknowledges it. They constitute its ceremonial or formal train.

Why, indeed, acknowledge the authority of Right? That many persons do not acknowledge it in fact, in action, and that all persons ignore it at times, is assumed by the argument. Just what is the significance of an alleged recognition of a supremacy which is continually denied in fact? How much would be lost if it were dropped out, and we were left face to face with actual facts? If a man lived alone in the world there might be some sense in the question "Why be moral?" were it not for one thing: No such question would then arise. As it is, we live in a world where other persons live too. Our acts affect them. They perceive these effects, and react upon us in consequence. Because they are living beings they make demands upon us for certain things from us. They approve and condemn—not in abstract theory but in what they do to us. The answer to the question "Why not put your hand in the fire?" is the answer of fact. If you do your hand will be burnt. The answer to the question why acknowledge the right is of the same sort. For Right is only an abstract name for the multitude of concrete demands in action which others impress upon us, and of which we are obliged, if we would live, to take some account. Its authority is the exigency of their demands, the efficacy of their insistencies. There may be good ground for the contention that in theory the idea of the right is subordinate to that of the good, being a statement of the course proper to attain good. But in fact it signifies the totality of social pressures exercised upon us to induce us to think and desire in certain ways. Hence the right can in fact become the road to the good only as the elements that compose this unremitting pressure are enlightened, only as social relationships become themselves reasonable.

It will be retorted that all pressure is a non-moral affair partaking of force, not of right; that right must be ideal. Thus we are invited to enter again the circle in which the ideal has no force and social actualities no ideal quality. We refuse the invitation because social pressure is involved in our own lives, as much so as the air we breathe and the ground we walk upon. If we had desires, judgments, plans, in short a mind, apart from social connections, then the latter would be external and their action might be regarded as that of a non-moral force. But we live mentally as physically only *in* and *because* of our environment. Social pressure is but a name for the interactions which are always going on and in which we participate, living so far as we partake and dying so far as we do not. The pressure is not ideal but empirical, yet empirical here means only actual. It calls attention to the fact that considerations of right are claims originating not outside of life, but within it. They are "ideal" in precisely the degree in which we intelligently recognize and act upon them, just as colors and canvas become ideal when used in ways that give an added meaning to life.

Accordingly failure to recognize the authority of right means defect in effective apprehension of the realities of human association, not an arbitrary exercise of free will. This deficiency and perversion in apprehension indicates a defect in education—that is to say, in the operation of actual conditions, in the consequences upon desire and thought of existing interactions and interdependencies. It is false that every person has a consciousness of the supreme authority of right and then misconceives it or ignores it in action. One has such a sense of the claims of social relationships as those relationships enforce in one's desires and observations. The belief in a separate, ideal or transcendental, practically ineffectual Right is a reflex of the inadequacy with which existing institutions perform their educative office—their office in generating observation of social continuities. It is an endeavor to "rationalize" this defect. Like all rationalizations, it operates to divert attention from the real state of affairs. Thus it helps maintain the conditions which created it, standing in the way of effort to make our institutions more humane and equitable. A theoretical acknowledgment of the supreme authority of Right, of moral law, gets twisted into an effectual substitute for acts which would better the customs which now produce vague, dull, halting and evasive observation of actual social ties. We are not caught in a circle; we traverse a spiral in which social customs generate some consciousness of interdependencies, and this consciousness is embodied in acts which in improving the environment generate new perceptions of social ties, and so on forever. The relationships, the interactions are forever there as fact, but they acquire meaning only in the desires, judgments and purposes they awaken.

We recur to our fundamental propositions. Morals is connected with actualities of existence, not with ideals, ends and obligations independent of concrete actualities. The facts upon which it depends are those which arise out of active connections of human beings with one another, the consequences of their mutually intertwined activities in the life of desire, belief, judgment, satisfaction and dissatisfaction. In this sense conduct and hence morals are social: they are not just things which *ought* to be social and which fail to come up to the scratch. But there are enormous differences of better and worse in the quality of what is social. Ideal morals begin with the perception of these differences. Human interaction and ties are there, are operative in any case. But they can be regulated, employed in an orderly way for good only as we know how to observe them. And they cannot be observed aright, they cannot be understood and utilized, when the mind is left to itself to work without the aid of science. For the natural unaided mind means precisely the habits of belief, thought and desire which have been accidentally generated and confirmed by social institutions or customs. But with all their admixture of accident and reasonableness we have at last reached a point where social conditions create a mind capable of scientific outlook and inquiry. To foster and develop this spirit is the social obligation of the present because it is its urgent need.

Yet the last word is not with obligation nor with the future. Infinite relationships of man with his fellows and with nature already exist. The ideal means, as we have seen, a sense of these encompassing continuities with their infinite reach. This meaning even now attaches to present activities because they are set in a whole to which they belong and which belongs to them. Even in the midst of conflict, struggle and defeat a consciousness is possible of the enduring and comprehending whole.

To be grasped and held this consciousness needs, like every form of consciousness, objects, symbols. In the past men have sought many symbols which no longer serve, especially since men have been idolators worshiping symbols as things. Yet within these symbols which have so often claimed to be realities and which have imposed themselves as dogmas and intolerances, there has rarely been absent some trace of a vital and enduring reality, that of a community of life in which continuities of existence are consummated. Consciousness of the whole has been connected with reverences, affections, and loyalties which are communal. But special ways of expressing the communal sense have been established. They have been limited to a select social group; they have hardened into obligatory rites and been imposed as conditions of salvation. Religion has lost itself in cults, dogmas and myths. Consequently the office of religion as sense of community and one's place in it has been lost. In effect religion has been distorted into a possession—or burden—of a limited part of human nature, of a limited portion of humanity which finds no way to universalize religion except by imposing its own dogmas and ceremonies upon others; of a limited class within a partial group; priests, saints, a church. Thus other gods have been set up before the one God. Religion as a sense of the whole is the most individualized of all things, the most spontaneous, undefinable and varied. For individuality signifies unique connections in the whole. Yet it has been perverted into something uniform and immutable. It has been formulated into fixed and defined beliefs expressed in required acts and ceremonies. Instead of marking the freedom and peace of the individual as a member of an infinite whole, it has been petrified into a slavery of thought and sentiment, an intolerant superiority on the part of the few and an intolerable burden on the part of the many.

Yet every act may carry within itself a consoling and supporting consciousness of the whole to which it belongs and which in some sense belongs to it. With responsibility for the intelligent determination of particular acts may go a joyful emancipation from the burden for responsibility for the whole which sustains them, giving them their final outcome and quality. There is a conceit fostered by perversion of religion which assimilates the universe to our personal desires; but there is also a conceit of carrying the load of the universe from which religion liberates us. Within the flickering inconsequential acts of separate selves dwells a sense of the whole which claims and dignifies them. In its presence we put off mortality and live in the universal. The life of the community in which we live and have our being is the fit symbol of this relationship. The acts in which we express our perception of the ties which bind us to others are its only rites and ceremonies.